Creative Activities for Young Children

Creative
Activities
for
Young Children

Eighth Edition

MARY MAYESKY, PH.D.

THOMSON

DELMAR LEARNING

Australia   Canada   Mexico   Singapore   Spain   United Kingdom   United States

THOMSON

DELMAR LEARNING

Creative Activities for Young Children, Eighth Edition
Mary Mayesky

Vice President, Career Education SBU:
Dawn Gerrain

Director of Editorial:
Sherry Gomoll

Acquisitions Editor:
Erin O'Connor

Editorial Assistant:
Stephanie Kelly

Director of Production:
Wendy A. Troeger

Production Manager:
J.P. Henkel

Director of Marketing:
Wendy E. Mapstone

Channel Manager:
Kristin McNary

Cover Design:
The Drawing Board

Library of Congress Cataloging-in-Publication Data

Mayesky, Mary.
    Creative activities for young children/ Mary Mayesky.—8th ed.
        p. cm.
    Includes bibliographical references and index.
    ISBN-13 978-1-4018-7245-8
    ISBN-10 1-4018-7245-X (alk. paper)
        1. Creative activities and seat work. 2. Early childhood education—Activity programs—United States.   3. Child development—United States.   I. Title.

LB1139.35.A37M365 2005
372.13—dc22   2005041405

NOTICE TO THE READER

DEDICATION

To Casper and Claire,

Thank you for listening, encouraging,
and putting up with yet another writing project.

You are the safe harbors in my rocky seas.

CONTENTS

**PART 2
(Continued)**

PART 2
(Continued)

SECTION 6
Creative Celebrations:
Holidays in the Early
Childhood Curriculum ℯ **514**

**PART 2
(Continued)**

Preface

Recently, a friend who was planning to return to early childhood teaching after raising her children told me about her plans for her first year back. She said she thought she'd use the lesson plans she usually used with four year olds for her class of three year olds. She reasoned that children today are far more "advanced" than they were ten years ago and this plan was, therefore, appropriate.

It's easy to assume that children are more "advanced" in today's technologic world. Children as young as two play with computers, totally unafraid of the machine that still plants fear in the hearts of many adults!

But technology or no technology, young children have *not changed developmentally*. A three-year-old child today has the same developmental needs of a three-year-old child in any age. Young children still grow physically in the same pattern. They learn language in the same way. They still learn to love and trust in the same way. Young children yesterday, today, and always need to learn how to get along with other children and adults. Our children today still need the "slow that it takes to grow" as children always will.

Therefore, while the world changes rapidly around us, the developmental needs of young children remain constant. So must our dedication to providing them the environment that nourishes each child *precisely* where they are in the developmental continuum. Our commitment to the development of their creativity must remain at least, or grow at best, as young children face the technologic pressures in today's world.

Besides the growth of technology, since the last edition of this text, an abundance of attention has been given to standards in education, both for teacher training and for children's learning.

Standards are a double-edged sword. On the positive side they have the potential to provide teachers a direction for what children should be learning. On the negative side is the fact that standards could lead to the identification of narrowly defined skills or facts. This may constrict the curriculum to those items that can easily be tested and ignore those items that cannot, such as children's creative development.

Standards, like technology, are here to stay and the No Child Left Behind Act has made standards a national issue. Wherever you stand on the issue, you *will* be dealing with more accountability as an early childhood teacher, whether you are at the preschool, kindergarten, or elementary level.

I have seen and experienced many such "standards movements" over the 30+ years of writing this book. My advice to you as an early childhood teacher is to remain steadfast to what you know is developmentally sound for young children. Let this knowledge be your "North Star" guiding your journey through this latest storm of standards.

Now, on to what makes this eighth edition more useful for you in your journey. The same purpose remains in this edition as in the first seven; it is designed for the person who is dedicated to helping children reach their full potential. It is written for people who want to know more about creativity, creative children, creative teaching, and creative curriculum and activities.

The eighth edition of *Creative Activities for Young Children* has been updated and revised to reflect an ever-increasing emphasis on creativity, including it in all the curriculum areas. In our world of rapidly changing technology, it is even more crucial to encourage and cherish the creativity in each and every child.

It is not enough to know how to use technology. It is not enough to know facts or how to test well. In our changing world, young children will need to know how to ask questions and to search for their own answers. They will need to know how to look at things in many different ways and how to create their own sense of beauty and meaning in life.

NEW FEATURES

Some specific features of the eighth edition are as follows:

- ⊙ A discussion of the No Child Left Behind Act and its effect on the creative arts has been added.
- ⊙ A section on effective teaching strategies that increase student performance such as attention to diversity, differentiated instruction, and process learning is included.
- ⊙ Increased information on learning styles is included. Also, activities for specific learning styles are provided in chapter end activities where applicable.
- ⊙ Teaching strategies for children with special needs are provided throughout.
- ⊙ Discussion on INTASC standards for teachers and accomplished teaching is included.
- ⊙ Former Chapter 14, *The Role of Creative Play in Development* from the seventh edition, has been moved to Section 2 as Chapter 7 in this edition.
- ⊙ Observation sheets for use in actual classroom settings are included in the Online Companion.
- ⊙ A new section entitled Helpful Web Sites is included at the end of each chapter in addition to the Web Sites referenced in the Online Companion.
- ⊙ New "This One's for You!" and "Think About It" sections have been added in every chapter.
- ⊙ Updated information and research on computers and their use with young children is included in Chapter 8.
- ⊙ A section on Technology & Multiple Intelligences in Chapter 8 has been added.
- ⊙ Additional information on digital cameras and their use in the early childhood classroom has been added.
- ⊙ New activities for preschool, kindergarten through grade 3, and grades 4 to 5 are included in every chapter.
- ⊙ New Additional Readings can be found at the end of every chapter.
- ⊙ New lists of children's books can be found in the Online Companion. The books are listed in three groups: preschool, kindergarten through grade 3, and grades 4 to 5.
- ⊙ New lists of software for children are included in each chapter, and software companies and contact information have been compiled in Appendix H.
- ⊙ More sugar-free and reduced-sugar recipes in Chapter 21, Creative Food Experiences have been added.
- ⊙ Activities at the end of Chapters 13 and 14, which were not included in the seventh edition, have been added.

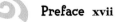

⊙ Dental health activities have been added to Chapter 23, Creative Health and Safety Experiences.

⊙ Chapter 26 has been revised to include a section on "Resources for Celebration," replacing Chapter 27 in the seventh edition. The new section contains online Web site references for children's books for celebrations to provide a source for the most current information on these materials.

INSTRUCTOR'S MANUAL

A key supplement to the eighth edition of *Creative Activities for Young Children* is the Instructor's Manual. The Instructor's Manual includes answers to review questions, multimedia resources, and discussion topics for every chapter of the text. In an effort to make teaching of the ideas in the text even more exciting and interesting for the student, the Instructor's Manual also includes Observation Sheets, Student Activity Sheets, Small Group Activity Sheets, and masters for Overhead Transparencies. These additional teaching aids are provided for each chapter of the text and are tied into the main ideas of the chapter. In addition to these teaching aids, each chapter of the Instructor's Manual provides many supplemental teaching ideas to expand on and enrich teaching of each unit. These teaching ideas range from traditional ideas such as activities using two- and three-dimensional media, to less traditional activities such as an outdoor scavenger hunt for textures.

COMPUTERIZED TEST BANK

Another supplement to the eighth edition of *Creative Activities for Young Children* is the computerized test bank (CTB) comprised of multiple choice, true/false, short answer, matching, and completion questions for each chapter. Instructors can use the CTB software to create sample quizzes for students. Refer to the CTB User's Guide for more information on how to create and post quizzes to your school's Internet or Intranet server. Students may also access sample quizzes from the Online Companion to accompany this eighth edition of *Creative Activities for Young Children* at http://www.EarlyChildEd.delmar.com.

PROFESSIONAL ENHANCEMENT BOOKLET

New to this edition is the Professional Enhancement booklet for students. This booklet, which is part of Thomson Delmar Learning's Early Childhood Education Professional Enhancement series, focuses on key topics of interest to future early childhood teachers and caregivers. Topics of interest include the No Child Left Behind Act and its impact on the Creative Arts; Reflective Practices; Differentiated Instruction; Special Topics in Language Arts and additional language arts activities; Special topics in Mathematics, Social Studies, and Nutrition; Information on appropriate art centers for different ages of children with examples of guidelines for use; and ideas for storing and maintaining art materials and equipment. Students will keep this informational supplement and use it for years to come in their early childhood practices.

ONLINE COMPANION

The Online Companion to accompany the eighth edition of *Creative Activities for Young Children* is your link to early childhood education on the Internet. The Online Companion contains many features to help focus your understanding of creative activities for the young child.

⊙ Critical Thinking Forum—In this section you have the opportunity to respond to "This One's for You" and "Think About It" concepts. Various creative activity scenarios and thought-provoking questions test your understanding of the content provided in the text. You can share your ideas with classmates and interact informally with your instructor online.

- Additional Activities—This section provides more activities in Language arts, Math, Social Studies, Nutrition, and Field Trips for elementary levels.
- Web Activities—These activities direct you to a Web site(s) and allow you to conduct further research and apply content related to creative activities for young children.
- Web Links—For each chapter, a summarized list of Web links is provided for your reference.
- Online Early Education Survey—This survey gives you the opportunity to respond to what features you like and what features you want to see improved on the Online Companion.
- Observation Sheets—These may be printed out and used for further observation of specific concepts in actual classroom settings.
- PowerPoint Presentations—These presentations cover the main points of each chapter and can serve as either an introduction to each chapter or a good tool for reviewing the chapter.

 The Online Companion icon appears at the end of each chapter to prompt you to go online and take advantage of the many features provided.
You can find the Online Companion at http://www.EarlyChildEd.delmar.com.

Creative Activities for Young Children is written for anyone who is interested in children, but since it is written especially for busy people who work with children in early childhood settings, the following points are emphasized:

- The approach to creativity is a practical one. A wide variety of activities is included in each chapter. All activities have been classroom-tested.
- Information on *why* activities should be carried out as well as *how* to carry them out is presented. Theory is provided where it is needed.
- Learning activities are included to help readers experience their own creativity.
- References for additional reading are given at the end of each chapter so students can explore each subject in more depth as desired.
- Each chapter begins with carefully worded, easy-to-understand objectives and ends with a summary. Review questions are in each chapter where appropriate.
- Each section starts with reflective questions linking together the chapters in the section.

Part 1 presents a general discussion of various child development theories. Included in Part 1 are chapters on creativity; aesthetic experiences; and social–emotional and physical-mental growth, as reflected in art development theories. Part 1 sets an appropriate theoretical stage for application of these theories in specific curriculum areas presented in Part 2.

Part 2 covers the early childhood curriculum in Section 5, Section 6, and Section 7. Section 5 covers creativity in curriculum areas. Section 6 addresses the place of holiday celebrations in the curriculum, and Section 7 covers the seasons of the year with aesthetic awareness as the unifying theme.

The author and Delmar affirm that the Web site URLs referenced herein were accurate at the time of printing. However, due to the fluid nature of the Internet, we cannot guarantee their accuracy for the life of the edition.

ACKNOWLEDGMENTS

The author gratefully acknowledges the contributions of the many people who helped make this eighth edition possible: Casper Holroyd for his unending patience with a writer's obsession, as well as for the many wonderful photos of children; Cindy Ferrell, Director, and the children and

staff at Highland Memorial Preschool and After School Program; Marcia Alford, Principal, Dawn Wade, art teacher, and the children at Lacy Elementary School, Raleigh, NC; Janet R. Sellers, Program Coordinator, Frankie Lemmon School & Developmental Center; Dr. Maureen A. Hartford, President of Meredith College; the library staff at Meredith's Carlisle Campbell Library; the Meredith College Parking Staff; Mrs. Rosalie Scott at Heards Ferry School in Atlanta, GA; and Lisa Coster, teacher, Leadmine Elementary School.

Sincere thanks to Alexis Breen Ferraro for her constant assistance in the process of publication. A hats-off salute to Erin O'Connor, my editor for so many editions, for her insight and appreciation for the entire process.

Unending thanks to my yoga instructors, Jane Barret and Sharri Gaines, for helping me get through the writing tasks undertaken thus far in my life. I would also like to say thank you to teachers around the world who everyday give the best of themselves to the youngest of our citizens.

REVIEWERS

The editors at Thomson Delmar Learning and the author wish to thank the following reviewers for their time, effort, and thoughtful contributions, which helped to shape the final text:

Deborah Ahola, MS
Schenectady County Community College
Schenectady, NY

Linda Aiken, M.Ed.
Southwestern Community College
Sylva, NC

Carol A. Anderson, MS
Colorado Community Colleges Online
Denver, CO

Audrey W. Beard, Ed.D.
Albany State University
Albany, GA

Jennfer E. Berke, Ph.D.
Mercyhurst North East
North East, PA

Elaine Camerin, Ed.D.
Daytona Beach Community College
Daytona Beach, FL

Kathleen T. Cummings, MS
Suffolk County Community College
Riverhead, NY

Pamela Davis, Ph.D.
Henderson State University
Arkadelphia, AR

Janet Imel, MA
Ivy Tech State College
Indianapolis, IN

Jennifer M. Johnson, M.Ed.
Vance-Granville Community College
Henderson, NC

Gloria Foreman McGee, Ed.D.
Tennessee Technological University
Cookeville, TN

ABOUT THE AUTHOR

Mary Mayesky, Ph.D., author of this eighth edition, is a certified preschool, elementary, and secondary teacher. She is a former professor in the Program in Education at Duke University, former director of the Early Childhood Certification Program, and supervisor of student teachers. She has served as assistant director for programs in the Office of Day Services, Department of Human Resources, State of North Carolina. She is also the former principal of the Mary E. Phillips Magnet School in Raleigh, North Carolina, the first licensed child care magnet in the Southeast. She has served several terms on the North Carolina Day Care Commission and on the Wake County School Board.

Dr. Mayesky has worked in Head Start, child care, kindergarten, and YWCA early childhood programs and has taught kindergarten through grade eight in the public schools. She has written extensively for professional journals and for general circulation magazines in the area of child development and curriculum design. She is a member of Phi Beta Kappa and was named Woman of the Year in Education by the North Carolina Academy of the YWCA. Her other honors include being named Outstanding Young Educator by the Duke University Research Council, receiving the American Association of School Administrators Research Award, and being nominated for the Duke University Alumni Distinguished Undergraduate Teaching Award.

A marathon runner, Dr. Mayesky has completed 19 marathons and received many awards in road races and senior games. She is an active member of the Raleigh Host Lions Club, having served as its first woman president. Her passions are sewing, reading on the radio for the blind, and studying and teaching yoga.

PART ONE

Theories Relating to Child Development

Part 1 presents a general discussion of various theories relating to child development. Beginning with the concept of creativity, theories, techniques, and basic program components and their relationship to the growth of creativity in young children are presented. Within this theoretical context of creativity, Part 1 provides basic information on planning and implementing creative activities for young children. Also included is a section on art and how it is related to the physical, mental, and social-emotional development of young children.

Practical information is included on how to set up an early childhood art program that encourages creativity, with chapters for both two- and three-dimensional activities. The concept of play and its relationship to a child's overall development, as well as development of creativity in play is covered in Section 1.

At the end of each chapter in Part 1 are many suggested activities designed to reinforce the concepts covered in each chapter. A wide variety of field-tested activities for young children up to and including grade 5 are also included in each chapter for use with young children.

The review questions and references for further reading provided at the end of each chapter further reinforce the main concepts. In essence, Part 1 sets the theoretical stage for application of these theories in the more specific subject and classroom areas presented in Part 2.

Fostering Creativity and Aesthetics in Young Children

REFLECTIVE QUESTIONS

After studying this section, you should be able to answer the following questions.

1. How could I change my current teaching strategies in order to better encourage the development of creativity in young children?

2. How do I encourage the development of a child's aesthetic sense in my classroom environment, lessons, and activities?

3. Are my teaching strategies based on the principles of creative development? How many of them encourage convergent thinking? How many encourage divergent thinking?

4. What thinking styles do my children have? Do I adapt my teaching to fit these individual differences?

5. Using the information on creativity and aesthetics, how will I now question my students about concepts and ideas?

6. As I plan classroom methodologies and management systems, am I keeping in mind the importance of cultivating creativity and the aesthetic sense in children?

7. What am I doing to help young children recognize their own uniqueness, creativity, and aesthetic sense?

8. What instructional strategies are best for the development of creativity and the aesthetic sense in young children?

9. What role will creativity have in my planning of curriculum for young children?

10. How will I talk with young children about their art and what they feel is beautiful?

11. How will I share with parents the importance of nurturing a child's creativity and sense of beauty?

12. How have I changed as a result of my learning about creativity and aesthetics?

Chapter 1

The Concept of Creativity

Objectives

After studying this chapter, you should be able to:

1. Define creativity.
2. List three ways in which children benefit from an environment in which creativity is encouraged.
3. List two ways teachers benefit from encouraging creativity in the classroom.
4. Name five things a teacher can do to help children develop a willingness to express creativity.
5. List several characteristics of creative children.

Take a few minutes to watch a four-year-old child in action. At one moment he is building a tower out of blocks. Suddenly he spots one of his friends playing with a homemade finger puppet. He wants to make one, too. A bit later he is playing with a guinea pig, stroking its fur and tickling its chin. Next, he is placing long, wide strokes of color on a piece of paper and getting spots of paint on everything in sight.

What is this? Now he is at the sand table building a sand castle with a high sand tower that keeps falling over. He seems to have discovered something. It is easier to build a tower out of blocks than out of sand; so he is back building with wooden blocks. It looks as though he is back where he started, except that the new block tower does not look anything like the one he started earlier.

It is exciting to watch active young children studying the world around them. A couple of things become clear almost immediately. First of all, children are full of curiosity. They seem to enjoy investigating and finding out things. Second, they seem quite capable of doing this successfully. They are very creative in finding answers to problems that arise from their curiosity. A child can figure out how to reach a needed block that somehow got thrown behind the piano. Another child selects interesting materials in order to make a finger puppet that is different from all the others. Young children seem to have a natural ability to come up with creative answers, creative approaches, and creative uses of materials.

People who work with young children need to understand creativity and have the skills to help and encourage children express their creative natures. They must realize the importance of creativity for both children and teachers. They need to be able to identify creativity in children and be able to help them develop a willingness to express this creativity.

WHAT IS CREATIVITY?

Perhaps the most important thing to realize about creativity is that everyone possesses a certain amount of it. Some people are a little more creative, and some a little less. No one is totally uncreative.

Preschoolers often ask parents 100 questions in a single day (Hoefferth, 1998). This behavior reflects the enormous power curiosity has on children's creativity and motivation to learn in early childhood (Strom & Strom, 2002a; Taylor, 2000). Young children tend to be highly open, curious, and creative. Unfortunately, many adults want children to conform. As outside pressures from adults grow, the children's environment closes in on them. They find it less and less rewarding to express interest in things, to be curious, to be creative in investigating their world. To avoid this, it is important to know ways of encouraging a child's creativity. To begin with, one should understand the meaning of the term **creativity.**

There are many meanings for this word:

- A definition by one writer on the subject, May (1975, p. 39), describes creativity as the "process of bringing something new into being."
- Paul Torrance (1970), a pioneer in the study of the creative process, suggests that creativity is the ability to produce something novel, something with the stamp of uniqueness upon it.
- More recently, creativity is further defined as a combination of abilities, skills, motivations, and attitudes.

Much like athletic ability, creativity is really a combination of many different abilities. It is more useful to think of many types of *creativities*. (Ripple, 1999, p. 629). There are many different senses of the term

creativity. One researcher separates the types of creativity in this way:

- **"Capital C" creativity,** which involves bringing into existence something genuinely new that receives social validation enough to be added to the culture. An example of Capital C creativity is the invention of the light bulb.
- **"Small c" creativity,** which involves ideas or products that are new to the person, but only to the person. An example of small c creativity is a child's new use of blending finger-paint colors (Ripple).

The following definition may help the student understand the concept better. Creativity is a way of thinking and acting or making something that is original for the individual and valued by that person or others. A person does not have to be the first one in the world to produce something in order for it to be considered a creative act. Creativity can be found anywhere, at home or school, as easily as in art or science.

Figure 1-1
Young children are naturally industrious and involved in learning new skills.

Figure 1-2
Children benefit from creativity as they experience the joy of developing their individuality.

The Creative Process

When someone is creating something, there are usually two parts to that person's activity. The first part has to do with originality—the discovery of an idea, plan, or answer. The second part has to do with working out, proving, and making certain that the idea or answer works or is possible. The first part, *discovering,* involves using the imagination, playing with ideas, and exploring. The second part, *process,* involves using learned skills, evaluating, and testing.

Thought Processes and Creativity

There are two kinds of thinking that produce solutions to problems. One of these types is called **convergent thinking.** The other type is called **divergent thinking.** Convergent thinking usually results in a single answer or solution to a question or problem. Divergent thinking opens things up and results in many answers to a single problem.

For example, if a child is asked to count the number of fish in an aquarium, there is only one correct answer. This is a question that leads children to convergent thinking. On the other hand, if a child is asked to tell as many things as possible about the aquarium, there are obviously many correct statements that can be made. Questions such as this encourage divergent rather than convergent thinking. Creativity requires both divergent and convergent thinking. Both types of thinking are

important to creativity. Consequently, the teacher's challenge is to avoid replacing one with the other. Another way to think about this is that children must learn the "way things are done" (convergent thinking) before truly experiencing the creative process. For example, a child needs to learn how to hold and use a paintbrush (convergent learning) before she can experience the process of painting. An older child must learn the rules (e.g., what are the parts of a book report?) before she can begin to break or change the rules to be creative (e.g., giving a book report as a board game).

In dealing with young children, the focus should be on the *process*—that is, developing and generating original ideas. This focus on the process encourages the development of creativity across the curriculum, instead of being confined to art and music activities.

Creativity and Older Children

With older children, creativity involves more of an emphasis on the criteria of high-quality, original products or solutions. The development of creative products emerges later in the child's development. An example of this is seen in the fourth and fifth grade science fair projects. It becomes very apparent that some projects are more creative than others. For example, a student who created and tested a new chair design may seem to have an idea of a different quality than another student who investigated which commercial cleaning product worked best on stains.

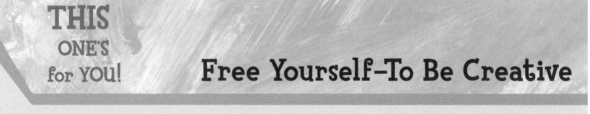

THIS ONE'S for YOU! Free Yourself–To Be Creative

One of the pioneers of research into children's creativity, Paul Torrance (1962), felt that we had to free ourselves to be creative before we can ever really be creative teachers. Here are some of his suggestions to free yourself to be creative.
- Don't be afraid to fall in love with something and to pursue it with intensity.
- Know, understand, take pride in, practice, develop, exploit, and enjoy your greatest strengths.
- Learn to free yourself from the expectations of others and to walk away from the games they impose on you. Free yourself to play your own game.
- Find a great teacher or mentor who will help you.
- Don't waste energy trying to be well rounded.
- Do what you love and can do well.
- Learn the skills of independence.

How many of these apply to you? Are you free to be a creative teacher? Pick one or two of the suggestions that you most want to work on and then go!

IDENTIFYING CREATIVITY

Creativity isn't always recognized by teachers and peers. Actually, history is full of examples of people whose creativity wasn't recognized in their school or work experience.

Did you know that . . .

⊙ Albert Einstein was four years old before he could speak and seven before he could read.

⊙ Beethoven's music teacher once said of him, "As a composer, he is hopeless."

⊙ F. W. Woolworth got a job in a dry goods store at age 21, but his employers would not let him wait on customers because he "didn't have enough sense."

⊙ Leo Tolstoy flunked out of college.

⊙ A newspaper editor fired Walt Disney because he had "no good ideas."

⊙ Abraham Lincoln entered the Black Hawk War as a captain and came out as a private.

⊙ Louisa May Alcott was told by an editor that she would never write anything that had popular appeal.

⊙ Winston Churchill failed the sixth grade.

⊙ Isaac Newton did poorly in grade school.

⊙ Thomas Edison's teachers told him that he was too stupid to learn anything.

⊙ Admiral Richard Byrd had been retired from the Navy, declared "unfit for service," when he flew over both poles.

⊙ A Western Union official, in a memo dated 1876, stated, "This telephone invented by Alexander Graham Bell has too many shortcomings to be seriously considered as a means of communication. The device is inherently of no value to us."

At this level with older children, creativity is seen as original products or original solutions. Creativity with older children is more than the generation of ideas. It involves the creation of products. Original products are one of the characteristics of creativity with older children.

Creativity goes beyond possession and use of artistic or musical talent. Creativity is evidenced not only in music, art, and writing, but throughout the curriculum, in science, social studies, and other areas.

Variety and Creativity

There is a kind of creativity that allows people to express themselves in a way that makes others listen and appreciate what they hear. There are creative abilities that enable human beings to discover meaning in nature—meaning that others had not understood before.

Creativity changes at different levels of development. Most people have ideas about what creativity is in adulthood, but what might we look for in a young child? It is crucial that early childhood teachers see creativity as part of the developmental process. For young children, a critical criterion for creative potential is *originality* (Tegano, Moran, & Sawyers, 1991). Thus, teachers of young children must understand the process that leads to original thinking.

Originality

Originality can be seen in a kindergarten classroom where children are making collages from pieces of torn tissue paper. Mary's experimenting with the material leads to her discovery of a way to make three-dimensional bumps in the collage. Mary's discovery of the three-dimensional aspect is a form of originality. Though making three-dimensional collages is certainly not a new idea in a kindergarten classroom, it is an *original* idea for that particular child at that particular time. Consider another kindergarten classroom where the children are embellishing full-size outlines of their bodies. Most children are adding hair, faces, and clothes to their outlines, while Todd is making an internal drawing of his skeleton. Todd's drawing of his skeleton is an original idea for him at that particular time.

Process over Product

Let's return to Mary and her three-dimensional collage. Teachers of young children need to be grounded in the **process over product** philosophy. The teacher's observation of the *process* that leads to originality (exploration and experimentation with the materials) is more valuable than any *judgment of the product* (the three-dimensional bump may have been imperfect and collapsed in the end). Remember that young children do not always have the skills to make a creative product (an elaborate painting or a workable invention), and so the process that leads to originality is the focus of creative potential.

Early childhood classrooms are full of examples of the process of original thinking. We see complex dramas unfold as children act out scenes of their own design, discover clever block building solutions, and demonstrate unique interpersonal problem solving (Tegano et al., 1991).

Figure 1-3
To be creative, children need time and space to create at their own pace.

Figure 1-4
Children enjoy activities in which they participate freely and openly.

IMPORTANCE OF CREATIVITY

Creativity is the mainspring of our civilization: from the concept of the wheel, through the steamboat, the telephone, the automobile, the airplane, radio and television, computers, automation, the electronics industry, nuclear power, and space travel. All the milestones of great inventions, scientific discoveries, painting, literature, music, drama, and all forms of artistic expression have depended on creative thinking of the highest order. Thus, the progress of civilization and humanity's present evolutionary stature are essentially due to creative thinking and innovations. Our inherent creativity contributes to the very quality of our lives.

The rapid changes of our present age require that problems be tackled creatively. The technological advances and discoveries during the next couple of decades could surpass all the past accomplishments in human history (Raudsepp, 1980). It is difficult to foretell exactly what knowledge we will need to solve future problems creatively. What the young are learning now will surely become obsolete. Everyone can and must continue to learn throughout life, but knowledge

alone is no guarantee that we will meet future problems effectively. Only a strong creative ability will provide the means for coping with the future.

Children want to express themselves openly. They want to bring out new ideas and have new experiences. They enjoy creativity and benefit from it in many ways, including:
⊙ learning to feel good about themselves.
⊙ learning to seek many answers to a problem.
⊙ developing their potential to think.
⊙ developing their individuality.
⊙ developing new skills.
⊙ experiencing the joy of being different.

Teachers also benefit from encouraging creativity, in such ways as:
⊙ being able to provide for more and greater variety in the program.
⊙ learning to recognize children for their unique skills.
⊙ being able to develop closer relationships with children.

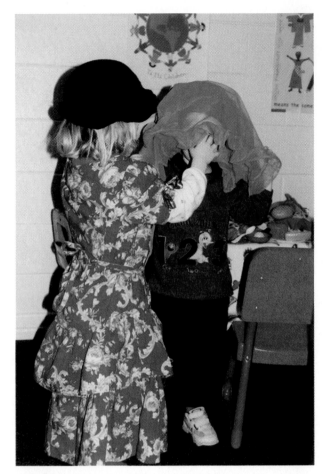

Figure 1-5
Young children have a natural ability to be creative in their use of materials.

Figure 1-6
Children develop a good self-concept when they are accepted for being themselves.

⊙ having fewer behavior problems.
⊙ using a minimum of standardized curricula and external evaluation.

CHARACTERISTICS OF CREATIVITY

Paul Torrance, a noted expert on creativity in children, has frequently emphasized that the kind of behavior teachers identify as desirable in children does not always coincide with characteristics associated with the creative personality. For example, teachers who think they value uniqueness may find that, when a child has spilled her milk because she tried the original method of holding the cup with her teeth, they don't like creative exploration as much as they thought they did!

> **There are certain things that our age needs. It needs, above all, courageous hope and the impulse to creativeness.**–Bertrand Russell

> **Imagination rules the world.**–Napoleon
> **Leap and the net will appear.**–Julia Cameron

This lack of conformity can be inconvenient, but teachers should realize that some creative individuals possess character traits that aren't always easy to appreciate. Some of the less attractive qualities include being stubborn, finding fault with things, appearing haughty and self-satisfied, and being discontented (Torrance, 1962). Yet it is easy to see that stubbornness might be a valuable quality when carrying through a new idea or that finding fault and being discontented could result in questioning and analyzing a situation before coming up with suggestions for improving it.

In all fairness, we must admit that we do not know at present if these less attractive attitudes lie at the root of creativity or if some of them are the result of mishandling by teachers, peers, and families as the child matures. On the other hand, Torrance also found that creative children possess many likable qualities, such

THINK ABOUT IT... Research on Creative Behavior

The following is a summary of two researchers' work on creative behavior in children (Strom & Strom, 2002b).

Everyone possesses creative abilities to some degree. Most of what preschoolers learn before they arrive at school comes from guessing, asking questions, searching, manipulating, and playing. These activities match most definitions of the creative process. Given the natural creativity of children, the main concern of adults should be to preserve and enrich this dimension of potential. Parents who over-schedule children to ensure they do not get into trouble inadvertently undermine creativity, because this practice prevents the solitude needed for reflection and to produce new ideas (Rosenfeld & Wise, 2000). Similarly, when imagination is discounted at school, children may unwittingly sacrifice their creative potential (Runco & Pritzker, 1999).

Teachers and parents should understand two observations based on a decade of research on creative behavior conducted at Brandeis University (McCabe, 1985). First, the best motivation for creativity is freedom. Something happens when the interests of students are accommodated, allowing them to periodically decide their goals and how to achieve these purposes.

Second, frequent evaluation and criticism smother creativity. This conclusion differs from the common assumption that students need continuous feedback. When creative behavior is desired, people do better if their productivity is reviewed less often. Adults who are the most inhibited and least capable of expressing themselves in imaginative ways are those in high-pressure occupations where they are subjected to weekly or monthly evaluations (Senge et al., 2000; Strom & Strom, 2002b).

as determination, curiosity, intuition, a willingness to take risks, a preference for complex ideas, and a sense of humor.

We point out these possible problems of encouraging creativity in children not to discourage teachers from fostering such behavior, but to enlighten them so that they will not subtly reject or discourage creative responses out of failure to recognize the positive side of such behavior. Ideally, understanding creativity will result in increased acceptance and valuing of creativity in young children. Acceptance is vitally important because it will encourage children to develop their creativity further. Let us now summarize the ways to encourage creativity in all young children.

HELPING CHILDREN EXPRESS CREATIVITY

There are at least eight things that can be done for children to help them express natural creative tendencies:

Help Children Accept Change. A child who becomes overly worried or upset in new situations is unlikely to express creative potential.

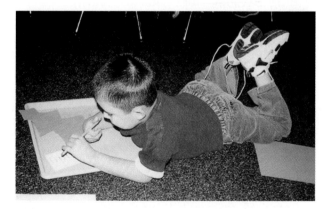

Figure 1-7

In all creative activities for young children, the process is more important than the product.

Help Children Realize that Some Problems Have No Easy Answers. This may help prevent children from becoming anxious when they cannot find an immediate answer to a question or problem.

Web Sites Relating to Creativity

THIS ONE'S for YOU!

For more information on the concept of creativity, check out some of the following Web sites:

BROKEN CRAYONS

http://www.cre8ng.com
Broken Crayons is the Web site by Robert Alan Black—speaker and author on creativity and innovation. This site is home to the weekly Creativity Challenges posted to several Creativity discussion lists. This site exhibits great use of color and the crayon motif. Make sure you read the "Cre8v Thoughts" newsletter and view the four quadrants of the M.I.N.D. Design questionnaire. You even get to break the crayons as you move the mouse over the graphics.

CREATIVITY POOL

http://www.creativitypool.com
This is an inspiring knowledge base full of creative and original ideas. It's the home of future innovation and tomorrow's most (in)famous inventions.

CREAX.NET

http://www.creax.net
An extensive and original resource for links on creativity and innovation on the Web. A selection of 690 good and actual links is divided into 67 categories for the visitor's convenience.

CREATIVITY FOR LIFE.COM

http://www.creativityforlife.com
This is a Web site for exploring creativity in our everyday lives. It features articles, newsletters, and personal creative activities.

ENCHANTED MIND

http://www.enchantedmind.com
This is a colorful, well-designed site with a great deal of information on creativity techniques, inspiring articles, and puzzles including some interactive Java puzzles. The site uses a lot of color, graphics, and background effects—complementing the creative nature of the site and creating the effect of a magazine.

ODYSSEY OF THE MIND

http://www.odysseyofthemind.org
Odyssey of the Mind promotes creative team-based problem solving in a school program for students from kindergarten through college. The program helps students learn divergent thinking and problem solving.

Help Children Recognize that Many Problems Have a Number of Possible Answers. Encourage them to search for more than one answer. Then they can evaluate all the different answers to see which ones fit the situation best.

Help Children Learn to Judge and Accept Their Own Feelings. Children should not feel guilty for having feelings about things. Create an environment where judgment is deferred and all ideas are respected, where discussion and debates are a means of trying out ideas in a nonthreatening atmosphere.

Reward Children for Being Creative. Let children know that their creative ideas are valued. In fact, the more creative the idea or product, the more greatly they should be rewarded. It is also useful to help children realize that good work is sometimes its own reward.

Help Children Feel Joy in Their Creative Productions and in Working Through a Problem. Children should find that doing things and finding answers for themselves is fun. The adult should establish the conditions that allow this to take place.

Help Children Appreciate Themselves for Being Different. There is a tendency to reward children for conforming. This discourages creativity. Children should learn to like themselves because they are unique.

Help Children Develop Perseverance—"Stick-to-Itiveness." Help children by encouraging them to follow through. Provide chances for them to stick with an activity even if everyone else has moved on to something different.

SUMMARY

Creativity is a way of thinking and acting or making something that is original for the individual and valued by that person or others. Young children are naturally creative. This means they behave in ways and do things that are unique and valued by themselves or others. Creativity in preschool children is stimulated when they are allowed to do divergent thinking. In many ways, both the child and teacher benefit from activities that encourage creativity. With older children, the criteria of creativity involves more of an emphasis on original products or solutions.

Some kinds of creative behavior are not seen by adults as desirable in children. The inconvenience and possible frustration caused by the constantly questioning and exploring child may lead even well-meaning

Figure 1-8
Help children feel joy in their creativity.

adults to discourage this behavior. Understanding and accepting these behavior traits can go a long way in encouraging creativity in children. Original thinking and the process that leads to it are also important criteria in understanding creativity in young children.

Children are being creative when they are solving problems, redefining situations, demonstrating flexibility, and being adventurous. Adults can help children develop a willingness to express creativity in many ways, such as by teaching them that change is natural in life and that many problems do not have easy answers. When children can go at their own pace and figure out their own way of doing things in a relaxed learning situation, they are likely to become more creative.

KEY TERMS

"Capital C" creativity
convergent thinking
creativity

divergent thinking
process over product
"Small c" creativity

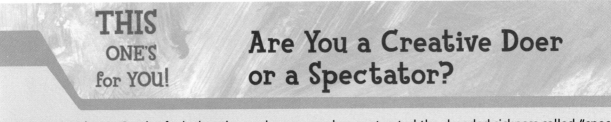

THIS ONE'S for YOU!

Are You a Creative Doer or a Spectator?

Painter Stanley A. Czurles feels that the modern person has contracted the dreaded sickness called "spectatoritis," which leads to increased feelings of boredom, lack of satisfaction, and apathy. In his view, only the creative person can experience true fulfillment in life. Czurles presents the following comparison of the two contrasting approaches to life. See if you can find yourself in either (or maybe both!) of the following two lists.

SPECTATOR

- Kills time
- Is an observer
- Has few self-sufficiency interests
- Seeks to have something happen to or for him or her
- Is involved in a merry-go-round of prestructured activities
- Has only temporary enjoyment, with little or no lasting product
- Is swept into activities
- Has fractionated experiences
- Is prone to boredom
- Experiences no deep challenge
- Accomplishes nothing very distinguished
- Curtails self by a focus on pessimistic personal concerns
- Has increased hardening of opinions and attitudes
- Achieves superficial trappings of culture
- Is subject to early spiritual-mental aging
- Experiences primarily what is

CREATIVE DOER

- Uses time to develop self
- Is involved; experiences personal achievement
- Is rich in self-enriching activities
- Is self-stimulating; is at home and in control of many conditions
- Enjoys selected relevant activities
- Experiences continuous satisfaction, achieves tangible results, and becomes a more efficiently functioning person
- Selects planned participation
- Has completeness and continuity of involvement
- Is stimulated by challenging interests
- Aspires more as he or she achieves new goals
- Grows in potential through unique achievements
- Is enlivened by a recognized freedom to pursue creative interests
- Continues being flexible through continuous new insights
- Experiences the essence of a culture
- Enjoys an extended youthful spirit
- Experiences what might be

(Adapted from *More Creative Growth Games* by Eugene Raudsepp. Copyright © 1980 by Eugene Raudsepp. Used by permission.)

LEARNING ACTIVITIES

CHANGING THE KNOWN

Although creative thinking can be hard thinking, that does not mean it cannot be fun. This activity is designed to prove it. Try it alone or with a few classmates. When the activity is completed, it may be enjoyable to compare lists with those of others.

A. Materials needed: paper, pencil, wristwatch (or clock).

B. Time allowed: two minutes.

C. Task: List as many uses as you can (not related to building or construction) for a standard brick. Do not worry if some of them may seem silly. The important thing is to think of using something in a new and different way.

D. It might be fun to try this exercise with a number of different objects: a nail, powder puff, paper clip, key, belt, cup, book, or other objects.

JUST SUPPOSE

Creative thinking occurs when one imagines what might be. It is a way of "playing" with the mind. Here is an exercise that allows you to experience this type of creative process. It can be done alone or with a few classmates.

A. Materials needed: paper, pencil.

B. Time allowed: unlimited.

C. Task: From the following fourteen possibilities choose any number of tasks.

1. "Just suppose" that there is nothing made of wood in the room. What would change? What would things look like? What dangers might exist? What would you be unable to do?

2. "Just suppose" (try this with other people) you cannot use words, either written or spoken, for an hour. How can you communicate? What is frustrating about it? What is pleasing about it? What would it mean if it continued for days?

3. "Just suppose" you receive a million dollars and must spend it within two minutes. Make a list of ways to spend the money and compare lists with others in the class.

4. "Just suppose" you were the first person to meet a man from Mars and could ask him only three questions. What would they be? Compare your questions with those of others in the class.

5. "Just suppose" you were with Julius Caesar when he met Cleopatra for the first time. If you could say only one sentence, what would it be?

6. "Just suppose" you could be any person in the world for one hour. Who would it be? What would you do? Compare responses with classmates.

7. What would happen if all people awakened tomorrow morning to find themselves twice as large?

8. IMAGINE!

Create seven sentences for which the seven-letter word "imagine" would be the acronym. All sentences should reflect in some way your thoughts about creative thinking, imagination, and ingenuity from what you have learned by reading this unit.

Example: **I**deas should not be hoarded or hidden.

Many small solutions are necessary to solve big problems.

All people are created creative.

Good ideas drive out bad ideas.

Innovative ideas are resisted by "spectators."

Never mind what others think—use your own judgment.

Enjoy your fantasies—that's what they are for!

Now, it's *your* turn!

9. Pick one or two characteristics associated with creativity that you would like to increase in your own life. For example, you might want to become more open to experience or more persistent. For a month, try to exercise that characteristic whenever you can. Record your efforts and see if you find that the characteristics can be changed.

10. Creativity is not always expressed in school-appropriate ways. For one week, pay careful attention to students causing disturbances in your room. Do you see evidence of creativity in their behavior? Propose and explain ways you could channel that originality in other ways. Get input from your fellow students on your ideas.

11. Begin collecting books and stories about individuals who display the characteristics associated with creativity in positive ways. Use the list on the Web site for suggested books. Share

these books with your students. Consider the kinds of models that are being presented in your language arts, science, or social studies curricula. Would students be able to tell from them that you value originality, independence, or persistence?

12. Read two biographies of the same creative person—one written for adults and the other for children (see the list of suggested books at the end of this chapter). Keep track of the emphases and information that are different. Do both books accurately describe the successes and failures in the person's life, the triumph and setbacks? How might these differences affect your students?

13. Divide a large piece of paper into squares and list one characteristic associated with creativity in each square. Leave the paper on your desk for two weeks. Each time a student does something to demonstrate a characteristic, put his or her name in that square. After the first time, just use tally marks. Be sure to mark the characteristic, even if it is displayed in a negative way. At the end of two weeks, see which students are listed most often. Are they students you expected?

14. Next week, plan one class activity that you believe is truly unusual or novel, something no one in your class would have experienced before. Observe how your students respond. What does this tell you about your teaching?

CHAPTER REVIEW

1. Discuss the following terms briefly:
   a. creativity
   b. convergent thinking
   c. divergent thinking
2. List five things a teacher can do to help children develop a willingness to express creativity.
3. List three ways in which children benefit from engaging in creative activities.

4. List several characteristics of creativity.
5. Discuss the concepts of original thinking and process over product.
6. What is the difference in the criteria for creativity in older children?
7. Why are both convergent and divergent thinking important to creativity?

REFERENCES

Hoefferth, S. (1998). *Children at work and play.* Ann Arbor, MI: University of Michigan Institute of Social Research.

May, R. (1975). *The courage to create.* New York: W. W. Norton.

McCabe, E. (1985, August 1). Creativity. *Vital Speeches of the Day. 51*(2), 628–632.

Raudsepp, E. (1980). *More creative growth games.* New York: Pedigree Books, G. P. Putnam's Sons.

Ripple, R. (1999). Teaching creativity. In M. A. Runco & S. R. Pritzker (Eds.), *Encyclopedia of creativity* (Vol. 2), San Diego, CA: Academic Press.

Rosenfeld, A., & Wise, N. (2000). *The over-schooled child: Avoiding the hyper-parenting trap.* New York: St. Martin's Press.

Runco, M., & Pritzker, S. (Eds.) (1999). *Encyclopedia of creativity.* San Diego, CA: Academic Press.

Senge, P., Cambron-McCabe, N., Lucas, T., Smith, B., Dutton, J., & Kleiner, A. (2000). *Schools that learn.* New York: Doubleday.

Strom, P., & Strom, R. (2002a, March). Too busy to play. *Parenting for High Potential,* 18–22.

Strom, R. D., & Strom, P. S. (2002b). Changing the rules: Education for creative thinking. *Journal of Creative Behavior. 36*(3), 183–200.

Taylor, M. (2000). *Imaginary companions and the children who create them.* New York: Oxford University Press.

Tegano, D. W., Moran, J. D. III, & Sawyers, J. K. (1991). *Creativity in early childhood classrooms.* Washington, DC: National Association for the Education of Young Children (NAEYC).

Torrance, E. P. (1962). *Rewarding creative behavior: Experiments in classroom creativity.* Englewood Cliffs, NJ: Prentice-Hall.

Torrance, E. P. (1970). *Encouraging creativity in the classroom.* Dubuque, IA: William C. Brown.

ADDITIONAL READINGS

Armstrong, T. (1998). *Awakening genius in the classroom*. Alexandria, VA: Association for Supervision and Curriculum Development.

Bredekamp, S. (Ed.). (1997). *Developmentally appropriate practice in early childhood programs serving children from birth through age one* (Rev. ed.). Washington, DC: National Association for the Education of Young Children (NAEYC).

Brittain, L. (Ed.). (1968). *Viktor Lowenfeld speaks on art and creativity*. Reston, VA: National Association of Educators of Art.

Dighe, J., Calomiris, Z., & Vanzutphen, C. (1998). Nurturing the language of art in children. *Young Children, 53*(1), 4–9.

Dobbs, R. (1998). *Learning in and through art: A guide to discipline-based art education*. Alexandria, VA: Association for Supervision and Curriculum Development.

Edwards, L. C. (1997). *Affective development and the creative arts: A process approach to early child-hood education* (2nd ed.). Columbus, OH: Merrill-Macmillan.

Eisner, E. W. (2002). *The arts and the creation of mind*. Reston, VA: National Art Education Association (NAEA).

Engel, B. S. (1999). *Considering children's art: How and why to value their works*. Washington, DC: NAEYC.

Feldman, E. (1997). *Becoming human through art*. Reston, VA: NAEA.

Feldman, E. (1994). *Teaching art and so on*. Reston, VA: NAEA.

Fineberg, J. (Ed.). (1998). *Discovering child art*. Princeton, NJ: Princeton University Press.

Fowler, C. (1996). *Strong arts, strong schools: The promising potential and strong shortsighted disregard of the arts in American schooling*. New York: Oxford University Press.

Guilford, J. P. (1968). *Intelligence, creativity and their educational implications*. San Diego, CA: Robert R. Knapp.

Jackson, P. W. (1998). *John Dewey and the lessons of art*. New Haven, CT: Yale University Press.

Jones, L. S. (1998). *Art information on the Internet*. Phoenix, AZ: Oryx.

McCutchan, A. (2000). *The muse that sings: Composers speak about the creative process*. New York: Oxford University Press.

Merrion, M. & Rubin, J. (1996). *Creative approaches to elementary curriculum*. Portsmouth, NH: Heinemann.

Ripple, R. (1999). Teaching creativity. In M. A. Reinco & S. R. Pritzker (Eds.), *Encyclopedia of creativity* (Vol. 2). San Diego, CA: Academic Press.

Rufer, L., Lake, B., Robinson, E., & Hicks, J. (1998). Stretching our boundaries and breaking barriers to the public mind. *Art Education, 51*(3), 43–51.

Runco, M. A., & Pritzker, S. (Eds.). (1999). *Encyclopedia of creativity* (Vols. 1 & 2). San Diego, CA: Academic Press.

Sacca, E., & Zimmerman, E. (1998). *Women art educators IV: Her stories, our stories, future stories*. Reston, VA: NAEA.

Sanders, T. (1998). *Strategic thinking and the new science: Planning in the midst of chaos, complexity and change*. New York: The Free Press.

Seefeldt, C. (1995). Art—A serious work. *Young Children, 50*(3), 39–45.

Tegano, D. W., Moran, J. D. II, & Sawyers, J. K. (1991). *Creativity in early childhood classrooms*. Washington, DC: NAEYC.

Torrance, E. P. (1973). *Is creativity teachable?* Bloomington, IN: Phi Delta Kappa.

Torrance, E. P. (1983). The importance of falling in love with something. *Creative Child and Adult Quarterly, 8*(2), 72–78.

Tyrell, J. (2001). *The power of fantasy in early learning*. New York: Routledge Falmer.

SOFTWARE FOR CHILDREN

ALPHABET

Reinforces: *creativity and alphabet*. This visually rich experience takes interactive alphabet books to a new level. Based on the artwork of famed Polish artist Kveta Pacovski, the software makes the alphabet come alive through screen after screen of dancing, twirling, and colorful letters. Ages 4 and up.

FLYING COLORS v.2.11

Reinforces: *creativity, drawing, and painting*. An alternative to Kid Pix, this draw-and-paint program allows all kinds of backgrounds and scenes for creating artwork.

FUN FOR BRAINS

Reinforces: *creativity, shapes, body parts, music, and counting*. This is an inexpensive, well-designed early learning CD-ROM that was created by a mom and dad for their 4-year-old daughter.

KID PIX DELUXE 3

Reinforces: *creativity, drawing, and painting*. This classic draw-and-paint program is easy for preschoolers to use and offers endless possibilities for creativity. Children can explore line, color, and texture, and their artwork can be made into slideshow presentations. Ages 4 and up.

HELPFUL WEB SITES

Web sites related to children's creativity and creative activities:

http://www.princetonol.com/groups/iad/lessons/ early/early.html

This site features dozens of child-friendly art projects submitted by teachers. Activities include painting to music, pipe cleaner sculpture, dough recipes, and primary color mixing.

http://www.first-school.ws/

Click on Preschool Materials for activities and on Themes for specific curriculum activities. This useful site is jam-packed with lesson plans and project ideas. Especially nice is the series of activities on Vincent Van Gogh and sunflowers.

http://www.everythingpreschool.com/

The craft pages on this site serve up hundreds of project ideas. Click on Themes for ideas on nature, seasons, animals, space, dinosaurs, and the circus.

For additional creative activity resources, visit our Web site at http://www.EarlyChildEd. delmar.com.

Chapter 2

Promoting Creativity

Objectives

After studying this chapter, you should be able to:

1. Describe the relationship between creativity and the curriculum.
2. Describe the role of play and exploration in promoting creativity.
3. Demonstrate four questioning strategies to encourage creative thinking in young children.
4. List three questions to consider when modifying the curriculum to encourage creative thinking.
5. List four beliefs associated with the philosophy of differentiated instruction in the early childhood curriculum.

Creative thinking is not a station one arrives at, but a means of traveling. Creativity is fun. Being creative, feeling creative, and experiencing creativity is fun. Learning is more fun for children in settings where teachers and children recognize and understand the process of creative thinking. Incorporating creative thinking into all areas of the curriculum contributes to a young child's positive attitude toward learning. As one student teacher commented, "I used to think that if children were having too much fun they couldn't be learning. Now I understand how they are learning in a more effective way." This unit addresses the relationship of creativity and the classroom environment, providing guidelines for encouraging creative thinking in the early childhood program throughout the day. In subsequent units, the same emphasis on creativity is applied to specific curriculum areas.

Creativity is an integral part of each day; it is part of circle time, reading time, and lunchtime—it is not limited to art, music, creative movement, or dramatic play. Creativity, the curriculum, and the overall learning environment should not be at odds with each other; they should all complement each other (Tegano, May, Lookabaugh, & Burdette, 1991). Children need knowledge and skills to be creative—the curriculum outlines *what* they need to learn, and this unit will help you understand *how* to attain these goals. Throughout this unit, keep in mind that creative thinking is contagious—from teacher to child, from child to teacher, and also from child to child and teacher to teacher.

PROMOTING CREATIVITY IN THE CURRICULUM

Young children need knowledge and skills to express their creative potential. Knowledge and skills are necessary before creative potential can have true meaning

Figure 2-1

A child who meets with unquestionable acceptance of her unique approach to the world feels safe expressing her creativity.

Figure 2-2

Dress-up games encourage children's creativity.

(Amabile, 1983; Barron, 1988). Children cannot develop high-level creative thinking skills without the basic knowledge and skills of a particular area, in the same way that a great chef must develop basic culinary skills before creating the gourmet recipe. The curriculum is the teacher's choice of what knowledge and skills are important and also developmentally appropriate for a particular group of children (Bredekamp, 1997; Katz & Chard, 1989).

An example of the need for a knowledge base emerged in the early pilot testing of a measure of creative potential for young children (Moran et al., 1985). The researchers were trying to adapt the classic "uses" task for preschool children. In this task, the children are asked to name all the "uses" they can think of for a common item. The number of original (i.e., unusual) answers serves as one measure of creativity (Wallach & Kogan, 1965; Torrance, 1962). The researchers were puzzled when a group of preschool children could think of only a few uses for common objects such as a clothes hanger and a table knife. The researchers realized that the reason for

the limited response was that the children had little or no knowledge and skill in the use of clothes hangers and table knives. In fact, most preschool children are not allowed to use these items. Knowledge and skills, then, are a prerequisite for creativity. Later research came up with better results when the children were asked to think of all the ways to use a box and paper, items about which the children had a working knowledge (Moran et al., 1985). As Barron (1988) asserts, creativity evolves from a knowledge base—*without knowledge, there is no creation.*

Thus, one important goal for the early childhood teacher is to provide an adequate base of knowledge and skills for children, while at the same time providing an environment that encourages creative thinking in the use of the knowledge and skills. The curriculum is the guide by which teachers determine *what* will be presented to children. Creativity is fostered according to *how* the curriculum is presented to the child (Tegano & Burdette, 1991).

Perhaps the greatest challenge for all teachers is to help preserve the sense of wonder that lives within the hearts of those who are very young.

PROMOTING CREATIVITY THROUGH PLAY AND EXPLORATION

Let's take a look at a preschool classroom where computers are available and observe the process of exploration as it leads into play. At first the computer is novel and children engage in random punching of keys—exploring what the keys can do. This leads to

THINK ABOUT IT... Right-Brained Children

I have always found children who "marched to a different drummer" a joy and a challenge to work with. They make me re-examine my teaching methods and open up my mind to alternate views. These children approach life and learning in a truly unique manner. One specific group of these special children has been named **right-brained** (or "alpha").

When we talk about a person who is right-brained or **left-brained,** we are referring to learning preferences based on functional differences between the hemispheres (sides) of the brain.

Children who are right-brained or "alpha" are those whose right hemisphere of the brain is dominant in their learning process. This is in contrast to the majority of children, whose left hemisphere is dominant in their learning style. As we will see later in this section, each hemisphere of the brain has distinctly different strengths and behavioral characteristics.

All of us use both hemispheres of the brain, but we may use one side more than the other. For instance, you might have a dominant right hemisphere, which simply means that it is your preferred or stronger hemisphere. It is the one in which you tend to first process most of the information you receive. That does not mean you don't use your left hemisphere. You may use your right hemisphere 60% of the time and your left hemisphere 40%. Similarly, when we talk about children who are right-brained or left-brained, we do not mean they use only one hemisphere but simply that they use one hemisphere to a greater extent than the other.

The right and left brain hemispheres have specialized thinking characteristics. They do not approach life in the same way. The left-hemisphere approach to life is part-to-whole. It sequences, puts things in order, and is logical. The right hemisphere learns whole-to-part. It does not sequence; it does not put things in order; it looks at things in an overall way or **holistically.** Let's consider specific skills and in which hemisphere that skill is best developed.

LEFT HEMISPHERE

The skills best developed in this side of the brain are handwriting, understanding symbols, language, reading, and phonics. Other general skills best developed here are locating details and facts, talking and reciting, following directions, and listening and auditory association. All of these skills children must exercise on a day-to-day basis in school. We give children symbols; we stress reading, language, and phonics. We ask for details; we insist upon directions being followed, and mostly, we talk at children. In short, most of our school curriculum is left-brained. We teach to the child who has a dominant left brain.

RIGHT HEMISPHERE

In the right hemisphere is a whole other set of skills. The right hemisphere has the ability to recognize and process nonverbal sounds. It also displays a greater ability to communicate using body language.

Although the motor cortex is in both hemispheres, the ability to make judgments based on the relationship of our bodies to space (needed in sports, creative movement, and dance, for instance) is basically centered in the right hemisphere.

The ability to recognize, draw, and deal with shapes and patterns, as well as geometric figures, lies in the right hemisphere. This involves the ability to distinguish between different colors and hues and the ability to visualize in color.

Singing and music are right-hemisphere activities. Creative art is also in debt to the right hemisphere. While many children who are left-brained are quite good in art, the "art" they make is structured; it must come out a certain way. They are most comfortable with models and a predictable outcome. Their pictures, or the things they create, are drawings made for Mother's Day or turkeys drawn for Thanksgiving. Children who are left-hemisphere dominant are good at other-directed art.

(Continues)

THINK ABOUT IT... (Continued)

Children who are right-hemisphere dominant create "mystery" pictures. They show the pictures to you, but they aren't quite sure what you are looking at until they start talking about it. For example, they may show raindrops falling and the sun shining at the same time.

After listening to a story, when you ask children who are right-brained what they heard, they can retell the story in their own words without any difficulty. However, they are so creative that they usually add their own details and ending. You think they are exaggerating, and they may be in adult terms. But in their terms, they are simply being what they are. They change stories, add details, and alter endings to meet their emotional needs. Feelings and emotions appear to be most dominant in the right hemisphere.

A further way to understand the child who is right-brained is by the behavioral characteristics associated with this group of children. Although not all children who are right-brained will display all of these characteristics, you will find many of these children easily recognizable. The following is just a sampling of right-brained behavioral characteristics:

- Appear to daydream
- Talk in phrases or leave words out when talking
- Have difficulty following directions
- Make faces or use other forms of nonverbal communication
- Display greater-than-average fine-motor problems (cutting, pasting, and so on) when asked to conform or do structured tasks; fine-motor problems rarely appear when children are doing something they have selected
- Are able to recall places and events but have difficulty recalling symbolic representations such as names, letters, and numbers
- Are on the move most of the time
- Like to work partway out of their chairs or standing up
- Like to take things apart and put them back together again
- Are much messier than other children
- Like to touch, trip, and poke other children
- Display impulsive behavior
- Get lost coming and going, even from familiar places such as the classroom
- May forget what they started out to do
- Will give the right answer to a question but can't tell you where it came from
- Often give responses unrelated to what is being discussed
- May be leaders in the group
- May chew their tongues while working

Now, armed with all of this information on children who are right- or left-brained, you need to reflect on your own work with children and ask yourself if your curriculum is directed toward only one type of learner. Are you in tune with the right-brained learners? You may find it helpful to go to the library and take out books with specific curricular ideas for children who are right-brained. At the very least, you need to be aware of yet another way in which each young child is uniquely different (Vitale, 1982).

the eventual realization that specific keys have specific uses. This process of *exploring* the computer to discover what it can do may take several months, depending on the frequency of the child's exposure to the computer. When the child has gained an understanding of what the computer can do, she may move on to another question: "What can *I* do with the computer?" Equipped with the skills gained through exploration (using a mouse, for example), the child truly begins to *play* with the computer.

Here again, it is important for the child to have basic knowledge of what a computer can do and the skills to operate it. But young children also need to explore the computer before any more formal experiences take place. Then, after they have acquired knowledge and skills, they can use the computer creatively.

As children explore and play with materials in the environment, they are also in a sense "shaping the brain" (Goleman, 1995). Researchers on the human brain make the point that "experience, particularly in childhood, sculpts the brain" (Goleman, 1995, p. 224). Therefore, the opportunities to learn actively in an environment provided throughout life and particularly in the early years help to create us as unique individuals. Another researcher put it this way: "Challenge and interaction (in the environment) are essential" (Abbott, 1997, p. 8). Passive observation in the early childhood program is never enough. As the ancient Chinese proverb states, "Tell me and I forget. Show me and I remember. Let me do and I understand." Thus, the role of exploration and play is central to the development of creativity—at all ages.

MODIFYING CURRICULUM TO PROMOTE CREATIVITY

Curriculum may be viewed as an outline of knowledge and skills to be learned, rather than a recipe for how they must be taught. The term "learn" implies that exploration and play are part of the process; the term "recipe" denotes a careful following of steps in a specific order and amount to come up with one precise product. As we know, young children are not all the same, so differing amounts and various combinations of ingredients are necessary for each child. Each child learns the same knowledge and skills in a unique way; therefore the recipe is continually modified. Keep in mind that developmental needs serve as a guide to the sequence in which all concepts are introduced.

When modifying curriculum to encourage creative thinking, consider the following points:

- The curriculum must be developmentally appropriate for young children. This means it will allow children to be both physically and mentally active, engaging them in active rather than passive activities.

- Be alert and aware of the children's interests. Choose materials and activities that are meaningful and relevant to the children in your group. Children, like you, are drawn to materials and activities that interest them. Be sure to involve the children in choosing materials and activities for the curriculum.

Figure 2-3
The child sets the pace in creative activities.

- Provide a variety of materials that encourage children's creative exploration. Allow the children ample time to not only physically explore but time to think about and mentally explore what they are doing.

- In planning curriculum, consider all the types of learning styles and multiple intelligences (ways of learning) of the children in your group. (More information on learning styles and multiple intelligences is found in Chapter 5.) Plan activities that meet the needs of these differences.

- Encourage children's divergent thinking and curiosity. Let them ask questions and search for solutions to their problems. The teacher ought to be only one of many members in a class who expresses their curiosity through questioning.

- With older children, encourage their curiosity by giving credit in the grading system for questioning.

Figure 2-4

With open-ended materials, children know how to create their own fun.

In this strategy, students are rewarded for curiosity in very real terms.

⊙ Be sure to provide opportunities for children to interact and communicate with other children and adults in an atmosphere of acceptance.

Integrated Curriculum and Creativity

The curriculum that encourages creativity the most in young children is an integrated, whole curriculum. In an **integrated curriculum** the artificial divisions among content areas are reduced. Although many teachers find it convenient to *think about* what the child will learn as separate categories of information, the curriculum is not designed in that way.

Most often an integrated curriculum is designed around a unit of study, centered around a specific theme or project. The unit of study contains a coordinated series of learning activities planned around a broad topic that will involve the whole group. A unit in an integrated curriculum will involve all of the content areas (reading, math, art, music, social studies, etc.) Integrated curriculum units provide the topics and framework for planning activities for children. The length of time for the unit may vary, taking weeks or months. The amount of time depends on the topic and the interests of the children.

In an integrated curriculum, children are able to experience learning as a whole. For example, they can explore the idea of neighborhood and community by reading books, hearing stories, drawing and painting a community mural, and planning and preparing foods from their neighborhood and community. In this broad approach to learning, they are able to express themselves creatively in many areas and not just in the area of the arts.

CREATIVE EARLY CHILDHOOD CURRICULUM AND DIFFERENTIATED INSTRUCTION

A term associated with effective curriculum for learners is **differentiated instruction.** Differentiated instruction is a way of thinking about teaching and learning. It is a philosophy. As such, it is based on a set of beliefs that relate to encouraging creativity in your children. The beliefs of differentiated instruction are as follows:

⊙ Children who are the same age are different in their readiness to learn, their interests, their styles of learning, their experiences, and their life circumstances.

⊙ These differences in children affect what they need to learn, the pace at which they need to learn it, and the support they need from teachers and others to learn it well.

⊙ Children will learn best when they can make a connection between the curriculum and their interests and life experiences.

⊙ Children will learn best when learning opportunities are natural.

⊙ Children are more effective learners when classrooms and schools create a sense of community in which children feel significant and respected.

⊙ The central job of teachers and schools is to maximize the capacity of each student (Tomlinson, 2000).

Differentiated instruction is a refinement of, not a substitute for, high-quality early childhood curriculum

THIS ONE'S for YOU!

Are You Challenging— Yourself, Not the Children?

Challenges are not just for the children. We can also challenge ourselves. One way to do this is to reflect on the ways you are providing challenges in your program. Ask yourself:

⊙ Do I take time to observe children in action before stepping in to "teach"?

⊙ Do I provide opportunities for children to use new understandings and skills in many different situations before moving to the next skill?

⊙ Do I provide open-ended activities for children each day?

⊙ Do I add or modify the materials in the centers as I perceive children are ready for change?

⊙ Do I feel comfortable being challenged myself? How can I challenge myself to grow as a learner and teacher?

Printed with permission: Church, E. B. (March 2002). "When to Challenge Children," *Scholastic Early Childhood Today,* pg. 34.

and instruction. Differentiated instruction is present in the early childhood classroom when the curriculum and instruction fit each child and the children have choices about what to learn and how. Also, children taking part in setting learning goals is further evidence of differentiated instruction. Finally, in the early childhood classroom, with differentiated instruction, the curriculum connects with the experiences and interests of individual children.

Differentiated instruction is not a new phenomenon in early childhood education. The one-room schoolhouses of the past offered teachers the challenge of finding ways to work with students with wide-ranging needs. The contemporary approach to differentiating has been shaped by the growing research on learning—drawing from the best practices in special education, gifted education, and multi-age classrooms; recent research on the brain and multiple intelligences; and developments in authentic assessment.

In summary, the aim of differentiating instruction is to maximize each child's growth by meeting each child where he or she is and helping the child to progress from there. In practice, it involves offering several different learning experiences in response to children's varied needs. More specific information on activities for different learning styles and multiple intelligences is presented in Chapter 5.

PROMOTING CREATIVITY THROUGH POSITIVE ACCEPTANCE

Adults who work with young children are in an especially crucial position to foster each child's creativity. In the day-to-day experiences in early childhood

settings, as young children actively explore their world, adults' attitudes clearly transmit their feelings to the child. A child who meets with unquestionable acceptance of her unique approach to the world will feel safe in expressing her creativity, whatever the activity or situation.

The following are guidelines on how to help transmit this positive acceptance to children, which in turn fosters creativity in any situation.

⊙ Openly demonstrate to young children that there is value in their curiosity, exploration, and original behavior.

⊙ Allow the children to go at their own pace when they are doing an activity that excites and interests them.

⊙ Let children stay with what they are making until they feel it's done.

⊙ Let children figure out their own ways of doing things if they prefer to do so.

⊙ Keep the atmosphere relaxed.

⊙ Encourage guessing, especially when the answers make good sense.

Working with Older Children

In the upper elementary grades, teachers have an even greater challenge to promote creativity because the curriculum often dominates the program. There are often state level guidelines for what to teach, at what level, with specific books and materials. Even in this situation, you can encourage creativity in your classroom. Here are some suggestions to help you get started.

To encourage creativity with older children:

◉ Use tangible rewards (stickers, prizes) as seldom as possible; instead, encourage children's own pride in the work they have done.

◉ Avoid setting up competitive situations for children.

◉ Downplay your evaluation of children's work; instead, lead them to become more proficient at recognizing their own strengths and weaknesses.

◉ Encourage children to monitor their own work, rather than to rely on your surveillance of them.

◉ Whenever possible, give children choices about what activities they do and about how to do those activities.

◉ Make intrinsic (internal) motivation a conscious factor of your discussions with children. Encourage them to become aware of their own special

interests and to take their focus *off* the extrinsic (external rewards).

◉ To build children's intrinsic (internal) motivation, help them build their self-esteem and help them focus on and appreciate their own unique talents and strengths.

◉ As much as possible, encourage children to become active, independent learners rather than to rely on you for constant direction. Encourage them to take confident control of their own learning process.

◉ Give children ample opportunities for free play with various materials, and allow them to engage in fantasy whenever possible.

◉ In any way you can, show children that you value creativity—that not only do you allow it, but you also engage in it yourself.

◉ Whenever you can, show your students that *you* are an intrinsically motivated adult who enjoys thinking creatively.

Just the way a question is phrased or asked sets the stage for creative replies. For example, the request, "Describe (or tell me about) the sky . . ." would certainly get different answers than "What color is the sky?" In the first, more open-ended (divergent) request, children are encouraged to share their personal feelings and experiences about the sky. This might be color or cloud shapes or even how jets, birds, and helicopters can fill it at times. The second question is phrased in such a way that a one-word (convergent) reply would do. Or even worse, it may seem to children that there is one and only one *correct* answer!

In asking questions, then, a teacher can foster children's creativity. Let us now consider more specific examples of activities that focus on creative questioning.

CREATIVE QUESTIONING FOR CHILDREN

The activities that follow suggest various ways of asking questions and are designed to draw out the creative potential in young children. Activities that deal directly with specific art forms and media are found in later sections of this book.

1. Making Things Better with Your Imagination.
One way to help children think more creatively is to get them to "make things better with their imagination." Ask children to change things to make them the way they would like them to be. Here are some examples of questions of this type.

◉ What would taste better if it were sweeter?

◉ What would be nicer if it were smaller?

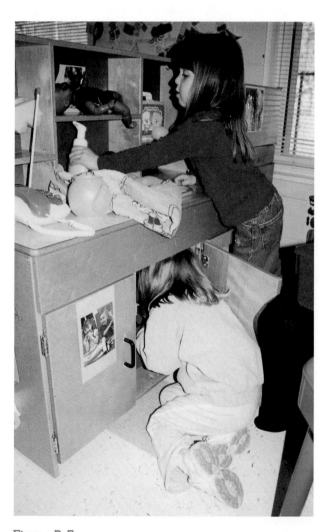

Figure 2-5

Young children actively explore their world in day-to-day experiences in early childhood settings.

⊙ What would be more fun if it were faster?

⊙ What would be better if it were quieter?

⊙ What would be more exciting if it went backwards?

⊙ What would be happier if it were bigger?

2. Using Other Senses. Young children can stretch their creative talents by using their senses in unusual ways. For example, children may be asked to close their eyes and guess what has been placed in their hands. (Use a piece of foam rubber, a small rock, a grape, a piece of sandpaper, etc.) Another approach is to have the children close their eyes and guess what they hear. (Use sounds like shuffling cards, jingling coins, rubbing sandpaper, or ripping paper.)

When doing this exercise, the children should be asked for reasons for their guesses. It makes it more fun and a better learning experience for the children.

3. Divergent-Thinking Questions. Any time you ask children a question requiring a variety of answers, you are encouraging their creative thinking skills. Here are some examples using the concept of water.

⊙ How can you use water?

⊙ What floats in water?

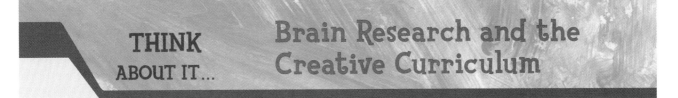

THINK ABOUT IT... Brain Research and the Creative Curriculum

Dan Goleman (1995) explained in his book *Emotional Intelligence* that people have two minds—a thinking mind and a feeling mind. These two minds work together, and sometimes against one another, in determining how we learn and how creative we become. Based on his research, he explains that the **emotional brain** is the first to receive input, and therefore is able to react first, before the **thinking brain.** This means that while we are still thinking about the logical response we should make, our emotional brain is already providing an emotional response. For example, your teacher announces a pop quiz. Your first response is emotional . . . "Oh, no, I'm not prepared." Or it may be, "Great, I can 'ace' it!" The logical response follows as your mind quickly goes over the information you think will be on the quiz.

Emotion, then, plays an important role in how we learn. Goleman indicated that students are more likely to recall and use information when it has an emotional context (i.e., when feelings are involved). In other words, our brains are better able to remember a concept if the concept is learned in an emotional setting. This means that teachers of art (or any subject) should liven up their classrooms by making lessons engaging and exciting; the classroom should be a stimulating place to be. For example, classroom simulations and role-playing activities enhance learning (and creativity) because they tie curricular memories to the kinds of real-life emotional contexts in which they will later be used.

According to researchers of the human brain, to best optimize brain growth, teachers need to plan activities that involve as many senses as possible. When objects and events are recognized by several senses (e.g., seeing, hearing, touching, tasting) they are stored in several inter-related memory networks (Sylwester, 1995). This same researcher goes on to state, "Such emotional, multi-sensory school activities as games, role-playing, simulations and arts experiences can create powerful memories" (Sylwester, p. 97). Thus, although it may be impossible to use all the senses in each area of teaching, the more senses incorporated into each lesson, the more likely it is that the concept will be remembered and later retrieved.

Finally, recent brain research supports the importance of self-direction in learning (Sylwester). From the research it is apparent that it isn't enough for students to be in a stimulating environment—they need to help create it and directly interact with it. They need to have many opportunities to tell *their* stories, not just listen to the teacher's stories. Formal schooling, thus, must start a process through which students are progressively weaned from their dependence on teachers and institutions and grow the confidence to manage their own learning.

Therefore, it should be your goal as an early childhood teacher to facilitate the growth of children to become their own teachers. When a student takes ownership by directing his or her learning in terms of what is personally meaningful, it is much more likely the student will be able to store the concept in memory and then retrieve the concept for later use.

- ⊙ How does water help us?
- ⊙ Why is cold water cold? Why is hot water hot?
- ⊙ What are the different colors that water can be? Why?
- ⊙ What makes water rain? What makes it stop?
- ⊙ What always stays underwater?

Divergent thinking questions using concepts such as sand, ice, smoke, cars, and similar topics are fun for children. They also encourage openness and flexibility of thinking.

4. What-Would-Happen-If Technique. The "What-would-happen-if?" technique has been used success-fully by many teachers of young children to spark good thinking-and-doing sessions designed to ignite imaginations. Some of the following questions may be used.

- ⊙ What would happen if all the trees in the world were blue?
- ⊙ What would happen if everyone looked alike?
- ⊙ What would happen if all the cars were gone?
- ⊙ What would happen if everybody wore the same clothes?
- ⊙ What would happen if every vegetable tasted like chocolate?
- ⊙ What would happen if there were no more clocks or watches?
- ⊙ What would happen if you could fly?

5. In How Many Different Ways. Another type of question that extends a child's creative thinking is one that begins, "In how many different ways . . . ?" A few examples are given to add to one's own ideas.

- ⊙ In how many different ways could a spoon be used?
- ⊙ In how many different ways could a button be used?
- ⊙ In how many different ways could a string be used?
- ⊙ In what *new* ways could we use this? How could it be modified to fit a new use?

All of these questioning strategies are intended to help an adult encourage creativity in young children. Children may also generate these types of questions once they have been modeled for them. Often, the use of these strategies is enough to begin a long-running and positive creative experience for the child as well as the teacher. They are limited only by the user's imagination.

MOTIVATING SKILLS FOR TEACHERS

Some children need help in getting started. The fact that the activity is labeled "creative" does not necessarily make the child "ready to go." A child may be feeling restless or tired or may feel like doing something else. All teachers, even those with good ideas, face this problem. There are several ways to help children become motivated for the creative process.

Physical needs. Make sure children are rested and physically fit. Sleepy, hungry, or sick children cannot care about creativity. Their physical needs must be met before such learning can be appealing.

Figure 2-6

Young children are happiest when they can be their creative selves.

Interests. Try to find out, and then use, what naturally interests the child. Children not only want to do things they like to do, they want to be successful at them. Whenever children feel that they will succeed in a task, they are generally much more willing to get involved. Parents may be good resources for determining the child's interests.

Friends. Permit children to work with their friends. This does not mean all the time. However, some teachers avoid putting children who are friends together in working situations. They worry that these children will only "fool around" or disturb others. When this does happen, one should question the task at hand because it is obviously not keeping the children's interest.

Activities for fun. Allow the activity to be fun for the child. Notice the use of the word "allow." Children know how to have their own fun. They do not need anyone to make it for them. Encourage child-initiated activities and self-selection of creative materials, and emphasize voluntary participation of the children in the activities presented. Teachers are giving children opportunities for fun if they honestly can answer "yes" to these questions:

- Is the activity exciting?
- Is the activity in a free setting?
- Can the children imagine in it?
- Can the children play at it?
- Is there a gamelike quality to it?
- Are judgments avoided?
- Is competition deemphasized?
- Will there be something to laugh about?

Goals. Permit children to set and reach goals. Most of the excitement in achieving a goal is in reaching for it. Children should be given opportunities to plan projects. They should be allowed to get involved in activities that have something at the end for which they can strive. If the completion of an activity is not rewarding to a child, then the value of that activity is questionable.

Variety. Vary the content and style of what the children can do. It is wise to consider not only what will be next, but how it will be done, too. For example, the teacher has the children sit and watch a movie, then they sit and draw, and then they sit and listen to a story. These are three different activities, but in each of them, the children are sitting. The content of the activity has changed, but not the style. This can, and does, become boring. Boring is definitely *not* creative.

Habit is one of the worst enemies of creativity. Teachers who set the standard for valuing creativity by taking a chance on a "crazy" idea may positively influence the expression of creative potential by many children.

Challenge. Challenge the children. This means letting them know that what they are about to do is something that will be exciting to try. An example of this is letting the children know that their next activity may be tricky, adventurous, or mysterious. It is the "bet you can't do this" approach with the odds in favor of the children.

Reinforcement. Reinforce the children. The basic need here is for something to come at the end of the activity that lets the children feel they would like to do it again. It could be the teacher's smile, a compliment, reaching the goal, hanging up the creation, sharing with a friend, or just finishing the activity. The main thing is that the children feel rewarded for and satisfied with their efforts.

Figure 2-7

Make sure children are rested, because sleepy children do not care about creativity.

The children's feelings. Try to make certain the children feel good about what they are doing. Some teachers feel if a child is working intensely or learning, that is enough. This may not be so. The most important thing is not what the children are doing but how they feel about what they are doing. If children feel bad about themselves or an activity while doing it, this is a warning. The teacher must be continually in touch with how the children are feeling. It is done by listening, watching, and being with the children in a manner that is open and caring.

SUMMARY

Creativity is fun. Incorporating creativity into all areas of the curriculum contributes to a young child's positive attitude toward learning. Teachers who encourage children to work at their own pace and to be self-directed in a relaxed, nonjudgmental atmosphere are fostering creative development.

Young children need knowledge and skills to express their creative potential. The curriculum is the guide by which early childhood teachers determine *what* will be presented to the children. Creativity is fostered according to *how* the curriculum is presented to the child. Differentiated instruction is a way of thinking about teaching and learning. Its aim is to maximize each child's growth by meeting each child where he or she is at and helping the child to progress.

Questioning strategies encourage creativity in young children. Even with creative activities, there may be motivational difficulties with some children. Appealing to natural interests, giving expectancies of success, reinforcing, and challenging are a few of the many ways to help children get started and keep going.

The learning environment needs to be a welcoming place. It must encourage exploration by its lack of strict time limits and stressful situations. It must be an environment that encourages children's self-expression and sharing of ideas.

KEY TERMS

differentiated instruction	left-brained
emotional brain	right-brained
holistically	tableaus
integrated curriculum	thinking brain

LEARNING ACTIVITIES

⊙ Examine today's newspaper. What evidence of creative thought do you see in the stories or advertisements? Look for original ideas that are appropriate to the situation. Are all creative ideas socially appropriate?

⊙ Think about the influence of culture on your conception of creativity. Do you consider some forms of expression or activity more creative than others? Why? What forms of creative expression are most valued by the cultures of students in your group? Are they the same as those you value?

⊙ Undertake a creative project of your own. This is one of the most interesting and effective ways to explore creativity. Identify a problem and invent something to address it. For example, an invention could include an enormous version of a dentist's mirror that allows the user to check leaves in the gutters without climbing a ladder, or a device that signals forgetful teenagers to retrieve their wet laundry. Look around for everyday annoyances or dilemmas that you might solve. What things around

you might be improved, simplified, or elaborated? Alternatively, you might want to undertake a creative writing project, artistic endeavor, or other creative task. Whatever you choose, record your thoughts, feelings, and activities. How do you feel about creativity as you contemplate such a project?

⊙ Make creative getting-to-know-you's. Assemble these materials: small paper plates or cocktail napkins, lemon slices or wedges, grapes, pretzel sticks, assorted small candy, raisins, peanut butter, banana slices, chocolate chips, small marshmallows, cereals of different shapes, string licorice (cut in short pieces), and any other small food items.

Instructions: You will have seven minutes to create a representation of the multiple "flavors" of your personality/self on your paper plate/napkin. You may use up to seven items to tell about various aspects of yourself. Be as creative as possible. Humor is a bonus, but be sure to be accurate in telling about yourself! At the end of the seven minutes, all the "selves" will be displayed and explained to the rest of your group. After all the explanations, if you have been creative enough, you will be allowed to eat your flavorful "self portrait!" (This activity could also be done on top of large sugar cookies.)

⊙ Sketch your ideas for illustrating this quote by Alice Walker: "In search of my mother's garden, I found my own."

⊙ With this quote in mind—"A house is a machine for living in" (LeCorbusier)—visually describe the kind of house you see yourself living in as an adult.

⊙ List three personal experiences that were challenging to you. Consider each and get in touch with the feelings experienced on those occasions.

1. Was there any chance of failure during these experiences?
2. What was the motivation?
3. How did it feel to succeed?
4. What does this mean for working with young children?
5. How does it relate to creativity?
6. List some of your reactions.

⊙ "Become" one of the following objects and dramatize its characteristics in class:

Bicycle   Wheelbarrow
Rake   Tire pump
Hose   Beach ball

Describe how you felt. Would children's dramatizations of these be similar? Different? Explain.

⊙ Tape 10–15 minutes of classroom interactions in which you play an instructional role. Analyze your interaction in terms of the kinds of questions you used, the amount of time you waited for children to respond after asking a question, and the way you responded to children's talk.

⊙ Observe a classroom and note the creative experiences available to children. To what extent do the experiences offered seem to contribute to the development of creativity? Describe your impressions and suggestions for improvement for the curriculum in creative expression.

⊙ Observe a teacher and describe the kinds of questions used, the amount of time allowed for children to answer, and the kinds of responses the teacher makes to the children. Do you think the communication you observed is effective in encouraging divergent thinking? Why or why not?

ACTIVITIES FOR CHILDREN

WATER PLAY ACTIVITIES FOR CREATIVE THINKING

Water play lends itself to the development of creative thinking in young children. A creative teacher can extend the play of young children by asking thought-provoking, divergent-thinking questions, posing simple problems to solve with water and play objects. Some of these divergent-thinking questions are as follows:

⊙ Can you make the water in your squeeze bottle shoot out like the water from the hose?

⊙ Can you make a water shower for the plants?

⊙ Can you catch one drop of water on something? How many drops of water can you put on a jar lid?

⊙ Can we think of some words to talk about what we do with water? (sprinkle, pour, drip, trickle, drizzle, shower, deluge, torrent, splash, spank, stir, ripple, etc.)

⊙ Could we collect some rainwater? How?

⊙ How far can you make the water spray?

⊙ Can you make something look different by putting it in water?

⊙ Can you find some things that float (or sink) in the water?

⊙ Can you make a noise in the water?

SPACE EXPLORERS

When the children need a "stretch," try one of these for fun.

⊙ Have the children pretend they are on a planet in space where they are much *heavier* than on earth. They lift their arms as though their bodies were twice as heavy as they are.

⊙ Have the children pretend they are on the moon, where their bodies are much *lighter* than on earth. They move body parts as though they were very light and walk as though their bodies were very light.

⊙ Have the children select a familiar activity such as dancing, moving to rhythms, etc., and do it on the strange planet, using slow motion because of increased weight.

BALLOON MOVES

Caution: Never use balloons with children younger than three years old.

Blow up a balloon for each child. If possible, use extra-thick balloons and blow them up only part of the way. Have extras on hand in case some balloons burst. Tie one end of a 3-foot piece of string or ribbon to each child's balloon. You can tie the other end of the string/ribbon to the child's waist, if the child wishes to do so.

Go outdoors with the children. Talk about the wind, how it makes the balloon move in different ways. Encourage the children to use their bodies to hit the balloon and make it move. Model new movements and make fun suggestions to extend children's movement exploration.

Indoors, allow the children to move in creative ways with the balloon. For older children, have the children work in pairs or in small groups to keep a balloon in the air on a calm day. See if children in the group can use movement different from their classmates to keep the balloon in motion.

MORE BALLOON MOVES

Go outdoors and have children pretend to be carrying a balloon. When you say, "Go!" children can pretend to let their balloons float off into the sky. Then ask the children to move as if they were these imaginary balloons, floating through space.

BOOKS ABOUT BALLOONS

Read one of the following books about balloons as a follow-up to the Balloon Moves activity:

Mansfield, F. (1986). *Air is all around you*. New York: HarperTrophy.

Dorros, A. (1990). *Feel the wind*. Reading, MA: Scott Foresman.

Curtis, J. L. (2000). *Where do balloons go? An uplifting mystery*. New York: HarperCollins.

FEEL CREATIVE WITH FEELY BAGS*

Turn the all-time favorite mystery game, the Feely Box (or Bag), into an activity to encourage creative thinking, as well as perception, analysis, and prediction.

*The Feely Bags activities are printed with permission from *Scholastic Early Childhood Today*. Church, E. B. "Feely Bag Games for Problem Solving," March, 2003, pp. 42–43.

It's easy to get started. Just put an item (more than one, if you want) in a bag and invite children to guess what it is. They can use tactile (touch), visual, or auditory clues or all of the above. Ask open-ended questions to spark children's thinking (e.g., What does this remind you of? How many ways can you describe it or use it?). Write down their ideas. This will help them make a connection between the spoken and the written word.

Begin with a Great Bag. Start with a colorful pillowcase or bag. Encourage multi-sensory learning by using bags with varying textures. (A burlap bag will feel very different from a satin pillowcase and will invite children to use different vocabulary in the game.) Consider an attractive gift box for larger items.

Children may like to help you decorate a special Feely Box to use for a new twist on Show & Tell, in which they hide their Show & Tell object in the box/bag and ask their classmates to guess what it is! Children love giving clues for others. Tactile, auditory, and/or verbal clues (their choice) can be used to solve the mystery.

Mix in Great Stuff! This is the fun part because the game changes when you change what's in the bag. Now is the time to think "out of the box" (or the bag) by presenting children with challenging objects and ideas. Look for objects that have an unusual shape or that children may not have seen before. Invite children to feel the objects and try to guess what they are. Then reveal the secret items and ask children to suggest many different ways to use them.

Shift the nature of the game from visual/tactile to auditory by adding objects that make a sound. Ask: What might make this sound? How many different things can we think of that make a similar sound? Write children's answers and predictions on chart paper, then pull out the item.

SCARVES

Have scarves available for children to use, letting the scarf be anything they want as they move with it in response to music. Use a record or tape of instrumental music, or put on the radio. Children may move to the music, explaining, if they like, what they are doing.

BECOMING AN OBJECT

The teacher names inanimate objects. Children show with their bodies the shapes of the various objects. If the object is moved by an external force, they show with their bodies how the object would move. For instance, they may move like:

- An orange being peeled.
- A standing lamp being carried across the room.
- A wall with a vine growing over it.
- A paper clip being inserted on paper.
- An ice cube melting.
- A balloon with air coming out of it.

- A cloud drifting through the sky, slowly changing shapes.
- Smoke coming out of a chimney.
- A twisted pin being thrust into paper.
- A rubber ball bouncing along the ground.
- A boat being tossed by the waves.
- An arrow being shot through the air.
- A steel bar being hammered into different shapes.

ACTIVITIES FOR OLDER CHILDREN (GRADES 4-5)

TELLING TABLEAUS

Tableaus are "frozen pictures" in which groups of students freeze or pose to act out a scene, a saying, a book title, etc. Before starting tableaus, discuss the skills necessary to be a good "freezer" (i.e., eyes staring blankly, no movement, frozen expression, etc.). Have students work in groups and give each group a caption (or better yet, have the students choose their own). Give students five to ten minutes (more, if needed) to develop their scene and practice their frozen poses. Don't allow any props.

To begin the performances, have the first group come to the front of the room. Turn off the lights and have the other students close their eyes as the first group sets up their scene. When the scene is set, turn on the lights and have the students open their eyes. Then you read the caption or have the class guess the title, whichever you feel is appropriate. Continue through the tableau scenes until all groups have had a chance to perform.

TELEVISION DRAMA

Pre-record a part of a television show that will interest your students. Students will be able to tell you which are their favorite shows if you aren't sure. Show students a couple of minutes of the tape and then turn it off. Discuss the creativity the characters are using. Show more of the program and stop it at a critical point in the story. Have students work in pairs to brainstorm decisions the characters could make. Then turn the show back on to see what decision the character actually made and what happened as a result of that decision. Have your students identify if the characters came up with creative decisions and why or why not.

FAIRY TALES–NOT JUST FANCY

Fairy tales are naturally creative and full of fantasy. Use fairy tales for these activities for older children's creative exercises.

Creative fairy tale puppet show. Create a puppet show to retell your favorite fairy tale to the class. Change one thing about the story and see if the class can guess the change.

Fairy tale rating. Read four fairy tales of your choice. Rate them in order of your most to least favorite and explain why you rated them as you did. Using your favorite fairy tale, write a short review explaining why everyone should read it.

Fairy tale journal. Pretend you have been put into one of the fairy tales, and in journal form discuss the events and characters you meet. Discuss what you like and dislike about the characters. Include at least eight entries.

Fairy tale logic. Choose a song that you think tells a story similar to one of the fairy tales you've read, and then write a short essay explaining why you chose this song and why it relates to your fairy tale.

Fairy tale music. Compose a song that tells the story of one of the fairy tales. Perform it for a group of students, and have them guess which fairy tale your song represents.

Fairy tale picture book. Create a picture book for your favorite fairy tale. Read it to another class.

Fairy tale day. Plan a Fairy Tale Day for the class, including activities for the entire day. This may include dressing up as your favorite character, eating fairy tale foods, playing games, and reading fairy tales.

Fairy tale rewrite. Rewrite a fairy tale from the perspective of one of the minor characters in the story. Read your story to the class.

Fairy tale game. Create a board game with a fairy tale theme. Include all of the main parts of the story in the game. Let students play the game and give you feedback. Make any changes that would make it more fun to play.

FIVE WHOLE MINUTES–A BRAINSTORMING IDEA

Brainstorm a list of different things the children think they can do in five minutes. Put the list aside. Have the children do various things in five-minute intervals (e.g., read, exercise, color, do math, walk, sit perfectly still, etc). Discuss their reactions. Talk about time management and how five minutes can be used most effectively.

CHAPTER REVIEW

1. Describe the relationship between creativity and the curriculum.
2. Describe the role of play and exploration in promoting creativity.
3. Demonstrate four questioning strategies that encourage creative thinking in the young child.
4. List three questions to consider when modifying curricula to encourage creative thinking.
5. Describe at least four characteristics of differentiated instruction.

REFERENCES

Abbott, C. (1997, March). To be intelligent. *Educational Leadership*, 6–10.

Amabile, T. (1983). *The social psychology of creativity*. New York: Springer-Verlag.

Barron, F. (1988). Putting creativity to work. In R. J. Sternberg (Ed.), *The nature of creativity*. New York: Cambridge University Press.

Bredekamp, S. (Ed.). (1997). *Developmentally appropriate practice in early childhood programs serving birth through age 8* (Rev. ed.). Washington, DC: National Association for the Education of Young Children (NAEYC).

Church, E. B. (2002, March). When to challenge children. *Scholastic Early Childhood Today, 34*.

Curtis, J. L. (2000). *Where do balloons go? An uplifting mystery*. New York: HarperCollins.

Dorros, A. (1990). *Feel the wind*. Reading, MA: Scott Foresman.

Goleman, D. (1995). *Emotional intelligence*. New York: Bantam Books.

Katz, L., & Chard, S. (1989). *Engaging children's minds: The project approach*. New York: Ablex.

Mansfield, F. (1986). *Air is all around you*. New York: HarperTrophy.

Moran, J. D., III, Milgram, R., Sawyers, J. K., & Fu, V. R. (1985). Original thinking in preschool children. *Child Development, 54,* 921–26.

Sylwester, R. (1995). *A celebration of neurons: An educator's guide to the human brain*. Alexandria, VA: Association for Supervision and Curriculum Development.

Tegano, D., Sawyers, J. K., & Moran, J. D. III. (1989). Play and problem-solving: A new look at the teacher's role. *Childhood Education, 66,* 92–97.

Tegano, D. W., & Burdette, M. (1991). Length of activity period and play behaviors of preschool children. *Journal of Research in Childhood Education, 5*(2), 34–38.

Tegano, E., May, G., Lookabaugh, S., & Burdette, M. (1991). Quality of teacher interactions in relation to creativity. Unpublished data.

Tomlinson, C. A. (1999). *The differentiated classroom: Responding to the needs of all learners*. Alexandria, VA: ASCD.

Tomlinson, C. A. (2000, September). Reconcilable differences: Standards-based teaching and differentiation. Educational Leadership, 57(8), 7–11.

Torrance, E. P. (1962). *Guiding creative talent*. Englewood Cliffs, NJ: Prentice-Hall.

Vitale, B. (1982). *Unicorns are real*. New York: Ablex.

Wallach, M., & Kogan, N. (1965). *Modes of thinking in young children: A study of creativity-intelligence distinction*. New York: Holt, Rinehart, & Winston.

ADDITIONAL READINGS

Armstrong, T. (1998). *Awakening genius in the class-room*. Alexandria, VA: Association for Supervision and Curriculum Development.

Dobbs, S. (1998). *Learning in and through art: A guide to discipline-based art education*. Los Angeles: The Getty Education Institute for the Arts.

Eisner, E. W. (2002). *The arts and the creation of mind*. Reston, VA: National Art Education Association (NAEA).

Engel, B. S. (1999). *Considering children's art: How and why to value their works*. Washington, DC: National Association for the Education of Young Children (NAEYC).

Fineberg, J. (Ed.). (1998). *Discovering child art*. Princeton, NJ: Princeton University Press.

Jackson, P. W. (1998). *John Dewey and the lessons of art*. New Haven, CT: Yale University Press.

Jones, L. S. (1998). *Art information on the Internet*. Phoenix, AZ: Oryx.

Owocki, G. (1999). *Literacy through play*. New York: Heinemann.

Runco, M. A., & Pritzker, S. R. (Eds.). (1999). *Encyclopedia of creativity* (Vols. 1 & 2). San Diego, CA: Academic Press.

Sacca, E. J., & Zimmerman, E. (1998). *Women art educators IV: Her stories, our stories, future stories*. Reston, VA: NAEA.

Sanders, T. (1998). *Strategic thinking and the new science: Planning in the midst of chaos, complexity and changes*. New York: The Free Press.

Schiller, M. (1995). An emergent art curriculum that fosters understanding. *Young Children, 50*(3), 33–38.

Seefeldt, C. (1995). Art—A serious work. *Young Children, 50*(3), 39–45.

Smith, R. (1995). *Excellence II: The continuing quest in art education*. Reston, VA: NAEA.

Strom, R. D., & Strom, P. S. (2002). Changing the rules: Education for creative thinking. *Journal of Creative Behavior, 36*(3), 183–200.

Tyrell, J. (2001). *The power of fantasy in early learning*. New York: Routledge/Falmer.

SOFTWARE FOR CHILDREN

Barbie as Rapunzel, 2002. Ages 5–8.
Curious George Downtown Adventure, 2002. Ages 3–6.
Disney Magic Artist Cartoon Maker, 2002. Grades 1 and up.
Disney Magic Artist Deluxe, 2001. Ages 5 and up.
Dogz 4, Catz 4, 2002. Ages 3–5.
Fisher-Price Little People Discovery Airport, 2002. Ages 2–4.

Freddi Fish 5: The Case of the Creature of Coral Cove, 2002. Ages 3–8.
Jump Start Artist, 2000. Ages 5–8.
Kingdoms & Castles, 4.0, 2003. Ages 5–12.
Moop and Dreadly in the Treasure on Bing Bong Island, 2002. Ages 5–10.
Mummy Mystery, 2002. Ages 5–8.
Putt-Putt Joins the Circus, 2002. Ages 3–8.
Secret Agent Barbie, 2002. Ages 6 and up.
Zoombini's Island Odyssey, 2002. Ages 8 and up.

HELPFUL WEB SITES

http://artsedge.kennedy-center.org/
Arts Edge—Marcopolo Teaching Materials, The Kennedy Center. Standards-based curricula lessons and activities. Click on Lessons in the Teach section.

http://www.VeryBestKids.com
Source for creative activities across the curriculum. Check out Teacher's Corner for art, language arts, math, social studies, and science activities.

http://www.pbs.org
PBS's website for creative activities across the curriculum and arranged by PBS characters (Arthur, Clifford, Dragon Tales, etc.). Click on PBS TeacherSource for Pre K–12 activities.

http://www.TeachingK-8.com
Excellent source for teacher resources.

For additional creative activity resources, visit our Web site at http://www.EarlyChildEd.delmar.com.

Chapter 3

The Concept of Aesthetics

Objectives

After studying this chapter, you should be able to:

1. Define aesthetics.
2. List three things a teacher can do to help children develop their aesthetic sensitivity.
3. List five benefits of aesthetic sensitivity in children.
4. List at least three art elements to discuss with children.

The term **aesthetics** refers to an appreciation for beauty and a feeling of wonder. Aesthetic experience begins with and depends on the senses. It is seeing beauty in a sunset, hearing rhythm in a rainfall, and loving the expression on a person's face. Each person has an individual personal sense of what is or is not pleasing.

Aesthetic experiences emphasize doing things for the pure joy of it. Although there can be, there does not *have* to be any practical purpose or reason. The goal of aesthetic experiences is a full, rich life for the child. Thus, you may take a ride in a car to feel its power and enjoy the scenery rather than to visit someone or run an errand. In the same way, a child plays with blocks to feel their shapes and see them tumble rather than to build something.

Young children benefit from aesthetic experiences. Children are fascinated by beauty. They love nature and enjoy creating, looking at, and talking about art. They express their feelings and ideas through language, song, expressive movement, music, and dance far more openly than adults. They are not yet hampered by the conventional labels used by adults to separate each art expression into pigeonholes. Young children experience the arts as a whole. They are creative, inquisitive, and delighted by art.

It is interesting to note that creative adults involved in the arts are finally catching up with young children. On the contemporary arts scene, there is a movement toward **multimedia artwork.** Examples of this multimedia movement are walk-in sculpture environments; a mix of live dance and films; and a mix of art exhibitions with drama, where actors move into the audience to engage it in the drama. All of these are new ways *adults* are integrating the arts.

This exciting development may be new for sophisticated adult arts, but it is a familiar approach for young children. For instance, in early childhood programs, it is a common occurrence to find young children singing original songs while they paint or moving their bodies rhythmically while playing with clay. Young children naturally and unself-consciously integrate the

Figure 3-1
Creating an original product is an aesthetic experience.

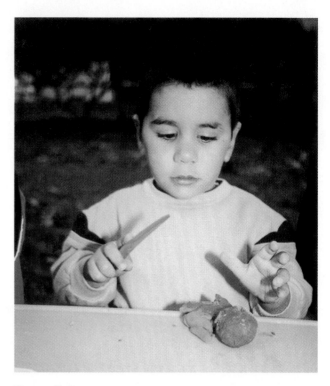

Figure 3-2
When children are given freedom to choose and evaluate, they are developing their aesthetic sense.

arts—weaving together graphic arts, movement, dance, drama, music, and poetry in their expressive activities.

The capacity for aesthetics is a fundamental human characteristic. Infants sense with their whole bodies. They are open to all feelings; experience is not separated from thinking. A child's aesthetic sense comes long before the ability to create. All of an infant's experiences have an aesthetic component—preferring a soft satin-edged blanket, studying a bright mobile, or choosing a colorful toy. These choices are all statements of personal taste. As infants grow into toddlers, the desire to learn through taste, touch, and smell as well as through sight and sound grows, too. The capacity to make aesthetic choices continues to grow through preschool. Preschoolers' ability to perceive, respond, and be sensitive becomes more obvious and more refined. They enjoy creating spontaneously with a wide variety of materials (Feeney & Moravcik, 1987).

To develop an aesthetic sense in children, one must help them continuously find beauty and wonder in their world. This is any child's potential. In fact, it is the potential of every human being. To create, invent, be joyful, sing, dance, love, and be amazed are possible for everyone.

Children sometimes see and say things to please adults; teachers must realize this and the power it

implies. Teachers who prefer that children see beauty as they themselves do are not encouraging a sense of aesthetics in children. They are fostering uniformity and obedience. Only children who choose and evaluate for themselves can truly develop their own aesthetic taste. Just as becoming literate is a basic goal of education, one of the key goals of all creative early childhood programs is to help young children develop the ability to speak freely of their own attitudes, feelings, and ideas about art. Each child has a right to a personal choice of beauty, joy, and wonder.

Children gain an aesthetic sense by doing. This means sensing, feeling, and responding to things. It can be rolling a ball, smelling a flower, petting an animal, or hearing a story. Aesthetic development takes place in secure settings free of competition and adult judgment.

AESTHETICS AND THE QUALITY OF LEARNING

Aesthetic learning means joining what one thinks with what one feels. Through art, ideas and feelings are expressed. People draw and sculpt to show their feelings about life. Art is important because it can deepen and enlarge understanding. All children cannot be great

Figure 3-3
Being outside and enjoying the beauty of nature are basic aesthetic experiences.

Figure 3-4
A happy balance must be established between structured and nonstructured activities.

artists, but children can develop an aesthetic sense, an appreciation for art.

Teachers can encourage the aesthetic sense in children in a variety of ways. For example, science activities lend themselves very well to beauty and artistic expression. Because children use their senses in learning, science exhibits with things like rocks, wood, and leaves can be placed in attractive displays for children to touch, smell, and explore with all of their senses. They can experience with their senses artistic elements such as line, shape, pattern, color, and texture in these natural objects.

Sensory awareness is nourished by teachers who help young children focus on the variations and contrasts in the environment: the feel and look of smooth bark and rippling rough bark, the heaviness of rock and the lightness of pumice stone, the feathery leaf and the leathery leaf, the slippery marble and the sticky tar. The rumble and roar of the subway train, the soft sound of leaves against a window pane, the loud clap of thunder—all these are opportunities for expression in the arts, poetry, sound, movement, and many other art forms (Lasky & Mukerji, 1980).

The arts are developed best as a whole. After hearing a story, some children may want to act it out. Some may prefer to paint a picture about it. Others may wish to create a dance about it, and some may want to make the music for the dance. These activities can lead to others. There should be a constant exchange, not only among all the art activities but among all subject areas. This prevents children from creating a false separation between work and play, art and learning, and thought and feeling.

There are three basic ways to provide young children developmentally appropriate aesthetic experiences in the early childhood program (Colbert & Taunton, 1992):

1. Provide many opportunities to create art.
2. Provide many opportunities to look at and talk about art.
3. Help children become aware of art in their everyday lives.

Of these three, the most often overlooked is the second. Many teachers mistakenly believe that if they are not artists themselves, they are not able to adequately discuss art with young children. Yet, most young children enjoy talking about art if they are given the opportunity, as evidenced in the following scenario:

A small, bright-eyed child named Risa arrived at my first preschool art class in the arms of her mother. She participated enthusiastically in the looking, talking, and making activities, and she especially liked our visits to the art museum. Risa clearly loved art, and I looked forward to our time together.

One Sunday afternoon, I was presenting an adult program in the museum. It was a tough crowd, and I sweated as I looked from one to another, waiting for someone to answer my question about a painting. Suddenly Risa appeared from nowhere, making her way to me through all those adult legs. Her mother said she heard my voice during their family outing and insisted on coming over for "class." Risa stared raptly at the artwork and then, in her baby voice, answered my question. We had a good conversation about the painting, its colors, shapes, and subject matter. Risa, at 3 years of age, was able to describe a work of art and have a conversation about it. She was also the highlight of my presentation that afternoon (Villeneuve, 2003).

The early childhood environment can be set up in such a way as to encourage this type of aesthetic discussion by implementing the following suggestions:

- In addition to the typical art center, include books about artists in the reading area (see the Web site for suggestions).
- Include "real" art books in the reading and quiet areas of the room. These do not necessarily have to be children's books; young children will enjoy looking at artwork in any book.
- Display fine-art prints on bulletin boards and walls so that children can easily see them. Be sure to change them regularly. If they are up too long, they will quickly fade into the background.
- Include art objects on the science table, where appropriate. Geodes, shards of pottery, and crystals are all good starting points.

THINK ABOUT IT...

Art Education Boosts Academic Achievement, Cuts Crime, and Reduces Taxes

Rivky's Arts Workshop, a New York–based art school, commissioned Expanding Horizons to conduct a comprehensive review of published research to assess the overall impact of art education and to determine if the socio-economic benefits of art education were further encouraged and more widely available. The main findings of the study are as follows:

- Art in school leads to higher academic achievements, better reading and writing skills, and more well-rounded individuals.
- Students who take art classes, irrespective of their socio-economic background, perform better in reading and math tests than those who do not.
- Art benefits children with learning difficulties—35% of students identified with a learning disability drop out of high school.
- Art training in the juvenile justice system encourages learning; boosts self-esteem; and helps offenders return to society, where they are less likely to re-offend.
- If art were more widely available in the juvenile justice system, it could save billions of dollars in incarceration costs and lead to a safe social environment.
- Art eases stress and boosts confidence levels.

Rivky's Arts Workshop, founded by Rivky Shimon, an internationally acclaimed artist, uses proprietary teaching techniques, which Shimon has developed over the past 15 years, that revolutionize the way art is taught. Her program has been successfully taught to thousands of students of all ages and abilities and has proved to have particular benefits for those with learning disabilities and physical handicaps (Art Education, 2003).

Figure 3-5
Children need alone time to develop their aesthetic sense.

⊙ Invite guest art educators into the classroom to show the children art objects to look at, touch, and talk about.

⊙ Give children an opportunity to choose their favorites from a selection of fine-art prints.

⊙ Display fine-art prints near the writing and art centers.

Suggestions for Aesthetic Experiences with Older Children

Children experience a developmental shift around ages 7–8 that allows them to deal with more abstract ideas (more information on this is in Chapter 10). At this point, older children not only are able to experience the arts aesthetically but are able to begin discussing their own opinions, aesthetic tastes, and experiences. Thus, the teacher can engage children in grades 4–5 in discussions about what is art and why they consider something to be art or not. The following is an example of a combination 4th–5th grade class involved in this type of aesthetics discussion:

> In their unit on art and history, prints of the work of Civil War photographer Matthew Brady were displayed and discussed. The fact was brought up by the teacher that Brady frequently repositioned and rearranged bodies of dead soldiers and other objects in composing war scenes to be photographed.

> The teacher used this fact to encourage the students' responses to her initial question: "Is there anything about Brady's practice that should disturb us?" The discussion led the students in many directions involving such issues as differences between "real" photographic art and "staged" art and which was art in the truest sense. They also questioned the worth of Brady's work in general, with students evaluating each in their own way. Some saw the work as "political" and of little artistic worth. Others saw it as an artist using his "props" just like any other artist does. One student compared it to a still life painting the class had seen earlier.

> Needless to say, this discussion led to a lot of research into Matthew Brady's life and work. But more importantly, the discussion helped the students learn how to reflect upon and present their own opinions of art and to consider the views of others.

The previous example demonstrates the type of environment for older children in which questioning is valued. In such an environment students will feel comfortable raising questions about art and their reactions to it. Teachers of older children need to encourage rather than suppress discussion of aesthetic questions as they emerge. This is done by providing them the time and environment for art-related experiences and inquiry.

BENEFITS OF AESTHETIC SENSITIVITY

An aesthetic sense does not mean "I see" or "I hear"; it means "I enjoy what I see" or "I like what I hear." It means that the child is using taste or preference. Aesthetic sensitivity is important for children because it improves the quality of learning and encourages the creative process. Aesthetic sensibility in children has many other benefits, too.

⊙ Children are more sensitive to problems because they have more insight into their world. This means they can be more helpful to other children and to adults.

⊙ Children are more likely to be self-learners because they are more sensitive to gaps in their knowledge.

⊙ Life is more exciting for children because they have the capacity to be puzzled and to be surprised.

THIS ONE'S for YOU!

Suggestions for Aesthetic Enhancement of Environments

For young children, giving special attention to the environment can help develop their aesthetic sense. Here are some suggestions on how to enhance the environment to develop children's aesthetic sense:

Color—Bright colors will dominate a room and may detract from art and natural beauty. If there is a choice, select soft, light, neutral colors for walls and ceilings. Color-coordinate learning centers so that children begin to see them as wholes rather than as parts. Avoid having many different kinds of patterns in any one place—they can be distracting and overstimulating.

Furnishings—Group similar furniture together. Keep colors natural and neutral to focus children's attention on the learning materials on the shelves. When choosing furnishings, select natural wood rather than metal or plastic. If furniture must be painted, use one neutral color for everything so that there is greater flexibility in moving it from space to space. Periodically give children brushes and warm soapy water and let them scrub the furniture.

Storage—Rotate materials on shelves rather than crowding them together. Crowded shelves look unattractive and are hard for children to maintain. Baskets make excellent, attractive storage containers. If storage tubs are used, put all of the same kind together on one shelf. If cardboard boxes are used for storage, cover them with plain-colored paper or paint them.

Decoration—Mount and display children's artwork. Provide artwork by fine artists and avoid garish, stereotyped posters. Make sure that much artwork (by both children and adult artists) is displayed at children's eye level. Use shelf tops to display sculpture; plants; and items of natural beauty like shells, stones, and fish tanks. Avoid storing teachers' materials on the tops of shelves. If there is no other choice, create a teacher "cubby" using a covered box or storage tub.

Outdoors—Design or arrange play structures as extensions of nature rather than intrusions upon it. If possible, use natural materials like wood and hemp instead of painted metal, plastic, or fiberglass. Provide adequate storage to help maintain materials. Involve children, parents, and staff in keeping outdoor areas free of litter. Add small details like a garden or a rock arrangement to show that the outdoors also deserves attention and care.

(Adapted with permission from the National Association of Young Children, S. Feeney and E. Moravcik, "A Thing of Beauty: Aesthetic Development in Young Children," in *Young Children,* Sept., 1987, 11.)

⊙ Children are more tolerant because they learn that there are many possible ways of doing things.

⊙ Children are more independent because they are more open to their own thoughts. They are good questioners for the same reason.

⊙ Children can deal better with complexity because they do not expect to find one best answer.

AESTHETIC EXPERIENCES

Aesthetic experiences for young children can take many forms. They can involve an appreciation of the beauty of nature, the rhythm and imagery of music or poetry, or the qualities of works of art. Far from being a specialized talent, the recognition of aesthetic qualities comes quite naturally to children.

Figure 3-6

Aesthetic development begins early in a child's life as he or she expresses personal preferences.

Figure 3-7

Children benefit from their aesthetic sensitivity as it generates more insight into their lives.

For instance, let us consider art appreciation. What adults have come to regard as strictly a "museum-type" experience—seeing and appreciating good artwork—is an enjoyable experience for young children whose fear of the "intellectual" is not yet developed. Art appreciation can occur in the early childhood program through the combined experiences of learning to look at and learning to create visual arts. Introducing young children to art appreciation should be a series of pleasurable experiences with time to look, enjoy, comment, and raise questions. It is a time when children learn to "see" with their minds, as well as their eyes. They begin to feel with the painter, the sculptor, or the architect and to explore their ideas and techniques.

As early childhood teachers, we don't ask ourselves whether language appreciation should be emphasized in our programs. We automatically encourage children to express themselves verbally and reflect on the words used by others. We want children to have fun with language, to appreciate its variety and its shades of meaning. Why should we not

LANGUAGE FOR TALKING ABOUT ART

The language of art is an expansion of the language of preschool. Both use terms like *color, shape, line,* and *size.* Descriptive words such as *empty* and *full* and comparison words such as *lighter* and *darker* are used by children and art critics alike. In encouraging art appreciation, teachers can help children expand the ways in which these common terms are used. Instead of focusing only on terms' *functional* aspects, such as clarifying that one wants the red cup, make observations about how features such as color evoke *aesthetic* responses: "The bright red dresses in that painting give the dancers a lively look."

Teachers can make children's art experiences meaningful through thoughtful dialogue. For example:

⊙ Use descriptive rather than judgmental terms when talking about art. Say "I see . . ." or "it makes me think of . . ." rather than "I like it" or "it's pretty."

⊙ After a small group art activity, encourage children to look at one another's work and ask them, "Why do you think they look so different from one another even though you all made them out of the same paper and markers?"

⊙ Introduce language to talk about the affect and aesthetics of the artwork. For example, "These colors look sad" or "All these little dots look busy on the page" or "This big, bright circle makes my eye keep coming back to it."

⊙ Ask children to reflect on artistic intentions and feelings. "Why do you think this artist makes little pictures but that one makes big pictures?" is a question that young children can ponder.

Connect children's natural desire to represent their experiences to comparable intentions of artists throughout the ages (Epstein, 2001).

Printed with permission by NAEYC, Epstein, A. "Language for Talking about Art: Encouraging Art Appreciation in Early Childhood Settings," *Young Children,* May 2001, pg. 40.

Figure 3-8

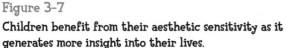

Language for talking about art.

do the same for visual imagery—that is, encourage children to go beyond art's functional aspects and find satisfaction in its aesthetic possibilities (Epstein, 2001)?

THINK ABOUT IT...   Research on Children's Aesthetic Abilities

Research in developmental psychology (summarized in Gardner, 1990) suggests that young children are more capable of art appreciation than we allow them to be. Although very young children do not naturally focus on aesthetics, they display sensitivity to the quality of artwork if engaged in meaningful conversation about it. Similarly, preschoolers can sort artwork on the basis of style rather than its content if they are encouraged and interested in doing so.

Children can also think about and reflect on the artwork they see. If adults ask young children open-ended questions rather than teaching them didactically, children can offer simple analyses of what they think the artist is trying to say or how the artwork makes them feel (Epstein, 2001).

Schiller (1995), for example, posted reproductions of fine artwork on classroom walls and made art books available to the preschoolers in her class. After giving children time to explore these materials, she engaged them in a discussion of what they saw and thought about the paintings. "The children instantly recognized that Matisse had a very different style than the realism of Michelangelo and da Vinci" (Schiller 1995, 37).

Preliminary accounts, therefore, indicate that young children can engage in art appreciation. They can regard artwork from the perspective of style and aesthetics, think about artists' intentions, and describe feelings and sensations evoked by viewing works of art (Epstein, 2001).

Early childhood teachers have a responsibility to provide the very best our culture has to offer by introducing young children to a range of good art, not merely what is easiest or most familiar.

Most children have plenty of exposure to cartoon characters; advertising art; and stereotyped, simplistic posters. These do not foster aesthetic development and are sometimes demeaning to children. Teachers often say, "children like them," but the fact that children like something—for example, candy and staying up late at night—does not necessarily mean it is good for them. Children might never have seen a Van Gogh sunflower, a mother and child by Mary Cassatt, or a sculpture by Henry Moore. Yet, young children can learn to appreciate these, as well as arts and crafts from many cultures, if introduced to them in the early years.

From such experiences, children also gradually learn the concepts of design (see Figure 3–8 on how to talk with children about this and other art elements). During group discussions, children should be encouraged to talk about the design qualities of a specific color, the movement of lines, the contrast of sizes and shapes, and the variety of textures. They should be helped to think and feel, as individuals,

about a certain art object or piece of music. Their understanding of aesthetics, and their willingness and ability to discuss its concepts, will increase with experience.

Aesthetic experiences for young children should be chosen according to their interests and level of understanding. Such details as dates and the social-political implications of a piece of art or music have no relevance for a child. Rather, a painting or a piece of music or a dance may appeal to them because of its familiar subject matter, its bold colors or rhythm, or its story. A variety of experiences in appreciation—paintings and sculpture, ballet and jazz dancing, marches and concertos—should be offered.

Art appreciation also includes the development of an awareness of the aesthetic qualities of everyday manmade objects. Children are surrounded daily by an endless number of objects such as furniture, clothing, toys, buildings, and machines and countless images in films, television, newspapers, books, magazines, advertisements, and exhibits. Examples of good and bad design can be found in all areas of the environment. With guidance and experience, children will become more sensitive to their environment and eventually will develop more selective, even discriminating, taste.

Art and Aesthetics Web Sites

THIS ONE'S for YOU!

The following sites are recommended for children from preschool through age 14 and their parents, teachers, and other caregivers. These sites have been reviewed and are recommended by the Children and Technology Commission of the Association for Library Service to Children, a division of the American Library Association.

A. Pintura, Art Detective. Outstanding, clever, and stimulating site using a detective style to explore art in some depth. http://www.eduweb.com/pintura

Albright-Knox Art Games. This interactive site engages children in art activities that help them to learn about artists and the works of art in the collection of the Albright-Knox Art Gallery in Buffalo, New York. http://www.kids.albrightknox.org

American Treasures. Divided into three main areas—Memory, Reason, and Imagination—with approximately twenty items in each, this site is exceptionally rich. It is to be a continuously updated exhibit at the Library of Congress. http://wwww.lcweb.loc.gov Click on the Especially for Teachers section.

The @rt Room. Provides a learning environment for exploring the world of art. Includes bibliographies of art books, exhibits of kids' art from different parts of the world, and facts about famous artists. http://www.arts.ufl.edu Click on Academic Units.

The Imagination Factory. This site provides art activities using recycled materials. Ideas and clear directions can be found for painting, drawing, sculpting, printmaking fiber art, and crafting from recycled media. http://www.kid-at-art.com

Inside Art. What if you were trapped inside a painting and had to solve a mystery to get out? An adventure inside art history. http://www.eduweb.com Click on the Kids and Teachers! section.

Metropolitan Museum of Art, New York. The page for young people includes family guides, museum hunts, and art games. http://www.metmuseum.org After pressing the Enter Here box, go to the Educational Resources Section.

SUMMARY

Aesthetics is an appreciation for beauty and a feeling of wonder. The purpose of aesthetic experiences for children is to help them develop a full and rich life.

Children gain an aesthetic sense by doing, sensing, feeling, and responding to things. As children learn and grow in the early childhood years, a sense of aesthetics can be developed as they learn to join what they think with what they feel. Such aesthetic experiences allow children to express their feelings about what they are learning and experiencing. In this way, there is no false separation between work and play, art and learning, and thought and feeling. After the ages 7–8, children are able to mentally deal with more abstract ideas. At this time children can engage in aesthetic discussions about their artistic opinions and ideas about what art is. Children with improved aesthetic sensitivity have a greater chance to be creative and have a more enjoyable learning experience.

Teachers can help develop children's aesthetic senses by involving them in the arts; introducing them to famous works of art, music, dance, or literature; allowing them to explore their environment; and avoiding single solutions to complex problems.

Children benefit from their aesthetic sensitivity because it generates more excitement in their lives as well as more insight. The ability to use one's taste or to know one's preference, which is basic to an aesthetic sense, can improve the quality of learning. Aesthetic sensibility in children also helps them develop their feelings of sensitivity, independence, and tolerance.

KEY TERMS

aesthetics
multimedia artwork

LEARNING ACTIVITIES

BEING AWARE

To use one's aesthetic sense, one must pay close attention to that which is personally interesting. This means being aware of oneself and one's surroundings.

A. Try to think a new thought or make a discovery by paying closer attention to yourself.

B. Begin by going to a place that is quiet and relaxing. Sit down and take a minute to rest. Then say, "Now I am aware of . . ." and finish this statement with what you are in touch with at the moment. Notice whether this is something inside or outside yourself.

C. Make the statement again and see what happens.
   1. Has your awareness changed?
   2. Are fantasies, thoughts, or images part of your awareness?

D. Make the statement again, but this time think of a person.
   1. Who comes to mind?
   2. What does it mean?

E. Try the same sentence, but change your awareness by thinking of different things such as a flower, a picture, someone from the past, a child, your favorite place, and so on.

F. Notice that when thinking of something outside, one cannot think of something inside at the same time.

G. What does this mean for working with children? Compare your answers with classmates, and find out how they feel about this activity.

FRUIT

This is an activity to make new discoveries by paying closer attention to everyday things.

A. Take three different types of fruit. Close your eyes and pick each one up. Feel them with your fingers from top to bottom.
   1. How are they different?
   2. How are they the same?

B. Place the fruits against your face.
   1. Do they feel different?
   2. What about the temperature of the fruit?

C. Smell the fruits, being sure to keep your eyes closed.
   1. How different are the aromas?
   2. Which is your favorite?

D. Open your eyes and look at the fruits.
   1. Hold them up to the light.
   2. See if you can see anything new about each fruit.

E. What have you discovered from this activity? (Notice you did not taste or eat the fruit.)
   1. Could you still receive pleasure from the fruit without eating it?
   2. What does this mean for working with children?

F. Compare your answers with those of classmates, and find out how they felt about this activity.

MUSEUM EXPLORATIONS

Plan a trip to a local museum for a group of young children. Help the children to focus in the gallery with activities such as the following:

⊙ Searching for a particularly interesting picture. For example, in a room filled with paintings ask children, "Can you find the painting where there is a bear, a house, a mother, and a baby?"

⊙ Asking, "What would it feel like to be in the painting?" "Where would you like to go?" "What would you like to do if you were there?"

⊙ Asking children to find two pictures that are the same in some way—the same colors, the same subject, the same feeling.

⊙ Grab your magnifying glass and enter the field of art investigation as the National Gallery takes you step-by-step through the examination of Picasso's *The Tragedy.* Sniff out the clues that led art historians to discover another artwork lurking just beneath the painting's surface. (http://www.nga.gov/feature/picasso/index.htm).

⊙ Explore your own environment. Pick a nearby location—a mall, a park, any area you enjoy exploring. Visit that location as an artist, writer, scientist, historian, or mathematician. Look carefully and jot down as many interesting ideas, problems, and questions as you can. Reflect on how your point of view affected your experience.

ACTIVITIES FOR CHILDREN

ART TALK

Using Van Gogh's famous painting *Starry Night,* ask young children the following questions about the painting.

- What do you see in the painting?
- What do you notice about the colors and lines?
- Show me in the painting what you think is the most important thing in it. Why?
- How does this picture make you feel?
- What do you think the artist was feeling when he was painting this picture?

Another kind of questioning about *Starry Night* might be to have the children imagine they are in the scene.

- If you were in the painting, where would you want to be?
- How would that feel?
- What kind of things do you think you would smell?
- What kind of animals might live there?

These questions could be used for any other painting of your choice.

ART IN NATURE

The beauty of nature is also a continuing source of inspiration for young children. It is through nature that many children acquire some of their earliest ideas and concepts of design. A variety of experiences can be planned to help children observe and discover color, line, form, pattern, and texture in natural objects.

- Make a bulletin board arrangement of natural objects and materials.
- Begin a collection of natural objects, such as flowers, weeds, twigs, stones, shells, seed pods, moss, and feathers, for a touch-and-see display.
- Take a walking trip to observe color, shape, and texture in the immediate environment. Share individual discoveries with others during class discussion.
- Show films, conduct dramatizations, or read stories and poems to develop these concepts.
- Arrange a shelf or corner table for things of beauty children can admire. Contributions can be made by parents, some of whom may have objects that represent art of their own heritage. Keep changing the collection! Variety and contrast encourage young children's interest.
- Give children an opportunity to arrange objects in an aesthetically pleasing manner: flower bouquets;

fruit and vegetable centerpieces; and collections of dried plants, leaves, and seed pods placed in a ball of clay or block of styrofoam.

- Offer equipment such as magnifying glasses, kaleidoscopes, prisms, and safety mirrors to help sharpen children's visual sensitivity.
- In describing the children's artwork to them, use terms that relate to the color, form, texture, patterns, and arrangement of space.
- Be enthusiastic about your own sensory awareness and share your perceptions with the children.
- What ideas can you add to this list?

PRIMARY AND SECONDARY COLORS PANTOMIME

Elementary children can work on color recognition and affective response to color through pantomime sentences. Have the children perform the following actions and then tell how each of the colors made them feel.

- You are the bright yellow sun shining in the summer sky.
- You are a blue wave crashing against the shore.
- You are an orange squirting your juice into a pitcher.
- You are a blue bird flying across the blue sky.
- You are a violet opening your petals.
- You are a red cardinal building your nest.
- You are an orange flame flickering atop a candle.
- You are a yellow jacket buzzing around a flower.
- You are a green leaf floating gently to the ground.
- You are a green bug crawling along the ground.
- You are a red fire engine speeding to the scene of a fire.
- You are an African violet growing in a pot.

Children will enjoy creating and playing their own pantomime sentences that incorporate primary and secondary colors. At the close of the activity, invite the children to tell how the colors in these new sentences made them feel.

LUCY'S SCIENCE PROJECT—BODY SCULPTURES

Science projects and school science fairs give children hands-on opportunities to examine, test, and operate technical devices. These experiences can be applied to the more fanciful invention in the following activity.

Children working in small groups create Lucy's new invention using their bodies and machine-like sounds after hearing the following scenario. They may adapt a device currently in use, such as a computer, or create a futuristic contraption with a real or fantastic purpose.

Lucy is a second grader in the year 2090. She has been assigned the creation of a new technologic device as her science project. As a group, you are to become Lucy's invention. Your task is to create the device, name it, show how it works, and tell the rest of the class what it does.

ACTIVITIES FOR OLDER CHILDREN (GRADES 4-5)

BIRTHDAY PARTIES FOR ARTISTS

Ask the children, "If you were planning a birthday party for a famous artist, what would you want the design, based on the style of that artist, to look like? How would you design a cup, plate, napkin, placemat, treat bag, party hat, and balloon to look as if they belonged together?"

Divide the class into teams of four. Each team votes on the artist for whom they would plan a party. Children review the artists they have learned about. List the names of those artists on the board. Display examples of their work, and provide folders with examples of each artist's work for children's review. Discuss the characteristic styles of these artists and how elements of those styles could be incorporated in the design of the party decorations.

As a team, students decide what the overall design is to look like to reflect the style of their artist. Each group also decides which art materials would best represent their artist.

Provide white napkins, balloons, paper plates, cups, treat bags, 12″ × 18″ white paper, colored markers, tempera paint, and watercolors for children to make their party accessories.

LOOK CLOSELY–PANTOMIME

Older children can be introduced to art history and gain insight into art criticism through this activity. By studying famous paintings, reproductions, or prints, children sharpen critical observation skills while analyzing artistic process and intent.

As an introduction to critical observation, have the children study prints of famous paintings and identify people or objects in each print that can be interpreted through pantomime. Several prints (or similar materials) should be selected for study, and children should be given ample time to view each. Prompt thinking with questions such as, "What was the artist trying to say in this work?" or "What does the artist want you to think or feel when you see this?" or "What do you think is the most important image in this picture?" The class can then generate a list of people or objects in the prints that appear significant to them. After an appropriate list has been developed, call out the subjects and ask the children to pantomime them.

WEB ACTIVITIES

Graphic artist M. C. Escher is known for his detailed drawings using patterns and optical illusions. View his work at the following Web sites:

⊙ http://www.mcescher.com/
⊙ http://www.worldofescher.com/gallery/
⊙ http://www.cs.unc.edu/. Click on Projects.

What is a metamorphosis? How does this artist organize line and shape to create his art? Describe the work you find most interesting. What is unique about it? How was he able to create such technical details? Besides artists and art viewers, who else may appreciate Escher's drawings?

Henri Matisse often used cut paper that he had painted to create collages. Look at reproductions of these collages in these Web sites:

⊙ http://www.artloft.com/. Click on Artist Directory.
⊙ http://www.museum.cornell.edu. Click on Collections.

Why would the artist choose collage instead of painting, drawing, or another media? Which artwork appeals to you the most? Describe the composition. What colors, shapes, and patterns do you see? How does your eye move through the image? What do you see first, and then which way do you proceed? Did you find balance and unity in the collage?

ARTISTIC OPINIONS

Aesthetic experiences for older children involve their opinions of art and their ability to express these opinions and to appreciate those of others. The following "Art Problems" are designed to capitalize on older children's ability to grasp more complex ideas and should encourage discussion on art and aesthetic appreciation.

A. The Problem of "The Pile of Bricks"

This problem involves the *nature of art* and such questions as "What is art?" and "Is it representation?" and "Is it the expression and communication of emotion?" Consider the following possibility, based on an exhibit at the Tate Gallery (London) in 1976. A famous artist, known to be a "minimalist" sculptor, buys 120 bricks and, on the floor of a well-known art museum, arranges them in a rectangular pile, 2 bricks high, 6 across, and 10 lengthwise. He labels it *Pile of Bricks*. Across town, a bricklayer's assistant at a building site takes 120 bricks of the very same kind and arranges them in the very same way, wholly unaware of what has happened in the museum—he is just a tidy bricklayer's assistant. Can the first pile of bricks be a work of art while the second pile is not, even though the two piles are seemingly identical in all observable respects? Why or why not?

B. The Problem of The Fire in the Louvre

The Louvre is on fire. You can save either the *Mona Lisa* or the injured guard who had been standing next to it—but not both. What should you do?

C. Is Shakespeare a Real Writer?

Lord Byron criticized Shakespeare as follows: "Shakespeare's name, you may depend on it, stands absurdly too high and will go down . . . He took all his plots from old novels, and threw their stories into dramatic shape, at as little expense of thought, as you or I could do." (Henderson, 1986). Is Shakespeare's use of familiar stories an aesthetic defect? Is Byron a good critic of Shakespeare?

CHAPTER REVIEW

1. Define aesthetics.
2. List three things a teacher can do to help children develop their aesthetic sensitivity.
3. List five benefits of aesthetic sensitivity in children.
4. List at least two specific ways to introduce young children to the work of an artist and to involve them in art appreciation in general.
5. List at least three art elements to discuss with children.
6. What aesthetic experiences are appropriate for older children (grades 4–5) and why?

REFERENCES

Colbert, C., & Taunton, M. (1992). *Developmentally appropriate practices for the visual arts education of young children*. NAEA Briefing Paper. Reston, VA: National Art Education Association (NAEA).

Epstein, A. A. (2001). Thinking about art: Encouraging art appreciation in early childhood settings. *Young Children, 56*(3), 38–43.

Feeney, S., & Moravcik, E. (1987, September). A thing of beauty: Aesthetic development in young children. *Young Children,* 6–15.

Gardner, H. (1990). *Art education and human development*. Los Angeles: The Getty Center for Education in the Arts.

Henderson, D. E. (1986). *Shakespeare*. New York: Vintage.

Schiller, M. (1995, March). An emergent art curriculum that fosters understanding. *Young Children, 50*(3), 33–45.

Villeneuve, P. (2003). A child named Risa. *Art Education 56*(4), 4.

ADDITIONAL READINGS

Ahlberg, L. (1999, spring). Understanding and appreciating art: The relevance of experience. *The Journal of Aesthetic Education, 33*(1), 11–23.

Aslin, E. (1969). *The aesthetic movement: Prelude to art nouveau*. New York: Praeger.

Bresler, L., & Thompson, C. M. (2002). *The arts in children's lives: Context, culture and curriculum*. Boston: Kluwer Academic Publisher.

Eisner, E. W. (2002). *The arts and the creation of mind*. Reston, VA: National Art Education Association.

Epstein, A. S. (2001). Thinking about art: Encouraging art appreciation in early childhood settings. *Young Children, 57*(3), 38–43.

Epstein, A. S., & Trimis, E. A. (2002). *Supporting young artists: The development of the visual arts in young children*. Ypsilanti, MI: High Scope Press.

Engel, B. S. (1998). *Considering children's art: Why and how to value their works.* Reston, VA: NAEA.

Engel, S. (1999). Looking backward: Representations of childhood literary work. *The Journal of Aesthetic Education, 33*(1), 50–55.

Feagin, S., & Maynard, P. (Eds.). (1998). *Aesthetics.* New York: Oxford University Press.

Holmes, C. (2002). *Monet at Giverny.* New York: Sterling Publishing Co.

In the News. Art education boosts academic achievement, cuts crimes and lowers taxes. *Art Education, 56*(4), 160–K.

Jones, L. S. (1998). *Art information on the internet.* Phoenix, AZ: Oryx.

Korsmeyer, C. (Ed.). (1998). *Aesthetics: The big questions.* Malden, MA: Blackwell.

Kulp, C. N. (1999, September). Looking for patterns. *Teaching K–8, 68–69.*

Lasky, L., & Mukerji, R. (1980). *Art: Basic for young children.* Washington, DC: National Association for the Education of Young Children (NAEYC).

Loebl, S. (2002). *America's art museums.* New York: W. W. Norton & Company, Inc.

Matravers, D. (1998). *Art and emotion.* New York: Oxford University Press.

Menke, C. (1998). *The sovereignty of art.* Translated by Neil Solomon. Cambridge, MA: MIT Press.

Merrion, M., & Rubin, J. (1996). *Creative approaches to elementary curriculum.* Portsmouth, NH: Heinemann.

Mulcahey, C. (2002). Art appreciation kits for kindergarteners and their families. *Young Children, 57*(1), 80–83.

Oxford University. (1998). *Encyclopedia of aesthetics,* 4 Vols. New York: Oxford University Press.

Sparshott, F. (1998). *The future of aesthetics.* Toronto, Canada: University of Toronto Press.

Szekely, G. (1991). Discovery experiences in art history for young children. *Art Education, 44*(5), 41–19.

Tyrell, J. (2001). *The power of fantasy in early learning.* New York: Routledge.

SOFTWARE FOR CHILDREN

Beauty or the Beast, 2003. Ages 8–11.

Disney Princess Cinderella's Castle Designer, 2003. Ages 5 and up.

Finding Nemo, 2003. Ages 6 and up.

Finding Nemo: Underwater World of Fun, 2003. Ages 4 and up.

Harry Potter and the Sorcerer's Stone, 2002. Ages 8 and up.

HyperStudio 4, 2001. Ages 8 and up.

Rescue Heroes Lava Landslide 4.3, 2003. Ages 4–7.

Rescue Heroes Mission Masters, 2003. Ages 4 and up.

Star-Flyers: Alien Space Chase, 2002. Ages 5–8.

Star-Flyers: Royal Jewel Rescue, 2002. Ages 5–8.

HELPFUL WEB SITES

http://www.artsconnected.org
Collaborative site involving four Minnesota museums and several teacher training sites. An exceptional online resource for use in classrooms. Click on For Your Classroom section.

http://www.artic.edu
Includes activities for children. Excellent opening page with animated changes of the art images. Includes exploring "A Mysterious Mummy" and "Thousands of Dots" (about a painting by Georges Seurat). Click on School Section, then on Programs and Resources.

http://www.nga.gov
European and American paintings, sculpture, decorative arts, and selected works on paper. Full-screen views of whole paintings and details allow close study. The site also includes information on artists and on the museum itself.

http://www.nga.gov/kids
Explore stories in art, take a post card tour of one of the galleries, get directions for art activities and projects, and more.

For additional creative activity resources, visit our Web site at http://www.EarlyChildEd.delmar.com.

Chapter 4

Promoting Aesthetic Experiences

Objectives

After studying this chapter, you should be able to:

1. Describe three types of sensing and feeling.
2. Choose materials that have good aesthetic potential.
3. List four guidelines to help children work with aesthetic materials.
4. List six guidelines to use in talking with children about their artwork.

People search their world for what is important to them. They look for what they need. They see what they want. This is as true of preschool children as it is of adults.

Imagine that a group of people are taken into a room and are asked to look at a table. On the table are some food, a glass of water, and a small amount of money. Those who are hungry are most likely to look at the food. Those who are thirsty will probably look at the water. Those who are in debt are apt to look at the money. Those who need furniture will probably take a closer look at the table.

Children also look for things they need and want. A tired child looks for a place to rest. A lonely child looks for a friend. The point here is that only when children are physically well, feel safe, and sense that they belong can they be ready to develop an aesthetic sense.

LOOKING AND SEEING

Children look in many different ways. Touching, patting, poking, picking, and even tasting are ways of looking for young children. Children look for what they need, but they also see what they find to be stimulating. Something can be stimulating to a child for many different reasons. It can be because it is colorful, exciting, different, interesting, changing, moving, weird, and so on. The list of stimulating things is seemingly endless. However, there are some basic guidelines for preparing a stimulating activity or object.

Can children experience it with more than one sense? Children enjoy what they can touch, see, and hear more than something they can only see or hear.

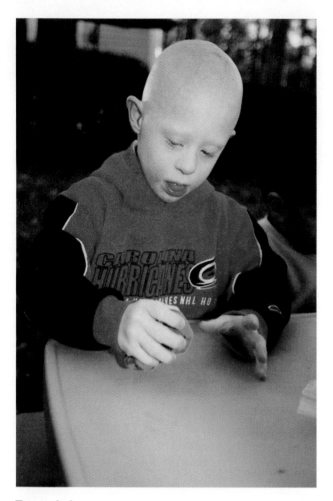

Figure 4-1
Molding clay, with no other purpose than to feel it in their hands, gives children the motivation to continue the activity.

Can children interact with it?   Children tend to enjoy what they can participate in. For children, the picture of a guinea pig will never replace a live guinea pig. For the same reason, an interactive computer game can never replace the fun and real-life learning experience of playing a game with friends.

Are the children interested in it?   Children relate to what is familiar to them and part of their life. Talking about a food that children have never eaten cannot produce the kind of discussion that comes when they talk about their favorite food.

Is the activity well paced?   Something that moves too quickly or too slowly eventually becomes boring. Watch how many children begin to fidget when the story is too long. Notice how children lose interest in toys that may appeal to adults but are too complex for children to use and enjoy.

Figure 4-2
Children explore things in many ways to learn how they work.

Does it promise to be rewarding?   Is the activity fun, adventurous, or exciting? Does it have something worthwhile at the end? If not, why should the children stick with it? Searching for a piece of a puzzle or looking for a hidden treasure is only fun if the children believe they can find it.

SENSING, FEELING, AND IMAGINING

There are basically three types of sensing and feeling. The first is contact with the world outside of the person—actual sensory contact with things and events. It is seeing, hearing, smelling, tasting, and touching. The second is what people feel within themselves. This includes what they experience under their skin. Itches, tensions, muscular movements, discomfort, and emotions are all a part of this type of sensing. The third type of sensing and feeling goes beyond the present and reality. It is usually called fantasy and includes dreams, memories, images, and guesses.

For a child, each of these types of sensing and feeling is very important. All three can take place during the same activity. Any one can become more important than the other two, depending on what the child needs or wants at the moment. Most teachers are concerned about the child's sensory contact with the outside world. Children do many things that involve touching, seeing, and hearing; yet, what they feel inside and what they fantasize about are also important. The teacher must give attention to these two processes

Figure 4-3

Provide children with materials that are open-ended and can be used in many ways.

Figure 4-4

A child's personal statement is more important than either the materials or the process.

as well. They are part of aesthetic sensitivity. Teachers should ask themselves two questions each day when working with preschool children. Both should be answered "yes," followed by the question, "How?"

The first question has to do with the inside feelings of the children: *Have the children done something today that has helped them feel good about themselves?* The second has to do with the fantasies of the children: *Have the children done something today that has helped them use their imagination in either the past, present, or future?*

Lesson plans, activities, and trips should be planned and evaluated with these two questions in mind. If teachers are sincere about answering yes to the two questions, their teaching will relate to all the ways children sense and feel.

FINDING AND ORGANIZING AESTHETIC MATERIALS

Every teacher has many ideas about what materials are best for children. Sometimes the desired materials are too expensive or difficult to find. Schools have limited budgets, and even ordinary items can seem impossible to obtain. There are three resources with great poten-

tial: salvage material, commonly known as "junk"; the hardware store; and things the children bring in.

Before describing the organization of these materials, it is helpful to have some guidelines for choosing materials with good aesthetic potential.

- ⊙ Choose materials that children can explore with their senses (touch, sight, smell).
- ⊙ Choose materials that children can manipulate (twist, bend, cut, color, mark).
- ⊙ Choose materials that can be used in different ways (thrown, bounced, built with, fastened, shaped).

Children enjoy finding materials because it suggests exploration and discovery. The discovery of materials can be celebrated and shared in a "beauty corner" where newly found leaves, ribbons, and other treasures can be placed (Chandler, 1973). A small collection of colored cloths; a few blocks or boxes; and a screen, pegboard, or tack board to fasten things on, all set in adequate light, can make a beauty corner. Children develop aesthetic skills in sensing and exhibiting

Studies in neuroscience tell us that a frequent change of materials, experiences, and environment provides novelty for the brain. Attention is drawn to things that are unusual or new (Church, 2002).

Because attention is needed for learning to take place, it is important to take a familiar activity or newly acquired skill and apply it to new situations and/or materials. In other words, an original activity can be experienced again and again in a modified form.

Doing activities in different ways also invites children to use flexible and fluent thinking skills. It also encourages their aesthetic senses, allowing them to see and experience many possibilities, objects, or situations in many different ways.

You can start with a wonderful activity and give it more meaning by inviting children to apply what they know with new materials or new settings. For example, change the paint tool. Replace brushes with corncobs, rollers, sponges, or even feather dusters. Change the paper. Surprise children by hanging wallpaper, paper bags, newspaper, or corrugated paper at the easel. Ask, "How can you paint on this?"

So take a moment now, stand back, and think of all the ways you can change the usual into the unusual. It will be an aesthetically pleasing experience for both you and the children.

by helping to build such a place. They can learn to ask such questions as, "Does it look better this way?" or "Should we put more light on it?"

Sometimes the children's search can be focused on something, as in finding things for painting or building. The search for aesthetic materials also includes seeking new uses for familiar materials. For example, change the paint by mixing things with it, such as sawdust, sand, rice, or confetti. Then ask children, "How many ways can you use the new paint?" As they find that their discovered materials make their day-to-day work more interesting, they become alert to new possibilities. For the teacher and the children, this can mean a constant supply of materials and new aesthetic experiences.

Older children will enjoy this same experience of collecting materials, but they can go further into associating materials with the elements of art. For example, the materials can be selected and collected according to their design possibilities. Objects can be classified into art categories such as those to be used for line, shape, texture, size, and color elements. The number and types of classifications will vary by the age level and interest of the children.

AESTHETIC USE OF MATERIALS

The uses of materials collected by the teacher and children are only limited by the collectors' interests and imagination. Of course, storage space and time to search can sometimes set boundaries on the exploration for aesthetic materials. However, what is most important is that the materials and what is done with them become personal statements of the children and teacher. This is not done by what is made but by how it is made—whether it is an art project, a building project, or another activity. The *process* of making and the child's personal involvement in it are the keys here—*not* the finished product.

Children must have the opportunity not only to find materials but also to try them out. This means much experimenting with the materials to determine what the children feel they need. A question such as, "What would you like to say with these things?" might help both the children and the teacher get started. Checking with the children's moods may be helpful, too. Do they seem to feel happy, dreamy, sad, gentle, aggressive? Such questioning can help the children reach their own purpose based on their experience and interests.

Another important consideration in the creative process is the number of materials. It is important to remember not to give children too many materials too often. Too much to choose from can overwhelm a child. The qualities of one material can be lost in the midst of so many others. An example of this would be to work with a certain color or a single material, such as clay or paper. In this way, the children can learn more about making their own aesthetic choices, as well as mastering specific skills.

While the *process* of exploring materials is the primary focus of aesthetic experiences, with older children (grades 4–5), the process usually involves the creation of more complex works of art. Children at this level pay greater attention to expressing specific ideas in their work. They are more intentional in their approach to using materials. Because they are not distracted by quantity of materials as younger children are, a variety of interesting materials needs to be available for their aesthetic experiences.

> A man who has no imagination has no wings.
> Muhammed Ali

GUIDANCE IN USING AESTHETIC MATERIALS

When children are exploring new materials of any kind, the teacher needs to provide guidance. With aesthetic materials, the guidance needs to be very gentle, supportive, and sensitive. This lets the child know that it is acceptable to take chances and be different. The following are some suggestions on how to give young children guidance when using aesthetic materials.

Ask questions aimed at helping the children reach out for and get the "payoff" they are seeking. A question teachers can ask themselves that will help them ask the right question of children is, "What can I ask the children that would help them better understand what they want?" When the children are working with paints, this question may be something about color. When they are working with paper, it may be something about form, such as "What shape would you like it to be?" Even better, ask how paper feels because just seeing a shape is only one way of sensing paper.

Avoid too many ready-made models or ways of doing things. Teaching children over and over to do something in only one way may ruin their aesthetic sense. Repetition tells them to stop thinking. For example, why always start to draw in the middle of a piece of paper? Why not sometimes draw from the edges or bottom? Or why not change the shape of the paper on which children draw, using paper in the shape of a triangle, parallelogram, or circle?

Be positive and creative when using models or examples. Occasional use of models and examples is not uncommon in many classrooms today. Their use need not be a negative experience for children if they

Figure 4-5

Children enjoy what they can touch or see.

are used positively—as a springboard to unlocking each child's own creative approach to a shared, common theme (or object). Many times, a brief look at one or two examples (which should *not* then be displayed for "copying" during the activity) can help motivate children to get started on making one of their own. Also, using a model produced by another child of the same age can encourage children in that it is something possible for them to do, too. Teacher comments throughout activities and the use of examples can help encourage each child to be creative in her approach. Statements like, "Claire, I like how you are using *so many* colors," or "Jeremy, you used that paper in a very nice and different way to make your own design," clearly communicate the positive acceptance of different approaches.

Help children select the materials they prefer. This may mean asking the children which materials they plan to use first, which materials they may not use at all, and which materials they may possibly use. Be patient with children and choices. Remember, the simplest choices for teachers become major decision-making opportunities for young children. What color paper to choose, what color crayons or paint, what shape and size of paper, and which way to hold the paper are all options children should have. Children may require more time to work if many decisions must be made, but it's time well spent aesthetically and creatively.

Help children "hunt" for aesthetic qualities. Help children get in touch with what they feel about differences. For example, ask children to show what

THIS ONE'S for YOU!

Create a Classroom Museum

Provide children (of all ages) a year-round aesthetic experience by incorporating a classroom museum in your program. It's "show and tell" in a more meaningful, aesthetic sense. Here are the basics to get you started.

WHAT IS A CLASSROOM MUSEUM?

A **classroom museum** is a collection of items and artifacts on a specific theme. Items and artifacts are brought in by the children for display. Using this approach for show and tell, the theme or topic is motivating and the exhibit grows gradually and joyfully. Decision making, problem solving, and communicating are skills practiced as the children share/add their special selections. Treasures from home, a family-crafted item, or an occasional purchase—each contribution is worthy. The sharing is educational and enjoyable. Museum topics change each month, with teacher/child interest sparking the choice.

ESSENTIALS FOR SUCCESS

⊙ Make a quality choice for the first museum of the year.
⊙ Determine a clear purpose and definite goals for the museum as a curriculum tool appropriate for children's development.
⊙ Invite family participation via an informative, friendly August newsletter, a September Parent's Night, and a special museum notice.
⊙ Plan a simple but attractive museum area in the classroom. A suitable physical set-up includes a backdrop for hanging pictures and a display table.
⊙ Highlight the children's artifacts and show and tell experience.
⊙ Select a child as a curator to encourage responsibility.
⊙ Guide children's selection for show and tell artifacts to help foster respect for all contributions and ensure their survival in the classroom (especially fragile or sentimental items).

A good place to start in the beginning of the program year is with a "Me Museum." This is a good topic to start with because it encourages a feeling of community as teacher and children learn more about each other.

STEPS TO SETTING UP THE "ME MUSEUM"

⊙ Awareness (with children)—Explore the concept of *museum*. Discuss possible items for a Me Museum. Plan ways that families can help. Frame a family museum notice. Establish routines for sharing.
⊙ Contributions (from children)—Me Museum artifacts are always surprises. Descriptions delight. Personal history in bits and pieces come alive. Students have shared stuffed animals, baby journals, family photos, toys, travel souvenirs, books or stories, ballet slippers . . .
⊙ Integration (with children)—Growth in vocabulary occurs. Expressive language expands. Thinking and problem-solving skills are nurtured.
⊙ Outcomes (for children)—Child by child, with each contribution, child-centered showing and sharing creates a caring community in which each child is important and friendships emerge.

TO CONTINUE THE MUSEUM

To create the next month's museum, brainstorm with the children some possible topics and themes. What do they want to learn about? What provokes their curiosity? What special interest do they want to share/explore with classmates? Inspired and motivated, many ideas are listed and voting follows (integrating math skills such as counting, graphing, predicting, and comparing).

First choice becomes the next museum, with second place a strong possibility for a future museum. The teacher also selects topics to coincide with curriculum or timely topics. Topics may vary from year to year. The steps of awareness, contributions, integration, and outcome all facilitate museum planning.

they like or think is better. Ask what is brighter, darker, happier, sadder. Encourage older children to identify and analyze more subtle and complex visual relationships such as how light affects our perception of colors, textures, and forms.

Help children use other senses when only one sense seems necessary. Children can be asked to hear what they see in a drawing or to draw what they hear in music. Colors can be related to feelings, music, and body movements, as well as to seeing. Older children can be encouraged to explore such ideas as how we perceive space and distance in art. They also need to be encouraged to continue to express in their art what they see, know, feel, and imagine.

Help children experience basic elements of art such as line, rhythm, and contrast in many art forms. Creative movements (or dance) display a strong relationship to the basic art element of line. For example, when children are moving in a wiggly or a twisting way, they can be given a signal to freeze or hold by the striking of a gong or stopping the music. The teacher might then appreciatively point out the different lines the body makes while it is held or frozen—the continuous curve from back toe through the body to the reaching, stretched fingers. The children can also make similar observations about each other's interesting body line designs in space. It is natural then to circle back from one's understanding of the body line to reaching, curving, or twisting lines in clay, crayon, or paint.

Figure 4-6

Has the child done something today that has helped him feel good about himself?

The element of **rhythm** is most frequently associated with music, dance, and poetry, but it can be just as much a quality in art. We find it in repeated shapes, colors, and textures that flow in a directional path, such as in children's nature print designs. We also sense rhythm in their block structures of repeated patterns. We know rhythm unmistakably in the pulse of movement and music. Good examples of rhythm in design can be found in the stylized geometric rhythmic patterns of traditional Native Americans in their weaving, pottery, beadwork, and sand painting, which often tell stories about mountains, rivers, sun, and lightning.

The element of **contrast** provides one of the most exciting characteristics in all the arts. Sensitive teachers frequently help children become more aware of the power of contrast by pointing out how two colors next to each other make the shapes stand out. They comment on the roughly textured bark of a tree in contrast to its smooth leaves. Children appreciate the exaggerated features of "evil creature" puppets in contrast to the more subtle features of the heroes and heroines.

The concept of contrast for older children can be expanded from that presented to younger children. Contrast can involve the introduction of the color wheel. They can see on the color wheel how colors that are opposite one another are called *complementary* colors. These complementary colors provide more contrast than colors next to each other on the color wheel, called *analogous* colors. The idea of warm colors (reds, oranges, yellows) and cool colors (blues, greens, purples) is another concept appropriate for older children as they learn about creating contrast in their work.

Displaying Children's Work

An important part of the teacher's role in developing children's aesthetic sensitivity is showing their work to parents and others. A good rule is that if the children feel good about their work, let them show it. The work does not have to be complete. It should be displayed at children's eye level so that they, as well as adults, may enjoy it. Not every child in the group has to have his or her work displayed.

Set up displays to show the different ways the children have used a medium, such as painting, collage, clay, and so on. Let the room reflect the children's diversity, their likes, their interests—much the way a well-decorated home reflects the interests and skills of the people who live in it. Children aren't clones, so we certainly don't expect to see 25 identical works of art with different names on them displayed in the room. How does this reflect the children's diversity?

Encouraging Aesthetic Development by Listening to Children

THINK ABOUT IT...

Really *listening* to children and encouraging their dreams and fantasies are basic to their developing aesthetic senses. In this excerpt, a young teacher and mother shares what she learned about children's questions, adult answers, and listening.

Several years ago a friend offered me a bit of simple advice that has contributed significantly to how I regard children and learning. When young children are inquisitive, my friend said, ask them what *they* think, rather than provide the all-knowing adult answer.

Soon afterward, on a spring day, 5-year-old Yara and I sat on the couch watching huge, lacy snowflakes falling outside. "Mom, did you ever wonder where those snowflakes come from?" she asked.

I started to remind her about the water cycle and what happens when the water freezes, but I remembered my friend's advice and instead asked her what she thought.

"Did you ever think," she asked, "that those snowflakes are pieces of angels' wings floating down from heaven?"

As soon as Yara spoke, I understood that those special spring snowflakes had inspired her to think metaphorically rather than scientifically. She already knew something about the water cycle but at this moment wanted to go beyond scientific knowledge.

Young children are curious and often ask us to explain how complicated things work. But most of the time they don't really want to know what we think. Instead, they want to share with us the ideas they are mulling over. A careful listener often learns more about the child than facts reveal (White, 2002).

Take time at the end of the day to show artwork to the children, letting them talk about each other's work. Model for the children how to make a positive comment.

Be sure to send all artwork home in a way that shows your respect for the artist and the art. For example, paintings folded rather than rolled, or rolled when wet and therefore stuck together, tell children their work doesn't matter (Clemens, 1991, p. 10). (More specific suggestions on displaying children's work are covered in Appendix D.)

Interpreting Children's Creative Work for Parents

Parents should be helped to see what the child liked about the creative work. All people have their own ideas of what creative talent is, parents being no exception. It is important, however, that they understand and know that what their children enjoy and feel about what they are doing is much more important than the finished product.

Parents should also know why some materials are used by their children and others are not. More importantly, parents should learn to approach their child's making of gifts, art exhibits, and displays as demonstrations of the child's aesthetic sense. With these displays, the child is saying, "This is how it is with me."

Parents want to know their children; children's creative work can help parents know more about their children. Teachers can assist parents by showing these visual examples of the creative *process* and pointing out that they are valuable for the process *alone*. Teachers can assist parents of older children to see and appreciate the progression of images that are growing more subtle and complex in their child's art.

Very few children will become professional artists, but given encouragement and experience they can learn to work with many media, enjoy beauty, and discriminate with aesthetic understanding. A person naturally responds to a lovely sunrise, painting, or piece of your spirit, and reflect your personality and philosophy. Indeed, it must be *your* personality and philosophy that determine how you use any activity. All of the ideas and activities in this book are to be shaped and modified to suit your own needs with a particular group of children. Any idea will only be successful if you like it and are excited to use it with young children. You must mix a lot of *you* into all of your work with young children. Do not hesitate to mix in your philosophy and personality along with those of the children, add a good portion of energy (yours and the children's), stir in a large measure of imagination, and you are on your way to a truly creative environment for young children.

SUMMARY

Children look for things they need and want. They are stimulated by things they find interesting and rewarding.

There are three types of sensing and feeling. The first is contact through the five basic senses; the second is what the person feels inside; and the third is fantasy.

Many materials with aesthetic potential can be found. Anything children can explore, manipulate, and use in different ways has aesthetic potential. What is most important is that these materials (and what is done with them) become personal statements of the children.

Teachers and parents can help children explore this aesthetic potential by concentrating on the importance of the *process* and *not* the product in young children's creative work. With older children (grades 4–5), the process usually involves the creation of a more complex work. With all ages of children, the teacher can give supportive and gentle guidance by asking helpful questions, avoiding models, and helping children "hunt" for aesthetic qualities.

Displaying children's work at their eye level is yet another way to show appreciation for their involvement in the creative process. Parents' appreciation for these displays must also concentrate on the importance of the child's creative process and not on the finished product. The teacher's role is to help interpret children's work for parents.

Figure 4-7
Teachers and parents can help children explore their aesthetic potential by concentrating on the importance of the process and not the product.

music. These aesthetic experiences help us live fully in the moment. Such responses do not need to be taught, but a child might need assistance and exposure to appreciate them fully. Aesthetic enjoyment provides an avenue through which people can find focus and achieve balance and tranquillity in an increasingly fast-paced world. Moreover, children who learn to love beauty in nature and in the arts are likely to want to support and protect these valuable resources.

Developing Your Sense of Aesthetics

Early childhood teachers need to protect the spirit, imagination, curiosity, and love of life and learning in young children as fiercely as we protect our environment. In a similar manner, early childhood teachers need to develop and protect their own aesthetic sense.

As you read through this book you will most likely find some activities that catch your attention, appeal to

KEY TERMS

classroom museum
contrast
rhythm

LEARNING ACTIVITIES

BEAUTIFUL THINGS

Everyone has had some experience with beauty and has a special idea about what is beautiful. It can be a very interesting experience to examine this concept with each of the five senses.

A. Write down the three most beautiful things (living or nonliving) that you have ever experienced with each of your five senses.

B. As you write your list, try as much as possible to relive the sensations.

C. Answer the following questions:
   1. Were most of your things living or nonliving?
   2. How many involved people?
   3. Did any of your answers surprise you?
   4. How often do you encounter beautiful things?
   5. Which sense seems to find the most beauty?
   6. How much does beauty in life depend on you?
   7. What does this mean for working with children?

D. Compare your responses with fellow students.

AMAZING JOURNEY

A. Find a quiet place and relax. Close your eyes and think of something that amazes you or produces wonder in you.

B. Think of yourself as that something. (Take some time to get the feel of being it.)

C. Write a description of yourself as this something. (Use plenty of adjectives.)

D. As a result of this experience:
   1. What emotions do you feel?
   2. How are you like what really amazes you?
   3. How are you unlike it?
   4. Would you like to change in any way?

E. Compare your answers with classmates.

F. Do you think children would enjoy using their imaginations like this?

CYBERSPACE AESTHETICS

Visit the Internet for some aesthetic experiences:

A. Visit one or more of these Web pages featuring paintings by Vincent van Gogh:
   http://www.vangoghgallery.com/.
   http://www.ibiblio.org/. Click on Arts and Recreation.
   http://www.artchive.com/. Click on The Artchive, then on Post-Impressionism.
   Look at several works by this artist. Pick the artwork that interests you most. What moods do you think the artist is trying to express in this painting? What features in the artwork made you think that? How was the artist able to convey these moods to the viewer?

B. Some artworks are not as easy to analyze because they are nonobjective—that is, they don't show any people, places, or things. Many modern artists work nonobjectively to express their unique ideas and feelings. How does an artist communicate this way? Can you explain how these artworks express ideas and feelings?
   http://www.ibiblio.org/. Click on Arts and Recreation.
   http://www.artchive.com/. Click on The Artchive, then on Abstract Expressionism.
   http://www.abstractart.20m.com/. Click on Jackson Pollock.

ACTIVITIES FOR CHILDREN

AESTHETIC THINKING THROUGH ART

Help the child to think of new ideas to create the following:

A. Say to the child, "If you could invent a new means of transportation, what would it be? Draw or construct how it would look."

B. Ask the child, "If you had a funny-shaped piece of paper, what could you make it into?"

C. Ask, "How do you think the world would look to a giant? Draw a picture (or make a model) of it."

D. Ask, "What could you do with this empty box, this stick, this cardboard (beautiful junk)? How could you place it or arrange it to make something that's your very own idea?"

SENSORY EXPERIENCES

Seeing

A. *Colors.* Have the children look for colors in the room, such as "How many red things can you see?" Or play a guessing game, such as "I am thinking of something green in this room. What is it?" Colors sometimes tell us important things, such as traffic lights that tell us when to go or stop. Red flags on a road mean danger. Red lights in a building mean an exit. We must obey these signals. We can make different colors by mixing them. (Allow children to experiment with mixing colors.) Show a prism to see the colors. Blow soap bubbles, and look for the rainbow colors in them.

B. *Shapes.* Show blocks or other objects that are circles, squares, rectangles, and triangles. Have children find things in the room that are these shapes. We can see color and shape at the same time. Find a red square, a blue circle, etc.

C. *Sizes.* Compare sizes of children and objects. Develop concepts of big, bigger, biggest; large, small; tall, short; thick, thin; wide, narrow; etc. Play riddles, such as "I am thinking of something that is white and round (clock)."

Listening

A. *Tape Recorder.* The children can listen to their own voices, to voices of others, and to classroom sounds. Take the recorder on field trips and record sounds of animals' environments. Replay to review the trip and to help children remember the sequence of events. Record sounds of the environment: cars passing; steps in the corridor or on the street; children skipping, hopping, running. Ask questions like, "Do any of the animals sound alike? Which of the sounds was loudest? How would you describe that sound? Can you draw that sound?"

B. *Street Corner.* Listen to sounds. Identify them: car turning corner, wind blowing past sign, click as light changes, dog barking, rain dripping, wheels on wet pavement, animal footsteps, high heels on pavement, sneakers on pavement, noises from buildings.

C. *Classroom Sounds.* Listen to sounds of different toys, clock ticking, blocks falling. Have children cover their eyes. "Where does the sound come from? What is the sound?" Have Mary walk (skip, run) across the back of the room, the front, or along the side.

D. *Stethoscope.* Listen to heartbeats of children, adults, and animals. Listen to someone's stomach after a snack. Scratch different objects on a table top (floor, rug, pipe) and listen to the sound through the stethoscope.

E. *Rhythms.* Beat out simple and then more complex rhythms with clapping hands. Ask the children to repeat them. Then have the children lead with their own sound rhythms.

TASTE AND SMELL

Be sure to teach children proper precautions in tasting or smelling strange substances.

A. *Cooking.* Make puddings, candy, cakes. Smell before, after, and during cooking. Identify what's cooking by smell. Taste brown sugar, white sugar, molasses, corn syrup, maple syrup. Make lemonade with and without sugar. Squeeze tomatoes, apples, oranges for juice. Question children about what smells best and what smells they don't like. Draw a picture about smells.

B. *Snack or Lunch.* Talk about differences in taste between hamburgers and bologna, between peanuts and peanut butter, between potato chips and mashed potatoes. (These discussions may also get into sense of touch as well as smell and taste.) Have children guess what they will have for lunch from smells coming from the kitchen.

Touching (Tactile Awareness)

A. *Rough or Smooth?* Discuss tactile sensitivity with the children. Objects of varying textures are available, such as silk cloth, burlap, feathers, rope, seashells, mirrors, balls, driftwood, beads, furry slippers, and so on. Children form small groups and each group receives an object. Each child shows how the object makes her feel. For example, a feather may stand in a straight line with arms and legs extended, and then move "softly," with arms waving gently from side to side.

B. *A Collage Made for Touching.* A texture collage is a bulletin board that all students can contribute to and use later for future projects. Have the children bring in materials of different textures—sandpaper, flannel, velvet, burlap, plastic, bottle caps, pebbles, and paper clips—to glue on the board. Once the collage is complete, the children can make "rubbings," using charcoal sticks on newsprint. This board should encourage use of vocabulary-expanding words like "coarse," "smooth," etc.

C. *Creative Movement.* Discriminate between various textures through movements. Have the children feel a texture such as that of silk and interpret it by moving the way it feels. Use a variety of textures that exhibit characteristics such as bumpy, smooth, coarse, prickly.

D. Outdoor Textures
1. Words to use: Rough, smooth, bumpy, soft, hard, sharp, cold, warm, wet, dry, same, different.
2. At the beginning of the walk, ask the children, "How do things feel?" Say, "Let's feel this building," or "Let's feel the back of this tree."
3. For the child who does not know the word "rough," say to her while she feels the tree, "The tree bark feels rough. Let's see if we can find something else that feels rough."
4. For the child who knows the word "rough," say, "Can you find something that feels different from this rough tree?" (Example: a smooth leaf.) Or, "Can you find something that feels the same as this rough tree?"
5. As you continue your walk, find new objects to touch, and name their textures. *Note:* For very young children, begin with two simple words such as rough and smooth, soft and hard, or wet and dry.

E. *Hidden Objects in Boxes.* Hide objects inside boxes and have children feel and describe them without seeing them. Have them match a given object by hunting for its mate in the box without seeing it. Have children match objects by size and shape, or only by shape, by pulling them out of the boxes. (Some children may be able to do this only if they have felt both objects with the same hand.) Put several objects in the boxes to make the task harder; more similar objects also make the task harder.

F. *Hidden Multisensory Objects.* A multisensory feely bag game is perfect for the development of aesthetic senses and descriptive vocabulary. Place an interesting object in a bag and invite children to use as many different words as they can to describe it as they feel it. Write their words down in rows like a poem—*big, squishy, soft, round . . . Pillow!*

G. *Sandpaper Letter Game—Early Elementary.* Provide children with letters cut from sandpaper. Have them work in pairs. Blindfold one child and have the other child give a letter to the blindfolded one to feel and guess its identity. Award one point for each correct identification. Then have the partners switch places.

H. *Touch the Alphabet—Early Elementary.* Make a collection of tactile objects for the various letters of the alphabet. Use cotton balls for "c," denim for "d," a brick for "b," etc. Children will experience the tactile relationship as well as the letter/symbol relationship.

COLORFUL BUBBLES

This activity will enhance children's visual perception and aesthetic skills by observing a variety of subtle color variations. They will also see how light can change these colors. Fine motor skills are also developed in this activity as children use eye droppers.

Materials: Bubble wrap, clear packaging tape, medicine droppers, food coloring, mixing cups, water, and scissors

Procedure:
1. Cut a piece of bubble wrap to a desired size. Use wrap that has at least 5/16″ height bubbles.
2. Using clear packaging tape, place bubble wrap onto the surface of a glass window that is at a level reachable for young children.
3. Cut tiny slits into the tops of bubbles. Let the child decide which bubbles to cut.
4. Fill medicine droppers with food color and place a bit of food coloring into each bubble, filling about ¾ of the bubble.
5. Water can be added to each color of food coloring in varying amounts to make a variety of shades.
6. The child can decide on the color choices and the arrangement of these colors on the bubble wrap. One color can be used and varying amounts of water can be added to investigate the subtle differences in color depending on the concentration of food coloring.
7. Various colors can be mixed together to make new ones.
8. When complete, small pieces of clear tape can secure each bubble.

MY FEELINGS

1. Have the children close their eyes and listen to words that evoke emotion: love, hate, cold, soft, fun, and laugh.
2. While their eyes are closed, ask them to move their markers to reflect the emotion/emotions they feel.
3. Do a series of emotions.
4. Ask students to talk about how each emotion made them feel. Older children can write a brief description of how each emotion made them feel on the back of each drawing.

MY IMAGINATION–KINDERGARTEN AND UP

Materials: string or yarn, scissors, paper, glue, washable markers or crayons

1. Children glue a 6–8-inch-long piece of string or yarn on a piece of paper.

2. Children pass their paper to the person sitting to his or her left.

3. Children take this piece of paper and imagine what the visual represents.

4. Students use markers or crayons to create something from the original string art.

5. Have children discuss what they saw and why it became what it did.

ACTIVITIES FOR OLDER CHILDREN (GRADES 4-5)

COLOR OPTICS

The following are some color optics phenomena older children will enjoy exploring individually.

⊙ **Afterimage.** This is probably the best known illustration of how our eyes react to color. Have the students stare at a page of solid color for about 30 seconds, then look at a dot on a page of white or gray. Our eyes will see *color* on the blank page—usually the complement or near complement of the color first looked upon. For example, we will see red if we first stare at blue-green. We will see blue/violet if we first stare at yellow.

⊙ **Juxtaposition.** Color pigments placed side by side in small repeated strokes are altered by our vision to appear to combine, thus forming a different hue. This new optical effect is more vibrant than if the same pigments were blended together. This technique has been used historically by mosaic and stained glass artists but most effectively by the nineteenth-century Post-Impressionists such as Georges Seurat. Use a print of his painting, *Sunday Afternoon on the Grand Jette,* to explore this concept. Then challenge the students to try their hand at this visual mixing of colors.

⊙ **Color Relativity.** The color gray appears much lighter when placed on a black background than it does against a white one. This dark/light effect holds true for many other colors as well. Yellow on a green background will appear to contain more red than it does on a white background.

Using pairs of colored sheets of paper, let the students make their own discoveries of color optics by placing two samples of the same color on a variety of different backgrounds. Then have them compare results.

ACTIVITIES ON THE CONCEPT OF LINE

Lines are basic to art. Lines can convey different moods. Before drawing and painting experiences, you might want to discuss the variety of lines that we encounter in our daily lives. Ask the students to think about telephone lines, clothes lines, lines of people, lines of music, the line of scrimmage. Then ask some of these questions to get them thinking: What do we associate with lines on a face? Where do you see long pairs of parallel lines? Where do you see more straight lines, in nature or in manmade objects? (Ask them to look around.) Where do you see more curves? Which conveys more movement, a straight line or a curvy one?

To encourage their creative use of line in their work, and to explore line and mood with students, ask questions like these:

A. Verticals
1. What do you see in our environment that is made up of vertical lines? (skyscrapers, trees, telephone poles, rain, Gothic cathedrals, soldiers standing at attention)
2. What moods or feelings do a series of verticals convey? (Heavenward, of the sky, strong, straight, dignified)
3. Have you ever leaned against a vertical? (yes, a wall, a tree, a lamppost)
4. When is your body vertical? (when standing)

B. Horizontals
1. What in the environment is predominantly horizontal? (the horizon, the floor, a bed, a table, a still lake or pond)
2. What moods do these horizontals convey? (grounded, of the earth, relaxed, at rest, calm, serene, expansive)
3. When is your body horizontal? (when lying down, asleep)
4. Can you stand or sit on a horizontal? (yes, a sofa, the floor)

C. Diagonals
1. Where do you see diagonals? (a slide, a plane taking off, a ramp)
2. What feeling is conveyed by diagonals? (action, movement)
3. When is your body at a diagonal? (when you are running, walking fast, leaning into the wind)

D. Wavy lines
  1. Where do you see wavy lines in the environment? (a wavy ocean, lake, river, snake, rolling hills)
  2. What feelings do they convey? (undulating movement, relaxed, rhythmic, fluid)
E. Zigzag lines
  1. Where do you see zigzag lines in the environment? (lightning, a jagged tear, the earth after an earthquake, crimped hair)
  2. What moods do they convey? (tense, anxious, frenzied)
  3. When does your body form a zigzag? (while jumping on a pogo stick)
F. Spirals
  1. What do you see that is shaped in a spiral? (a spring, a slide, water going down a drain, a tornado, a coiled snake)
  2. What feelings do spirals convey? (spinning, swirling, energetic)
  3. When is your body in a spiral? (while twirling on the dance floor or doing a pirouette)

CYBERSPACE AESTHETICS

Have students use the Internet for the following aesthetic experiences:

⊙ Kcho (pronounced as KA-cho) is a well-known artist from the island of Cuba. Check out some of his large three-dimensional works, which are displayed around the world:
  http://www.artnewsonline.com/. Click on Back Issues, go to June 2000 issue, and search for Kcho or click on Making Waves.
  http://www.walkerart.org/education/. Click on Collections and Resources. Type in Kcho on Search box.

⊙ What did you learn about the artist's background? How would you describe Kcho's work? What subjects and themes do you see in most of Kcho's art? What messages do you think the artist is communicating about his culture? How does he use different materials to express himself?

⊙ Ramona Sakiestewa is a Hopi Indian fabric artist. Learn about the artist and her work at the following sites:
  http://www.lewallencontemporary.com. Click on Browse by Artist.
  http://www.dsg-art.com/s/sakiestewa/.

⊙ Describe the design of Sakiestewa's art. What colors, lines, shapes, and textures can be seen? How do you think the work would be different if you saw it in person? Why do you think she uses this media? What could she want viewers of her tapestries to know about her?

ARTISTS LIKE US

Exposing children to the work of famous artists can help them find the artist within.

Materials: white drawing paper; markers; colored pencils; crayons; books or art prints of famous artists such as Picasso, Cezanne, Seurat

1. Present the work of a great master such as Picasso for the children to observe and discuss.

2. Invite children to notice specific qualities of the works and techniques used. For example, children might notice the unusual Cubist portraits of Picasso. You might ask, "How are these different from other portraits you have seen or even drawn?"

3. Provide art materials for children to create their own portraits in the Cubist style.

4. Encourage children to give a title to their works and create a Picasso-inspired art show or class art book.

Variation: Present the Pointillism style of George Seurat. Show how he preferred not to make brushstrokes but to paint by applying small dots of unmixed colors. Provide cotton swabs as painting tools and watercolors for children to paint their own Pointillism painting.

WATER DESIGNS USING AN OVERHEAD PROJECTOR

This is a wonderful way for children to explore the different aesthetic properties of materials—transparent, opaque, and semi-transparent. It also encourages experimentation with a variety of materials.

Materials: Overhead projector, glass tray or glass baking dish filled with water, string, yarn, lace, food coloring, cooking oil, eye/medicine droppers, netting, pipe cleaners, feathers, and any other transparent or semi-transparent materials.

1. Place the glass tray filled with water on top of the overhead projector.
2. Turn on the projector to project light onto a screen or wall.
3. Invite the children to experiment with different materials by placing them into the water tray and watching the projected image on the screen.
4. Encourage children to use drops of color and oil to see and document interesting results.
5. Small pieces of string and yarn can be added along with pipe cleaners twisted into interesting shapes

to further manipulate the image and see the aesthetic nature of the art materials.
6. Add other materials for further explorations of transparent properties, semi-transparent properties, opaqueness, and color mixing.

Variation: More than one projector can be used. Images can be projected as large as the wall to create interesting environments for children. These environments could change on a daily basis depending on the project theme (underwater, forest, sunsets, storms, etc.). Musical selections accompanying these themes can be played while imagery is projected.

CHAPTER REVIEW

1. List three types of sensing and feeling.
2. Give three guidelines to use in choosing materials that have aesthetic potential.
3. List four suggestions to help children work with aesthetic materials.
4. Discuss how to involve parents in their children's aesthetic experiences.
5. List some points to cover when discussing with parents how to interpret their children's creative works.
6. List some points to consider when displaying children's creative works.
7. List six guidelines to use in talking with children about their artwork.
8. What are some differences to expect in the aesthetic experiences of older children?

REFERENCES

Chandler, M. (1973). *Art for teachers of children* (2nd ed.). Columbus, OH: Charles E. Merrill.

Church, E. B. (2002, March). When to challenge children. *Scholastic Early Childhood Today, 33–38.*

Clemens, S. C. (1991, Jan). Art in the classroom: Making every day special. *Young Children,* 4–11.

White, M. (2002, May). A lesson in listening. *Young Children,* 43.

ADDITIONAL READINGS

Althouse, R., Johnson, M. H., & Mitchell, S. T. (2003). *The colors of learning: Integrating the visual arts into the early childhood curriculum.* Washington, DC: National Association for the Education of Young Children (NAEYC).

Barrett, T. (2003). *Interpreting art: Reflecting, wondering, and responding.* New York: McGraw-Hill.

Bresler, L., & Thompson, C. M. (2002). *The arts in children's lives: Context, culture and curriculum.* Boston: Kluwer Academic Publisher.

Epstein, A. S. (2001, May). Thinking about art: Encouraging art appreciation in early childhood settings. *Young Children,* 38–43.

Epstein, A. S., & Trimis, E. A. (2002). *Supporting young artists: The development of the visual arts in young children.* Ypsilanti, MI: High/Scope Press.

Loebl, S. (2002). *America's art museums.* New York: W. W. North & Company, Inc.

Seefeldt, C. (2002). *Creating rooms of wonder: Valuing and displaying children's work to enhance the learning process.* Beltsville, MD: Gryphon House.

SOFTWARE FOR CHILDREN

Animals in Art 1: Art History. Ages 8 and up.

Animals in Art 2: Artists and Illustrators Today. Ages 8 and up.

Fun for Brains. Ages 2–6.

Hoyle Puzzle Games, 2003, Ages 7 and up.

I SPY Series. Ages 5–9.

Milo and the Magical Stones. Ages 3–8

Ollo and the Sunny Valley Fair. Ages 3–6.

HELPFUL WEB SITES

http://www.artbma.org/
Click on Education.
Young children will enjoy using this entertaining, interactive program on the Baltimore Museum of Art Web site. Teachers who introduce their students to Matisse should definitely check out this site.

http://www.EnchantedLearning.com/
Click on English Dictionary on the site index. Click on a letter of the alphabet and connect to, not one, but many, many pictures of works with that letter and hot links to Web sites about that work.

http://www.sanford-artedventures.com/
This Web site has resources for creative individuals from beginner to advanced. It has sections entitled "Create Art, "Study Art," "Play Art Games," and "Teach Art."

For additional creative activity resources, visit our Web site at http://www.EarlyChildEd. delmar.com.

SECTION 2

Planning and Implementing Creative Activities

After studying this section, you should be able to answer the following questions.

1. What do I know about the attention span and activity levels of the young children in my group? How will I include this information in my lesson planning?

2. What can I do to improve the classroom environment for young children in my care by focusing on developmental levels and individual needs and interests of young children?

3. Is my classroom reflective of the individual differences present in the group of children using it?

4. In planning lessons, do I include activities that address the learning styles (multiple intelligences) of children in my group?

5. Do I use methods of differentiated instruction in my classroom that are designed to meet the children's individual learning styles?

6. Have I created a positive and safe physical environment for the young children in my care? What strengths and weaknesses are evident in my classroom arrangement and management practices?

7. Have I included all of the media I can that are developmentally appropriate for young children in my classroom? What changes do I need to make to improve my use of media with young children?

8. Does my classroom reflect all of the ethnic and cultural groups appropriate for my group of children?

9. How do I encourage independent learning and exploration in the arrangement of my room? In my lesson planning? In my choice and use of media?

10. Do I enjoy being in and teaching in my classroom the way it is currently arranged? Do the children enjoy being there? How can I rearrange it to make it more enjoyable for both myself and the children?

11. Are my room arrangement, choice of media, interest centers, and presentation of lessons enticing to the children's interests? Do they encourage convergent or divergent thinking?

12. How will the needs of children from varying backgrounds be addressed in planning a creative and safe environment?

13. Am I aware of the national standards in the content areas and the approach my state has taken to meet the No Child Left Behind Act?

14. Am I working to develop my teaching skills to become as accomplished a teacher as I can be?

15. Does the environment I create for young children provide space, time, and opportunities for all types of play?

16. What role does play have in the total development of young children?

17. How can I plan and arrange the classroom environment so young children are encouraged to play in a way that emphasizes problem solving and exploration?

18. Have I included enough dramatic play materials for all the developmental levels and multicultural backgrounds of my children?

Chapter 5

Children, Teachers, and Creative Activities

Objectives

After studying this chapter, you should be able to:

1. Discuss the terms **differentiated instruction, process learning,** and **multiple intelligences.**
2. Ask a series of questions to better understand and work with young children's developmental levels.
3. Discuss attention span and activity patterns as they relate to young children.
4. Discuss three aspects of the teacher's attitude that have an impact on children's creativity.
5. Explain the teacher's role as facilitator in children's creative activities.
6. List the general planning guidelines for creative activities.
7. Discuss strategies for handling transition times.
8. Discuss national standards for teachers and curriculum content.

Planning creative activities always begins with the child. Each child is unique; each has his own way of being and his own way of responding to the world. The teacher must know what each child is like and should be aware of each child's level of development, strengths, abilities, and special personality. With this knowledge, teachers can relate their own personalities and unique skills to those of each young child. Thus, an atmosphere is created in which both adult and child remain themselves in order to help and respect each other.

Watching a child at play helps an adult understand this young person. A teacher is able to see how the child uses materials and relates to other children. In many educational experiences, and especially in creative activities, the teacher is a facilitator. To **facilitate** means to help along, to guide, to provide opportunities, and to be sensitive and caring without interfering. The meaning as used here is that the teacher allows the young child to deal directly with the materials, with the teacher acting as an aide rather than a leader or judge. Because the emphasis is on divergent thinking and not on right answers in creative activities, judging is not necessary. Yet guidance and feedback are helpful. Because creative activities are open-ended, there are no simple standards for evaluating them. The teacher's role, then, is one of encouraging, questioning, and experimenting.

> I never teach my pupils; I only attempt to provide the conditions in which they can learn. Albert Einstein, 1879-1955, German physicist

CONSIDER THE CHILD

Developmental Level

In many early childhood books and journals, we often see the phrase **developmental level.** Generally, when we speak of a child's development, we are referring to four major areas of growth: physical, social, emotional, and intellectual. These areas serve as a framework on which we organize our knowledge and observations of children. These four areas combined make up the

Figure 5-1

Watching a child play can give a teacher a better understanding of that child.

individual child. When the needs of a child are met in each of these areas in any particular activity, we can be fairly well assured that the overall growth of that child is being encouraged.

Another aspect of a child's development refers to **individual differences.** For example, two children may be exactly the same age but they may be performing at different levels in one or more areas of development. Both children may be within the normal range of development. Therefore, a teacher must not only have a knowledge of developmental levels but must also tune in to the different levels of each child's progress in the four major areas.

A child's ability is closely related to his level of development. If a teacher understands this, failure and frustration can be avoided when planning creative activities. Answers to the following questions can help adults better understand and work with a young child.

- ⊙ What is special about the child?
- ⊙ What are the child's interests?
- ⊙ What are the child's strengths?
- ⊙ What abilities and skills are already developed?
- ⊙ What is the child's home life like?
- ⊙ How does the child relate to adults?
- ⊙ How does the child respond to other children?
- ⊙ What are the motor skills (large and small muscle) of the child?
- ⊙ How does the child express himself?
- ⊙ How does the child speak?
- ⊙ How are problems solved by the child?
- ⊙ With what materials does the child enjoy working?
- ⊙ How does the child learn?

When you have answers to these questions, you are then able to plan creative activities that meet the specific needs of young children.

DIFFERENTIATED INSTRUCTION

The term differentiated instruction is often associated with individualized planning and teaching strategies for young children. Quite simply, it means providing different types of learning experiences and environments to suit the children's individual needs.

Even a beginning teacher will soon discover that no two children learn at the same pace or in the same way. Some need lots of practice; others "get it" immediately. Some take to new materials easily; others are slower to accept them. In early elementary levels, some children can learn from reading, while others get more from listening or from visual aids. Some elementary children have trouble writing clearly, but others express complex ideas in art or music.

Figure 5-2

Differentiated instruction involves planning activities that meet the developmental level of each child.

When using differentiated instructional strategies, a teacher learns how to spot what "works" for each child. She checks to be sure that lessons contain activities and content that will connect for each child in the group.

Characteristics of a Differentiated Classroom

The most obvious feature of a differentiated classroom is that it is child-centered. The following are other indicators that differentiated instruction is present:

⊙ Teachers and students accept and respect one another's similarities and differences.

⊙ The teacher is primarily a coordinator of time, space, and activities rather than a provider of information. The aim is to help students become independent, self-reliant learners.

PARTICULAR STRATEGIES TO INDIVIDUALIZE OR DIFFERENTIATE

Directions: Individualize lessons for particular children by altering lesson and classroom *structure,* the number and kinds of *practices,* the kind and amount of *feedback,* the amount and kind of *choice and control* given to students, the *teaching strategies* used, the nature of *examples* provided, and the kind of *motivational strategies* (i.e., encouragement strategies, such as belief statements).

Place. Change the environment or amount of space. Use carrels, centers, music, different desk arrangements, carpet squares, lower or brighter lighting.

Amount. Give more or less time (e.g., to explore materials). Use more repetition and break into smaller steps. Reduce or increase the number of things to be learned. Alter amount of examples and feedback given. Give additional practice.

Rate. This is the "oftenness." Change the pace. Give more breaks. Create more or less structure for the activity (e.g., intensity of teacher-directed lessons).

Target objectives. Make sure students are clear about goals or outcomes. Consider alternative goals or alternative means of reaching goals. Decide what a child can realistically achieve (know and be able to do). Make objectives life-centered and connected to interests.

Instruction. Use more or less direct instruction (models, demonstration, examples, descriptive feedback, reassurance). Cause students to be mentally and physically active, engaged, and involved with questions. Use Gardner's multiple intelligences to plan each day and monitor the week. Use multisensory approaches: visual, auditory, kinesthetic, tactile, and humor.

Curriculum materials. Give easier materials to read or adapt (e.g., highlight, tape record, rewrite). Use hands-on materials such as games or art media.

Utensils. Use visual and auditory aids. Teach meaning-making tools and strategies (i.e., ways to learn to comprehend, such as shortcuts, cue sheets, cue cards, mnemonics). Don't just teach strategies: teach *when* to use them and *how.*

Level of difficulty. Make the lesson easier or harder to challenge appropriately. Highlight text essentials. Allow notes during tests. Change amount of structure or supervision.

Assistance (from other people). Use peer tutoring, grouping, structure changes, and prompts.

Response. Allow students to show what they know in a variety of ways. Use projects that call for a product or piece to perform. Give exemptions (e.g., from oral reading).

Printed with permission from *The Arts as Meaning* by Claudia E. Cornett, pg. 70, Merrill/Prentice Hall, Inc. (2003).

Figure 5-3

PARTICULAR strategies to individualize or differentiate.

- Children and teachers work together in setting group and individual goals.
- Children work in a variety of group sizes, as well as independently. Flexible grouping is evident.
- Time is used flexibly in the sense that pacing is based on student needs.
- Students have choices about topics they wish to study, ways they want to work, and how they want to demonstrate their learning.
- The teacher uses a variety of instructional strategies to help target instruction to student needs.
- Students are assessed in multiple ways, and each student's progress is measured at least in part from where that student begins.
- Assessment is an ongoing diagnostic activity that guides instruction. Learning tasks are planned and adjusted based on assessment data.

In differentiated instruction, learning, activities, and materials may be varied by difficulty to challenge children at different readiness levels. They may be varied by topics in response to children's individual interests. Activities and materials may also be varied by student's preferred ways of learning or expressing themselves.

Differentiated instruction is a way of thinking about teaching and learning. Some further suggestions for strategies to differentiate instruction are found in Figure 5–3.

> "Many of us have learned to teach with sort of a frontal approach to teaching. In a differentiated classroom, a teacher's role shifts." Tomlinson, 1996.

DIFFERENTIATED INSTRUCTION AND PROCESS LEARNING

Another term associated with differentiated instruction is process learning. Process learning conceives of learning in terms of its processes rather than its products. In process learning focus is on providing children experiences that promote thinking and problem solving without specifically identified outcomes. The early childhood classroom abounds with opportunities for children to actively engage in learning activities rather than listening unquestioningly as they receive the knowledge of others. In process learning, not only do children learn by doing, they reflect on the learning process itself. By doing so, they are able to transfer the information learned in one process or learning situation to another. For example, as the child builds with blocks, continually building up and breaking down

structures, he is learning the process of balance. This process involves size, weight, and object placement. These concepts, in turn, can be applied in the science/discovery center with "sink or float" experiments.

Explaining Process Learning to Parents/Caregivers

To a casual observer, a child's process learning experiences may appear to be simply "playing" or just "messing around." Yet, this type of learning is crucial in that it is self-initiated, ongoing, and transferable to other learning situations. Early childhood teachers need to explain the importance of process learning to parents and caregivers to encourage children's continued and active involvement in process learning. What may seem aimless is active processing, storing and receiving information by a child's exploration. Process learning helps children develop information processing skills that can be applied across the curriculum. Most importantly, process learning emphasizes information discovered by the *learner*. This type of independent, active learning is key to acquiring knowledge all through life.

DIFFERENTIATED INSTRUCTION AND MULTIPLE INTELLIGENCES

When planning early childhood activities using differentiated instructional strategies, an understanding of multiple intelligences is essential if you are to meet the individual needs of children. According to Howard Gardner's multiple intelligence theory, each of us possesses eight "intelligences," or ways to be smart (Gardner, 1999). Some of us are more adept at using our hands; others are good at making rhymes or singing songs. Each type of intelligence gives us something to offer the world. What makes us unique is the way each intelligence expresses itself in our lives.

By recognizing multiple intelligences, we can help children enhance their individual strengths. Yet understanding multiple intelligences means more than focusing on individual characteristics. Just imagine a grown person who could do nothing but write poetry or solve algebra problems. To do everyday things like drive a car or follow a recipe, a person needs to be smart in more than one way.

Each of us is smart in all eight ways. Here's how to recognize these multiple intelligences in ourselves and in children:

Word Smart (Linguistic Intelligence)

At younger ages, children who are word smart enjoy listening and telling stories. They are effective in expressing themselves and convincing others by using language and their rich vocabulary. They like word games and puzzles. These children are often successful learners by listening and hearing because they sort information through their listening and repeating skills.

Older children who are word smart have a rich vocabulary and are sensitive to the meaning of words, grammar rules, and the function of language in writing and orally. Journalists, lawyers, and storytellers often demonstrate this type of intelligence.

Logic Smart (Logical/Mathematical Intelligence)

Children with high logical/mathematical intelligence are curious about how things work. They like to ask questions and investigate. They use numbers easily and enjoy solving problems. They have the ability to understand logical patterns, categories and relationships, and causes and effects. They enjoy strategy games, logical puzzles, and experiments. They like to use computers. Scientists, accountants, and computer programmers generally have this ability.

Picture Smart (Visual/Spatial Intelligence)

People with high visual intelligence are able to visualize three-dimensional objects. They take the information and translate it into images and pictures in their mind. When they need to, they have the ability to retrieve the information through the images and pictures they made earlier.

Older children who are picture smart have the ability to understand geometry and recognize the relationships of objects in space. Children with visual intelligence in schools are successful in geometry. They also are very good in visual arts, sculpture, architecture, and photography.

These children enjoy mazes and jigsaw puzzles. They like to spend their free time drawing and building with Legos. These children are also known as daydreamers.

Music Smart (Musical Intelligence)

Music smart is the capacity to understand and express oneself musically. Children with this ability can keep time with music, sing in tune, and tell the difference between types of music. They can appreciate melodies.

People with musical intelligence have ability to hear and recognize tones, rhythms, and musical patterns. These people enjoy listening to music and singing to themselves.

Musical children often play a musical instrument. They participate in the school choir or school band.

They like to sing or drum to themselves. They can remember and repeat a melody after listening to it only once. They learn through rhythm and melody. They need music to study or learn. They learn new things more easily if sung, tapped out, or whistled.

Body Smart (Bodily/Kinesthetic Intelligence)

Body smart is the ability to use the body skillfully and express oneself. People with bodily intelligences use their body to communicate and solve problems. They are good with objects and activities involving their body, hands, and fingers.

People with bodily intelligence prefer to learn through their body or feelings. These people are more successful in learning if they can touch, manipulate, and move or feel whatever they are learning.

Children with high kinesthetic intelligence learn best with activities such as games, acting, hands-on tasks, and building. These children process the information by applying it and through bodily sensation (e.g., in a classroom where people from history are acted out or an assignment that allows them to build something such as Lego towers, etc.).

Children with bodily intelligence like being physically active, playing sports, dancing, and acting. They like doing crafts and working on mechanical projects.

Person Smart (Interpersonal Intelligence)

Person smart is the ability to understand people and relationships. People with interpersonal intelligence understand and care about people and their feelings and interact effectively with them. They approach people with empathy and recognize differences among people and value their points of view with sensitivity to their motives, moods, and intentions. These people are sensitive to facial expressions, gestures, and voice. They get along with others and they are able to maintain good relationships with one or more people among family and friends.

Children with interpersonal intelligence often have more than one friend. They care about their friends and like to help to solve their problems. These children like to teach other children and take part in school organizations and clubs. They have the ability to influence people and are natural leaders.

Self-Smart (Intrapersonal Intelligence)

Being self-smart is having the ability to think about and understand oneself. People with intrapersonal intelligence are aware of their strengths and weaknesses and moods and motivations. They have the ability for self-discipline to achieve personal goals.

These children are self-motivated. They can monitor their thoughts and feelings and control them effectively. Intrapersonal children need their own quiet space most of the time. They prefer to study individually and learn best through observing and listening. They like to play by themselves. They use self-knowledge to make decisions to set goals. They are sensitive to their own feelings and moods.

Nature Smart (Naturalistic Intelligence)

Nature smart is the ability to recognize plants, animals, and other parts of the natural environment. These people may like doing activities related to nature such as fishing, hiking, or camping.

Children with naturalistic intelligence enjoy outdoor activities and have a strong connection to the outside world or to animals. They notice patterns and things from nature easily. They love collecting flowers, rocks, leaves, etc. They may enjoy stories, shows, or any subjects that deal with animals or natural happenings. They are interested in the care of animals and zoology. These children also show an interest in endangered species. They easily learn the characteristics, names, and any information about species found in the world.

By exploring all of the intelligences, children become well-rounded individuals who are successful in many aspects of life. Early childhood teachers need to recognize these different strengths in children as they emerge. Some children may respond more to words, and others to music—the point is to plan activities that allow children to express themselves in the way that suits them best. If children have the opportunity to learn in the areas they prefer, and to improve in those areas that are not as strong, they will grow to become intelligent in more ways than one. See the Online Companion for observation sheets to help you in understanding your own intelligences and how to use them in your teaching.

In summary, the multiple intelligences theory can be a useful way to help children learn and truly *understand* what they are learning. Although the multiple intelligence theory has powerful implications for teachers, it is not an educational prescription (Nicholson-Nelson, 1998). You must decide how best to use it in your own classroom setting.

DIFFERENTIATED INSTRUCTION AND CHILDREN WITH SPECIAL NEEDS

Adapting a classroom to accommodate children with special needs is a similar process to the basic idea of differentiating instruction. In both cases, the teacher provides activities and content that is appropriate for each student. The following are some specific ways to adapt (or differentiate) instruction in the early childhood classroom for children with special needs.

⊙ Meet each child at his own level of development, foster that stage, and enable the child to move on to the next level. For example, children have individual differences when it comes to motor development. Some children will be able to carry out complex actions such as tying their shoes or doing a complicated drawing, while others may barely be able to draw a line. A child with special needs in the motor area may barely be able to communicate preverbally with pointing, while other children without special needs may have lots of words but differ in the complexity of their thinking. Each needs to be worked with at her own level and then helped to advance.

⊙ Tailor the environment to each child's strengths and weaknesses and help all the children, special needs or not, to build greater competency.

⊙ Interact with children in ways that help them to think and problem-solve at their own levels. These interactions need to be a part of an ongoing, trusting relationship that children have with you and with each other. Having dynamic relationships is essential while climbing up the developmental ladder (Greenspan, 2001).

⊙ Make sure that the child is gradually using most of his senses. For example, if a child has a visual-processing difficulty, begin by offering activities that draw on other senses, including hearing, smell, or touch, as a way to engage him or her. Gradually introduce simple visual-processing experiences. As the child comes to recognize that he or she can succeed, the child will feel more competent and be more inclined to participate in activities he or she finds challenging.

⊙ Increase challenges in manageable, easy steps so children are successful 70% to 75% of the time. Again, keep in mind that it is important to use warm and caring words of encouragement and lively praise as children attempt to meet each new challenge (Greenspan, 2001).

ADAPTING INSTRUCTION FOR OLDER CHILDREN WITH SPECIAL NEEDS

Some suggestions for differentiating instruction and adapting a classroom for older children with special needs are as follows:

⊙ Adapt the number of items that the learner is expected to learn or complete. For example, if the student is to know the 50 states, have students only be responsible for remembering a certain number at a time. This would be dependent on the student's level of disability.

⊚ Adapt the time allotted and allowed for learning, task completion, or testing. For example, allow the student additional time to complete timed assignments. However, if the total project is due by a particular time, have the student complete each portion of the project over various intervals with the required finished project due at a later time.

⊚ Increase the amount of personal assistance with a specific learner. For example, allow for peer teaching. Pair the special learner with the more advanced students to provide support.

⊚ Adapt the way instruction is delivered to the learner. For example, provide students with an audiotape and/or videotape of the lesson. Allow for field trips, guest speakers, peer teaching, computer support, or video productions performed by students.

⊚ Adapt the skill level, problem type, or rules on how the learner may approach the work. For example, allow the student to be creative, providing that the task is completed according to the teacher's specifications. For example, the student may draw a picture of the assignment, do an interview, etc., depending on the subject. Allow the student to come up with the idea.

⊚ Adapt how the student can respond to instruction. For example, allow students to draw pictures, write an essay, or complete specific computer software programs relating to the lesson.

⊚ Adapt the extent to which a learner is actively involved in the task. For example, tailor the student's participation in a task to his or her abilities, whether intellectual or physical.

⊚ Adapt the goals or outcome expectations while using the same materials. For example, in a writing assignment, alter the expectations for a student with disabilities who takes longer to write a paragraph.

⊚ Provide different instruction and materials to meet a student's individual goals. For example, instead of reciting the 50 states, have the student with special needs work on a puzzle of the United States.

Developmentally Appropriate Early Childhood Classrooms

Using their knowledge of developmental levels and using the previously mentioned information on teaching strategies, early childhood teachers are able to design developmentally appropriate environments for young children. Developmentally appropriate early childhood classrooms are those that demonstrate, among other important characteristics, maximum interaction among children as they pursue a variety of independent and small-group tasks. The teacher prepares the environment with challenging and interesting materials and activities and then steps back to observe, encourage, and deepen children's use of them. In a developmentally appropriate environment, teachers ask thought-provoking questions and make appropriate comments (Barclay & Breheny, 1994).

The National Association for the Education of Young Children (NAEYC), in its position statement on developmentally appropriate practices in early childhood education, calls for a curriculum of active learning organized around learning centers for four- to eight-year-olds. These strategies include the following:

⊚ Children select many of their own activities from among a variety of learning areas the teacher prepares, including dramatic play, blocks, science, math, games and puzzles, books, recordings, art, and music.

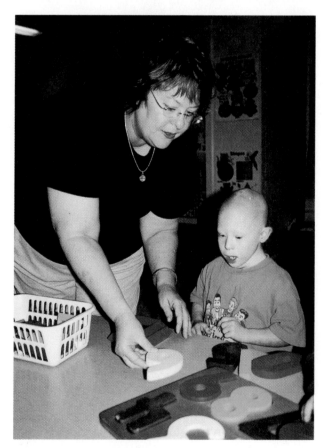

Figure 5-4

Children with Down's syndrome often can surprise you with very strong feelings.

Figure 5-5

According to Gardner's multiple intelligence theory, some children learn best in a group setting.

- Children are expected to be physically and mentally active. Children choose from among activities the teacher has set up or the children spontaneously initiate.
- Children work individually or in small, informal groups most of the time.
- Children are provided concrete learning activities involving materials and people relevant to their own life experiences (Bredekamp, 1997).

Thus, a developmentally appropriate environment for young children is one that empowers children to be curious, to inquire, to experiment, and to think for themselves.

Attention Span and Children's Physical Needs

One must also consider a child's attention span and activity patterns when planning creative activities; it may

Figure 5-6

Freedom to explore materials in his or her own way aids the child's creative development.

mean the difference between successful creative learning experiences and creative activities that dissolve into chaos.

Attention span. A general rule to remember on the length of a child's interest (**attention span**) is this: The *younger* the child, the *shorter* the attention span. It is not unusual for toddlers and two-year-olds to have a maximum attention span of two to three minutes on the average. Attention span gradually increases as a child gets older, and a child of six years of age can be expected to attend for an average of 15 minutes maximum. A teacher may come to expect a longer attention span than is really possible, simply because the child maintains the *appearance* of attention. More often than not, however, young children make it quite obvious when their attention span is waning—by a yawn, a turned head, fidgeting, excess wiggling, or even by physically leaving—giving clear signs that attention to the task is "turned off."

Figure 5-7

In differentiated instruction, a teacher works with children's specific developmental levels, adapting as necessary to meet their changing needs and interests.

Figure 5-8

An observant teacher knows when a child is ready to move from tearing and pasting to trying out scissors.

An early childhood teacher needs to be able to read these obvious signs of lessening (or lost) attention. When they appear, it is time to move on to another topic, suggest a new activity, ask a question, do some "body stretching," or use any other change of pace to get back the child's interest. However, if a teacher has planned developmentally appropriate activities—those that are not too easy and present just enough of a challenge—even very young children will attend longer. Noting which activities keep the children's interest longer and planning for their frequent inclusion in the program are good ways to work *with* children's developmental needs and interests. Including activities that appeal to the children's multiple intelligences is also part of planning developmentally appropriate activities for young children.

In direct contrast, many teachers feel compelled to "forge ahead" on their lesson plans despite the children's lack of interest or involvement. Although it may be difficult to scrap one's lesson plans in midstream, it is even more difficult to try to "make" children pay attention when the activities just do not match the children's needs and interests. As many experienced teachers have found, it is far easier to work *with* children's specific needs and interests, adapting as necessary to meet their changing developmental needs. If, for instance, the interest at the art center is waning and children choose to go elsewhere when given the choice, a teacher needs to reevaluate the activities in that center to see if they are, in fact, a suitable match for the developmental needs of the children.

The children might be ready to move from tearing and pasting to trying out scissors because their small motor skills are better developed from all the previous tearing experiences. Or they may be ready for colored markers as a change of pace from crayons. The point is that by changing activities and equipment to keep them "matched" to their present developmental levels, you are helping the children attend to activities longer *on their own.* Young children will, however, never be bored using the same media over and over again if they have new, interesting, and exciting ideas,

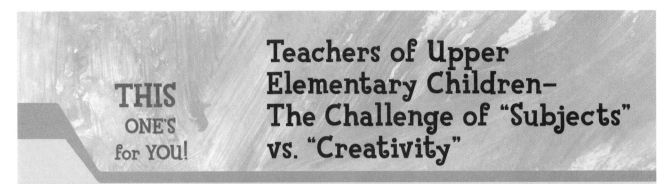

Teachers of Upper Elementary Children— The Challenge of "Subjects" vs. "Creativity"

Teachers of children in the upper elementary grades have an especially challenging situation with regard to creativity in the classroom. There is much ado about what we should be teaching children. We hear, "Teach them basics." "Teach them to test well." "Teach them to resolve conflict." "Teach them about sex." Teach them, teach them, teach them—and make sure that their test scores show they have been taught well.

But, it isn't *what* should be taught that's important. It's what should be kept *alive* that deserves equal attention. And for these children—it's their sense of wonder.

Rarely have I known a child who enters his or her first school situation without a natural sense of wonder. If, while we teach, we simultaneously fan the embers of wonder and hope that existed in them as small children, can we go wrong?

Ask yourself some questions. Do I teach children to read so they can test well? Or do I teach them to read so that they can have direct lines to the thoughts, hopes, and dreams of thousands of writers?

Do I teach children to write so that they can have a nice piece of writing in their portfolio for next year's teacher? Or, do I teach them to write to help them sprout wings and access new avenues for self-expression? Question the reasons why you teach the things you teach.

Our jobs are important. The implications of what we do go beyond the next test scores. If we lift up our reasons for teaching into what I see as the higher realms of wonder—hope and possibilities—wouldn't test scores rise with our reasons?

It's not a question of whether or not we should teach the basics. Of course we should teach them. But let's not sell ourselves or our students short with our reasons for teaching them.

thoughts, and feelings to express. With a store of continual, meaningful experiences to think or feel something about, children's stores of ideas, feelings, and imagination will be constantly enriched.

When there is a new thought or feeling pushing to be expressed, children will continually be challenged to find new and different ways to use the same paints, clay, crayons, paper, and markers to give form to their ideas. Think about it. Adult artists use the same materials for decades. What changes is how they use the materials and what they want to communicate (Seefeldt, 1995).

Another approach to working with short attention spans is to plan *around* the expected attention span of the children in the group. For example, for a 10–minute circle time, a teacher of a group of three year olds would plan an average of four activities taking about two to three minutes each. This could be four different finger plays; two poems, one finger play, and one song; or two "Simon Says" games and two fingerplays.

The point is to work with what you know about the group of young children with whom you are working.

Another important point about attention span is its highly individual nature. Some young children of three may attend to a very favorite activity for longer than three minutes, or a first grader of six may not be able to attend to a language arts lesson for five minutes! In this case, you need to consider the match between the individual child and the specific activity.

Activity patterns.   A young child will generally attend better to new activities that are a good match to his present level of development—that is, activities that are neither too difficult nor too easy. It is also important to vary activities so that the new and the old are in an interesting as well as developmentally appropriate pattern for young children. A good **activity pattern** is one that begins with the familiar (or favorite), reviews some other related activities, then moves on to introduce the new and different. For example, in intro-

THINK ABOUT IT... Why Coloring Books?

Many early childhood teachers would have to admit that they use pre-drawn images that they ask the children to either add to or complete by coloring in. One 4th grade teacher I know requires an intensive book report for his class and then gives them a picture to color in for the cover! Where does creativity enter into that?

Whenever I discuss this "coloring book problem," whether with students or colleagues, many of them share their experiences with coloring books and dittos and remark that coloring was, and still is, a very relaxing activity. Why would this be bad for children?

Dittos and coloring books are adult-generated images designed to occupy children's time. There are times when occupying children's time is exactly what we want to do—for example, during long car trips. Coloring in coloring books can be relaxing because children are not required to think to complete the work. In school, do we want children *not to think?* Activities such as these often reduce children's ability to think for themselves and result in dependence on the teacher at a time when children should be learning independence.

Teachers sometimes use these methods so they can accomplish work of their own, such as correcting homework and classroom papers. Children can become so accustomed to seeing adult-generated images that when asked to create drawings of their own, they become frustrated because their work resembles that of a child rather than that of an adult. If children become frustrated, they lose interest in drawing and the creative process.

ducing the letter "B," the teacher may begin with a favorite song about "Buttons, the Clown." Then she has the children identify picture cards of foods that begin with "B," and later introduces the phoneme "b" and related written words. In a similar activity pattern, a teacher of four year olds begins with a favorite finger play about five little monkeys; has five children act out the monkeys; and then introduces a new book he plans to read about monkeys and their babies which is part of a new animal unit.

An activity pattern for young children also must take into account their physical characteristics. Children develop large muscle skills first and enjoy practicing these skills. They also need practice to develop small motor skills. So, activity patterns should include time for both large and small motor tasks. In the previous example, the teacher of four year olds included a large motor task (jumping like monkeys) with a small motor task (a finger play). Activities planned to include both types of activities in one session also help increase attention span because they include favorite large-motor activities.

Creative activities for young children must also have a good balance between active and quiet activities. All of one type activity would not be appropriate for the developmental needs of young children. A good rule to

remember here is as follows: The younger the child, the greater the tendency to become overstimulated. So, the amount of activities for toddlers and young two year olds should be limited to avoid overstimulation. Activities should be added as the children can handle them.

Also, in a single instructional setting (or lesson), young children of all ages need active as well as quiet activities because they have a difficult time sitting quietly for extended periods. In the previous first-grade example, the teacher could provide an appropriate balance of active-quiet activities by having children go to the board and write a "B" on it or even walk to an object beginning with the letter "B." This way, children's physical inability to sit quietly is considered in the lesson. In the example of the teacher of four year olds, we see similar planning for the active (jumping) and quiet (listening to a story). By following the more active with a more quiet activity, the teacher is working with the physical needs of young children to be active and to rest after exertion.

Transitions from group times. Transitions from group times to the next activities can be chaotic if group times are uninteresting, too long, or too demanding. If children in a group become wiggly and uncomfortable, you can expect a difficult transition.

Even a short, interesting group time can end with a mad exodus if precautions are not taken. Consider how the teacher in the following scenario took such precautions:

> The teacher is showing slides to the children. Between shows, she suggests the children get up to jump and stretch to get their wiggles out. Just as she is about to start the projector again, Christine and three friends come running up to her. The teacher looks at Christine and asks, "What is it?" Christine reports, "John is bothering us. He didn't get all his wiggles out."

This teacher has a delightful way of labeling the process through which young children settle down and become quiet after active play or after a period of concentration. Getting rid of wiggles on demand is seldom an easy process. Each child has her or his own way and time to achieve quiet, as this scene so nicely demonstrates. A group of young children without wiggles would be cause for concern. A healthy group of children needs a patient teacher, one who can accept the various ways in which individual children respond to the request for quiet.

Another suggestion for preventing chaotic transitions from group times is to share the day's schedule with the children at the beginning of the day. This way they know what will happen. Any special rules may need to be reviewed. Then as each activity begins and ends, reminders will suffice. "Do you remember what we are going to do after our story today?" "When we get ready for our walk we will need to get our coats. How can we do that without bumping into each other when we leave the circle?" When children help with the plans and participate in setting the limits, they are more apt to understand, remember, and be willing to help enforce the rules. Do not forget to give positive reinforcement when things go well, not just reminders when someone fails to remember. However, positive reinforcement should not become so automatic or mechanical that children begin to doubt its sincerity. Some genuine response—a smile, pat, or word—is always more effective than a stock phrase.

Transitions to free choice times. A key strategy for avoiding mad dashes at the beginning of free choice times is the assurance that children will have

THINK ABOUT IT...

Teaching Children with Special Needs—Truth or Fiction?

Many adults have had little or no experience with people who are handicapped in some way because, usually, people who are handicapped have been separated from the mainstream into programs especially designed for them. For teachers with little or no previous experience with people with disabilities, having children with disabilities in their classrooms may provide them with the opportunity to learn to value such children for their unique strengths as well as to understand better their disabilities. Teachers and other adults may find that as they become acquainted with children who are disabled, former beliefs about the handicaps are changed. For example, they may find the following:

⊙ Children who are blind do not use alternative sensory channels for information automatically; they must learn to use hearing, smell, and tactile senses as well as movement to replace sight. Adults must help them develop these skills.

⊙ Children with loss of hearing, even with severe or profound loss, are not necessarily quiet. They may be constantly babbling, chattering, or using jargon and other forms of unintelligible speech.

⊙ Children with Down's syndrome typically appear to be cheerful, compliant, and loving, but they are not always so. They may surprise you with anger and stubborn resistance.

⊙ Children with severe and multiple physical handicaps such as cerebral palsy may have normal or superior cognitive ability masked by their inability to express themselves readily.

ample time for their favorite activities. If free choice time is too short or few activities are interesting, some children will run to grab their chosen activity. Others will flit about aimlessly and not bother to start anything because they know they will have to stop soon. It is important to have enough interesting things to do and to use a system that allows children to select a second activity if the first is not satisfactory. Children who are bored or frustrated during free choice time are rarely cooperative when it is time to clean up. A free choice time that is too long, however, will give you tired children who are no longer constructively busy and are ready to misbehave. It takes flexibility and a good eye for the quality of work and play to know the right amount of time for free play.

Transitions to group times: back together. Moving into a group time is often facilitated by a little advance publicity. It builds interest to have something in a bag and as the children ask about it, say, "I'll show you at group time." Children will look forward to group times in which they have a chance to show their block building, artwork, or the book they have drawn and stapled. The morning planning time can give advance notice of exciting things to come, and reminders can keep interest alive throughout the day.

From the first arrival at group time, there should be a teacher or classroom assistant in place to be with the children. Trying to control behavior at a distance is always hazardous and never more so than during a transition.

Sometimes teachers let children look at books until all are ready for storytime or music. When the last things are put away at cleanup time, the teacher walks over to the rug and says, "Time to collect the books." Some children have just arrived and have opened the cover of their favorite storybook. Some children are in the middle of reading their favorite book. Some children may resist and some might cooperate, but they will all be left with the feeling that the teacher does not value books except as a tool to keep them quiet.

Figure 5-9

The child with an intrapersonal intelligence learning style often prefers to work alone.

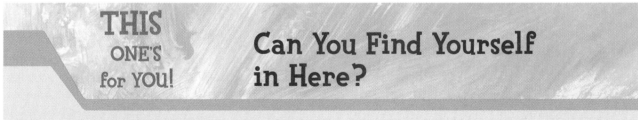

THIS ONE'S for YOU!   Can You Find Yourself in Here?

Asking young children the question, "What do you think teachers do in the teacher's lounge?" resulted in some interesting answers. Here are three of them:

"Chew the gum they take away from you!"

"Tell each other who the worst kids are."

"Think up more rules."

How close to the truth are their answers? Can you find yourself in any of these answers? What do you think children would say about what *you* do in the teacher's lounge?

Figure 5-10
Children with a logical/mathematical learning style are curious about how things work.

Figure 5-11
Teachers encourage creativity by letting children discover their own best way of doing something.

You might try this different approach. When all the children are seated and looking at books, sit down with the children. You may share books with some of the children or just wait for a reasonable period of time. Then you may give a warning that it will soon be time to put the books away. As children finish, collect their books and allow others to finish while you begin the discussion or possibly a fingerplay to occupy those who are through. When most books have been collected, then you may have your group activity. This process respects children and their interest in books.

CONSIDER THE TEACHER/CAREGIVER

Attitude

Attitude is basic to facilitating creative activities with young children. Some teacher attitudes and ideas that help facilitate creative behavior in young children include the following.

Tolerate small mistakes. When children do not have to worry about being perfect, they have more energy to be creative.

Avoid telling the child the best way to do things. To tell a child the best way implies, first, that the teacher knows it; second, that the child does not know it; and third, that the child has to ask the teacher to know the next time.

Be concerned about what children are doing–not about the final product. In creative activities, young children are in a process—playing, drawing, painting, building. Although they are interested in mastering tasks and producing things of which they are proud, they are not like adults. The final product may not be as important as experimenting, as using their minds and senses while doing it. That is why young children often build a complex structure with blocks and then take great joy in knocking it over. They want to see what happens!

Older children enjoy the process of creating as well as younger children. However, older children will show more concern for the product, which is natural at this developmental level. Encouraging an open, "what-if?" approach to creative activities will help the older child concentrate on the process as well as the product.

Resist the temptation to always have quiet and order. Silence may not be the spirit of joy. Cleanliness may not be the companion of discovery. Timing and flexibility are all important in these matters.

Get involved. The teacher who is painting, drawing, and working beside the children, or accompanying them on a field trip or a walk, is a companion and friend. To the children, the activity must be worth doing if the teacher is doing it too. This helps motivation and is a legitimate entry into the children's world. Besides, it's fun! Be careful, however, not to cause the children to copy what you are doing. Be sure to "slip away" before this happens.

STRATEGIES FOR SUCCESS

Teachers plan creative activities with the children's needs and interests in mind. In addition to assessing whether the planned activity is developmentally appropriate for a particular group of children, there are some general planning guidelines to follow that will help ensure the success of these activities.

Preparation

Often, teachers attempt a creative activity that they have not experienced before. They may have read about it in a book, heard about it from a friend, or seen it at a workshop. They try it because they feel it should work and the children should gain something from it. Often it does succeed, but sometimes it does not. The unfortunate part is that when it does not, the teacher may not know whether it was because of the activity itself or the way it was prepared for and offered. For any activity, especially for a first-time experience, the following suggestions may be helpful.

Try the activity before presenting it to the children. Do this physically, if possible, or else mentally. Sometimes things sound better than they really are. The children should experiment, not be experimented on.

Figure 5-12
An early childhood environment should encourage children's free expression.

Make sure all necessary equipment is present. Too few scissors, paints without brushes, and paper without paste can cause a great deal of frustration. Creativity and frustration don't mix well.

Think through the activity. Review in your mind (and on paper) the best way to present the activity, step by step.

Modify the activity, if necessary, to meet the developmental needs of the children. Few activities are right for all cultures, all situations, or every type of child. Be sure to include appropriate materials for children with special needs. All teachers must be sensitive to this.

In as little time as possible, explain the activity so that the children know how to begin and proceed. For this part, rules are not necessary but understanding is.

THIS ONE'S for YOU!

Fragile! Speak to with Care

The way a teacher speaks to and with a young child can mean the difference between the child's positive feelings of self and those not-so-positive feelings. The following suggestions may be helpful to you as you work with young children, helping them grow. Cherish their uniqueness.

⊙ Before speaking to children, get their attention. Putting your hand on a child's shoulder or speaking the child's name helps. Always get on the child's eye level.

⊙ The younger the child, the simpler your statement should be.

⊙ Act as if you expect your words to be heeded. Young children are influenced by the confidence in the adult's tone and action.

⊙ Give children time to respond—their reaction time is slower than yours. Try not to answer your own questions!

⊙ Tell children what they can do rather than what they cannot do. Use positive rather than negative suggestions or statements.

⊙ Give only as much help as is needed, and give simple directions. Use manual guidance to aid verbal suggestions with young children.

⊙ Use encouraging rather than discouraging statements: "You can do it," not "Is it too hard?"

⊙ Use specific rather than general statements: "You need to put on your socks, and now your shoes," not, "Put on your clothes."

⊙ Use pleasant requests rather than scolding: "You will need to pick up your materials now," not, "Get those things picked up."

⊙ Use substitute suggestions rather than negative comments: "Use that pencil from the drawer over there," not, "Don't use that."

⊙ Give a choice between two things when possible. You may say, "Will you wash your face, or shall I help you?" This means the child will be washed in any case. Never give a choice where there is none, such as, "Do you want to wash?" when washing is necessary. Try not to say, "Would you like to _____?" if you do not intend to abide by the child's choice.

⊙ Remember to show disapproval in what the child *does* when necessary, but never disapproval of the *child.* You can say, "You are a good climber, but you will need to climb on the jungle gym. This roof is not solid enough."

⊙ Working *with* a child—trying to tell or show the child how to do it alone—is better for learning than doing it for the child.

⊙ Keep your promises to children. For example, if you say you will let someone have a turn later, be sure to offer that turn as soon as you can, even though the child may have found another activity. Let the child decide whether to leave the present activity to take a turn.

⊙ Encourage children to use language (to replace physical force, crying, whining, etc.) to communicate their problems, needs, and wishes.

⊙ Children learn through example. Many things, such as manners, are "caught," not always necessarily "taught."

After the children have started, circulate among them. Offer suggestions where helpful, and answer questions as needed. Try to let the children answer their own questions as well as solve their own problems. The teacher's role remains that of a facilitator.

Presentation of Creative Activities

The success of any creative activity is influenced by how it is presented, which in turn is affected by how prepared the teacher is for guiding the children in the activity. In planning for each activity, the teacher should do the following:

⊙ identify goals for the activity.

⊙ identify possible learning from the activity.

⊙ list the materials necessary for the activity.

⊙ determine how to set up the activity.

⊙ decide how to stimulate the children and how to keep their interest alive.

Figure 5-13

A young child is always learning new ways to approach materials. Always allow time for children to explore new media and repeat activities with familiar materials.

- anticipate questions the children might ask.
- plan ways to evaluate the activity.
- consider follow-up activities.
- consider cleanup time and requirements.

A broad range of creative activities should be included each week. This gives children a variety of choices to suit their many interests. Not only should each curriculum area be highlighted, but certain types of behavior should also be considered. Dramatic play, creative movement, singing, outdoor activities, and small-group projects should all take place within each week.

Do not move too fast when presenting new ideas or activities for young children. As we learned earlier, when using methods of differentiated instruction, time is flexible and is based on the needs of the child. Children need time to create and explore with new materials. For the very young child, even more time may be needed. Activities should be repeated so that the children learn new ways of approaching the material and expand their understanding through repetition. Purposely leave out specific art activities in the classroom for several days so that if a child does not want to try it the first day or the second day, she has another chance.

Proper sequencing should be given close attention. Activities should build upon each other. For example, some children may want to taste, feel, and smell an apple before they draw or paint one. Once a child is

involved in a creative activity, a few words of encouragement may be all that is needed to keep the child interested. It is useful to watch for children who are having problems. A little help may be needed to solve a small problem. Children need enough time to finish an activity. Be sure children are not stopped just when they are beginning to have fun.

Completing a Creative Activity

At the end of each day, the teacher evaluates the day's activities. Ideas for the next day can be revised or created based on what then appears best. What were the successes of the day? How interested were the children in what they were doing? What did their conversation and play indicate? What does the teacher feel like doing? The key words are *question, think, feel, decide.* A person who works with young children must always be open to new information and feedback.

STRATEGIES FOR SUCCESS— THE NATIONAL LEVEL

All of the information in this chapter so far has centered on the developmental approach to teaching young children. This is, and will continue to be, the most basic and direct approach to working with young children in creative activities and in all other areas. However, anyone who teaches young children in the United States today needs to be aware of the three-prong national focus on (1) legislation in education, (2) content standards, and (3) standards for teachers. What follows is a brief description of each of these three areas. More in-depth information on these issues can be found in the references listed at the end of this chapter.

Legislation and Education

In 2001 the **No Child Left Behind (NCLB) Act** was authorized by Congress. This particular act has been highly publicized for its dramatic emphasis on improving American schools to create more equitable educational opportunities for all children. NCLB is intended to provide *all* children with a fair, equal, and significant opportunity to obtain a high-quality education. One of the most significant (and controversial) provisions of NCLB is the requirement that states set standards and conduct annual assessments to gauge school districts' progress in improving students' academic achievement. This leads us directly to the second focus in our discussion—content standards.

INTERSTATE NEW TEACHER ASSESSMENT AND SUPPORT CONSORTIUM STANDARDS

Standard #1—Knowledge of Subject Matter
The teacher understands the central concepts, tools of inquiry, and structure of the discipline(s) he or she teaches and can create learning experiences that make these aspects of subject matter meaningful for students.

Standard #2—Knowledge of Human Development and Learning
The teacher understands how children learn and develop and can provide learning opportunities that support their intellectual, social, and personal development.

Standard #3—Adapting Instruction for Individual Needs
The teacher understands how students differ in their approaches to learning and creates instructional opportunities that are adapted to diverse learners.

Standard #4—Multiple Instructional Strategies
The teacher understands and uses a variety of instructional strategies to encourage students' development of critical thinking, problem solving, and performance skills.

Standard #5—Classroom Motivation and Management Skills
The teacher uses an understanding of individual and group motivation and behavior to create a learning environment that encourages positive social interaction, active engagement of learning, and self-motivation.

Standard #6—Communication Skills
The teacher uses knowledge of effective verbal, nonverbal, and media communication techniques to foster active inquiry, collaboration, and supportive interaction in the classroom.

Standard #7—Instructional Planning
The teacher plans instruction based on knowledge of subject matter, students, the community, and curriculum goals.

Standard #8—Assessment of Student Learning
The teacher understands and uses formal and informal assessment strategies to ensure the continuous intellectual, social, and physical development of the learner.

Standard #9—Professional Commitment and Responsibility
The teacher is a reflective practitioner who continually evaluates the effects of his or her choices and actions on others (students, parents, and other professionals in the learning community) and who actively seeks out opportunities to grow professionally.

Standard #10—Partnerships
The teacher fosters relationships with school colleagues, parents, and agencies in the larger community to support students' learning and well-being.

NBPTS Standards for Accomplished Teaching
In most states, teachers in kindergarten and up must be state certified to teach in public schools. In addition to state certification, there is a national certification that recognizes exemplary practice or **accomplished teaching**. The National Board for Professional Teaching Standards (NBPTS) has created a set of standards for a system of national certification for teachers.

National Board Certification complements, but does not replace, state systems of mandatory licensing. Whereas mandatory state licensing is designed to assure that beginning teachers meet certain basic requirements, National Board Certification is voluntary. Unlike licensing standards, which vary from state to state, National Board Certification is uniform across the country. It also attests to a level of accomplishment far surpassing basic state licensing requirements.

A Board Certified teacher receives the title of accomplished teacher. The National Board recognizes accomplished teachers at four developmental levels: early childhood (age 3–8); middle childhood (age 7–12); early adolescence (age 11–15); and adolescence and young adulthood (age 14–18+).

Accomplished teaching involves meeting the following five standards:
1. Teachers are committed to students and their learning.
2. Teachers know the subjects they teach and how to teach those subjects to students.
3. Teachers are responsible for managing and monitoring student learning.
4. Teachers think systematically about their practice and learn from experience.
5. Teachers are members of the learning community.

These standards summarize quite nicely all of the information we have covered in this chapter on creative teachers. They also provide a good lead-in to the next chapter where they are put into practice in creative environments.

Figure 5-14

INTASC Standards (Interstate New Teacher Assessment and Support Consortium)

THIS ONE'S for YOU!

Getting Started with Multiple Intelligences— Try These Ideas

Here are a few classroom activity suggestions that can get you started with multiple intelligences.

⊙ For musical or bodily-kinesthetic learners who persist in drumming, humming, and tapping during quiet work time, provide thin plastic straws for them to tap on desks. This is much less distracting to others!

⊙ For bodily-kinesthetic students who tear paper, scribble on desks, and gouge textbooks, provide a small piece of clay for them to keep in their desks. Allow them to manipulate while working, listening—anytime.

⊙ For musical students, provide a set of headphones with a music tape to aid concentration.

⊙ Before reading a story to your group, take a moment to imagine how you could turn it into a participatory reading event for your children who are musical or bodily-kinesthetic. For example, before you read a story about a particular animal, instruct students that every time you read the animal's name, they are to make a noise like that animal.

⊙ Assign a different mouth noise to represent each punctuation mark you are teaching. When you put sentences on the board that need punctuation, students will vie for the privilege of reading a sentence with the appropriate noisy punctuation, while you or a student adds the marks to the sentence. (If you can't handle the mouth noises, you might try instruments like a cymbal or rattle.)

⊙ When practicing vocabulary words, let children who are musical make up a rap or song about the spelling (or meaning) of a word/set of facts. Have your spatial learners draw a "word picture" or "math fact picture." First write the word or math fact in the middle of the paper; then draw a picture around it that will help them remember the word. For your linguistic learners, have them create a crossword puzzle using vocabulary words. Both linguistic and musical learners would enjoy creating a rhyming poem using vocabulary words or math facts.

Content Standards

NCLB requires state Departments of Education to develop challenging academic content standards and academic assessments. This means you can expect to hear a lot about state academic standards in basic subjects and new or revised state "standards tests." Many states already have such standards and testing programs, but NCLB will require more consistency on how tests are used, who takes the tests, and how results are reported for both individual students and schools. The law requires annual testing of children in at least grades 3 through 8 in reading and math by 2005–2006; science must be assessed by the 2007–2008 school year. This means children in grades 3–8 will be taking state standards tests every year. Many states and districts will include younger and older children in their testing programs.

The content standards are important for preschool teachers as well as K–5 teachers. Although most **national standards** are written for grades K–12, they are often written in broad language, making them applicable in some cases to prekindergarten. Some national standards written for the primary grades begin with pre-K. Also, most states have developed or are developing their own content standards, and these often include pre-K content standards. Head Start has developed its own set of standards, the Head Start Child Outcomes Framework (2002). It is based on the Head Start Program Performance Standards, which serve as a framework of building blocks that are important for school success.

As a result of the development of content standards, many early childhood teachers have been increasingly integrating the subject matter standards into their programs for several years and have been involved in the standards movement in many states. Most teachers recognize that we must have expectations and standards for our early childhood programs. But they also know the nature of learning at this age, and they carefully define how content standards are most appropriately and effectively incorporated into preschool and kindergarten programs. Because a program uses playful ways to build children's success does not mean the curriculum is not rigorous or content-based. It means that it is just right for what's best for three-, four-, and five-year-old children.

With regard to the emphasis on assessment that is part of the NCLB Act, observation of young children is at the heart of early childhood practice. As we have seen earlier, the early childhood curriculum grows out of an understanding of the young child. Knowing as much as possible about each child's uniqueness, strengths, and needs, educators can create an effective environment to support development and learning for *all* ages.

In this standards issue, once again as early childhood professionals, we must create our *own* definition of assessment rather than yielding to others. Owning the word, we can keep its meaning from narrowing to the domain of standardized tests or high-stakes evaluation. Owning the word in our developmental sense, we can keep the conversation focused on the *uses* of assessment—not assessment as an end in itself but as a means of helping young children and families reach valuable goals.

The third and final focus in our discussion directs the issue of standards for the teacher herself.

Standards for Teachers–INTASC Standards

Interstate New Teacher Assessment and Support Consortium (INTASC) standards are model standards for licensing new teachers. Drafted by representatives of the teaching profession, along with personnel from 17 state education agencies, these standards represent a common core of teaching knowledge and skills that will help all students acquire 21st century knowledge and skills. An important attribute of these standards is that they are performance-based—that is, they describe **key indicators,** or what teachers should know and be able to do, rather than listing courses that teachers should take in order to be awarded a license. Figure 5–14 presents these standards with a brief description of each.

developmental levels, and (3) the available materials and resources. Differentiated instruction involves providing different types of learning experiences and environments to meet children's individual needs. Multiple intelligence theory provides further insight on how to meet children's needs by knowing how each child is "smart."

Other considerations in planning creative activities are children's attention spans and activity patterns. A teacher should have reasonable expectations of how long young children can be attentive in certain activities and should know how to supervise these activities so that there is a good balance between active and quiet ones.

Although young children naturally compare their work with other children, competition is not necessary or helpful in creative activities. It is important that young children learn that personal feelings are normal and acceptable. Sometimes the expression of these feelings may cause problems and, therefore, may need modification. Sensitive answers to the questions, "How is the child being creative?" and "How does the child feel about it?" can help guide the teacher in facilitating creative behavior.

Teachers also need to consider their own needs, interests, skills, and abilities when planning activities for young children. Their attitude is crucial to the success of any creative activity.

In creative activities, the teacher's role is to facilitate creative expression. This generally means having a knowledge of children's developmental levels and skills, a sensitive and caring attitude toward them, and a willingness to help them interact with materials. It means guidance without interference or judgment.

To ensure the success of creative activities, careful planning is essential. Also, attention and thought must be given to the manner in which the activity is to be presented, the children's interest sustained, and the activity completed. Once the creative activity is finished, its success should be evaluated in terms of individual and program goals. The NCLB Act, National Board Certification, and INTASC standards are all national approaches to ensuring excellence in teaching.

SUMMARY

Planning creative activities for young children begins with an awareness of the young child. There are many questions to ask about the child, the child's environment, and the teacher's own feelings in order to plan properly. The teacher's plans need to take into consideration: (1) the children's needs and interests, (2) their

KEY TERMS

accomplished teaching
activity pattern
attention span
developmental level
differentiated instruction
facilitate

individual differences
key indicators
multiple intelligences
national standards
No Child Left Behind
process learning

LEARNING ACTIVITIES

A. Check the list of attitudes found in this unit that facilitate creative behavior in young children.
   1. Choose one example of each from your personal life in which you demonstrate the attitude.
   2. Decide whether this is an attitude you already possess or one that you need to work on in order to improve.
   3. For those attitudes that need improvement, consider how you plan to go about doing this.
B. There are strategies that teachers use to create a good climate for creative activities. There are other factors that may cause a child's creativity to be hindered by a teacher.
   1. Make a list of five do's and don'ts for creative activities in the early childhood setting.
   2. If possible, compare and discuss your list with those of your classmates.
   3. Observe a head teacher who is supervising a creative activity in an early childhood classroom. What does he or she do to facilitate the children's expression of creativity?
C. Using the information in this chapter on planning and presentation of creative activities, plan a creative activity for one of these pairs of groups: (a) three year olds and 3rd graders or (b) four year olds and 4th graders.
   In your activity plan, include the following:
   ⊙ developmental needs of the children
   ⊙ attention span
   ⊙ physical ability
   ⊙ activity level
   ⊙ appropriate materials
   ⊙ appropriate motivation
D. Use the observation sheet in the Online Companion to assess your own multiple intelligences. Were you surprised by anything you learned about yourself? Can you apply this learning to your teaching? How?
E. Use the observation sheet in the Online Companion to help you reflect on your personal teaching style. Which intelligences are the strongest in you? Which are the weakest? Are you neglecting types of activities because of your own weaknesses?
F. Log onto the NCLB Web site at http://www.teachersandfamilies.com/. Click on the Parents section, then on Parenting Features. Click on the Your Child and No Child Left Behind. Find out what students will be included in state assessments. According to the Web site, what are the benefits of testing?
G. Find out the National Standards for Arts Education at the Artsedge Web site at http://www.artsedge.kennedy-center.org/. Click on the Standards line under the Teach Section. Find curricula, lessons, and activities linked to these national standards that you can use with children in your group.

CHAPTER REVIEW

1. Discuss the ways you can plan activities to match a child's attention span.
2. List at least two ways you can plan activities to match the young child's activity level.
3. List 10 important questions that should be asked to better know and work with young children.
4. With regard to young children, discuss the difference between having feelings and expressing feelings.
5. Define *facilitator* as it applies to the teacher involved in creative activities for children.
6. List the necessary steps in preparing for a creative activity.
7. Discuss strategies for handling transition times.
8. Discuss the term *developmental level*.
9. Define the terms *differentiated instruction, process learning,* and *multiple intelligences.*
10. Discuss the national standards for curriculum content, teacher certification, and the NCLB Act.
11. Describe accomplished teaching by listing the five standards associated with it.

REFERENCES

Barclay, K. H., & Breheny, C. (1994, Sept.). Letting the children take over more of their own learning: Collaborative research in the kindergarten classroom. *Young Children, 33–39.*

Bredekamp, S. (Ed.). (1997). *Developmentally appropriate practice in early childhood programs serving children from birth through age 8* (Rev. ed.) Washington, DC: NAEYC.

Cornett, C.E. (2003). The arts as meaning makers. Upper Saddle River, NJ: Merrill/Prentice Hall.

Gardner, H. (1999). *Intelligence reframed: Multiple intelligences for the 21st century.* New York: Basic Books.

Greenspan, S. I. (2001, Sept.). Creating an inclusive classroom. *Scholastic Early Childhood Today, 33–34.*

Head Start Bureau (2002). *The Head Start Child Outcomes Framework.* Online: http://www.headstartinfo.org.

Nicholson-Nelson, W. (1998). *Developing student's multiple intelligences.* New York: Scholastic.

Seefeldt, C. (1995, March). Art: A serious work. *Young Children, 39–44.*

ADDITIONAL READINGS

Greenspan, S. I., & Wieder, S. (1998). *The child with special needs.* Reading, MA: Addison Wesley.

Greenspan, S. I. (2000). *Building healthy minds.* New York: Perseus Books.

Helm, J. H., & Beneke, S. (Eds.) (2003). *The power of projects: Meeting contemporary challenges in early childhood classrooms.* Washington, DC: NAEYC.

Helm, J. H., & Katz, L. G. (2001). *Young investigators: The project approach in the early years.* New York: Teachers College Press.

Hemmeter, M. L., Maxwell, K. L., Ault, M. J., & Schuster, J. W. (2001). *Assessment of practices in early elementary classrooms.* Washington, DC: NAEYC.

Isbell, R., & Exelby, B. (2001). *Early learning environments that work.* Beltsville, MD: Gryphon House.

Lombardi, J. (2003). *Time to care: Redesigning child care to promote education, support families, and build communities.* Washington, DC: NAEYC.

Perry, C., Steele, C., & Hilliard, A. III (2003). *Young, gifted, and black: Promoting high achievement among African American students.* Boston: Beacon Press.

Reynolds, A. J., Wang, M. C., & Walberg, H. J. (Eds.) (2003). *Early childhood programs for a new century.* Washington, DC: NAEYC.

Saab, J. F. (2001, May). How do we know when we're there? One school district's journey toward developmentally appropriate practice. *Young Children, 88–94.*

Sandall, S. R., & Schwartz, I. S. (2002). *Building blocks for teaching preschoolers with special needs.* Baltimore, MD: Paul H. Brooks.

Seefeldt, C., & Wasik, B. (2002). *Kindergarten: Fours and fives go to school.* Upper Saddle River, NJ: Merrill/Prentice Hall.

Stephens, P., & Walkup, N. (2001). *Bridging the curriculum through art: Interdisciplinary connections.* Glenview, IL: Crystal Productions.

Tertell, E. A., Klein, S. M., & Jewett, J. L. (Eds.) (2002). *When teachers reflect: Journeys toward effective inclusive practice.* Washington DC: NAEYC.

Tomlinson, C. A. (2000, Sept.). Reconcilable differences? Standards-based teaching and differentiation. *Educational Leadership, 7–11.*

HELPFUL WEB SITES

http://www.ldpride.net/
Click on Learning Styles and then on Multiple Intelligences Explained.

http://www.ascd.org/
Click on Education Topics, then on Differentiated Instruction.

http://www.eduref.org
Click on Teaching.

http://learnweb.harvard.edu
Click on Active Learning Practices for Schools (ALPS).

For additional creative activity resources, visit our Web site at http://www.EarlyChildEd.delmar.com.

Chapter 6

Creative Environments

Objectives

After studying this chapter, you should be able to:

1. Describe an appropriate physical environment for creative activities for young children.
2. Describe some things to consider when arranging appropriate environments for creative activities for children with special needs.
3. Discuss the main considerations involved in setting up activity centers.
4. List and describe interest centers that encourage children's creativity and developing skills.
5. List six factors that are important when selecting equipment to be used in creative activities for young children.
6. List five safety factors to be considered in the early childhood environment.

The setting in which a creative activity takes place is very important. Young children are very aware of negative mood and environment. A dark room or crowded space can have much more effect on them than a rainy day. The arrangement of space and the type of equipment provided have dramatic impact on a child's creative experiences. The impact is even greater on children with special needs.

PHYSICAL SPACE: GENERAL GUIDELINES

A positive physical environment is one of the keys to the success of the creative activities that take place within it. Some basic guidelines to consider when evaluating the physical space in early childhood programs are the following:

⊙ Satisfactory acoustics help communication. Therefore, curtains and carpets should be used to help eliminate noise, as well as add beauty and comfort. Select wall colors that add to the light available in the room. Yellow and other light colors are good. It is best if walls are washable at least as far up as children can reach.

⊙ Floors should be easily cleaned, suited to hard wear, and comfortable for children to sit on; they also should deaden sound. Some suitable floor coverings are linoleum, carpets, and rubber or plastic tiles. A carpeted section of the floor makes possible a comfortable arrangement for group activities without the need for chairs.

⊙ Proper heat, light, and ventilation are important. Remember that children live closer to the floor than do adults and that warm air rises and is replaced by cooler air. It may be helpful to install a thermostat or thermometer at their level so you can be aware of the temperatures they are experiencing. However, it must also be remembered that children of all ages are more active than adults and that they may not feel cool at temperatures that may be uncomfortable for you.

⦿ Consider the source of natural light in the room. Children are likely to be more comfortable if they do not face directly into strong sunlight when they work. For children with visual difficulties, or those who have limited vision, make sure the room has plenty of light to help those children who have some useful vision.

⦿ Running water and sinks are a must for preparing and cleaning up after some creative activities. They should be near the area where they are needed. In spaces where sinks are not available, a fresh bucket of soapy water and a sponge along with paper towels for cleanup will suffice.

⦿ Easy-to-reach storage space for equipment that is in daily use should be provided so that children learn to put their things away.

⦿ Chairs should be light enough for the children to handle and move without too much noise. Because the chairs are used at tables for creative activities, the kind without arms should be used. For children in wheelchairs, provide small stools for the child's feet when placing the child at a table.

⦿ There should be some tables that accommodate from four to six children for group activities. Rectangular tables are better for art activities involving large sheets of paper. Some small tables designed to be used singly or in combinations are quite versatile. Tables with washable surfaces such as formica are best.

⦿ Shelves should be low and open and not too deep, so that children have a chance to see, touch, and choose materials independently. Shelves that are sturdy but easy to move are more flexible in room arrangement and help create interest centers.

Safety Factors

Special consideration should be given to safety in the physical environment. Some important safety checks are the following:

⦿ Be sure that all low window areas are safe.

⦿ Beware of and remove toxic, lead-based paints and poisonous plants, particularly berry-producing plants.

Figure 6-1

Organizing materials so that they are easily accessible to young children encourages children's creative use of materials.

⦿ Be sure that commercial or teacher-made materials are safe for children. Read labels—they may indicate the materials are toxic. Ask yourself: Will the item be likely to cause splinters, pierce the skin, or cause abrasions? Will the attractive glitter stick under fingernails? Are the fumes from a spray irritating? Will a two-year-old child's tongue-test transfer color from the object to the mouth?

⦿ Teachers who first try new materials for creative activities will become aware of applicable safety factors. Most young children can learn to be careful workers when they understand hazards. A teacher, when discussing how to use scissors, might ask, "How can you hide the point in your fist so that it cannot hurt anyone while you are walking with it?" Two- and three-year-old children will usually need to have adults set rules—for example, "Clay is for modeling, not for eating." Children four years of age and older can cooperatively decide on rules and regulations for safe handling of tools, materials, and equipment. However, older children may still need verbal reminders or simple signs.

◉ Cover hot pipes and radiators. Insert protective coverings over all electrical outlets. Pronged covers made especially for this purpose are readily available at drug stores, grocery stores, and most discount stores.

◉ Install door knob locks that only adults can use in areas prohibited to young children. These are available at hardware stores. Also, install high knobs on cabinets within prohibited areas.

◉ Check the facility to make sure that there are no hooks, hangers, or other sharp objects that protrude, especially at child's level.

◉ For children with visual impairments, keep the arrangement of furniture stationary until the child is familiar with the room. Be sure to warn the child when changes are made in the arrangement of the room and/or equipment.

◉ Make sure that there are adequate exits provided in the event of a fire or other emergency.

◉ Check to see that fire exits, fire alarms, smoke detectors, and fire extinguishers are in working order and are placed appropriately in the classroom.

ARRANGEMENT OF SPACE AND EQUIPMENT

The arrangement of the space in an early childhood program also has an effect on the safety and success of the creative activities for which it is used. Adults need to consider a number of factors in planning for the arrangement of equipment (Figure 6–2).

Children's Age and Developmental Levels

The age and developmental levels of the children using a room dictate how that room should be arranged. A group of two- and three-year-old children, for example, would do quite nicely in a simple, small, enclosed space. At this age, children may be overwhelmed by too large a space or too much equipment in it. Yet, as their large motor skills are developing rapidly, the space should be big enough for active, large motor activities. Here is where balance is very important. Also, since coordination is not well developed yet, the space should be as uncluttered as possible because children aged two to three years fall, stumble, and slip quite a bit.

In contrast, a five year old has better coordination because of a more centralized center of gravity and doesn't

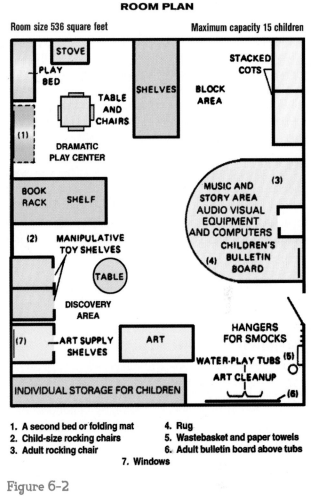

ROOM PLAN

Room size 536 square feet — Maximum capacity 15 children

1. A second bed or folding mat
2. Child-size rocking chairs
3. Adult rocking chair
4. Rug
5. Wastebasket and paper towels
6. Adult bulletin board above tubs
7. Windows

Figure 6-2

Sample classroom arrangement using interest centers.

fall as frequently as a two- or three-year-old child. More equipment in a room will not present a space or safety problem for the five year old. Yet the space still needs to be large enough to allow for five year olds to run, jump, climb, and pretend. In organizing space for young children, then, there should be enough open space for the children to move around safely and comfortably at their level of physical coordination and to work together cooperatively and freely. Approximately 40 to 60 square feet per preschool child is recommended. Middle and upper level elementary students can and need to work in a much larger area than younger children. A larger working space allows for their larger physical size and provides room for various student groupings that naturally arise out of project work, which is an appropriate instructional method for this age group.

Supervision

Another consideration in arranging space for young children is the supervision of that space. Open play spaces should not be so large that it becomes difficult to supervise the children properly. A common technique is to divide the space up into interest centers or activity areas with limited numbers allowed at each center. (Interest or activity centers are discussed later in this chapter.) When breaking up the space in such a way as to facilitate supervision, using low, movable barriers, such as child-level bulletin boards, bookshelves, or room dividers, provides a clear view of the area and permits a more flexible use of the space itself.

In supervising a group that includes children with special needs, the teacher needs to be aware of the special limitations of these children and to check throughout the day that their needs are being met. For example, with children in wheelchairs, the teacher should watch that the child is not in the same position for long periods (more than 20 to 30 minutes). The teacher also should be aware of when to move the child to the proximity of ongoing activities.

Flexibility

Space should be kept as open and flexible as possible so it can be adjusted as the children grow, develop, and change in their needs. Your early childhood program certainly should not look the same on the last day of the year as it did on the first day of the year! The early childhood environment must reflect the young children in it—changing and developing along with them. In response to children's growing ability to deal with more concepts, additional equipment, supplies, and interest centers need to be incorporated in

the room. Conversely, materials, equipment, and even whole centers need to be removed to storage when the children have outgrown them. This same idea holds true for older children in middle and upper elementary grades. The classroom that never changes is boring and a less-than-stimulating learning environment for these children. In a flexible environment, space can easily be rearranged to fit these new centers without major renovations.

This same flexibility holds true when working with children with special needs. For example, at the beginning of the school year children who are visually impaired need to be in a room where there is assigned seating. This will aid in helping them learn their classmates' voices and names. The reason for assigned seating needs to be clearly explained to the class so they can understand the importance of the seating arrangement. Another helpful suggestion is to make sure that the children understand that they should identify themselves before speaking.

Traffic Flow

Even when increasing activity options in a room, space should be as free as possible to allow the traffic to flow between activities. For example, the traffic flow should not interfere with activities that require concen-

Figure 6-3
Equipment in the early childhood program should encourage children to work together as well as alone.

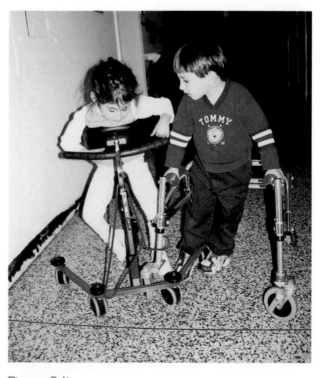

Figure 6-4
Children need space for movement in creative activities.

tration. A language arts/reading or book corner is more likely to be used by children if it is away from the noise of people coming and going. The block corner, too, will be used more often if it is planned for a space that is free from interruption and traffic.

Older children will enjoy an arts center that is situated in an area where they can concentrate and work without a lot of interruptions (i.e., away from the door or other heavy traffic areas).

Involve children in arranging space. Sometimes children as young as four years of age, as well as older, may help determine where particular centers should be located and the reasons for such decisions. For example, a kindergarten teacher, introducing the woodworking bench, held a discussion with the children about where it should be placed. They wisely considered safety and noise factors in making their decision. Older children can actually help move desks, tables, and other equipment to carry out their own space reorganization plan.

Figure 6-5

Working on the floor with materials nearby is a favorite activity for many children.

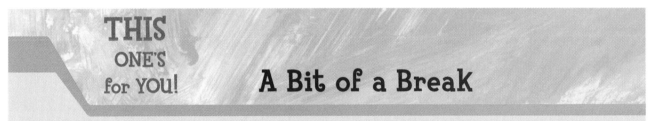

THIS ONE'S for YOU!

A Bit of a Break

Reading about all of the things you need to keep in mind when setting up the environment for creative activities can be overwhelming. You can get lost in all of the details and lose sight of all the positive things that are part of being a teacher of young children. So stop now and take a break from the details and read the scenes below to help you regain your focus.

SCENE 1

A teacher in line at a movie theater was recognized by a man in his mid-20s. He said he had been in that teacher's first-grade class during her first year of teaching. "Do you still go out under the tree and sing songs on Friday afternoons?" he asked. "We sure do," she replied. "Thanks, Mrs. Anderson, I'll never forget that."

SCENE 2

After watching her first high school football game, a kindergarten teacher went down to the hallway outside the locker room to find the star quarterback. "Do you remember me?" she asked. "Sure, but what are you doing here?" "I promised," she said. "One day back when you were in kindergarten, you and two of your buddies wouldn't settle down, and I was so mad I could spit. I blurted out that if you'd only sit still for a while, I'd come and watch you play football some day. Well, you sat still, and here I am." Without saying anything, the young man gave her the sweatiest, smelliest hug she'd ever gotten.

SCENE 3

A first-grade teacher at a wedding reception was approached by a young man and his wife. "You're Mrs. Douglas," he said, "and you used to teach fifth grade, right?" The teacher agreed that he was right about both things. "You were my teacher then," he continued, "and it was a hard year for me. My parents were getting a divorce, and it was nasty. You said a lot of things that really helped. I still quote you. Thanks."

Printed with permission by NAEYC, Hunter, T. "Taking the Long View," *Young Children,* March 2001, p. 82.

Figure 6-6

Activity centers with materials in good condition, neatly arranged, and placed far apart on open shelves tell a child that materials are valued and important enough to be well cared for.

Figure 6-7

Organizing materials in plastic bins or boxes makes them easily visible and accessible for children's use.

Personal Space

In the early childhood years, children are growing physically and intellectually and developing their sense of self. For this reason, it is very important to plan space in such a way that each child has a place of her own. Having a place of one's own to keep personal belongings, extra clothes, artwork, and notes to take home helps encourage a child's developing sense of self. A snapshot of the child used to label the personal space is a good way, too, of assisting the growth of a sense of self. A snapshot removes all doubt that the place is *private property* even before a child has learned to recognize her name. Each child needs to be able to count on having a place belonging only to her.

It is only by firmly establishing an understanding of ownership that a young child learns about sharing. Having a *cubby* of one's own helps the child learn about possession and care of self, which are both basic to a growing sense of independence.

If there is not enough space for individual cubbies, labeled dishpans, clear plastic shoeboxes, large round ice cream containers, or even plastic milk crates can be used. Making personal space important recognizes each child's personal needs. This says to the child, "You are important."

In developing a positive self-concept, young children also need privacy. Besides respecting a child's

private cubby, the space should be arranged so that there are quiet places to be alone. Especially as a child grows intellectually, she or he needs space and time to reflect and think. Quiet places to be alone encourage this reflection where a child can enjoy his or her own thoughts and mental perceptions of the world. Older children have no less need for privacy and personal space. The classroom needs to have a designated space where a student's need to be alone is respected.

For children with attention deficit disorders (ADD), personal space is a basic need. This is because children with ADD tend to be most successful when they have their own materials and spaces to work (Karnes, 2003).

ACTIVITY/INTEREST CENTERS

One approach to fostering creative activities and use of materials is to provide as part of the environment **activity** or **interest centers** and to identify activities and materials for each, based on the group of children in the class.

CLASSROOM PLANNING FOR ARTWORK

The way you plan for and display children's artwork tells the children a lot about how much you value their work. Here are some suggestions on how to manage children's artwork in a way that shows children you value their work.

Plan your artwork exhibits so they reflect children's ideas and experiences. Ask children to help select the items to be displayed. They may want to (or have you) write down why this particular work is meaningful to them. For instance, they like the medium, color, or subject.

Make interesting groupings of children's art work. Feature a specific theme, stress a particular color, or highlight a special medium.

Display artwork outside, as well as inside, the classroom. Use the hallway and stairwell walls and other flat surfaces, such as doors, for your gallery.

Exhibit artwork in various stages. Include photos of the work in progress for documentation so others can enjoy the process, too.

Place artwork at children's eye level. Label the displays with large, easy-to-read letters and make up simple but catchy titles. Older children can make up these titles as well as cut out or write them out for the display.

Handle work respectfully. Let the children know that you appreciate and value their skills and creativity. Frame or mount their work attractively. (Use backgrounds with contrasting colors and interesting textures, such as burlap or corrugated cardboard.) Encourage the young artists to sign their own names. Be sure not to write on their work without permission. Take dictation on a separate strip of paper. Older children may want to write a short statement to accompany their work.

Showcase work in exciting ways. Instead of stapling work to bulletin boards, hang pictures with clothespins from clotheslines. You can use tree branches to display mobiles. Create a free-standing kiosk with four display sides from a cardboard refrigerator carton. A cardboard, folding, pattern-cutting board can be used to display art on both sides.

Arrange special areas for fragile or three-dimensional work. Supply stable shelves or low tables to display wire and clay sculptures or woodwork. Use cardboard "shadow boxes" for added emphasis and protection.

Provide individual display space. Have each child choose her own small area of a bulletin board that has been divided into sections. Let her select and change dated samples to document her growth.

Organize a space where parents can collect artwork. Designate the top compartment of the child's cubby as the "art shelf" or create an art "mailbox" from a large, partitioned, cardboard beverage carton turned on its side. Use cardboard mailing tubes to send home rolled-up artwork to prevent folding, creases, and tears.

Figure 6–8

Classroom planning for artwork.

An activity or interest center is a defined space where materials are organized in such a way that children learn without the teacher's constant presence and direction. It is a place where children interact with materials and other children to develop certain skills and knowledge. Activities in each activity center are planned by the teacher according to the developmental needs of the children (Patillo & Vaughan, 1992).

Learning centers are a place where children learn through direct interaction with other children and their environment. In centers, children learn through doing in an environment carefully prepared for their personal and active exploration.

An early childhood program organized around activity centers encourages creativity by giving children many opportunities to play, experiment, and discover as they engage in activities that help them with problem solving, learning basic skills, and understanding new concepts. In activity centers, young children can manipulate objects, engage in conversation and role-playing, and learn at their own levels and at their own pace.

For the young child, most educators and experts recommend the following interest centers:

Art area. A place for painting, collage making, cutting, pasting, chalking; it should be located near water and light and away from large motor areas (Figure 6–8).

Housekeeping/dramatic play center. A place for acting out familiar home scenes with pots, pans, and dishes. A place to "try out" social roles, real-life dialogues, and "grown-up" jobs.

Block-building area. A place where children can create with both large and small blocks, tinker toys, logs, Legos, etc.

Manipulative area. A place to enhance motor skills, eye–hand coordination, mental, language, and social skills through the use of play materials such as puzzles, pegboards, and games.

Science/discovery center. A place to learn about nature and science. Here, children can display what they find at home or on nature walks, for example. It is a place to discover, explore, and ask questions.

Music center. A place for listening to audiotapes, singing, creating dance, and playing musical instruments.

Books and quiet area. A place to be alone, quiet in one's thoughts, and to explore the world of books.

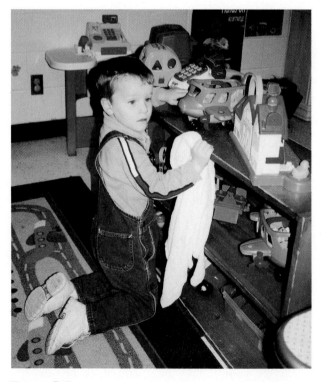

Figure 6-9
Shelves should be low, open, and not too deep so that children have a chance to see, touch, and choose materials independently.

Sand and water play area. A place to learn through sensory experiences with sand and water, such as floating and sinking experiments; weighing, measuring, and comparing quantities; building boats; drawing letter shapes and numbers in the sand; experimenting with food coloring and water; and making buildings in the sand.

The social studies center: people and places. A special area to study about families, different cultures, ethnic groups, community awareness, specific occupations, and lifestyles.

Woodworking center. An area that provides the opportunity to develop large and small muscles by working with wood in sanding, gluing, fastening, drilling, and sawing.

Outdoor play area. A natural learning environment where activities from indoor learning areas can be extended.

Appendix C lists materials for each of these centers. A teacher can certainly add other interest centers to this list. The sample room arrangement in Figure 6–2 shows how interest centers can be designed. Again, it is a suggestion, to be adjusted to the needs of the children.

Decisions About Activity Areas: Where and When

Before setting up activity centers, you have to make a number of decisions about which centers to use, when to use them, and where they can best be placed in the classroom. Some of the questions to be addressed include the following:

⊙ Will centers be offered all day, every day; part of the day; or only some days of the week? The ideal choice is to offer activity centers for a large block or blocks of time every day at approximately the same time. This lets children plan ahead, make choices, and get involved in activities. It allows teachers initially to structure learning centers throughout the room and gradually add centers, remove centers, or modify centers during the year.

⊙ What room features offer potential settings for centers? You can make creative use of walls, floor, chalkboards, tables, and nooks and crannies.

⊙ Should there be limits on the number of children using any specific center? If so, how will this be determined, and how will children know what the limits are? Activity centers need to be planned so children can work individually or in small groups of various numbers. The size of a small group of children at any center is determined by the amount of materials available, the purpose of the center, physical space considerations, and the need to avoid overstimulating confusion. Signs with stick figures and numbers can indicate the number of children who can use a specific center. For some children with ADD who may wander from center to center, make a photo display of the centers so the child can select from the photos to make an individual schedule of what she plans to do.

⊙ What kinds of centers will provide a workable balance in terms of content? This will depend on the characteristics of the children and staff.

⊙ How free should movement in and out of the centers be? Ideally, children should move at their own pace, guided by the teacher. This allows for more individualization within the program.

⊙ How will children know what to do in each center? Some centers will require more direction than

others. You may want to use pictures or symbols for routine directions (hands with a faucet of running water to remind children to wash; aprons on pegs to facilitate art and cooking cleanup without having to mention it). Be sure your centers have the appropriate equipment for children with special needs. For example, children with physical disabilities may need to use art materials in different ways, such as lying on the floor over a bolster pillow to draw. For children who are visually impaired, be sure to provide in your centers many activities that use senses other than hearing. For the child who uses a wheelchair, which places him at a different height than the other children, it may be possible to use a beanbag chair for floor-time activities. For a child who does not have the strength to stand for long periods, a tabletop easel will let the child sit in a chair while painting.

Condition and Organization of Materials within the Activity Center

Activity centers with materials that are in good condition, arranged and placed far apart on open shelves, tell a child that materials are valued and important enough to be well cared for. What kind of message does a child get from crowded, open shelves with a mixture of materials and broken or missing pieces? What kind of message does she get from torn books?

Young children work best in a predictable environment where materials are organized and can be found repeatedly in the same place. Organizing materials can help children develop self-help skills and self-control, as well as help them learn to respect materials and use them well. For example, cutouts of tools or other equipment help children learn to identify materials and return them to the proper place. Organizing open storage shelves by labeling them clearly with pictures and words makes it possible for children to find materials they want to work with. When shelves are clearly labeled with few objects on them at a time, putting things back in place becomes an easier task for young children.

Labeling, too, can be done in the block area by cutting out the shapes of the blocks in colored Con-Tact® paper and pasting them on the back and shelves. Clear labeling of shelves helps even very young children become independent in the use and maintenance of their environment. For children who are visually impaired, cut out tactile shapes and attach them to shelves to assist them in finding and replacing blocks in the manipulative area.

Figure 6-10

The age and developmental levels of the children in the group dictate the type of equipment that should be available for children's use.

MATERIALS FOR MULTI-INTELLIGENCES–PRESCHOOL TO KINDERGARTEN

Word Smart	**Picture Smart**	**Body Smart**	**Person Smart**
Books	Legos/blocks	Audiocassette tapes	Art supplies
Maps	Colored pencils/markers/	CDs and CD player	Sports equipment
Magazines	crayons/paint	Bean bags	Musical instruments
Pipe cleaner letters	Puppet theatre	Large-motor equipment	Puppet theatre
Chalkboard	Tongue depressors	Dress-up clothes and	Books
Dry erase board	Glitter	other props for	Video recorders
Rice/sand/shaving	Manipulatives	dramatic play	Seeds/gardening tools
cream/finger paints	Clay	Manipulatives	Computer
Texture letters	Posters	**Self Smart**	Cooking supplies
Construction paper	Puzzles	Books	**Nature Smart**
Laminator	Sand/water	Puzzle	Terrarium
Pencils/pens/markers	**Music Smart**	Art supplies	Microscope
Overhead projector	Musical instruments	Cassettes/cassette	Ant farm
Letter puzzles	Headphones	players	Seeds
Logic Smart	Cassette/record/CD	Computer	Soil
Manipulatives	player	Microscope	Bird feeders
Counters	Keyboard	Reference material	Bird guides
Abacus	Music books	Writing materials	Gardening tools
Legos/blocks	Video camera	Clay	Magnifying glass
Geo boards	Kitchen utensils for	Musical instruments	
String art	making sound effects	Tape recorder	
Cuisenaire rods	Recordings of nature		
Blocks	sounds		
Play money	Toy microphones		
Puzzles	Posters of composers		
Marbles/beans	Tape recorders/blank		
Geometric shapes	tapes		
Straws/string/clay			
Pattern blocks			

Figure 6-11
Materials for Multi-Intelligences–Preschool to Kindergarten

Organization of Activity Centers in Convertible Spaces

Many early childhood programs operate in multipurpose facilities. In family day care homes, day care centers in churches, and public school day care programs, equipment must be packed up for storage after school or over the weekend. If materials are packed up and stored frequently, movable shelves that are ready for use as soon as they are rolled into place and unlocked are helpful. If shelves are not available for material storage, tables or boxes may be used. Whatever the arrangement, children should understand the system for selecting toys and replacing them in the right containers. Visual cues, such as putting red oilcloth on the storage tables and white oilcloth on the play tables, help children remember the organizational principles and keep the environment functional.

Convertible or multipurpose spaces will have to make use of many portable activity boxes. This is also the case in small classrooms or in day care programs in public schools where space is shared. An individual activity box includes all the materials needed for a particular activity—related books and pictures, reminder cards with relevant questions for the teacher, rhymes, games, and songs. For example, a firefighter prop box might include firefighters' hats, hose sections, several books about firefighters, and a ball. The children would use the props and other items in the box as a mini-center of sorts. The teacher would integrate the center into the program by using the questions, books, reminder cards, and other activities prepared as part of the instructional plans for that particular activity.

Activity boxes can be used outdoors or indoors, either in response to requests by the children or as part of the teacher-prepared activities. Activity boxes can

THINK ABOUT IT... Hints for a Smoother Daily Program

If you, like most teachers, are always looking for ways to improve the daily operation of your program, you may want to think about using some of the following general hints:

- Store small books easily and neatly in plastic napkin holders. These can be found at discount stores and even at garage sales.

- When odd parts of toys and games turn up around the room during the day, forget trying to return them to their proper place each time they are found. Instead, make a special container just for toy and game parts. A zipper-type plastic bag works well for this purpose. Not only will this save time during the day, but you will always know where to look if a part is missing.

- To preserve posters, pictures, and other items you want to last from year to year, cover them with clear Con-Tact paper. The items will be easier for the children to handle, and dirt and finger marks can be wiped off easily.

- Spray new puzzles and gameboards with clear varnish (outdoors and away from the children, of course). You'll find they last much longer.

- Empty food boxes used in the housekeeping corner and for other learning games will be sturdier if you stuff them with newspaper and then tape them shut. Be sure to brush all crumbs out first.

- When sanitizing furniture and fixtures with bleach and water, put the mixture into an empty spray bottle that has been thoroughly washed and dried. The spray bottle is easy to use, and it will protect your hands from the harsh bleach.

- Instead of using tape to hang paper shapes on a wall with a hard finish, try sticking them on with dabs of toothpaste. The toothpaste can be washed off the wall when you change decorations.

- When a child paints a picture that you want to display on a wall, attach the paper to the tabletop with masking tape. The tape keeps the paper from sliding during painting, and when the child has finished, you can unpeel the ends of the tape from the table and use them to retape the painting to the wall.

- To make taking home artwork and notes to parents easier and more efficient, have the children make Pringles can "purses." (You may have to make them for younger children.) Use a Pringles can for each child. Cover the can with Con-Tact paper. On opposite sides of the can make two small holes ¾ inch from the top. Take the ends of the string and push through the inside of the can. Tie a big knot on each end. Replace the lid. Have each child write his or her name on their can. Teachers just roll papers and place inside the can. Children place the can around their neck like a necklace, or hold it like a "purse." No more lost papers!

---

be made up with all the materials needed for science experiences, such as a sink-float game or a cooking activity. Various objects commonly found in an early childhood center environment, such as blocks and beads, can be organized into sorting, matching, or seriation games and kept in separate boxes.

SELECTION OF EQUIPMENT FOR CREATIVE ACTIVITIES

The kinds of equipment available to young children can either promote or discourage creative expression.

If equipment is to encourage creative activities, it should have certain characteristics.

Characteristics of Appropriate Equipment

Simple in design. Too much detail destroys children's freedom to express themselves. Crayons, blocks, clay, sand, paints, and even empty cardboard boxes are examples of simple, but useful, equipment for young children.

Versatile. Equipment should be usable by both girls and boys at their developmental level for many kinds of activities.

Take Your Cue from Colors: Using Color Coding in Activity Centers

THIS ONE'S for YOU!

A tried-and-true method for helping children function independently and successfully with activity centers is the systematic use of color and symbols. Children can quickly learn a color-coding system even if they do not yet know how to read. Colors and symbols can be used to identity activity centers, to manage children's movement in and out of centers, and to let children independently find and replace assigned materials.

Special symbol and color codes help children identify and locate each center. The symbol identifies what is learned in the center. The color code helps children easily locate the center in the classroom. For example, the art center's symbol might be a paintbrush, and its color code might be red. A card would be hung at the entrance to each center with its corresponding symbol and color code.

To manage traffic in and out of the centers, the card at the center's entrance would also indicate the number of children allowed in the center at one time. It could be a number of stick people or the actual numeral, depending on the children's knowledge of written numbers. That corresponding number of color-coded clothespins would be attached to the bottom of the card. For example, the art center might allow 10 children and thus have 10 red clothespins. The clothespins are children's "tickets" to the centers. Children must pin on the clothespin when they enter the center, wear it while using the center, and replace it on the card when they leave. When no clothespins are on the card, the center is full, and children must choose another activity until a clothespin is available.

Stimulating. The equipment should be the kind that allows children to do things and motivates them. If adults must supervise children every minute that they are using the equipment, this may hinder creativity. Long explanations on how to use the equipment should not be necessary.

Large and easy to use. Because of the growth of muscles during this time, very small equipment can cause young children to become anxious. Big trucks and wagons are just right. Large, hollow blocks are better than small, solid ones.

Durable. Breakable equipment soon is broken by two- to five-year-old children. Equipment made of hard wood such as maple is less likely to splinter than equipment made of soft wood such as pine. Rubber-wheeled riding toys are preferred to those with wooden wheels.

For older children as well, durability of equipment is important. For example, a higher quality roller will last far longer through vigorous printing use by this age group.

In proper working order. Nothing impedes creativity more than things that don't work. Do a daily quick

checkup on equipment to see that it's in good working order. Older students can help with this inventory and write down a "To Do" list of specific repairs needed. Even better, select materials that are the best quality you can afford. It's cheaper in the long run.

Available in proper amounts. Too many toys or too much equipment can decrease the effectiveness of those materials. Too many blocks can overwhelm a child and he or she may never start to build. Equally frustrating is too few blocks to complete a creation. Work for a balance in amount of equipment.

Designed to encourage children to play together. Many pieces of equipment are designed for one child to use alone. However, children need to work together and find out what others are thinking and doing. Therefore, equipment designed to get children together should also be provided.

Safe. Safety is a key consideration in selecting equipment for young children. Among the safety factors to consider are whether the equipment is developmentally appropriate (for instance, you would not select for 1½ year olds toys that are small enough to be swallowed easily), whether nontoxic and nonflammable

MATERIALS FOR MULTIPLE INTELLIGENCES—GRADES 1 TO 5

Word Smart
Reference books
Glue
Encyclopedias
Scissors
Computer
Desktop publishing software
Bulletin board
Thesaurus
Dictionary
Letter stencils

Logic Smart
Pattern blocks
Protractors
Unifix cubes
Balance scales
Tape measures
Puzzles
Rulers
Strategy games
Construction sets
Objects to serve as counters
Dice
Cuisenaire rods
Collections for sorting/classifying
Science equipment

Picture Smart
Markers
Art prints
Crayons
Video equipment
Collage materials
Videotapes
Pastels
Graphic software
Colored pencils
Computer
Stencils
Puzzles

Music Smart
Tape recorder
Recording equipment
Headphones
Musical software
Tapes/CDs
Keyboard with headphone
Homemade instruments
Books on musicians and music
Instruments

Self Smart
Private, quiet place
Journals
Writing materials
Stories, books, and articles dealing with character
  development
Independent projects

Sentence strips
Variety of paper
Newspapers
Notebooks
Magazines
Bookmaking materials
Student-made books
Writing utensils
Books on tape

Body Smart
Costumes
Puzzles
Miscellaneous props
Sand
Hats and scarves
Craft supplies
Construction sets
Tools
Stacking blocks
Building materials
Puppets
Sports books and magazines
Tactile learning materials
Scissors

Rubber stamps
Art prints
Graphs
Drafting supplies
Posters
Architectural supplies
Charts
Paints
Clay
Variety of drawing paper
Lego sets

Person Smart
Large table for students to sit around
Group games and puzzles
Autobiography and biography books
Conflict resolution materials and posters
Tutoring activities
Group projects
Board games
Comfortable chairs/rugs
Writing paper

Personal collections
Bulletin board/small chalkboard
Posters/pictures of individuals strong in this
  intelligence.
Self-checking materials

Figure 6-12

Materials for Multiple Intelligences—Grades 1 to 5

Figure 6-13

Middle and upper elementary students can and must work in a much larger area than younger children.

materials were used in the manufacture of the equipment, whether the materials have any sharp edges or rough areas that could cause injury, and whether the physical environment allows for the safe use of the equipment. (Appendix F provides more complete information on appropriate toys and equipment for early childhood programs.)

Other considerations. In selecting equipment and materials for creative activities, keep these additional considerations in mind:

- Do not choose a material or piece of equipment because it looks "cute" to you. Instead, select each item with some developmental purpose in mind. For example, ask yourself, "What contribution will the item make to the growth of small or large motor skills of the children? How will it help a child's intellectual growth? Self-esteem? Will it encourage the growth of social skills?"

- Resist the temptation to buy inexpensive merchandise as a matter of course. Select equipment that is sturdy and durably constructed because it will get hard use. In the long run, one high-quality, durable item will last longer and be more cost effective over time than an item that is less expensive but poorly constructed.

- Consider each new item of equipment in light of what you already have. Work toward a balanced environment, one with many sources of creative expression: working alone, in pairs, in small or large groups. In addition to equipment for large and small motor skills, select items that appeal to the sensory motor explorations of young children. Equipment should be stimulating to see, interesting to touch, and satisfying to maneuver. This applies to equipment for older children as well.

- Purchase all major equipment in child size, rather than doll or toy size. It is also important to have real-life and adult-sized equipment where appropriate. Real hammers and screwdrivers in a smaller adult size (not toy tools) work best in construction projects.

- Consider the total number of children and how many at a given time are to use the equipment. Ten two- or three-year-old children need a basic supply of equipment. Add several more children, and you may need more blocks, more cars and trucks, etc. Also consider the age of the children in the group. Because two- and three-year-old children spend much of their time in egocentric (solitary) play or parallel play (playing *next to* but *not with* another child), there must be enough blocks, people, animals, cars, and dishes to allow several children to engage in similar play at the same time. Yet another strategy is to have duplicate or very similar copies of favorite items on hand.

Interest Centers and Multiple Intelligences

As we learned in the previous chapter, young children have many ways of learning. You can incorporate what you've learned about these multiple intelligences by including appropriate materials and equipment in your activity centers that appeal to multiple intelligences. Figure 6–12 presents a list of materials and activities for preschool and kindergarten children. Figure 6–13 has the same information for grades 1–5. You don't need to include all of these items in each center, but it is important to have a variety of materials for the multiple intelligences of children in your group.

SUMMARY

To ensure the proper environment for creative expression in young children, careful attention must be given to safety, amount and organization of space, light, sound, and furniture. Planning the environment in the early childhood program involves knowledge of children's needs, as well as attention to traffic flow in the room, children's developing skills, and safety. Arrangement of personal space for each child also needs to be planned.

A balance between teacher planning and children's self-direction is necessary. Interest or activity centers help children make their own choices. The placement and organization of the various activity centers have an impact on how creative materials within them are used by children, how safe the environment is, and how children's self-help skills are encouraged.

Because creative activities are so important in promoting children's development, careful attention must be directed toward the selection and care of creative materials and equipment. The best equipment is simple in design; versatile; easy to use; large; durable; working properly; available in needed amounts; designed for group play; and, above all, safe.

It is also important that equipment be stored properly so that children can reach it easily, thereby developing their self-help skills. Materials that appeal to the multiple intelligences should also be included in activity centers.

KEY TERMS

activity centers   interest centers

LEARNING ACTIVITIES

A. Choose one activity center from the list provided in this chapter. Design your own unique version of this activity center. Describe it in detail. List the items and activities it would include.
B. Draw an ideal room plan for creative activities. Imagine you have all the money, materials, and space necessary. Be creative. After drawing it, list what you feel is important in it, starting with the most important feature. Share this list with classmates and discuss it.
C. Using small blocks or any other similar object, show how you would arrange space in a room to ensure smooth traffic flow and noninterference among interest centers in the room.
D. Go through a school supply catalog. Find examples of furniture, shelving, and play objects that you would include in planning your "ideal room" in the activity preceding.
E. Obtain a toy and equipment catalog or go to a toy store. Make a list of materials that would be useful for children's play. Imagine that you have $1,250 to spend on equipment. Make a list of items you would purchase. Assume you may not go over the $1,250 amount.

CHAPTER REVIEW

1. List 10 items to consider in creating a positive physical environment for young children.
2. Discuss the considerations and requirements involved in setting up activity centers, including convertible centers.
3. List the major considerations involved in arranging space in the early childhood setting.
4. List five interest centers that early childhood experts recommend be available for the creative expression of young children. Describe what skills are developed in each.
5. Name at least five important factors when selecting proper equipment for young children's creative activities.
6. Discuss some safety precautions to consider in choosing equipment.
7. Discuss some ways to adapt the environment for children with special needs.
8. List types of materials that appeal to each of the multiple intelligences.

REFERENCES

Hunter, T. (2001, March). Taking the long view. *Young Children,* 82.

Karnes, M. (2003, May). Art for children with special needs in All About Art Inside and Out. *Scholastic Early Childhood Today,* 33–39.

Myers, B. K., & Maurer, K. (1987, July). Teaching with less talking: Learning centers in the kindergarten. *Young Children,* 20–27.

Patillo, J., & Vaughan, E. (1992). *Learning centers for child-centered classrooms.* Washington, DC: NAEYC.

ADDITIONAL READINGS

Bronson, M. B. (2000). *The right stuff for children birth to 8: Selecting play materials to support development.* Washington, DC: NAEYC.

Carter, M., & Curtis, D. (2003, May). *Designs for living and learning: Transforming early childhood environments.* St. Paul, MN: Redleaf.

Dodge, T., Colker, L. J., & Heroman (2002). *The creative curriculum for preschool,* 4th ed. Washington, DC: NAEYC.

Hewes, D. W. (2001). *W. N. Hailmann: Defender of Froebel.* Grand Rapids, MI: Froebel Foundation.

Hill, D. M. (2001). *Mud, sand & water.* Washington, DC: NAEYC.

Hirsch, E. S. (Ed.). (2002). *The block book,* 3rd ed. Washington, DC: NAEYC.To

Isbell, R., & Exelby, B. (2002). *Early learning environments that work.* Washington, DC: NAEYC.

Miller, S. A. (2000, Jan.) Managing children's artwork. *Scholastic Early Childhood Today,* 16.

Vergeront, J. (2000). *Places and spaces for preschool and primary (indoors).* Washington, DC: NAEYC.

HELPFUL WEB SITES

http://nccic.org
National Child Care Information Center Online Library.
http://www.pbs.org/wholechild and
   http://www.naeyc.org
Child Observation Web Sites for Busy Early Childhood Teachers.

http://teacher.scholastic.com/
Information on Materials and Supplies by Activity Center; click on Products.

For additional creative activity resources, visit our Web site at http://www.EarlyChildEd. delmar.com.

Chapter 7

Play, Development, and Creativity

Objectives

After studying this chapter, you should be able to:

1. Name and discuss the four kinds of human growth that are influenced by play.
2. Define solitary, parallel, associative, and cooperative play.
3. Discuss ways the environment can be adapted to encourage social play experiences for children with special needs.
4. Discuss some reasons children engage in violent play and how to deal with this type of play.

Some children are busily involved in activities in an early childhood program. One group of children is removing the wheels from the wooden trucks in the room. Now they are having races by pushing the wheelless trucks along the floor. One child notes the scraping sound being made, while another discovers that the trucks without wheels make marks on the floor.

One child is preparing a tea party for three friends. The child has baked an imaginary cake and has just finished putting on icing. Now the table is being set and the chairs arranged. Another group of children is carefully observing several small furry animals on the other side of the room.

Are these children working? Are they playing? Is there a difference between work and play for a young child? Must children be involved in games to be playing? Must toys be involved? Is play natural, or can children be taught to play?

The answers to these questions are important. They help define the meaning of the word *play*. The answers lead to an understanding of how children benefit from creative play. They give direction for the purchase and placement of creative materials that guide children's play. They help adults plan activities that help children grow through creative play.

WHAT IS PLAY?

For adults, play is what they do when they have finished their work. It is a form of relaxation. For young

Figure 7-1
A young toddler often engages in solitary play.

children, play is what they do all day. Playing is living, and living is playing.

Young children do not differentiate between play, learning, and work. Children are by nature playful. They enjoy playing and will do so whenever they can. Challenges intrigue them. Why do children love to play? Because play is intrinsically motivated—that is, no one else tells them what to do or how to do it. An activity ceases to be play, and children's interest dwindles, if adults structure or even interfere inappropriately with play.

For older children, learning may be work. When they complete their work, then they can play. For young children, mental development results from their play. Growth of their ability to deal with the problems of life—social development—results from play. Growth of their imaginations results from play. Muscles develop in play, as well.

Play is an activity. It does not necessarily result in a product. It may involve one child or groups of chil-

dren. It may be built around toys and tools or may involve nothing more than the child's imagination. A play period may last a few minutes or go on for days.

Types of Play

There are two main types of play: **free** (or **spontaneous**) **play** and **organized play.** In either type, children may work alone or in a group. Each type may involve materials and equipment, or it may not. Basically, *free play,* as its name suggests, is flexible. It is unplanned by adults. It is a self-selected, open exercise. The following scene depicts free play.

Two teachers I know regularly take their class to a park where there is no equipment. At first the children were disoriented, thinking there was nothing to do. The adults purposely got busy preparing food, and in time the children began to lead each other into forays of discovery. They climbed trees and fences and hills; hid from each other in the bushes; chased each other; and collected sticks and discovered pinecones, pebbles, feathers, and wonders of all sorts. They brought treasured items back and came for help when others got stuck in hard-to-get-out-of places. The adults limited them to a large, but visible, area. This was excellent teaching—nonintervention to let children find their own fun.

Organized play is also open and flexible. However, some structure is provided in terms of materials and equipment.

Teachers can promote organized play by providing representational toys and dress-up clothes. Representational toys are toys that strongly resemble real objects, such as dolls, toy vehicles, dishes, cooking utensils, stoves, telephones, and doctor kits. Dress-up clothes can include handbags, lunch boxes, briefcases, hats of various kinds, and jewelry. These representational toys prompt children to pretend to engage in the activities of others, to do the things they see adults do. This is often called "dramatic" play as children act out the roles of grownups in their lives. (More specific information on dramatic play is provided in Chapter 15.) They pretend to feed the baby, drive to work, cook dinner, talk on the telephone, and so forth. Props relevant to the children's culture and community can enrich the children's efforts to construct and express their understanding of significant events and people in their lives.

Figure 7-2
Children are by nature playful.

Figure 7-3
For young children, play is a way of life.

Sequence of Play

There is a general sequential order of play activities that may be observed in young children. These types of play activities may be classified according to stages.

In early toddlerhood, a child at first generally plays alone. This stage is termed **solitary play.** Using all of their senses, children explore long before they use any objects in their play. They touch, smell, see, and listen. Manipulating and handling materials are important parts of play experiences. In these early play experiences, children are more involved with the manipulation of materials than they are with the uses of them. Gradually, as the toddler's social realm expands, he or she will engage in **parallel play.** Parallel play occurs

when a child plays side by side with other children, with some interaction but without direct involvement.

As the number of relationships outside the home increases, the child's ability to play with other children develops further. At this point, the child may engage in **associative play.** This type of play may take the form of a child merely being present in a group. For example, a child who participates in fingerplays during circle time or group time would be said to be engaging in associative play. Common activities occur between children. They may exchange toys and/or follow one another. Although all the children in the group are doing similar activities, specific roles are not defined, and there is no organized goal (such as building something or pretending to have a tea party). Eventually, as they grow more comfortable with their social ties, young children will begin to talk about, plan, and carry out play activities with other children. This type of play, marked by mutual involvement in a play activity, is called **cooperative play.** Children cooperate with others to construct something or act out coordinated roles.

IMPORTANCE OF PLAY IN CHILD DEVELOPMENT

Creative play activities influence children's total growth, including physical, mental, emotional, and social growth.

Physical Growth

Play contributes to muscle development in many ways. Throwing a ball or lifting objects helps children's muscles develop. Placing an object on top of another and grasping tools also add to a child's muscle development and hand–eye coordination. Play that requires children to look for objects, feel textures, smell various odors, hear sounds, and taste substances help them develop their senses.

Children spend hours perfecting such abilities in play and increasing the level of difficulty to make the task ever more challenging. Anyone who has lived or worked with one year olds will recall the tireless persistence with which they pursue the acquisition of a basic skill such as walking. In older children, this repetitious physical activity is also a major characteristic of play. It is evident on playgrounds, where we see children swinging, climbing, or playing ball with fervor.

As a child gains control of his or her body, self-concept is enhanced. When a child runs, she or he feels exhilarated. When a child uses the last bit of strength to accomplish a goal he or she has set, he or she gains a better sense of self. As the child discovers his or her own strength, the child develops a concept of himself or herself as a competent individual. A young child is quite physical in play, playing with his or her whole being. As the child plays, she or he decides what to do and how to do it; he or she does his

Figure 7-4

Imaginative play permits the child to fit the reality of the world into his or her own interests and knowledge of the world.

Figure 7-5

Play activities help children develop a positive self-concept.

or her own planning and implements plans in his or her own ways.

When children have a chance to be physically active, they continually gain strength. As they become more adept, they become more adventurous and learn to take reasonable risks to test their strength. When children set their own challenges, they are less likely to have accidents. Without predetermined goals, they can pace themselves and discover what they can and cannot do.

A child aged five to eight years in the middle childhood years develops physically in his or her play. At the beginning of this period of growth, the child is almost continuously active, whether standing or sitting. Toward the end of this period, however, movements of

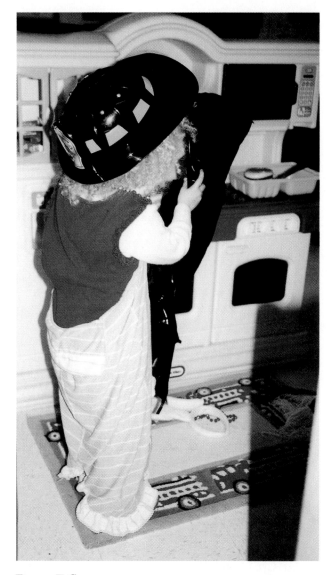

Figure 7-6

In creative play, the child has control of the situation, using props he or she chooses and in the manner he or she prefers.

the eight-year-old child have become fluid and graceful. He or she has developed poise. In fact, he or she is continually on the go—jumping, running, chasing, or wrestling. There is an increase of speed and smoothness in fine motor movements. The child approaches objects rapidly and smoothly, and releases them with sure abandon. Organized games with rules to follow are beginning to be popular with this age group.

During the later childhood years (in grades 4–5), the need for vigorous play is still important for children. A glance at children of this age group reveals one factor that stands out above all others. Children of this age vary widely. The group may be about the same age, even in the same grade, but there the similarities end. They vary widely in their size, interest, activities, and abilities, and these differences, in turn, influence every aspect of the child's development. The child, other children, parents, and teachers should realize that these differences are quite normal.

This age group has good muscular control, has a general increase in strength, is particularly sturdy, is keenly interested in sports, and acquires the skills for games readily. Watching them at play, one often wonders if they ever get tired. They have a lot of stamina. Arms grow longer, and hands and feet grow bigger. Some children at this stage are clumsy and awkward as a result of the uneven growth of the different body parts.

Children who are eight to twelve years old select increasingly demanding physical play, which gives them a greater opportunity to develop muscle control and coordination. At this age, boundless amounts of energy and enthusiasm are hallmarks of their play. Children in this group enjoy running, tumbling, climbing on jungle gyms, and swinging. As they grow in motor skills and confidence, they begin more advanced forms of play such as roller skating, skipping rope, skate boarding, and throwing and catching. Children's increased physical abilities and improved coordination also allow participation in team sports and other organized activities in which one's physical ability affects the outcome of the game.

Mental Growth

Play helps children develop important mental concepts. Through play activities, a child learns the meaning of such concepts as up and down, hard and soft, and big and small. Play contributes to a child's knowledge of building and arranging things in sets. Children learn to sort, classify, and probe for answers. Playing outdoors children learn to sense differences in their world as the seasons change and as they observe other subtle changes every day.

Figure 7-7

For young children, play is what they do all day long.

Figure 7-8

Ten- to twelve-year-old children develop the social skills necessary to participate in complex, cooperative forms of play.

Piaget (1962) feels that **imaginative play** is one of the purest forms of symbolic thought available to the young child. According to Piaget, it permits the child to fit the reality of the world into his or her interest and knowledge of the world. Thus, imaginative play contributes strongly to the child's intellectual development. Some researchers even maintain that symbolic play is a necessary part of a child's development of language (Dyson, 1991; Kagan, 1990; Monighan-Nourot, 1990).

Play also offers the child opportunities to acquire information that sets the foundation for additional learning. For example, through playing with blocks a child learns the idea of equivalents (that things can be equal) by discovering that two small blocks equal one larger one; or through playing with water or sand, the child acquires knowledge of volume, which eventually leads to developing the concept of reversibility.

A child gains an understanding of his or her environment as he or she investigates stones, grass, flowers, earth, water, and anything else around. Through these experiences, the child eventually begins to make his own generalizations: Adding water to earth makes mud. A puddle of water disappears in sand. The inner part of a milkweed pod blows away in the wind. Wet socks can be dried out in the sun.

As children play, they develop spatial concepts; as they climb in, over, and around the big box in the yard, they clarify concepts of "in," "over," and "around." They hear someone call the box a "gigantic" box and "gigantic" becomes a new word. In the sandbox, words such as "deep," "deeper," and "deepest" begin to have meaning.

Older Children's Play and Cognitive Development

Older children learn many concepts through play. They learn about such things as rules of the game and strategies in play. They begin to learn about their own

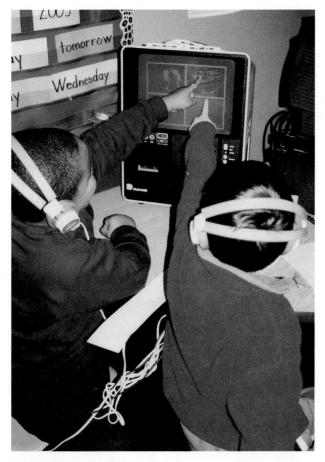

Figure 7-9

Working at the computer can be a chance for cooperative play.

skill levels in various activities and develop preferences for specific sports and activities.

Children's increasing cognitive abilities allow them to participate in more advanced forms of organized games and team activities where rules guide actual behaviors. Although younger children often play together (actually, they may only be playing near each other), they also often play alone. Children who are eight to twelve-years old might also play alone either by choice or by necessity. However, their increasing cognitive abilities (especially in those ten to twelve years of age) allow them to play with others in situations requiring consistent or complex rules. The cognitive abilities of ten to twelve year olds also allow for more advanced forms of play such as word games, riddles, and other literacy-related play.

Today's technology allows older children many new forms of play. Children can play a wide array of computer games either alone or with another child. Software, such as for chess, requires that children think and participate in active decision making, while other software requires writing and complex thinking. As techno-

logic advances become commmonplace in our society, children will have even greater access to problem-solving programs, CD-ROMs, videodiscs, and simulation programs. Many eight- to twelve-year-old children who have benefited from computer use in schools are sufficiently computer literate to "play" with the many technologic advances.

Emotional Growth

One of the keys to the quality of children's emotional health is how they feel about themselves. Creative play activities help a child develop a positive self-concept. In play activities, there are no right or wrong answers. Children are not faced with the threat of failure. They learn to see themselves as capable performers. Even when things do not go well, there is little pressure built into play. Thus, young children learn to view themselves as successful and worthwhile human beings through creative play. This is an important first step in developing a positive self-concept.

Children also learn to express and understand their emotions in creative play experiences. They may be observed almost any place in the early childhood setting expressing their feelings about doctors by administering shots with relish or their jealousy of a new baby by reprimanding a doll, but creative play is not necessarily limited to the expression of negative feelings. The same doll that only a moment ago was being reprimanded may next be lulled and crooned to sleep in the rocking chair.

Another emotional value of creative play is that it offers the child an opportunity to achieve mastery of his or her environment. The child has control of the situation, using what props he or she chooses and in the manner he or she prefers. The child is in command. He or she establishes the conditions of the experience by using imagination and exercises his or her powers of choice and decision as the play progresses.

Play is a safe and acceptable way to test out the expression of feelings. Through play children can recreate experiences that have been important to them and elaborate on experiences that have special meaning. The child can relieve anxiety or stress through play activities and feel perfectly safe in doing so. For example, Susan gets pleasure out of hammering on a piece of wood. She feels strong as she swings the hammer and sees the deep indentations she is making in the wood. Woodworking, thus, is providing a medium through which she can release tension or aggression in an acceptable way.

Children in the middle and upper elementary grades grow emotionally when engaged in play with their peers. Playing together, children learn to accept each other's styles and personalities and learn how it feels to be accepted for their own. Once the child gains acceptance among the peer group, he or she begins to have self-respect and feels confident and adequate in attempting new problems and activities.

Social Growth

Children learn social skills as they relate to others during play. As a child becomes proficient in his or her social relating, he or she learns to deal with more than one person at a time. As a group participant, he or she finds not everyone behaves in the same way and that some forms of behavior are not acceptable. When Claire takes a block from Jimmy's building, Jimmy pushes her away. Next time, she does not try that. In one situation, Claire learns that crying will get her what she wants, while in another it does not work at all. Children establish social relationships as they sit side by side playing with clay, dough, and other manipulative materials. A child discovers that he or she can make some decisions about what he or she will or will not do. If a child does not wish to push a wagon, he or she can play somewhere else. The child cannot, however, always be the one to tell others what to do. Sometimes the child takes the role of leader and sometimes he or she finds the role of follower satisfying.

When children play together, they learn to be together. The development of common interests and goals takes place among children during creative play. They must learn to "give a little" as well as "take a little" when involved in creative play activities. Whether two small children are arguing over the possession of a toy or a group of children are playing together on a jungle gym, play helps children grow socially.

Ten- to twelve-year-old children, in particular, develop the social skills necessary to participate in complex, cooperative forms of play. Their enhanced social skills allow them to see others' perspectives and allow them to realize the benefits of playing socially and cooperatively with other children. At this age, play that requires social skills might consist of games, team sports, and organized activities.

Children, especially ten- to twelve-year-old children, shift allegiance from parents and teachers to peers. They are beginning to seek freedom and independence, which results in their playing away from home and often away from direct adult supervision. Children might visit ball fields, playgrounds, and recreation centers where others play or where special equipment is available to them.

At school, teachers can assist older children through play activities at recess, noon, or during class time to become more proficient in skills for ordinary games. Yet, the acquisition of physical skills needed in ordinary games involves more than physical maturation. It is a matter closely tied to social adjustment.

A child who is socially comfortable with other children will try and try until he or she can participate without ridicule from others. The teacher needs to help children feel socially comfortable in the area of games. This developmental task is actually enhanced when facilities, equipment, and play space are made available for children of this age group. Too often, the importance of vigorous play for children of this age group is overlooked because they seem so "grownup."

Figure 7-10

Given the times in which we live, we should afford children every opportunity to store as many happy recollections as they can.

ADAPTING ENVIRONMENTS TO ENCOURAGE SOCIAL DEVELOPMENT FOR CHILDREN WITH SPECIAL NEEDS

One purpose for including children with special needs in typical early childhood settings is to provide these children opportunities to interact with children who do not have disabilities (Haring, 1992). The ultimate goal is to have these interactions lead to friendships. Even when first enrolled in an inclusive classroom, some children who are developing typically seem very comfortable around children who have special needs. These children may show a strong desire to nurture or touch children with special needs (Bergen, 1993) and/or show great interest in any adaptive equipment their peers use (Diamond & Stacey, 2000). They may spend a great deal of time observing how adults interact with the children who have special needs but may appear unsure about how to approach or interact with these peers themselves. These children may delight in pleasing others and may even forego play opportunities to "help" the children with special needs. In these situations, teachers should provide ample opportunities for children to interact. Young children usually describe "friends" as the people who play with them that day.

Teachers should arrange the physical environment and daily schedule to facilitate opportunities for children to interact and continue to model appropriate behaviors for these children (Taylor, Peterson, Murray-Schwarz, & Guillou, 2002).

One way to arrange the physical environment to promote social interaction is to use specific toys. When social toys (e.g., blocks, balls, miniature cars) rather

THINK ABOUT IT...   What Play Really Is

Play is a characteristic of children at all times and places. Nonetheless, it varies with social class and culture. Sara Smilansky initiated a new line of play research studies with her finding that sociodramatic play was more common among children of advantage than it was among those with less advantage (1968). Although some writers (Weinberger & Starkey, 1994) contest this conclusion, they remain in the minority.

There are also cultural differences in play. One general finding is that the more complex the culture, the more complex the competitive games engaged in within that society (Sutton-Smith, 1980).

At the early childhood level, however, there is likely much more similarity in children's play than difference across both culture and social class. This is true because young children are less socialized and more apt to create their own play than to adopt socially transmitted play activities. For the young, and to a degree all ages, play has personal meaning and value not dealt with in traditional theory and research. Although there has been a great deal of research on play since these theories were offered, we really have no new theories of play (Elkind, 2003).

David Elkind, noted child developmentalist, feels that all the research on play simply represents one side of the issue—the adult side. Adults in his opinion look at children's play as, in one way or another, facilitating healthy development. Although he does not deny the developmental value or meaning of children's play, Elkind maintains that play has a personal, experiential value of equal, if not greater, importance (Elkind, 2003).

We, as teachers of young children, need to resist the pressures to transform play into work—into academic instruction. We encourage true play by making certain that we offer materials that leave room for the imagination—blocks, paint, paper to be cut and pasted—and that children have sufficient time to innovate with these materials.

The vital importance of play is obvious in Elkind's words:

Given the times in which we live, we should afford children every opportunity to store as many happy recollections as they can. If we encourage and facilitate children's true play, we bequeath them an important and priceless gift, an *album of joyous memories*. Years from now these memories are what our young charges—grown up—will remember us by, and thank us for (Elkind, 2003, p. 50).

Figure 7-11

Play is very much an activity of the mind. Children may become deeply engrossed in their play and find it difficult to stop when asked.

than isolate toys (e.g., crayons, modeling dough, puzzles) are used during playtimes, children engage in more interactions and less solitary play (Beckman & Kohl, 1984). Also, limiting the space available to children during playtime and placing children with special needs in close proximity to peers during group time and play sessions increase social interactions (Brown, Fox, & Brady, 1987).

Increasing the proximity of children and limiting the space available to children can be accomplished by creating play centers and by assigning seats during group times, ensuring that children with special needs always have peers who are typically developing on both sides of them (Guida, Pirsos, Schempp, & Cuthbertson, 1994). These strategies can be designed around individual children's Individual Educational Plans (IEP) goals and can be made part of the general curricular and daily activities.

VIOLENT PLAY

Many early childhood teachers are concerned about how to deal with war and superhero play in their classrooms. Concern with this type of play seems to increase when violent world events dominate the news.

Play, as we have discussed in this chapter, is viewed as an essential part of the early childhood program. In our world today, however, play often is a problem because of the frequency of war and superhero play in the early childhood years. Some teachers wonder why play is so important when it is so focused on fighting. Some teachers resort to planning other activities that

are easier to manage. Another solution some teachers use is to reduce playtime. This may seem to reduce problems in the short term, but it deprives children of the wide-ranging developmental benefits play provides. Before we consider how to deal with the problem of war and superhero play, it is important to consider some of the reasons for this type of play.

Some Reasons for Violent Play

Children are exposed to far more violence today than their teachers have experienced in their lives. Yet teachers must help today's children face and deal with this exposure to violence. Let us consider what impact the presence of violence has in a child's life.

Violence in Everyday Life. Simply looking around in today's world, it's obvious that violence is something young children are exposed to in their lives. Young children may see violence in their homes and communities as well as in entertainment and news on the screen. It's hardly surprising that children are bringing it into their play.

If you watch children's violent play, you will see that they often focus on the most graphic, confusing or scary, and aggressive aspects of violence. It is this context they are struggling to work out and understand in their play. Usually, the children who seem most obsessed with war play have been exposed to the most violence and have the greatest need to work it out (Levin, 2003).

Feelings. Most young children look for ways to feel powerful and strong. Play can be a safe way to achieve a sense of power. From a child's point of view, play with violence is very seductive, especially when connected to the power and invincibility portrayed in entertainment. The children who use war play to help them feel powerful and safe are the children who feel the most powerless and vulnerable (Levin, 2003).

Media, Toys, and Violence. Many action-figure toys so popular today are highly structured toys. Just by the way they look and work, they give children powerful messages about the content and direction of play. In contrast, open-ended toys such as blocks and stuffed animals can be used in many ways that the child controls.

Many of the action and war games toys are linked to violent movies, TV shows, and video games. These toys have strong appeal because they promise dramatic power and excitement. Often, these toys cause children to replicate violent stories they see on the

THIS ONE'S for YOU!

More Information on Play

Play is the natural and best way for children to learn as they investigate for themselves and observe others at play and work. They are natural explorers who have a need and desire to investigate their world through real experiences and natural environments. There are five qualities that distinguish play for young children from other activities:

- It is a process. The outcome is not as important as the process itself.
- Play is child-initiated. The activity is done for no other reason than the child wants to do it.
- In play, everything and anything can happen; a sheet over a table becomes a castle and the little girl inside is the princess.
- Play becomes the arena for testing rules, both logical and illogical. Rules freely appear and disappear in children's play; they may be simple or complex, and they are created from children's previous knowledge. An example of rules in play is the "rule" of roles. For example, when young children play in the housekeeping center, you will often hear one of the children assigning roles to each of the other children ("You be the mommy.").
- Play is very much an activity of the mind. Children may become deeply engrossed in their play and find it difficult to stop when asked. Play involves the mind in an active process as a child investigates, explores, and inquires during play (Hurwitz, 2003).

Within the early childhood classroom, play and the curriculum should be deeply connected. A quality curriculum for young children should rely heavily on play.

Learning to identify different types of play may give you further understanding of their importance. Types of play categories include the following:

- Practice play—play that children do repeatedly, solely for pleasure, such as playing in sand and pouring it through their fingers.
- Constructive play—play where children construct or create something, such as block building.
- Rough and tumble play—play that involves laughing and pretending; as the name implies, it can get a little rough (it is *not* aggressive play and, when done in a safe area, is an acceptable form of play).
- Dramatic play—play that gives children the opportunity to take on the role of another person or an animal or even an object.
- Games with rules—play governed by a set of rules, such as a game of "Duck, Duck, Goose."

Understanding these categories helps teachers plan appropriate play activities to meet the developmental needs of the whole child (Hurwitz, 2003). So the next time you see children engaged in play, remember that they are practicing and developing the skills necessary to be successful students and members of the community. Let them have fun and play!

---

screen. Many young children get stuck imitating media-linked violence instead of developing creative and imaginative play.

Working with Children's Violent Play. There are no simple or perfect solutions to children's violent play. However, here are some ways to approach the problem:

- Wherever possible, reduce the amount of violence children see. Most of young children's exposure to violence occurs in the home, so family involvement is crucial. Teachers can help families learn more about how to protect children from violence through parent workshops and family newsletters. Teachers can also help parents learn to deal with

the violence that still gets in. In addition, teachers can provide parents information on how to choose open-ended toys and toys with nonviolent themes (Levin, 2003).

- Promote imaginative and creative play. Be aware of the difference between *imitative* play and creative or imaginative play. Imitative play is when children engage in the same play with violence day after day and bring in few new or creative ideas of their own. Piaget called this kind of behavior *imitation,* not play (Carlsson-Paige & Levin, 1987). In imitative play, children are less likely to work out their needs than in imaginative play.

⊙ Take time to observe children's play and learn what children are working on and how. Use this information to help children move beyond their imitative play that focuses on violent actions. Help children learn new ways to work out the violent content of their play. For example, children can work out their feelings by pounding nails into wood, rolling and pounding out clay, and knocking down stacks of blocks.

⊙ Encourage children to deal with issues of violence by expressing their feelings in painting, drawing, or telling stories. Older children can write down their thoughts in stories or poetry.

⊙ Talk with children about violent play. As children struggle to feel safe and make sense of violence, they need to know adults are there to help them in the process (Levin, 2003). Talk with children to learn what confuses and scares them. When a child raises an issue about something that frightens him, it helps to ask an open-ended question. For example, simply ask, "What have you heard about that?" That way you can respond more exactly to what is troubling the child.

⊙ It is important to keep in mind that children do not always understand violence as adults do. They may have misconceptions. Try to correct these misconceptions. ("The planes that go over our school do not carry bombs.") Help children sort out fantasy from reality. ("People in real life can't change back and forth like the Power Rangers do.")

⊙ Encourage children to engage in creative play so they can transform violence into positive behavior. Provide them props, time, and a positive environment in which to act out violent ideas in more positive ways. Guide them in their approach so they might learn firsthand how to treat each other in peaceful ways. Praise them for their efforts. ("I'm glad that in real life you could solve your problem with Scott by. . .") These real-life experiences can help defuse some of the harmful lessons children learn about violence.

Given the state of our world, young children now more than ever need to find ways to work out the violence they see. For many, play helps them do this. We have a crucial role in helping meet young children's needs through play.

SUMMARY

Play is a central part of the lives of young children, not something to do when work is finished. Play may be organized (structured) or spontaneous (free). It may involve dramatics or special equipment, or it may take the form of a game. Play usually develops in a natural sequence that evolves from a child's level of socialization. The sequential stages of play include solitary, parallel, associative, and cooperative play.

The needs of children are met through creative play. They learn about themselves, others, and the world around them through their play activities. Creative play has specific purposes in the early childhood program—to promote physical, mental, social, and emotional growth. Observation of children engaged in creative play will reveal some differences (stages) of play. Play is quite different for three year olds than it is for five year olds. Three-year-old children often cannot separate the real from the pretend. They prefer to be characters about whom they know something. Four year olds tend to be aggressive and play characters that enable them to display their aggressive feelings. Five year olds can separate the real world from the world of their imaginations. They are better able to control their emotions. Teachers can adapt the environment so that it encourages the play of children with special needs. They also need to be aware of the reasons for children's violent play and how to deal with it in the early childhood program.

Older children enjoy games that allow them to perfect skills achieved at earlier ages. They enjoy games with rules. In games and other play activities, social and emotional development are as important as physical development to this age group.

KEY TERMS

associative play	organized play
cooperative play	parallel play
free play	solitary play
imaginative play	spontaneous play

LEARNING ACTIVITIES

A. Observe children of various ages at play. Without letting them know you are watching, observe one or more children from each age group at play for periods of at least 10 minutes for each group. How are the play activities similar? How are they different? Observe children in these two groups: (1) kindergarten–grade 3 and (2) grades 4–5. How are their play activities similar? How are they different? What were the most prevalent forms of play observed in each group? Were you surprised by what you saw? Why or why not?

B. Select one play activity and discuss how it contributes to a child's growth in each of four areas of development discussed in this chapter (physical, mental, social, emotional). Choose an activity for each of the age groups discussed in this chapter. Compare and contrast the activities for each age group.

C. Observe the dramatic play of a group of three year olds and a group of five year olds. In what ways is their play different? How is it similar? Observe dramatic play for a group of children in each of these age groups: (1) kindergarten–grade 3 and (2) grades 4–5. In what ways is their dramatic play different from each other? How is it similar? Did you observe anything that surprised you? Share your observations with your fellow students.

D. Try the Animal Cracker game. It is an example of a game that children enjoy and one that helps the student develop a better understanding of the creative possibilities of games.
1. Obtain a box of animal crackers. Stand before a full-length mirror and, without looking, take one of the crackers from the box. Look at and then eat the cracker. With that action, you "become" the selected animal for two minutes. Observe your behavior as that animal. Do this a number of times.
2. Answer the following questions about this activity:
   a. How did you feel about doing this?
   b. How is creativity different from silliness?
   c. How do games help people develop creativity or become more creative?

ACTIVITIES FOR CHILDREN

EXPANDING PLAY EXPERIENCES

One way to encourage and expand children's play is by changing the materials they normally use in activity centers. Add some of the following materials to your interest centers to expand children's play experiences.

Dramatic Play Center

⊙ Add open-ended materials such as sheets and scarves or a large cardboard box. Ask children, "What can you do with this?"
⊙ Have a box of unusual items (tools, beach ball, funny glasses and hats) that children can choose from when they want to add a new element to their play.
⊙ After reading a favorite story, provide props to go with it and let them retell the story in their own way.

Block Center

⊙ Add rope and small balls. Ask the children, "What can you do with these?"
⊙ Add aluminum foil and flashlights to inspire new types of building.
⊙ Have pictures of unusual buildings in the center to inspire children's building.

Shadow Play. In a group, perhaps outdoors on a bright day, encourage children to make silly movements and observe their own shadows. Introduce a quick "copy cat" (follow-the-leader) game: "Everybody jump! Everybody hop! Now, everybody dance!"

On the playground, play a shadow touch game. Have the children in the group make one connecting shadow by having their shadows touch each other's. Then, play shadow tag.

IMAGINATION EXERCISES

Children enjoy "being" animals or other "pretend" things. These activities are good for large-muscle development as well as for creative play. In these activities, encourage children to move slowly and quietly. Once they interpret the object or animal in their own way, suggest that they hold the positions while continuing to breathe slowly.

A. *Tree.* Together, close your eyes and think about different trees you've seen. Then stand up and raise your arms to look like a tree. Breathe slowly in and out and try to hold the pose for about 30 seconds.

B. *Mountain.* Begin by sitting on the floor, legs crossed, or sitting in any position that's comfortable. Then, slowly raise your arms to create a mountain peak. As you hold the position, ask the children to pretend they are a huge, quiet mountain. You, or someone in the group, can describe the peaceful scenes you might see below.

C. *Cat.* Find a comfortable way to curl up like a cat and pretend to be sleeping in a warm, comfy place, such as near a fireplace or in a sunny place. Then wake up and stretch.

D. *Turtle.* Pretend you are a turtle by rounding your back like a shell and tucking your head, arms, and legs under the shell. Hold this pose for a bit, then very slowly stretch out your neck, arms, and legs (Church, 1993).

The following are some creative play activities that require the use of large muscles and that promote large (gross) motor skills.

Guess What I Am. Without saying a word, a child tries to act out the movements of some object. This may be an airplane making a landing, a rooster strutting around the barnyard, a cement truck dumping its load, or a clock telling the time of day. The child may think up things to do, or the teacher may whisper suggestions.

Water Play. A water table or a large tub is filled with water and used for creative water play. Children pour, mix, and stir the water. Soap may be added so they can create suds, too. They may also enjoy using water and a large paintbrush to "paint" a fence or the school building. A variety of objects can be put together to make a boat that floats. (Aluminum foil works well for this.) Creative cleanup can be developed by children as they find how water, tools, and materials can help them clean up messes.

Playing with a Hose. A child enjoys playing with a hose connected to an outlet with the water on strong. The children learn about what happens when they put their thumbs over the nozzle. They discover the push effect as water leaves the hose. They make rain by sprinkling water into the air. They create a rainbow. They hear different sounds as the water strikes different materials.

For a realistic gas pump hose to use outdoors with riding toys, fit an old piece of garden hose with a pistol grip nozzle. These nozzles are available at hardware stores.

Toddler's Play

⊙ Cardboard boxes offer toddlers the opportunity for a great deal of beneficial play. Take sturdy cardboard boxes of different sizes and tape them together with packing or duct tape to form long "trains." Make segments of varying heights by propping some boxes on sturdy pillows or padding. Then place the trains in a padded area or surround them with pillows. Encourage the toddlers to climb on top of the train at one end and crawl the length of the train. Moving up and down onto the different levels promotes motor planning, eye–hand coordination, and balance. You can also have them crawl through open boxes taped together in "tunnels," which will increase their body awareness.

⊙ Stuff an empty tissue box with scarves or large pieces of nylon or similar fabric. Toddlers enjoy pulling the fabric out. Turn on some music and let the children dance with their scarves.

⊙ Add materials to a water or sand table. A large plastic tub or box can be a portable sand table. Put in foam packing "peanuts," cotton balls, shredded paper, or even dirt. Hide some small plastic toys in the box. Give a child some scoops, funnels, or cups to dig for fun and good hand–eye coordination.

Using Empty Cartons. Many children receive toys that come in large cartons. After a short time, many of these children put aside the fancy toys and play with the empty cartons. In view of this, it makes sense to provide such boxes for children to play with. The boxes can be used in many creative ways—they can be arranged into trains, serve as houses and stores, and used as a cave or hideaway. Children can paint the outsides and insides.

ACTIVITIES FOR OLDER CHILDREN (GRADES 4–5)

ELECTRONIC PLAY

Software companies have put back the "fun" in learning fundamentals, releasing dozens of computer games that teachers can adopt for classroom use. Here is a brief list of some of the best and most popular electronic educational games.

Language Arts

Hoyle Word Games 2001, Sierra On-Line, Inc., http://www.sierra.com; 800–757–7707; ages 8 and up, 2001.

Turbo Twist Vocabulator and Turbo Twist BRAIN QUEST, LeapFrog, http://www.leapfrog.com; 800–701–5327; ages 8 and up, 2001.

Logic

Chessmaster 8000, Mekada, http://www.mekada.com; 804–327–8444; ages 8 and up, 2002.

Gearhead Garage, Mekada, http://www.mekada.com; 804–327–8444; ages 8 and up, 2002.

Scooby Doo: Showdown in Ghost Town and **Phantom of the Knight,** The Learning Company/Broderbund, http://www.broderbund.com; 800–395–0277; ages 6–12, 2001.

Zoombinis Mountain Rescue and **Zoombinis Logical Journey,** The Learning Company/Broderbund, http://www.broderbund.com; 800–395–0277; ages 8 and up, 2002.

Math

Math Arena, Sunburst Communications, http://www.sunburst.com; 800–338–3457; ages 8–10, 2001.

On Track: Multiplication & Division 3–4, School Zone Interactive, http://www.schoolzone.com; 800–253–0564; 2001.

CHAPTER REVIEW

1. List the four areas of development that are enhanced by play activities.
2. Explain the sequence in which play develops and the characteristics for each stage.
3. Describe and compare the characteristics of play for an infant, toddler, two and one half year old, and four year old.
4. Describe the characteristics of play of children in kindergarten–grade 3 and grades 4–5.
5. Discuss some adjustments teachers can make in the environment to encourage the play of children with special needs.
6. Discuss some possible causes of children's violent play and ways to deal with it in the early childhood program.

REFERENCES

Beckman, P., & Kohl, F. (1984). The effects of social and isolate toys on the interactions and play of integrated and nonintegrated groups of pre-schoolers. *Education and Training of the Mentally Retarded, 19,* 169–174.

Bergen, D. (1993). Facilitating friendship development in inclusive classrooms. *Childhood Education 69,* 234–236.

Brown, W., Fox, J., & Brady, M. (1987). Effects of spatial density on three- and four-year-old children's socially directed behavior during free play: An investigation of a setting factor. *Education and Treatment of Children, 10,* 247–258.

Carlsson-Paige, N., & Levin, D. E. (1987). *The war play dilemma: Balancing needs and values in the early childhood classroom.* New York: Teachers College Press.

Church, E. G. (1993, Feb.). Moving small, moving quiet. *Scholastic Pre-K Today,* 42–45.

Diamond, K. E., & Stacey, S. (2000). The other child at preschool: Experiences of typically developing children in inclusive programs. In S. Sandall & M. Ostrosky (Eds.), *Young Exceptional Children monograph series no. 2: Natural Environments and inclusion.* (pp. 59–68). Longmont, CO: Sopris West.

Dyson, A. H. (1991). The roots of literacy development: Play, pictures, and peers. In B. Scales, M. Almy, A. Nicolopoulou, & S. Ervin-Tripp (Eds.), *Play and the social context of development in early care and education.* (pp. 98–116). New York: Teachers College Press.

Elkind, D. (2003, May). Thanks for the memory: The lasting value of true play. *Young Children, 58,* 46–50.

Guida, J., Pirsos, S., Schempp, K., & Cuthbertson, D. (1994). Making inclusion work: Angela is supported by a circle of friends. *Exceptional Parent, 24,* 43–46, 84.

Haring, T. (1992) The context of social competence: Relations, relationships, and generalization. In S.L. Odom, S.R. McConnell & M.A. McEvoy (Eds.), *Social competence of young children with disabilities.* (pp. 307–320). Baltimore: Paul H. Brooks.

Hurwitz, S. C. (2003). To be successful—Let them play! *Childhood Education Winter 2002/2003,* 100–101.

Kagan, S. L. (1990). Children's play: The journey from theory to practice. In E. Klugman & S. Smilansky (Eds.), *Children's play and learning: Perspectives and policy implications,* (pp. 173–185). New York: Teachers College Press.

Levin, E. D. (2003). *Teaching young children in violent times: Building a peaceable classroom.* 2nd. ed. Cambridge, MA: Educators for Social Responsibility.

Monighan-Nourot, P. (1990). The legacy of play in American early childhood education. In E. Klugman & S. Smilansky (Eds.), *Children's play and learning: Perspectives and policy implications.* (pp. 59–85). New York: Teachers College Press.

Piaget, J. (1962). *Play, dreams, and imitation in childhood.* New York: W. W. Norton.

Smilansky, S. (1968). *The effects of socio-dramatic play on disadvantaged preschool children.* New York: Wiley.

Sutton-Smith, B. (1980). Children's play: Some sources of play theorizing. In Rubin, K. H. (Ed.). (1980). *Children's play.* San Francisco: Jossey-Bass.

Taylor, A. S., Peterson, C. A., Murray-Schwarz, P., & Guillou, T. S. (2002). Social skills interventions: Not just for children with special needs. *Young Exceptional Children, 50,* 19–23.

Weinberger, L. A., & Starkey, P. (1994). Pretend play by African American children in Head Start. *Early Childhood Research Quarterly, 9,* 327–43.

ADDITIONAL READINGS

Bergen, D. (2002). The role of pretend play in children's cognitive development. *Early Childhood Research and Practice, 4,* 11–15.

Brown, C. T., & Marchant, C. (Eds.). (2002). *Play in practice: Case studies in young children's play.* St. Paul, MN: Redleaf.

Fromberg, D. P. (2002). *Play and meaning in early childhood education.* Boston: Allyn & Bacon.

Harris, T. (2002). *Shane's inspiration: Creating boundless playgrounds for children of all abilities.* Valley Village, CA: Shane's Inspiration.

Koralek, D. (2002). Let's go outside! Outdoor settings for play and learning. *Young Children, 57,* 8–9.

Rivkin, M. S. (2000). *Great outdoors: Restoring children's rights to play outdoors.* Washington, DC: NAEYC.

Rogers, C. S., & Sawyers, J. K. (2000). *Play in the lives of children.* Washington, DC: NAEYC.

Sawyers, J. K., & Rogers, C. S. (2001). *Helping young children develop through play: A practical guide for parents, caregivers, and teachers.* Washington, DC: NAEYC.

HELPFUL WEB SITES

http://www.earlychildhoodtoday.com
http://www.abcteach.com
Good sources for play activities, lesson plans, outdoor activities, and center equipment.

For additional creative activity resources, visit our Web site at http://www.EarlyChildEd. delmar.com.

Chapter 8

Using Technology to Promote Creativity

Objectives

After studying this chapter, you should be able to:

1. List at least five characteristics of developmentally appropriate computer software.
2. List four reasons why technology should be used with young children.
3. List the four basic types of children's Web sites.

Elmo has e-mail. Barney and his friends use interactive compact discs (CDs) on their computer. Even characters on children's television are using technology as a matter-of-fact, everyday part of their lives.

It's the same in early childhood programs today. Computers are a part of many children's preschool experiences. You can generally find at least one computer available for children's use during learning center or free choice time.

Technology—computers, digital cameras, videos, video games, interactive CDs and digital video discs (DVDs)—is definitely here to stay in the early childhood program.

With the growing use of technology in the early childhood program, teachers more than ever need to know the best ways to use technology with young children. This chapter provides a basic framework of information on using technology in developmentally appropriate ways in the early childhood program.

IMPORTANCE OF USING TECHNOLOGY

Technology serves a number of purposes in the early childhood program.

It provides variety in the program. Some children's learning is enhanced when they view a video or DVD or use the computer. The total early childhood program must meet the needs of a variety of children. Therefore, the program must have a variety of activities for each child. Using technology is one more means of meeting the children's needs.

It provides children with highly interesting learning experiences. Technology helps children learn facts, learn to enjoy the school setting, and develop skills—particularly creative skills.

It gets children involved in the creation of materials. Experiences with technology involve children in hands-on activities creating materials with cameras, computers, tapes, recorders, and other such technology.

It builds on and reinforces other activities. Working with technology allows children to express, as well as practice, what they are learning in yet another way. This helps reinforce a child's learning.

ACTIVITIES TO DEVELOP CREATIVITY

Technology provides variety, interest, involvement, and reinforcement. One of the most important things it provides is a chance for a child to develop creativity. The creativity comes when children design, manipulate, and express themselves using technology.

Videotapes

It is possible for children to plan and produce videotapes of class activities. They can videotape dramatic presentations, dancing, field trips, and other activities in and around the school.

Today, fairly inexpensive videotape equipment is available to schools. It is lightweight, portable, and easy to use.

Videotape can do all the things that movies and slides do, and it is less expensive to use. Videotape can be reused. Mistakes may be erased. Children see the results of their work right away. Video can be used with dramatic play activities: a play can be videotaped, and a children's art show can be recorded. Some children enjoy telling stories or retelling favorite events. Playtime games can be created and taped.

Many portable units can be taken on field trips. Videotapes made on field trips can be used to spark creative storytelling and the creation of new games.

When children get tired of a videotape, it can be erased and reused. Thus, although the cost of the video camera is high, the cost of tapes is low.

Videotape movies can be obtained by renting them or on a free loan basis. These movies can then be used to introduce creative activities. Creative dramatics can begin with a movie. The movie can introduce a story and some characters. At the proper time, the movie is turned off, and children take the parts of the characters. The children then create their own ending to the story, painting and drawing their own creative versions.

Photography

Young children enjoy taking pictures. Using an inexpensive camera, they can take shots of many different activities, objects, people, or whatever they find interesting. A 35-mm camera with a built-in flash for indoor and outdoor use is the least expensive and easiest for children to use.

Taking photographs is yet another way for children to experience their world. It is especially interesting and challenging for children in the middle and upper elementary grades. An interesting approach to photography with upper elementary grade children is to focus on common themes generated by the teacher or the children. Some of these might be pictures of special people or places or pictures of people or places that make you happy or even unhappy. Children can journey around the school to document the images in their mind's eye.

> As teachers watch young children taking their first photos, they can't help but reminisce about their own first experiences taking pictures. Do you remember the excitement you felt when you took your first pictures of your world? As almost by magic, you had a way to capture those special people and events in your life. With your camera you could make memories from today for tomorrow and forever. Photography has been described as a medium that is partly a language, but it creates a resonance with thoughts, feelings, and creativity that goes beyond verbalization (Savage & Holcomb, 1999).

Photography is an outlet for self-expression that has potential for all ages. This is due in large part to the low cost and simplicity of many cameras, which allow even the novice to take well-focused pictures. Children can share the special world of their school with others through pictures and words.

It is important, especially with younger children, to keep responsibilities simple. Explain that taking pictures is a fun activity and children can take pictures of whatever they would like to remember about their experiences at school. For example, a class of second graders came up with these ideas: happy places, happy people, special places, and special people. With older children, you may be a bit more abstract. For example, a class of 4th graders could be asked to take pictures of friendship in as many images and ways they can find. However, don't provide specific guidelines for what they photograph. Let the child be the leader.

Plan to spend some time explaining and demonstrating how to take a picture—how to load the film, frame the picture, activate the flash, and so forth.

Leave the cameras (without film) in the art center, and let the children practice with them. After they have practiced taking pictures (without film) for a while, the children will be ready to really use the cameras.

When children are taking photos for the first time, a teacher or another adult needs to be on hand to help if needed, with the mechanics of opening the case, loading the film, looking through the viewfinder, advancing the film, and answering questions as they may arise.

When children are out taking pictures, be sure they have notebooks and pencils with them to record where each picture was taken and its significance. So that the children do not forget what they have photographed, they need to write a note keyed to the exposure number about each picture right after they take it. The notes can become stories later. Be certain that the students understand that *their* personal impressions are what you want them to describe.

Although children will need some help, it is important to remember that you are just an observer. Have children move independently as they photograph their school world. If they prefer to stay inside, be sure the flashes work. Be prepared to provide technical assistance, which with most inexpensive cameras is minimal. Finally, share in the children's enthusiasm as they enjoy the newfound pleasures of a unique learning opportunity (Savage & Holcomb, 1999).

Digital Cameras

Digital cameras make it possible to instantly see the picture you've just taken (and erase it if you don't like it). This camera has incredible educational possibilities, from making labels for your classroom to showing parents their children's creations during parent–teacher conferences.

The power of a digital camera is measured in something called *megapixels*—the more it has, the sharper your picture. A classroom camera should have at least 2.1 megapixels and strong rechargeable batteries. Of course, you'll need a computer to use with your digital camera.

The computer acts as your darkroom. Once you load the picture disc into your computer, it lets you alter pictures to your liking. You can also store thousands of photos for later use.

A digital camera is a great tool for teachers. You can take pictures of children's artwork throughout the year to create a portfolio of each child's work. You can take pictures of each child, print them up, and post the photos on each child's cubby or personal space area.

Some other ways to use a digital camera include the following:

⊙ Do some time-lapse photography. Take a picture of the children in front of the same tree each month to see the seasons change.
⊙ Preserve memories. Next time a child cleans up, snap a picture.
⊙ Decorate the bulletin boards with photos of active, happy children.

Children, too, can use a digital camera. Inexpensive, throw-away digital cameras are available that are well suited for children's use. You will be amazed and delighted as you see the world through children's eyes.

"Smart" Toys

You don't have to have the most expensive computer to offer high-quality interactive learning opportunities, thanks to a new generation of **smart toys** with microprocessors as brains. Here are some favorites, available in most toy stores.

⊙ Music Blocks (http://www.neurosmith.com) lets children experiment with the structure of music.
⊙ LeapPad (http://www.Leapfrog.com) is an outstanding early language experience. Children can touch each letter or sound to hear it spoken in a clear voice. Multiple language options are also available.
⊙ Pixter (http://www.fisher-price.com) is an electronic sketching device.
⊙ Question-Air (Educational Insights, http://www.edin.com) is like a game of hot potato but with educational questions tossed in.
⊙ GeoSafari Talking Microscope (http://www.edin.com) lets children learn about magnified bugs.

Cassette Tape Recorders

Small cassette tape recorders that are inexpensive and easy to use are available to all schools. Young children use these recorders with few problems, recording their own voices just for the fun of it. They can also record common sounds, creative plays, and made-up stories and songs.

Using cassette tape recorders can help children better understand each other and develop an appreciation for diversity. Let the child take home a cassette tape recorder or use one they may have at home. Encourage children to record the sounds of family members who may speak a different language, the music they enjoy, foods sizzling on the stove, and family activities. When you play the tape in the classroom, see if children can identify the different languages spoken. See if they can guess what kinds of foods are cooking in the kitchen.

Compact Discs and Disc Players

Compact discs (CDs) and disc players are becoming more and more common in early childhood classrooms. CDs are played on a CD player, much like a cassette tape is played on a cassette tape player. CDs are also used in computers, providing sound effects and narration on early childhood computer software. Music played on a CD is of a higher quality sound than most cassette tapes. Playing recorded music, then, on a CD is an excellent source of musical experiences for young children.

TECHNOLOGY AND MULTIPLE INTELLIGENCES

Technology can help meet the needs of various learning styles. The multiple intelligences, as discussed in Chapter 5, can be enhanced with the use of technology. The list in Figure 8–1 covers the types of technology and software suitable for each of the multiple intelligences. When integrating technology in the early childhood program, teachers need to make sure to keep in mind the needs of all learners and use various methods and techniques suitable for each.

VALUE OF COMPUTERS IN EARLY CHILDHOOD PROGRAMS

Computers, as we have seen, have found their way into the preschool setting, taking their place beside the finger paints, play dough, books, and other media found within the early learning environment. Computer programs have been developed for young children that allow them to produce colorful graphics, music, and animated graphics.

Children of the 21st century *will* use computers as an integral part of their daily life. Yet, children who are plugged into computers to do drill and practice engage in convergent thinking. In fact, these programs are just another version of convergent ditto sheet–like work. It is important to realize that using computers with young children is a process of exploration and discovery for both you and the children.

How you use computers the first year in your classroom will probably be very different from how you use them five years later.

Based on recent research, some general conclusions about the value of computers with preschool and other children in early childhood programs may be made:

⊙ *Computers can be used effectively with young children.* Researchers have consistently observed high levels of spoken communication and cooperation as young children interact at the computer. Compared with more traditional activities, such as puzzle assembly or block building, the computer elicits both more social interaction and different types of interaction. Children in comprehensive, technology-enhanced programs make progress in all developmental areas, including social–emotional, fine motor, gross motor, communication, cognition, and self-help skills (Hutinger et al., l998; Hutinger & Johanson, 2000).

"When they use these new (software) programs, children are thinking, doing all the things we would like children to do," says Sue Bredekamp, director of professional development at the National Association for the Education of Young Children in Washington. "And for young children, computers are really a social activity. Children will interact in pairs, even in threes and fours. It's very different from the adult experience of computing" (Mills, 1994).

⊙ *Computers can be interactive.* The term **interactive** here means that the computer used with young children provides a vehicle for two types of interaction: child-to-computer and child-to-child. Child-to-computer interaction depends to a great extent on the software. Some software requires children to choose one response, which is then corrected. Other programs have been developed that allow children to use information on the screen to make more than one response.

Child-to-child interaction at the computer depends on the arrangement of the environment. When children work near each other by the computer, they discuss what they are doing and assist each other as they work. Some software is also designed for, or lends itself better to, participation by more than one child. (See the end of the chapter for suggested software for children.)

The teacher and the software together also make a difference. By placing two child seats in front of the computer and one at the side for adults, the teacher is encouraging cooperation between

TECHNOLOGY AND MULTIPLE INTELLIGENCES

Following Howard Gardner's theory of multiple intelligence, teachers can encourage development by providing enrichment opportunities in each of the areas of the intellect. The following are suggestions on how to integrate technology with each of the multiple intelligences.

Linguistic Intelligence (Word Smart)

Use of word-processing programs can help teach language, writing, editing, and rewriting skills. Also, the Internet is invaluable for learning. Through e-mail children can improve their language skills.

Other technologies children may benefit from are as follows:

- Desktop publishing programs
- Programs that allow children to create stories, poems, essays, etc.
- Multimedia authoring
- Videodiscs to create presentations
- Tape recorders

Logical–Mathematical (Logic Smart)

Computer programs can teach logic and critical thinking skills. These are also in game formats that could motivate children's thinking, for example, math programs that allow drilling and practicing. Database programs help explore and organize data and information.

Other technologies children may benefit from are as follows:

- Problem-solving software
- Computer-aided design programs
- Strategy game software
- Graphing calculators
- Multimedia authoring programs
- Spreadsheet programs

Visual/Spatial (Picture Smart)

Graphics programs help develop creativity and visual skills. Also, browsing the Internet and organizing files and folders will develop some spatial understanding.

Other technologies children may benefit from are as follows:

- Drawing programs
- Image-composing programs
- Paint programs (Photopaint, Microsoft Paint)
- Reading programs with visual clues
- Web page programs
- Three-dimensional software
- Software games
- Spreadsheet programs that allow children to see charts, maps, or diagrams
- Multimedia authoring programs

Musical Intelligence (Music Smart)

Some computer programs help write or play music.

Other technologies that children may benefit from are as follows:

- Music-composing software
- Videodisc player
- Programs integrating stories with songs and instruments
- Reading programs that relate letter/sound with music
- Programs that allow children to create their own music
- CD-ROMs about music and instruments
- Tape recorders
- Word processors to write about a movie or song

Figure 8-1

Technology and Multiple Intelligences.

(Continues)

Bodily–Kinesthetic (Body Smart)
Using computers will help develop hand–eye coordination. Working with a computer will allow children to become actively involved in their learning.
   Other technologies children may benefit from are as follows:

- Software games that allow contact with the keyboard, mouse, joystick, and other devices
- Programs that allow children to move objects around the screen.
- Word-processing programs
- Animation programs

Interpersonal (Person Smart)
Students can work in groups of two to four on the computers. Working in groups will strengthen children's communication and cooperation skills.
   Other technologies children may benefit from are as follows:

- Computer games that require two or more people
- Programs that allow children to create group presentations (Power Point)
- Telecommunication programs
- E-mail
- Distance education
- Help others with any programs

Intrapersonal (Self Smart)
The computer can help children build individual skills. It allows for differences in children's learning styles and abilities. Children may work at their own pace with computers.
   Other technologies children may benefit from are as follows:

- Any programs that allow children to work independently
- Games involving only one person
- Brainstorming or problem-solving software
- Instructional games
- Word processors for journaling and recording feelings
- Developing multimedia portfolio
- Video editing

Figure 8-1 (Continued)

children as well as interaction with an adult. Such an arrangement encourages children to work cooperatively and to converse as they work on the computer.

Computer work can instigate new instances and forms of collaborative work—such as helping or teaching, discussing and building on each others' ideas, cooperating, and praising. It can also increase social interaction between children with disabilities and their typically developing peers (Hutinger & Johanson, 2000; Clements & Sarama, 2003a).

- *Placement of computers can encourage childrens' learning.* The ideal placement of the computer center is in a visible location. The monitors are situated so that they can be seen from throughout the classroom (Haugland & Wright, 1997). Children

are interested in what's happening in the computer center, although they may be working in another center. All of this stimulates peer mentoring, social interaction, language development, and cooperative play. In addition, a highly visible computer center enables you to supervise the computer center without leaving the area in which you are working. You need to move to the computer center only when it is necessary to assist children, or you can ask another child who is not busy if he or she is willing to help. This help encourages children's independent learning as well as peer teaching. Strive for a 10:1 ratio (or better) of children to computers to encourage computer use, cooperation, and equal access by girls and boys.

- *Age and computer use.* Age doesn't appear to be a limiting factor in computer use. Even two-year-old

Figure 8-2

Playing with new software on the computer is fun for children.

Figure 8-3

By placing two child seats in front of the computer and one for adults nearby, the teacher is encouraging cooperation between children as well as interaction with an adult.

children can work proficiently on the computer using age-appropriate software that requires only simple keypresses or pointing with a mouse. Preschoolers can easily start the computer, load disks, type on the keyboard, and understand pictorial cues.

During the preschool years, children should have many opportunities to explore open-ended, developmentally appropriate software programs in a playful, supportive environment. These experiences will help them develop the basic skills needed to use technology equipment, such as opening and closing programs, saving and printing documents, and navigating the screen using a mouse.

This will help children become confident in their ability to use a computer and will provide the foundation skills needed to use more advanced applications for purposeful work as they grow older.

As children enter the primary years, they can begin to use familiar technology tools as a part of their academic program. At the same time, adults should model the use of technology in support of the curriculum and learning experiences children are engaged in. For example, adults can model the use of technology for communication by using e-mail and word-processing programs with children to communicate with families and others important to the classroom community. There are many other ways adults can model the appropriate use of technology, such as documenting events in the classroom using digital still or video cameras and creating multimedia electronic portfolios that document children's learning (Murphy, DePasquale, & McNamara, 2003). This way, children can see firsthand the purposeful use of technology and benefit from exposure to more advanced applications that they will eventually use independently.

⊙ *Children prefer action.* Just as in other aspects of their play, children like action with computers, and they do not necessarily choose to follow the rules of games. They watch what happens when they press new keys, and they purposely may try to squash all the keys at one time. One of the strengths young children bring to computer use is their fearless experimentation!

A good environment for young children includes many experiences that involve the senses, adult–child and child–child conversation, and a host of other age-appropriate activities. Computers can supplement, but do not substitute for, experiences in which children can discover with all their senses. Technology is a tool, and as such it should be used because it is the best tool for the job (Murphy, DePasquale, & McNamara, 2003).

Only after a sound, basic program has been developed should teachers consider buying a computer. First should come blocks, sand and water tables, art materials, books, and all other proven elements of a good program for young children.

CHOOSING SOFTWARE FOR YOUNG CHILDREN

Care must be taken to select computer software that is developmentally appropriate for the children who will use it. Research shows that different types of software have different effects (Clements & Samara 2003b). Open-ended programs foster collaboration. Drill-and-practice programs encourage turn-taking but also may encourage a competitive spirit. Violent programs can lead to aggressiveness (Clements & Samara, 2003b). The following 10 criteria distinguish software that is developmentally appropriate:

1. *Age appropriateness.* The concepts taught and their method of presentation reflect realistic expectations for young children.

2. *Child control.* Children are active participants, initiating and deciding the sequence of events, rather than reactors, responding to predetermined activities. The software needs to facilitate active rather than passive involvement (Clements & Swaminathan, 1995). The pace is set by the child, not the program.

3. *Clear instructions.* Because the majority of preschool children are nonreaders, spoken directions are essential (Yelland, 1995). If printed instructions are used, they are accompanied by spoken directions. Directions are simple and precise. Graphics accompany choices to make options clear to the children.

4. *Expanding complexity.* Entry level is low; children can easily learn to manipulate the software successfully. The learning sequence is clear; one concept follows the next (NAEYC, 1996). The software expands as children explore, teaching children the skills they are ready to learn. Through the expanding complexity of the software, children build on their knowledge.

5. *Independent exploration.* After initial exposure, children can manipulate the software without adult supervision.

6. *Process orientation.* The process of using the software is so engaging for children that the product becomes secondary. Children learn through discovery rather than being drilled in specific skills. Motivation to learn is intrinsic, not the result of praise, smiling face stickers, or prizes.

7. *Real-world representation.* The software is a simple and reliable model of some aspect of the real world, exposing children to concrete representation of objects and their functions.

8. *Technical features.* The software has high technical quality that helps the young child pay attention. It is colorful and includes uncluttered, realistic animated graphics. There are realistic sound effects or music that corresponds to objects on the screen. The software loads from the disks and runs fast enough to maintain the child's interest.

9. *Trial and error.* The software provides children many chances to test alternative responses. Through resolving errors or solving problems children build structures and knowledge.

10. *Visible transformations.* Children have an impact on the software, changing objects and situations through their responses (NAEYC, 1996).

In this list, it is important to note that software may have a developmental approach to learning without having all of the criteria. Some software has more developmental criteria than other software. You need to choose the software that includes as many of these criteria as possible.

Figure 8-4

Computer work can instigate new forms of cooperative work among children.

CHOOSING DEVELOPMENTALLY APPROPRIATE SOFTWARE

Teachers basically have two options to assist them in selecting developmentally appropriate software. First, they can use a software rating scale to evaluate software themselves. Many evaluation forms, such as the Haugland/Shade Software Developmental Scale (Haugland & Wright, 1997), can help teachers understand the key component of quality software.

Second, several individuals and organizations have designed systems that teachers can use to evaluate software. The advantage of using a preexisting software evaluation system is that previewing software is unnecessary because it has already been extensively field-tested by teachers, parents, and children. Table 8–1 presents a list of online sources of educational software reviews.

THE INTERNET AND EARLY CHILDHOOD PROGRAMS

Many rich educational opportunities await children on the Internet, and its potential is primarily untapped. While the Internet has been researched less extensively than software, it provides children with a variety of learning opportunities that appear to enhance problem-solving, critical thinking skills, decision-making, creativity, language skills, knowledge, research skills, the ability to integrate information, social skills, and self-esteem (Haugland, 2000, p. 13).

THIS ONE'S for YOU! Computer Maintenance

You don't need to be a technology "guru" to know how to keep your computer running smoothly. Here are some maintenance steps and commonly recommended procedures to protect your computer and prolong its life.

- Turn on your computer when you begin each day and don't turn it off until you finish for the day. Some people turn their personal computer (PC) on and off throughout the day. This causes a computer's innards to frequently expand and contract, creating stress that can lead to premature component failure.
- Defragment your hard disk periodically. The operating systems of typical PCs and Macs scatter file fragments over the hard disk. Specific software programs combine these fragments, which reduces hard drive wear and tear and increases system performance. Some programs signal you to defragment when your hard disk reaches a specified level of fragmentation, such as 90 percent. Alternately, you can defragment weekly, monthly, or semiannually, depending on how often you use your PC. Don't use a program that defragments your hard disk continually. It will create more wear and tear than it prevents.
- For maximum safety, unplug your PC and any phone line leading to it during a thunderstorm, unless you need to keep it on for work purposes. A nearby lightning strike will blow right past a typical surge protector and can fry a PC. Use a surge protector or uninterrupted power supply for smaller surges.
- Use a disk drive cleaning kit when you experience problems with your disk drive, or at most, once a year as preventive maintenance.
- Do not use a cleaning kit every week as some kit manufacturers suggest. This just overstresses your disk drive's read/write head.
- Your PC should be plugged into a three-pronged grounded outlet, preferably on a dedicated circuit. Don't move a PC or connect or disconnect its cables while it is on unless they are plugged into a universal serial bus port.
- Clean your monitor if it becomes smudged. Stay away from glass cleaners, as they can remove a monitor's antiglare finish. Use isopropyl alcohol or distilled water along with a lint-free cloth. Wet the cloth first, then the monitor.
- Keep CD-ROM discs inside a caddy or jewel case when not in use to avoid scratches. If dirt or fingerprints sully a disc, gently wipe it with a soft lint-free cloth or use an audio CD cleaning kit.

Table 8-1

Educational Software Reviews on the Internet

SITE	INTERNET ADDRESS	INFORMATION AVAILABLE
AOL@School	http://www.school.aol.com	Offers a collection of resources for teachers, including software reviews, lesson plans, and links to other technology-related sites.
California Instructional Technology Clearinghouse	http://www.clearinghouse.k12.ca.us	Contains the searchable California Technology in the Curriculum Evaluation database on 3,000+ technology products.
Children and Computers	http://www.childrenandcomputers.com	Includes the Haugland/Shade Software Development Scale for evaluating software for children and sample evaluations.
Northwest Educational Technology Consortium (NETC)	http://www.netc.org/software	Provides information about software selection and links to software review sites.
Superkids Educational Software Review	http://www.superkids.com	Provides reviews and ratings of software and practical and fun tools for online and offline use.
Technology & Learning	http://www.techlearning.com	Offers a searchable database of software and Web site reviews, as well as information about professional development activities and grants.
Worldvillage	http://www.worldvillage.com	Provides reviews of software, Internet content, and more.

The sheer volume of Internet sites is overwhelming. Because most have not been reviewed in print, you will need to check out any sites before you use them with children. There are four basic types of children's Web sites: information, communication, interaction, and publication.

Information Sites

Enhanced with sound and videos, information sites are rich reference resources that teachers and parents can use to model or assist children in answering questions, making new discoveries, and building knowledge. For example, a virtual trip to the zoo gives children opportunities to see pictures, hear animal sounds, and view movies of animals exploring their natural habitats. The National Zoo (http://www.si.edu/natzoo/) from the Smithsonian Institute is such a Web site. A virtual tour

of a dinosaur museum (http://wf.carleton.ca/Museum/7.html) is another possibility. Another example is taking an online tour of Italy to learn more about the children's electronic pen pals from Rome.

Communication Sites

At communication sites children interact with friends, relatives, or classrooms across the street, in another city, or even across the globe. Using simple e-mail addresses, children and classroom groups write letters, compose stories, create poems, or work on a class project such as a virtual monster. At the virtual monster Web site (http://www.2cyberlinks.com/monster.html), four classrooms provide descriptions of one physical feature each of a creature. Then they draw their monsters—composites of the four features—and compare the results! Afterward, some of the classrooms continue to learn

THIS ONE'S for YOU!

Assistive Technology for Children with Special Needs

For young children with disabilities, technology offers a wide range of equipment to support participation and learning. Some devices—voice synthesizers, Braille readers, switch-activated toys, and computers—are truly high tech. Yet many simple, low-tech tools are equally valuable in early childhood classrooms. For example, special handles on utensils and paintbrushes, or a handle attached to a stuffed animal, allow a child to grasp without help.

Using technology to help a child with special needs may not be as simple as providing a utensil with a handle. We must consider the level of technology necessary for the child to fully participate, what technology is best suited to the child's needs and abilities, and what can reasonably be used in the environment given available space and resources (Mulligan, 2003).

It is equally important to match the technology to the needs and abilities of the child. With so many options available today, it is essential that those adults most familiar with the child work closely with professionals who have special expertise in assistive technology. This type of collaborative process can ensure that the supports used will help the child achieve more independence and that technology benefits everyone.

Assistive technology options are exciting and full of promise, but not every device fits in every environment. Some might be too expensive, too cumbersome to transport between home and school, or too specialized to be used in multiple environments.

Carefully analyze each environment to determine what equipment or technology is needed to support the child's participation (Mulligan, 2003). Even the most advanced device won't help unless it matches the child's abilities *and* the demands of the environment. The challenge is to find the device that helps a young child with special needs take part in every routine and activity. The right match of assistive technology can be magical if it allows a child to be more independent and expressive.

The following Web sites provide more information on assistive technology:

⊙ **The Tots 'n' Tech Research Institute,** http://www.tnt.asu.edu. This site offers ideas for equipment and materials that can help children with special needs to be more independent in caring for themselves, making friends, communicating, and doing the things that other young children do in child care and community activity settings.

⊙ **The National Early Childhood Technical Assistance Center,** http://www.nectas.unc.edu/. Click on Topics, then go to Early Childhood Practices and click on Special Practices. This site provides information on various types of assistive technology, funding resources, and current legislation.

⊙ **Child Care plus+:The Center on Inclusion in Early Childhood,** http://www.ccplus.org. This site offers a number of free and inexpensive resources, including an Adapting Toys Tool Kit that contains materials and instructions for adapting toys, adding sensory input, and promoting independent play.

cooperatively, exploring other topics such as weather patterns, summaries of their favorite stories, and so on.

Also through e-mail children can ask "experts" questions in various disciplines. One example is Ask Dr. Math (http://mathforum.org/dr.math). This provides classrooms not only with the answers to questions, but also with the opportunity to explore a variety of math-related occupations.

Interaction Sites

Interaction sites are similar to software programs, using sound; animation; sound effects; and high-quality,

realistic graphics. Unfortunately they sometimes run slowly. The Internet, however, is improving. *Internet Safety* (2003) by Josepha Sherman provides descriptions of sites for children three to eight years of age. A tremendous variety of Internet sites are arranged by topic. As you explore them you will find some to be more developmentally appropriate than others.

Publication Sites

The Internet can be used as a resource for actually publishing children's work. Even three year olds can

Figure 8-5

Thanks to a new generation of toys with microprocessors, you don't have to have a thousand-dollar computer to offer children interactive learning opportunities.

understand that when their work is displayed on the Internet everyone in the world can see it. Imagine their pride! Motivation for learning is sparked as they create new pictures and stories. There are a number of Web sites that post children's work, such as KidPub (http://www.kidpub.org/kidpub/).

A Note of Caution!

Although the potential of the Internet is tremendous, some precautions need to be addressed. Anyone can place anything on the Internet, some of which may be harmful to young children. A screening device is essential, such as Kid Desk: Internet Safe (1998), Net Nanny (http://www.netnanny.com), or Cyber Patrol (http://www.cyberpatrol.com).

THINK ABOUT IT... Can Video Games Make Children Smarter?

A recent study "Action Video Game Modifies Visual Selection Attention" by Green & Bavelier of the Department of Brain and Cognitive Sciences at the University of Rochester found that videogame players scored significantly higher on a series of tests designed to measure their ability to screen out distractions.

Here are some facts to consider that were not mentioned in many news reports on this study. First, the subjects of the study were not children—they were a group of 16 college-age students, between 18 and 23 years of age, and nearly all were males. They were divided into groups—videogame players and non–videogame players. The players spent six months (1 hour/day) playing teen and mature-rated action games. The non–videogame players had little, and preferably no, videogame time in the same period. The two groups were given five types of visual tests to see how well they could visually filter distractions, in the form of shapes on printed charts. The researchers conclude that videogame players are better able to filter outside distractions.

That the game players scored better on these visual tests makes sense. After all that time spent intensely concentrating, carefully watching for enemies crouching behind pillars, timing kicks and jumps, and driving on a crowded racetrack, one is bound to develop some sort of increased competency. But is enhanced visual attention the only thing that is learned? What about what *isn't* learned, if the players spend significant amounts of time alone, rather than socializing with other children?

There are still many questions for researchers to examine, such as does this study's conclusion generalize to children, as many news reports imply? Perhaps more importantly, what else do children learn from video games? Visual attention might be enhanced, but are video games the purveyors of lower forms of culture, where children first get ideas about cheating, gender stereotyping, stealing cars, and using violence?

For now, when you see "Video games will make children smarter. . ." remember that there are a lot of ways to define "smarter" and there are a lot of action video games such as Finding Nemo (on the PS2, Game Cube, and Xbox) that require problem solving and visual acuity, minus the car theft and violence.

And most importantly, don't let "videogame player" become synonymous with "socially isolated child." Remember to keep your eyes open, play alongside the child, and read the news with an extra grain of salt.

It is critical that children understand they cannot share any personal information such as their last name, address, phone number, or parents' names for their own safety. It is probably best for children to use a pen name when on the Internet—the name of their dog, cat, or favorite stuffed animal (Haugland, 2000).

RESEARCHING THE INTERNET

Children, Families and the Internet 2003, a national survey on technology and children, was conducted in partnership with the Corporation for Public Broadcasting with underwriting from BellSouth, the Educational Testing Service, and Kodak. This survey examined how children ages 2 to 17 used the Internet. The survey was based on interviews with 2,300 children ages 6 to 17 and 1,000 parents of children ages 2 to 17. Some of the findings follow.

⊚ Parents and families have a much more balanced view of the benefits and threats presented by technology than is commonly assumed by the media

Figure 8-6

With the growing use of technology in the early child-hood program, teachers more than ever need to know the best ways to use technology with young children.

and Washington policymakers. In the survey, when parents were asked to describe their role in their children's Internet use, they had to choose between two different views: (1) either a watchdog to guard against danger or (2) as a guide to finding good content. The survey reported that more than 85% of parents viewed themselves as a guide to good content.

⊚ Digital technology use has increased for girls. As of the survey date (2003), use of the Internet in terms of the proportion of girls and boys is essentially equal. Uses of the Internet are different for girls and boys, but one cannot claim that boys dominate.

⊚ There is a striking increase in the number of children who are online. Growth is coming from sectors that have been previously underrepresented, such as young children, children from lower income families, and minority children.

⊚ The use of the Internet on an hours-per-day basis is rapidly approaching the use of television. Among online teenagers, the use of interactive media in total hours/day actually exceeds television. More information on this study can be found at http://www.grunwald.com.

SUMMARY

Technology enhances the early childhood program because of the following:

⊚ It provides variety in the program.
⊚ It leads to interesting learning experiences.
⊚ It leads children to create materials or develop new ideas.
⊚ It builds on other things children have experienced in the preschool program.

Computers are rapidly becoming more common in early childhood programs. It is important to choose developmentally appropriate software that includes 10 characteristics: age appropriateness, child control, clear instructions, expanding complexity, independent exploration, process orientation, real-world representation, technical features, trial and error, and visible transformations. There are four basic types of children's Web sites: information, communication, interaction, and publication.

KEY TERMS

digital camera
interactive
smart toys

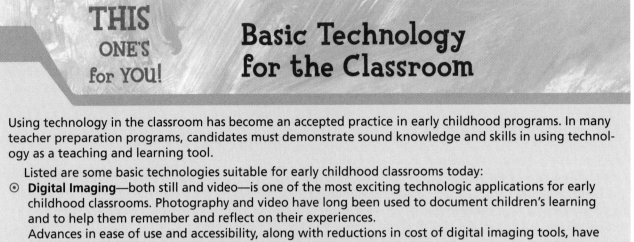

THIS ONE'S for YOU!

Basic Technology for the Classroom

Using technology in the classroom has become an accepted practice in early childhood programs. In many teacher preparation programs, candidates must demonstrate sound knowledge and skills in using technology as a teaching and learning tool.

Listed are some basic technologies suitable for early childhood classrooms today:

⊙ **Digital Imaging**—both still and video—is one of the most exciting technologic applications for early childhood classrooms. Photography and video have long been used to document children's learning and to help them remember and reflect on their experiences.

Advances in ease of use and accessibility, along with reductions in cost of digital imaging tools, have greatly simplified the use of these tools in the classroom. Using digital images, records of children's experiences can be loaded onto the computer where children can seek them out and review them at will. The images can lead children to discuss the events with adults and peers and then perhaps use them as a basis for writing, drawing, or other forms of processing and expression.

⊙ **Word processing and writing tools,** for example, WriteOn (Software Production Associates), allow children to express themselves, free from the fine motor demands of letter formation. For many children these tools can serve as adaptive or assistive technology to make the physical act of writing less frustrating. For others the excitement of seeing their stories and ideas in formal print is extremely motivating and can spur them to revise and edit their work in order to see it "published."

⊙ **Computer art programs** such as Kid Pix (Broderbund) are an excellent way to introduce children to open-ended exploration of the computer. Children's art programs generally provide a wide range of choices for expressing ideas, from freehand drawing to the use of stamps, text, or other special effects that can be combined to create a complex visual display. Many of these programs also provide multimedia options such as sounds, animation, and voice recording to allow children to create multimodal work. Some of these programs are simple enough for three-year-old children to use with ease and have the capability to expand and grow as children's expertise with a program increases.

⊙ **Presentation software** such as HyperStudio (Robert Wagner Publishing), which is often part of art programs, can allow children to create multimedia presentations that express their ideas, experience, and understanding to others. Children can create slides in the art part of the program and then import them into a slide show to be shared with others.

⊙ **Research tools,** both age-appropriate Web sites and software programs that provide information, such as Nature-Virtual Serengeti (http://www.disney.com) and Encarta Encyclopedia (http://www.encarta.msn.com/), can be used formally and informally to research topics in which children are interested. These applications can augment the classroom library and provide multimedia databases on a huge range of topics (Murphy, DePasquale, & McNamara, 2003).

LEARNING ACTIVITIES

TAKING CREATIVE PHOTOS

A. Obtain an inexpensive camera. Shoot a roll of color film, trying to make each picture creative.

B. Try to get pictures of:
1. a beautiful sunset
2. an ugly, broken-down house
3. a beautiful building
4. interesting-looking people
5. a flower in bloom
6. an animal
7. a brightly colored bird

C. Use the pictures to tell a creative story about some experience.

D. Use a digital camera for this same activity.

Figure 8-7
Playing with new software on the computer is fun for children.

DIGITAL CAMERA ACTIVITIES

Make a Face Gallery. Take pictures of each child in your group with a digital camera. Turn off the flash, and zoom in close on each child's face. Capture every detail, and then print out each picture on an 8–1/2″ × 11″ sheet of paper and make a "face gallery" bulletin board. If you don't have a color printer, don't worry—the pictures look great in black and white.

Bringing Home to School. Offer parents a classroom camera (or a disposable camera) to take home for the weekend. Provide a "shot list" of ideas that includes their children's bedroom, pets, favorite toys, etc. Any 2.1 megapixel or digital camera works fine. Use the photos to make a poster or bulletin board that features that child. If you don't have a digital camera, you can use a disposable camera. They even have disposable digital cameras you can use for this activity.

ADDITIONAL ACTIVITIES

A. Using a tape recorder, make tape recordings of interesting sounds. Try to get fellow classmates to recognize the sounds. Try any or all of the following sounds:
  1. a computer keyboard
  2. a door closing
  3. a car starting
  4. a jet plane taking off
  5. voices
  6. music
  7. popcorn popping
B. Choose one of the Web sites listed at the end of this chapter. Visit the Web site. Evaluate it for potential use with young children. List its strengths and weaknesses. In what way would you use this Web site in your work with children?
C. Preview a computer software program designed for preschoolers. Does it allow for individual creativity? Is it developmentally appropriate? Was it easy to use?
D. Choose one of the research references from the list provided at the end of this chapter and report on its findings with regard to young children's use of computers. Apply what you have read to your own experience with children.

ACTIVITIES FOR CHILDREN GRADES K-3

HARDWARE/SOFTWARE MOVEMENT ACTIVITY

This activity is designed to assist young children in contrasting the hardware and software used in computers. The children walk clockwise in a circle. Whenever the teacher calls out the word "hardware" the children walk stiffly with hands held in front of them. Whenever they hear the term "software," they

relax their bodies and walk limply, like rag dolls, around the circle. Once children appear to be good at listening, increase the speed at which the terms are used.

Add other calls to those of hardware and software. When the children hear "together," they find a partner and link arms. One walks stiffly as hardware and other limply as software. To resume walking individually, call "remove disk," an instruction for the "software child" to leave the other. After this activity, children can describe how their movements contrasted when they walked individually and how they moved when walking with a partner.

TECHNOLOGY CHOREOGRAPHY MOVEMENT ACTIVITY

In this activity, children can learn about technology and interpret their understandings through creative movement. Begin by preparing a tape recording (no more than three minutes) of the sounds of various

Figure 8-8
Computers are part of many children's preschool experiences today.

machines, such as an electric can opener, microwave, coffee maker, or mixer. It is not necessary to have many sounds. Rather, juxtapose the sounds of different lengths and repeat them during the three-minute recording.

Play the tape. After the students identify the source of the sounds, discuss the ways in which technology (in the kitchen, garage, or other places) helps us do our work. Assign children to work in pairs or alone to prepare a choreographed interpretation of the sounds on the tape. Ask the children to think about the function of the technology as they select movements.

Play the tape three or four times for rehearsal and preparation. Encourage students to select appropriate movement, depending on the function and "feeling" of the technology. The interpretation may take the form of finger movements, a hand jive, dance, or creative movement. Perform the choreographs and critique the movements as to their connection with the function of technology.

INTERNET ACTIVITIES–GRADE 3 AND UP

⊙ Teach your students how to be safe on the Internet by visiting http://www.SafetyClicks.com. They can play games to become "Internet savvy," visit other sites, watch a cartoon, and get tips on how to use the World Wide Web.

⊙ Have your class create a story at http://www.eduplace.com/. Click on Kids Place, then on Brain Power. Using 10 to 15 of their own words such as a plural noun, a large number, an adjective, and so on, students create a story. They can also publish their own "Wacky Web Tales" and read tales that other students have written.

⊙ Invite students to find the basics of surfing the net at http://www.albion.com/. Click on Netiquette. After exploring this site, ask them to define *netiquette, online, behavior,* and *cyberspace.*

⊙ Find a directory of games at http://www.surfnetkids.com/. Click on Games. The games are listed by type (such as crossword or jigsaw) and topic (such as science or history). Play the Harry Potter games and do the word searches, quizzes and crossword puzzles related to the Harry Potter books.

⊙ Learn about animals at http://www.zoobooks.com where they'll find games and artwork by other students and lots of other fun activities.

CHAPTER REVIEW

1. List four reasons why using technology is important to preschool programs.
2. Name several kinds of technology that are appropriate for use with young children.
3. List at least five factors to consider when evaluating computer software for young children.
4. List four potential values of computers for young children.
5. What are the four basic types of children's Web sites?

REFERENCES

Clements, D. H., & Samara, J. (2003a). Young children and technology: What does the research say? *Young Children 58*(6), 34–40.

Clements, D. H., & Samara, J. (2003b). Strip mining for gold: Research and policy in educational technology—a response to "Fools Gold." *Educational Technology Review 11*(1). Online: http://www.aace.org/pubs/etr/issue4/clements.cfm.

Clements, D. H., & Swaminathan, S. (1995, Sept.). Technology and school change: New lamps for old? *Childhood Education, 72*(1).

Cordes, C., & Miller, E. (2000). *Fool's gold: A critical look at computers in childhood.* College Park, MD: Alliance for Childhood.

Haugland, S., & Wright, J. (1997). *Young children and technology: A world of discovery.* New York: Allyn & Bacon.

Haugland, S. W. (2000). What role should technology play in young children's learning? Part 2. Early childhood classrooms in the 21st century. Using computers to maximize learning. *Young Children, 55*(1), 12–18.

Healy, J. (1998). *Failure to connect: How computers affect our children's minds—for better and worse.* New York: Simon & Schuster.

Hutinger, P. L., & Johanson, J. (2000). Implementing and maintaining an effective early childhood comprehensive technology system. *Topics in Early Childhood Special Education 20*(3), 159–173.

Hutinger, P. L., Bell, C., Beard, M., Bond, J., Johanson, J., & Terry, C. (1998). *The early childhood emergent literacy technology research study. Final report.* Macomb, IL: Western Illinois University. ERIC ED 418545.

Mills, J. (1994, Feb. 13). Tots use computers before they learn to read. *The New York Times* (Reprinted in *The News and Observer*).

Mulligan, S. A. (2003). Assistive technology: Supporting the participation of children with disabilities. *Young Children 58*(6), 50–51.

NAEYC (1996). NAEYC Position Statement: Technology and young children—ages three through eight. *Young Children 51*(6), 11–16.

Savage, M. P., & Holcomb, D. R. (1999). Children, cameras and challenging projects. *Young Children, 54*(2), 27–28.

Savetz, K. (2003). Ergonomics for the littlest computer user. Online: http://www.sesameworkshop.org/parents/solutions/information/0,6412,74305,00.html.

Sherman, J. (2003). *Internet safety.* New York: Scholastic.

Yelland, N. J. (1995, Spring) Encouraging young children's thinking skills with LOGO. *Childhood Education, 71*(3), 152–155.

ADDITIONAL READINGS

Bitter, G., & Pierson, M. E. (1999). *Using technology in the classroom,* (4th ed.). Needham, MA: Longwood. (Contains annotated list of recommended videos arranged by title & subject with vendor information.)

Clements, D. H., Natasi, B. K., & Swaminathan, S. (1993, Jan.). Young children and computers: Crossroads and directions from the research. *Young Children, 56*–64.

Cortes, C. E. (2000). *The children are watching: How the media teach about diversity.* New York: Teachers College Press.

Cuban, L. (2001). *Oversold and underused: Computers in the classroom.* Cambridge, MA: Harvard University Press.

CyberStart (2003). Cyberstart initiative/digital divide. Online: http://www.cyberstart.org.

Entz, S., & Galarza, S. (1999). *Picture this: Digital and instant photographic activities for early childhood learning.* Thousand Oaks, CA: Corwin Press.

Fischer, M., & Gillespie, C. (2003). Computers and young children's development: One Head Start Classroom's experiences. *Young Children 58*(4), 85–91.

Heroman, C. (2003). Using technology for ongoing assessment. Online: http://www.teachingstrategies.com/pages/page.cfm?pageid=183.

Hohman, C. (1998). Evaluating and selecting software for children. *Child Care Information Exchange, 123,* 60–62.

Joseph, L. C. (1999). *Net curriculum: An educator's guide to using the Internet.* Medford, NJ: Information Today.

Kay, H., & Delvecchio, K. (2003). *The world at your fingertips: Learning research and Internet skills.* Ft. Atkinson, WI: Upstart Books.

Moore, C. (2003). With computer, children learn the 3Rs plus the S: Self-esteem. Online: http://www.americaconnects.net/field/F7abcd.asp.

Murphy, K. L., & DePasquale, R. (2003). Meaningful connections: Using technology in primary classrooms. *Young Children 58*(6), 12–18.

Papert, S. (1999). Child power: Keys to the new learning of the digital century. On-line: http://www.connectedfamily.com.

Tobin, J. (2002). *Good guys don't wear hats: Children's talk about the media.* New York: Teacher's College Press.

VonBlanckensee, L. (1999). *Technology tools for young learners.* Larchmont, NY: Eye on Education.

Figure 8-9

Research shows that girls are just as interested in computers as boys are.

THINK ABOUT IT...

Computer Screens, Young Children, and Vision Problems

Many parents caution their children not to sit too close to the television. Should this warning apply to computer screens also? Sitting too close to a screen can cause eye strain as a result of screen glare and lack of blinking (Cordes & Miller, 2000). Savetz (2003) mentions in his "Ergonomics for the Littlest Computer User" that children's eyes should be positioned anywhere from 18 to 22 inches from the computer screen. Additional tips to reduce eye strain include providing enough light in the area, reducing glare on the screen, and taking five-minute breaks every half hour. Young children should not spend as much time using a computer as an adult because their vision centers are still developing (Cordes & Miller, 2000). Recommendations for total screen time per day for preschool children range from one to two hours with frequent breaks; this includes television viewing and computer use. However, as long as the ergonomics mentioned previously are considered, computers will not post a significant risk to children's vision.

Specific research concerning computers and children's brains has not yet been released. However, Jane Healy examines the effects of computer use in terms of what is known about brain development during the early childhood years (1998). One aspect that is considered is the plasticity of the brain in the early years. A younger child's brain is more flexible than that of an older child or adult; therefore technology needs to be used in a way that encourages active learning habits and connections to develop. Another important aspect of brain development is that different brain systems develop at different times. These developmental stages need to be a factor in computer use and software selections. The relationship between brain development and technology is one that continues to be explored.

HELPFUL WEB SITES

http://www.mediafamily.org
National Institute on Media and the Family. This site is designed to help families and educators maximize the benefits and minimize the harm of mass media on children through research, education, and advocacy. It has many online tools and resources.

http://www.ivyjoy.com/
Click on Search Engine. This web portal for students not only gathers a significant number of search engines designed specifically for kids, it also offers a comprehensive list of Web Guides for Kids, Specialized Searches for Kids, and Family-Friendly Search Engines.

All of the popular student search engines are listed, and there are even some great search engines such as iThanki for Kids and Family Friendly Search.

http://www.safetyclicks.com
This is a free, flash-based Internet site that contains a cartoon introduction to Internet safety, along with a simple quiz that a child can take to test his Internet knowledge.

http://www.ajkids.com
This Ask Jeeves Kids site is a fast, easy, and kid-friendly way for kids to find answers to their questions online. This site combines human editorial judgment with filtering technology to enable kids to find both relevant and appropriate answers on the Web.

http://www.yahooligans.com
This is a Yahoo Website for kids. It provides a wealth of information on school subjects, world geography and customs, sports and recreation, science and nature, and computers and games. Fun features are the Yahooligan Poll and the Joke of the Day.

These are two excellent search engines for children's use.

http://www.everythingpreschool.com/
Click on Themes. This site contains more than 150 themes and activities for preschoolers. Choose from pets, dinosaurs, the grocery store, Dr. Seuss, shapes, and more. Each theme contains related songs and activities as well as ideas for art projects, snacks, bulletin boards, field trips, etc. Recipes and articles are also included.

http://www.netc.org/
Click on Early Connections. From the Northwest Educational Technology Consortium this site provides generic advice on using computers in a wide variety of early childhood settings.

http://www.techandyoungchildren.org
This is the NAEYC's site containing advice on how to lead discussions, share research and information, and demonstrate best practices regarding technology so it can be used to benefit children aged birth through eight years.

http://www.ala.org
This is the American Library Association Web site. It contains a Guide to Cyberspace for Parents and Kids, which includes many safety tips on children's use of the Internet.

SOFTWARE FOR CHILDREN

Clifford Thinking Adventures, 2003. Pre-K.
Does it Belong?, 2003. Pre-K.
Dogz 4, Catz 4, 2003. Pre-K.
Freddi Fish 5: The Case of the Creature of Coral Cover, 2003. Pre-K.
Krazy Art Room, 2003. Pre-K.
Reader Rabbit's Toddler, 2002. Pre-K.
Sesame Street Baby & Me, 2003. Pre-K.
Disney's Magic Artist Deluxe, 2002. Grades K–3.
Disney's/Pixar's Monsters, Inc. Scare Island, 2001. Grades K–3.
Flying Colors v. 2.11., 2002. Grades K–3.
Math Missions: The Race to Spectacle City Arcade, 2003. Grades K–3.
Mummy Mystery, 2002. Grades K–3.

Powerpuff Girls Mojo Jojo's Clone Zone, 2002. Grades K–3.
Rugrats Go Wild, 2003. Grades K–3.
Walt Disney's Snow White and the Seven Dwarfs, 2002. Grades K–3.
What's Her Face!, 2003. Grades K–3.
Dance Dance Revolution, 2002. Grades 4–5.
HyperStudio 4, 2002. Grades 4–5.
Jak and Daxter, 2002. Grades 4–5.
Scooby Doo: Showdown in Ghost Town, 2001. Grades 4–5.
Spider-Man, 2002. Grades 4–5.
Turbo Twist Vocabulator and **Turbo Twist BRAIN QUEST,** 2002. Grades 4–5.
Zoombini's Mountain Rescue, 2002. Grades 4–5.
Zoombini's Logical Journey, 2003. Grades 4–5.

For additional creative activity resources, visit our Web site at http://www.EarlyChildEd.delmar.com.

SECTION 3

Art and the Development of the Young Child

REFLECTIVE QUESTIONS

After studying this section, you should be able to answer the following questions.

1. How am I encouraging the development of self-concept in young children in my classroom management and teaching practices?

2. What are the strengths and weaknesses of my art program as it relates to the development of self-concept? What can I do to improve it so that it is more conducive to the development of a positive self-concept for young children?

3. Do I have sufficient and appropriate art materials for both large and small motor activities? What can I add to improve my program? What can I remove? Have I made appropriate changes for children with special needs?

4. Are the young children in my group able to fully develop their physical and mental potential in the room and the activities I have planned?

5. Does my classroom reflect the range of individual differences in social–emotional and physical–mental development present in the group? How can it be improved?

6. At what levels in the development of art are the children in my group? Have I planned activities and lessons to fit these levels?

7. Are my teaching practices based on a knowledge of social–emotional, physical–mental, and art development levels? Is this knowledge reflected in my choice of materials, supplies, and interest centers?

8. Am I aware of each child's individual schema? Can I recognize them? How do I speak with children about their art?

9. How can I assist parents in their understanding of children's development of art? Of a child's physical–mental development? Of a child's social–emotional growth?

10. Do I encourage young children to verbalize their feelings? Do I encourage this process by modeling consideration of their thoughts and actions?

11. What can I do to improve my current teaching practices in the art program?

12. Am I satisfied that the social–emotional, physical–mental, and developmental levels of art are being appropriately addressed in my teaching strategies? What can I change to better meet the individual needs of young children in all of these areas of development?

Chapter 9

Art and Social–Emotional Growth

Objectives

After studying this chapter, you should be able to:

1. Define the terms *self-acceptance, self-concept,* and *social competence.*
2. Describe how the art program can add to a child's self-concept and self-acceptance.
3. Discuss how the art program helps a child in child-to-child relationships, child-to-teacher relationships, and child-to-group relationships.

The term **social–emotional growth** refers to two kinds of growth. Emotional growth is the growth of a child's feelings, and social growth is the child's growth as a member of a group.

Learning to be a member of a group involves many social skills. Young children, for example, must learn to relate to other children and adults outside the family. Often, a child's first experience of sharing an adult's attention with other children occurs in the early childhood setting. Of the social skills involved in learning to work in a group, children have to learn how to share materials, how to take turns, how to listen to others, and how and when to work on their own—to mention just a few!

This chapter covers both the social and emotional growth of the child as it occurs in the early childhood art program. Although social–emotional growth occurs at the same time as physical–mental growth, the two are covered in separate chapters within this text for the sake of clarity. *The developmental concepts learned and applied in this and the following two chapters are applicable to all other creative activities and materials.*

We are *teaching children about art,* rather than *teaching art to children.* The child comes first. There is a subtle but important difference in this statement. The emphasis is on children and how they learn, rather than on art. Art plays an important role in the well-being and the education of the whole child. The objective, then, of all creative activities is to promote the development of the child in all areas, thus maximizing his or her full potential.

This chapter is divided into four main sections: (1) self-concept and self-acceptance, (2) child-to-child relationships, (3) child-to-teacher relationships, and (4) child-to-group relationships.

SELF-CONCEPT AND SELF-ACCEPTANCE

Self-concept can be defined as the child's growing awareness of his or her own characteristics (physical appearance as well as skills and abilities) and how these are similar to or different from those of others.

All children like to feel good about themselves. This good feeling about oneself is called *self-acceptance* or self-esteem. Children who feel good about themselves and believe they can do things well have a good sense of self-acceptance.

Children who have positive self-concepts accept their own strengths and limitations. The early childhood program provides an environment that nurtures the development of a positive sense of self and a good self-concept in each child.

Children learn to accept themselves from birth all the way throughout life. They learn about themselves by the way they are treated by others. The way parents hold their baby makes the baby feel accepted. A baby who is being held closely with tenderness learns to feel loved and good. The only way babies understand this is by physical touch because they do not yet understand words.

As babies grow into young children, they continue learning to accept themselves. When toddlers are encouraged and praised for messy but serious attempts to feed themselves, they learn to accept themselves and feel good about what they do. If children are accepted as they are, they learn to accept themselves.

In the early childhood art program, children must continue to learn to accept and feel good about themselves. The art program can be of special help in this area. When children feel they can do things well in art, they grow in both self-confidence and self-acceptance.

In the art program, young children learn more about themselves and their capabilities and affirm their sense of self. For example, a child at the easel used many bright colors and was proud of his accomplishment. "I'm Harry and I like to paint pretty colors. Write

Figure 9-1

Children learn about themselves by the way they are treated by others.

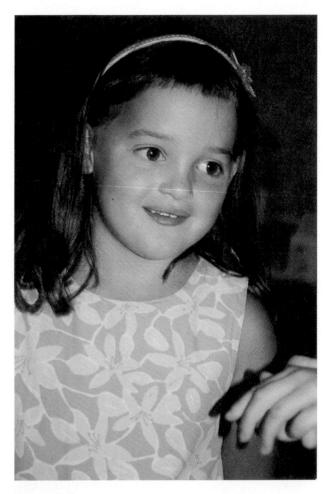

Figure 9-2

Self-acceptance is learning to feel good about oneself.

my name at the top," he calls out to a teacher. This three-year-old child's growing concept of self is evident as he views what he has painted. The good feelings about oneself, which can be fostered through art, are essential for positive development of self-concept.

The importance of a good self-concept is equally as important to middle and upper elementary students. They, too, need the same encouragement and emotionally safe environment in which to express themselves creatively. Just because they are physically bigger and appear more sure of themselves doesn't mean that a teacher can overlook the development of their self-concept in creative activities.

At the primary level and above, state and national standards often overpower teachers with lists of objectives, goals, and mandated learning experiences. Often in this situation with older children, teachers may impose art activities on children from a prescribed curriculum without consideration for the child's interest or concerns for the learner's personal experiences. This approach takes less time than it takes to listen to children, to get to know them, and to adapt the curriculum with the child at the center. It is far easier for adults to dictate to children.

In this adult-directed model, children learn primarily to follow directions. They are directed through one activity after another, activities that often are related to the seasons of the year or holidays. Then, children are evaluated primarily by how well they are able to follow directions.

The importance of changing such an adult focus is clearly explained by the renowned art educator, Viktor Lowenfeld:

Because every process involves the _whole_ child, and not only a single segment, art education may well become the catalyst for a child-centered education in which the individual and his creative potentialities are placed above subject matter, in which the child's inner equilibrium may be considered as important as scientific achievements (Lowenfeld, 1957, p. 11).

This approach is one that obviously builds the child's self-acceptance.

An early childhood teacher needs to plan the art program in such a way that it gives each child a chance to grow in self-acceptance. To do so, the program should be _child-centered,_ which means that it is planned for the age and ability levels of the children in it.

Naturally, if it is child-centered, it is, in turn, developmentally appropriate—meeting the specific individual needs of each child. The art program is planned around the developmental needs of the child. In this way, the teacher has clear guidelines for selections of appropriate materials and activities for the level of each child in the program. (Developmental levels in art and related activities for these levels are covered in Chapter 11.)

Encouraging Self-Acceptance through the Art Program

A climate of psychological safety is essential to the growth of a child's self-acceptance. This safe, accepting environment doesn't just happen. It is carefully planned with the following points included in the planning.

Accept children at their present developmental level.
If the adult accepts the child in a positive way, the child feels this acceptance. This does not mean that the child should not be challenged. Art activities can be planned that are a slight challenge for the child's present level. But they must not be so hard that they frustrate the child. By feeling successful in art activities, children learn to feel more sure about themselves and their skills.

Self-confidence is built on a circular relationship between child and teacher. When the teacher shows confidence in a child, it helps that child develop greater self-confidence.

When four-year-old Rathnam was sweeping broad, free strokes of blue, red, and white paint across his paper, the colors inadvertently mixed at various places.

Figure 9-3

Children feel secure when they feel accepted by the adults caring for them.

Suddenly he stopped, his brush in midair, as he squinted hard at his painting. "Look, it's pink up here and look at this," pointing to a hazy lavender area. "Yes," said his teacher, catching the excitement of the moment, "and you made them—you made those special colors."

The teacher had a hunch that there was more learning potential in that event than the pleasure of discovery. "Which two colors did you mix to make the pink?" she asked. Without hesitation Rathnam responded, "Oh, that's red and white, mixed." "So now you can make pink whenever you want," summarized the teacher. "Yeah," whispered Rathnam with a touch of pride and awe, "I'll mix red and white."

In this way the teacher made clear her confidence that he could repeat purposefully a technique for changing color that he discovered accidentally. Rathnam's response highlighted a moment of self-confidence in his ability to control this responsive art medium.

Provide an environment that is comfortable for the age level of the group.   Plan the room so that it is a place where children can feel at home. It should have tables and chairs that are the right size for young children. A room for older children needs the same care in planning. This age group needs chairs and tables of the appropriate size and strength. There is often a widening difference in physical size in grades 4–5, so a mixture of sizes is often necessary if equipment is to be appropriate for this age group. For example, small-sized desks and chairs often aren't the right size for 5th-grade children who have had a growth spurt. It's hard to feel good about oneself when you feel too big for your chair! If necessary, there should be covering on the floor and work areas so that the children can work freely without worrying about spills. It is hard for children to feel good about themselves and their work when they are always being told they are "too messy." If sponges and towels are within reach, children can clean up their own mess. A little thing like this is fun for them, as well as a good way to help them develop independence and confidence. By being in charge of keeping their own area clean, children learn to feel good about how they can take care of themselves. This strengthens their self-acceptance and personal pride.

Provide an environment that is appropriate for children with special needs.   Adapt the environment so that children with special needs can successfully function in the program. Figure 9–4 presents some ideas on how to make these changes for children with physical disabilities.

SOME SUGGESTIONS ON ADAPTING THE ENVIRONMENT FOR CHILDREN WITH PHYSICAL DISABILITIES

- Use plenty of verbal activities for students whose body movements are limited.
- Use a "buddy system." A partner can quietly explain points that may be confused by children with hearing impairments, help move a wheelchair, or make an area accessible for those with limited mobility. With a sighted partner, space can be explored gradually.
- Use touch to calm, direct, and assist children. Don't let a wheelchair act as a barrier; give tactile encouragement to children who are wheelchair-bound as often as you do other students.
- Focus on dance and pantomime activities that can be done with a child's most mobile part. Facial expressions can be a focus for those whose arms and legs are impaired, or gestures can be emphasized if hands and arms are mobile.
- Paint word pictures and give clear details. Describe art materials, tools, pictures, and props and tell stories with great detail to create mental images for those with visual impairments.
- Let children with visual impairments explore through touch as often as possible.
- Place children with hearing impairments close to the music source to feel the vibrations.
- Be sure children with hearing impairments can see your face, especially the lips, if they are lip readers. Don't stand against a window, or a shadow will be cast on your face. Don't exaggerate your speech; in fact, this distorts the sounds children are taught to observe.
- Repeat comments by children if they are too soft to be heard by those with hearing loss.
- Use visual cues, pictures, props, gestures, and directions on cards for those with hearing loss or speech/language delays.

Printed with permission from *The Arts as Meaning Makers* by Claudia E. Cornett, Merrill/Prentice Hall, Inc. (2003).

Figure 9-4

Some Suggestions on Adapting the Environment for Children with Physical Disabilities.

Provide materials and activities that are age appropriate. By giving children tools they are able to work with at their age and skill level, the teacher helps them have more success in art projects. Success helps them grow with pride and confidence and know that they can do things well. Success breeds success.

Provide creative materials and activities that the children can work on and complete by themselves. Activities that children can finish themselves help them feel more self-assured and confident about their art ability. To do this, teachers need to be good observers to know exactly what materials and activities are developmentally appropriate for each child. This match between children's developmental levels and appropriate activities and materials is an ever-changing one, as children continue to grow and develop in the early years. The creative process offers opportunities for children to gain a spirit of independence and a sense of personal autonomy when the choice of medium, process, or kind of expression is their own.

CHILD-TO-CHILD RELATIONSHIPS

It is only after a child has developed self-acceptance that it is possible for her to accept other children. In the early childhood art program, there are many chances for a child to be with other children of the same age. Children who have had positive creative experiences are the ones who can honestly accept their own abilities and those of other children.

The art program is a good place for child-to-child relationships, where children can work, talk, and be together. If the art activities are developmentally appropriate for the children, they provide a relaxed time for exploring, trying new tools, and using familiar ones again. They also allow children many chances to interact with each other.

The freedom of art itself encourages children to talk about their own work or the work of other children. Working with colors, paint, paper, paste, and other materials provides children an endless supply of things to talk about.

Sharing Ideas and Opinions

Art activities also provide endless opportunities for a child to learn how other children feel about things. For example, a three-year-old boy may hear for the first time how another child his own age feels about his painting. At home, this child may hear mostly adult comments; in the early childhood setting, he can experience the ideas and feelings of an age-mate. An action

Figure 9-5
Learning to be with an adult other than a parent is important social learning.

as simple as putting easels side-by-side encourages this type of social learning. In the same way, 4th and 5th graders will learn a lot about each other's ideas and opinions as they work together planning and creating a class mural for a Martin Luther King Day project.

Although this sharing can be a new and exciting thing for a child, it can also be hard for some children to accept at first. Children may have good feelings about themselves and their work in art; likewise, they can learn to accept ideas about their work from others.

The chance to share ideas and talk about one's own work or the work of others is the beginning of a new type of relationship. It is a sharing relationship. The child begins to see that other children have different ideas and feelings. This type of sharing makes the child see that people can have different feelings and ideas and still be friends. A child can learn that everyone does not have to agree all the time and can share ideas and opinions.

By the time children are in the 4th grade, they are capable of developing rather strong friendships. It is good to encourage these friendships because the social development of the children is furthered as they gain feelings of inner security in having a friend. By the time children are in the 4th or 5th grade, they are being prepared socially for peer group participation. It is this association with a peer group that is the focus of social development of this age group. Within a peer group the needs of the child are met in the following ways:

1. The child finds models for behavior and achievement among peer group members and their activities.

2. The peer group makes it possible for the child to get the attention that he or she discovers he or she needs and wants.

3. The child learns to view himself or herself in different ways as he or she identifies with the group.

4. The group furnishes a support in asking or doing certain things.

5. The child is growing toward maturity with the help of the peer group as he or she learns to rely less on his or her parents.

SOCIAL COMPETENCE

Social competence, the ability to get along with others, is another important factor in child-to-child relationships. During the last two decades a large body of research has accumulated that indicates that unless children achieve minimal social competence by about the age of six years, they have a high probability of being at risk throughout life. These risks are many: poor mental health, dropping out of school, low achievement, and other school difficulties (McClellan & Katz, 2003).

Peer relationships contribute a great deal to a child's social development. As one researcher states:

> Indeed, the single best childhood predictor of adult adaptation is <u>not</u> IQ, <u>not</u> school grades and <u>not</u> classroom behavior but, rather the adequacy with which the child gets along with other children. Children who are generally disliked, who are aggressive and disruptive, who are unable to sustain close relationships with other children, and who cannot establish a place for themselves in the peer culture are seriously "at risk" (Hartup, 2002).

Working together in the early childhood program, children learn how to get along with each other. Sharing materials and ideas, children learn the give and take of being in a group, the skills of social competence. See the Online Companion for a checklist on children's social competence.

Expression of Feelings

The creative art process allows children to visually translate personal feelings as well as ideas (Dewey, 1958; Lowenfeld & Brittain, 1987). Art thus becomes an emotional catharsis. The use of color and the size or placement of representations frequently reflect healthy emotions that are difficult to express in words.

It is not unusual for a teacher to notice that children vigorously pounding clay or energetically hammering nails seem to be relieving tension or frustration. Children who are afraid of the dark may paint some brown or black or purple renditions to express this feeling. Bright colors or symbols of smiling faces may express happy experiences. Art as a vent for feeling is universally acknowledged for artists of all ages (Lowenfeld & Brittain, 1987).

Expressing strong feelings through art rather than through destructive acts may provide catharsis for emotions. Teachers who accept the reality of children's feelings can understand children better and help them cope with distressing feelings. In the same way, teachers who accept children's expressions of their desires and delights can share, and thus intensify, children's joy.

Figure 9-6

Learning to get along with others is important social learning at any age.

Cooperation and Sharing

Working together with other children in creative activities gives a child the chance to learn about being with others. Being with others teaches a child the value of sharing and cooperation.

Working with limited amounts of crayons, paint, and paper means that a child has to share. The child soon learns that sharing is a part of being in a group. One can of red paint for two young painters is a real-life lesson in sharing. Likewise, sharing woodworking tools in the creation of three-dimensional structures teaches 4th and 5th graders how to deal with limited equipment in a cooperative way.

Cooperation among children is also part of the art program. A child learns the meaning of cooperation while helping another child glue seeds on a paper, clean a brush, or button a painting shirt. This is truly learning by doing. This is actively learning social competence.

CHILD-TO-TEACHER RELATIONSHIPS

The teacher in the early childhood program is a very important person in the child's eye. Children look up to their teachers and tend to take them very seriously.

A child learns new ways to be with an adult in the early childhood program. The teacher is an adult, but not the child's parent; therefore, a new type of relationship opens up. Of course, it is different in several ways from the adult-child relationship at home.

The school setting is unlike the home situation. Children learn how to be and act in a place other than the home. They learn how it is to be in a larger group than the family and how to share an adult's attention with other children.

The children learn about art as well as about themselves from the teacher. The teacher helps them feel that it is safe to be themselves and to express ideas in their own way. The sensitive teacher lets the child know that the fun of participating in and expressing oneself in art or other creative activities is more important than the finished product. With older children, the teacher encourages them to explore the many ways to

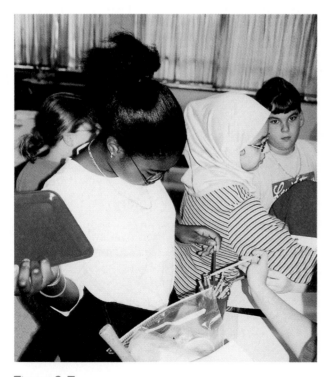

Figure 9-7
The early childhood program provides many opportunities for cooperation and sharing.

Figure 9-8
Learning to feel competent in one's physical abilities is part of social-emotional development.

express their ideas in the growing complexity of their work, which is characteristic of this age group. A teacher opens up many new art skills and feelings for the child and is thus a very important person in the eyes of the child.

The teacher may be the first real adult friend for the child. It is, therefore, important for a good child-teacher relationship to develop during the art program. A happy feeling between teacher and child affects the child's school days to come.

Building Rapport

Building a warm and friendly feeling, a **rapport,** between teacher and child is not always easy; it does not happen quickly. The best learning and teaching take place, however, when the child and teacher have this feeling for each other.

The following are some ways in which the child–teacher relationship may be enhanced:

⊙ Welcome each child into the room. Make the child feel wanted and special.

⊙ When speaking to children, look into their eyes.

⊙ When speaking to children, use their names.

⊙ Understand that children like to feel proud of themselves.

⊙ Talk with and listen to every child as much as possible.

⊙ Use a normal speaking voice.

THINK ABOUT IT... Research on Teachers' Nonverbal Clues

Children are quick studies when it comes to their teachers' body language, and the messages they get about their teachers' feelings toward them can have a profound effect on their classroom, a University of Florida researcher has found.

"Not only what we teach, but how we teach and the learning community we create in the classroom, are going to become the evidence for not only what you think of the students but what they think of themselves," said Vicky Zygouris-Coe, an assistant professor in the University of Florida's College of Education. Zygouris-Coe did the research for her dissertation at the University of Florida.

Zygouris-Coe found that students often interpret things such as their teachers' body language, the order in which they are called on, and the intensity with which they are listened to as signs of their teachers' feelings toward them. Many students even cast a skeptical eye on teachers' compliments, she said.

She studied 60 students in two fourth-grade classes at a local elementary school for 5 1/2 months to gather data for her dissertation. She observed the classroom environment at least twice a week, and gave the children written response questions during the class "journal" time four times a month. The questions were open-ended statements such as, "My teacher thinks that I am. . . ," and the students were encouraged to write several paragraphs to explain their answers.

Each question session was followed a few days later with individual interviews in which Zygouris-Coe asked some of the children to expand on their answers.

One of the most important things teachers can do is to make an effort to know their students as well as possible. Positive nonverbal feedback from teachers—in the form of making eye contact, paying attention when students speak, and letting them know that you understand their strengths and weaknesses—can make all the difference in the world in removing barriers to the learning process.

"I hope that this will make teachers a bit more aware of how children interpret what happens in the classroom," Zygouris-Coe said. "I definitely recommend to teachers to give very specific feedback to children, not necessarily about every aspect of their behavior, but to make frequent attempts to let children know what they think about their progress, their behavior, and other specific elements of their lives."

If teachers take the time to listen to how their students feel and think about how their actions might affect students' perspectives, the classroom learning environment could be greatly improved, Zygouris-Coe said (Harmel, 1999).

> A little girl had just finished her first week of school. "I'm just wasting my time," she said to her mother. "I can't read, I can't write, and they won't let me talk."

Acceptance

In addition to accepting children at their individual developmental levels when planning the arts program, teachers have countless opportunities to model an accepting attitude for children. When Meg derisively called three-year-old Sharon's crayon picture a "scribble scrabble mess," the teacher matter-of-factly commented, "Sharon is hard at work trying out many different crayons. That's exactly how everybody begins—with big, colorful lines." Sharon smiled contentedly; Meg said, "Oh," and went off thinking her own thoughts but perhaps somewhat responsive to the teacher's casual yet positive acceptance of the legitimacy of scribbling in that classroom.

From such small incidents, which collectively reveal an attitude, Meg may realize she is accepted as a person

who warrants an explanation, while Sharon may feel the teacher accepts her as she is. When children feel accepted by people who are important to them, they are better able to develop a sense of trust in those people.

When the teacher accepts and respects each child's physical and artistic abilities, the children then accept each other. By accepting each other, they learn about ideas, opinions, and feelings different from their own peers. These new ideas make the art program richer and more exciting for the children.

Provide an Environment that Respects Individuality

Teachers appreciate how differently children respond to new art activities just as to any other new experiences. Some children eagerly plunge into new activities,

Figure 9-9
Sharing ideas while working on the computer is an activity that encourages social development.

Figure 9-10
The teacher in the early childhood program is a very important person in the child's eye.

attracted perhaps, to new materials or the newness of the venture, while other children temporarily hold back. Still others retreat to the safety of the familiar and are reluctant to take risks with new materials or processes.

Sensitive teachers, trying to provide a climate in which children can take risks in their own ways, will accommodate the differences they observe in children. Three-year-old Mary refused her teacher's invitation to try finger painting. She apparently had the same conflicting feelings she had expressed when clay was introduced. She wanted to play with messy materials but was anxious about getting carried away in her play and becoming too dirty. Her response to the invitation was to run away and play with the little cars across the room.

Eventually, she drove her car toward the finger painting area while accompanying herself with a

steady, persistent engine sound of rhum-rhum-rhum. She barely glanced at the children who were finger painting, then turned and raced back to the block area. Once again, Mary approached and stopped her engine sounds. She looked at the painters with side-long glances, pretending to examine the wheels on her car at the same time. The teacher, noting Mary's interest and reluctance, decided to give her more time. His only comment that day was, "When you decide you want to finger paint, you can pick the color you want." After a few days, Mary announced, "I want blue." The teacher had read Mary's nonverbal behavior correctly; her individual pattern of response had been respected.

This similar approach works with older children as well. For instance, some children may be reluctant to

THIS ONE'S for YOU!
Collaborating with Children: Another Way to Build Self-Concept

Involving young children in decorating their room is a fun, productive way of building their self-concept and improving the room's appearance at the same time! Designing a bulletin board (or wall decoration) can involve many skills and can be a learning experience unlike any other. Here are some tried-and-true bulletin board ideas to involve children while building their self-concept, too.

⊙ **Hands On**—Cover one wall with brown kraft (wrapping) paper. With bright paint (one color for each letter), write the title, "Hands On!" at the top of the paper. Children then place handprints randomly on the board by first pressing hands on a paint-coated sponge and then pressing directly on the paper. Label each print with the child's name and date.

⊙ **Pattern Prints**—Prepare the bulletin board by measuring off horizontal lines on backing paper to create one horizontal stripe/space for each child. At the left end of the stripes, list the children's names. Then, offer the children a variety of materials for printing (cut fruits and vegetables, rubber stamps, printing letters, etc.) and an inked pad (or sponge soaked in tempera paint). Allow the children to create any pattern or design they would like to make.

⊙ **Names**—Cover a large bulletin board with a bright, solid background. Divide paper evenly into a grid design, thus providing each child with a 12–inch square space on the board. With a marker, print each child's name in large letters at the top of the space, leaving at least 11 inches of paper exposed under each name. First, use the board as a basis for a matching game—children must match namecards to their name printed on the board. Children are then invited to decorate their name with markers, crayons, or paints. As the year progresses, children can copy their names in a variety of other materials (older preschoolers may enjoy using yarn, sparkles, etc.).

⊙ **Artwork**—Children are always being told not to write on the walls, but now they can have the freedom and the fun to write on at least one board in the room. Once again, cover a large bulletin board with kraft (or wrapping) paper. (You may want to tack several layers at first so that you can tear off the top layer to expose a fresh piece when needed.) Then, invite the children to draw to their hearts' content. If you share a special story, event, or trip, expose a fresh piece of kraft paper to create an instant mural!

Decorating the room with your children develops a sense of pride in them toward themselves and their environment. They will be proud to show off their room and the bulletin boards they all shared in creating!

work with a new art technique such as printing using a roller for the first time. A sensitive teacher accepts this and allows alternative activities for all students.

CHILD-TO-GROUP RELATIONSHIPS

When taking part in creative activities, a child learns to be in a group. Being in a group at school is not the same as being in a family. In school, the child is a student as well as a member of the group.

As a member of a group, the child learns many things. In art, a child learns how to follow—for example, learning to use a paintbrush by following directions. When making a mural with a group of children, a five year old learns to follow and work with group ideas in planning the project. Learning to follow rules about cleanup is another way a child learns to follow in a group.

Figure 9-11

Building a warm and friendly feeling, a rapport, between teacher and child is essential in the early childhood program.

A child learns how to lead in a group, too. For example, a six-year-old boy who is in charge of his group's paint learns to be a leader with responsibility. Children who can go ahead with ideas on their own are learning the qualities of a leader, too. Thus, in art projects, children have many chances to learn to sometimes be leaders and sometimes be followers.

Being a member of a group is a social learning experience. A group of children engaged in a creative project is a little social group for the child. In such a group, children learn how to share and cooperate. They learn that being in a social group has advantages, such as being with other children their own age, working, sharing ideas, and having fun with them. Children also learn that it is sometimes a disadvantage having to work with the group's rules and that it is not always easy to take turns or to play with others each day in school.

A child learns to respect the rights and ideas of others by being a member of a social group. Learning to respect others is also a part of the child's life outside the school. The things children learn about being members of a group in school help them as members of social groups outside the school.

Because young children are naturally egocentric, they face the difficult, yet necessary, task of moderating their self-interest to cope with group living. Young children must learn the self-discipline inherent in cooperating, in taking turns, and in adapting when necessary to group interests and needs. Skill in resolving interpersonal conflicts gradually develops. Creative art activities that take place in an open and flexible atmosphere provide a valuable setting for these psychosocial learnings.

How fortunate that creative experiences that give children so much pleasure should also be so effective in helping them to learn about themselves, other people, and how better to negotiate the real conditions of group living.

KEY TERMS

rapport   social competence
social–emotional growth

SUMMARY

Well-planned creative activities help children develop good feelings about themselves and their abilities. In these activities, a child learns to be with other children, to be with adults other than parents, and to be in a group. The social skills learned in the early childhood art program help children adapt to other groups outside the school.

LEARNING ACTIVITIES

A. Your first peer group may have been made up of children in your neighborhood or classmates in school. Can you remember their names? What did they look like? How did they behave toward you? How did you feel about your involvement with this group?

B. During these early years, who were the popular, amiable, rejected, or isolated children with whom you came into contact? How would you rate yourself?

C. What happened to this group? What caused it to break apart? Can you remember how you felt about this change?

D. You have a time machine. Would you go back to your childhood to give the child you were a message? Or would you go forward to the future and give your own child a message? What would those messages be? Share them with your classmates.

E. Think about teachers you have had who helped you feel good about yourself. Write down a list of single words describing this teacher. Make a collage using these words. Share your memory collage with fellow students.

F. Going back in your school-day memories, can you remember being afraid, worried, anxious? Write down these memories, including the situation that created this feeling. Now think about your work with children. Have you created similar situations for children? Share your memories and thoughts with your classmates.

G. Psychological safety requires that every child in your room feel accepted, important, and valued. Examine the images of children and adults found in your room. Consider those in textbooks, posters, calendars, and any other available materials. Think about the mixture of genders and races portrayed. Will it support psychological safety for all your students?

ACTIVITIES FOR CHILDREN

The following activities can be used with classmates or with children in laboratory situations. Remember them for real-life classroom use.

"I CAN" BOOK

Show parents of young children the specific skills their children have learned. Make an "I Can" scrapbook using samples of the child's work. Show "I Can Paint," "I Can Color," and "I Can Paste" with samples of work. Illustrate "I Know Colors," for example, with samples of the colors the child can recognize and "I Can Count" with drawings of the number of objects that the child can count.

TEACHERS ARE PEOPLE, TOO

A teacher who was late one day and was explaining to the children that she'd had a flat tire was surprised to hear one four-year-old child say, "But don't you sleep here?" A teacher was obviously part of the equipment that came with the room! How much do

Figure 9-12

Art activities provide children a relaxed time for exploring and learning new skills.

your children know about you? Do you live in a house, an apartment? Do you come to school by car, by bus? Are you married? Do you have children? Talk with the children about *your* life. It will help broaden their understanding of the world.

GROUP EFFORT ACTIVITY

To encourage and develop children's self-esteem, co-operation, and group effort, try this activity. You will need a table, crayons, markers, paper, and tape. Cover the top of the table with paper, attaching it with tape. In the middle of the paper write the title of the picture—for example, "Our Group Art." Allow the children to draw pictures on the paper during group or free choice time. When the picture is finished (to everyone's liking), take it off the table and tape it to the wall or put it on a bulletin board. As a variation, use different shapes or colors of paper. Use a round table or a rectangular table, or an animal or tree shape. Or try to have a special theme for the group artwork: nature, families, animals, etc.

MIRROR ACTIVITIES

Use a large, full-length or small, hand-held mirror to encourage self-awareness with toddlers, preschoolers, and children in grades kindergarten through grade three and grades 4 through 5.

⊙ With toddler—Bring each child to the mirror. Encourage them to look at the mirror. Have them point to the parts of the body you name. "Show me your nose." "Where is your tummy?" "Point to your mouth."

⊙ With kindergarten–3rd grade students—Ask them as they look at themselves such questions as, "Why do people look in mirrors?" "Why do people look at themselves?" "What do you like about you that you see in the mirror?" Then have two children look in the mirror together. Have one child tell the other what is special about him or her or what he or she likes about her or him.

⊙ With 4th–5th graders—Have them look in the mirror. What features do they see that are like their parents, siblings, a famous person, other relatives? What is special about what they see? What lines and shapes do they see in their image? Then have two children look into the mirror. Have them compare the lines and shapes they see in each other's face. Ask them to tell each other what is special about their images. Does either one look like a famous person?

MAKING A PHOTO ALBUM

A. Objectives: To see oneself and others. To learn to admire oneself and others.

B. Procedure: Have each child bring in a photo of himself or herself.

  1. Use large pieces of colored paper. Punch holes in the side of each sheet of paper. Tie yarn through the holes to hold the pages together.

  2. Paste each child's photo on a page. Print the child's name under the photo.

C. Leave the photo album out so the children can look at and enjoy the pictures.

D. A personal picture sequence chart can be made for each child using photos taken at different times of the year (birthday, outings, holidays, etc.). Children will gain a sense of time, change, and growth in these photo charts.

E. During the year, children may want to dictate stories or short descriptive statements to accompany these photos. These "story pages" can be added to the book throughout the year.

ACTIVITIES FOR SELF-AWARENESS, SELF-ACCEPTANCE, AND COOPERATION

Clothes Encounters. Gather together the spare clothes that were stored at the school for the year or packed away the previous year. Use a full-length mirror for this activity. At the end of the school year, encourage each child to try on his or her old spare clothes and examine himself or herself in the mirror. This activity provides a concrete measurement experience that is full of surprises. Talk about the "tight squeeze" of the clothes now and why this is so.

Body Shapes

A. Objectives: To encourage children's positive feelings about themselves and their bodies. To encourage cooperation among children.

B. Equipment: Large pieces of brown paper, crayons, and paints.

C. Procedure: Have a child lie down flat on a piece of paper. Another child uses a crayon to trace the first child's body outline on the paper. Then the first child paints or colors in his or her own body shape outlined on the paper.

D. Encourage the children's self-awareness by having them notice what they are wearing and the colors before they paint their outline.

PATTY-CAKE (FOR THREE YEAR OLDS)

A. Objectives: To learn to use body parts. To learn other children's names.
B. Procedure: Teacher begins by singing and clapping: "Patty-cake, Patty-cake, Baker's Man, Bake me a cake as fast as you can, Roll it and pat it, Mark it with (use a child's initial), Put it in the oven for (use a child's name) and me."
   1. Use all the children's names in the song. (Or each child can have a turn to sing the song and name another child in the group.)
   2. Repeat it often so that children learn each other's names.

Murals

A. Make up a mural after a field trip. It can be made by all of the children working together on one large piece of paper, or it can be made by pasting separate paintings together on a large piece of paper.
B. Variations: Decorate some windows in the school. Plan and give a puppet show. Have the children make the puppets.

I Like. You will need a tape recorder. Individually ask children to name something they like or are interested in. Record these statements and create a pause on the tape. After the short pause, ask each child to say his or her name and record it. During group meeting time, play the tape for the children, asking them to identify the child after each statement of interest. The children can check their guesses when they hear the name of the child recorded on the tape. As a follow-up to this activity, play the tape in the art center. Some children may want to express what they heard on the tape with paint, markers, clay, etc. Another possible use of the tape is in the book corner. Have earphones on the tape player so children can listen quietly to their own and their friend's voices and comments. Some children might want to dictate a story about something they heard on the tape.

THIS MAKES ME FEEL HAPPY

A. Working in a small group, bring an object to the group and say, "I would like to share something with you that makes me happy." Explain why the object makes you happy. For example, "Here is a necklace that someone I like very much gave to me. When I wear it, it reminds me of that person and I get a good feeling." Then, "I would like to give you a chance to share something with us and tell us how it makes you happy."
B. Ask the children to obtain something to bring back to the group. One by one, they are given an op-

portunity to share their object with the group. This can take place over several days as children bring sentimental objects from home. (See Chapter 7 for ideas on making a "Class Museum" to display these special objects.)

Me-Mobiles (Older Four Year Olds). You will need: (1) a selection of magazines (school and department store catalogs, nature, sports, as well as any popular family magazines); (2) scissors; (3) paste; (4) construction paper; (5) wire hangers; (6) yarn (or string); and (7) name tags large enough to fit in the central triangle of the hanger.

Tie the child's name tag to the central portion of the hanger and allow at least three strings to dangle from the bar of the hanger. Have the children look through the magazines and cut (or tear) out three or more pictures that reflect a favorite thing or activity. The children then past the pictures on the construction paper. The children tie or staple the mounted pictures to the strings attached to the hanger. Encourage the children to talk about their selections. Hangers can be hung on a "clothesline" in the classroom or in any other appropriate place.

Fill Your Talent Plate! In this activity, you are giving children the opportunity to discover that there are many talents that people all around them possess. This activity also works with language and fine motor skills.

Discussion: Discuss the meaning of "talent" and emphasize that everyone has special talents. Talk about personal talents of people the children know that will help them connect the meaning of "talent" with their own experiences.

Materials: Magazines, newspapers, photographs, scissors, glue, paper plate.

Procedure:
⊙ Look at all the pictures that show people doing things that they are good at.
⊙ Cut them out and glue them all on your paper "talent plate."
⊙ Show someone else your "talent plate" and help them make one, too.

Faces Charades. Start by singing songs such as "If You're Happy and You Know It" and play Simon Says to introduce the idea that facial and body expressions can convey meaning. Focus on changes in mouths, eyes, and eyebrows.

Preparation: With a small group of children in front of a wall mirror (or small, unbreakable hand mirrors) suggest that they make faces with these or other expressions: you mean yes, you mean no, you are very tired, you are very excited, you are angry, you are happy, etc. When they are able to read each other's expressions, they are ready for Faces Charades!

Procedure: Write one word or idea on an index card. Draw a picture to illustrate the feeling, or use pictures cut from magazines.

Mix up the cards. The children choose a leader to pick the first card. The leader then makes a face according to the directions on the card. The other children try to figure out what feeling it is. The one that guesses correctly gets to pick the next card. Variations: Cards could be of animals, favorite story characters, or any other topic that appeals to children and can be acted out.

With toddlers, you might begin with two or three very different feelings. They could tear pictures from recycled magazines to help distinguish facial expressions.

Half of Me. Materials: Pieces of lightweight cardboard; old magazines and catalogs; markers, crayons, or paint and paintbrushes; blunt tip scissors; glue.

Procedure:

⊙ Children go through the magazines and catalogs to find a picture of something they like. They then cut it out and glue it to a piece of cardboard and cut the picture in half. An adult or older child can help the younger ones with the cutting.

⊙ Put the halves in a box or bag.

⊙ Pass around the box or bag of half pictures and ask each child to take out one of the pieces. Continue passing the box or bag until all the pieces have been taken.

⊙ Ask a child to hold up one of his half pictures. Ask the other children to look through their pieces to see who has the other half. Invite those children to come together to fit the pieces together. The children can leave the completed piece on a table.

⊙ Ask which child selected this picture. Then ask this child to talk about why this was a picture she liked. Continue the activity until all the children have had a chance to talk about their chosen pictures.

ACTIVITIES FOR OLDER CHILDREN (GRADES 4–5)

A. Older children can use cameras and take each other's pictures. They may take photos on a field trip or during a special project, or at whatever time they want. A "documentary" of their experience can be created by arranging the photos in a special order and then writing an explanatory text to go with the photos. Or have older children take pictures of each other according to a specific idea or theme, such as lines/shapes in faces; dark-hair/light-hair friends, etc.

B. Older children can sketch the body outline of another student by projecting a light onto a blank wall, which has a large sheet of paper taped on it. Students can trace each other's "standing shadow" with a large dark marker. They may want to decorate the outline or fill it in with words and phrases describing that person. The point is to do another person's outline to learn more about that person. Asking questions about favorite foods, clothes, TV or movie stars, cars, etc. is a good way to learn information to "fill in" the outline.

C. With older children, make a mural after a field trip. Have them work as a group to decide which part of the field trip they want to feature as the topic of their mural. Encourage them to include as many art techniques as possible in their mural (i.e., collage, finger paint, tempera painting, printing, three-dimensional add-ons, etc.).

D. For older children, give them a chance to learn more about each other in "Talk Time." A talk time break gives them an opportunity to visit with their friends. As we know, the development of strong friendships and a peer group are characteristic of this age group. They can talk about what they did last night, their new item of clothing, what they are going to play at recess, a book they have been reading—just anything they feel is important to share with their classmates. This type of experience also provides an opportunity for developing social interaction and for finding out that their friends have special interests and mutual concerns. Teachers who use this technique find that when the children know they are going to have a time to visit freely, they refrain from visiting at inappropriate times. Teachers can join in the conversations, thus using this "break" as an information-gathering time.

E. **Celebration of Life.** Set aside a day to celebrate life. The purpose of this day is to help each child feel good about themselves and to recognize how precious the gift of life is. Provide each student with several blank business cards. Have them fill in their own name, address, and phone number. Then ask them to draw pictures of or list their special talents, their place in the family, or their favorite things. In group time have them share and explain their cards.

F. **Personal Trophies.** Challenge the students to make a trophy for a family member that honors something they do well. Use clay, gold tempera paint, and paintbrushes.

Look at reproductions of Greek sculpture and a variety of commercial trophies featuring athletic forms. Explore different ways of modeling figures. Try working flat from clay slabs, like gingerbread men. Flattened clay balls make good bases for the clay figures.

Let the clay figures dry and then paint them with gold tempera paint.

G. **Personal Memories.** Motivate your students to create art and writings based on their personal memories. Share with them the following Web sites.

Online Resources: Two contemporary artists who make art based on their personal memories are Carmen Lomas Garza and Faith Ringgold. Both have strong online presences with their personal Web sites: Carmen Lomas Garza: Chicana Artist, available at http://www.carmenlomasgarza.com/ and Faith Ringgold at http://www.faithringgold.com/. Lomas Garza, a self-described Chicana narrative artist, creates images about everyday events in the lives of Mexican Americans based on her own childhood memories and experiences in South Texas. Her Web site includes an artist statement, images of her artwork, a biography, and much more.

Ringgold is an African-American artist well known for her illustrated children's books such as *Tar Beach*. Her Web site offers many features, including a biography, a test about prejudice, a story to read and illustrate, frequently asked questions, and a link to send a message to the artist.

Another artist who painted from personal experience who older students could explore is the Mexican painter Frida Kahlo. Web sites about this artist include Frida Kahlo & Contemporary Thoughts, http://www.fridakahlo.it/index.html; Artocyclopedia: Frida Kahlo, http://www.artcyclopedia.com/; and Frida Kahlo, National Museum of Women in the Arts, http://www.nmwa.org/.

Encourage your students to write autobiographies including artwork, photographs, and any other images they choose to include.

CHAPTER REVIEW

1. Define the terms *self-acceptance, self-concept,* and social competence. Describe a child with a good sense of self-acceptance and self-concept and good social competence skills.

2. Decide whether each of the following statements helps develop self-acceptance, does not help develop self-acceptance, or does not apply to the situation:
   a. holding a baby closely with tenderness
   b. giving a baby enough vitamin C each day
   c. encouraging a baby who tries to feed herself
   d. teaching a child to feed himself when the parent wants the child to do it
   e. leaving an infant alone as much as possible because too much touching spoils the baby
   f. having early dental care
   g. praising a child who dresses himself or herself
   h. discouraging the child's messy eating habits
   i. getting yearly eye examinations
   j. making a child ashamed of an inability to walk well

3. Choose the answer that best completes each of the following statements about an art program and a child's self-acceptance.
   a. An art program should be planned so that it is
      (a) adult-centered
      (b) child-centered
      (c) year round
   b. With each child in the program, a teacher must
      (a) encourage the child to do more advanced work
      (b) praise only successful work
      (c) accept the child's present level
   c. To challenge children, the teacher must provide activities that are
      (a) a bit beyond their present level
      (b) two or three years advanced
      (c) for some children only

d. A well-planned art room
 (a) is best on the north side of the building
 (b) has child-sized chairs and tables
 (c) has mostly large chairs and tables

e. A teacher should choose art materials on the basis of the
 (a) age group using them
 (b) price of materials
 (c) type of distributor

f. A good reason for buying high-quality art materials is
 (a) the low cost of the materials
 (b) children prefer quality materials
 (c) the good results children get with quality materials

g. In planning art activities, a teacher must consider each child's
 (a) ethnic origin and sex
 (b) age
 (c) age, ability, and interest level

h. Success in art projects
 (a) depends on having high-quality materials only
 (b) helps the child's pride and self-confidence
 (c) depends on the teacher's daily attitude

i. One good guide to help children's self-confidence is to tell children
 (a) what they are doing right
 (b) to improve their drawing
 (c) to copy other children's work

j. Another good guide to help children's self-confidence is to
 (a) tell them what they are doing wrong
 (b) guide their hands to help improve their drawing
 (c) encourage them to try again after mistakes

4. Complete the statement in column I about child-to-child relationships by selecting the letter of the best choice from column II.

Column I	Column II
1. A child can accept other children	A. see that not all people have the same ideas
2. Sharing ideas helps children	B. affects all the other school days to come
3. Helping another child clean a brush	C. makes the child feel good about herself
4. Getting along with other children	D. has no effect on a child
5. A good preschool experience	E. is an example of learning to cooperate
	F. only after she accepts herself

5. Discuss why the teacher is so important in the preschool art program or any preschool program.

6. List two ways a teacher can help a child feel accepted.

7. List three things children learn by being part of a group.

8. List some advantages for the child in a group.

9. List some disadvantages for the child in a group.

REFERENCES

Cornett, C. E. The arts as meaning makers. (2003). Upper Saddle River, NJ: Merrill/Prentice Hall.

Dewey, J. (1958). *Art as experience.* New York: Capricorn Books/G.P. Putnam's Sons.

Harmel, K. (1999). UF researcher: Teachers' nonverbal clues affect student's performance. Online: http://www.sciencedaily.com/releases/1999/01/990122130911.htm.

Hartup, W. W. (2002). Having friends, making friends, and keeping friends: Relationships as educational contexts. Urbana, IL: ERIC Clearinghouse on Elementary and Early Childhood Education, ED345–854.

Lowenfeld, V., & Brittain, W. L. (1987). *Creative and mental growth* (8th ed.). New York: Macmillan.

Lowenfeld, V. (1957). *Creative and mental growth* (3rd ed.). New York: Macmillan.

McClellan, D., & Katz, L. G. (2003). Young children's social development: A Checklist. Urbana, IL: ERIC Document EDO-PS–93–6.

ADDITIONAL READINGS

Blanenmeyer, M., Culp, R. E., Hubbs-Tait, L., & Culp, A. M. (2002). A tool for identifying preschooler's deficits in social competence: The preschool taxonomy of problem situations. *Education and Treatment of Children, 25*(2), 208–223.

Blankenmeyer, M., Flannery, D. J., & Vazsony, A. T. (2002). The role of aggression and social competence in children's perceptions of the child-teacher relationship. *Psychology in the Schools 39*(3), 293–403.

Brown, W. H., Odom, S. L., & Buysee, V. (2002). Assessment of preschool children's peer-related social competence. *Assessment for Effective Intervention 27*(4), 61–71.

Close, N. (2002). *Listening to children: Talking with children about difficult issues.* Boston: Allyn & Bacon.

Fisher, M., & Meyer, L. H. (2002). Development and social competence after 2 years for students enrolled in inclusive and self-contained educational programs. *Journal of the Association for Persons with Severe Handicaps 27*(3), 165–174.

Glanville, D. N., & Nowicki, S. (2002). Facial expression recognition and social competence among African American elementary school children: An examination of ethnic differences. *Journal of Black Psychology 28*(4), 318–329.

Greenberg, P. (2000). *Character development: Encouraging self-esteem and self-discipline in infants, toddlers and two-year-olds.* Washington, DC: NAEYC.

Guralnick, M. J., Connor, R. T., Neville, B., & Hammond, M. A. (2002). Mother's perspectives of the peer-related social development of young children with developmental delays and communication disorders. *Early Education and Development 13*(1), 59–80.

Kaiser, B., & Rasminsky, J. (2002). *Meeting the challenge: Effective strategies for challenging behaviors in early childhood environments.* Washington, DC: NAEYC.

Katz, L. G., & McClellan, D. (2000). *Fostering children's social competence: the teacher's role.* Washington, DC: NAEYC.

Landy, S. (2002). *Pathways to competence: Promoting healthy social and emotional development in young children.* Baltimore, MD: Paul H. Brooks.

McGuire, B. A. (2001). *Embracing child art.* Iola, WI: Krause Publications.

Rolfa, S. A. (2002). Promoting resilience in children. *AECA Research in Practice Series, 9*(2), 113–128.

SOFTWARE FOR CHILDREN

Arthur's Preschool, 2002. Pre-K.

Arthur's Preschool, 2000. Pre-K.

Blue's Clues Preschool, 2002. Pre-K.

Blue's Clues: Blue Takes You to School, 2003. Pre-K.

Disney Learning Preschool, 2003. Pre-K.

Franklin the Turtle Goes to School, 2000. Pre-K.

I'm Ready for Kindergarten: Huggly's Sleepover, 2003. Pre-K.

Jump Start Advanced Preschool, 2002. Pre-K.

LEGO My Style: Preschool, 2003. Pre-K.

My Little CD Tots, 2003. Pre-K.

Pencil-Pal Preschool, 2002. Pre-K.

Publix Preschool Pals, 2003. Pre-K.

Sesame Street Preschool Learning Basics, 2002. Pre-K.

Freddi Fish 5: The Case of the Creature of Coral Cove, 2003. Grades K–3.

Furreal Friends, 2002. Grades K–3.

Spot and His Friends, 2002. Grades K–3.

Stories and More: Animal Friends, 2002. Grades K–3.

The Little Raven and Friends: The Tricycle Story, 2002. Grades K–3.

Thomas & Friends: Thomas Saves the Day, 2003. Grades K–3.

Thomas & Friends: Building the New Line, 2002. Grades K–3.

Arty the Part-Time Astronaut, 2000. Grades 4–5.

Bugs Bunny & Taz Time, 2000. Grades 4–5.

Casper: Spirit Dimensions, 2002. Grades 4–5.

Code Head: X-treme Culture, 2002. Grades 4–5.

Dear America: Friend to Friend, 2000. Grades 4–5.

I Spy School Days, 2000. Grades 4–5.

Liberty's Kids EEV, 2003. Grades 4–5.

HELPFUL WEB SITES

http://www.fci.org
Family Communications. Includes information provided by elementary educators and other professionals on helping children to manage angry feelings.

http://www.childdevelopmentinfo.com
Excellent Web site for general development information and research on social–emotional and intellectual development. It also has links to research articles on developmental issues.

http://www.teachersandfamilies.com
Good source for information to share with parents on development. The site is sponsored by the Network for Instructional television.

For additional creative activity resources, visit our Web site at http://www.EarlyChildEd.delmar.com.

Chapter 10

Art and Physical–Mental Growth

Objectives

After studying this chapter, you should be able to:

1. Explain how art aids a child's physical (motor) development.
2. Describe how art aids a child's mental development.
3. Discuss the place of art in the total early childhood program.

This chapter presents the ways in which art relates to physical and mental growth. Physical, mental, social, and emotional growth all occur together in a child, but physical and mental growth are discussed separately here for the sake of clarity.

ART AND PHYSICAL (MOTOR) DEVELOPMENT

The term **motor development** means physical growth. Both terms refer to growth in the ability of children to use their bodies.

In an early childhood program, activities like dance, drawing, painting, pasting, and other activities that exercise muscles aid a child's motor development. Exercising muscles in creative activities aids both small- and large-muscle development. Before we consider each of these types of motor development, let us look at the overall pattern of growth and development.

Pattern of Development

The process of human development follows a general pattern that includes growth in three basic directions (Figure 10–1). The first of these is called large to small muscle or **gross** to **fine motor development.** Large (gross) to small (fine) motor development means that large muscles develop in the neck, trunk, arms, and legs before the small muscles in the fingers, hands, wrists, and eyes develop. This is why young children can walk long before they are able to write or even scribble.

The second direction of growth, from head to toe (or top to bottom), is called **cephalocaudal development.** This growth pattern explains why a baby is able to hold up his head long before he is able to walk because the muscles develop from the head down.

The third pattern of development is from inside to outside (or from center to outside) and is called **proximodental development.** This explains the ability of a baby to roll over before he is able to push himself up

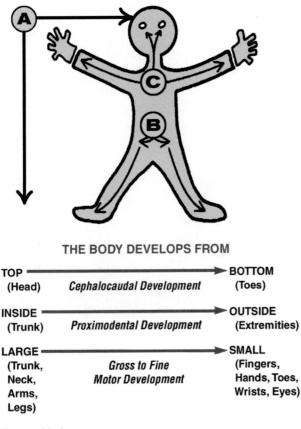

THE BODY DEVELOPS FROM

TOP	➤	BOTTOM
(Head)	*Cephalocaudal Development*	(Toes)
INSIDE	➤	OUTSIDE
(Trunk)	*Proximodental Development*	(Extremities)
LARGE	➤	SMALL
(Trunk, Neck, Arms, Legs)	*Gross to Fine Motor Development*	(Fingers, Hands, Toes, Wrists, Eyes)

Figure 10-1

The pattern of development.

Figure 10-2

Small motor skills develop in art activities.

with his arms. Because the inner muscles of the trunk develop first, rolling over comes before pulling or sitting up. Understanding these basic principles of development, especially large to small motor development, is important in planning appropriate art activities for young children. Let us now consider large and small motor development.

Large-Muscle Development

A child's proportions are constantly changing as he or she grows because different parts of the body grow at different rates. Physical disproportions are common from birth to approximately age six as the upper body is generally longer and not in proportion to the lower body. As a consequence of these body proportions in which the legs and body are not developed in proportion to the upper body region, toddlers and preschoolers have a high center of gravity and are prone to falls.

By age six, however, body proportions are more similar to those of an adult. When the child has matured to adultlike proportions, his or her center of gravity is more centrally located so that he or she achieves a greater sense of physical balance and is able to be more purposeful in movements.

Because large muscles in the arms, legs, neck, and trunk develop first, by the time children reach the preschool age, they are able to use large muscles quite well. They can walk, run, sit, and stand at will. They can use their arms and hands quite easily in large movements like clapping and climbing. Younger children enjoy large motor play activities. Most three year olds and many four year olds are actively using their large muscles in running, wiggling, and jumping. They are not yet as developed in small motor skills (like cutting, tying, or lacing) as five year olds.

The early childhood art program gives the child a chance to exercise large motor skills in many ways other than just in active games. Painting with a brush on a large piece of paper is as good a practice for large-muscle development as dancing. Whether it be wide arm movements made in brush strokes or arms moving to a musical beat, it is only by first developing these large muscles that a child can begin to develop small motor skills.

Creative activities in the early childhood program provide many opportunities for exercising large-muscle

Figure 10-3

A child's small muscles are exercised by using blunt scissors in art activities.

Figure 10-4

This child is using the small muscles in her hands, fingers, and wrists.

skills. Activities that exercise large muscles include group murals, tracing body shapes, easel painting, clay pounding, and crayon rubbings. (See end of chapter for more specific activities.)

Small-Muscle Development

Small muscles in fingers, hands, and wrists are used in art activities such as painting, cutting, pasting, and clay modeling. These small motor art activities and any other activity that involves the use of small muscles help exercise and develop a child's fine motor control.

Small muscle skills are different for a child at different ages. For example, many three year olds do not have good small muscle development, so the muscles in their fingers and hands are not quite developed enough to enable them to use scissors easily.

In the following report, a teacher found out that the planned art activity was, in fact, too difficult a small motor task for some of the children in the group.

Making masks out of paper bags was a good experience for many of the children. However, I found that many other children had difficulty handling the scissors and became frustrated. They were eager to have the masks, but couldn't handle the problem of not being able to manipulate the scissors [easily] enough to make a mask quickly. I tried to overcome this problem by helping them make the first holes, or cutting out part of an eye, and letting the child finish the job. Perhaps many theorists would say that I should have let them do it by themselves completely. But I just felt that their eagerness to make the mask and to complete the cutting once I had helped them was not to be overlooked. The children all wanted to take home their masks and ran to put them in their lockers so they wouldn't forget them. One little girl wore hers all day and had to be convinced that she couldn't eat with it on! (Author's log)

Practice in crushing and tearing paper, and later practice in using blunt scissors, all help small muscles develop. The better the small muscle development, the easier it will be to cut with scissors. Small muscles can grow stronger only by practice and exercise. A teacher encourages a child to exercise these small muscles in small motor artwork, such as tearing, pasting, working with clay, making and playing with puppets, and finger painting.

A teacher also encourages a child to exercise small muscles by providing the right small motor tools. The teacher in the following report managed to use clay as the medium for helping children practice small motor skills.

In my activities I wanted to emphasize fine motor development, so I used clay with different-sized soda straw pieces, toothpicks, buttons, etc., to stick in the clay. The children made animals, designs, and monsters. They kept up a running commentary on how they were making a monster and could smash it if they wanted to. It seemed that the clay was a good means of having them release their fears, ideas, and emotions on many things. This clay activity went over very well. During the day, many different, as well as the same, children came back to play at the clay table. (Author's log)

Small muscles are often better developed in four and five year olds. However, small motor activities are still necessary for continued small-muscle development. Drawing with pencils, crushing paper into shapes, modeling figures with clay, and making mobiles are examples of more advanced small motor activities.

Working with small muscles in small motor art activities helps make learning to write much easier for the child. The control over hand and finger movements used for finger painting and clay modeling is the same control the child needs to be able to write. Early childhood art activities give the child a chance to practice and develop the small motor skills needed in schoolwork to come.

Large and Small Motor Activities

The early childhood art program should have a good mixture of both small and large motor tools and activities. A child needs to develop both large and small muscles, and artwork provides this chance.

The teacher needs to respect each child's need to develop both large and small muscles at any age. This means a teacher needs the right equipment but, more important, the right attitude for the level of each child. The right attitude is one that lets the child know it is all right to try many large and small motor activities at any age. In this type of art program, not all four year olds are expected to cut well, to button a shirt successfully, or to be able to do either at all. Five year olds, as well as younger children, may enjoy pounding clay for no other purpose than the fun of pounding. Older children should also be allowed this same freedom of expression with both large- and small-muscle activities. Just because they may appear more grown, middle and upper elementary children still enjoy "messing around" with clay and even fingerpaints.

Art activities provide both fine and gross motor experiences. As children create—thrusting sticks into plastic foam, forming small shapes with a marker, using a paint brush at an easel—they move back and forth between large, sweeping motions and small, discrete movements. These movements help children develop control and coordination of both fine and gross muscles. Both types of development are important for the child's growth, not only for forming letters and

Figure 10-5

Small muscles in the fingers and hands develop later than those in the legs and arms.

SKILLS AND CHARACTERISTICS	SUGGESTED ACTIVITIES

The Two Year Old

Skills and Characteristics	Suggested Activities
Very active, short attention span	Provide pushing and pulling toys. Encourage play with pounding bench, punching bags, and soft clay. Provide opportunities both indoors and outdoors for active free play that involves climbing, running, sliding, tumbling.
Interest in physical manipulation; ability to stack several items; pull apart, fill, and empty containers	Provide stacking cups or blocks for stacking and unstacking. Provide pop-apart toys, such as beads, for taking apart. (Large enough *not* to swallow.) Provide opportunities for filling and emptying containers with sand, water, rice, beans, rocks, etc.
Increased development of fine motor skills	Provide crayons, chalk, paint, and paper for scribbling and painting. Be sure all materials are lead-free and nontoxic. Allow the child to "paint" the sidewalk, building, wheel toys, etc., with clear water and a brush large enough to handle. Provide opportunities to play with play dough, finger paint, paper for tearing, etc.
Increased development in language skills	Encourage the child to talk with you. Use pronouns such as "I," "me," "you," "they," "we." Encourage the child to use these words. Talk with the child about pictures. Ask her to point to objects or name them. Always give the correct name for objects. Give directions to follow: "Close the door," "Pick up the doll." Be sure to make this a fun game. Teach the child the names of unusual objects such as fire extinguisher, thermometer, screwdriver, trivet.
Likes to imitate	Encourage finger plays. Recite nursery rhymes. Encourage the child to repeat them. Play "I am a mirror." Stand or sit facing the child and have him copy everything you do.
Shows interest in dramatic play	Provide dolls, dress-up clothes, carriage, doll bed, toy telephones for pretend conversations.

The Three Year Old

Skills and Characteristics	Suggested Activities
Increased development of large motor skills	Provide opportunities for vigorous free play indoors and outdoors. Provide opportunities for climbing, jumping, riding wheel toys. Play "Follow-the-Leader," requiring vigorous body movements.
Greater control over small muscles	Provide opportunities for free play with blocks in various sizes, shapes. Provide a variety of manipulative toys and activities such as pegboard and peg sets, tinker toys, puzzles with 3–8 pieces. Encourage children to dress and undress themselves, serve food, set the table, water the plants.
Greater motor coordination	Provide art activities. Encourage free expression with paint, crayons, chalk, colored pens, collage materials, clay, play dough. Be sure all materials are lead-free and nontoxic.
Increased development of language skills and vocabulary	Provide opportunities each day for reading stories to children in a group or individually. Encourage children to tell stories. Tape record their stories. Encourage children to talk about anything of interest.
Beginning to understand number concepts. Usually can grasp concepts of 1, 2, and 3. Can count several numbers in a series but may leave some out.	Count objects of interest, e.g., cookies, cups, napkins, dolls. When possible, move them as you count. Allow children to count them. Display numbers in the room. Use calendars, charts, scales, and rulers.

Figure 10-6

Motor skills and characteristics of children ages two through 10 years, with suggested activities to encourage physical development.

(Continues)

SKILLS AND CHARACTERISTICS	SUGGESTED ACTIVITIES
Enjoys music and is beginning to be able to carry a tune, express rhythm	Provide music activities each day. Sing songs, create rhythms. Move body to music. Encourage children to make up songs. Tape record them and play them back for the children to dance to or to sing along with.
Curious about why and how things happen	Provide new experiences that arouse questions. Answer the questions simply and honestly. Use reference books with the child to find answers. Conduct simple science activities: What will the magnet pick up? Freeze water, make ice cream, plant seeds, make a terrarium, fly a kite on a windy day.

The Four Year Old

Good balance and body coordination; increased development of small and large motor skills	Provide opportunities each day for vigorous free play. Provide opportunities for the child to walk on a curved line, a straight line, a balance beam. Encourage walking with a bean bag on the head. Games: "See how fast you can hop," "See how far you can hop on one foot," "See how high you can jump." Provide opportunities to throw balls (medium-sized, soft), bean bags, yarn balls.
Small motor skills are developing most rapidly now. Drawings and art express world around them. Increasing hand–eye coordination	Provide opportunity for variety of artwork. Encourage children to tell a story or talk about their finished projects. Encourage children to mix primary colors to produce secondary colors. Name the colors with them. Encourage children to unzip, unsnap, and unbutton clothes. Dressing self is too difficult at this point. Encourage children to tear and cut. Encourage children to lace their shoes.
Ability to group items according to similar characteristics	Play lotto games. Group buttons by color or size. Provide a mixture of seeds. Sort by kind. At cleanup time, sort blocks according to shape. Play rhyming word games.
Increased understanding of concepts related to numbers, size and weight, colors, textures, distance and position, and time	In conversation, use words related to these concepts. Play "Follow Direction" games. Say, "Put the pencil beside the big block," or "Crawl under the table." Provide swatches of fabric and other materials that vary in texture. Talk about differences. Blindfold the children or have them cover their eyes and ask them to match duplicate textures.
Awareness of the world around them	Build a simple bird feeder and provide feed for birds. Record the kinds of birds observed. Arrange field trips to various community locations of interest (park, fire station, police station).
Has a vivid imagination; enjoys dramatic play	Provide variety of dress-up clothes. Encourage dramatic play through props such as cash register and empty food containers, tea set, and child-sized furniture.

The Five and Six Year Old

Good sense of balance and body coordination	Encourage body movement with records, stories, rhythms. Encourage skipping to music or rhymes. Teach them simple folk dances.
A tremendous drive for physical activity	Provide free play that encourages running, jumping, balancing, and climbing. Play tug-of-war. Encourage tumbling on a mat.

Figure 10-6 (Continued)

Motor skills and characteristics of children ages two through 10 years, with suggested activities to encourage physical development.

(Continues)

SKILLS AND CHARACTERISTICS	SUGGESTED ACTIVITIES
Development and coordination of small muscles in hands and fingers	Encourage opportunities to paint, draw, cut, paste, mold clay. Provide small peg games and other manipulative toys. Teach sewing with large needle and thread into egg cartons or punched cards. Provide simple carpentry experiences.
Increased hand–eye coordination	Allow children to copy designs of shapes, letters, and numbers. Show a child how his name is made with letters. Encourage catching small balls.
Ability to distinguish right from left	Play games that emphasize right from left. Games can require responses to directions such as "Put your right hand on your nose" or "Put your left foot on the green circle."
Can discriminate between weights, colors, sizes, textures, and shapes	Play sorting games. Sort rocks by weight; blocks by weight or shape; marbles or seeds by colors. Match fabric swatches.
Increased understanding of number concepts	Count anything of interest—cookies, napkins, cups, leaves, acorns, trees, children, teachers, boys, chairs, etc. Identify numbers visible on a calendar, clock, measuring containers, or other devices.
Enjoys jokes, nonsense rhymes, riddles	Read humorous stories, riddles, nonsense rhymes.
Enjoys creative, dramatic activities	Move body to dramatize opening of a flower, falling snow, leaves, rain, wiggly worms, snakes, blowing wind. Dramatize stories as they are read. Good stories to use are: *Caps for Sale, Three Billy Goats Gruff, Three Bears.*

The Six to 10 Year Old

Good sense of balance and body coordination.	Encourage movements that challenge the child such as horizontal and vertical jumps. Introduce more complex motor skills such as relay runs, obstacle courses, etc.
More directed in their drive for physical activity	Encourage free play that allows running, jumping, balancing, throwing and catching. Introduce basic sports such as baseball, basketball and soccer.
Good development and coordination of small muscles in hands and fingers	Provide many challenging and diverse art activities that allow for fine motor exercise. Encourage three-dimensional projects such as woodworking, papier mâché, costume-making, etc.
Improved hand–eye coordination	Continue to encourage tossing, throwing, and catching skills. Use activities that incorporate several skills such as dodge ball.
Learns to apply and refine perceptual skills developed earlier	Challenge children in art activities to see and express shape, form, color, and line in a variety of media. Provide activities that allow them to learn to identify and analyze relationships such as how light affects perception of colors, textures, and form.
Growing facility with use of numbers; can think more flexibly	Introduce the use of calculators for math problems. Challenge them with basic probability and estimation activities/problems. Allow them to work in small groups for problem-solving.
Has an increasingly sophisticated sense of humor	Provide jokebooks, humorous books, nonsense riddle and rhyme books. Encourage them to write their own humorous pieces.
Enjoys dramatic activities, but self-consciousness is becoming an issue	Encourage children to express themselves in short performances such as sketches, vignettes, "freeze-frame" scenes, and pantomime. Provide opportunities for them to see dramatic activities of other students (i.e., middle school play, dance rehearsal, etc.). Provide books, music, and artwork of great artists for children to experience. (Gallaghue & Ozmun, 1997)

Figure 10-6 (Continued)

Motor skills and characteristics of children ages two through 10 years, with suggested activities to encourage physical development.

numbers later in school, but for overall physical movement. Offering children a variety of different materials, such as crayons, easel paint, scissors, recycled materials, and clay, helps them develop the various muscles in their arms and fingers.

Hand-Eye Coordination

In the early childhood program, as children exercise their small and large muscles, they also improve their hand–eye coordination. **Hand–eye coordination** refers to the ability to use hand(s) and eyes at the same time. Painting is a good example. When children paint, they use their eyes to choose the colors and their hands to hold and use the brush.

Hand–eye coordination is also used in clay modeling, making a mobile, pasting, and finger painting. In all of these art activities, the child is receiving practice in *coordinating* (using together) the hands and eyes.

Art Activities and Reading Readiness

Hand–eye coordination is important for future schoolwork. Many reading experts feel that good hand–eye coordination helps a child learn to read. They feel that the ability to use hands and eyes together in activities like painting or playing ball helps a child learn the motor skills needed in reading. Holding a book in two hands and using the eyes to read from left to right is simple hand–eye coordination.

Reading experts feel that the growth pattern of large to small muscles affects reading ability. In other words, a child must have a chance to develop large muscles before being able to use small muscles—such as the eyes in the right-to-left movements of reading. The side-to-side or lateral movements developed in such activities as painting and printing are also helpful in developing left-to-right tracking in reading. Thus, art activities are important for future reading as they exercise and develop hand–eye coordination and left-to-right tracking.

Explorations with art materials also offer opportunities to sharpen perceptions of form. Children note relationships between artistic two- and three-dimensional forms and the environment. "My clay is round like a pie," "I drew a square like that book," or "Look at the funny shape of my puppet's head; it's not like my head." These expressions indicate that children are learning about form while being involved in creative activities. **Visual acuity**—the ability to see and recognize shape and form—is implicit in all art activities. It is also an ability that needs to be developed for beginning reading.

Motor Control

All that we have discussed thus far about muscle growth and hand–eye coordination falls under the general category of motor control. As children grow, they gain progressive control over their bodies.

Children growing in small- and large-muscle skills and in hand–eye coordination are growing in total motor control. (Figure 10–6 contains suggested activities in art and other curriculum areas to enhance overall motor control for children ages 2 through 10.) The child's work in various activities demonstrates this growing motor control. An observant teacher can assess an individual child's motor skills in one activity and make judgments about his likely skill or ability in another area. For instance, when considering art activities, a teacher recognizes that early scribbling is the beginning of motor control. The child holds the crayon and scribbles with very little motor control. As children grow in motor control, they can control the direction of their scribbles, then control lines to make basic forms, and finally draw pictures.

Therefore, a teacher can assess children's general motor control by knowing their artwork. For example, the teacher who knows that a certain five year old cannot yet cut with scissors knows how to reply to parents who ask if this child is ready for piano lessons. Thus, observing each child's motor control in artwork helps the teacher know each child's motor control in other areas as well.

ART AND MENTAL DEVELOPMENT

Art and Thinking Skills

Art activities involve children mentally as well as physically. They involve both the physical ability to use art tools as well as the thinking processes involved in the creation itself. Let's now consider how art and thinking skills are related in art activities.

Creating art is a complex mental process that requires children to use many skills, such as problem solving, predicting, geometric design, and cause and effect. For example, think about a child who wants to draw a person. First, she needs to remember what she knows about how people look, then identify the important features and represent them on paper through shapes and lines. That is no small achievement for a three or four year old!

Just as art reflects children's thinking, it also enhances it. Consider an older child who wants to draw an ant and a mosquito. He or she learns about the similarities and differences between the two insects by

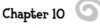

observing; then, through drawing, the child clarifies and reinforces what he or she has learned.

Art helps children gain a great deal of knowledge in more direct ways as well. As children experiment and investigate, they learn about the physical nature of tools and materials. What will the brush do if I hit it on the paper this way—or that way? How can I make the foil plate stick to the wood? How much glue is OK to use on the tissue paper? When you offer a wide variety of materials for children to investigate freely, you broaden their opportunities for learning.

Art and Sensorimotor Development

As children grow physically, they also grow mentally. This is because young children learn by doing. Jean Piaget, in his work with young children, describes a child's learning by doing as "sensorimotor" development.

The word **sensorimotor** derives from the two words *sensory* and *motor*. Sensory refers to using the five body senses and motor refers to the physical act of doing. Sensorimotor learning involves the body and its senses (sensori) as they are used in doing (motor).

Figure 10-7
Young children learn mentally as they do things physically.

For Piaget (1955), the foundation of all mental development takes place in physical knowledge, the knowledge that comes from objects. Children construct physical knowledge by acting on objects—feeling, tasting, smelling, seeing, and hearing them. They cause objects to move—throwing, banging, blowing, pushing, and pulling them. They observe changes that take place in objects when they are mixed together, heated, cooled, or changed in some other way. As physical knowledge develops, children become better able to establish relationships (comparing, classifying, ordering) between and among the objects they act upon.

Sensorimotor Learning in Art

An example of sensorimotor learning in art is modeling with clay. In using clay (the motor activity), children use their senses (sensory), such as feel and smell, to learn about clay and how to use it. A teacher can tell the children how clay feels and how to use it; but children truly learn about clay by physically using it themselves. A child needs this sensorimotor exploration with clay and many other art materials.

In the art program, children learn many things in this sensorimotor way—learning by doing. Many ideas and concepts are learned from different art activities. Just as children exercise different muscles in art activities, they also learn new concepts in many kinds of art activities. Exploring and creating with art materials encourages children to use their senses to become more aware of the environment.

Creative Activities and the Senses

Touch. Art activities that use the sense of touch teach children many important concepts. For example, working with clay helps them learn the concepts of hard and soft. The children feel the softness of clay in their hands as they work with it. When the clay is old and needs water, they feel how hard it has become. In using clay this way, children learn not only that clay is soft, but that it can be hard, too.

Increased ability to discriminate among textures develops through creative activities. Children use a variety of papers and fabrics for collages, rub crayons over different materials, and print with many objects on diverse surfaces. Opportunities to learn about texture abound at the workbench: the roughness of sandpaper, the smoothness of the dowel, and the sharpness of the wood splinter. Textured art materials help children reinforce knowledge about the physical appearance of people and animals. Yarn, cotton, and fur fabric may be used for people's hair, beards, and mustaches or for

Figure 10-8
Seeking answers and finding new ways to approach problems are part of the mental growth in early childhood programs.

Figure 10-9
Young children learn about their world in active ways.

animal coats. You may want to try some of the activities suggested at the end of this chapter to help develop children's sense of touch.

Sight. Art activities involve the sense of sight as well as touch. A child sees and feels the art material being used. The sense of sight in artwork helps the child learn many important concepts.

The child sees the sameness and the difference in size, color, shape, and texture when working with different materials. He learns concepts like big/small and wide/thin by using many types of art materials. A child sees that different sizes of crayons make different sizes of lines. Wide brushes make paint strokes that look different from strokes made with a thin brush. He or she learns that a figure drawn with a felt-tip pen looks different from the same figure made with paint and a brush.

Ideas about basic shapes are learned by cutting with scissors, working with clay, painting, and drawing. A child also sees many basic shapes in the scrap materials used for a collage.

In artwork, the child sees that things can look alike but feel different. Sand and cornmeal may look alike, but they feel different to the child as they are glued onto paper. In this way, she learns that the sense of sight alone is not enough to really learn about a material.

In art activities, older children learn to see and use the elements of art in their work. For example, they learn to use line and shape to express a certain mood or feeling in a drawing.

Color concepts. Concepts about colors are learned in the art program. While painting and drawing, children learn the names of colors, how to mix colors, and how to make colors lighter or darker. In such a

sensorimotor experience, the child learns that colors are not set things, but things that the child himself can change.

When children start to perceive differences in color, they experiment with light and dark hues and tints and mixtures. Contrasts of brilliant and dull and warm and cool colors are juxtaposed for effect. Linear patterns are created with two- and three-dimensional art media. Children can make sharp lines, curved lines, coils, and squiggles with paint, crayon, string, yarn, and wire. In rural areas children observe the slant of tall wheat and grasses, while city children notice the sharp contrasts in city skylines. Older children learn that colors can be cold or warm and use these colors to express a mood in their paintings.

Concept of change. The idea of change is an important thing for the child to know and is a concept that develops slowly. Piaget (1955), in his writings about the growth of intelligence in young children, emphasizes the fact that mental growth is aided by a child's active exploration of the environment. The child, according to Piaget, gradually comes to understand about how things can change as he or she experiences different materials in various situations in his environment. For example, by using color, mixing colors, and making color lighter or darker, the child learns that things can change. Clay can change from hard to soft. Plaster can change from liquid to solid.

"Learning by doing" in art helps a child grow mentally, as he or she grows more flexible in his or her thinking. The child learns to think of things in the context of change and that not all things are permanent. The ability to think this way is called **flexible thinking** (Figure 10–11).

Figure 10-10

Physical activity abounds in an early childhood program.

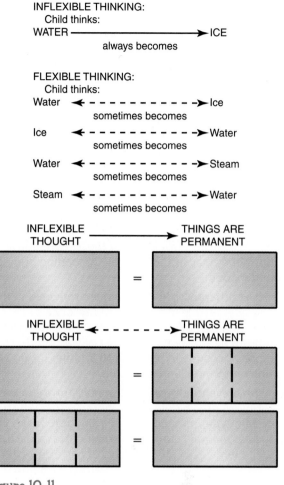

Figure 10-11

Flexible and inflexible thinking.

Art activities with a variety of materials encourage flexibility of thought. In making a collage, the characteristics of different items are compared and relationships are discovered between the new and the familiar items. Flexibility of thought is encouraged as children associate particular tools with certain processes and learn which tools work best with various materials. For example, a thin brush will make a thin line with paint, and a thick one creates a broader stroke. A sharp needle is needed to sew through felt, but a blunt one works well for open-weave fabrics.

Being able to think flexibly helps children become mentally prepared for later school experiences. Math, spelling, and science all require thinking that can deal with change. In science, for example, a cooking lesson involves changes that ingredients go through in the process of becoming a cake. In math activities, a child learns how numbers can change by such things as addition and subtraction. In spelling, children learn how words change with plurals, suffixes, and prefixes. Flexibility in thought processes is, therefore, basic to most of a child's subsequent learning experiences.

Vocabulary and Art

An expanding vocabulary about creative materials and processes is a natural partner to the activity itself. Children working with art materials will use descriptive terms for the media and the resulting creations. The teacher's use of particular words to compare size, weight, color, texture, and shape influences children's descriptions of their artwork. Previous knowledge is combined with new information as oral language develops. "Gushy, mushy, wet paint," chanted three-year-old Laura as she pushed the finger paint around on the tabletop. "Gushy, mushy, *red* paint," responded one of her tablemates.

THINK ABOUT IT...

Boys' and Girls' Brain Development . . . Are There Any Differences?

Yes, but they are subtle differences and a product of both nature and nurture.

Electrical measurements reveal differences in boys' and girls' brain function from the moment of birth. By three months of age, boys' and girls' brains respond differently to the sound of human speech. Because they appear so early in life, such differences are presumably a product of sex-related genes or hormones. We do know that testosterone levels increase in male fetuses as early as seven weeks of gestation and that testosterone affects the growth and survival of neurons in many parts of the brain. Female sex hormones may also play a role in shaping brain development, but their function is currently not well understood.

Sex differences in the brain are reflected in the somewhat different developmental timetables of girls and boys. By most measures of sensory and cognitive development, girls are slightly more advanced: vision, hearing, memory, smell, and touch are all more acute in female than male infants. Girl babies also tend to be somewhat more socially attuned—responding more readily to human voices or faces or crying more vigorously in response to another infant's cry—and they generally lead boys in the emergence of fine motor and language skills.

Boys eventually catch up in many of these areas. By age three, they tend to out-perform girls in one cognitive area: visual–spatial integration, which is involved in navigation, assembling jigsaw puzzles, and certain types of hand–eye coordination. Males of all ages tend to perform better than females on tasks such as mental rotation (imagining how a particular object would look if it were turned 90 degrees), while females of all ages tend to perform better than males at certain verbal tasks and at identifying emotional expression in another person's face. It is important to emphasize that these findings describe only the average differences between boys and girls. In fact, the range of abilities within either gender is much greater than the difference between the "average girl" and the "average boy." In other words, there are plenty of boys with excellent verbal skills and girls with excellent visual–spatial ability. Although it can be helpful for parents and teachers to understand the different tendencies of the two sexes, we should not expect all children to conform to these norms.

Genes and hormones set the ball rolling, but they do not fully account for sex differences in children's brains. Experience also plays a fundamental role. Consider, for example, the "typical" boy, with his more advanced spatial skills; he may well prefer activities like climbing or pushing trucks around—all of which further hone his visual–spatial skills. The "typical" girl, by contrast, may gravitate more toward games with dolls and siblings, which further reinforce her verbal and social skills. It is not hard to see how initial strengths are magnified—thanks to the remarkable plasticity of young children's brains—into significant differences, even before boys and girls begin preschool.

But this remarkable plasticity also provides parents, teachers, and other caregivers with a wonderful opportunity to compensate for the different tendencies of boys and girls. For example, it is known that greater verbal interaction can improve young children's language skills. So the "typical boy" may especially benefit from an adult who engages him in lots of conversation and word play. However, the "typical girl" may benefit from an adult who engages her in a jigsaw puzzle or building a block tower—activities that encourage her visual–spatial integration.

The point is not to discourage children from sex-typical play but to supplement those activities with experiences that encourage the development of many competences (ZERO TO THREE, 2003).

THIS ONE'S for YOU!

Motor Development and Movement

As you are reading this chapter, have you sat still for an uninterrupted time? Or did you get up to move around some? Did you take a break for a while during your reading? Did you get up to call and talk with a friend on the phone?

Consider how adults learn. Sometimes when they are working, adults need to spread out materials on a floor or table. At other times, adults retreat to a "snug spot" to read and reflect. At other times, adults need to talk with friends to chat about work and ideas.

None of these facts are surprising to you. Yet they are surprising when we start to apply these same facts to children.

With children, do we allow the same flexibility in space and preferences that we, as adults, take for granted in our learning environment?

Children need the same access—access to a range of working spaces, access to materials, access to other children and adults. We need to provide environments for children that have different working spaces to meet the demands of a child's particular task and way of making meaning.

Especially for older children, rather than having their own assigned seat or desk, children can be members of a wider creative workshop community, sitting where and with whom they need to for the task at hand.

In early childhood classrooms, children need the flexibility to change where they are working depending on the varied needs and nature of their tasks. Socially it allows them to work alone when they need undisturbed time or to seek out spaces that accommodate two or three others when they need to share ideas or to help each other. This in turn leads to far greater independence within the class. Children know they can turn to others besides the teacher for help and feedback, and they are likely to work toward solving their problems as part of a community rather than passively sitting at their desks, waiting for a teacher's help.

A classroom with this kind of flow and movement can be disconcerting to parents—and some teachers—the first time they experience it. But having watched this type of environment over the years, it is clear that these conditions add to children's abilities to work for longer periods of time than many adults imagine.

Just like adults, children need spaces to work, not one designated space. Assigning children to one work spot day after day doesn't give them the chance to learn how they work best. Children, in their workplaces and creative environments, need the same tools adults do. This doesn't mean that there is one magic formula for the physical layout of the classroom. Teachers create different environments with their children that set the stage for stimulating learning.

For example, one teacher used this arrangement: She set up her room with a variety of areas rather than centers. Over one small round table hung a sign, "Quiet! Genius at work." This was a place designated for children to work where they wouldn't be disturbed. Other tables were pushed together, in fours or twos, and there were several longer tables that would seat up to six children for larger group work. At one point in the year, this teacher's classroom included a listening area with many books created by the children and "published" in class as well as recordings of children reading their stories; a bird feeder outside the window with pads of paper and pencils for observations; and a long publishing table with enough room to spread out covers, glue, binding materials, and labels. Organizing the classroom with areas like these shows the thought this teacher put into planning for the resources that children might need. What a difference from an assigned seat and a set schedule!

As children grow and develop through art, they begin to use words such as *thick, thin, hard, soft, straight, curved, dark, light, smooth,* and *sticky.* Vocabulary that indicates direction is also quickly assimilated into the children's arena of understanding when they work with art materials. Five-year-old children show how much they have learned with statements like these: "I wrote my name at the top," "I put a board under the clay," and "I drew smoke coming out of the chimney."

The teacher introduces words like *soft* and *smooth* to describe the feel of velvet material. Scraps of burlap are called *rough, bumpy,* or *scratchy.* Even the word *texture* is one that can be used with young children. As they feel the different kinds of cloth, the different "feels" can easily be called "textures." Children then put together in their minds the feel of the velvet with the words soft, smooth, and texture. This is sensorimotor learning—learning through sensing as well as by association.

Learning to notice the different way things feel teaches a child about concepts that are opposite, which are important in subjects like math and science. The difference between hard and soft is similar to the difference between adding and subtracting in math; both ideas are opposites. A child learns in art that soft is not the same as hard. In math, a child learns that adding is different than or the opposite of subtracting. Mastering opposite concepts used in doing artwork thus helps the child learn the mental concepts needed later in other school subjects.

ART AND THE TOTAL PROGRAM

The early childhood art program helps a young child grow in social, emotional, physical, and mental ways. It gives children a chance to be themselves and grow at their own individual paces.

Art should not be the only part of the early childhood program where this growth can occur, however. Freedom for growing at the child's own pace should be part of the whole early childhood program. The exploring, creating, and relaxing parts of artwork should be part of all the other early childhood activities. (Activities in these other program areas are included in subsequent chapters.)

Art helps a child grow through creative thinking and feeling, not only about art but about all other things. The confidence and good feelings about themselves and their work that children develop in art apply to other things in and out of school. Seen in this way, art cannot be thought of as a separate part of the program. It is and always must be an approach to learning inseparable from all the rest.

SUMMARY

Young children learn mentally as they do things physically. In the art program, they learn many important concepts that are used later in other learning experiences. Art activities involve children in sensorimotor learning through the use of the body, senses, and mind. Involving all the senses in art activities helps provide a complete learning experience for young children.

Young children learn important concepts such as hard/soft and same/different by doing artwork. Artwork also helps in developing their mental abilities: learning to think flexibly; being able to see fine differences; being able to hear, listen, and follow directions; and learning new words. Finally, art helps them develop a creative mental attitude that will help in all school subjects. The creative aspects of art cannot and should not be separate from the total early childhood program.

KEY TERMS

cephalocaudal development	motor development
fine motor development	proximodental
flexible thinking	development
gross motor development	sensorimotor
hand–eye coordination	visual acuity

LEARNING ACTIVITIES

1. Observe children in a preschool program. Include observations in these program areas: (a) art center; (b) block center; and (c) housekeeping center. Describe the small and large motor development of children as demonstrated by their play in each of these areas.

2. Using the information in Figure 10–6, create your own suggested activities for each of the age groups presented in this chart.

3. Listen to a group of children painting. Record or take notes on their conversations. Compare your observations to the information in this chapter on

vocabulary and art. Discuss your findings with your classmates.

4. Observe in an early childhood classroom. Survey and describe the equipment and materials in the room for suitability for the following:
(a) small and large motor activities
(b) hand–eye coordination activities

(c) reading readiness activities
(d) motor coordination activities

5. Using your observations from #4, describe the strengths and weaknesses of the supplies and equipment in the classroom you observed. What would you suggest as ways to improve it?

ACTIVITIES FOR CHILDREN

The following activities are designed to help the child exercise both small and large muscle skills and develop hand–eye coordination. Students should try the activities themselves, with classmates, and with children.

SMALL MOTOR ACTIVITIES

Box Weaving. Weaving teaches children about patterns and the basic idea of how fabric is made. It also encourages small-motor skills, sequential thinking, and understanding spatial relationships.

Materials: lid of a box (preferably cardboard), a variety of colorful yarn, hole punch, plastic needle, scissors

Preparation: Prepare the box lid for weaving by punching holes around the entire edge of the box approximately ½ inch apart.

Procedure: With two or three children watching, demonstrate how to put the end of the yarn through a hole and tie it securely (make the knot on the inside of the box lid). Put the yarn through a needle and let the children thread the yarn across the box lid, going back and forth into different holes. Patterns may begin to appear. Show how a second colored yarn will add more pattern and color to the weavings. A third colored yarn can be added in the middle by weaving it in with the fingers. Let the children make their own patterns.

As the children become more experienced at handling yarn on a plastic needle, they can be encouraged to move on to the next kind of weaving. String yarn from the top to bottom of box lid. Using a piece of yarn threaded on a needle, the children will weave over and under, over and under, experiencing how real fabric is woven. Start at one end, leaving a tail to tie later. Make sure the yarn is stretched evenly and stays taut and rigid. Children will need help threading the yarn. They can do finger weaving using thicker yarn, which is less frustrating for little fingers.

Variations: For more artistic expression, beads and feathers can be incorporated into the weaving.

Tearing, Punching, and Stapling. Children love to just tear, punch, and staple. Keep a stack of old magazines and newspapers on hand for this purpose. It is great small motor practice and lots of fun for young children. If you do not have a paper punch or if the child is too young to use it, the child can use the handle of a wooden spoon to punch large holes in the paper.

If a paper punch is used, save the circles that the child punches from white waxed paper and put them in a jar full of water. After you fasten the lid on tightly, he or she can shake the jar and make a "snowstorm" inside.

Give the child a variety of paper, such as smooth, bumpy, heavy, and tissue-thin, all in different colors. Challenge the child to tear a tiny shape, an enormous shape, a wide shape, and so on. The child might enjoy pasting or stapling all of the interesting, ragged shapes on a long piece of paper for a big, colorful mural. Tape the mural on an empty wall for all to see!

ADDITIONAL SMALL MOTOR ACTIVITIES

A. Decorate a Shirt
Using wax crayons, have children color a picture on a white or light-colored shirt. Press with newspaper over the picture and on the ironing board. The picture will stay indefinitely.

B. Watercolors and Salt
Children love to paint with watercolors, but sometimes the colors seem too subtle and quiet. Once a picture is done (using enough water to make it a moist picture), bring out table salt and sprinkle a little over the picture while it is still wet. The salt causes the paint to separate and gives the painting a completely new look. This is a good activity to talk about *change* in objects and to discuss what the child *sees* as a change.

C. Printing with Feet and Hands
1. Equipment: Finger paint and finger paint paper.

2. Procedure: Children step in finger paint and print their right feet and left feet and then their hands. This work could be saved and used in social studies for a book "all about me."

D. Shaving Cream Art

An easy-to-do favorite is to take shaving cream and put a few squirts of it in an empty water table. Take food coloring and dye the shaving cream the color the children choose. Watching the shaving cream turn color is half the fun; the other half is to fingerpaint with the dyed shaving cream and save the design on paper. To save the design, put a clean sheet of white paper over the design drawn by the child, rub the paper, and lift. Hang to dry.

Shaving cream is also great to use when there are a few minutes until cleanup time and the children are bored with what they are doing. Squeeze a little dab of shaving cream on a table in front of each child. Show how it grows, changes, and how designs, mountains, and squeezy-feely shapes can be made from the cream. When time allotted is over, each child can clean up with a sponge. The children and the table will shine and smell good.

E. Creative "Find" Sculpture

On a neighborhood walk, on a field trip, or from a child's weekend trip with his family, collect an assortment of wood scraps such as driftwood, weathered boards, seashells, stones, twigs, dried flowers, pine cones, and leaves. Use either a flat stone or piece of wood for the base of the sculpture. The rest is up to the child's imagination; animals, designs, birds, etc., can be created. Simply assemble your creation and glue it together in place on the base. Markers can be used to draw in faces, make decorations, or add necessary details.

HAND-EYE COORDINATION ACTIVITIES

A. Water Pouring

Set up a pan filled with water. Provide different-sized plastic containers, squeeze bottles, funnels, and strainers. The children enjoy pouring water from one container to another.

B. Block Bowling

Set up a long unit block on the floor. The children sit in a circle around it. Each child has a chance to knock it down by rolling the ball at it.

C. Music and Painting

Play music while the children paint.

D. Ball Rolling

Play catch with the children who are able, or roll the ball to the children who cannot catch yet. Notice which ones can catch and return the ball. Compare this ability with their motor control in art.

E. Painting with Water (Outside Activity)

Fill a bucket with water and let the children "paint" the building or sidewalk with water. The children should use large paintbrushes (one to two inches wide) and buckets of water small enough to be carried around.

ACTIVITIES FOR CHECKING MOTOR CONTROL

A. Artwork Samples

Collect examples of artwork from children aged two to six years. Divide up the examples into the degree of children's motor control as seen in the examples.

B. Obstacle Course

Make an obstacle course of chairs, tables, or blocks to climb under, over, or around. Notice how easy or difficult it is for children aged three, four, and five.

C. Action Songs

Sing an action song, such as, "If You're Happy and You Know It," using different directions: "clap your hands," "clap your hands and tap your head," "clap your hands and shake your head." Notice which children can do the combined actions and which can do the single actions. Note their ages.

D. Rope Games

Put a long rope on the floor in a zigzag pattern and have the children walk on it. Note how many of the children can do this and how well they can do it. Put the rope in a straight line and pretend it is a tightrope. The children "walk the tightrope" with a real or pretend umbrella in their hands for balance. Note the balancing ability of each child. Two children take turns holding the rope very high at first and then gradually lower and lower. The rest of the children go under the rope without touching it. Place the rope straight out on the floor. The children walk across it, hop on one foot across it, hop on two feet across it, crawl across it, jump across it, and cross it any other way they can think of. Note each child's physical control.

LARGE MOTOR ACTIVITIES

A. Blanket Statues/Shapes (suitable for kindergarten and up)

Have children make shapes using their bodies. Have them experiment with as many shapes and forms they choose. Then involve the children in making "blanket statues." A child stays frozen in one position, and a blanket is placed over her to create a statue. Two children can create partner statues: one child rests on hands and knees and a second child rests on his back. Or two children stand three or four feet apart, facing one another, with their arms raised and reaching across, fingertips touching in an arch. These are just suggestions. Let the children's creativity direct their movement. This activity is a good opportunity for photographs that can later be displayed. Older children may want to write captions for their photographs, creating their own documentary of the activity.

B. Can You Guess What I Am?
Collect about 15 to 20 different animal pictures. Place these in a box on a chair over to one side. From a group of children (a small group of 4–5 children works best) seated on the floor, the teacher chooses one child to pick out a picture from the box. The child then acts out the animal in the picture for the others to guess. Whoever guesses the animal is the next to pick out a picture to act out. As a variation, use transportation pictures such as a train, truck, jet, car, boat, bus, etc.

C. Body Creations
Invite children to create different shapes by using their bodies. For example, three children might stretch out on the floor, joining their bodies in a way that creates a triangle. Later, four children can position their bodies to create a square, four others can create a rectangle, and so on. Ask others in the group if they know the names of the shapes their classmates are creating. Introduce terms such as *square, triangle,* and *rectangle.* Continue the activity until all children have had an opportunity to participate. Photograph the activity and post the photos where visitors can see them.

ACTIVITIES FOR THE SENSES

The following activities are designed to exercise the senses. Students should try the activities themselves, with classmates, and with children.

Seeing Activities
A. Exploring with a Magnifying Glass
Provide children magnifying glasses and a tray full of different objects—stamps, coins, rocks, leaves, etc. Encourage young children to talk about what they are seeing. They might also want to draw or paint what they've seen.

With older children, talk about the qualities of color, line, shape, and other visual elements they see magnified in the objects. Provide opportunities to sketch what they see. Challenge them to draw a pattern or design using what they've seen in the magnifying glass.

Use the magnifying glass outside on a nature walk. Encourage the children to talk about what they see. Provide them opportunities to express their reactions to "nature under glass" in two- and three-dimensional activities.

B. Paper Towel Telescopes
Collect paper towel rolls for telescopes. The children use the paper towel roll to see their world in a sharper focus. Looking through a tube such as this helps children concentrate on a single area of focus.

Encourage children to talk about what they see. Maybe later they will want to draw or paint about what they have seen. Older children can be challenged to see if they can see specific elements of design through their telescope.

C. Examining Objects in Different Colors
(Silverblatt, 1964)
1. Use different-colored pieces of transparent plastic or colored cellophane.
2. The children look at the things around them through transparent, colored material. They can see how the brown table looks through "yellow" or how the blue sky looks through "red," for example.
3. When the children seem to understand how the color of different objects changes when seen through another color and have been satisfied using just a single color, they may look through two colors at once (superimpose red over blue) and see still another change.

D. See Through Colors
Looking through color strips will help children learn how colors combine to make new colors—specifically, how the combination of two primary colors creates a secondary color. The children can relate the colors to familiar objects.

Materials: scissors; red, yellow, and blue cellophane papers. (You can find colored cellophane paper in the wrapping paper section of a variety store. It is most readily available at Easter time when it is used to cover baskets.)

Preparation: Cut the red, blue, and yellow cellophane into strips about 4 inches long and 2 inches wide.

Procedure: Gather four children together. Give each child a color strip. Have them first look through their individual color strips by holding them up to the light. Each child names something that is the color of the strip—for example, blue is the color of water or the sky. Each child should have a turn.

Put children with different color strips into pairs. Each child in the pair looks through the two strips to see what new colors are made. The teacher then gives each pair another strip, making sure that each pair has a set of red, blue, and yellow. Allow children to explore and exchange color strips. When the interest is waning, call the children together. Let each pair name the colors produced, and name something that is that color.

Variations: Allow children to cut up pieces of cellophane to make their own color combinations. They could tape the pieces together to make stained glass designs.

Encourage the expression of emotional and impressionistic responses of the children caused by colors. For example, yellow is the color of sunshine and it makes me feel happy. Blue is the color of the ocean and I like the waves in the ocean.

E. Shadow Guessing

In this activity, children learn about the interaction of light, shadows, and distance. Shadow play also encourages creative expression.

You will need a flashlight or lamp, a sheet, and different kinds of fruit for this activity.

Hang a sheet up in the room in front of a table. Put several kinds of fruit on the table.

From behind the sheet, shine a light on the fruit one at a time. Bananas, grapes, apples, and other fruits will puzzle the children as they try to guess the type of fruit and to figure out how they are appearing on the sheet.

Then, again with a small group, shine a flashlight or other light source on a wall in the dramatic play area. Children use their fingers to produce shadow figures. They will enjoy making rabbit ears, a duck, a dog, a monster, or just abstract forms. Children can also use puppets, and the teacher can add music to allow for rhythmic movements and self-expression. Have the children move their puppets closer and farther from the light source and observe how the shadows change.

In a large group outdoors, on a bright day, encourage children to make silly movements and observe their own shadows. You can even introduce a quick "copy cat" (follow-the-leader) game: "Everybody jump! Everybody hop! Now, everybody dance!"

HEARING ACTIVITIES

A. Room Noises
  1. The children close their eyes and name the different sounds they hear in the room.
  2. Make up noises and sounds (birds singing, blocks dropping, sawing wood, bells, drums and other instruments, tearing paper, water splashing, for example). Have the children guess what they are.
  3. A child closes both eyes while another child speaks. The first child tries to guess who is speaking.

B. Rattlesnake
  You will need a small plastic bottle with beans inside. The group closes their eyes and the "leader" walks around shaking the bottle. The group then points to the direction from which they hear the sound and identifies the level of sound (i.e., "high" or "low"). This can be played with one child as well.

C. Sound Cans
  Place four different substances—a small block, a piece of clay, a piece of cotton, small amount of sand—in four identical cans. When all the lids are on, shuffle the cans. The child guesses what is in each can by the noise made as the can is shaken.

D. Parrot Talk
  Use a paper bag puppet of a parrot, or just use your hands and fingers to look like the mouth of a parrot talking. Discuss with the child how parrots like to repeat everything they hear. Let the child speak first while you are the parrot and repeat everything the child says. Then you speak first and the child repeats. Begin with a single word and build up to a full sentence.

  Nonsensical words may also be used. Variation: Talk with the child about echoes and how they repeat the sounds two or three times. After you have echoed something the child has said or a noise the child has made, by tapping for instance, let the child be *your* echo.

SMELLING AND TASTING ACTIVITIES

A. Painted Toast
  Make "paint" with 1/4 cup of milk and a few drops of food coloring. Paint designs or faces on white bread with a clean paintbrush. Toast the bread in a toaster. The bread can be buttered and eaten or used as part of a sandwich. This is a very popular tasting experience!

B. Community Fruit Salad
  1. To further experiment with how things taste, the children may help make a community fruit salad. Each child brings a different fruit: apples, peaches, pears, seedless grapes, tangerines.
  2. The children help peel bananas and oranges, wash grapes, and cut the fruit with blunt or serrated knives.
  3. The children should taste each fruit separately as they are preparing the salad. Then they should taste how the fruits taste together.

4. Talk about how each fruit tastes, looks, and smells different from the others.

ACTIVITIES FOR OLDER CHILDREN (GRADES 4–5)

A. Link Art to Dance and Physical Movement
Older children have well-developed large and small muscles as well as good overall motor coordination. Challenge them to use these skills in creative ways. Choose several artists' works that have a good deal of movement in the composition. Some suggestions are Van Gogh's "Starry Night," Jackson Pollock's "Water Birds," Jacob Lawrence's "Strike," or Edgar Degas' "Ballet Scene." Review with the children the elements of line and movement in art, while viewing one of the prints. Have them discuss the ways the artist used lines in the painting to show movement. Tell students that they will take turns modeling and drawing different movements. Then have volunteers pantomime individually or in small groups various kinds of movements such as those in dance, in a sport, or in a type of exercise. Have students observing the movement draw lines that represent or reflect the movements they are seeing. Continue the activity until students have filled their sheet of drawing paper with colorful lines. Then have students exchange roles.

B. Understanding Composition by Posing a Picture
One of the most effective ways to help students understand the overall composition or structure of a work of art is to have them pose as a painting or sculpture. This requires some advance preparation on the part of the teacher. Scour your attic, basement, closets, the local resale shop for old items of clothing and props that resemble those depicted in the artwork you have chosen to pose. Some suggestions for this posing activity would be Diego Rivera's "The Flower Carrier," Jan Van Eyck's "Arnolfini Marriage," George Caleb Bingham's "Wood Boatmen on a River," Pieter de Hooch's "Interior with People," or Van Gogh's "The Bedroom of Van Gogh at Arles."

Be creative. For example, posing "Washington Crossing the Delaware" by Leutz, you might borrow oars from a boat store.

Assign clothing, props, and their position to your students and have them really study that part of the painting to notice facial expressions, body positions, relationship to other figures, the background, and so forth. If you have a large group, split it in half or thirds and have an audience comment on the accuracy of each group's pose. Everyone gets to participate, and students remember the artwork better by recalling their own part in it. Posing is not only great fun but also of value in increasing understanding. For example, ask students which poses were easier to hold in order to point out how some paintings create a feeling of motion or imbalance, while others give the impression of equilibrium or stability.

C. Recreating a Still Life
A similar activity to posing can be done for still life painting. This involves having the children recreate with real objects one of the paintings they have been studying. The teacher brings in as many items as possible that are found in the artwork.

Ask each child to identify an object and place it in its proper position so that the finished arrangement approximates the original as closely as possible. This exercise enables students to comprehend some of the basic concerns of the still life painter: the use of light, the concepts of balance and harmony, the question of focus, and the problem of rendering three-dimensional objects on a two-dimensional surface.

Some suggestions of art to use with this activity are William J. McCloskey's "Wrapped Oranges," Albert Dummouchel's "Still Life," Margaret Burroughs' "Still Life," Laura Wheeler Waring's "Still Life," and Gustave Caillebotte's "Fruit Displayed on a Stand."

D. Shadowplay
Students often have difficulty determining the source of light in a painting. A simple way to demonstrate how shadows help us determine where light is coming from is to shine a flashlight on a ball from a variety of angles (behind the ball, to the left of the ball, above the ball, below the ball). Place the flashlight in the position before turning it on and ask the students if they can guess where the shadow will fall. (This exercise works best if the area around the ball is fairly plain and darkened somewhat so that the shadows can be seen clearly. Also the flashlight beam should be smaller than the ball.) One school did this activity near Groundhog's Day and substituted a toy stuffed animal for the ball.

E. Matching Colors Under Different Lights
To demonstrate to students that light influences the way we see color, bring in various paint chips or cloth swatches. Be sure to have multiples of the same color available. Have the students view identical color samples under different light sources (fluorescent, incandescent, and natural). They will soon discover that it is almost impossible to match colors under different lighting conditions. The most accurate light for viewing colors is daylight.

F. More Telescopes

Visual perceptiveness is an important skill that comes into use not only when looking at a painting, but when reading a book, examining a map, even doing a math problem. To hone this ability, encourage students to look carefully for details in a painting. One way to accomplish this is to use "telescopes." These are simply four-by-six-inch index cards that students roll up into tubes and look through. The teacher can ask them to find certain things in a painting and will be able to tell by the angle of the telescopes if the child is looking in the correct place. This is a technique artists have used themselves. Frederic Church handed out a rolled up piece of cardboard to everyone who came to see his painting "Heard of the Andes" when it was exhibited in 1864.

G. Magnification—Once Again

The use of a magnifying glass can heighten the enjoyment for older children when looking at certain paintings, especially those that are extremely detailed. Allow the students to use the magnifying glass one at a time and give them specific instructions as to what they should find. Explain to them that artists use very thin brushes in order to paint the tiniest details. The sixteenth-century Flemish master, Pieter Brueghel the Elder, supposedly used only a few cat's hairs as a brush for his miniscule figures. Thus, a magnifying glass enables us to appreciate the artist's creation more thoroughly. It also intrigues students to see even more than the eye alone can see.

H. Creative Color Thinking

Ask the children to gather in small groups. Ask a recorder in each group to write down, in columns, the names of the basic colors on the color wheel. Have the students identify adjectives that are often used to describe varieties of each color such as "sky" blue, "fire engine" red, and "grass" green. While the students work, set up columns on the board so students can compile the unique adjectives and place tally marks by those identified by more than one group. Discuss the connotations of the adjectives for yellow, red, and orange in relation to ideas or experiences of warmth. Discuss the connotations of the words listed for blue, green, and violet in relation to experiences of coolness.

I. Online Learning: Enlighten Me

Check out the Web site http://www.superpages.com/enlightenme, sponsored by Verizon and Fablevision. Play the Peetnik Mystery using a phone book, a *Who's Who,* and a map to help Penn Peetnik and his friends solve a mystery. In this activity, students make "phone calls" and find locations, which helps them practice mapping skills, research, and real-life problem solving to find clues that lead to a solution. Also on this site, children can make a book, write a book review, or print Super Thinker posters. Super Thinkers also has games, stories, and many more activities.

CHAPTER REVIEW

A. Physical Development
   1. Define motor development.
   2. List three examples of locations of small muscles.
   3. Define small motor activities and give three examples.
   4. Define large motor activities and give three examples.
   5. List three examples of locations of large muscles.
   6. Tell whether each of the following activities helps a child develop a small or a large motor skill.
      a. tracing body forms
      b. using scissors
      c. pounding clay
      d. finger painting
      e. finger puppets
      f. painting with a brush
      g. pounding nails
      h. clay modeling
   7. Choose the answer that best completes each statement describing a child's motor development in art.
      a. Most three year olds
         (a) have good small muscle development.
         (b) do not have good small muscle development.
         (c) have good small and large muscle development.
      b. One way to check small motor skill is by having a child
         (a) pound on clay.
         (b) walk a balance board.
         (c) cut paper with blunt scissors.

c. Development of the body goes from
(a) small muscles to large muscles.
(b) large muscles to small muscles.
(c) arms to legs.

d. In order to be able to use small muscles, a child must first be able to use
(a) finger muscles.
(b) large muscles.
(c) eye muscles.

e. By the time children are in preschool, they can use
(a) small muscles quite well.
(b) both large and small muscles quite well.
(c) large muscles quite well.

f. An art activity that exercises large motor skills is
(a) painting on large-sized paper with a wide brush.
(b) cutting paper with scissors.
(c) finger painting.

g. In planning the art program, a teacher should include
(a) mostly large motor activities for four year olds.
(b) mostly small motor activities for three year olds.
(c) both large and small motor activities for all ages.

h. The age group that uses mostly large muscle activity is the
(a) three year old.
(b) four year old.
(c) five year old.

i. A teacher in the art program should let children know that they are free to
(a) use only small motor activity.
(b) try all types of activities.
(c) try only large motor activity.

8. Define hand–eye coordination and give two examples of it.

9. Discuss what reading experts say about the importance of hand–eye coordination.

10. Describe how one can see motor control develop in a child's artwork.

B. Mental Development

1. Define sensorimotor learning and give one example of it.

2. Which of the following mental concepts does a child learn in art by the sense of touch?
a. new words
b. hard/soft
c. true/false
d. large/small
e. smooth/rough

f. names of colors
g. feel of clay
h. difference in shades of color
i. feel of play dough
j. sweet/sour

3. Choose the answer that best completes each of the following statements about how art helps mental development.

a. Concepts are
(a) phrases.
(b) songs.
(c) ideas.

b. The mental concept of opposites learned in art is also used in
(a) math.
(b) finger plays.
(c) cooking.

c. Introducing new words in art activity
(a) often confuses the children.
(b) helps improve the child's vocabulary.
(c) has little effect on young children.

d. An example of an activity that improves the sense of touch is
(a) a piano lesson.
(b) work on a collage.
(c) a seeing game.

e. Some concepts of color a child learns in art are
(a) how to erase color errors, paint over, and choose colors.
(b) how to choose colors, mix colors, and color over.
(c) names of colors, how to mix colors, and how to make colors lighter or darker.

f. An important new way of thinking that a child learns in art is
(a) flexible thinking.
(b) inflexible thinking.
(c) permanent thinking.

g. Seeing and learning that clay can have many shapes and textures helps the child develop
(a) inflexible thought.
(b) flexible thought.
(c) permanent thinking.

h. In artwork, very young children often use the senses of
(a) touch and sight only.
(b) smell, taste, touch, sight, and hearing.
(c) touch and smell only.

4. Discuss development of a creative mental attitude as a goal in the art program for young children.

5. Discuss what other aspects of the school program should be like the art program.

6. Should art be considered a separate part of the preschool program? Explain your answer.

REFERENCES

Gallaghue, D. L., & Ozmun, J. (1997). *Understanding motor development: Infants, children, adolescents, adults* (4th ed.). New York: McGraw Hill.

Piaget, J. (1955). *The child's conception of reality.* London: Routledge & Kegan.

Silverblatt, I. M. (1964). *Creative activities.* Cincinnati, OH: Author.

ZERO TO THREE Brain Wonders (2003). Boston University School of Medicine, The Erickson Institute, http://www.zerotothree.org/brainwonders/FAQ-body.html.

ADDITIONAL READINGS

Andrews, A., & Trafton, P. R. (2001). *Little kids—Powerful problem solvers.* Portsmouth, NH: Heinemann.

Berk, L. E. (2001). *Awakening children's minds: How parents and teachers make a difference.* New York: Oxford University Press.

Bronson, M. (2000). *Self-regulation in early childhood: Nature and nurture.* New York: Guilford.

Efland, A. D. (2003). *Art and cognition.* Richmond, VA: National Art Education Association.

Katz, L. G., & Chard, S. C. (2000). *Engaging children's minds: The project approach.* Norwood, NJ: Ablex.

Piaget, J. (1955) (2001). *The language and thought of the child* (2nd ed.). Reprint. New York: Routledge.

Piaget, J. (1977). *The development of thought: Equilibration of cognitive structures.* New York: Viking.

Shore, R. (1997). *Rethinking the brain: New insights into early development.* New York: Families and Work Institute.

Wasserman, S. (2000). *Serious players in the primary classroom: Empowering children through active learning experiences* (2nd ed.). New York: Teachers College Press.

HELPFUL WEB SITES

http://www.rie.org
Resources for infant educators.

http://www.highscope.org
The High/Scope Educational Research Foundation.

http://www.ericec.org/
Information center on Gifted Education and Disabilities.

http://www.worksamplingonline.com
Online checklists designed at the University of Michigan.

http://www.zerotothree.org
Boston University School of Medicine, the Erikson Institute.

http://www.project-approach.com
Background information on projects for preschool through grade 6.

For additional creative activity resources, visit our Web site at http://www.EarlyChildEd.delmar.com.

Chapter 11

Developmental Levels and Art

Objectives

After studying this chapter, you should be able to

1. Describe the scribble stage, including appropriate materials for use in this stage.

2. Explain the basic forms (preschematic) stage, including appropriate materials for use in this stage.

3. Discuss the pictorial (schematic) stage, including appropriate materials for use in this stage.

4. Discuss appropriate art activities and materials for toddlers, young preschoolers, older preschoolers, kindergartners, and grades 1 through 5.

As children grow older, they change in height and weight and gain new skills. They also develop different abilities in art. The artwork of a three year old is different from that of a four or five year old. It is different in the way it looks, as well as in the way it is made.

For many years people have been trying to explain why all children the world over draw in the way they do. There are many theories of children's art, each of which offers an explanation for why children produce art and suggests strategies for teachers. Basic to all of these theories are two facts. The first is that all children go through definite stages in their development of art. The second is that the pace of each child's development in art varies with the child.

DEVELOPMENTAL LEVELS/STAGES OF ART

Just as young children experience various stages of physical development, they also develop art abilities in a gradual process, going through specific stages. These stages are called **developmental levels.** A developmental level is a guide to what a child can do in art at different ages, but it is not a strict guideline. Some children may be ahead or behind the developmental level for their age. Developmental levels tell the teacher what came before and what is to come in the artwork of the young child.

There is no exact pattern for each age level. Not all three year olds behave alike, nor are they completely different from four year olds. But there is a gradual growth process, called *development,* that almost every child goes through. An understanding of developmental levels helps an adult accept each child at the child's present level, whatever it is.

From 1830, when Ebenezer Cooke first drew attention to the successive stages of development found in children's drawings, to Rhoda Kellogg's *Analyzing Children's Art* (1970), and Viktor Lowenfeld's *Creative and Mental Growth of the Child* (1987), teachers have based their objectives for art activities on the idea that children's art is developmental. Ability in art develops as the child grows and matures. Each stage is a part of the natural and normal aspects of child growth and development. These stages are sequential, with each stage characterized by increasing progress. Even though stages in art have been identified and accepted, the age at which children progress through these stages is highly *individual*. As children's bodies and minds mature, so does their art ability. Children learn to paint, model, and build as they learn to walk—slowly, developing in their own way. They learn each new step in the process as they are ready for it. As a general guide, art development progresses from experimentation and exploration (the scribble stage in drawing), to the devising of basic forms, to the forming of symbolic figures and their naming.

Older children continue to develop and refine their abilities in art as they create more complex works of art and give greater attention to their expressive intentions. Children ages nine to 11 are in what Lowenfeld calls the **gang stage.** The title of this stage reflects the fact that children of this age are more independent of adults and more anxious to conform to their peers.

The following discussion of the development of children's drawing is intended to serve as a general guide to the overall process development in art. The basic developmental levels, or stages, apply to all art media. For the sake of clarity, children's drawing will be the primary focus of the discussion.

CHILDREN'S DRAWING

There are three developmental levels in drawing that are of concern to the early childhood teacher: the **scribble stage,** the **basic forms stage,** and the **pictorial** (or first drawings) **stage.** The realism stage, generally covering children ages 9 years and above, is of concern for teachers in the upper elementary levels.

THE SCRIBBLE STAGE

Most children begin scribbling at about one and one-half to two years of age. Children can be given a crayon or marker as soon as they no longer put everything in their mouth. They will scribble with anything at hand and on anything nearby. Their first marks are usually an aimless group of lines. Yet these first scribbles are related to later drawing and painting. They are related to art just as a baby's first babbling sounds are related to speech.

The crayon may be held upside down, sideways, with the fist, between clenched fingers, or with either hand. Children may be pleased with this scribbling and get real enjoyment from it. They enjoy the physical motions involved in scribbling. It is the act of doing—not the final product—that is important to the child. When they get their hands on materials, they begin to manipulate and explore randomly. This exploration delights the child, therefore leading to further manipulation and discovery.

If you watch a baby draw or a toddler scribbling, you know it is a sensorimotor activity. As a child draws or paints, every part of the body moves, all working to move the crayon or brush across the paper. Once the child begins the movement, it's difficult to stop! As a consequence, whatever surface the child is working on often becomes covered with paint and crayon.

⊙ **Every child is an artist. The problem is how to remain an artist once we grow up.** Pablo Picasso

⊙ **It took me 4 years to paint like Raphael, but a lifetime to paint like a child.** Pablo Picasso

Early Scribble Stage: Disordered or Random Scribbling

During the early scribble stage, the young child does not have control over hand movements or the marks on a page. Thus this stage is called **disordered** or

Figure 11-1

Small muscles of the hands are used in scribbling.

random scribbling. The marks are random and go in many directions. The direction of the marks depends on whether the child is drawing on the floor or on a low table. The way the crayon is held also affects how the scribbles look. But the child is not able to make the crayon go in any one way on purpose. There is neither the desire nor the ability to control the marks. (See Figure 11–2 for some examples of random scribbles.)

Because it is the sensory experience of making marks that's important at this stage, the child doesn't even realize that she is producing these scribbles. The connection between herself and the scribbles isn't made by the early scribbler. In fact, these children receive as much satisfaction from just handling the materials—dumping the crayons out of the box, putting them back in again, rolling them across the table or in their hands—as they do from scribbling!

Art is such a sensory experience at this age that children may use crayons in both hands as they draw, singing along in rhythm to the movements they are making. They may not even notice the crayon they're working with isn't leaving marks on the paper.

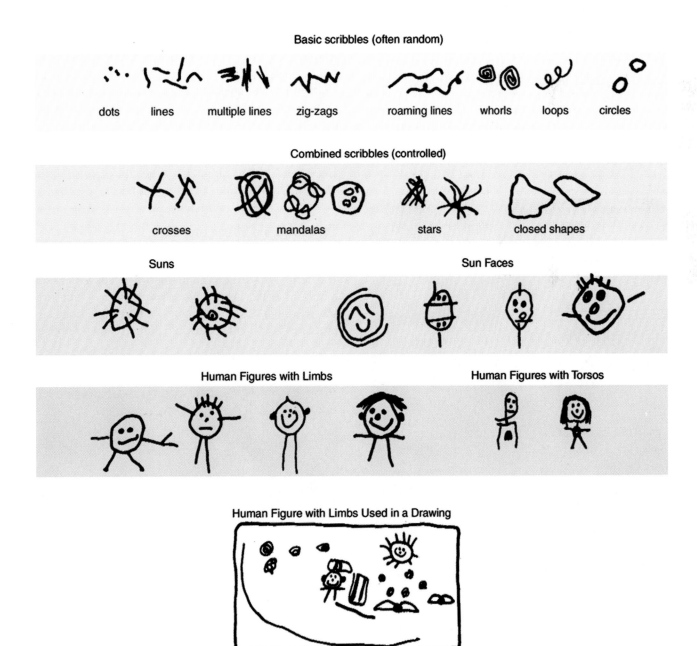

Figure 11-2
Examples of development in children's drawing (from Feeney et al., 1995). Printed with permission from Prentice Hall.

Because it is the process that is important to children when they're toddlers, there's no need to label their scribbles with their names or ask for stories or titles to accompany the scribbles. For young children in the early scribble stage, it is appropriate for adults to comment on the process. Focusing on the process, you might say, "You covered the entire paper," "Your whole arm moved as you worked," or "You moved your crayon all around and around." These are the kinds of comments appropriate in the scribble stage. They are *specific* and they are geared to the developmental level of the child. Be sure to save samples of scribbles from time to time, using portfolios to keep a visual record of the child's progress. (Portfolios are discussed in detail later in this chapter.)

Later Scribble Stage: Controlled Scribbling

At some point, children find a connection between their motions and the marks on the page. This may be about six months after the child has started to scribble, but the time will vary with each child. This very important step is called **controlled scribbling.** The child has now found it possible to control the marks. Many times, an adult cannot see any real difference in these drawings. They still look like scribbles—but they are different in a very important way.

The child's gradual gaining of control over scribbling motion is a vital experience for the child. She or he now is able to make the marks go in the direction desired. Most children scribble at this later stage with a great deal of enthusiasm because coordination between seeing and doing is an important achievement.

Because children enjoy this newfound power, they are encouraged to try new motions. They now may scribble in lines, zigzags, or circles. When they repeat motions, it means they are gaining control over certain movements. They can become very involved in this type of scribbling.

In this later scribbling stage, repeated movements among the scribbles begin to appear. At a basic level, the child is beginning to organize his or her environment. One universal form seen most often in this stage is the *mandella*. They are a variety of circular patterns (see Figure 11–2). During this stage children also make sweeping, wavy, bold, and rippling lines.

The Scribble Stage and Two-Dimensional Media

The term **two-dimensional media** refers to any art form that is flat. Art in two dimensions has only two sides, front and back. Examples of two-dimensional art processes are painting, drawing, printing, and scribbling.

Figure 11-3

Small motor development may be observed in other activities such as sewing with yarn.

Figure 11-4

A two-finger grip on a crayon is a sign of good motor control.

Children just beginning to scribble need tools that are safe and easy to hold and use. For a child between the ages of one and one-half and three years, large, nontoxic crayons are good tools for two-dimensional artwork. Pencils are dangerous for the young child and are also too difficult to hold and use. A good-quality, kindergarten-type crayon is the best tool. Crayon quality is determined by how much wax can be scratched off the paper—the more wax, the poorer the quality. The child will have to press so hard to get a good color that his fingers (and the resulting drawings) will become cramped. The smaller the child, the better (and bigger) the crayons should be. The crayon should be large and unwrapped so it can be used on both the sides and ends. Good-quality crayons are strong enough to hold up to rough first scribbles. They also make bright, clear colors, which are pleasant for the child to use.

Because motion is the chief enjoyment in this stage, the child needs large blank paper (at least 18″ × 24″). This size allows enough room for wide arm movements and large scribbles in many directions. The paper should always be large enough to give the child a big open space for undirected, random scribbles. Paper can be in a variety of shapes, such as triangular, circular, oval, etc.

If possible, a child in the scribble stage should use large white paper. Crayon scribbles show up better on white paper, so the child can see more easily the results of the scribbling. The classified section of the newspaper is also appropriate paper for beginning artists. The small print of the advertisements makes a neutral, nonintrusive background for scribbling, and this section of the paper provides a generous supply of material for young scribblers, which encourages the frequency of their scribbling.

The child needs only a few crayons at a time. Because motor control is the main focus in the early period of the scribbling stage, too many different crayons may distract the child in the scribbling process. A box of 32 crayons, for example, would become an object of exploration itself and hence a distraction from the act of scribbling. This type of interruption breaks up arm movement as well as total physical involvement. New crayons may be added when a new drawing is started. The tools should mark clearly and flow easily.

Painting is another good two-dimensional art activity for children in the scribble stage because it offers children the most fluidity. Paintbrushes for two and three year olds need to have 12-inch handles and ¾-inch to 1-inch bristles. Paint for two- and three-year-old children should be mixed with a dry soap so it is thick enough to control. The paper for painting may need to be heavier than newsprint because children will repeatedly paint the paper until it disintegrates. For these first painting activities, beginners should paint while seated at a flat table rather than stand at an easel. It is difficult for young painters to control drips on an easel. Also, these beginning artists are likely to become distracted if they are standing at an easel and wander off. Pasting, tearing paper, and soap and finger painting are also two-dimensional art activities enjoyed by most children of this age. A good deal of monitoring is required with toddlers because they are tempted to taste the materials and carry them about the room. For toddlers the major value lies in simple experimentation with the colors and textures.

Observation of the Scribble Stage

The student observer of young children (ages one and one-half to three years) should keep in mind the following points in observing scribbling. A copy of the observation sheet (Figure 11–5) may be used to record your observations.

Age. Note the age of the child. Keep in mind the average range for the scribble stage (one and one-half to three years). See how the child fits in the range. There may be an overlap between stages.

Motor control. Note how the child holds the crayon: with two fingers, clenched fingers, or a fist. If the child uses a two-finger grip, this is the start of good motor control. The other methods of holding the crayon show less motor control. See if the child can hold the crayon without dropping it during the entire drawing. This also shows good motor control. Note any other things that might show the child's degree of motor control.

Arm movements. In scribbling, a child may use one type of arm movement or a variety. Note if movements are wide, long, short, jabbing, or of other kinds. The type of arm movement used affects the basic forms the child will make in the future. For example, if circular scribbles are being made, later these scribbles become circles.

Types of scribbles. Note the kind of scribbles the child is making. They may be controlled or uncontrolled, circular, lines, or others mentioned earlier.

Use of paper. There are many ways of using paper for scribbling. Some are moving across the paper from left to right, moving across the paper from right to left, scribbling on only one part of the page, and moving

CHILD	AGE	MOTOR CONTROL	ARM MOVEMENTS	TYPES OF SCRIBBLES	USE OF PAPER	EARLY PERIOD	LATER PERIOD

COMMENTS:

Figure 11-5

Scribble stage observation form. (See the Online Companion™ for an example of how to complete this form.)

Figure 11-6

When young children practice new skills, allow enough space and time for their total involvement.

Figure 11-7

Controlled scribbling may not appear much different than random scribbling.

the paper to make marks in the other direction. See if the child seems to know how to use the paper. Older scribblers often have more control over the paper.

Try these activities, observing and noting what happens:

⊙ Provide the child with some soft, colored chalk. See if this new tool causes any differences in the way the child scribbles.

⊙ Change to smaller paper. See if there are any differences in the child's arm movement, type of scribbles made, and use of paper.

⊙ Place two extra colored crayons in the child's view. See if the child uses them. Then see if scribbles look different when the child uses many colors. Compare an all-one-color drawing with a many-color drawing.

THE BASIC FORMS/PRESCHEMATIC STAGE

Basic forms like rectangles, squares, and circles develop from scribbles as the child finds and recognizes simple shapes in the scribbles. More importantly, they develop as the child finds the muscle control and hand–eye coordination (use of hand(s) and eyes at the same time) to repeat the shape.

At this stage, the drawings look more organized. This is because the child is able to make basic forms by controlling the lines. A child in the age range of three to four years is usually in the basic forms stage. This stage is also referred to as the **preschematic stage.** This means that in this stage basic forms are drawn in and of themselves and not to represent a particular object. For example, the child draws a rectangular form over and over in a variety of sizes. At this point, this rectangle is *not* the child's schema or idea of a house. It is simply a controlled drawing of a basic form.

During this stage children hold their tools more like adults do and have a growing control over the materials. Children can now control their scribbles, making loops, circular shapes, and lines that are distinguishable and can be repeated at will. Children at this age value their scribbles. By age three or four, children will not draw if their marker is dry. Children now ask to have their names put on their work so it can be taken home or displayed in the room.

It is important to note, again, that there may be an overlap between developmental levels in art. For example, one three-year-old child may be drawing basic forms and an occasional scribble. Another three-year-old child may still be totally in the scribble stage. Developmental levels are meant merely as guidelines, not as set limits on age and ability levels.

Early Basic Forms Stage: Circle and Oval

Generally, the first basic form drawn is the oval or circle. This marks the **early basic forms stage.** It develops as children recognize the simple circle in their scribbles and are able to repeat it. Both the oval and the circle develop from circular scribbles. Following the discovery of the oval or circle, the child will begin to elaborate it by adding dots and perhaps lines.

Another early basic form in this stage is the curved line or arc. This is made with the same swinging movement of an arm used in the early scribble stage. Now, however, it is in one direction only. This kind of line gradually becomes less curved, and from it come the horizontal and vertical lines. Making an intentional arc-shaped line reflects more developed motor control.

Figure 11-8

For older children, many software programs allow them to continue creating in a different media.

Later Basic Forms: Rectangle and Square

As muscle control of three to four year olds continues to improve, more basic forms are made in their drawings. The rectangle and square forms are made when the child can purposefully draw separate lines of any length desired. The child joins the separate lines to form the rectangle or square. This indicates the **later basic forms stage.**

The circle, oval, square, and rectangle are all basic forms made by the child's control of lines.

The Basic Forms Stage and Two-Dimensional Media

Children in the basic forms stage have enough motor control and hand–eye coordination to use different tools. In addition to crayons, the child may now begin to work with tempera paint. Tempera paint is the best kind for children because it flows easily from the brush onto the page. Liquid tempera in 16-ounce squeeze bottles is a convenient way to provide paint for beginning painters. Powdered tempera is also appropriate because it can be mixed with water to the desired consistency (very thick for beginners). Be sure to mix dry tempera well out of children's reach because it contains silica, which is not safe for children to breathe.

Large lead pencils are good for children in the later period of this stage; there is less danger of injury with these older children. A variety of papers can be supplied, from newsprint to construction paper. These children should be allowed plenty of time with the basic tools of drawing, painting, modeling, cutting, and pasting and should not be rushed into other media. The basic developmental goal for this age is the control of the media and tasks of drawing, painting, or modeling. (A complete list of proper materials is included in Chapter 12 on selecting materials.)

Felt-tip pens or colored markers are excellent tools for this stage. They provide clear, quick, easily made, and nice-looking marks. In the basic forms stage, when the child really enjoys seeing the marks come out as desired, these pens are best. They require little pressure to make bold marks. Felt-tip pens should be nontoxic and water-soluble so that most spots can be washed out of the child's clothes. (See "Think About It . . . Marker Maintenance" for suggestions on prolonging the life of colored markers.)

Figure 11-9
Good motor control is shown by the child who uses more hand than arm movement.

Figure 11-10
Children in the basic forms stage enjoy repeating the forms over and over again in their work.

Figure 11-11
Basic forms drawings might look simple, but they represent a great motor achievement for the child.

The largest paper size is not as necessary in this stage as in the scribble stage. Because the child now has better motor control, it is easier to keep marks on a smaller space. Room for wide, uncontrolled movements is not as necessary. Make available paper of many sizes and shapes.

Also make available different colors and textures of paper and a variety of colored pencils and markers. Children in this stage like to make basic forms in many colors and ways as an exercise of their skill.

Student observers should realize that children of this age like to repeat forms and should not try to force them to "make something else" to fill up the paper. It is important that children practice making their own basic forms. The forms may look simple, but each drawing is a great motor achievement for them. The children may rightly be quite proud of their basic form drawings.

Observation of the Basic Forms Stage

The student observer of young children in the basic forms stage should keep in mind the following points when observing children. The points may then be recorded on a copy of the observation form, Figure 11–12. If students are observing children in both the scribbling and basic forms stages, observations of each stage may be compared to help highlight the differences in these two stages.

Age. Note the age of the child. Check Figure 11–25 for the average age range for the basic forms stage. See how the child fits in the range. See if there is an overlap between stages.

Motor control. See how the child holds the crayon. Note if it is held very tightly or if the child can draw with sureness and ease. Also note if the child draws with a lot of arm movement or uses just the hand to draw. The child who uses more hand movement and less arm movement is showing good motor control. In the basic forms stage, children use fewer unnecessary arm movements.

Types of basic forms. Write down the number and type of basic forms mentioned earlier that the child can draw. See if the shapes are well drawn or rough

THINK ABOUT IT... Why Children Draw

The most obvious reason children draw is for the sheer pleasure of it. How many times have you witnessed a small child completely engaged in drawing and humming a joyful tune? We can probably remember our own spontaneous experiences as being pleasurable ones. Spontaneous drawing is a type of drawing that is free and without rules or limitations for the artist. Spontaneous drawings encourage children to explore and experiment with their own thoughts and ideas while leaving a record of these on paper. This type of spontaneous drawing should be nurtured at all ages.

More reasons for drawing:

⊙ Children interact with their world and often use drawing as the medium to describe their experiences. Children's literacy skills are still developing; drawing allows them the means to communicate complex thoughts. Children's drawings tell us what they think and feel. One particular seven-year-old child drew a picture showing his mom coming home from the hospital with his new baby brother. The brother was drawn with a large smiling head and his mother was carrying him. The brother and mom were colored with bright colors and drawn with detail. Off to the side were the artist, his dad, and sister. They were drawn on a much smaller scale with little detail. It seems the message the artist was trying to convey in the drawing was that the new baby brother would become the center of attention and take much of his mother's time.

⊙ Drawing empowers children to experiment and practice various drawing techniques and processes. This, of course, can be achieved by art activities in school. The art program teaches children to observe, create, express, and experiment with the principles and elements of drawing.

⊙ Drawing allows the child to invent. In their drawings children create objects, characters, and worlds that erupt from the child's imagination. These drawings are essential and help develop a sense of self, what they like and dislike.

CHILD	AGE	MOTOR CONTROL	ARM MOVEMENTS	TYPES OF BASIC FORMS	USE OF PAPER	EARLY PERIOD	LATER PERIOD
COMMENTS:							

Figure 11-12
Basic forms stage observation form. (See the Online Companion™ for an example of how to complete this form.)

THINK ABOUT IT...   Marker Maintenance

Markers are wonderful for young artists. But busy artists frequently lose caps from these markers, often resulting in dried-out markers. Replacing dried-out markers can be expensive, so here are a few hints on "marker maintenance" to help preserve markers as long as possible.

- Solve the lost cap/dry-out problem by setting the caps with *open ends up* in a margarine or whipped topping container filled with plaster of Paris. Make sure the plaster does not cover the holes in the caps. When the plaster dries, the markers can be put into the caps and will stand up-right until ready for use again.

- Give new life to old, dry felt markers by storing them *tips down with the caps on.* When the mark-ers become dried out, remove the caps and put in a few drops of water. This usually helps "re-vive" them.

- Recycle dried-out markers by having children dip them in paint and use them for drawing.

- Make your own pastel markers by adding dry tempera paint (or food color) to bottles of white shoe polish that come with sponge applicator tops.

- Purchase empty plastic roller-top bottles from a school supply store. Fill them with watery tem-pera paint and use them as a different type of marker.

Figure 11-14

Notice how the child puts basic forms together in a drawing.

Figure 11-13

Observing how a child uses his or her hands and fingers in art activities is one way to learn about small motor development.

and unclear. Rough, less clear forms are made in the early stage. A child in the later basic forms stage draws clear, easy-to-recognize shapes.

In drawings with a variety of forms, see if one form is clearer than another. Clearer forms are the ones that the child first began to draw. The less clear forms are in the practice stage and eventually become clearer.

Use of paper. Use the same checkpoints for the use of paper that were used in the scribble stage section. In addition, see if the child fills the page with one or many basic forms. If the same shape is made over and over, it means the child is practicing a new basic form. Practice like this occurs at an early point in the stage.

THE PICTORIAL/SCHEMATIC STAGE

With the two earlier stages complete, the children now have the ability to draw the variety of marks that make up their first pictures; this occurs at the next developmental level in art—the pictorial stage. Many four year olds and most five year olds are at this level. The schematic stage refers to the child's ability to use his own special variety of marks or *schema*. More details on schema follow later in this section.

Pictures or first drawings are different from scribbling in that they are not made for pure motor enjoyment. Instead, they are made by the child for a purpose. The basic forms perfected in the preceding stage suggest images to the child that stand for ideas in the child's own mind. A new way of drawing begins. From the basic forms the child is able to draw, only particular ones are chosen. Miscellaneous scribbling is left out. In this way, children draw their first symbols. A **symbol** is a visual representation of something important to the child; it may be a human figure, animal, tree, or similar figure. Art in which symbols are used in such a way is called **representational art.** This means there has been a change from kinesthetic, or sheer physical, activity to representational attempts. The child realizes that there is a relationship between the objects drawn and the outside world and that drawing and painting can be used to record ideas or express feelings.

The ability to draw symbols in representational art comes directly from the basic forms stage. The basic forms gradually lose more and more of their connection to body motion only. They are now put together to make symbols, which stand for real objects in the child's mind. In scribbling, the child was mainly involved in a physical activity, trying out the materials to see what she could do with them. Now the child is expressing in the scribble something of importance to her. It may seem to be a scribble, but it is now a "man"

THIS ONE'S for YOU!

Portfolios for Developmental Assessment

Artists generally keep a **portfolio,** or a representative collection of their work. The artist's portfolio usually has samples chosen from various periods, showing how the artist's talent has developed over time. Samples chosen from different media are also included in the portfolio to reflect the artist's versatility and range of talent. For example, you may find works done in pastels, chalk, fine line drawings, and watercolors in the portfolio.

In the early childhood art program, many teachers find the use of portfolios (or individual art files, as it is more generally called) for young children—most often children four years and older—quite helpful. There are many advantages to this practice for the young child, teacher, and parents.

The most obvious advantage of a portfolio/file is the fact that it is visible evidence of the child's development in art. From the earliest selections in the portfolio to the most recent, one can see the child's progress in art.

A portfolio/file can greatly aid the teacher during parent–teacher conferences, by showing examples of how the child is developing in this area. It reduces the subjectivity of discussions by helping both teacher and parent focus objectively on the portfolio.

Another excellent advantage of the portfolio is that it encourages growth of the child's aesthetic sense of choice. By involving the child in selection of pieces for the portfolio, the child learns about the *process of selection.* Of course, learning to be selective is a very complex skill and will take time for the child to develop. But like any other skill, given the time, opportunity, and guidance to make selections of one's own work for the portfolio (or file), the child will develop his or her own personal preferences. Be sure to date and label and write a short comment on each piece added to the portfolio. The label would describe the media/materials used, and a comment would be on some significant aspect of the piece. For example, "First time Jorge named an object in a drawing. This one he called 'Daddy.'"

For all of these reasons, then, using a portfolio in the early childhood art program has definite merits. Alongside these merits are some pitfalls one needs to keep in mind. Most importantly, if you plan to use portfolios for developmental assessment, *stick to it for the whole year.* There is nothing particularly advantageous to having a half-done portfolio. Beginning a portfolio with good intentions and then only sporadically filling it with work reduces its importance as the year goes on—this type of portfolio is best left out of the program entirely. To be of use in developmental assessment, the portfolio needs to be as complete as possible, reflecting the process of artistic development *as a whole.* Many teachers find it helpful to include in their monthly planning a week set aside for portfolio selection. This way, they are sure to have it on their list of priorities. Of course, there should always be time for spontaneous inclusions whenever they occur.

Also keep in mind to include the child in portfolio development, even if it "takes longer that way." Don't forget that the development of personal preference is on a par with developmental assessment as a reason for using portfolios.

Finally, in the spirit of "celebrating" one's artwork, be sure to have an attractive place to keep each child's work. Many teachers use donated (unused) pizza boxes, some use file folders, and others use pocket folders. Find the one best method that works best for your own organizational style. Of course, the child should be involved in decorating the file, box, or whatever other form is used to "house" the collection. Precious art deserves special treatment.

or a "dog"—a definite symbol representing something in the child's life.

The human form is often the child's first symbol. A man is usually drawn with a circle for a head and two lines for legs or body. These are often called "tadpole" figures because of their large heads on a tiny body with extended arms. Other common symbols include trees, houses, flowers, and animals. The child can tell you what each symbol stands for in the drawing.

Further attempts to make symbols grow directly from the basic forms the child can make. Flowers and trees are combinations of spiral scribbles or circles with attached straight lines for stems or trunks. Houses, windows, doors, flags, and similar objects are simply made up of rectangles and straight lines.

It is a common adult practice to label these first drawings "children's art" because they contain rec-

ognizable objects. If children's drawings appear to be mere scribbles to an adult, they are not considered "children's art" because they don't look like "something." Yet being able to identify objects in a child's work does *not* make it "children's art." Art is self-expression and has value in any form and at any stage.

Because art is now representational, children need tools that can be easily controlled and thus facilitate their ability to produce the desired symbols. Thinner crayons and paintbrushes and less fluid paints can now be made available so children can express their ideas and feelings with greater realism. Children over age five will want to be able to select representational colors, so a variety of colors of paint, crayons, and markers are necessary.

Naming and owning the art produced are also important to children in this stage. These children may ask you to record the names of their paintings or drawings as well as write stories to go with their drawings. These children recognize other children's work at this point. They will want to take their work home, as well as contribute some to display in the classroom.

This is an excellent stage to begin keeping a portfolio of the child's work, if you haven't started yet. Samples of the child's early, initial representational artwork will be a record of the development of the child's first symbols. As representational development proceeds, this may be forgotten, without the portfolio sample. For example, when Claire first made a scribble that she called "doggy" her teacher noted it down on the sample and kept it in Claire's folder. Over the year a collection of these various samples gave quite a graphic story of Claire's progress in art.

Keeping portfolios does not mean, however, collecting and keeping all of the child's work. Items in a child's portfolio should reflect how the child is progressing in art. Each piece in the portfolio needs to be selected with this question in mind: "What does *this* piece tell me about *this* learner?" For example, selected samples of scribbles from the early and later scribble stages tell a great deal visually how a child is progressing. In contrast, keeping all of the child's scribble work samples in the file would make it difficult to clearly see the child's development. Digital cameras are very useful in keeping portfolios of children's artwork. See Chapter 8 for details on digital portfolios.

Early Pictorial (First Drawings) Stage

In the **early pictorial (first drawings) stage,** a child works on making and perfecting one or many symbols. The child practices these symbols, covering sheets of paper with many examples of the same subject. For

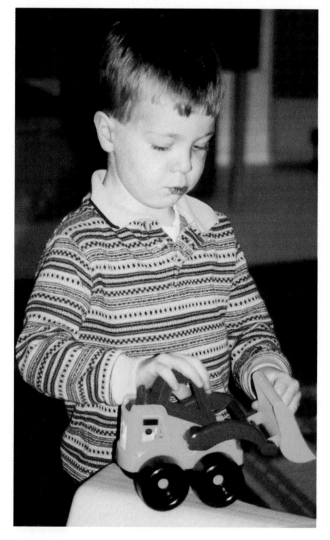

Figure 11-15

Many types of toys in the early childhood program help children develop the small muscles in their hands and fingers.

Figure 11-16
Cutting and pasting are excellent small motor activities.

Figure 11-17
Children will vary in their developmental levels in art. There is no exact pattern of development for each age level.

example, a child may draw windows and doors over and over in each drawing. Also at an early point in this stage, a child's picture may be a collection of unrelated figures and objects. This type of picture is a sampling of the child's many tries at making different symbols. At this point, pictures are done very quickly.

During this early pictorial stage, the child is searching for new ideas. Symbols change constantly. A picture of a man drawn one day differs from the one drawn the day before. In this stage, there is often a great variety of forms representing the same object. Early first drawings are very flexible in appearance. Children are assigning meaning to the shapes they make. The shapes will stand for whatever the child wishes regardless of whether it truly looks like it.

Later Pictorial (First Drawings) Stage: Use of Schema

In the **later pictorial (first drawings) stage,** through practice, a child draws symbols easily and more exactly. Many four year olds and most five year olds perfect to their own liking and take pride in producing a series of many symbols. A child at this point often likes to see these symbols set clearly and neatly on the page. They are now drawn one at a time with few or no other marks on the page. They are clear and well drawn. If children can draw the letters of their name on the page as well, they may feel this is all that belongs in the picture.

For a while, children are content to make these finished yet isolated examples of their drawing skill, but it is not long before more complex drawings are made. Children four to five years of age are able to use their symbols in drawings to tell a story or describe an

event. The naming of these symbols is an important step in that the artwork becomes a clear form of visual communication. It may not look any different, but the child now calls the circle a "sun" as it represents a specific object to the child.

By five and one-half to six years of age, children generally are ready to make a picture of many things in their experience or imagination. Their drawings are made up of combinations of symbols they are familiar with and that have meaning to them. Children create new symbols as they have new experiences and ideas. However, children at this point can't be expected to make pictures of the unfamiliar or of things they have not personally experienced. Another common error by well-meaning teachers is a misunderstanding of this stage by expecting all children five years old and older to be able to use symbols in their art. This is not a valid expectation since the age at which children begin to use symbols is as highly individual as the age at which they learn to walk. Children use symbols when they are ready—and no sooner. Creative expression is the goal at this and all ages; a child's art does not have to include specific symbols, like a house, tree, or animals, unless the *child* chooses to include them.

Children need to repeat art processes over a period of time in order to become competent with and feel secure about using materials to express ideas and feelings. Four- and five-year-old children who have had many opportunities to paint will frequently move easily from manipulative scribbling to expressive symbolic or representational art.

In the later pictorial stage, each child has a special way of drawing the human form, houses, and other

Figure 11-18

A schema, or individual pattern, often can be seen in drawings by the age of six.

Figure 11-19

Older children enjoy further developing fine motor skills in drawings.

symbols. This individual way of drawing is called a **schema.** A schema, or individual pattern, often can be seen in drawings by the age of six. A schema comes after much practice with drawing symbols. As the child becomes a more sophisticated drawer, his or her drawing begins to show the child's direct experiences coming from his or her mind onto the paper. Once the child has a schema, symbols become special marks. A schema is special for each child just as a signature is unique for each adult. One child may tell another, "That's Chad's drawing, I recognize his trees," or "I know it's Zarina's painting because she paints her skies that way." These children have developed a schema that is clearly their own, easily recognizable by others.

Importance of schema. The schema drawn by a child represents something important to the child, something that is part of the child's environment and experience. Things of emotional importance to the child are included in the picture.

Children draw schema in a picture not according to actual size, but in a size that shows the emotional importance of the object to them. For example, people and things important to a child might be drawn large and with many details. If a tree is drawn, the limbs may be made larger because the tree is used for climbing. If it is an apple tree, the apples may be drawn very large.

Children express other responses to their environment in their drawings. A painting showing a child walking on wet grass may show the feet and toes large in size. This may show how the child felt after a walk in the early morning.

Importance of First Drawings

At about the same time children develop their own schemas, they begin to name their drawings. Naming a

Figure 11-20

In the later pictorial stage, each child has a schema—a special way of drawing the human form, houses, and other symbols.

Figure 11-21

In the early childhood art program, young children participate in many activities that help develop their small motor control.

drawing is really an important step for children. It is a sign that their thinking has changed; they are connecting their drawings with the world around them. This is the beginning of a new form of communication—communication with the environment through art.

Figure 11-22

The early childhood teacher needs to show her positive acceptance of the young child's developmental level in all activities.

Soon a five year old may think: "My daddy is a big man; he has a head and two big legs." She then draws a head and two big legs and names her drawing, "Daddy." Through drawing, the child is making a clear relationship between father and the drawing. The symbol of a man now becomes "Daddy." Of course, a child will not verbally name all objects every time a picture is made.

In their use of schemas, children express their own personalities. They express not only what is important to them during the process of creating, but also how aware they have become in thinking, feeling, and seeing. From early drawings to the most complex, they give expression to their life experiences.

Observation of the Pictorial (First Drawings) Stage

The student should keep in mind the following points when observing children in the pictorial stage. You may want to use a copy of the observation form (Figure 11–23) to record your observations. (See also Figures 11–24 and 11–25).

Age.   Write down the age of the child. Check to see what the average age range is for the pictorial stage. See

CHILD	AGE	COMBINATION OF BASIC FORMS	SIZE OF FIGURES	NUMBER OF FIGURES	DETAILS	USE OF FIGURES	NAMING DRAWINGS	EARLY PERIOD	LATER PERIOD
COMMENTS:									

Figure 11-23

Pictorial (first drawings) stage observation form. (See the Online Companion™ for an example of how to complete this form.)

AGE	DEVELOPMENTAL CHARACTERISTICS	CHARACTERISTICS AS AN ARTIST
Birth to two years (infants and toddlers)	Work in creative expression is sensory and exploratory in nature.	Reacts to sensory experience. Explores media through *all* senses. Draws for the first time from 12–20 months. Begins to follow a universal developmental sequence in scribbling (see Figure 11–2.)
Two to four years (young preschoolers)	Work in creative expression is manipulative and oriented toward discovery and skill development.	Explores and manipulates materials. Experiences art as exploratory play. Often repeats action. Begins to name and control symbols. Views final product as unimportant (may not be pleasing to adults). May destroy product during process. Sees shapes in work.
Four to six years (older preschoolers and kindergartners)	Work in creative expression becomes more complex and representational.	Creates symbols to represent feelings and ideas. Represents what is *known*, not what is seen. Gradually begins to create more detailed and realistic work. Creates definite forms and shapes. Often preplans and then works with care. Rarely destroys work during process.

Figure 11-24

The development of art in young children (Courtesy Feeney et al., 1995).

STAGE	AGE RANGE	MOTOR CONTROL	PURPOSE OF ARTWORK	CHARACTERISTICS OF STAGE
Scribble, random/ disordered scribbling	One and one-half to three years (toddlers)	Lacks good motor control and hand–eye coordination.	Scribbles for pure physical sensation of movement.	1. Lacks direction or purpose for marks. 2. Does not mentally connect own movement to marks on page.
Controlled scribbling	Young preschoolers	Improving motor control and hand–eye coordination.	Scribbles with control.	1. Explores and manipulates materials. 2. Tries to discover what can be done—explores color, texture, tools, and techniques. 3. Often repeats action. 4. Makes marks with intention and not by chance.
Basic Forms	Three to four years	Has more developed motor control and hand–eye coordination. Has control over direction and size of line.	Enjoys mastery over line.	1. Masters basic forms: circle, oval, lines, rectangle, and square. 2. Discovers connection between own movements and marks on page.
Pictorial (First Drawings)	Four to five years and up	Has most advanced motor control and hand–eye coordination.	Communicates with outside world through drawing. Expresses personality and relation-ship to symbols drawn.	1. Combines basic forms to create first symbols. 2. Names drawings as a form of true communication.

Figure 11-25

Developmental levels in children's art.

how the child fits in this range. There may be an overlap between stages. For example, the student may see figures as well as simple basic forms in one drawing.

Combination of basic forms. See how the child puts basic forms together to make figures. Very simple combinations mean the child is at an early point in the stage. An example would be a flower made up of a single circle and one-line stem. On the other hand, a

flower of many circles with oval petals and a stem of many leaves is a more complex combination of basic forms and would show that the child is at a later point in the stage.

Size of figures. A child in both the early and later periods of this stage may use size to show importance. The large figure represents something important to the child. Note, for example, children may draw themselves

THIS ONE'S for YOU!

Stages of Art Development– Grades 1-5

With elementary students, one of the major goals of art experiences is to cultivate students' abilities to create original and expressive art. At this level, children are usually able to produce pictorial drawings at will. Art experiences for children in grades 1 through 5 need to focus on prior creative experiences and build on these.

In order to set appropriate expectations and guide artistic growth, you should be familiar with the typical stages of development in creating artwork for this level of students.

The stages of artistic growth outlined here focus on skills portraying space, proportions, and movement or action. Each stage is typical of many children at a particular grade level; however, it is not unusual to find a range of developmental levels within a class or within the work of single students during a year.

Similar variations can be expected in students' ability to respond thoughtfully to artwork. At each stage of development, some students will have greater interest and skill in responding to art than in creating art (or the reverse).

Stage 1 (usually Grades K-2). Children begin to create visual symbols to represent figures such as people, houses, and trees. The figures often seem to "float" in space. Proportions are related to the importance of a feature in the child's experience. Movement is often suggested by scribble-like lines. Three-dimensional artwork reflects the level of prior instruction and practice in using media and the physical coordination students have developed.

Stage 2 (usually Grades 1-3). In picture-making, lines or borders are often used to represent the ground below and sky above. Figures may be placed along a line or at the lower edge of the paper. Proportions are shown through relative size—a house is larger than a person. Action is implied by the general position of lines and shapes, rather than subtle shifts in direction. Students who receive instruction will show general improvement in using three-dimensional media and applying design concepts as they work.

Stage 3 (usually Grades 3-6). Students try out new ways to portray space in the pictures they draw and paint. These explorations often reflect remembered functional or logical relationships more than visual recall or observation. General proportions improve, as well as the use of diagonals to suggest action. Many students develop a strong affinity for three-dimensional work and are willing to try out new media and techniques that require several steps.

Stage 4 (usually Grades 4-6). In picture-making, students search for ways to portray recalled or observed space. Some students begin to use perspective to imply near and distant objects. Movement is suggested through more subtle angles and curves. Individual styles and preferences for two- or three-dimensional work become more evident, along with increased skill in applying design concepts to create expressive work.

or other figures such as their mother in a very large size. Extra-large heads on a small body are found mainly in the early period of this stage.

Notice the relative size of certain things in the picture. For a child who likes animals, a dog may be far larger than the human form. Here, too, size indicates that the object is important to the child.

Number of figures. Mark down the number of figures in each drawing. A drawing with few figures or a single figure means that the child is at an early point in the stage. The child making this type of drawing is working on developing a symbol.

At a later point, the child can draw many types of symbols and figures in one drawing. Also, drawings at a later point look as if they tell a story with the figures.

Details. Note the type and number of details a child uses in a drawing. They indicate at what point the child is in the stage.

Figures with only a few details are made in the early pictorial stage. For example, a circular head, round body, and stick arms and legs make up an early human form. A picture of a man with details such as full arms, hands, and fingers is a sign that the child is at a later point in the pictorial stage.

THINK ABOUT IT...   Research on Children's Art

"Along with other data, children's drawings can be used as measures of intellectual growth, emotional maturity, and mental well-being," says Dr. Marlene Cox-Bishop, associate professor of human ecology at the University of Alberta. After collecting the artwork of more than a thousand children from around the world, Cox-Bishop knows children's pictures transcend language and cultural barriers. "We learn to communicate through drawing long before we can read or write about our ideas and our response to the world," she says.

In a cross-cultural study, Cox-Bishop compared Inuit children's drawings with those of American midwestern children. Item by item she examined the drawings of each child, noting technique, line quality, use of color and space—and tried to statistically determine any gender differences. What she found surprised her: there were very few differences. A child's art is reflective of his or her culture, she says, and maybe each of the children had been similarly influenced by satellite television, common textbooks, and teachers educated in a southern culture.

What surprised her more, however, was discovering that no matter where children live, their visual consciousness develops at the same rate. "All kids learn to draw, learn to represent the world at about the same stages, which is incredible. Although the cultural information such as specific games, costumes, and houses may change, generally how kids organize space, forms, stick figures, or Mr. Potato Heads—happens at about the same age everywhere."

Developing visual literacy is important, Cox-Bishop says, because 80 percent of the messages that bombard us are visual, not written. "Visual literacy is the ability to read the images, the visual environment," she says, and children have it naturally, if briefly. "We lose those skills. They atrophy."

The ability to represent the world visually comes from the intuitive, emotional, right hemisphere of the brain, she says. Our culture emphasizes the more logical, linear, left hemisphere. In the process, we squelch a child's creativity. "We pin their notion of whether they're successful on good grades in reading and math and forget about the kid who could write a poem that would knock your socks off, or paint a picture—what about those kids and that part of the brain?"

Renowned artists have had the same appreciation of children's art. Picasso was known to have collected children's art. He didn't collect it because he wanted to go back and copy the children's artistic solutions; he loved its spontaneity.

Ironically, that original and personal quality cherished in a child's drawing is often scorned in an adult's. "On one hand, we appreciate children's art because it's lovely and unsophisticated," Cox-Bishop notes. "Then we judge a modern artist by the fact that his art doesn't appear to be sophisticated. When we say, 'Ha! My six-year-old kid could do that,' we have forgotten something important. Perhaps that artist is yet a child, still has that child-like ability to look at the relationships of line and color and shape." What's more, we forget that a child's drawing captures a wondrous and fleeting moment in time (Johnson, 1998).

See if certain objects are drawn in greater detail than others. A child's experience with certain objects can cause this increase in detail. As an example, tree limbs may be unusually large in the drawings of children who love to climb trees. Special sense experiences can also cause increase in detail. For example, a child may draw large raindrops in a drawing after a walk in the rain.

Use of figures. Note how the child uses figures. See if the paper is filled with many unrelated figures that just fill space and look like practice forms. If there is no real connection between figures, it can mean the child is at an early point in the stage; the child is practicing a symbol and is not yet ready to tell a story with it.

If there seems to be a connection between figures, the child is at a later point. This type of drawing is a narrative drawing, one that tells a story. It is a visual form of communication for the child.

Naming drawings. Be sure to listen to the child who wants to talk about a drawing. Note if the child names certain things, figures, or the whole thing, but never force the child to tell you "what it is." Naming must come only through the child's own idea. It is an important step in the child's ability to communicate. It is only worthwhile if the child sees the meaning in the work and *wants* to name it.

THE GANG STAGE

Children ages nine through 12 fall into the *gang stage* of art development according to Viktor Lowenfeld. At this point, the child becomes more aware of how things look in his drawings. This awareness is often expressed with more detail in his or her schema. Drawings are still far from naturalistic. Children at this age discover space in their drawings and it is often depicted with overlapping objects in the drawings. Children of this age also begin to draw the horizon line to separate land from sky.

Because children of this age are becoming more social minded, they are beginning to compare their work with other children's. They often become critical of their own work, wanting their images to be very realistic. Children at this point often become frustrated if realism can't be achieved. The "I can't draw" syndrome typically starts to emerge at this stage.

Teachers of children in this stage need to encourage a self-accepting attitude. They can help children realize that they can still express themselves by exploring new uses for familiar media. For example, printing using brayers (rollers) and wood blocks is one way to encourage exploration at this stage. Group projects such as murals are also appropriate at this age because they allow children to "pool" their talents. In such a project, each child can contribute at his or her own level.

SUMMARY

As children grow older and change in height and weight, they also develop different abilities in art. There are three developmental levels in art that are of concern to the preschool teacher: the scribble, basic forms, and pictorial stages. Teachers of children in middle and upper levels of elementary school need to build and expand on the pictorial skill that children have achieved at each level.

The scribble stage ranges from about one and one-half to three years of age. It covers the time from the child's first marks to more controlled scribbles. The child enjoys the pure motion involved in scribbling.

Wide, good-quality crayons are the best tools for the scribble stage. Large paper should be given to the child to allow room for wide arm movements. Age, motor control, use of paper, and type of scribbles should be noted in scribble stage observations.

The basic forms stage covers approximately ages three to four years. The child develops more muscle control and hand–eye coordination through scribbling. Basic forms come when children can see simple forms in their scribbles and are able to repeat them. The oval or circle is usually the first basic form, followed by the rectangle or square. Children now enjoy seeing forms emerge out of their own will.

A wider variety of art materials can be used with children in the basic forms stage. Age, motor control, use of paper, and basic forms used should be noted in observations of the basic forms stage.

The pictorial stage generally occurs from ages four to six. Basic forms made in the prior stage are put together to make up symbols. The human form, birds, flowers, and animals are examples of some symbols. Naming drawings is an important part of first drawings. Children can now communicate outside themselves and with their world. A child's artwork is very individual and expresses the child's own personality.

In the pictorial stage, children make the most varied and complex drawings. Points to note in observing this stage are the age of the child and figures and details in the drawings. Children ages nine to 12 are in the gang stage of art development. This term, developed by Viktor Lowenfeld, refers to the fact that the peer groups assume more importance to the child than ever before.

These basic stages of art development parallel the overall development of children at particular periods. In planning the early childhood art program, the teacher must choose appropriate activities for the ability and interest levels of the age group of children in the program. Each age group has its own special considerations that must be included in a teacher's planning.

KEY TERMS

basic forms stage	pictorial stage
controlled scribbling	portfolio
developmental levels	preschematic stage
disordered or random scribbling	representational art
early basic forms stage	schema
early pictorial (first drawings) stage	scribble stage
	symbol
gang stage	two-dimensional
later basic forms stage	media
later pictorial (first drawings) stage	

LEARNING ACTIVITIES

SELECTING APPROPRIATE MATERIALS FOR ART EXPERIENCES

A. Examine the tools that are available for the children to work with in a preschool classroom—paintbrushes, scissors, crayons, to mention a few. Inventory these in terms of how many are available, the condition of the various tools, and their suitability in terms of design and quality for young children.

B. Using toy and equipment catalogs that can be cut up, compile a catalog with classmates that pictures appropriate materials in terms of the many areas covered in this chapter. Select and annotate each entry in each category in terms of age level, appropriateness, appearance, versatility, durability, and safety.

Consider the quote below:

When my daughter was about seven years old, she asked me one day what I did at work. I told her I worked at the college—that my job was to teach people how to draw. She stared back at me, incredulous, and said, "You mean they forget?" Howard Ikemoto.

How would you answer this child? Why do you think "we forget" how to draw? What can you as a teacher do to help children continue drawing?

SCRIBBLE STAGE EXPERIENCES FOR THE STUDENT

A. Exercise 1. Goal: To experience some of the lack of motor control of a young child in the scribble stage.
1. The student is to use the hand opposite the writing hand to "draw" a crayon picture. Using a large crayon in the hand that is not usually used for drawing, the student should experience difficulties like those of the young child.
2. Consider and discuss the following:
   a. clumsy feeling of the crayon in hand
   b. lack of good control over finger and hand movements
   c. inability to draw exactly what is desired
   d. difficulty in controlling crayon, paper, and hand movements all at once
3. Try painting on your knees at an easel. Discuss how it felt and how it may have affected your painting. After this experience, what would you change about your approach to easels and painting for young children?

B. Exercise 2. Goal: To experience the pure motor pleasure of scribbling.
1. The student is to close both eyes and do a crayon scribbling.
2. To experience feelings similar to the young child, consider and discuss the following:
   a. difficulty of overcoming the adult need for seeing as well as doing
   b. how it feels to move hand and fingers for movement's sake alone
   c. what forms are seen in the scribbles
   d. feelings about how the drawing looks

RECOGNIZING AND EVALUATING THE THREE ART STAGES

Obtain samples of drawings from children one and one-half to five years of age. Separate the samples into three groups (one for each stage). Give reasons for the stage selected for each sample, especially for the samples that are not clearly defined.

A. Note and explain the differences in scribble stage examples:
1. early or later scribbling period
2. type of scribbles (circular, jagged)
3. control of crayon

B. Note and explain the differences in basic forms examples:
1. type of basic forms used
2. how clear and exact the forms are
3. control of crayon
4. early or later basic forms period

C. Note and explain the differences in pictorial examples:
1. early or later period
2. what basic forms are combined into symbols
3. observable symbols

D. Use the same drawings and see if you can determine why some people believe children draw what they feel, know, and see.

E. Make a list of children's books with outstanding illustrations that could be used to introduce children to the concept of the artist as well as to different techniques and a wide variety of art materials.

F. Work with a small group of children (or even one child) to try to motivate art with a firsthand experience, such as touching a tree or kitten or observing a moth. Then ask the children to draw a picture. Identify how this experience influenced the drawings.

G. Obtain samples of drawing from children in grades 1 through 5. Separate them by grade level. Using the stages presented in the "This One's For You!" box, discuss how each sample fits (or doesn't fit) the general characteristics of that grade level/stage.

H. Collect samples of drawing from one grade level only (grades 1 through 5). Sort them according to how they represent the grade level stage. For ex-ample, sort them out by grouping the samples most near the characteristics of the grade level stage down through those with the least characteristics of the grade level stage. Discuss the ranges of abilities represented in these samples. Share your ideas on how you would work with each of the children whose samples you have in your collection.

ACTIVITIES FOR CHILDREN

A. Display prints of famous artworks. Examples: Mondrian's "Composition with Red, Blue, and Yellow," Pollock's "Detail of One (#31, 1950)," and Van Gogh's "Cypress Trees." See if these examples affect the children's choice of colors, type of figures made, and amount of details in their pictures.

B. Play music during part of the art period. Compare the drawings made with music to those done without music.

SOME VARIATIONS ON EASEL PAINTING

⊙ use a number of shades of one color
⊙ use colored paper—colored newsprint comes in pastel shades or the backs of faded construction paper can be used
⊙ use the same color of paint with same color paper
⊙ use black and white paint
⊙ use various sizes of brushes, or both flat and floppy ones, with the same colors of paint
⊙ paint objects the children have made in carpentry, or paint dried clay objects
⊙ paint large refrigerator-type boxes
⊙ work on a long piece of paper (computer paper) together to produce murals
⊙ paint the fence with water and large brushes
⊙ draw firmly on paper with crayons, and paint over it to produce "crayon resist" art
⊙ use all pastel colors (start with white and add color a bit at a time when mixing)
⊙ set up a table with many colors of paint and encourage the children to select the colors they prefer
⊙ paint to music

CRACKED PAINT AND CRAYON DRAWINGS

The child draws with crayons an image or design on a piece of paper. Crumple up the picture, but don't tear it. Smooth out the drawing and brush over it with watery tempera paint. The paint will go into all the little cracks in the paper. After it dries, brush a coat of thinned white glue onto the drawing. This gives it a shiny effect.

PAINTING WITH SOFT OBJECTS

The child dips a cotton ball in a shallow dish of wet paint. She or he can smear it or squish it on paper or another surface. Try dipping a cotton ball into dry powdered paint. Rubbing it across dry paper creates an interesting soft effect.

COTTON SWAB PAINTING

Dip cotton swabs into paint, and use as a brush.

BUTTON PRINTING

Glue buttons onto small wooden dowels for children to use in printing. Vary the sizes, shapes, and designs of buttons.

SPONGE PAINTING

Cut sponges into different shapes. Children may dip each shape in paint. Then dab, press, or rub it on paper.

PAPER TOWEL PAINTING

Wad a paper towel into a ball. Children may want to dip it in paint. Then dab, press, or rub it on paper.

CRAYONS

Try a variety of surfaces for crayon drawings. Children may enjoy drawing with crayons on these surfaces for variety:

fabric	sticks and stones
egg cartons	spools and clothespins
paper towel rolls	cardboard
sandpaper	styrofoam trays
wood scraps	

PRINTING

A. Toy Prints

Dip the wheels of an old toy car, truck, or other toy in paint. Children then make tracks on the paper.

B. Plastic Alphabet Letters and Numbers

Dip plastic alphabet letters and numbers in paint and print them on paper.

C. Paper Cup Printing

Dip the rim of a paper cup into paint. Press the rim on the paper to make a design.

D. Comb Printing

Dip the teeth of a comb into paint. Print with it by drawing it along the paper.

E. Printing with Clay

Children pound clay into small flat cakes about an inch thick. Then they may want to carve a design on the flat surface with a bobby pin or popsicle stick. If desired, the design is either brushed with paint or dipped in paint and pressed onto paper to print the design.

FABRIC PAINTING

Wrap small pieces of burlap, nylon netting, or other textured fabrics (2 ½ × 3 inches square) over a sponge that has been attached to a clothespin or secured to a dowel with a piece of string or elastic. Dip fabric into paint and press onto a surface.

PINECONE PRINTING

Roll whole or pieces of pinecones in paint. The large ones with flat bottoms can be dipped into paint and used to print images and designs.

COMBINATION PAINTING

Thicken tempera paint with liquid starch. Divide the paint up into individual portions. Have the children use this paint in their paintings. While the paint is still wet, the children can sprinkle the painting with any of the following for attractive combination paintings: salt, coffee grounds, eggshells, glitter, colored rice, tiny styrofoam balls, seeds, cornmeal, sequins, tiny beads. The media dries in the paint for interesting effects.

SMALL-GRAINED PASTING ACTIVITIES

The child paints an area of paper with either a white glue mixture or liquid starch. Then, the child shakes on any small-grained media such as sand, salt, flour, or cornmeal. These can be put into shakers with large or small holes. (Dry tempera can also be added to granular material.)

IDEAS TO ENCOURAGE DRAWING

Try some of the following ideas to encourage children in kindergarten to grade 3 to use imagination in expressing their observations through drawing.

⊙ Draw a picture of something that can't be seen.
⊙ Draw as many animals as you can on one page.
⊙ Draw a map for a brain surgeon or for a heart surgeon.
⊙ Design a special machine or device to help the President.
⊙ Draw a picture showing how you would improve human beings.
⊙ Draw a picture of an angry sea or a noisy city.
⊙ Draw a picture that shows how you would make your school a better place.
⊙ Draw a picture that shows how you would weigh an elephant.
⊙ Design an underground city or an underwater city.
⊙ Design a dog-exercising machine.

DRAWING FOR BREAK TIME

When you have five to 10 minutes to kill, encourage children to draw some of the following:

⊙ Your shoe
⊙ Your lunch
⊙ The teacher
⊙ A friend
⊙ Draw your hand holding something
⊙ Draw a small object big
⊙ Draw a car
⊙ Draw a dream
⊙ Draw a nightmare
⊙ Draw a leaf
⊙ Draw yourself

ACTIVITIES FOR OLDER CHILDREN (GRADES 4-5)

SCRIBBLE ART

Have each child make a scribble line on a piece of paper. The child then passes the paper to another child on the left. The child receiving the scribble is challenged to turn the scribble into an image or a design. Challenge the children to be as creative as they can be in transforming the scribbles.

VARIATION ON A SCRIBBLE

Give each student a 6- to 8-inch long piece of string or yarn, glue, and a piece of paper. Students glue the string or yarn into a scribble-type shape. Students pass their paper to the person sitting to his or her left.

Students take this piece of paper and imagine what the string brings to mind. Students use markers or crayons to create something original from the string. Have students discuss what they saw and why it became what it did.

DIRECTION DRAWING

The purpose of this activity is to help children see how with just one set of directions everyone will come up with their own unique works of abstract art. There are two basic steps in this activity: (1) teacher calls out directions for the children, and (2) children draw what they hear.

Here are some ideas on directions to call out for this activity. Of course, you can make up your own.

- ⊙ Draw five circles—any size—anywhere on your paper.
- ⊙ Draw four straight lines from one edge of your paper to the other.
- ⊙ Draw two more straight lines from one edge of your paper to the other, only this time make the lines cross over the lines you have already drawn.
- ⊙ Draw two curved lines beginning at the edge of the paper and ending up somewhere in the middle of the paper.
- ⊙ Fill in three of the five circles.
- ⊙ Fill in four areas of your paper however you would like.

Once the drawings are complete, students sign their work. Display the work in the classroom. Discuss how the drawings look the same. Discuss how they are different.

Come up with more directions and try this again. You will be amazed at the unique qualities of all of the drawings.

LINE SHAPE AND SPACE: MAPS FROM THE AIR

Discuss students' experiences in seeing actual or televised views of the earth from high in the sky. Have students describe any differences between extremely high views (many weather reports have satellite views) and views closer to the ground (hot air balloon or low-flying aircraft).

You may want to explain that some artists are fascinated with map-like views of the earth. They have created original artworks to suggest the special arrangements of lines and shapes that people cannot see from the ground. Good examples of artwork to use for this are Clause Herbert Breeze's "Canadian Atlas: Position of London," Judith Wittlin's "Cincinnati," or "Late Evening Traffic" by Yvonne Jacquette.

If you can't obtain artwork prints, have a city map available to show the grid-like structures common to many cities and rural areas where the land is flat. From the air, and on maps, you can see graceful curves made by freeways. Point out the differences between an actual map and the paintings. (A map is more complex and has labels).

Discuss the similarities and differences between the simple map and a painting. Guide students to see how the organic lines and shapes—those with complex, irregular curves—are related to natural forms such as the rivers, borders of an island, and surrounding land. Have students identify geometric lines and shapes that suggest the human-made environment (grid lines, long lines that might be highways) in the maps.

Bring in old maps that can be cut apart and used for artwork. Have students work in small groups to identify sections of the maps where interesting organic or geometric lines and shapes occur on the map. Ask the students to offer explanations for these designs in relation to concepts from this lesson. Then have the students change the map into an abstract design by adding crayon or oil pastels or by cutting along lines and creating new shapes. Compare and contrast the results.

INTEGRATED ART ACTIVITY: SCIENCE/INDEPENDENT RESEARCH

Have the students look through science books for illustrations of linear structures (snowflakes, bones, blood circulation, plants, geological formations, and the like). Have them select a small section of one of the illustrations and draw a similar structure on a large sheet of paper. After they have completed the drawing, have them use dark colors of crayons or oil pastels to increase the width of lines, making an abstract design. Shapes between the lines might be colored as well. Display the work and discuss relationships between the "artistic structure" and the structure shown in the scientific illustration.

INTEGRATED ART ACTIVITY: LANGUAGE ARTS/AESTHETIC AWARENESS

Explore the connotations of phrases such as "the blues," "I'm feeling blue," "green with envy," and the like. Ask the students to give additional examples of the use of color-related words to describe moods or feelings. Write the phrases on the chalkboard, in two columns, so students can compare and contrast phrases for warm colors and cool colors. Have the students select one of these phrases and create an artwork that uses the phrases as a title and is dominated by variations on the color in the title.

INTEGRATED ART ACTIVITY: LANGUAGE ARTS/ART CRITICISM

Ask the students to speculate on reasons why many artists like to create paintings that portray flowers in vases. There are many reasons. Flowers in general are symbols of a cycle of life. Cut flowers are often symbolically related to the concept of enjoying moments of beauty. The colors, lines, textures, and other qualities provide a challenge for artists to interpret. The paintings are also enjoyed by many people, especially in homes, where the image of a vase of flowers can add a feeling of warmth or happiness. You might want to include prints of flower paintings, such as Van Gogh's "Sunflowers" for students or any of Georgia O'Keeffe's flower paintings, in this discussion. Provide students an opportunity to create their own flower paintings.

AESTHETIC AWARENESS

Have students cut out, from old magazines or newspapers, some black-and-white photographs. Provide them with viewfinders. (See telescope activity in Chapter 10). Have them place the viewfinder over the photograph and look for the darkest area of the photograph. Show them how to trace around the edges of the hole of the viewfinder to mark the place on the photograph, then cut out and save the piece. Have them continue to identify and cut out four or five other pieces that differ from each other in value. Have students arrange the pieces in a light to dark sequence. Ask pairs of students to check each others' arrangements.

CHAPTER REVIEW

1. Describe a young child in the scribble stage in the following areas:
   a. age
   b. degree of motor control
   c. reason for scribbling
2. List three basic forms that a child in the basic forms stage may be able to draw.
3. Describe a schema.
4. Give four examples of symbols.
5. Discuss the importance of children naming their pictures.
6. Define the term two-dimensional media and give an example of a two-dimensional process.
7. List the materials that are right for children in the scribble stage and basic forms stage.
   a. For the scribble stage, what are the best (a) crayon size and type; (b) paper size and type?
   b. For the basic forms stage, what are the best (a) tools for drawing; (b) paper size and type?

8. Give an example of an early and a later combination of basic forms.
9. In the following, decide which period of the pictorial stage best shows each listed characteristic.

Period	Characteristics of Drawing
1. early pictorial stage	a. few, unrelated figures
2. later pictorial stage	b. greater degree and amount of detail
	c. narrative or story drawings
	d. greater size to show importance
	e. larger head size for figures

10. Choose the answer that best completes these statements about the basic forms stage:
    a. The child with good motor control
       (a) drops the crayon often.

(b) uses a clenched grip.
(c) uses more hand than arm movement.
  b. An early type of basic form is
  (a) well drawn.
  (b) a less clear form.
  (c) combined to make a symbol.

  c. In the later period of basic forms, a child
  (a) cannot draw good basic forms.
  (b) easily draws clear forms.
  (c) fills the page with practice forms.
11. Describe a child in the gang stage of art development.

REFERENCES

Feeney, S., Christensen, D., & Maravcik, E. (1995). Who am I in the lives of children? *An introduction to teaching young children* (5th ed.). Upper Saddle River, NJ: Prentice Hall.

Kellogg, R. (1967). *The psychology of children's art*. New York: CRM, Inc.

Kellogg, R. (1970). *Analyzing children's art*. Palo Alto, CA: National Press Books.

Lowenfeld, V. (1987). *Creative and mental growth of the child* (8th ed.). New York: Macmillan.

ADDITIONAL READINGS

Adejumo, C. O. (2002). Improving the teaching of art. *School Arts 102*(4), 39–41.

Alter-Muri, S. (2002). Viktor Lowenfeld Revisited: A review of Lowenfeld's preschematic, schematic and gang age stages. *American Journal of Art Therapy 40*(3), 170–176.

Chadwick, W. (2002). *Women, art and society*. London: Thames & Hudson.

Counihan, J. (2003). Young artist. *Arts and Activities 133*(2), 29–34.

Cox, M. V., & Wright, R. (2000). Relative heights of males and females in children's drawings. *International Journal of Early Years Education 8*(3), 217–226.

Edwards, B. (1979). *Drawing on the right side of the brain*. Los Angeles, CA: J. P. Tarcher.

Edwards, L. C. (2001). *The creative arts: A process approach for teachers and children*. Upper Saddle River, NJ: Pearson Education.

Enstice, W., & Peters, M. (2003). *Drawing: Space, form and expression*. Upper Saddle River, NJ: Prentice Hall.

Erickson, E. H. (2000). *Erik Erikson reader*. New York: Norton.

Geist, A. L. (2003). Children's art in wartime. *Journal of Higher Education 41*(8), 49–52.

Golumb, C. (2003). Art and the young child: Another look at the developmental question. ERIC Document ED352163.

Jensen, E. (2003). *Arts with the brain in mind*. Washington, DC: Association for Supervision and Curriculum Development.

Johnson, D. Folio Back Page, February 6, 1998. Online: http://www.ualberta.ca/~publicas/folio/35/11/10.htm.

Kimball, M. (2002). *The web portfolio guide: Creating electronic portfolios for the web*. Upper Saddle River, NJ: Pearson Education.

Marantz, K. (2003). What is an artist? *School Arts 102*(5), 72–75.

Sisto, F. F. (2000). Relationship of the Piagetian Cognitive Development in the human figure drawing. *Child Study Journal 30*(4), 225–232.

Striker, S. *Young at art: Teaching toddlers self-expression, problem-solving skills, and an appreciation of art*. New York: Henry Holt.

Watson, M. W., & Schwartz, S. N. (2000). The development of individual styles in children's drawings. *New Directions for Child and Adolescent Development 90*(1), 49–63.

HELPFUL WEB SITES

http://www.scribbleskidsart.com
  Click on Articles under the References icon.
http://www.fresnofamily.com/
  Click on Parenting Articles then on Miscellaneous Articles, and then on Developmental Stages of Art.

http://www.creativity-portal.com
  Click on Newsletter, and go to February 2004 for article on Developmental Stages in Art.

For additional creative activity resources, visit our Web site at http://www.EarlyChildEd.delmar.com.

SECTION 4

The Early Childhood Art Program

REFLECTIVE QUESTIONS

After studying this section, you should be able to answer the following questions.

1. How do my classroom art activities reflect the emphasis of process over product?

2. When I set up art activities for young children, what activities and materials do I plan to use for each different age and developmental level present in the group?

3. How do I avoid falling into a routine when planning, setting up, and using art activities with young children?

4. Am I keeping the early childhood program basic goals in mind as I plan lessons and activities?

5. Am I planning developmentally appropriate two- and three-dimensional art activities for all of the children in my group?

6. How are children using the two- and three-dimensional materials I have provided for them? Do they appear motivated and involved in exploring them?

7. How can I improve the appeal as well as range of two- and three-dimensional activities I currently use with young children?

8. What skills do the young children in my group already possess with regard to two- and three-dimensional media? Have I planned lessons and activities to match these skills?

9. What instructional strategies are best for young children's learning and enjoyment with two- and three-dimensional media?

10. How will I modify my lessons and activities as children become more proficient in their use of art materials?

12

Program Basics: Goals, Setting Up, Materials, and Strategies

Objectives

After studying this chapter, you should be able to:

1. Discuss goals for the early childhood art program.
2. Describe the basic set-up for the early childhood art program.
3. List the basic materials, equipment, and their uses in the early childhood art program.

Art experiences are an essential part of the early childhood curriculum. Yet, creative experiences do not just happen. They are the result of careful planning. This chapter covers three major areas of concern in planning for children's creative art experiences: (1) program goals; (2) setting up for art activities; and (3) using basic art materials and equipment.

BASIC GOALS OF THE EARLY CHILDHOOD ART PROGRAM

The early childhood art program provides the time and place to express thoughts, ideas, feelings, actions, and abilities in a variety of media and activities.

Process, Not Product

Art programs provide young children many opportunities to work with a variety of materials and techniques to express themselves creatively.

The first and main goal in all art experiences is not the end product but the process of creating. It is in the process that the child expresses experiences and feelings. The expression of one's self is what is important here, not what the finished product looks like. Lowenfeld expresses the importance of the *process* of creating as follows:

> Art activity cannot be imposed but must come from a spirit within. This is not always an easy

process, but the development of creative abilities is essential in our society, and the youngster's drawing reflects his creative growth both in the drawing and in the process of making the art form (Lowenfeld & Brittain, p. 5, 1987).

Another reason that it is better to emphasize the process is that young children are not yet skillful users of materials. Much of their creative effort is expended in the manipulative experience of trying materials out and becoming acquainted with them. Also, young children are more interested in doing than in producing and rarely, if ever, betray a planned intention when they take up their paintbrushes or select collage materials. This sort of advance planning belongs to children on the verge of kindergarten age. Older children in middle and upper elementary levels will be more purposeful in their creative activities. However, this does not change the fact that the main objective of their artistic endeavors is self-expression.

Children take paints, bits of cloth, clay, wood, and stone and put them together into products that express their own ideas. In the art program, emphasis must be on continued satisfying experiences with many kinds of materials and a continued involvement in the process of making. Creative activities provide opportunities for self-expression by allowing children to construct something that is uniquely their own.

Needs of the Children

A second major objective of the art program is to meet the needs of the children. This means that it must be designed for their age, ability, and interest levels. Thus, a program for three year olds is set up to have the right materials and activities for a group with a limited interest span and limited motor control. It has materials and activities that interest them and that they can use without a lot of adult help. Two year olds are at the point of learning how to tear and paste and do not require scissors, whereas three and four year olds are able to use scissors independently. The same applies to art activities for four-, five-, and six-year-old children. In a mixed age group, the program must be set up with a variety of materials and activities available to all children in the group. For middle and upper elementary students who are beginning to create more complex works of art, there needs to be an increased supply of materials and equipment for their creative expression. The teacher's job at this level is to maximize students' use of these resources as they continue to develop their imaginations in art experiences.

Another way a teacher meets the individual needs of children is to provide art materials appropriate for the multiple intelligences of the children in the group. (See Chapter 5 for more information on multiple intelligences.)

Originality and Independence

A third important objective of the early childhood art program is to give each child the chance to think originally and to learn to work independently. In artwork, a child can use and explore all kinds of materials. This encourages original, divergent thought. Also, giving children material that they can control at their physical level encourages independent work. Materials that appeal to a child's multiple intelligences encourage exploration. For example, providing a child who is logic smart blocks and clay encourages this child to create models and structures, which are a natural expression of his or her logical/mathematical skills. These two things (originality and ability to work on their own) are basic to children's creativity.

With older children, you can expect and plan for a higher degree of independence in use of materials. With ready access to a variety of materials, if allowed, children are able to be self-directed and choose the materials they need to express ideas. At this level, instead of relying on the teacher to pass out supplies and leading a lesson, self-directed independent children are able to get their own materials needed for creative work.

Creative Thinking

Another goal in the early childhood art program is for children to be creative thinkers. Creative children work freely and flexibly. They attack each problem without fear of failure. Children in an art program that is right for their developmental level are able to work creatively, freely, and flexibly. They can handle the material in the setting, which helps them feel more sure of themselves.

If children do not feel secure, safe, and comfortable with themselves, the teacher, and the other children, they will not be able to take the risk or meet the challenge involved in producing art.

As we have learned, all children have multiple intelligences or ways of learning. These individual learning styles will influence how each child will work in art activities. See Figure 12–1 for a summary of these learning styles and appropriate art activities for each style.

A STUDENT WHO IS . . .	WILL ENJOY ART PROJECTS THAT . . .	AND WILL ENJOY HELPING OUT IN THE CLASSROOM BY . . .
Person Smart *"The Socializer"* ⊙ interactive ⊙ communicative ⊙ group-oriented ⊙ extroverted	⊙ are group projects ⊙ require giving/receiving feedback ⊙ require group leaders	⊙ distributing and collecting materials ⊙ mediating
Self Smart *"The Individual"* ⊙ individualistic ⊙ solitary ⊙ self-reflective ⊙ introverted	⊙ are individual projects ⊙ focus on feelings, dreams, or self ⊙ are goal-oriented	⊙ arranging items in storage spaces ⊙ assisting teacher before or after class
Body Smart *"The Mover"* ⊙ physically active ⊙ hands-on ⊙ talkative	⊙ involve physical motion such as dancing or acting ⊙ involve touching various objects, materials, and textures	⊙ running errands ⊙ role-playing safety rules ⊙ distributing and collecting materials
Word Smart *"The Word Player"* ⊙ oriented toward language, words, reading, and writing	⊙ involve spoken or written words ⊙ involve storytelling	⊙ reading instructions aloud ⊙ labeling storage spaces ⊙ creating "rules" posters
Logic Smart *"The Questioner"* ⊙ inquisitive ⊙ experimental ⊙ oriented toward numbers, patterns, and relationships	⊙ involve patterns, relationships, or symbols ⊙ require problem solving	⊙ arranging or classifying materials for distribution ⊙ helping solve problems
Picture Smart *"The Visualizer"* ⊙ imaginative ⊙ creative ⊙ oriented toward colors, pictures	⊙ involve colors and designs ⊙ involve painting, drawing, or sculpture ⊙ require active imagination	⊙ creating displays of artworks ⊙ designing charts and posters
Music Smart *"The Music Lover"* ⊙ oriented toward music, rhythmic sounds, and environmental sounds	⊙ involve rhythmic patterns, singing, humming, responding to music, keeping time, or listening for sounds	⊙ thinking of cleanup songs ⊙ thinking of safety songs ⊙ creating displays about music or musicians

Figure 12-1

Learning styles and art activities (Gardner, 1993, 1999).

(Continues)

A STUDENT WHO IS . . .	WILL ENJOY ART PROJECTS THAT . . .	AND WILL ENJOY HELPING OUT IN THE CLASSROOM BY . . .
Nature Smart *"The Outdoors Lover"* ⊙ interested in the outdoors ⊙ oriented toward animals, insects, and nature in general	⊙ involve collecting objects of nature ⊙ involve observing and recording weather ⊙ involve identifying plants and insects ⊙ involve tree rubbings ⊙ involve creating his or her own animal or insect	⊙ working in the garden ⊙ caring for classroom pets and aquarium ⊙ arranging collections of natural objects
Acquiring English	⊙ require limited word usage ⊙ involve terminology from their first language ⊙ involve simple name/word games	⊙ creating labels and posters in their first language ⊙ creating images or icons for bulletin boards ⊙ sharing elements of their culture with other students

Figure 12-1 (Continued)

Individualized Progress

Finally, the art program must allow children to grow at their own speed. Activities may be planned to stimulate children, but true growth comes only at their own pace. Just as children learn to walk on their own, they learn to paint by painting in their own way.

In the art program, young children are given time to grow, explore, and experiment with materials at their own pace. Two and three year olds, barely out of the sensorimotor stage of development, are respected for being two or three. These young children are expected to explore materials; to enjoy feeling, tasting, and playing with crayons; to scribble and mess around; and to find out how paint feels on their hands and faces or what they can do with soft clay. Children are not hurried or pressured into representing their ideas or feelings through art, nor to be interested in the product, much less to produce one.

Children who have had the opportunity and time to explore and experiment with materials as toddlers are ready at three, four, or five to find out how they can gain control over the materials and use them to express themselves. In turn, preschoolers who have had the time and freedom to develop their art ability will then enjoy using these skills to express themselves visually in a wide variety of media.

Individual growth rate must also be a consideration when working with children with special needs. Figure 12–2 summarizes the ways a teacher can respond to students' special needs in art activities.

Respecting each child's rate of growth helps them feel good about themselves. Children who feel good about themselves will be successful in the art program and in other learning situations.

SETTING UP FOR ART ACTIVITIES

Whether setting up an art center or an entire room for art experiences, there are certain basic guidelines for arranging the environment. The age of the group will always be a major consideration in planning, as each age group has varying abilities and interests requiring different arrangements. Specific requirements for different age groups are covered in Chapter 6. At this point, our discussion covers basic guidelines that cross age levels. The following are basic to setting up art activities:

General considerations.   The art area needs to be arranged for ease in cleaning up and dispensing materials. One type of arrangement that works well is to separate wet from dry materials. For example, clay

CHILDREN WITH SPECIAL NEEDS

All students benefit from a balanced program of creative work in two- and three-dimensional media and from the opportunity to try out different approaches to art. It is essential for you to encourage original thinking and authentically creative work for all children with special needs.

Creativity is one of the most important considerations as you conduct creative activities and adapt instruction to meet the needs of individual students and groups who have special needs. Artwork that is traced, copied from adult art, or based on ditto patterns does not involve the student in significant creative activity and should not be encouraged.

Talent plays a role in students' interest and skill in art, just as it does in other subjects. During the elementary and middle school years, encourage varieties of artistic accomplishment and understanding, not just skill in representational drawing. It is unwise to identify a few students as "class artists" or to compare students' artwork in a manner that discourages further interest. Always respect each student's unique effort and insights about art.

Students with *visual impairments* can respond to discussions of artwork, especially themes portrayed in artworks that are related to the student's experience. In art activities, provide materials to create tactile, kinesthetic artwork—clay, textured paper, cloth, small boxes, or wood blocks to arrange.

Students with *speech and hearing impairments* respond slowly to verbal communication. Use nonverbal communication: Have students point out what they see or use pantomime to express responses. Present information through diagrams, charts, and other visual aids. Nonverbal communication can be valuable for all students.

Students who have *impaired mobility* may need to use alternate tools and materials for some activities. Rehabilitation specialists may help you solve unique problems. A number of special tools are available for students with physical impairments (scissors, a mouthpiece that holds a pencil or brush).

Students who are *mentally challenged* have difficulty grasping complex ideas in art and other subjects. Even so, they often respond to art in a direct and insightful manner. They are often able to portray their ideas or feelings more successfully through art than through words. Simplify and separate into specific steps any more difficult activities. Encourage independent thinking about the ideas to be expressed.

Students who *do not speak English* benefit from many of the same nonverbal teaching strategies already noted. Introduce the whole class to the arts and culture of the students. This will broaden the art background of all the students and help them communicate with each other.

Respect *other cultural differences.* An important aspect of art is learning about the arts of cultural groups. Identify individuals and groups in your community who can help familiarize students with unique cultural traditions in the arts and crafts. All students can benefit from learning about these examples of "living cultures" within their own community.

Figure 12-2

Responding to students' special needs.

and paint centers can be placed near the room's water source.

To work creatively with art materials, children need to be free from constraints and worry related to keeping themselves and their work spaces clean. Children will need smocks to protect clothing, supplies for covering work surfaces, and tools for cleaning. Men's shirts with the arms cut off make good smocks, or children can wear an old set of clothes for art activities. These "art clothes" will be like an art journal because the various spots and splashes on them are reminders of past art projects. Children will also need to know where to place work in progress for safekeeping and where wet items can be left to dry. Providing these

arrangements is part of the teacher's responsibility as a guide and facilitator.

Sharp materials such as scissors must be placed out of reach of children who have not yet mastered handling them independently and safely. Usually such materials are dispensed from a teacher-height counter placed in a location convenient to children's work tables. Easels are placed out of the way of traffic so that children can work without being jostled. Next to the easels are places for children to hang paint smocks and a rack to drape paintings to dry. The rack where children's paintings are hung is situated so that the children do not have to carry their wet paintings through areas where other children are working to hang them.

THIS ONE'S for YOU!

Teacher Tips

The way a teacher sets up her own materials, supplies, and space can make or break the child's and teacher's successful experiences in art. The following are some suggestions for arranging supplies for art experiences as well as displaying children's artwork.

- Scissors holders can be made from gallon milk or bleach containers. Simply punch holes in the container and place scissors in holes with the points to the inside. Egg cartons turned upside down with slits in each mound also make excellent holders.
- Paint containers can range from muffin tins and plastic egg cartons to plastic soft drink cartons with yogurt containers in them. These work especially well outdoors as well as indoors because they are large and not easily tipped over. Place one brush in each container; this prevents colors from getting mixed and makes cleanup easier.
- Crayon containers can be made from juice and vegetable cans painted or covered with contact paper.
- Crayon pieces may be melted down in muffin trays in a warm oven. These, when cooled down, are nice for rubbings or drawings.
- A card file for art activities helps organize the program.
- Airtight coffee cans and plastic food containers are excellent ways to keep clay moist and always ready for use.
- By keeping two or more boxes of scrap paper, children will be able to choose the size paper they want more easily.
- Cover a wall area with pegboard and suspend heavy shopping bags or transparent plastic bags from hooks inserted in the pegboard. Hang smocks in the same way on the pegboard (at child level, of course).
- Use the back of a piano or bookcase for hanging a shoe bag. Its pockets can hold many small items.
- Paint a large cardboard box to use as a three-dimensional kiosk to hang pictures on. Use shoeboxes to display children's clay work.
- For clay sharing, mold clay in the shape of a cake. Place the "cake" on a small table and use a plastic knife to slice it. Children can each work with a "slice" of clay.
- Show off young children's creative work at their eye level on classroom walls or bulletin boards. Keep bulletin boards low so children can help tape on materials. Toddlers can safely touch displays if you slide drawings down behind clear Plexiglas frames.
- To keep artwork accessible, use press-on cork tiles to create low bulletin boards for toddlers. Use different levels of paper or cloth-covered boxes as pedestals to display clay sculptures. Display delicate clay miniatures in the partitions of a beverage six-pack carrier placed on its side.

Drying racks are convenient to have in early childhood classrooms. However, the commercial type can be expensive. An inexpensive substitute can be assembled in the same manner as a bookshelf. Cardboard is placed on top of four brick or block supports (one in each corner). Several layers are built so paintings can be left on the shelves for drying. Two other methods for drying paintings are (1) hanging paintings on a clothesline suspended above the head of the tallest adult and (2) using a portable, folding clothes-drying rack. However, paintings can drip in both of these methods. Windowsills can also be used, especially for drying three-dimensional artwork.

Masonite boards cut in 10–inch squares are convenient for transporting wet or unfinished clay work and

assemblages to a place where they can dry. The children can work directly on the boards when they start their modeling and construction. These boards can frequently be obtained from scrap piles at a lumberyard or purchased inexpensively. Foam core board or heavy corrugated cardboard can also be used. To enlarge table surfaces for drying artwork, cover the table top with large pieces of cardboard. You can find these at warehouse-type stores where they are used to hold large lots of merchandise on pallets. They are generally discarded everyday and are available for the asking.

A place for children to wash after using wet materials must also be nearby. If you don't have the convenience of a sink in your room, a plastic kitchen tub half filled with water and placed on a low stand next to the paper

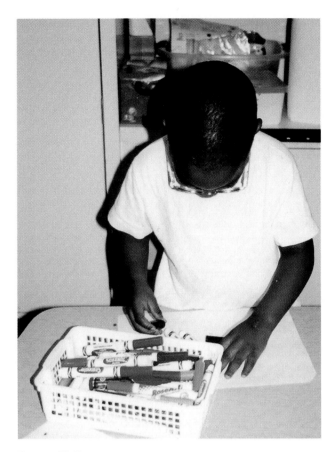

Figure 12-3

Markers in many colors and tip widths are basic drawing materials.

towels and wastebasket works well. Include a bucket of small sponges near the art area. They are easy for children to use and can be rinsed and used again.

Set up art materials so that children have daily art experiences.   A teacher should make sure every day that there are designated places, equipment, and materials for art experiences. For example, every day the teacher prepares easels with paper and paints for children's use. This way, there is a smooth movement through the easel area instead of the teacher rushing around to get paint ready amid waiting children.

Have a supply of paper, crayons, pencils, and clay available in a set place every day for the children's use. Tearing, cutting, and pasting supplies should be ready and easily available, too. (Specific suggestions on supplies and their care follow later in this chapter.) As part of this preparation, the teacher guides the children in learning the necessary use and care of all equipment as it is set up.

Being prepared in all these ways ensures that children will have the supplies they need, will know where to get them, and will know how to use them—

which encourages them to pursue independent, creative activities on a daily basis.

Set up for weekly art activities.   To enhance children's creative experiences, the teacher plans for and sets up weekly art activities in addition to the children's daily experiences. For example, a teacher might plan a unit on printing (see Chapter 13 for more information on printing), using each week to introduce a specific technique of printing. This, of course, would be in addition to and *not* in place of the children's regular art experiences. The teacher plans in advance to set up a table or other area with printing supplies and equipment. Scurrying around for "things to print with" at the last minute can be avoided in this planned weekly approach.

Work of the previous week is evaluated before new plans are prepared. Even though plans have been carefully thought through, a teacher must be prepared to make changes due to unexpected events. For example, a sudden snow storm extends the amount of time the children will play outdoors. Or one morning the road outside the building is being repaired and huge machines appear on the street. The teacher obviously recognizes this scene as a good learning experience and arranges time for children to observe the workers.

In weekly plans, teachers plan for a balance between the familiar and the new as they make decisions about how materials and equipment are to be used. Teachers need not be concerned that children may lose interest if the same activities are offered week after week. If children have freedom to use materials in their own ways, they do not tire of working with the same ones. After children have gained success in using a material, they enjoy repeating the experience.

Since some activities require more supervision than others, a teacher needs to consider how many activities will be available for a given period. The number of activities chosen that require close supervision depends upon the number of adults assigned to the room. After a teacher has made careful observations and has decided upon the activities for the week, he or she must think through what would be the best use of his time—for example, whether to give special attention to the block area or to the art area. If a new material or technique is being introduced, it generally requires teacher supervision. In this case, the teacher usually sits with a small group and participates in the activity with them. Unless there are several teachers in a room, it is unlikely there would be more than one group activity requiring close supervision.

In weekly and monthly planning, consideration must be given to the time of the year and to the developmental levels of the children. At the beginning of a

Figure 12-4

In choosing drawing materials, keep in mind the motor control, coordination, and overall developmental level of the child.

school year, too many choices and too much open space may be upsetting to children because they are not yet familiar with the room or the school. At a time when a teacher's goal is to help children feel comfortable in the school, too many new and exciting materials can be overwhelming and distracting. The same is true for older children at the beginning of a new school year. Children will feel more comfortable as the year begins by using familiar media and equipment they have used the previous school year. Therefore, materials offered at the beginning of the year should be those that are familiar to most children. For example, even a very shy child can feel secure at a table with crayons and paper. As children begin to know each other, feel more comfortable in the room, and become aware of the daily routines, additional materials can be introduced and activities can be expanded.

Set up the art area so that it facilitates children's creative experiences. While specific materials and their use are discussed individually later in this chapter, there are some general ideas that apply to the use of materials for young children.

Children work better in art activities in a predictable, organized environment where materials can

always be found in the same place. For example, art materials on open storage shelves at child level make it possible for children to find the materials they want to use easily and independently. Also, when materials such as paper or paste are spaced far apart on shelves, putting things back in place becomes an easier task for young children. Using placemats or trays on child-size tables helps organize space into individual work areas. (More information on setting up centers is found in Appendix C.)

Art activities in the early childhood program work best on child-level tables and easels. Although some children may occasionally enjoy working on the floor, it is important to have a table set up for regular art activities. It is a good idea to have a limit on the number of children for each art activity/area to ensure the proper space for children as well as sufficient materials for each child.

SETTING UP FOR ART ACTIVITIES–SPECIFIC AGES

In addition to the general considerations discussed earlier, there are some specific, age-related considerations for setting up art activities for young children.

Planning Art Activities for Toddlers

Very young children benefit from a program divided into well-defined areas in which they have freedom to move, explore, and make decisions about activities and materials. However, when planning for this age range, special considerations must be kept in mind. Since toddlers and young two year olds are very active and instinctively want to explore everything, the materials they use must be sturdy, must be practically indestructible, and should not include tiny pieces that might be swallowed.

Put only a few materials out at a time so that young children are not overwhelmed with too many choices. Materials should be rotated often, and children should learn to work on the floor or table area nearby and not carry materials across the room.

Art materials, such as crayons, play dough, colored markers, chalk, and paint, as well as materials such as sand and water, should be frequently available to children of this age. These materials are presented under the supervision of an adult so that appropriate use is encouraged. Also, since children of this age have difficulty sharing, duplicates of materials will help cut down on competition for the same items.

Figure 12-5

Making a collage is easier if materials are organized and easy for children to find and use.

Figure 12-6

Be sure to have both right- and left-hand scissors for children's use in art activities.

Traffic patterns and the children's distractibility also need to be considered when art or any other interest areas are arranged in the room. Place activities requiring running water, such as play dough and painting, convenient to sinks. Walking babies and younger toddlers are prone to falling, grabbing, and running; therefore they need clear, open spaces. They are also easily distracted by other activities, making task completion or cleanup difficult unless areas are visually divided. (See Appendix C for more information on dividing the room into centers.) The need for occasional solitude and quiet is especially important at this age. Toddlers can easily become overstimulated if exposed to too many activities at once. In view of all these considerations, dividing and organizing a room becomes an art in itself. Several arrangements should be tried to determine which one best fits the children's needs.

Art Activities for Young Preschoolers, Age Two to Four Years

Most young preschoolers two to four years of age have a limited span of interest and attention. Many activities, even the most interesting, hold their interest for less than 10 minutes. However, it should be remembered that each child is different and interest spans may be shorter or longer for each individual child.

The point is that the teacher must, first of all, plan activities that appeal to the interests of the young preschooler. Simple, basic art activities are most interesting to the child of this age group. Second, the teacher must be prepared to accept the fact that the activity may hold the child's interest for only a short time. It helps to remember that a period of time that seems short to an adult may be quite long to the young preschool child. Finally, alternative and extra activities

Figure 12-7

When a child gets involved in painting, the process of creating is more important than the product.

Figure 12-8

Creative activities are often a social time.

should always be available for those children who may not be interested in the first activity planned.

Because two- and three-year-old children require considerable supervision, many teachers prefer to introduce or arrange for only one supervised art activity each day. Sometimes they will divide the whole class into small groups for simultaneous participation. Unless there are several adults, this can be a difficult undertaking. In such a set-up, one-to-one interaction between teacher and child, which is so necessary in the early years, will be limited. In addition, whole-group participation in art can frequently lead to conformity of response rather than individuality of expression.

In one popular method for organizing supervised art activity, the teachers have the children take turns coming to an area where materials for art are arranged. The space will usually accommodate four to six children and provides opportunities for peer interaction as well as for interaction with the teacher. This arrangement allows for freedom of choice and gives children

a chance to grow toward autonomous decision making about the kind of art they will do.

With the young preschool group, it is usually best to use only the basic materials at first. This helps keep the art program from being too confusing for the child. Using only a few crayons or paints or pasting one or two kinds of things at first is a good idea. It encourages children to experiment with each new tool and medium. They learn to use the basic tools and materials first. When they have acquired the basic skills, more colors and variety can be added.

Why and when to provide a variety of materials for early childhood art deserves thoughtful consideration. After children have had opportunities to explore the basic expressive materials, varieties of the basics can be introduced, providing the children do not become overwhelmed. Two- and three-year-old children and some less secure older children may still need consistency because sameness and simplicity provide a sense of security. Observant teachers will notice when a child begins to lose interest in using art materials or when a child keeps repeating the same crayon or paint symbols daily. Then it may be time to offer that child the stimulation contained in a change of medium or novel material. Let us now consider specific activities for the interest, ability, and skill levels of young preschool children.

Collage.   (For more information on the techniques of collage, see Chapter 13.) Making a collage is a good activity for young preschoolers because it can be completed quickly and is within the interest span of most young preschoolers. It also encourages the use of small muscles as children tear and paste. Young preschoolers also benefit mentally as they learn to choose items and to arrange them in a collage. As they paste together a collage, they learn about the feel, shape, and color of many things and develop the ability to use things in unusual ways.

At times, it may seem as if young preschoolers focus more on the paste than on the items being pasted, but that is part of the fun. The teacher must be sure that the objects available are suitable for the child who is using them. For example, it is important to keep tiny, inedible objects away from children who still put things in their mouth.

With young preschoolers who are new to this activity, begin with just one thing to paste. A good idea is for them to make a tear-and-paste collage. To do this, provide the children with pieces of newspaper, colored tissue, or any colored scrap paper that tears easily. The teacher shows them, if necessary, how to tear large and small pieces. Then they paste these torn bits of paper on colored construction paper in any way they choose. This is a good activity for young preschoolers who do not want or are not yet able to use scissors. Some scissors should be available for children who want to try cutting the pieces to paste on the collage. However, children should not be forced to practice cutting.

As the children master the basic technique of pasting, more objects can be added to the collage. Some good things to add are large buttons; bits of cloth and paper in different colors, textures, and shapes; and bottle caps. Care must be taken to be sure the materials are not sharp, not painted with lead paint, and not small enough to swallow.

For a change of pace, different materials may be used for the backing of the collage. The children may use pieces of cardboard to paste things on, or shoe box lids, or even pieces of burlap. The teacher and children use their imaginations to come up with ideas for new and different collage materials.

Painting. Young preschool children also get much satisfaction from working with paint and experimenting with color and form. Painting at an easel is not as easy for young preschoolers as painting on a table. It is difficult for this young artist to control drips at an easel. Also, while standing at an easel, the young child may be easily distracted and wander away. Often, young children of this age paint one color on top of the other and enjoy the effect. But most of all, they enjoy the movement involved in painting. Finger paint is an especially good medium for this age group, as it can be manipulated over and over again. In this way, the process is stressed, not the product. This is very important for

children, who at this age are learning the basic ways to use paint. This age group enjoys the feel (and sometimes the taste) of the paint. They may even use their upper arms and elbows to help them in their designs.

To save on the cost of finger paint paper and to try something new, have the children finger paint on a formica table top, an enamel-top table, a sheet of smooth formica, or even linoleum. When this is done, a print can be made from the child's finger painting by laying a piece of newsprint paper on the finger painting and gently rubbing it with one hand. The painting is transferred in this way from the table top to the paper. More finger paint activities are suggested later in this chapter.

There may be some preschool children who do not like the feel of finger paint. If this is so, the child should never be forced to use it. Instead, another art activity can be found that the child will enjoy.

Printing. Printing with objects is an art activity that is appropriate for the age, ability, and interest level of young preschool children. In a basic printing activity, the child learns that an object dipped in or brushed with paint makes its own mark, or print, on paper. Children use small muscles in the hand and wrist as they hold the object, dip it in paint, and print with it on paper. They learn that each object has its own unique quality since each thing makes its own imprint.

For the young preschool child, stick prints are a good place to start. In this type of printing, children dip small pieces of wood of various sizes and shapes into a thick tempera paint and press them onto a piece of paper. Twigs, wooden spools, wood clothespins, and bottle caps are objects suitable for three year olds to use in printing.

After stick printing is mastered, printing with vegetables is good with this age group. Some teachers are opposed to the idea of using food in any art activities. However, many teachers feel that using vegetables past their "shelf life" is a good use for food that is not useable for other purposes. There are many printing activities presented in this book for teachers on both sides of this issue. For those who don't object to food printing, green peppers, carrots, turnips, and potatoes are some vegetables to try. The vegetables are sliced in half, making two smooth surfaces for printing. A good way for young preschoolers to begin printing is to "walk" the inked vegetable across the paper in even "steps." When it gets to the other side, they walk it back again. By making three or four lines, or walks, the child has made a pattern.

After one color is used, the vegetable can be wiped clean and another color can be used. Three year olds like to try many colors with the same printing object.

They may even print over their first prints in a different color. More printing activities for young preschool children are found in Chapter 13 and at the end of this chapter.

Crayons.   Crayons are the most basic, most familiar, and easiest tool for young preschoolers to use. Large crayons are easy to hold and can be used to make attractive colored marks on paper. Most young preschoolers have crayons, but often drawings on paper are the only use made of them. There are, however, several other ways to use crayons that the teacher might try to vary the program for young preschoolers.

⊙ *Crayons and a Variety of Materials.* Crayons can be used to draw on many surfaces. Cardboard in any form (including corrugated cardboard, paper gift boxes, and food trays) is a good surface for crayon drawings, as is styrofoam. Crayon drawings on sandpaper have an interesting effect.

⊙ *Crayon Rubbings.* Drawing pictures with crayons is only one of the uses for crayons. Crayon rubbing is a technique that young preschool children can easily master. To make a crayon rubbing, the child puts a piece of paper over a textured surface and rubs the sides of a peeled crayon over the paper.

The crayon picks up the texture on the paper in a design. Some surfaces that can be used are bumpy paper, food trays, bark, leaves, the sidewalk, bricks, and corrugated cardboard. This is a good activity for developing both small and large muscles.

⊙ *Crayon Resist.* Another way to use crayon is in crayon resist drawings. To make a resist drawing, the child first draws a picture on paper with crayons, pressing hard. She then paints over and around the crayon drawing with thin paint (tempera paint diluted with water). A dark-colored paint works best. The dark color fills in all the areas that the crayon has not covered. In the areas covered with crayon, the crayon "resists," or is not covered by, the paint. Crayon resist gives the feeling of a night picture. It is a thrilling experience for the child to see the changes that come when the paint crosses the paper.

See Chapter 13 for additional activities and techniques for using crayons.

Art Activities for Older Preschoolers and Kindergartners (Four to Six Years)

Just as in the case of the younger preschool child, there are preferred and suitable materials and activities for older preschoolers. Although there may be considerable overlap, children in this age group generally differ significantly from younger preschool children.

There are some general traits of preschoolers and kindergartners four to six years old. Small-muscle development in the fingers, hands, and wrists is much improved. Whereas younger preschool children may have great difficulty buttoning their clothing or using scissors, most in this older group do not. Use of crayons; colored markers; and, in some cases, pencils and pens is quite possible.

Since these children are very interested in life beyond home and school, art activities including outside environments (e.g., television characters) can be stimulating. Youngsters of this age paint and draw with more purpose. Designs and pictures are within their abilities. These will probably be somewhat simple but nonetheless fun and exciting for the children to do.

If a variety of materials is available, especially to children five years of age and older, they can discover alternative ways of accomplishing similar tasks. For example, if glue does not hold, children may try tape or a stapler. If other fibers are available in addition to yarn, children will experiment and discover possibilities for knotting, stitching, or weaving with each. Children, finding some materials more satisfying than others, are more apt to use them to express ideas. With variety, older children come to understand that color, line, form, and texture can be expressed through different materials.

The first cooperative or group art projects will usually take place in kindergarten. In most cases the children discuss the joint effort but work individually. Then the teacher helps arrange the individual contributions into a whole. (See Chapter 13 for discussion of a group mural as an example of this group activity approach.)

Older children, in grades 1 through 5, will continue to express their creative potential if appropriate art activities are provided for them. See the Think About It: Summary of Art Curriculum Goals/Activities—Grades 1–5 Box on page 227 for a summary of appropriate curriculum goals and activities for older children.

Let us now consider some specific art activities and the required materials and strategies for each.

BASIC EQUIPMENT, MATERIALS, AND USE

What follows are lists of basic art materials needed in the early childhood art program and related strategies for their use. Basic recipes for making finger paint, paste, play dough, and other related materials are found in Appendix C. In choosing from the lists, the teacher must keep in mind the motor control, coordination, and overall developmental level of children in the group.

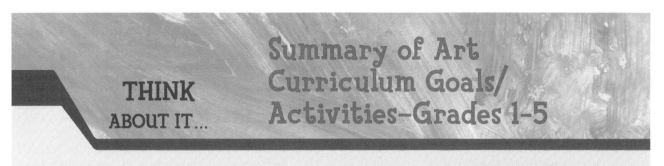

THINK ABOUT IT...

Summary of Art Curriculum Goals/ Activities–Grades 1-5

When planning art activities for older children, the following summary may provide you with some ideas to help plan age-appropriate activities.

Grade 1: Students learn to identify visual elements such as lines, colors, shapes, textures, and their sensory qualities. Perceptual skills and a vocabulary for art are developed through role-playing, physical movement, visual searches, and game-like activities.

Students create art based on imagination, personal interpretations of nature, familiar places, and activities with family or friends. They learn to plan their use of visual elements to create original artworks. They acquire basic skills in using media for drawing, painting, collage, printmaking, sculpture, and other three-dimensional art.

Students see and discuss styles and types of artwork from varied cultures and periods. They learn about places to see art in their community, where artists work, and the kinds of art they create. Students become aware of art in everyday life through lessons on architecture, clothing, and other environmental arts.

The process of looking at art is presented as an enjoyable and integral part of learning about art. Students learn to perceive and describe the subject matter, visual elements, and mood in their own art and the work of adults. Students learn to express their opinions about art and to respond thoughtfully to others' opinions.

Grade 2: Students learn that observations of the environment—changes in weather, animals, the city by day and night—have inspired adult artists and can be sources of inspiration for their own art. Perceptual skills and a meaningful art vocabulary are developed with an emphasis on imagination, sensory awareness, and visual recall.

Students continue to create art based on imagination and personal interpretations of varied themes related to their environment, activities, and events. They learn to make intentional choices of lines, colors, and other visual elements. They use familiar media in new ways and combinations to create two- and three-dimensional art.

Students continue to learn about varied styles and types of art with greater emphasis on the cultural origin and functions of artworks. They expand their knowledge of types of artists, where they work, and reasons people create or display art. Lessons on architecture and product design and related art forms focus attention on art in everyday life.

Students continue to learn that looking at art is an enjoyable and thoughtful process. They perceive, compare, and contrast the subject matter and visual elements in artworks. They learn that judgments about art—their own and others'—should be based on features they perceive in the artwork.

Grade 3: Students become aware of and develop an ability to use different vantage points (e.g., side views, top views) for observing objects and scenes. They learn to perceive and describe subtle visual qualities such as lines, colors, shapes, textures, and patterns within the natural and constructed environment.

Students continue to create art based on imagination, recall, and observation. They learn to portray details, depict action, use different vantage points, and plan their use of visual qualities to express an idea, feeling, or nonverbal message. Activities develop flexibility and problem-solving skills in two- and three-dimensional media and art forms.

Artworks are selected to help students appreciate themes, types, and styles of art. The functions, cultural origin, and relative age of selected artworks are studied along with methods and reasons for creating art. The concept of living with art is developed in lessons about crafts, architecture, and related art forms.

(Continues)

THINK ABOUT IT... (Continued)

Positive attitudes about the process of looking at art are reinforced and extended. Students learn to perceive more subtle visual qualities in their own art and the art of adults. They use art terms to describe, analyze, and interpret visual qualities of artworks. They develop skill in talking about specific features in an artwork to explain their judgment of it.

Grade 4: Increased visual awareness is developed as students learn to identify subtle visual qualities in the natural and constructed environment and artworks. Greater emphasis is placed on perceiving implied paths of movement, interactions of colors and shapes, moods of places at different times of day, and different seasons or weather.

Students create more complex works of art and give greater attention to their expressive intentions. They use design concepts for specific purposes, such as color to express a mood and repetition to create visual rhythms. Efficient and inventive uses of media are emphasized to build skills and flexibility in creating expressive two- and three-dimensional art.

Students contrast and compare the functions, cultural origin, and relative age of artworks from different eras. Students learn that creating and studying art can be a life-long pursuit or career. Lessons about innovative and traditional art reinforce the concept of art as a "living heritage" that brings artistry to daily life.

Students learn to be art "detectives" who seek answers to questions, such as "How is the work planned (designed)?" "What materials were used?" "What ideas or moods are expressed?" Students learn that thoughtful judgments about art are related to qualities in the work and how they can be interpreted.

Grade 5: Students learn to apply and refine perceptual skills developed in earlier grades. They learn to identify and analyze more subtle and complex visual relationships such as how light affects our perception of colors, textures, and forms and how we perceive space and distance.

Students continue to create art in order to express what they see, know, feel, and imagine. They make sketches to develop ideas and to try out design concepts. Skills in using media are developed by problem solving and planned experiments. Multistep techniques are introduced in two- and three-dimensional media.

Students learn about selected styles and historical changes in art of the Americas as well as world cultures. They learn more about careers in art, the use of computers for art, and the role of museums. Lessons acquaint students with art in public places and 20th century art forms such as photography and filmmaking.

Students learn that criteria for judgments of their own and others' work should be relevant to its general style or purpose—expressive, imaginative, representational, abstract, or functional.

Drawing Materials and Use

1. Sturdy sheets of paper (manila or newsprint, 8″ × 12″ or 12″ × 18″). Spread the paper on a table or on the floor, or pin it to a wall or easel. Paper of different shapes and colors may be used for variety.

2. A basket of jumbo crayons about three quarters of an inch in width. These are a good size for the muscle control of small fingers. Unwrap the crayons so they can be used on both the sides and the ends.

3. Colored markers in many colors and tip widths. (Be sure they are not permanent markers.)

Colored markers come in beautiful, clear colors. Compared with paint, they have the additional ad-

vantage of staying bright and unsullied until the children use them up.

Most schools set out crayons or pens jumbled together in a basket. However, you might try assembling them in separate boxes so that each user has an individual, complete set. This cuts down on arguments and means that all the colors are available to each child as the children require them.

Another alternative is to store crayons in wide-mouth containers according to color—all red crayons in one container, all blue in another, etc.

Crayons are an ideal medium for children; they are bold, colorful, clean, and inexpensive. They consist of an oily or waxy binder mixed with color pigments. They are of various types, some soft, some semihard, some for general use with young children (kindergarten or "fat" crayons). Crayons work well on most papers. They do not blend well; if attempts are made to do this, the wax often "tears."

Chalking Materials and Use

1. A blackboard and eraser, and/or a stack of wet or dry (or both) paper.

2. A container full of colored and white chalk.

Chalk is inexpensive and comes in a variety of colors. Its most typical use is with chalkboards, but young children do not seem to use it very effectively there. They do better if they can mark on the sidewalk with it—perhaps because the rougher texture of the cement more easily pulls the color off the stick, and the children seem more able to tell what they are doing as they squat down and draw. It is, of course, necessary to explain to them that they may "write" with chalk only on special places.

Some young artists apply chalks in separate strokes, letting the color blending take place in the viewer's eye. Others are not reluctant to blend the colors and do so successfully, although the colors may get muddied. Of course, there is no need to caution children against this; they should be encouraged to explore by rubbing with fingers, a cotton swab, or anything available. Most children will select and use chalks easily.

Chalk drawing is best done on a paper with a slightly coarse, abrasive surface. This texture helps the paper trap and hold the chalk particles. Many papers have this quality, including inexpensive manila paper.

Chalks are brittle and easily broken. They are also impermanent, smearing very easily. Completed works should be sprayed with a "fixative" (ordinary hairspray works well); this should be done with proper ventilation.

Chalk strokes can be strengthened by wetting the chalk or paper. Various liquids have also been used with chalks for interesting results. These include dipping the chalk sticks in buttermilk, starch, and sugar water. Liquid tends to seal the chalk, so teachers must occasionally rub a piece of old sandpaper on the end of the chalk in order to break this seal and allow the color to come off again.

Fat, soft chalk of different colors mixes with ease and provides a great beginning for small-motor, free expression. Chalk discourages tight, inhibited work and makes free expression easy. Covering each piece of chalk with a piece of aluminum foil, leaving about half an inch of the chalk exposed, prevents smearing. It also prevents the transferring of colors from one piece of chalk to another while they are stored.

Figure 12-9

Painting at an easel is a naturally appealing activity for the visual/spatial learner.

If a slippery surface is desired, liquid starch may be applied to the paper before the dry chalk. There is less friction with starch, and the paper is less likely to tear.

Soaking pieces of large chalk in sugar water (one part sugar and two parts water) for about 15 minutes and then using the chalk on dry paper is another method of application. Sugar gives the chalk a shiny look when dry.

Brush Painting Materials

1. Two easels (at least) with two blunt-tipped nails sticking out near each upper corner to attach the paper. (Paper can also be held on the board with spring-type clothespins.) Easels must be at the right height so that a child can paint without stretching or stooping. Children can also paint seated at a table covered with newspapers or an old shower curtain.

2. Sheets of paper (18″ × 24″ plain newsprint), white or in assorted colors.

3. Three or four jars of tempera paint. These may be mixed with powdered detergent for proper consistency.

4. Paint containers. These must have flat bottoms so they will not tip over easily. Quart milk cartons (cut down) are good since they can be thrown away

after using. Also, plastic fruit juice cans with lids work well when unused paint needs to be stored.

5. Large, long-handled brushes in each jar. Those with 12-inch handles and ¾-inch bristle length are easy for young children to use. Soft, floppy, camel-hair brushes allow the child to swoop about the paper most freely. The stiff, flat kind of brush makes it harder to produce such free movements. See Figure 13–13 for more information on paintbrushes.

6. Smocks. An old shirt with the sleeves cut to the child's arm length makes a practical smock. Oilcloth or plastic aprons are also good. Extra art smocks can be made easily from either large plastic trash bags or newspaper. Cut openings for the child's head and arms at the end of a plastic trash bag. Instead of a smock, a set of old clothes can also be used as "art clothes."

7. A place to dry finished paintings.

THIS ONE'S for YOU!

Sand, Art, and Exploration

The traditional sand table is often limited to preschool programs where young children develop coordination and visual perception by scooping, patting, smoothing, pushing, and packing sand. The sand table is actually better termed a sensory table because of the many sensory experiences it affords young children. It is also a place for art explorations.

The sand or sensory table in preschool programs is generally a low table containing sand; vehicles; animals; shovels; and assorted funnels, cups, and spoons. Because of limited budgets, many preschools and kindergartens unfortunately don't feel they can afford sand/sensory tables. However, a large, plastic tub with a removable lid filled with sand can provide children the tactile and creative experiences with sand so valuable in a child's development—at a fraction of the cost of a sand table!

Sand provides children an abundant source for creative expression in forming shapes and making sand-based creations. Activities at the sensory table also cover many tactile experiences across the curriculum. Consider some of the following tactile experiences using the sensory table or tactile tub:

⊙ During a lesson on flowers, place sand and plastic flowers in the sensory table. Place several flower pots and hand shovels in the table. Provide spray bottles filled with water. The children can pot the flowers and make flower beds in the sensory table.

⊙ Put shredded paper in the sensory table; add magnetic items and magnet wands. The children can go on a treasure hunt for different items. Make sure to give them a cup to place their discoveries in!

⊙ Try this "magical" experiment at the sensory table. Clean 1–liter soda bottles and the caps. With a drill (or an awl) make 3 small holes in the bottom of the bottle. Fill with water and cover. When you unscrew the cap, the water comes out of the bottle. When you tighten the cap, the water stays in the bottle. For younger preschoolers, this is almost "magical" and they will repeatedly twist the cap to open and close it, which will help their small motor skills. For older children, this is a great introduction to a discussion of air and pressure.

⊙ Add rubber fish from the bait department of a store to water in the sensory table. Add a couple of small aquarium nets for catching the plastic fish. The addition of blue food color to the water makes it even more fun!

⊙ During a pet unit, fill the sensory table with stuffed animals, dog bones, dog food dishes, measuring devices, etc. The children love feeding their "animals."

⊙ For bugs in the grass, place green Easter grass in the sensory table, and add plenty of plastic bugs, snakes, butterflies, etc. The children love looking for the critters, then trying to identify them. Books about insects can be placed close by so they can look up the bugs and try to match them with the ones in the sensory table.

⊙ Put Mardi Gras beads into the table. Add scissors, bowls, and big tweezers to pick up the different-sized balls that were cut from the beads. The children measure lengths of the bead strings and sort beads by size and color with the tweezers. Scissors provide wonderful eye–hand coordination with cutting the little strings in between the beads.

Mixing paint. Although mixing paint in large quantities saves teachers time, the children enjoy making it so much, and this is such a good learning experience for them, that mixing a fresh batch each day with one or two children helping stir is generally preferred. A surprising amount of tempera is needed in relation to the quantity of water to make rich, bright, creamy paint; thus it is best to put the tempera into the container first and then add water bit by bit. Instead of water, some teachers prefer using liquid starch because it thickens the paint mixture. However, it does increase the expense. It is also helpful to add a dash of liquid detergent, since this makes cleaning up easier. Another hint to easier cleanup is to cut a posterboard to fit the easel and laminate both sides of the posterboard. Tape the laminated posterboard over the easel so that as the students paint on the easel and get ready for the next child, the student can easily wipe off the paint with a damp cloth, rag, or paper towel. It helps the student learn how to cleanup, keeps the center clean, and develops more eye–hand coordination in a fun way.

At the easel, it may help children to see that if they wipe the brush on the side of the jar the paint does not drip or run. An adult can show the children that keeping each brush in its own paint jar keeps the color clear.

It will expedite matters if several pieces of paper are clipped to the easel at once. Many teachers prefer to write the child's name on the back of the paper to avoid the problem of having him paint over it. If a developmental portfolio is kept at school for each child, dating a few paintings and saving them delights parents at conference time because it enables them to see how the child's skills have developed during the year. You can use a digital camera to take photos of selected pieces of each child's artwork for a video presentation of her painting experiences throughout the year.

Easel painting. With easel painting, teachers like to start with only the three primary colors (red, blue, and yellow) in the beginning of the year and then add others in the second month or so. Each jar of blue tempera paint should be labeled with a strip of blue paper clearly printed BLUE. (Use the same label idea for each color.) Brushes should be thoroughly washed and kept in good condition. Teach the children how to wipe up and wash the art area after its use.

At the end of each day, all paintbrushes are washed thoroughly in running water and dried, bristles up, before being put away. Easels and aprons are washed with a wet cloth and soap if necessary. Paint containers are washed and put away. Leftover paint must be covered with a tight lid or aluminum foil. Aprons and smocks are hung up.

Finger Painting Materials and Use

1. Paper that has a shiny surface. This can be butcher paper, shelf paper, special finger paint paper, freezer wrap, or glossy gift wrap paper.

2. A water supply to make the paper damp. A damp sponge or rag works best. Water may also be sprinkled directly onto the paper.

3. Finger paint. This can be special finger paint or dry tempera paint mixed with liquid starch or liquid detergent to make a thick mixture.

4. Racks to dry the finished work.

5. A smock for each painter.

6. A nearby sink and running water for washing hands and cleaning up or a bucket of soapy water, sponges, and paper towels.

For finger painting, the tables are covered with linoleum, formica, or plastic, and the children wear smocks. Plenty of paper towels and clean rags are provided. Smooth-surfaced paper is dipped in a pan of water and spread flat on a table.

The quickest, simplest way to make finger paint is to combine liquid starch with dry tempera. This may be done by pouring a generous dollop of starch onto the paper and then sprinkling it with dry tempera. Alternatively, some teachers like to stir the dry pigment into an entire container of starch base. No matter how the paint is originally prepared, you need to be ready to add more ingredients as the children work. The results to strive for in mixing are rich, brilliant color and sufficient paint to fill the paper completely if the child wishes. Children must be allowed to experiment with

Figure 12-10

It is important to have printing equipment such as a brayer available for older children.

There are so many more ways to display children's artwork than just on the bulletin board. Here are some ideas to help get you started on new ways to display the work of young artists.

- ⊙ Personalize displays. On a large bulletin board, mark sections off for each artist. Take children's photos and invite them to draw self-portraits to hang in their own gallery. Encourage the children to discuss and select the rest of the artwork they wish to display in their section of the bulletin board.
- ⊙ Make interactive displays. Have the children make and display a group collage of materials that encourage children to touch it when they see it. Make peephole covers for pictures. Tape the peephole cover on one side of the picture. Encourage children to guess what's under the peephole. Then lift it up to see if they guessed correctly.
- ⊙ Suspend wire sculptures from clear fish line.
- ⊙ Make floor display cubes with cardboard boxes with taped on, clear cellophane tops for peek-a-boo viewing.
- ⊙ Make an elastic "clothesline" for displaying artwork. Stretch a length of ¼-inch elastic along the wall chosen for display. Staple it in place. Use miniature clothespins to hang the children's artwork. The elastic stretches slightly, and the clothespins are always in place as instant hang ups for new artwork.
- ⊙ For an interesting display method, place a huge sheet of clear, shatterproof Plexiglas over children's artwork on the classroom floor. Encourage the children to observe the artwork on their tummies for a "closer look."

the paint as they wish, using their fingers, the palms of their hands, wrists, and arms.

Prepared finger paints may be used, or the children may help mix a recipe from Appendix C. If the recipe is used, the mixture may be separated into three or four parts and coloring added—either food color or the powdered tempera used for easel painting. Children like to add their own color; they may use salt shakers containing powdered paint and mix in the color with their fingers. Adding soap flakes (not detergents) to the paint mixture increases variety. Finger painting can also be done with interesting materials such as pudding, cold cream, and shaving cream. Be sure to check the list of ingredients on the label for any ingredients children may be allergic to.

Variations.   Another method of finger painting is to cover a table with white oilcloth and let the children work on the oilcloth. The mixture can later be washed off with a hose or under a faucet. This activity is good for all ages.

Use waxed paper for a change, instead of regular finger painting paper, because of its transparent quality. A combination of any liquid dishwashing detergent and a dark-colored tempera paint (one part paint, one part soap) can be applied onto waxed paper. Cover the surface evenly so the painter can make a simple design with his or her fingers.

Finger painting without paper is another variation. The children finger paint directly onto plastic trays or a table top. When each child finishes, place a piece of paper on top of the finger painting and rub across the back of the paper. Lift the paper from the tray or table top and a print of the finger painting is made. The trays are easily rinsed off in the sink.

Pasting Materials and Use

1. Small jars of paste. (Or give each child a square of waxed paper with a spoonful of paste on it. This prevents waste.) A wooden tongue depressor is a good tool for spreading the paste, or paste can be spread with the fingers. Glue sticks can also be used.

2. Sheets of plain or colored manila or construction paper in many sizes.

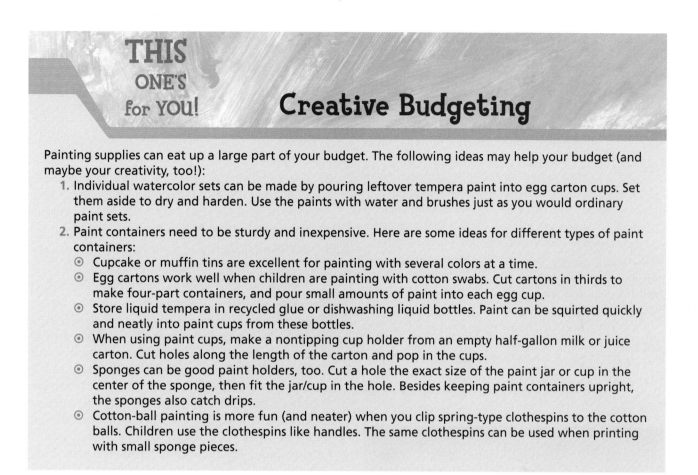

THIS ONE'S for YOU!

Creative Budgeting

Painting supplies can eat up a large part of your budget. The following ideas may help your budget (and maybe your creativity, too!):

1. Individual watercolor sets can be made by pouring leftover tempera paint into egg carton cups. Set them aside to dry and harden. Use the paints with water and brushes just as you would ordinary paint sets.

2. Paint containers need to be sturdy and inexpensive. Here are some ideas for different types of paint containers:
   - Cupcake or muffin tins are excellent for painting with several colors at a time.
   - Egg cartons work well when children are painting with cotton swabs. Cut cartons in thirds to make four-part containers, and pour small amounts of paint into each egg cup.
   - Store liquid tempera in recycled glue or dishwashing liquid bottles. Paint can be squirted quickly and neatly into paint cups from these bottles.
   - When using paint cups, make a nontipping cup holder from an empty half-gallon milk or juice carton. Cut holes along the length of the carton and pop in the cups.
   - Sponges can be good paint holders, too. Cut a hole the exact size of the paint jar or cup in the center of the sponge, then fit the jar/cup in the hole. Besides keeping paint containers upright, the sponges also catch drips.
   - Cotton-ball painting is more fun (and neater) when you clip spring-type clothespins to the cotton balls. Children use the clothespins like handles. The same clothespins can be used when printing with small sponge pieces.

3. Collage materials. Some of these can be paper shapes in different colors, scraps of cloth, feathers, yarn, tinfoil, string, beans, sawdust, bottle caps, buttons, styrofoam packing pieces, rock salt, bits of bark, and any other things that look interesting.

4. Blunt scissors, for both left- and right-handed children.

Pasting should be done away from climbing toys, building blocks, and similar large motor activities. All the materials for pasting should be on a shelf at child level. Collage and pasting materials should be placed on a separate table and sorted into shallow containers, such as baskets or clear plastic boxes, so that children can readily see the kinds of things that are available and consider how they will look when arranged together. Some children will enjoy tearing and pasting, while others will prefer cutting and pasting. Of course, the children should learn about safety rules for using scissors early in the year. The teacher must also be sure that all young children have only blunt scissors.

Keep paste in small plastic containers or jars. To help children learn to keep lids on jars, mark the bottom and top of each jar with a number or a colored X. The children are shown how to match up the jar with its lid by matching colored Xs or numbers. In this way, children learn to keep the lids on the jars and to recognize numbers and colors as well. Show the children how to rinse out paste brushes and where to return all pasting material. A place to put finished work to dry should be set up.

Using common recycled household disposables will make cleanup easier. Aluminum pie tins and frozen food trays are both excellent for holding paint, paste, or glue for table activities. At the end of the activity, you may want to recycle the aluminum. Another way to make cleanup easier after pasting is to fold over the top edges of a large paper bag, then tape the bag to one end of your work table. When the children have finished their projects, scraps can easily be swept off the table into the bag. Then, just toss the bag in the trash.

Scrap Art Materials and Use

1. Paste, glue, tape, and stapler.

2. Colored tissue paper.

3. Colored sticky tape, gummed circles, stars, and designs.

4. Tempera paint, chalk, crayons, and colored markers.

5. Odds and ends of scrap material—egg cartons, styrofoam pieces, plastic containers and lids, pinecones, feathers, and buttons.

For scrap art activities, all material needs to be in good order. This is because this type of activity requires a large supply of materials. A special place is needed for all supplies within the child's reach and at eye level.

Scraps of cloth may be kept in one box with scrap pieces glued on the outside to show the child at a glance what is in the box. Clear plastic shoe boxes are excellent for scrap art storage, as children can easily see the contents. Buttons may be kept in a muffin tin, feathers in a plastic bag, and old bits of jewelry for puppets in a plastic shoe box. The point is to keep each material in a specific place so that it is ready for planned or spontaneous projects.

Organizing material in this simple, easy-to-find way helps children learn to work on their own. Having glue, scissors, paper, and all other materials on shelves at the child's height also encourages independent work. Cleanup time is much easier, too, when the chil-

Figure 12-11

Although some children may occasionally enjoy working on the floor, it is important to have a table set up for regular art activities.

dren can see "what goes where" and can reach the places where materials are supposed to go.

Potter's Clay and Play Dough Materials and Use

1. Potter's clay or play dough (mixed from the recipe in Appendix C and kept in an airtight container).

2. Clay or play dough table. Use a table with a formica top or any table that is easy to clean. (Or use large pieces of plastic spread out on the table, or cut one for each child's use.)

3. Tools for clay work like toy rolling pins, cookie cutters, spoons, and blunt plastic knives.

Working with clay and play dough requires a place away from all active centers such as building blocks, wheel toys, and climbing toys. The tables should be covered with formica or oilcloth to make cleaning easier. Young children also enjoy working with clay on individual vinyl placemats, Masonite boards, burlap squares, or brown paper grocery bags. Newspaper does not work well because when it gets wet, bits of paper may mix with the clay. For clay projects that are meant to be hardened and possibly painted later, a good place for drying must be set up. Since these objects may take a few days to dry, this place must also be away from frequently used areas.

Before starting any three-dimensional projects that require several stages such as molding, drying, and then painting, the teacher must be aware of the children's interest spans. Some of these projects take longer than other art activities, and some children may lose interest and not finish the project. The teacher must also consider the time needed for preparing the material, making the objects, drying them, and painting them. Then it must be decided if the children's interest is strong enough to last through the time needed for the whole project. It is an unpleasant experience for both teacher and children when a project is too rushed. This takes the joy out of the activity for all involved.

Potter's clay.   Potter's clay may be purchased at any art supply store in moist form. This is much easier to deal with than starting with dry powder. It is available in two colors—gray and terra cotta. (Terra cotta looks pretty but stains clothing and is harder to clean up.) Clay requires careful storage in a watertight, airtight container to retain its malleable qualities. When children are through for the day, form it into large balls, press a thumb into it, and then fill that hole with water and replace in container. If oilcloth table covers are used with potter's clay, they can simply be hung up to dry, shaken well, and put away until next time.

Making play dough. Children should participate in making dough whenever possible. If allowed to help make the dough, children learn about measuring, blending, and cause and effect and also have the chance to work together.

The doughs that require no cooking are best mixed two batches at a time in separate deep dishpans. Using deep pans keeps the flour within bounds, and making two batches at a time relieves congestion and provides better participation opportunities. Tempera powder is the most effective coloring agent to add because it makes such intense shades of dough; adding it to the flour before pouring in the liquid works best. Dough can be kept in the refrigerator and reused several times. Removing it at the beginning of the day allows it to come to room temperature before being offered to the children—otherwise it can be discouragingly stiff and unappealing. The addition of flour or cornstarch on the second day is usually necessary to reduce stickiness.

Dough variations. All the dough recipes in Appendix C have been carefully tested and are suitable for various purposes. In preschool centers where process, not product, is emphasized, the dough and clay are generally used again and again rather than the objects made by the children being allowed to dry and then sent home. For special occasions, however, it is nice to allow the pieces to harden and then to paint or color them. Two recipes included in Appendix C serve this purpose particularly well: ornamental clay and baker's dough.

For dough to be truly satisfying, children need an abundance of it rather than meager little handfuls, and they should be encouraged to use it in a manipulative, expressive way rather than in a product-oriented way.

Cleanup. For clay cleanup, sponge off tables, mats, and boards. Burlap squares can be stacked and shaken when dry, and grocery bags can be thrown away. Clay-caked hands and tools should never be washed in the sink because clay can clog the drain. Instead, have the children wipe off their tools and hands with paper towels, then wash them in a basin filled with soapy water. When the clay particles settle, you can let the soapy water down the drain and throw the sediment in the trash can. Children may rinse their hands in the sink, and the tools may be left to dry on paper towels.

The cooked cornstarch recipes are the only ones that are particularly difficult to clean up because they leave a hard, dry film on the pan during cooking. However, an hour or two of soaking in cold water converts this to a jellylike material that is easily scrubbed off with a plastic pot-scrubbing pad. If pans are soaked during nap time, the children will be quite interested in the qualities of this gelatinous material when they get up. You might even have one or two of them work on scrubbing the pot clean!

Woodworking Materials and Use

1. A bin of soft lumber pieces (leftover scraps of lumber).
2. Supply of nails with large heads.
3. Wooden spools, corks, and twigs.
4. Wooden buttons, string, and ribbons to be nailed to wood or tied to heads of nails already hammered into the wood.
5. Bottle caps.
6. Small-sized real tools. Hammer and nails are best to start with. Saws, screwdrivers, a vise, and a drill may be added later.
7. Workbench.
8. Sandpaper.
9. A vise or C-clamp placed near the corner of the workbench, flush with the table top.
10. Safety goggles.

For older children:
11. Screws and screwdrivers—standard and Phillips.
12. Pencils, rulers, and tape measures.
13. Files, planes, levels.
14. Crowbars.

Figure 12-12

It is best to work with clay on a surface that is easily cleaned.

Carpentry needs to be done in a special area away from other activities. Provide children plenty of good wood and satisfactory tools. A sturdy workbench of the right height is helpful.

The most basic woodworking tools are hammers and saws. The hammers should be good, solid ones—*not* tack hammers. The saws should be crosscut ones so that they can cut with or across the grain of the wood, and they should be as short as possible. A well-made vise in which to place wood securely while sawing is invaluable. Preferably, there should be two of these, one at each end of the table. (C-clamps can also be used for this purpose and are less expensive, or a board can be nailed to the table while the child saws it, but this leaves the troublesome chore of removing the nails afterward.)

Very young children enjoy sawing up the large pieces of styrofoam that come as packing for electronic equipment. Hammering into such material or into plasterboard is also quick and easy and does not require more force than two- and three-year-old children can muster. Older children need plentiful amounts of soft wood to work with.

Cabinet shops are a good source for scrap lumber. Only smooth lumber should be used. Pieces of various lengths and sizes add interest. The greater the variety of wood, the greater the challenge for building. An old tree stump is great fun for children to pound countless nails into.

Woodworking needs careful adult supervision, since children can easily hurt themselves or each other with a hammer and saw. General guidelines for adult supervision include the following:

- Stay very close to the woodworking activity. Be within reach of each child.
- There should be no more than three or four children for one adult to supervise. Only one child at a time should use a saw.
- Show the children how to saw away from their own fingers and from other children. Show them how to avoid hitting their fingers with the hammer.
- Hand out nails a few at a time.
- Never turn your back on the activity for even a few seconds.
- Make a wall-mounted toolboard to store frequently used tools. (Less-used tools can be stored in a cupboard.) The outline of each tool can be marked on the board so children can figure out where to hang each tool. (More woodworking information is found in Chapter 14.)

Some variations for woodworking.

- Remember to vary the tools the children use as their skill (and self-control) increases.
- Purchase a variety of nails by the pound, not by the little box, from a hardware store. Children love an assortment of these. They can be set out in small foil pie plates to keep them from getting mixed up. These pie plates can be nailed to a long board to prevent spilling.
- Offer various kinds of trims to go with woodworking, such as wire; thick, colorful yarn; and wooden spools (with nails long enough to go through the spool).
- Have children wear safety glasses.
- Offer round things for wheels, such as bottle caps, buttons, or the lids of 35-mm film containers.
- Provide dowels of various sizes that will fit the holes made by the different sizes of bits.
- Younger children may use a rubber mallet with golf tees to pound into styrofoam.

SAFETY

For all the activities in this chapter and in any art activities for young children, be sure that you are not using any unsafe art supplies. Potentially unsafe art supplies include the following:

- Powdered clay. It is easily inhaled and contains silica, which is harmful to the lungs. Instead, use wet clay, which cannot be inhaled.
- Paints that require solvents such as turpentine to clean brushes. Use only water-based paints.
- Cold water or commercial dyes that contain chemical additives. Use only natural vegetable dyes, made from beets, onion skins, and so on.
- Permanent markers, which may contain toxic solvents. Use only water-based markers.
- Instant papier-mâché, which may contain lead or asbestos. Use only black-and-white newspaper and library paste or liquid starch.
- Epoxy, instant glues, or other solvent-based glues. Use only water-based white glue (Clemens, 1991).

The teacher should:

- Read labels.
- Check for age-appropriateness. The Art and Creative Materials Institute labels art materials AP (approved product) and CP (certified product) when they are safe for young children, even if ingested. These labels are round. A product bearing the

square "Health Label" is safe only for children older than 12 years.

⊙ Check for ventilation requirements. In most cases, one open window or door is not sufficient ventilation.

⊙ A list of materials safe for young children is available from the Art and Creative Materials Institute, Inc., P.O. Box 479 Hanson, MA 02341-0479, or visit their Web site at http://www.acminet.org/Safety. htm. Write to the National Art Education Association, 1916 Association Drive, Reston, VA 22091 for an updated, detailed list of safety guidelines.

⊙ Always use products that are appropriate for the individual user. Children in grade six and lower and adults who may not be able to read and understand safety labeling should use *only nontoxic materials.*

⊙ Do not eat or drink while using art materials. Wash up after use. Clean yourself *and* your supplies.

⊙ Never use products for skin painting or food preparations unless indicated that the product is meant to be used in this way.

⊙ Do not transfer art materials to other containers. You will lose the valuable safety information that is on the product package.

⊙ Know your students.

⊙ Be aware of students' allergies. Children with allergies to wheat, for example, may be irritated by wheat paste used in papier mâché. Other art materials that may cause allergic reactions include chalk or other dusty substances, water-based clay, and any material that contains petroleum products.

⊙ Be aware of students' habits. Some students put everything in their mouths. (This can be the case at any age.) Others act out or behave aggressively. Use your knowledge of individual students' tendencies to help you plan art activities that will be safe for all students.

ADAPTING PROGRAM BASICS FOR CHILDREN WITH SPECIAL NEEDS

Many early childhood programs today include in their classrooms children with special needs. Although this book is not intended as a resource for teaching special education, this section is intended to provide some very basic information on how to adapt the art program for children with special needs. References are provided at the end of this chapter and in the Online Companion for more in-depth information on this topic.

Developmental Delays

It takes many repetitions for the child with developmental delays to fully learn a new skill. For this reason, some children will appear to have mastered the task one day but then be unable to perform the same task on another day. This type of inconsistency is common for children with developmental delays (Gould & Sullivan, 1999).

Open-ended art activities are most appropriate for children with developmental delays. Some effective techniques to use are demonstration, task breakdown, and hand-over-hand assistance as needed. It also helps to demonstrate the activity by doing it first while the child watches. Another approach is to break down an activity into a series of small steps. It is most important to help the child complete one step before going on to the next. In addition, you may find that some children will need you to physically guide their hands. For example, this would involve placing a crayon in the child's hand and then gently moving the child's hand and crayon across a sheet of paper.

Some children with developmental delays may have weak hand muscles and a poor grasp. For these children, short, stubby art instruments are frequently easier to grasp than commercially available crayons, markers, and brushes. You can adapt materials by breaking chalk and preschool crayons into small, short pieces.

Some other suggestions for working with these children are to do the following:

⊙ Place masking tape or colored tape or draw colored lines with a permanent marker about one inch from the end of the paintbrush end to show the child where to place his fingers on the brush.

⊙ Use large pieces of paper for art activities to allow for large arm movements characteristic of children with developmental delays.

⊙ In art activities, place the paper on a horizontal surface such as a table or the floor, or tape it to a large easel, door, or wall. Be sure to place a large sheet of plastic, such as a shower curtain or plastic tablecloth, underneath the paper to protect the surface.

⊙ Stabilize the paper with tape, clips, clothespins, etc., to prevent excess slippage. At the same time, encourage the child to use his or her nondominant hand to hold the paper down.

⊙ Children with cerebral palsy will benefit greatly from consistent physical and/or verbal cues to use the less functional hand as a stabilizer while painting with the other.

⊙ Place paper inside a sturdy shirt-size box that will provide walls to contain extraneous movements of the paintbrush or other tool.

⊙ Use thickened paint to provide more resistance and feedback. Paint can be thickened with cornstarch, salt, sugar, flour, sawdust, or sand.

Physical Impairments

In working with children with physical impairments that affect the upper body, arms, hands, or fingers you will need to make some modifications for art activities. For these children, you may find the following strategies helpful:

⊙ Stabilize paper with tape, clips, clothespins, etc., to prevent the paper slipping.

⊙ Encourage the child to use his or her nondominant hand to hold the paper down.

⊙ Place paper inside a sturdy shirt-size box to contain extraneous movements of the art tool.

⊙ Mix paint to a thick consistency to provide ease of use as well as more resistance and feedback.

⊙ Thicken paint with cornstarch, salt, sugar, flour, sawdust, or sand.

Visual Impairments

The term visual impairment is a general term that includes all levels of vision loss from partially sighted to complete blindness. The child with visual impairments learns about the objects and people around him through the senses of touch, smell, taste, and hearing. A child with a visual impairment is unable to observe and imitate others as they explore the environment. Because of this, he or she will need to learn how to investigate the world around him or her. You can help by offering verbal descriptions about what the room looks like, where furniture and playthings are located, and what other people in the room are doing.

Although some children with visual problems prefer dimmed lighting, most need bright, even lighting. To help reduce glare, use a table with a dull finish on it. If you don't have this type of table, tape light-colored construction paper on top of the table. Place the table in an area of the room where the lighting is optimal to reduce glare and shadows. Another way to reduce glare from reflection of light is to use pastel paper instead of white paper for art activities.

Some other suggestions for working with children with visual impairment are as follows:

⊙ Use high-contrast materials, such as dark or bright colors on light paper. Red, yellow, and orange are the easiest colors for a child with low vision to see, especially on a dark blue background.

⊙ Place a piece of mesh or screening under the paper the child is coloring with a crayon so that the child can feel the raised finished product.

⊙ Show the child how to hold a crayon or marker and what to do with it if he or she has never held a crayon or marker before.

⊙ Hang paper at eye level, either at the easel or taped to the wall. Placing the paper on a vertical allows the child's head and eyes to remain in a neutral position while he or she is working.

⊙ Use markers or crayons instead of paint. When using paint, the child has to constantly change his visual orientation as he or she looks from the paper to the paint and back to the paper. Markers and crayons reduce the amount of visual shifting.

⊙ Add materials to paint such as thickeners and fragrances so the child will experience the smell as well as the paint itself. Try sand, salt, flour, cornstarch, sawdust, lemon juice, vanilla extract, and ground cinnamon.

⊙ Allow extra time to complete projects; encourage frequent breaks; and suggest a low-key, relaxing activity to follow. Doing art activities can be extremely fatiguing for a child with visual impairments (Gould & Sullivan, 1999).

Attention Deficit/Hyperactivity Disorder and Behavioral Issues

Students with attention deficit hyperactivity disorder (ADHD) can be a challenge for any teacher. ADHD is also referred to as ADD, or attention deficit disorder. Children with ADHD display signs of the short attention span along with hyperactivity. Children with ADD only display signs of the short attention span, but they do not display signs of hyperactiveness.

Some techniques to use with these children are as follows:

⊙ Plan freeform art activities such as painting, finger painting, and drawing to hold the child's interest for extended periods. These activities allow them to enjoy expressing themselves in a nonverbal, nonthreatening manner.

⊙ To transition this child out of an art activity and into another, use a timer or give the child another type of cue that marks the end of an activity. Another way is to use an end-of-playtime song before the cleanup song. The end-of-playtime song gives the child a few minutes to get used to the idea that cleanup time is only a short time away.

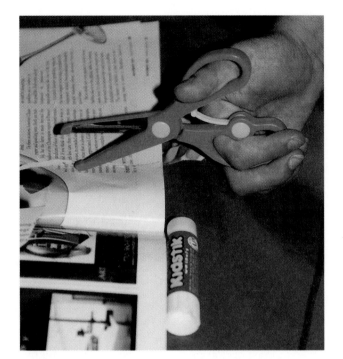

Figure 12-13

Developmental or "learning" scissors help children master cutting skills.

⊙ Give the child clear expectations before he or she begins the activity. For example, you might state that the child will have 15 minutes to work on the activity and that you will give an advance warning when that time is almost up.

⊙ Allow the active child to either stand at the art center table or kneel on a chair. These positions are sometimes easier to maintain than sitting in a chair. If the child prefers to sit, however, make sure that the chair is the appropriate height, with the child's feet flat on the floor.

⊙ Allow the child to lie on the floor while working on an art project. This position allows most of the child's body to come into contact with a hard surface, providing the type of pressure touch that can be calming to the child who is active or agitated.

⊙ Provide the child with as many choices as possible to reduce noncompliant behavior. Offer choices that are acceptable to you but that give the child the sense that he or she is in control. As an example, ask the child whether he or she would like to use a fat paintbrush or a skinny one, the blue paper or the white.

⊙ Provide an adequate work area with well-defined boundaries. If possible, move the easel next to the art table and allow the child to work there alone. Another possibility is to place the child's paper onto a cookie sheet at the table. This provides a clear, separate area for the child to concentrate on in the activity.

SUMMARY

The early childhood art program is a part of the early childhood curriculum in which children have the chance to work with many kinds of materials and techniques. It provides a time and place for children to put together their thoughts, ideas, feelings, actions, and abilities into their own creations.

Toddlers are very active and want to explore everything. For this reason, they need materials that are sturdy, are practically indestructible, and do not include tiny pieces that might be swallowed. Only a few materials should be put out at a time so toddlers are not overwhelmed by too many choices. Art materials, like crayons, play dough, chalk, and paint, need to be frequently available to toddlers. These materials should be presented under the supervision of an adult to encourage their appropriate use. In setting up art (and all other) centers for toddlers, a teacher should arrange lots of space and clear traffic patterns, since toddlers are prone to falling, grabbing, and running.

Young preschool children, two to four years of age, have a limited interest span. Even the most interesting activities hold their interest for only approximately 10 to 15 minutes. Thus, the teacher must plan several activities and alternative activities for this age group. Some appropriate art activities for children of this age are easel and finger painting, printing, collage, coloring with crayons, using play dough, making simple puppets, and sculpting.

Older preschool children and kindergartners (four to six years of age) have begun to develop better small-muscle control in the fingers, hands, and wrists. For this reason, they enjoy cutting with scissors, using smaller paintbrushes, and trying out a wide variety of colored markers. All of these activities are also appropriate for middle and upper elementary level students.

The objectives of the art program must consider the interest, age, and ability levels of the children. An important goal of the art program is the growth of a child's creativity and ability to work independently. But the main goal is to let children grow at their own individual rates.

Teachers play an important role in the success of the early childhood art program. They must choose the right materials, as well as know the right way to set up and use the materials for each activity. Teachers need to adapt the early childhood program so that the program basics meet the needs of young children with special needs.

LEARNING ACTIVITIES

A. It is hard to really appreciate the individual merits of the dough recipes unless they are actually available for inspection and experimentation. As a class project, have volunteers make them up and bring them to class to try out.

B. Suppose a bad fairy has waved her wand and ruled that you could only select three basic types of creative self-expressive activities to use for a whole year in your preschool. Which three would you select and why? Answer the same question for a group of older children, grades 1 through 5.

C. Suppose that same bad fairy has waved her wand again, and now you are allowed to *purchase* only paint and glue (no paper even!) for your creative activities. How limiting is this? What self-expressive activities would you actually be able to offer under these circumstances? How might you go about acquiring the necessary free materials to make them possible? Be specific.

D. Visit one or possibly several early childhood programs and observe the arts activities. Keep in mind these points in observing:
  1. Are the equipment and activities right for the age, ability, and interest levels of the children?
  2. Is the area well planned for each activity?
  3. Are the children free to make what they want with the material?

E. Set up a classroom, real or imagined, for one or more of the following activities:
  1. finger painting
  2. collage
  3. making puppets
  Consider the following in setting up the activity:
  1. location of water source
  2. preparation of area
  3. preparation of materials
  4. preparation of children
  5. teacher preparation
  6. activity itself
  7. cleanup
  8. drying and storage space for work in progress or finished

F. Draw up a plan of a room set up for art activities for three-, four-, and five-year-old children.
  1. Include the following areas:

brush and finger painting	papier-mâché work
clay	crayon and chalk work
puppetry	woodworking
	scrap art

  2. Show on the plan where the following areas would be found:

storage space	water source(s)
child-level shelves	light source(s)
drying areas	

G. Ask children what they think is the hardest part about cleaning up. Record their answers. See if there is one thing that is mentioned more than others. Check on the problem to see if it is caused by room set-up, supply set-up, water source, or something else.

H. Go on an odds-and-ends hunt.
  1. See how many different kinds of things can be found for use in art projects. Things to look for include spools, styrofoam, feathers, buttons, and foil.
  2. Sort the material and store it in the best way possible. Label each container so that children will know what is inside.

I. Choose a grade level from grades 1 through 5. Draw up a room plan for art activities for this grade level. Include the same areas and requested information as in question F.

J. In 105 AD paper was invented by Ts'aiLun, an official of the Chinese Imperial Court at the Han Dynasty in China. Lun's paper was made from bamboo and mulberry fibers, fishnets, and rags.

  What did people use before paper? Can you name 10 uses of paper? What else can paper be made with? Do you know what paper is made of now? Does your school recycle its paper?

CHAPTER REVIEW

1. Is the product or the process more important in the art program? Explain your answer.
2. Choose the statements that describe an important purpose of art in the early childhood program:
   a. Art gives the child a chance to try new materials and techniques.
   b. Art helps the child make perfect artwork.
   c. The child has a chance to express experiences and feelings.
   d. The emphasis in art is on continued good experiences with many kinds of materials.
   e. In art, the child learns how to copy models.
   f. Learning to judge one's own work and other children's work is very important in art.
   g. Being successful in art helps develop a child's self-confidence.
3. Select the items that should be included in a list of equipment for each of the following activities:
   a. Crayoning
      (a) newsprint or manila paper, 8″ × 12″ or 12″ × 8″
      (b) lined white paper
      (c) colored tissue paper, 18″ × 24″
      (d) colored markers in many colors
      (e) jumbo crayons, unwrapped
      (f) jumbo crayons, all wrapped
   b. Chalk work
      (a) colored chalks, white chalks
      (b) colored tissue paper
      (c) paper, wet and dry
      (d) chalkboard
      (e) eraser
      (f) pencils
   c. Brush painting
      (a) easels
      (b) lined 9″ × 12″ paper
      (c) newsprint, 18″ × 24″, plain or pastel
      (d) construction paper
      (e) tempera paint
      (f) finger paint
      (g) glue
      (h) brushes, long (12″) handles and ¾″ bristles
      (i) smocks
      (j) a place to dry finished paintings
   d. Finger painting
      (a) dull, porous paper
      (b) shiny-surfaced paper
      (c) water supply
      (d) crayons
      (e) finger paint
      (f) colored tissue paper

   (g) smocks
   (h) racks to dry finished work
   e. Pasting
      (a) glue in small jars
      (b) paste in small jars
      (c) lined 9″ × 12″ paper
      (d) colored tissue paper
      (e) plain or manila construction paper
      (f) scissors, blunt, left and right types
      (g) collage materials
      (h) stapler and staples
   f. Puppets and scrap art
      (a) paper bags
      (b) boxes
      (c) scissors, paper, paste, paints
      (d) sticks
      (e) play dough
      (f) colored sticky tape
      (g) cardboard rolls
      (h) odds and ends
      (i) airtight container
      (j) socks and mittens
   g. Clay and play dough
      (a) plasticene
      (b) real clay
      (c) open containers
      (d) airtight containers
      (e) formica-top tables
      (f) oilcloths
      (g) paint
      (h) scissors
      (i) tools for clay work
      (j) play dough, purchased
      (k) play dough, made with help from the children
   h. Woodworking
      (a) paint
      (b) workbench
      (c) supply of soft lumber pieces
      (d) bottle caps
      (e) sandpaper
      (f) wooden spools, corks, twigs
      (g) clay
      (h) supply of nails
4. Choose the answer that best completes each of the following statements describing the basic objectives of the early childhood art program.
   a. The most basic objective of the art program is to
      (a) produce the best artists possible.
      (b) meet the age, ability, and interest levels of the children.

(c) fit into the total preschool program.

b. Learning to be a creative thinker is

(a) more important in the elementary grades than for younger children.

(b) not an objective in art.

(c) an important objective in art.

c. The art program must allow children the freedom to

(a) grow at their own individual paces.

(b) do anything they please.

(c) go against safety rules.

5. Choose the answer that best completes each of the following statements describing techniques for using material in arts and crafts.

a. With very young children, it is best to begin with

(a) a great variety of materials.

(b) the basic essentials.

(c) only small motor activities.

b. A teacher must avoid

(a) making models for the children to copy.

(b) helping the children with the material.

(c) giving suggestions at cleanup time.

c. Painting work should be done

(a) in an area near the quiet activities.

(b) in an area away from climbing toys.

(c) only if sunlight is available.

d. Finger painting works best with

(a) dull, porous, dry paper on wood tables.

(b) shiny paper on the floor.

(c) shiny paper on a table covered with formica or oilcloth.

e. It is best to keep pasting supplies

(a) out of child's reach.

(b) on a shelf at child-level.

(c) in a locked cabinet.

f. Scrap art activities require

(a) a good deal of organization of supplies.

(b) no special order in supplies.

(c) a small amount of supplies.

g. Woodworking is an activity that

(a) needs very little supervision.

(b) needs careful adult supervision.

(c) is too dangerous for young children.

h. In woodworking and all art activities, it is important to encourage children to

(a) copy the teacher's models.

(b) copy the ideas of the other children.

(c) do what they want with the materials.

6. List some special considerations for setting up art areas for toddlers.

7. List the skills, interests, and abilities of older preschool children and kindergartners.

8. List appropriate art activities for older preschool children and kindergartners.

9. Choose the answer that best completes each of the following statements describing the skills and abilities of the young preschool child (aged two to four).

a. The young preschool child often has

(a) better small- than large-muscle development.

(b) better large- than small-muscle development.

(c) good large- and small-muscle development.

b. The interest span for a young preschool child is usually

(a) long, more than 20 minutes.

(b) short, not more than one minute.

(c) short, between 10 and 15 minutes.

c. In lesson plans for young preschool children, the teacher plans

(a) only one main activity for the whole group.

(b) alternative activities for those who have different interests.

(c) only challenging activities to stimulate interest.

d. Some good art materials for young preschoolers are

(a) blunt scissors, wide brushes, and large crayons.

(b) narrow brushes, ballpoint pens, and clay.

(c) Plasticene, play dough, and colored markers.

10. Name at least two appropriate (adapted) art activities for the following children with special needs:

a. children with developmental delays

b. children with visual impairments

c. children with attention deficit disorders

d. children with physical impairments

REFERENCES

Clemens, S. G. (1991). Art in the classroom: Making everyday special. *Young Children, 46,* 4–111.

Gardner, H. E. (1993). *Multiple intelligences.* New York: Basic Books.

Gardner, H. E. (1999). *Intelligence reframed. Multiple intelligences for the 21st century.* New York: Basic Books.

Gould, P., & Sullivan, J. (1999). *The inclusive early childhood classroom: Easy ways to adapt learning centers for all children.* Beltsville, MD: Gryphon House.

Lowenfeld, V., & Brittain, W. L. (1987). *Creative and mental growth of the child* (8th ed.). New York: Macmillan.

ADDITIONAL READINGS

Althouse, R. (2002). *Colors of learning.* New York: Teachers College Press.

Engel, B. S. (2000). *Considering children's art: Why and how to value their work.* Washington, DC: NAEYC.

Greh, D. (2002). *New technologies in the artroom: A handbook for teachers.* Worcester, MA: Davis Publications.

Hayes, K., & Creange, R. (2003). *Classroom routines that really work for pre-k and kindergarten.* New York: Scholastic.

Jensen, B. J., & Bullard, J. A. (2002). The mud center: Recapturing childhood. *Young Children 57*(3), 16–20.

Koh, M. F. (2002). *First art.* Beltsville, MD: Gryphon House.

Mayesky, M. (2003). *Creative art & activities: Painting.* Clifton, NY: Delmar.

Mayesky, M. (2003). *Creative art & activities: Clay, play dough and other modeling materials.* Clifton, NY: Delmar.

Mayesky, M. (2003). *Creative art & activities: Crayons, marker and chalk.* Clifton, NY: Delmar.

Mayesky, M. (2003). *Creative art & activities: Paper art.* Clifton, NY: Delmar

Mayesky, M. (2003). *Creative art & activities: Printing.* Clifton, NY: Delmar.

Molter, C. (2003). *Silent L as in chalk.* Edina, MN: ABDO Publishing.

Prince, E. S. (2002). *Art matters.* Tucson, AZ: Zephyr Press.

Snyder, J. (2001). *Caring for your art.* New York: Allworth Press.

Vande Griek, S. (2002). *The art room.* Berkeley, CA: Publishers Group West.

Van Hoorn, J., Scales, B., Nourot, P., & Always, K. (2002). *Play at the center of the curriculum.* Upper Saddle River, NJ: Prentice Hall.

HELPFUL WEB SITES

Everything Preschool, http://www.everything-preschool.com/
Click on Arts/Crafts.

Kinderart, http://www.kinderart.com

Gayle's Preschool Rainbow,
http://www.preschoolrainbow.org

ADD, http://www.kidsource.com
Click on Search and type in ADD.

Cerebral Palsy, http://www.kidsource.com
Click on Search and type in Cerebral Palsy.

Downs Syndrome, http://www.cdss.ca

Physical Impairments, http://www.pecentral.org
Click on Adapted Physical Education.

American Arts Therapy Association, http://www.arttherapy.org/

American Dance Therapy Association, http://www.musictherapy.org

Arts Education Partnership, http://www.aep-arts.org

National Art Education Association, http://www.naea-reston.org

Very Special Arts, http://www.vsarts.org/

For additional creative activity resources, visit our Web site at http://www.EarlyChildEd.delmar.com.

Chapter 13

Two-Dimensional Activities

Objectives

After completing this chapter, you should be able to:

1. Describe the tools, materials, techniques, and strategies involved in the two-dimensional activities of picture making, printmaking, and collage.

2. Define collage.

Using as a framework the basic information presented thus far on developmental levels, creativity, aesthetics, and planning and implementing creative activities, let us now take a closer look at the general processes of picture making, printmaking, and collage. You will note that specific ages are not listed for many of the activities in sections of this chapter. This is because many of the activities are designed to be springboards for art experiences and not limited to certain age groups. Use your knowledge of the developmental levels of the children in your group as a guide to choosing and using activities in this and all chapters of the book. You will, however, find the developmental information provided in the previous sections helpful in determining which activities to initiate with children. Children's reactions to the suggested activities will determine the appropriateness of the choice. Their interest, enthusiasm, and ability to do the activity should be your guide to each activity's appropriateness.

PICTURE MAKING

The term **picture making** in this chapter refers to any and all forms of purposeful visual expressions, beginning with controlled scribbling. A common error associated with picture making is to equate it with artwork that contains recognizable objects or figures. Yet children's pictures (artwork) may take any form, just as long as the child is expressing herself visually in a nonrandom way.

To young children, the act of drawing and painting comes naturally. It is a means by which they communicate visually their ideas and feelings about themselves and their world. They may work in paint, crayon, or chalk; each material has its own distinct characteristics for the child to explore.

The sensitive teacher understands and appreciates the charm and freshness of children's early drawings and paintings. He or she motivates children by helping them recall their experiences and record these in art media. Because the teacher respects their individuality, the teacher inspires and encourages each child to express his or her own personal reactions about the world as they understand it. In this way, children discover and build their own unique style of expression. Each child's picture is different from the others in the class, just as his or her appearance and personality are different.

When properly motivated the child eagerly examines materials and looks forward to proceeding with the activity. Most young children are eager to express themselves in their drawings. However, some children may need more encouragement than others to express themselves in drawings. Also, sometimes a few motivating ideas from the teacher can liven up a child who seems to be less motivated than usual.

Reading a familiar story or singing a song can stimulate art. Such stimulation is most successful when children are able to associate themselves with the story, poem, or song. They might be asked to think about the character they liked the best, a new ending for the story, or the part that frightened them or pleased them the most and to draw or paint what they thought.

There are many ways of motivating that awaken the child to the world of color, shape, size, texture, action, and mood. Some of the following ideas may help stimulate children's spontaneity and experimentation:

⊙ Take a walking trip using careful observation.
⊙ On the trip, gather a collection of objects for a "touch-and-see" display.
⊙ Put up an interesting bulletin board or case display of children's and your artwork.
⊙ Dramatize stories, animals, birds, etc.
⊙ Encourage children to try using materials in different ways if children do not discover them on their own. For example, you might say, "I wonder if the back and side of the crayon will make the same kinds of marks as the pointed end?"
⊙ Exhibit sincere pleasure when a discovery is announced and share it with others in the group.
⊙ Encourage children to bring materials from home to incorporate into their art.
⊙ Share the works of several artists that represent the same or similar theme. This will help children understand that they can draw in many different ways.
⊙ Display the work of each child at some time during the year and call attention to the fact that everyone sees thing differently (nonrealistic use of color included).
⊙ Offer found materials that can be used as accessories or tools for artwork. Children will find a variety of ways to create with them. For example, they will use buttons for stringing, glued designs,

wheels on toys, or eyes for a puppet or as shapes for print making.
⊙ Add new materials that match the group's interest at particular times. Children who live in snowy areas may need lots of white paint. Temperate spring seasons will stimulate use of pastel colors. Gold and silver papers will spark experimentation with holiday decorations. Furry fabrics may intensify interest in animals and pets.
⊙ Make papers available in many kinds, shapes, and colors. The variety will lead to more responses and experimentation with techniques.

Children's growing awareness is gradually reflected in their pictures as the ability to interpret their environment increases. As the process continues the teacher and children can evaluate their progress and consider how pictures may be varied, different media to use, and any other changes the children suggest.

Painting with a Brush

Painting with a brush encourages the spontaneous use of color. Finger painting, covered in Chapter 12, is another form of painting that is enjoyable for children.

Figure 13–1

A variety of brush sizes need to be available for children's use.

Materials. Basic materials for painting with brushes include the following:

⊙ Watercolor paint sets. These are actually dehydrated tempera colors in concentrated cakes. They provide easy and convenient paint for individual use or group activity in the classroom. *To use paints in cakes:* Place a few drops of water on the surface of each cake of color to moisten the paint. Dip brush in water and brush surface of moistened cake of paint to obtain smooth, creamy paint. *To use powder paint* (**tempera**): Fill a can ¼ full of dry paint. Add water slowly, stirring constantly until the paint has the consistency of thin cream. A small amount of liquid starch or liquid detergent may be added to the mixture as a binder. Use enough paint to make good rich colors. For best results, prepare paint when needed; large amounts kept over a period of time have a tendency to sour. Containers for use with powder paint include milk cartons, juice cans, yogurt containers, coffee cans, plastic cups, and cut-down plastic bottles. A set of paints can be carried easily if containers are placed in tomato baskets, soft-drink carriers, boxes, or trays (See Figure 13–2).

ART TOOL HOLDER

Heavy paper, folded several times, will make a holder that keeps tools from rolling. Also good for drying cleaned paintbrushes.

DRYING RACK

Drying racks for wet artwork are ideal if space is at a premium. A number of wooden sticks of the same size tacked or stapled to pieces of corrugated cardboard of the same size will make a drying rack. If pieces of wood are not available, substitute two, three, or four pieces of corrugated cardboard taped together. Tape stacked pieces to the cardboard base.

PAINT CONTAINER

Paper milk cartons stapled together or taped together with duct tape (with tops removed) and with a cardboard handle make an ideal container for colored paint and water.

PAINT DISPENSERS

Plastic mustard or ketchup containers make good paint dispensers. An aluminum nail in the top of each will keep the paint fresh. In some cases the plastic containers can be used for painting directly from the container. Syrup pitchers also make good paint dispensers and are ideal for storing paint.

PLASTIC SPOONS

Keep plastic spoons in cans of powdered tempera for easy paint dispensing.

Figure 13-2

Some helpful hints for storing and handling painting materials.

- Individual pieces of paper, at least 12″ × 18″: roll paper, manila paper, newspaper, wallpaper, newsprint, freezer paper.
- Water containers for painting and rinsing brushes: coffee cans, milk cartons, juice cans, cut-down plastic bottles. Half-gallon plastic containers with handles (the kind used for milk) are light and can be filled to carry water during the painting lesson.
- Paper towels or scrap paper for blotting brushes while painting.
- Newspapers to protect painting area. Painting may be done on paper-covered tables or desks, pinned to a bulletin board, fastened to a chalkboard, or on the floor if protected with newspaper.
- A bucket of child-sized moist sponges for cleanup.

See Figure 13–2 for additional hints on painting materials.

Care and Storage of Materials

- Lay paintings horizontally to dry before stacking. An unused floor space along the wall is suitable for this purpose. (See Chapter 12 and Figure 13–2 for directions on making a drying rack.)
- Wipe paint sets clean with paper toweling. They can be stored conveniently in a cardboard carton.
- Rinse brushes in clean water, blot, gently point bristles, and leave to dry standing upright in a container.
- Clean brushes after each use. Neglect will cause the brush to lose its shape. Never rest a brush vertically on its bristles. Suspend it, if possible; if not, rest it on its side.

Processes.   Painting with brushes may require some demonstration of the following techniques:

- How to prepare paint trays for use. A drop or two of water is placed in each paint color to moisten it.
- How to use a variety of brush strokes. Encourage children to paint directly, using full free strokes. Use the point, side, and flat surface of the brush. Try wide lines, thin lines, zigzag lines, and dots and dabs.
- How to mix colors on the paper as they paint. Try dipping one side of the brush in one color, the other side in a second color to blend paint in one stroke.
- How to create textures. Paint with bits of sponge, crushed paper or cloth, cardboard, string, sticks, or an old toothbrush. A stiff brush with most of the paint removed creates interesting textural effects.
- How to handle excess paint or water on a brush.
- How to clean paint trays.
- How to rinse and dry brushes.

More Painting Hints

- Thicken easel paint with liquid starch to cut down on drips.
- To help paint stick better to slick surfaces such as foil, waxed paper, styrofoam, or plastic, mix dry tempera with liquid soap.
- To keep paints smelling fresh and sweet, add a few drops of mint extract or oil of wintergreen or cloves.
- For an added sensory experience, try adding lemon flavoring to yellow paint, mint to green, vanilla to white, and peppermint to red paint. You might want to caution the children not to taste the paint, especially with younger children.
- Keep dated examples of each child's work through the year in the child's portfolio, to reflect the growth and development in creative expression. The children will enjoy seeing their progress in control and expression over the year.
- Use a digital camera to create a digital portfolio of children's artwork. One day every month, put a reminder on your calendar to carry a fully charged digital camera throughout the day. Snap the highlights of the day but especially zoom in on their artwork. At the end of the day, empty the camera into a dated folder to keep on your hard drive. After about four months, select about 10 pictures from each folder and print them, grouped by month. This is a fun way for parents and children to see how much they've developed over the course of the year and their progress in art. See Chapter 11 for more suggestions on using portfolios with children's artwork.

More ideas on painting activities for children are found at the end of this unit.

Crayons

Most young children are introduced to using crayons before starting school. (See Chapter 12 for further information on crayons).

Materials.   Crayon drawings may be done on a wide assortment of surfaces, such as newsprint, wrapping

Figure 13-3
Crayon drawings are one of the most popular two-dimensional art activities.

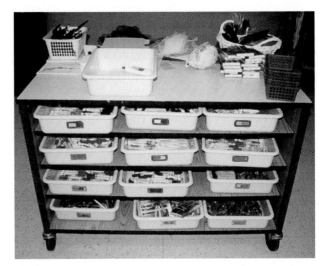

Figure 13-4
Storing markers by colors makes it easier for children to access colors when making drawings or designs.

paper, newspaper, construction paper, corrugated board, cloth, and wood. This is an ideal medium for all children; it is bold, colorful, clean, and inexpensive. Crayons work well on most papers. They do not blend well; when attempts are made to do this, the wax often "tears." Crayons can be applied thinly to produce semi-transparent layers of subtle color, and these layers can be coated with black crayon and scratched through for crayon etchings.

Processes. Encouraging children to experiment with crayons and to explore the use of different parts of the crayon leads to their discovery of new methods that satisfy the needs for expression. The wax crayon has great versatility and can be used in many different ways.

The best way to get bright, rich color from the crayon and onto the paper is by pressing hard. A cushion sheet placed underneath the drawing will assist children in creating bright colors easily.

- Make thin lines with the point of the crayon, heavy lines with the blunt end or side of the crayon.
- Vary the pressure to create subtle tints or solid, brilliant colors.
- Make rough texture by using broken lines, dots, jabs, dashes, and other strokes with the point.
- Create smooth texture by using the flat side or by drawing lines close together in the same direction with the point.
- Twist, turn, swing the crayon in arcs, and move it in various ways to achieve different effects.
- Repeated motions create rhythm.

Figure 13-5
Scissoring is a developmental skill.

Avoid using coloring books or ditto sheets. Children who are frequently given such patterns to color are in fact being told that they and their art are inadequate. A pattern of a dog for children to color says to them—more clearly than words could—that "This is what your drawing should look like; this is the RIGHT way to make a dog" (Seefeldt, 1995). Instead of dittos and coloring books, provide children a variety of art supplies, media, large blocks of time, and the freedom to work at one's developmental level.

The crayon offers new areas of creative interpretation when used in combination with other materials:

- Use crayon and white chalk on colored construction paper.
- Make a crayon rubbing by placing shapes or textures under paper and rubbing over the surface.
- Make a crayon resist by first drawing in brilliant color, then cover the drawing with watercolor paint.
- Paint a colorful background, allow to dry, and then draw directly over the painted surface with chalk or crayon.
- Use white crayon underneath a color to make a brighter color.
- Use craypas (oil pastel crayons) on colored construction paper. Apply the oil pastels thickly to get rich colors.

More crayon activities are found at the end of this chapter.

Pasting

Paste serves a functional purpose, and its properties also make it a valuable medium for creative expression. The stickiness, texture, odor, and changes that take place as paste is used provide children with opportunities for many discoveries. When a young child picks up paste in his or her hands, the child will almost automatically spread it over his or her fingers and squeeze it or roll it between his or her fingers and feel

its stickiness. Before long, the child spreads paste over his or her hands, sometimes even rubbing it into his or her palms. As paste dries, a child feels a different sensation. When the child begins to wash his or her hands, the paste is transformed from hard to sticky to slimy, a phenomenon of great interest to a child. Paste is a medium that can stimulate a child to repeated explorations of the properties of matter.

Given sufficient paste and a piece of paper, a child almost invariably smears the paste on the paper as though it were finger paint. He or she moves his hand across the page with sweeping motions. In some places on the paper he or she smooths the paste until it is slick and shiny. In other places the child forms lumps of paste and then enjoys pressing down on the lumps to smooth them out. The paste-smeared paper becomes an artistic creation for the child.

Having explored paste in this manner, a child reaches for small pieces of paper and pastes piece upon piece, using large quantities of paste in the process. He or she is excited by what he or she can accomplish with the medium. When the child attempts to lift the mound of paper he or she has created, very often the paper tears. The child discovers that paste is heavy.

Adults should avoid instructing children on the uses of paste and allow them to make their own discoveries. Eventually a child will begin to create a collage,

Figure 13-6

Two-dimensional activities provide children opportunities for social learning.

Figure 13-7

Two-dimensional drawings often combine the use of crayons and markers.

arranging random shapes of varied colors on large paper. At first he or she pays no attention to design but will later learn to carefully arrange the pieces to achieve a balance that is pleasing to him or her.

By adult standards, it may appear that the amount of paste children use is exorbitant, but their explorations are limited if they cannot have as much paste as they need.

Although most paste for children is nontoxic, a teacher should be certain that the commercial paste used in the classroom is safe, because children put paste in their mouths. Paste can also be made by the child and/or the teacher. (See Appendix C for paste recipes.)

Torn Paper and Pasting

Materials

- Kinds of paper: construction paper, wallpaper, gift wrappings, metallic paper, tissue paper, newspaper, illustrated magazine pages.
- For mounting: newsprint, construction paper, cardboard, wallpaper, newspaper (classified ad pages), cardboard box lids.
- Paste, glue sticks, scissors, brushes.

Process

- Demonstrate cutting and tearing paper shapes.
- Have the children cut and tear paper shapes.
- Show a variety of papers different in color and texture and encourage children's suggestions on how to use them.

Figure 13-8

When a child puts his or her name on his or her work it shows how important it is to the child.

- Demonstrate pasting the torn pieces to the background.
- Torn paper creates a textured edge. Cut edges appear smooth.
- In tearing paper, greater control of the paper is achieved by tearing slowly with fingers close together.
- Encourage children to choose light and dark colors for interesting contrast and different sizes or shapes and a variety of papers for textural effects.
- Paper shapes can be overlapped or grouped to produce new shapes and new combinations of colors and textures.
- Cut paper can be textured by wrinkling, crumpling, slitting, and folding out.

Older children who have mastered scissoring skills will enjoy cut paper activities. Some suggestions for working with cut paper artwork are as follows:

- Encourage children to think about the shape of an object and its edges before cutting.
- Plan the composition. Cut the big, important shapes first. Cut details, patterns, and textures later. Glue last.
- Use a variety of shapes. Repeat shapes and change their size for variety. Repeat colors by changing their intensity or value for variety.
- Create textured areas by folding, fringing, pleating, curling, and weaving the paper.
- Overlap shapes to give depth and distance to a cut paper composition. Create distance in cut paper by working from the background forward.
- Glue small shapes, details, patterns, and textures to larger shapes before gluing them to the background.
- Glue around the outside edge of the shapes, not over the entire back of the shape.
- Create identical shapes by folding the paper once and remembering that the fold is the middle of the shape.
- Use positive and negative shapes in the composition. The positive shape is the cut shape. The remaining paper is the negative shape.
- Use the lightest colors first when creating with tissue paper. Cut and arrange all the big important shapes before gluing. Change the arrangement of the shapes until a pleasing composition is found.

Suggested projects

- Paper collage: Use papers of various textures, colors, sizes, and shapes to create a design or picture. See section on collage later in this chapter.

Figure 13-9
Children with an interpersonal learning style enjoy working alongside others.

- All-over design: Cut or tear related shapes of different sizes and colors to form a design.
- Cut-paper mural: Select a topic. Each child may cut shapes and combine them in a group mural.
- Three-dimensional picture: Parts of the picture may be modeled, curled, fringed, or fastened only at the edges to allow them to protrude from the background.
- Pasting can involve anything and everything that can be stuck to paper, wood, cardboard, or together: tissues, scraps, corks, feathers, popcorn, styrofoam pieces, yarn, paste, colored paste, white paste, even pasting with glue on brushes or glue on figures.

Murals

A storytelling picture or panel intended for a large wall space is called a **mural,** another form of picture making. A suitable topic for a mural may come from children's personal experiences at home, at school, or at play, or it may relate to other school subjects. In the classroom, mural making is a versatile art activity; it may involve a large group or just a few children, depending on the size of the mural. Mural-making projects are excellent for "person smart" children who enjoy activities involving other children. Of course, murals are a natural fit for children who have the picture smart (visual) learning style. With young children, it should be a simple, informal, spontaneous expression with a minimum of preplanning. Tedious plan-

ning destroys much of the intuitive quality and reduces interest. In contrast, older children will enjoy planning a group mural almost as much as making it. With older children you can have them think about the composition of the mural—what they could include in it. Some design elements to consider when making a mural with older children are as follows:

- Varied sizes and shapes
- Varied breakup of foreground and background space
- Overlapping shapes
- Shapes extending out of the picture
- Quiet areas to balance busy ones
- Large objects or figures at the bottom and smaller ones at the top to create the illusion of distance

Materials

kraft paper	paste
roll paper	newspapers
wallpaper	collage materials
crayons	brushes
paint	scissors
water and container	colored construction paper

Processes

- Watercolor paint allows for spontaneous bold design and brilliant color, ideal for murals.
- Cut or torn paper is a flexible medium suitable for murals, permitting many changes and parts as the mural progresses. Other techniques for manipulating paper are folding, curling, pleating, twisting, fringing, and overlapping. Place background paper on a bulletin board, then plan, pin, and move parts before attaching. Various papers such as tissue, wallpaper, illustrated magazine pages, and metallic paper add interest. Topics for group murals are limited only by the imagination of the children. Providing children a variety of experiences both in and out of the classroom will stimulate them to express their ideas visually in a mural. Sometimes an ordinary group discussion will nudge children to become interested in creating a mural.

PRINTMAKING

Long before they enter the classroom, most children have already discovered their footprints or handprints, made as they walk or play in snow or wet sand. In a basic printing activity, the child learns that an object dipped in or brushed with paint makes its own mark or *relief* print on paper. This process can be repeated over and over again to create a design. Children use

THINK ABOUT IT... Art Activities Online

How often have you felt the need for some new ideas to use with your students? Sometimes you just need a spark to jumpstart your thinking to develop fresh ideas into lesson plans and instructional units. Although the following Web sites do not offer comprehensive lessons or units, they do offer many ideas that you can further develop to meet your needs.

KINDERART

KinderArt, http://www.kinderart.com, claims to have the largest collection of free art lessons on the Internet. Addressed to teachers, parents, children, homeschoolers, and museum educators since 1996, it has grown into a collection of resources featuring more than 800 free lesson plans. In addition to lessons for grades K through 12, KinderArt offers printable activity pages, an interactive bulletin board, art trivia, educational links and articles, and early childhood education resources. The "Lessons" section lists categories from Architecture, Artists/Art History, and Crafty Ideas to Cross Curriculum, Drama, Painting, and Recycling. Users can also contribute lessons to be posted and participate in an online bulletin board.

ANTI-COLORING BOOKS

The Anti-Coloring Books by author Susan Striker, http://www.susanstriker.com, features visual image "starters" that can spur children's imaginations to create original pictures and designs. Designed to stimulate creativity and encourage problem solving and critical thinking, her books help children draw their own pictures. Under the section Teacher Resources, Striker integrates art and literature by recommending a number of children's storybooks to use as motivation for art activities in the classroom.

KATHY SCHROCK'S GUIDE FOR ART EDUCATORS: ART AND ARCHITECTURE

The Web site http://www.school.discovery.com/ (Click on Kathy Schrock's Guide for Educators) is part of the DiscoverySchool.com site. It provides a noteworthy gateway to sites of interest to art teachers researching and developing instructional materials.

GEM.

Visit the Gateway to Educational Materials (GEM) at http://www.thegateway.org/. GEM offers one-stop access to high-quality lesson plans, curriculum units, and other educational resources available on the Internet. The site includes resources from the Smithsonian American Art Museum, NASA, UNICEF, numerous universities, and other organizations.

---

small muscles in the hand, wrist, and fingers as they hold the object, dip it in paint, and print with it on paper. They learn that each object has its own unique quality—that each thing makes its own print.

Techniques range from a simple fingertip printing to carving a styrofoam plate and printing with it. Emphasis should be on the free manipulation of objects and experimentation with color, design, and techniques.

The teacher may begin by encouraging children to search for objects from the home or classroom.

Household items, kitchen utensils, hardware, discarded materials, and many objects of nature are useful in relief printing. Gradually, the child learns to look and discover textures, colors, and patterns that exist all around.

In their first attempts to organize shapes into a design, young children usually work in a random fashion. These early experiments help them develop a better understanding of the printmaking process and of the possibilities for variety of design.

THIS ONE'S for YOU!

Painting—It's Great Outdoors!

Break away from traditional thinking about painting inside at a table or an easel. There are many exciting painting adventures awaiting you and the children in the great outdoors. Here are a few ideas to get you started:

WATER PAINTING

Preschoolers enjoy painting the side of a building or on the sidewalk with large paint brushes and buckets of water. The broad strokes enhance gross motor development and hand–eye coordination. This activity can also lead to a rudimentary discussion of evaporation.

WEED PAINTING/PRINTING

Go outside and collect a variety of weeds to use as paintbrushes. Queen Ann's lace is one that works especially well. Children dip the weed in a small, shallow container of paint. Then they can either print with the weed or use it as an interesting paint brush.

ROOT PAINTING

Help children dig up dead plants and save the roots (with the stems attached). Or ask families to gather roots that children can use. (Be sure that you have nontoxic roots that are bushy, with stems sturdy enough to serve as root brush handles.) Mix a variety of tempera paint to a medium consistency and pour it in juice cans, paint cups, or ready-to-use frosting containers. Gather paper—any kind will do—and put it in a bag or basket to take outside. Set up easels on a grassy area, or cover a picnic table with newspapers. Put out the paper and paint. Give the children lots of time to experiment and create designs and pictures with their root brushes.

MUD FINGER PAINTING

Fill a dishpan with dirt (high clay content works best, but any "clean" soil will do). Fill another dishpan with water. Provide several large, washable trays and several plastic scoops for the soil and the water. Set up a table (preferably near a faucet with a hose). Place the trays, dishpans, and scoops on the table with smocks nearby. Children put on smocks and scoop soil and water onto their trays. Let the children enjoy experimenting with this new "mud finger paint" they create by mixing water and soil together.

OUTDOOR WEAVING

Gather long scarves, pieces of ribbon, cording and ropes in many colors and rolls of crepe paper in as many colors as possible. Locate a nearby chain link fence. Children weave the ribbons, crepe paper, and other materials in and out of the links on the fence to create a colorful woven design on the fence. (This is not painting, but it's a fun outdoors activity!)

SUN PRINTS

Collect a variety of items with interesting shapes such as spools, forks, cookie cutters, seashells, and stray puzzle pieces. Gather several sheets of bright construction paper. Be sure not to use construction paper guaranteed not to fade. Dark blue, purple, and green construction paper work well. Attach the construction paper to one side of a large flat sheet of cardboard. Children choose shapes from the collection and place them any way and where they like on the paper. Then leave everything in the sun. In a day or two, go outside and remove the objects. When the objects are removed, the sun will have bleached the paper, leaving dark silhouettes in an interesting design.

Helping Children Get Started in Printmaking

The following suggestions are some ways to introduce printmaking activities.

⊙ Paint hands and feet and then "print" them on paper as a natural beginning to printmaking.

⊙ Children may observe and discuss examples of repeat design in clothing, wrapping paper, and wallpaper in which objects appear again and again, up and down, across the whole material.

⊙ Children print repeat designs using found objects, such as a sponge, rubber eraser, stick, and bottle cap, or natural materials, such as leaves, twigs, stones, and bark.

⊙ In potato printing, carve out a section of the potato, making simple designs on the flat surface by notching the edges or carving holes with dull scissors, split tongue depressors, or a small plastic knife. Older children are able to carve with a plastic knife, but younger children will require teacher assistance.

⊙ The creative teacher demonstrates any necessary processes of using materials and tools without dictating what the final product will look like. He or she provides stimulation and guidance in the use of children's original ideas and encourages children to experiment with various objects and techniques.

Gradually, through their printmaking experiences, children discover for themselves the following:

⊙ The amount of paint needed to obtain clean edges.

⊙ The object must be painted each time it is printed. Print by pressing slowly and firmly.

⊙ The amount of pressure needed to get a print.

⊙ How the shape and texture of an object determine the shape and texture of the print.

⊙ How to repeat a print over and over to create a design.

Printmaking Materials

Materials for printmaking may include the following:

⊙ *Paint.* Any of the following are suitable: tempera paint in sets of eight colors, powder paint in a thin mixture, food coloring, water-soluble printing ink.

⊙ *Stamp pad.* Discarded pieces of felt or cotton cloth inside a jar lid, cut-down milk carton, frozen food tin, or similar waterproof container saturated with color.

⊙ *Paper.* Absorbent papers suitable for printing include newsprint, manila paper, wallpaper, tissue, construction paper, classified pages of the newspaper, plain wrapping paper, or paper towels. Avoid using paper with a hard slick finish because it does not absorb paint and ink well.

⊙ *Cloth.* Absorbent pieces of discarded cloth can also be used to print on, such as pillow cases, sheets, men's handkerchiefs, old shirts, and napkins.

⊙ *Other items.* Newspaper for covering tables, brushes for applying paint when not using a stamp pad, and cans for water.

Printmaking Techniques

The following are some common printmaking techniques suitable for young children.

Found object printing. With a few familiar objects, such as forks, spools, sticks, buttons, bottle tops, some paper, paint, and a brush, children can learn to print their own designs. Objects of nature such as leaves, weeds, seeds, and stones can be used similarly.

Fingerprints. Get a sheet of newsprint. Press one of your fingers onto a stamp pad or onto a tray filled with thickened tempera. Press your finger onto the newsprint. Experiment. Use different fingers, singly or in combinations, etc. Add details with markers and crayons.

Vegetable printing. Cut a potato, carrot, or other firm vegetable into sections for ease of handling. Keep the design simple, avoiding thin lines. Older children can draw the design on the flat cut surface and carve the design about ¼–inch deep, leaving the area desired to be printed. Paint the raised part of the design and press on paper or cloth.

Monoprinting. To create a **monoprint,** apply paint to paper. Carefully place a sheet of paper over the painting and rub smoothly from the center out to the edge. If desired, children can draw in crayon on the top sheet of paper, pressing the lines into the paint on the bottom sheet. Pull the print gradually, starting from one corner.

Styrofoam prints. Get a flat piece of styrofoam. Draw a picture or design using permanent markers. These markers will dissolve the foam. Use a brush or sponge to apply a thin layer of tempera to the surface of the tray. Place a piece of construction paper over

Figure 13-10
When introducing a new tool for printing, like a brayer, a teacher may need to demonstrate its use.

the tempera. Rub. Another way to print with styrofoam is to make a pattern, picture, or design by squeezing glue onto the styrofoam. After the glue has dried, tempera paint is applied to the entire surface. Place a piece of construction paper over the paint and rub. Because this is a two-step process, it is more appropriate for children in the middle and upper elementary grade levels.

Pieces of styrofoam can also be used as printing plates by cutting them into shapes and pasting them on a background. The same applies to heavy cardboard.

Older children, as we have seen in Chapter 12, continue to refine their creative skills throughout the elementary grades. In printing experiences, children in the middle and upper elementary levels are usually able to use a **brayer** (an ink roller) with a printing plate. Brayers in various sizes can be purchased at art supply stores.

The brayer is rolled in a shallow pan filled with a small amount of water-soluble ink or tempera paint. A metal or plastic tray or small cookie sheet works well for this. The child rolls the brayer over the ink to spread an even coat on the brayer. Then the ink-coated brayer is rubbed over the printing plate (e.g., a cut out design on styrofoam) until the whole surface is covered with ink. It works best to roll the brayer in one direction, then in another at right angles.

The child then places paper on top of the inked plate and presses it down gently with the palm of the hand. Then, she or he rubs the back of the paper with the fingertips or the back of a spoon, being sure to cover all areas including the edges. Finally, the child pulls the paper away from the block. This is called "pulling the print." Now the print is ready to dry. Some hints for working with older children and printing with brayers are as follows:

- Set up three printing centers in a classroom. You may want to use a different color of ink at each center, keeping it neat and well stocked with paper and ink.
- As students are ready to print, they go to a center and roll the ink on their blocks with the brayer. They take their inked blocks and papers to their desks and do the actual printing there. This will prevent long lines at the centers.
- For clean up, drop a folded piece of newspaper in the pan filled with ink. Roll the brayer on the newspaper. This will remove a great deal of the ink from both the pan and the brayer. Unfold the newspaper and refold it with the dirty side inside. Crumple and throw away the newspaper. Once most of the ink is out of the pan, it is easy to rinse both it and the brayer at the sink.

Paper stencils.   The four- to five-year-old child can begin to use stencils in a most creative manner. Each child is given four or five pieces of drawing paper about four inches square. With scissors, the child cuts holes of various sizes and shapes in the center of each piece. It is a good idea to cut more than one hole per piece. When the holes have been cut, each child is given a tissue, small piece of cotton, or patch of cloth. This is rubbed on a piece of colored chalk to pick up enough dust to stencil. Then the child selects a shape and places it on the paper on which the design is to go. The child rubs the tissue across the hole, making strokes from the stencil paper toward the center of the opening. This is continued around the edge of the opening until the paper under the stencil has a clear print. The same shape can be continued across the paper, or other shapes and colors may be added according to the child's preference.

A child can choose the shapes and combinations desired. The same technique can be used with wax crayons instead of chalk. The crayons are rubbed directly on the stencil. Unbleached muslin or cotton material can be used to print on as well.

The spatter technique.   Simple spatter or spray printing is both fascinating and fun for children. It also has the advantage of allowing for a wide variety of patterns and shapes. Children can work individually or with partners on this project.

Have several of the children bring in old toothbrushes. Beside toothbrushes, only a small amount of watercolor paint and paper is needed. The method is to "spray" the paint with a toothbrush. This is done by dipping the brush in paint and gently pulling a straight-edged object (ruler, emery board, or tongue depressor) across the ends of the bristles. This causes

THIS ONE'S for YOU!

Bits of History– Art Materials

You might like to know a little about the history behind some of the familiar art media you use with children. Here are bits of history on these everyday materials:

Chalk–The original chalks for drawing, some still in use today, were pure earth, cut and shaped into implements. The addition of a binder created a fabricated chalk that we know today as a pastel chalk. Chalks used by the early master painters were generally limited to reds (sanguine), black, and white.

Crayons–Of the many art materials, probably none is more familiar than wax crayons. The fact that most of us were introduced to them at a tender age may influence us to think that they are beneath the dignity of more mature artists. Such is not the case; examples abound of distinguished drawings executed in this humble medium (Miro and Picasso, for example). Examples of the use of crayons begin in the nineteenth century. Crayons consist of an oily or waxy binder impregnated with pigments or color. Records exist of a variety of prescriptions for binders, involving soap, salad oil, linseed oil, spermaceti, and beeswax.

Ink–The earliest ink known, black carbon, was prepared by the early Egyptians and Chinese. This was followed by iron-gall (made from growths on trees), bistre (burnt wood), and sepia (a secretion from cuttlefish). Today, there is a wide variety of inks available, but the best known is India ink, which is really a waterproof carbon black.

Pens–Those of us who take for granted our familiar metal pen points of various kinds may not realize that they are fairly new, not having been successfully developed until the last century. Until that time, the reed pen had been the pen of the ancients, and the quill pen was the principal instrument from the medieval period to modern times. Most of us probably remember the use of quill pens in the drawings of Rembrandt and in the historical documents drawn up by the founders of our Republic.

Brushes–Bristle is obtained from the body of hogs and boars found in Russia, Japan, Formosa, Korea, France, and Central and Eastern Europe. While all animal hair has "points," bristle has "flags." The individual bristle splits into two or three tiny forks on the end, which are called "flags."

the bristles to snap forward, throwing small particles of paint onto the paper.

The children create designs by placing small, flat objects on the paper. When the bristles snap the small particles of paint forward, the object prevents the spray from striking the paper directly under the object. This leaves the shapes free of paint spray while the rest of the paper is covered with small flecks of paint.

This technique has endless possibilities. Not only can a variety of shapes be used, but colors can also be superimposed on one another. Natural forms such as twigs, leaves, and grass are excellent for this activity. Several forms can be combined, leading to interesting arrangements with unlimited variety. A field trip is a good way to find new print forms and shapes, thus encouraging children to find and learn about beauty in their own environment. Another strength of this project is that it avoids stereotyped designs and ready-cut patterns. The children create beauty for themselves.

Suggestions for Printmaking Experiments

With Color

- Alternate thin transparent watercolor with thick, opaque tempera paint.
- Use a light color to print on dark paper or vice versa.
- Use transparent paint on colored paper or cloth so that the color of the background shows through.
- Combine two sizes of objects of the same shape.
- Combine objects of different sizes and shapes.
- Use one object in various positions.
- Try overlapping and grouping objects.

With Texture

- Vary the amount of paint used in printing.
- Use objects that create different textures, such as sponges, corrugated paper, wadded paper or cloth, stones, vegetables, and sandpaper.

Figure 13-11
Two-dimensional art activities can be integrated into the entire elementary curriculum.

With Background Paper

⊙ Try using a variety of shapes and sizes of paper.

⊙ Paint background paper and allow to dry before printing.

⊙ Paste pieces of tissue or colored construction paper onto background paper, allow to dry, then print.

⊙ Print a stippled design on background with a sponge, allow to dry, then print with a solid object.

With Pattern

⊙ Print a shape in straight rows or zigzag. Repeat design to create an all-over pattern.

⊙ Use a different shape for each row and add a second color in alternate rows.

⊙ Print in a border design with a single shape or group of shapes.

More ideas for print making are found at the end of this chapter.

COLLAGE

Collage, a French word meaning "to paste," is the product of selecting, organizing, and arranging materials of contrasting color and texture and attaching them to a flat surface.

One way children become aware of things around them is by touching. Through manipulation of everyday objects, they grow in sensitivity to shapes and textures and discover ways to use them in creating new forms and images. With added experience, the tactile sense becomes an instrument of knowledge and a tool of expression. Unlike the *imitation of texture* in drawing and painting, the textural materials in collage are *real.*

Figure 13-12
Middle and upper elementary level children enjoy working with two-dimensional media, perfecting skills learned in earlier years.

Helping Children Get Started in Collage Activities

The following suggestions are designed to help motivate children in their initial collage activities:

⊙ Arouse children's awareness of texture by passing various materials for them to touch and examine. Discuss the qualities of various textures by asking: How do these materials feel? Are they smooth? Hard? Soft? Fuzzy? Sharp? Round? How can we use these materials?

⊙ Arrange a "touch-and-see" display.

⊙ Discuss sources of collage materials and encourage children to collect them.

⊙ Demonstrate making a collage; selecting and arranging materials on a background; and ways of fastening, using paste, thread, and staples.

⊙ Assess qualities of materials in relation to ideas to be expressed (e.g., gold paper is bright and "shiny like the sun" and cotton is soft and white "like snow").

Materials

- *Background:* Manila paper, construction paper, cardboard, and shirtboard.
- *Collage materials:* Paper and cloth scraps, magazine pages, yarn, string, ribbon, lace, and any other items the children and teacher collect.
- *Natural materials:* Leaves, twigs, bark, seed pods, dried weeds, feathers, beans, ferns, sands, small stones, and shells.
- Scissors, brushes, paste, glue sticks, stapler, and staples.

Sort and keep materials of a similar nature in boxes to facilitate selection.

Processes

- When working with beginners, limit the number of collage materials; this lessens the confusion in selection.
- Encourage children to use materials in their own way. Instead of giving exact directions, suggest ways of selecting materials for variety of shape, size, color, and texture.
- Materials may be cut, torn, or left in their original shapes.
- As children arrange and rearrange the shapes on the background, they may form a representational picture or compose an abstract design.
- Throughout the work period, emphasize thoughtful use of space by overlapping and grouping shapes, trying different combinations of colors and textural surfaces.
- Create three-dimensional effects by crumpling flat pieces of material and attaching them to the background in two or three places. Other techniques include overlapping, bending, folding, rolling, curling, and twisting paper.
- Include buttons, braids, tissue, or yarn for added interest and accent.
- Use glue or staples to fasten heavy materials and plastics.
- A collage may be displayed in a shadow box, using a box lid as a frame; it can be mounted in an old picture frame or on a sheet of colored construction paper.
- Create a nature collage using all natural materials.
- Make a paper or cloth collage, exploring a variety of one kind of material. Do the same with leaves, buttons, or one kind of material children enjoy.

Since older children enjoy creating more complex works in their art experiences, collage is an excellent

FLAT-TIP AND ROUND-TIP BRUSHES–BASIC INFORMATION

The best brushes are made of natural hairs from animals such as hogs.

Basic FLAT Brush Sizes

Length	Width of Bristles	Ages Appropriate
8″	1″	Toddler & up
12″	½″	4 years and up
6″	½″	4 years and up
12″	¾″	3–4 years
6″	¾″	3–4 years
12″	¼″	5 years and up
8″	¼″	5 years and up

Basic ROUND Brush Sizes (With Pointed Tips)

8″	¾″	6 years and up
8″	½″	6 years and up

Figure 13-13
Flat-Tip and Round-Tip Brushes–Basic Information

medium for this age group. Here are some collage ideas for this age group:

- Keep a collection of old picture magazines on hand. Have students tear or cut out sections of pages with large areas of interesting colors, textures, or patterns that might be used for collages. Have them create collages with these. Allow them to trade magazine pages with one another.
- Collages can often send the viewer a very strong message. Have students make a collage mural about littering. Discuss how litter pollutes the school grounds and the environment. Talk about the types of items that define litter. Have students cut pictures from magazines of things that could litter the playground or cause environmental pollution. Students can also draw objects for the mural. Give the mural a title that reinforces the message of the artwork.
- After students have completed the collage activities, have them write about their art work.

SUMMARY

Picture making is a term that refers to any and all forms of purposeful visual expressions, beginning with controlled scribbling. Painting is a method of picture making, which can be done with a brush or with the fingers (finger painting). Other appropriate activities in the early childhood art program are drawing with crayons, printing, and working with clay. Children enjoy collage activities, which involve selecting, organizing, and arranging materials and attaching them to a surface.

KEY TERMS

brayer   mural
collage   picture making
monoprint   tempera

ACTIVITIES FOR CHILDREN

PAINTING

Bubble Wrap Painting. Take a piece of bubble wrap and lay it on a table so that the bubbles are facing up. Have the child cover the bubbles with tempera paint. Then place a piece of construction paper on top of the bubbles. Press down on the paper so that all of the bubbles are able to make a print. Lift up the construction paper and see the design. See what happens when some of the bubbles pop when pressing down on the construction paper. How do the bubbles print differently than the ones with air still in them? If you use more than one color of paint, how do the paints blend?

Rainbow Painting. Use white crayons to draw simple pictures or designs on white paper. Then make a rainbow of lines over the picture, using different colors of watercolor paints. Watch as the drawings magically appear through the rainbow.

Variety Painting. For a change, try using household implements to paint or print with. Try a comb, an old toothbrush, string, an old wheel toy, sponges, a wadded bit of paper towel, alphabet letter magnets, and other safe items from the kitchen drawer. Try different motions, such as pulling the object across the paint, or quick dabs onto the paper.

String Painting. You will need two pieces of white drawing paper for each child, tempera paint in bowls, and 12″ lengths of string (at least three per child). Provide several lengths of string for each bowl of tempera paint. Hold one end, and dip string into paint. Lay string onto paper to create a design. Redip and repeat, or use a new string and a new color. For a variety, try dropping the string onto paper. For a print design, press a second sheet of paper on top of the string design and lightly press.

Pulled String Painting. You will need yarn or string, bowls of tempera paint, construction paper or drawing paper, and a damp rag or sponge. Dip the string or yarn into a bowl of tempera paint. Do not squeeze paint out of the string. Lay the string on a sheet of paper in any design, leaving the tail end of the string off the edge of the paper. Place another piece of paper over this. Lay a hand gently over the paper and string. Pull the string from the paper, keeping the hand pressing gently on the top of the paper. Remove the top paper and see the string design! For a variation, try a folded sheet of paper and place the string inside. Try several colors, one at a time, adding each color after the first is done. Try a rope dipped in paint and place it between very large sheets of paper. Many hands can help this time!

Smash Painting. You will need white construction or drawing paper (let the children cut or tear it into interesting shapes), plastic cling-type wrap cut a bit larger than the pieces of paper, plastic eye droppers, tempera paint in three colors (white, dark blue, and light blue), and markers.

Children pick up one color of paint with an eye dropper and drip it onto the paper. Repeat with the next two colors. Then the children place the plastic wrap on top of their paper and rub, using the paints underneath to blend and swirl. Talk about the colors being created. When the child is pleased with the blended colors, remove the plastic wrap and enjoy the design. After the paintings are dry, children can add details and designs with markers and crayons.

Splotch Paintings. Mix some paint in a small cup of water. Make sure it is dark enough to show up on the paper you are using. The child "spills" some paint onto his paper. Watch as the puddle of paint forms an organic or free-form shape. The children can tilt the paper in different directions to spread the spill if they like. Allow the organic shape to dry. The child can use his imagination to turn the shape into a picture or a design.

Flashy Painting. You will need black or very dark construction paper, glitter, white glue, and newspapers. Cover the work area with newspapers. The child spreads the glue on the paper in shapes and designs. Sprinkle glitter on the paper. Slide the excess glitter off the picture and back into the glitter container. Repeat the glue and glitter process with different colors of glitter. Let the glue dry.

PRINTING

Line Printing. You will need 2″-wide strips of various lengths of manila tag paper, 1 sheet of 9″ × 18″ white drawing paper per child, paper clips, staplers, and three plates of tempera paint per group (e.g., hot/cold colors). Students fold, curve, pleat, etc., their strips of manila tag paper and either paper clip or staple the form. Students dip each strip form into different colors of tempera paint, then print onto their drawing paper to demonstrate the element of line.

Bubble Prints. You will need 1 cup of water, food coloring, ¼ cup liquid detergent, ¼ cup liquid starch, straws, printing paper, and a 6- to 8-inch bowl. In the bowl, mix the water, drops of food coloring, liquid detergent, and liquid starch. Let the children blow bubbles in the bowl using a straw. (Poke a hole in the top of the straw to prevent children accidentally sipping with the straws.) Blow until the bubbles form a structure above the rim of the bowl. Make a print by laying a sheet of white paper across the bowl rim and allowing the bubbles to pop against the paper. Talk about the lines, shapes, and patterns the bubbles make on the paper.

Berry Nice Prints. You will need plastic berry baskets, construction paper, tempera paint, a container large enough to dip the berry basket in, and paper. Talk about the lines children see in the plastic berry basket. Discuss how the lines cross and how they make squares. Talk about which kinds of prints the children think the baskets will make on paper.

Dip the berry basket in paint. Press the basket onto the paper. Repeat, overlapping the shapes. Continue until the pattern or design is completed. For variety, make contrasting designs by printing with white paint on black paper. Print with different colors of primary colors and watch the colors mix.

Circle Challenge. You will need paper cups of various sizes, Lifesavers candy, round paste, and any other circular shapes to print, tempera paint, shallow container for paint, brushes, and paper.

Talk about circles. Have the children identify as many circles as they can in the room. Discuss which things in a circle shape the children can think of to use in print making. Challenge the children to bring from home as many of these items as they can.

Begin by printing with one circular printing object. Print this on the page, making a pattern or a random design. Use another circular object and print with it on the page. Try printing one line with one size circle. Do another with a differently sized circle. Alternate large and small circular shapes in one line. Print zigzag, horizontal, and vertical lines with circle shapes.

For variety, repeat the activity with another shape—square, rectangle, even triangles!

Pinecone Prints. You will need pinecones, thin mixture of tempera paint, a container for the paint, and paper. Talk with the children about pinecones, their shapes, how they feel, and how they smell.

Give each child a piece of paper. Dip a pinecone in tempera paint. Press the pinecone onto the paper. Use all sides of the pinecone to make prints.

Plunge Into It! You will need new plungers of various sizes, large sheets of butcher paper, various colors of tempera paint, and foam trays or plates.

Cover the art area with newspaper. Tape the newspaper to the floor. Lay out butcher paper, and tape it to the floor as well. Prepare paints in trays. Set plungers in paint trays.

Dip the plunger in paint. Press the plunger onto the butcher paper to make a print. Continue printing to create a design or pattern. Add other round objects to print such as paper cups or towel rolls. Use two plungers at a time, each with a different color or paint. Use the paper as a giant class mural. Use the print as wrapping paper or book covers.

Recycled Puzzle Prints. You will need old puzzle pieces, white glue, cereal box cardboard, scissors, tempera paint, paintbrush, paper, and construction paper.

Talk about print making and how you can make several of the same image. Discuss what a pattern is—a repeat design. Talk about how patterns can be made of repeated lines of the same object (e.g., lines with alternating objects). Cut cereal boxes into pieces about 6″ × 8″.

Take several puzzle pieces and arrange them on the nonprinted side of the cereal box cardboard. The pieces can be arranged to create a picture, a random design, or a pattern.

Once happy with the way the pieces look, glue them down and let the glue dry. Use a paintbrush to cover the puzzle pieces with paint. Lay a sheet of paper on top of the painted puzzle pieces. Rub gently with the palm of the hand. Peel off the paper to see the print.

What Can It Be? You will need long pieces of newsprint paper (18″ × 24″) or classified ad sections from the newspaper, tempera paint in shallow pan or cookie sheet, crayons, markers, pail of soapy water, and paper towels.

Cover the floor by taping down newspapers. Tape long sheets of paper onto newspapers. Have the children step into a pan of paint and put their hands in the paint, too. Step out of the paint onto the paper to make foot and hand prints. Let the prints dry completely. Using crayons and markers, use the foot and hand prints to make a design or any kind of original creation.

Yarn Prints. You will need yarn, glue, scissors, cardboard or oaktag, paper, tempera paint, and crayons. Talk about how designs can be repeated to make patterns. Discuss how lines can be zigzag, horizontal, vertical, and so on.

Use crayons to draw a pattern, design, or picture on the cardboard. Outline parts or all of the picture with white glue. Apply glue to the yarn. Let the yarn and glue dry thoroughly. Brush tempera paint over the picture. Place another piece of paper over the picture. Press lightly with the palm of the hand. Peel off the paper to see the string print.

CRAYONS, MARKERS, AND CHALK

Chalk Blend Backgrounds. Rub and blend light pastel colors of chalk on a plain sheet of heavy paper. Dip a small comb in black tempera paint and use the comb with paint to make interesting repeat patterns on the paper. Spray the entire picture with hair spray to prevent smearing. Be sure to spray in a well-ventilated area.

Using Chalk in Picture Making. Don't overlook the creative possibilities of chalk as a medium for young children's drawing and picture making. Here are some creative ways to use chalk:
- Texture: Place thin paper, such as copy paper or tracing paper, over a surface with a unique texture

like sandpaper, bricks, or corrugated cardboard. Then rub over the paper with the side of the chalk so that the texture of the object appears. Numerous textures can be used for many interesting effects.
- Chalk on wet paper: Using colored chalk on wet paper (construction paper or toweling), glide the chalk over the damp surface to give a flowing motion to the drawing. This process provides bold and colorful pictures.
- Starch and chalk: Pour a small amount of liquid starch on a sheet of paper. Dip the colored chalk in the starch and create a unique art experience.
- Wet chalk: Soak chalk in water for several minutes before using it on a dry surface. The wet chalk can be used on windows, paper, ceramic surfaces, and numerous other slick areas. This chalk medium reacts much like a finger painting activity and provides a leaded glass appearance.

Aquarium Crayon Resist. Children draw a crayon picture of a fish or something else that might live in the ocean. They need to mark heavily with the crayons as they draw. After the drawing is finished, give each child a small cup of watered down blue tempera paint. The child brushes the tempera over the crayon drawing. The blue makes the water for the aquarium scene.

Line Stories. Create a story using different types of lines. For example, a line is a dot that went for a walk in the snow. Each set of subsequent lines can be different things (e.g., thin parallel lines are sled tracks, thin curvy lines are bike tracks, spiral lines could be a snake, etc.).

Scribbles. Discuss scribbling, how it looks, and how much fun it is to do. Explain that this activity begins with scribbling.

The child makes a large scribble on the paper. Outline with a marker parts of the scribble. Fill the outlines with crayons. Leave some areas uncolored. Some variations: Make rules for filling the scribbles (e.g., "You can't put the same colors next to each other." "You can only use primary colors." "Use only complementary colors.") Challenge the children to make scribbles using straight lines and angles. Have a group of children make a scribble picture mural. Scribble using crayon, then paint the spaces using tempera paint.

Chalk and Sand Painting. You will need sawdust or sand, pieces of broken chalk, dry tempera paint, water, bowl, construction paper, and glue. Shave chalk with a knife (adults only). Put sawdust or sand with chalk shavings mixed with tempera paint (dry) in a bowl of water (just enough water to cover). Stir and allow to dry overnight. This will make a colorful sand (or sawdust) material.

Apply glue or paste to a piece of construction paper in a design or random fashion. Sprinkle colored sand or sawdust over the glued area to create a sand painting.

Disappearing Line Drawings. You will need hard soap (the type from hotels works well), black construction paper, crayons, water, and sink or large tub of water.

Talk with the children about lines in drawings and how they can be straight, curvy, horizontal, vertical, zigzag, and so on. This project is messy, so you may want rubber gloves and a newspaper-covered drying area.

Give each child a piece of black paper. Do a line drawing with the soap. The drawing should have lots of outlined areas in which to color. Note that the soap will not work for areas the children want white; for these areas the children must use white crayon. Color in the drawing. Light colors work best. Rinse the drawing until the soap lines disappear. Allow to dry. Variation: Draw a design using only shapes. Repeat the process.

Crayon-Rubbing Pictures. You will need crayons, textured surfaces (e.g., sandpaper, pieces of screen, cardboard), and newsprint or another thin-type paper.

Discuss the pieces of textured surfaces with the children. Use descriptive words like *coarse, bumpy,* and *crisscross.*

Make an outline drawing with a pencil on thin paper. Hold the drawing against a surface that has a definite texture. Rub the crayon over all areas of the drawing, filling the area with an interesting texture pattern. The texture will transfer to the paper by the crayon. Place the paper against another texture and transfer this texture to another part of the drawing. Textures may be repeated or overlapped. Continue until all areas are filled with texture rubbings.

Crayon Batik. You will need crayons, paper, water, container for water, thin solution of tempera paint, brushes, and paper towels.

Discuss the fact that the term *batik* is a design with wrinkles in the paper. This is part of the design. Talk

about which kind of picture or design the children would like to make in this activity.

The child makes a drawing or design with the crayons on paper. Soak the paper in water. Crumple the paper into a ball. Uncrumple the paper. Flatten it out. Blot off excess water with paper towels. Flow diluted tempera paint over the surface with a wet brush. Let the batik dry thoroughly. Variations: Draw with light-colored crayons and cover the drawing with dark tempera paint. Draw with dark-colored crayons and cover the drawing with light tempera paint. After the batik has dried, add more design elements or details with markers.

Stained-Glass Chalk Designs. You will need black construction paper, white glue, colored chalks, and examples of stained glass (pictures or the real thing).

Show the children pictures of stained glass (or the real thing). Discuss the colors. See how the colors are in separate sections. Talk about the colors and shapes the children see in the stained glass.

Create a stained glass design and draw it on the construction paper using white glue. Experiment with different shapes and image. When the glue is dry, color between the glue lines using colored chalks. An adult sprays design with hairspray to prevent chalk from smudging off the paper.

Squares. Talk about squares and how we know things are square because they have four even sides. Discuss how squares are all over the place and find some.

On a piece of paper, draw squares. Draw the squares in different sizes. Try stacking the squares. Draw a design or an object made totally of squares. Color the squares different colors. Variations: Do the same activity using only circles, triangles, rectangles, ovals, and so on. Use markers to add details to the design. Glue on scraps of fabric or cloth for added effect.

Line Collage. You will need 1- to 3-inch wide strips of various lengths of colored construction paper, one sheet of 9″ × 18″ white drawing paper per child, glue, and scissors.

Students glue the strips of construction paper to their piece of drawing paper, using the edge of their strip to demonstrate the element of line (e.g., twisting, looping, chaining, rolling, curling, folding, pleating).

CHAPTER REVIEW

1. Discuss how to mix, store, and use paint for picture making.
2. List some variations to include in crayon pictures.
3. Explain how to introduce children to torn-and-cut pictures.
   a. List some materials needed.
   b. List some possible demonstration strategies.
4. Discuss the importance of murals as two-dimensional art activities.
   a. List some topics for murals.
   b. List some materials for murals.

5. Discuss the various printing techniques.
6. List the basic materials needed for each printing technique.
7. Define the word *collage* and give specific examples of collage activities.
8. List specific materials and techniques used in collage activities.

REFERENCES

Seefeldt, C. (1995, March). Art: A serious work. *Young Children, 39*–44.

ADDITIONAL READINGS

Althouse, R. (2002). *Colors of learning*. New York: Teachers College Press.

Althouse, R., Johnson, M. H., & Mitchell, S. T. (2004). *The colors of learning: Integrating the visual arts into the early childhood curriculum*. New York: Teacher's College Press.

Braun-Reinetz, J. (2001). *The mural book: A practical guide for educators*. Glenview, IL: Crystal Productions.

Engel, B. C. (2000). *Considering children's art: Why and how to value their works*. Washington, DC: NAEYC.

Gould, P., & Sullivan, J. (1999) *The inclusive early childhood classroom: Easy ways to adapt learning centers for all children*. Beltsville, MD: Gryphon House.

Greh, D. (2002). *New technologies in the artroom: A handbook for teachers*. Worcester, MA: Davis Publications.

Hayes, K., & Creange, R. (2002). *Classroom routines that really work for pre-kindergarten and kindergarten*. New York: Scholastic.

Jensen, B. J. (2002). The mud center: Recapturing childhood. *Young Children 57*(3), 16–20.

Kawamura, M. (2002). *Polyhedron origami for beginners*. New York: Japan Publications Trading Co.

Kohl, M. F. (2002). *First art*. Beltsville, MD: Gryphon House.

Mackenzie, R., & Mackenzie, G. (2003). A bridge to learning: The life and work of Eric Carle. *School Arts 102*(8), 29–32.

Mayesky, M. (2004). *Creative arts and activities: Painting*. Clifton Park, NY: Delmar.

Mayesky, M. (2004). *Creative arts and activities: Crayons, markers & chalk*. Clifton Park, NY: Delmar.

Mayesky, M. (2004). *Creative arts and activities: Print making*. Clifton Park, NY: Delmar.

SOFTWARE FOR CHILDREN

Amazing Book of Colors, 2003. Pre-K.
Art Safari (Pixter), 2003. Pre-5.
Caillou's Birthday Party, 2001. Pre-K.
Dinosaurs Dino Draw (Pixter), 2003. Pre-3.
Kaleido Draw, 2003. Pre-K.
Kid Pix Deluxe 3, 2003. Pre-K.
Krazy Art Room, 2002. Pre-K.
Action Art (Pixter), 2003. Grades K–3.
Arthur's Kindergarten, 2002. Grades K–3.
Barbie as Rapunzel: A Creative Adventure, 2002. Grades K–3.
Cinderella's Castle Design, 2003. Grades K–3.

Disney Learning Kindergarten, 2003. Grades K–3.
Disney Magic Artist, 2002. Grades K–3.
Disney's Magic Artist Deluxe, 2001. Grades K–3.
Finding Nemo: Nemo's Underwater World of Fun, 2003. Grades K–3.
Pencil-Pal Kindergarten, 2002. Grades K–3.
Action Art (Pixter), 2003. Grades 4–5.
Disney's Magic Artist Deluxe, 2002. Grades 4–5.
Kid Pix Deluxe (3rd ed) 2003. Grades 4–5.
What's Her Face!, 2002. Grades 4–5.
LEGO Creator, 2003. Grades 4–5.

HELPFUL WEB SITES

EduPuppy, http://www.edupuppy.com
Art ideas for preschool and kindergarten teachers.
Gayle's Preschool Rainbow,
http://www.preschoolrainbow.org/
Ideas for pre-kindergarten and kindergarten teachers.
Kinderthemes, http://www.kinderthemes.com
Thematic units created by a kindergarten/1ˢᵗ grade teacher with 15 years teaching experience. Units contain poems, ideas, recipes, and activities.

Crayola Crayons, http://www.crayola.com/
Web site sponsored by the Crayola Company presenting hundreds of activities for parents, educators, and "Crayola Kids."
Pencils! Pencils! Pencils!, http://www.pencils.com/
Web site sponsored by the Incense Cedar Institute containing information on pencil history, pencil making, kinds of pencils, renewable resources, and pencil trivia.

For additional creative activity resources, visit our Web site at http://www.EarlyChildEd.delmar.com.

Chapter 14

Three-Dimensional Activities

Objectives

After studying this chapter, you should be able to:

1. Describe how young children work with clay.
2. Define modeling and describe its benefits for children.
3. Discuss some guidelines to follow for successful modeling activities.
4. Define assemblage and give specific examples of assemblage activities for children, including the necessary materials and tools.
5. Discuss how cardboard may be used for three-dimensional activities, and describe the materials and tools used in constructing with it.
6. Describe woodworking supplies and strategies, and its benefits for young children.
7. Discuss how to adapt assemblage activities for children with special needs.

The term **three-dimensional art** refers to any art form that has at least three sides. Three-dimensional art is "in the round," which means that one can look at it from many sides. Modeling with clay, working with play dough, making creations with paper boxes, and creating other sculpture forms are examples of three-dimensional art activities.

Just as in drawing, there are basic stages of development in working with three-dimensional material, much the same as for two-dimensional media. While the names of stages in two-dimensional art do not apply (a child does not "scribble" with clay), the same process of growth and basic ideas for each stage apply.

DEVELOPMENTAL LEVELS AND THREE-DIMENSIONAL MEDIA

When young children first learn to use a three-dimensional material like clay, they go through much the same process of growth as in the scribble stage.

Random manipulation. At first, clay is squeezed through the fingers in a very uncontrolled way. This **random manipulation** is comparable to the early scribble stage. With both clay and crayons, the child in this age range has little control over hand movements. The feel of the clay in his or her hand while squeezing,

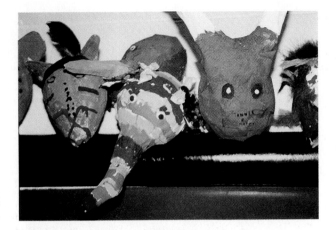

Figure 14-1

Three-dimensional art refers to any art form that is "in the round," which means that one can look at it from many sides.

Figure 14-2

Play dough offers young children many opportunities to enjoy three-dimensional work.

the sheer physical pleasure alone, is what the child enjoys about the clay.

Just as children make early scribbles in many directions, they also make early clay forms in many ways. A child of this age beats and pounds clay for no special purpose, just like scribbling in all directions. The child does not try to make anything definite with the clay. What is made depends on whether the child pounds, flattens, or squeezes the clay.

Although a child may occasionally identify a mound of clay as a house or a ball of clay as a car she or he is usually more interested at this point in the manipulation of the material and discovering what he or she can do with it than in the object created.

Potter's clay is a very good three-dimensional material for young children. Clay is an exciting manipulative experience. It is pliable; it is a very different experience from working with paint. Preschoolers and children in all grade levels enjoy working with it. It is easy to use because it is soft and elastic. It is best bought in moist form, because the dry powder is difficult to prepare and the silica dust is unhealthy for children to inhale. Plasticene, a plastic type clay, is more expensive and is much harder for the young child to use because it is not as soft and elastic as real clay. To make it easier for young children to use, warm and soften cold or hard plasticene by rolling it between your hands.

To make the play dough and clay area satisfying for toddlers in their first experiences with modeling clay, use a small, low table. While many different props can be used (animals, cookie cutters, play dishes), most of the activity with the media comes from the use of hands and fingers. Squeezing, patting, pulling apart, and rolling all help develop small muscles and make the experience relaxing and successful for toddlers. Many young children like to watch and vocalize to their friends while they use dough. If the housekeeping area is nearby, toddlers may even initiate simple imaginative games around themes of cooking, eating, and birthday parties. Play dough can be made from water, flour, and salt; the colors can be varied each time. (See Appendix C for recipes for various doughs for three-dimensional activities.) Toddlers enjoy helping mix the dough, which can be refrigerated when not in use.

Patting and rolling. As children's muscle control develops, they begin to pat and roll the clay with purpose. This matches the controlled scribbling stage. In both scribbling and clay work, the children now enjoy seeing the effects of their movements. They find that they can use their hand movements to make the clay go in desired ways. At this point, a child may roll the clay into thin lengths (ropes), pound it, or shape it into balls. Lines drawn with crayon and rope lines made of clay are proof of the child's growing motor control.

Circles and rectangles. An older preschool child able to draw basic forms can also make clay into similar forms. Rolling clay to make balls is an example of a basic form (circle) in clay. Boxes made of clay are examples of basic forms (rectangles) in a three-dimensional material.

In drawing and in working with clay, the circle is one of the first basic forms made. In both two- and

Figure 14-3
Clay is an excellent material for three-dimensional objects.

Figure 14-4
Paper can be used to create three-dimensional artwork.

Figure 14-5
Creating three-dimensional objects can be done with many objects.

three-dimensional media, the child is able to make this form by controlling the material.

The rectangular form usually comes after the circle. Just as in scribbling, the rectangle is made with clay when the child can shape it into whatever length desired.

Forming clay figures. Many children aged four to five can put together basic clay forms to make up figures. This is equivalent to the pictorial stage in two-dimensional media.

Most children in this age range like to make specific things with clay. They combine basic forms to build objects that are like figures in drawing, by making simple things out of basic forms. The child working with clay puts together a round clay ball (circle) for a head and a clay stick-type line or lump for a body. This is an early combination of basic forms in clay. It is a lot like the stick figure made in early first drawings.

Later, in working with clay, children five years and older may put these forms together in more complex ways. They may make a person with legs, arms, fingers, and feet. This is like the later pictorial stage when a child draws with more details.

Children at this stage do not make the same forms over and over again for practice as in the stage before. This is because a child of four or five has the motor control and hand–eye coordination to easily make any form desired. Clay is now used to make a definite object, a symbol for something important to the child. These forms are made in the child's own special way, just as in drawing.

Development of schema. This special way, or schema, of working with clay is the same for two- and three-dimensional media. It comes from much practice in making symbols and is the child's own special way of making these symbols.

In developing their personal schemas, just as in drawing, children may make things that are more important to them (symbols) larger than things that are less important. They may also use more details for an important clay figure. At this stage, these details may be made by putting other pieces on the clay, like buttons for eyes, straws for legs, and cotton for hair.

Children start to name their clay objects at about the same time they start to name their drawings. This is just as important with clay as with drawing. In both cases, it means the children are expressing their ideas in art. The children now can tell other people just what these ideas are by naming their work.

THE VALUE OF CLAY

At all ages, work with clay gives the child many chances for creative experiences. Most children like the damp feel of clay. They like to pound it, roll it,

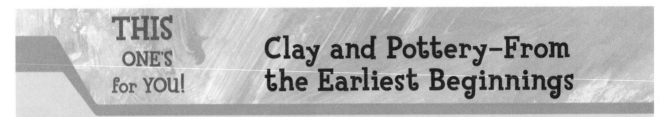

THIS ONE'S for YOU!

Clay and Pottery–From the Earliest Beginnings

Clay, a material that is found all over the world, has served as both an aesthetic and utilitarian form of expression since the beginning of civilization. The making of pottery dates back to the sixth or seventh millennium B.C., during which time, in Europe and in Asia, food containers were made from pure clay earth and fired in the sun.

The story of earth vessels, or pottery, is as ancient as humanity itself. Concerns with proportion, design, decoration, and color are visible in the earliest Chinese red vases of the fifth to fourth millennium and the contemporary forms produced by the artist/potter/sculptor today. Fine prehistoric examples are found in Mesopotamia, Egypt, and Crete. The potter's wheel, developed about 2000 B.C., provided the craftsman with a means of making more precise shapes and thinner walls than were possible using the coiled slab methods used previously.

The pottery from Crete is called *Minoan,* after King Minos, and is well known for its decoration, which consists of stylized natural forms of seaweed, waves, and octopus. The *amphora* vase was a tall, two-handled jar that held wine or oil and was placed over the graves of loved ones for nourishment, with small holes permitting the contents to seep slowly into the grave. The amphora funerary was often more than 5 feet tall. Many examples were found in a cemetery in Athens, dating back to 750 B.C. The golden age of the 5th century B.C. produced designs of Black and Red Figure styles in pottery. Each area of Europe and the Orient produced distinctive styles of pottery, with great artists contributing to the fascinating history of pottery.

Clay is the name used for mineral substances that are mainly aluminous silicate. Impurities may range from iron (which adds yellow, brown, or red), lime, magnesia, free silica, and alkali. Carbonaceous matter gives clay a gray or black color—most clays are pure white. Clay is the remains of rocks that have broken up over millions of years, and the exact composition depends on the rock from which it was formed. Clay is also formed from the fine rock powder that was created by the grinding of the glaciers. All clays are not alike, and some are better for pottery and sculpture. The two basic features of clay are the degree of fine individual particles as well as the plasticity that permits the clay to be molded into the shapes it retains after drying.

Clay is used in a moist form, but as it comes from the earth, it is sandy and sometimes rocklike. When clay is hard, it is ground and crushed for use. For thousands of years, man has devised ingenious ways of working with clay and many of them are still used today.

The primitive potter probably made his or her bowl or jar by pressing out the sides of a ball of clay. The potter may have used a rock to press into the ball for the basic form and then added coils for larger shapes. To make the pottery hard, the primitive potter probably placed it out in the open air to sun dry and bake. The potter's wheel was first used in ancient cultures. The formation of clay from a ball into a pot shape achieved by turning it on a wheel is a skilled technique and is aesthetically exciting to watch. Visit a craftsperson's studio to see a pot "thrown" on a wheel. Enjoy watching yet another phase in the long history of pottery and clay.

poke holes in it, and pull it apart. Just as in drawing, it is the fun of working with the clay that counts. The end product is not as important as using it; a child becomes really involved in the process.

The following scene from an early childhood program emphasizes this value of clay experiences.

> In my activities I wanted to emphasize fine motor development, so I used clay with different sizes of soda straw pieces, toothpicks, buttons, etc., to stick in the clay. The children made animals, designs, and monsters. They kept up a running commentary on how they were making a monster and could SMASH it if they wanted to. It seemed that the clay was a good means of having them release their fears, ideas, and emotions on many things. This clay activity went over very well. During the day many different children, as well as the same children, came back to play at the clay table (Author's log).

Children who perceive clay as "messy" or "slimy," however, may not want to work with it. Never force the issue! Be patient and give these children lots of time and plenty of opportunities to see the fun others have with clay. Some teachers find that involving timid children first in a "cleaner" aspect of clay work, such as mixing up play dough, helps involve them on a gradual basis. Hesitant children might feel more comfortable sitting near you as you pat the dough and describe how it feels. Acknowledge these simple participations. As children feel more comfortable, they may eventually try patting clay gently with you or a friend.

STRATEGIES FOR WORKING WITH CLAY

Working with clay requires planning and forethought. A lack of planning can result in a teacher's constantly having to remind the children about the right use of clay. Proper set-up will make this unnecessary. Some tips for clay set-up are as follows:

⊙ The tables used for working with clay should be placed away from wheel and climbing toys. They should be covered with linoleum or formica to make cleaning easier. If the tables in the room are formica-topped, additional covering is not usually needed.

⊙ The number of children at a table at one time should be limited, allowing each child enough room to spread out and use as much arm and hand movement as he or she needs.

⊙ Each child should be given a lump of clay at least the size of a large apple or a small grapefruit. The clay may be worked with in any way the child wants. These basic guidelines help: the clay may not be thrown on the floor, and no child may interfere with another child's work.

⊙ The teacher may sit at the table and play with clay, too; this adds to the social feeling. But the teacher should avoid making objects for the child to copy. This discourages the child's creative use of the clay.

⊙ When the children are done, clay needs to be stored until its next use. It is best to form it into balls, each about the size of an apple. A hole filled with water in each ball helps keep the clay just right for use the next time. Keep the clay in a container with a wet cloth or sponge on top of the clay. The container should be covered with a tight-fitting lid. (Margarine tubs with plastic lids work well.) Clay becomes moldy if it is too wet and hard to handle if it becomes very dry. If clay should dry out, it can be restored to a proper consistency by placing the dried-out clay in a cloth bag and pounding it with a hammer until it is broken into small pieces. After soaking this clay in water, it can be kneaded until it is the proper consistency again. If clay does become moldy, there is no need to throw it away. Simply scrape off the moldy area and drain off any water collected in the bottom of the container.

MODELING

Modeling—manipulating and shaping flexible material—has many benefits for young children. It helps them develop tactile perception, the understanding and appreciation of the sense of touch. Modeling also helps develop the child's adaptability to change, by use of an ever-flexible material. In modeling three-dimensional objects, the child's concepts of form and proportion are strengthened as he or she learns to make objects with his or her hands. With older children, the appreciation for sculpture and pottery as they appear in our environment may also be enhanced as they have experiences modeling their own original sculpture and simple pottery.

Three-dimensional art is generally an under-explored area of the arts in many early childhood programs. And yet, the main ideas of sculpture (one of the most basic of three-dimensional arts) are form, space, and materials—qualities that are seen every day by everyone whatever they are doing.

Clay and play dough are excellent materials for developing and enhancing children's individual learning

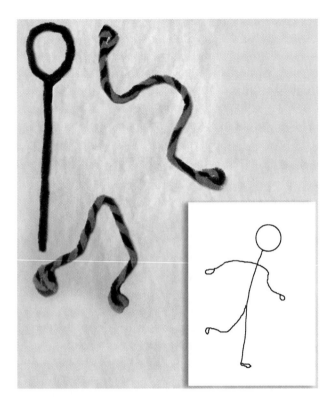

Figure 14-6

Older children enjoy making a simple "skeleton" of a person using three pipe cleaners. They can bend the wire sculpture into different poses. Then they may draw some of the action poses.

Figure 14-7

Older children enjoy creating unique three-dimensional objects.

styles. It has appeal for the body-smart learner because it involves tactile experiences such as squeezing, shaping, and physically manipulating it. The child with an interpersonal learning style finds working with clay alongside other children a very natural learning environment. The child with the visual–spatial learning style will find clay an ideal material for making models and other similar projects involving measurement. Clay also makes a great base for a natural objects display piece for the child with a nature-smart learning style.

Materials

The soft, plastic quality of natural clay has a strong appeal for children at any age. In addition to the types of clay referred to earlier in this chapter, salt clay may be substituted for modeling; it is quite a suitable modeling material for young children. To prepare salt clay, mix together ⅔ cup of salt, ½ cup of flour, and ⅓ cup of water. Add a small amount of dry powder paint or food coloring, if desired, while the mixture is moist. When the clay is left white, the dried piece has a crystalline sheen or "snow" effect caused by the salt. Finished objects dry to a durable hardness.

Paper pulp (papier-mâché), another modeling material, is easy to work with, does not crack or break readily, and is inexpensive. It can be made in either of two forms: as a pulp or in strips applied to a base. It can be molded into various three-dimensional shapes when it is wet and painted when it is dry. This medium is not appropriate for very young children because it is a two-step process that involves a sustained span of interest.

To prepare paper pulp. Shred pieces of soft paper, such as newsprint, paper towels, newspaper, or facial tissue, into small bits or thin strips. Soak several hours in water. Then drain, squeeze out the extra water, and mix the pulp with prepared wheat paste to the consistency of soft clay. Let the mixture stand for an hour before beginning to work with it. Use the pulp to form shapes.

To prepare paper strips. The second type of papier-mâché involves the use of paper strips. Tear newspaper or newsprint into long, thin strips about ½″ wide. Dip the strips into a wheat paste or starch and white glue mixture, and then put down a layer of wet strips over the shape to be covered. Continue putting

Figure 14-8

Using cardboard rolls to make bird binoculars is a favorite three-dimensional activity.

Figure 14-9

Three-dimensional activities allow children to express their unique, individual ideas.

strips on the form until there are five or six layers. This thickness is strong enough to support most papier-mâché projects.

Foundations. Good forms that can be used as foundations for papier-mâché include the following: rolled newspapers secured with string or tape, blown-up balloons, plastic bottles, paper sacks stuffed with newspapers and tied with string, and wire or wooden armatures used as skeletal forms.

Encouraging the Use of Modeling Materials

The following suggestions are intended to encourage children's modeling activities.

◉ Clay interests and absorbs children. As with painting, use clay with young children for the process—the feelings it generates, the pleasure of discovery, putting one's mark on it, and making it change. Very rarely should clay be used with young children to make something permanent. Rather, clay is used at a table with others and to make back into a ball once you are through, storing it for the next time.

◉ Introduce new tools for modeling to add variety to clay activities. Include sticks, tongue depressors, a garlic press, popsicle sticks, nails, combs and paper clips. Of course, any tools small enough to put in the mouth should *not* be used with any young children (especially toddlers) who still put things

in their mouth. All young preschoolers need to be supervised in their use of modeling tools.

◉ Some children find satisfaction in manipulating a modeling material without making anything. Others, in the symbolic stage, give names to objects such as balls, pancakes, and coils. The teacher, recognizing different stages of growth, encourages children's efforts on all levels.

◉ One child may pull, pinch, or squeeze the material into a desired shape with head, arms, and legs extended. Another may make each part separately, then put them together into the whole figure. Some children may combine the two ways of working. It is best not to block the child's thinking by diverting him or her from one method to the other.

◉ When children are ready for other techniques, the teacher may demonstrate how to do the following:

—moisten both parts when joining pieces of clay together, then pinch and work them together so they will not separate when the object has dried.

—avoid delicate parts that break off.

—smooth the material to prevent cracking.

Figure 14-10

Recycled egg cartons can become unique three-dimensional creations.

—create texture using fingernails or carving tools.

—depict action by bending the head or twisting the body.

⊙ If a child has difficulty with this method, you might demonstrate how to "pull" a smaller piece of clay out of the larger mass, rather than add an attachment. Just be sure your suggestion helps the child accomplish his own goal for his clay.

⊙ Unfinished clay work may be wrapped in plastic bags or aluminum foil or placed in covered cans with the child's name attached, if the child wants to continue work on it at a later time.

⊙ A small lump of modeling material can be used as a magnet to pick up crumbs at cleanup time.

Encouraging Older Children's Modeling Activities

Children who are in the middle and upper elementary grades enjoy more exploration and challenge with modeling activities. This is a good age to introduce the work of potters to the children. Having a potter visit your class to demonstrate how pottery or clay sculptures are made can motivate children's work in clay. As an alternative, a teacher or parent can arrange a field trip to a potter's studio so that the children can see a potter's wheel, kiln, and other special ways of working with clay.

Bring in beautiful earthenware serving pieces to show the children that these "common" dishes, bowls, and cups are made from clay. Explain that for thousands of years people have used clay to make utensils for eating.

Children of this age can also begin to learn about and appreciate the work of sculptors. Art prints of the sculpture work of Henry Moore are a good place to begin discussing the qualities of form, subject, and theme in sculpture. Obtain samples of sculpture pieces from a museum gift shop or from local art stores. En-

courage children to view these pieces from all sides. Have them identify basic geometric forms they see in sculpture examples. Encourage the children to create sculpture pieces of their own. Suggestions for more activities involving clay and play dough are at the end of this chapter.

ASSEMBLAGE

As an art form, **assemblage** refers to placing a number of three-dimensional objects, natural or manmade, in juxtaposition to create a unified composition. Materials are combined in a new context to express an abstract, poetic, or representational theme. Assemblage makes use of three-dimensional space, resembling a still-life arrangement as objects are first selected, then grouped and regrouped.

There are many ways to make an assemblage. One way is to put things together. Matchboxes, a paper cup, a cardboard roll, and an egg carton can be glued together. Another way to make an assemblage is to build *up* a form, using materials you can shape yourselves. For older children, cardboard is a good material for shaping an assemblage with building up a form. Cardboard can be found anywhere and it is easy to work with. All the children need are scissors and glue to cut and stick the cardboard shapes together. You can bend, twist, fold, cut, or glue shapes to make a sculpture.

Encouraging Assemblage Activities

Try some of the following suggestions to introduce children to an assemblage activity.

⊙ Encourage children to bring objects from their environment and containers for assemblages.

⊙ Display and discuss collected items.

⊙ Explore ways of arranging various objects emphasizing variety of shapes, sizes, colors, textures, and methods of fastening the objects.

⊙ Explore ways of making items for an assemblage.

⊙ Some materials for an assemblage:

Containers: Wooden boxes, cardboard boxes, cigar boxes, matchboxes, suitcases, egg cartons and crates, packing cartons. These may be painted or decorated if the children desire.

Mounting boards: Pasteboard, corrugated cardboard, wood, crates, picture frames.

Objects: Wooden forms or scrap lumber, driftwood, screening, corks, cardboard boxes, discarded toys, household items, articles of nature (such as seeds, weeds, stones, twigs), and any other interesting items.

THINK ABOUT IT...   Cornstarch

Believe it or not, a fascinating modeling medium is plain old cornstarch. Use the following recipe to mix up cornstarch for children's three-dimensional play.

CORNSTARCH AND WATER

2 cups warm water
3 cups cornstarch

Put ingredients in a bowl and mix with your hands. This mixture will solidify when left alone, but turns to liquid from the heat of your hands. Magic!

Involve the children in making the cornstarch recipe. Have them feel the dry cornstarch. Encourage their reactions to it, using their senses of sight, smell, touch, and even taste. Add a little water, and then let the children mix it and feel it again. It is lumpy. After this lumpy stage, you can add a little more water until it's all moist. Wet cornstarch forms an unstable material, which is fun because of its unexpected behavior—it breaks, but it also melts. It doesn't behave like glue, or like milk, or like wood; it's a liquid, and it's a solid, too. If you rest your fingers lightly on the surface of the cornstarch–water mix, it will let your fingers drift down to the bottom of the container. If you try to punch your way to the bottom, it will resist.

Cornstarch works well in a baby bathtub set on a table, with a limit of two or three children using the entire recipe. If you leave it in its tub overnight, by morning it's dry. Add some water, and it becomes that wonderful "stuff" again. Be sure to invite the children to watch this event.

It's a clean sort of play: the white, powdery mess on the floor can be picked up easily with a dustpan and brush or a vacuum cleaner.

Children come back to this cornstarch and water mix again and again, because it feels good and behaves in an interesting way (Clemens, 1991).

Adhesives: Paste, glue, staples, tape.

Tools: Scissors, stapler, hammer, nails, pliers.

Encourage children to collect objects that are meaningful to them. Almost any area of interest or everyday experience is a possible theme for assemblage.

⊙ Objects may be selected according to an idea; topic; size of container; or variation in line, form, color, and texture. Use multiple items for repetition of shapes.

⊙ Three-dimensional forms may be altered or transformed so that they lose their original identity and take on a new meaning. They can be bent, twisted, stretched, crumpled, or painted.

⊙ Objects also can be made by cutting out pictures or illustrations and pasting them over cardboard, wood, or other substantial material.

⊙ Objects can be glued, stapled, taped, or even nailed together or onto a mounting board.

⊙ Arrange and rearrange objects until the desired effect is achieved. Distribute paste and other

fastening materials *after* the arrangement is satisfactory in the child's opinion.

CARDBOARD CONSTRUCTION

Cardboard, an indispensable material for construction projects, stimulates and challenges the imagination of children on all levels. It is readily available in various forms. Such commonplace objects as milk and egg cartons, apple-crate dividers, toweling tubes, and assorted sizes of boxes offer unlimited possibilities for creative art projects.

Encouraging Cardboard Construction Activities

Gather together an assortment of cardboard materials. Some suggestions follow:

⊙ assorted cardboard boxes, cartons, corrugated cardboard, paper cups and plates of all sizes

Figure 14-11

A teacher's enthusiasm for three-dimensional art encourages children's creativity

⊙ recycled materials: paper bags, yarn, string, buttons, feathers, cloth, tissue paper, scraps of construction paper, and wrapping paper

⊙ paste, glue, tape, crayons, colored markers, paint, brushes, scissors, stapler, and staples

Most topics of interest to young children can be adapted to cardboard construction projects. Creations are as endless as the imaginations of young children. Some possibilities for creative construction projects include using boxes for making various buildings, houses, cities, and even neighborhoods. Young children also enjoy making such things as imaginary animals, people, and favorite characters from a story out of various cardboard rolls and containers. Some children have even made costumes out of boxes large enough to fit over the child's body. Cars, trucks, and trains are some other favorite construction projects with young children. Cardboard construction provides a wealth of possibilities for creative expression in arts and crafts projects as well.

Some suggestions for facilitating cardboard construction include the following:

⊙ Have the cardboard construction materials out and available for the children to explore on their own.

Encourage the children to stack materials or combine them in different ways. Encourage children to explore the possibilities for creating they may discover while playing with the materials.

⊙ Discuss with the children and demonstrate (if needed) ways of fastening boxes together, covering them with paint or paper, and adding other parts or features.

⊙ Encourage the children to select as many objects as they need for their construction.

⊙ Boxes with waxed surfaces can be covered with a layer of newspaper and wheat paste and allowed to dry before painting. Powder paint mixed with starch adheres well to box surfaces.

⊙ Textured surfaces can be created by using corrugated cardboard, shredded packing tissue, or crinkled newspaper.

⊙ Shapes and sizes of cardboard objects may suggest ideas for a project, such as using an oatmeal box for the body of an elephant or a milk carton for a tall building.

⊙ Use a variety of materials to complete the design, such as pieces of ribbon, buttons, sequins, spools, etc.

⊙ Older children are able to appreciate lessons combining three-dimensional assemblage projects with architectural ideas. For example, after drawing their plans for a building or structure, the students might like to use boxes, cardboard, or cut-and-fold paper techniques to make three-dimensional models of their buildings. Students who are particularly excited by such projects may wish to create realistic settings for their structures as well, using sand, pebbles, dried moss, and the like to create their own miniature scene.

More assemblage activities are found at the end of this chapter.

WOODWORKING

Woodworking involves a range of activities from hammering nails to sanding, gluing, and painting wood. As with other three-dimensional activities, woodworking can be an excellent medium for fostering a child's creativity if the *process,* and not the product, is emphasized.

There are many valuable reasons for including woodworking in the early childhood art program.

⊙ Woodworking provides opportunities for children to strengthen and control their large and small muscles through participating in vigorous activities such as sawing and nail pounding.

- Through participation in woodworking experiences, children improve social and communication skills as they share ideas, talk over problems, or help one another handle tools.

- Woodworking provides opportunities for children to release tension. Experiences that allow a child to work off his tension, either consciously or unconsciously, help build an emotionally healthy child.

- Skills learned through woodworking furnish the basis for developing scientific thinking. Woodworking materials provide opportunities for young children to investigate, experiment with, and develop problem-solving skills. Through fitting, fastening, connecting, and cutting, children learn basic mechanics—the foundation for understanding math and physics.

- Woodworking provides children with opportunities to become aware of textures and forms. Senses are sharpened as children explore the field of construction. Fingers explore many textures, ears pick out the sounds of different tools, noses test the different smells of various woods, and eyes see the many hues of wood.

- Working with tools and materials allows the child to express herself or himself. What a child chooses to play with and how the child uses play materials reflects his or her feelings about and reactions to the people around him or her.

Planning for the Woodworking Experience

Planning for the woodworking area and related experiences is the key to success. Thought needs to be given to time allotment, location of the woodworking area, limits, number of children working at one time, and the role of the teacher. The following criteria need to be considered.

- Enough time should be allotted for children to explore materials without feeling rushed. If the woodworking area is a popular one, the teacher may find it necessary to set up time allotments to give all children a chance to participate.

- The workbench should be situated so that several children can move around and work without bumping into one another. It should be located out of major traffic patterns to avoid interruptions and accidents and away from quiet areas, so the noise will not disturb others. Weather permitting, and with adequate supervision, woodworking can be provided out-of-doors.

- A specific limit should be set in advance regarding the number of children working at one time.

Usually, one teacher can comfortably supervise three or four children. No more children than the set limit should be allowed in the woodworking area at one time. Teachers can enforce this number by requiring all children who are woodworking to wear an apron and safety goggles and only have the set limit available.

- Tools and materials need to be geared to the ability level of the children using them.

- The teacher needs to familiarize himself or herself with the use of woodworking tools and materials in order to give effective guidance and set reasonable limits. To create enthusiasm in the children for woodworking, it is important that the teacher be excited about its possibilities. The carpentry area must be constantly supervised to avoid accidents.

Guidance for Woodworking Activities

In guiding children in woodworking activities, the teacher must first help them become familiar with the tools. In introducing the saw, for example, show the children how to hold the saw at a 45–degree angle and gently move it back and forth rhythmically. Children do not have to use a great deal of force or power for sawing; the saw will do the work on its own. Demonstrate how to fasten the wood in a vise, hold the wood with the left hand and saw with the right hand, or vice versa for left-handers.

The rules of saw safety must be emphasized, including where to keep the hands, how to carry the saw, and where to lay it down.

In introducing the hammer, show the children how to set a nail by gently tapping it into the wood. It can be driven using more vigorous strokes while holding the hammer by the end of the handle. Make a series of holes in various pieces of wood, showing how to set nails into these premade holes.

Avoid too many detailed instructions or making models or patterns because all of these things limit the children's initiative, independence, and creativity.

To prevent children from becoming frustrated, show them how to make handling wood easier by laying it flat and securing it with a vise. Allow the child to try out his or her own ideas, but guide the child in choosing the proper tools to use for carrying out those ideas.

Selecting Tools for Woodworking Experiences

When buying tools and equipment for woodworking, choose adult-type tools of good quality to withstand hard use. Tools should also be able to be resharpened, be reconditioned, and have broken parts replaced.

⊙ *Saws*. Three types of saws are generally sold for woodworking purposes: the rip saw, the crosscut saw, and the coping saw. The rip saw has coarse teeth for cutting wood in the direction of the grain. The crosscut saw is designed to cut across the grain, while the coping saw is designed for use on thin wood and for cutting curves. Of the three saws available, the crosscut saw is the easiest for young children to manage. An 8– or 10–point saw (teeth per inch) is the most satisfactory size for children's use.

⊙ *Hammers*. A 10– to 13–ounce claw hammer, with a broad head, is the most satisfactory for use by young children.

⊙ *Plane*. A plane may be provided for children's use. If it is available, the blade should be adjusted to make small cuts, and children should be cautioned to use it only on surfaces free from nails, screws, or knots.

⊙ *Workbench*. The workbench used must be strong, sturdy, and stable. An old door or heavy wooden packing box are ideal for homemade workbenches. Or a pair of sawhorses connected with a heavy board can be easily set up. All workbenches should be about 16″ to 18″ high, just under a child's waist height, for the most convenient work.

Optional tools

⊙ pliers for holding nails as children are "setting" them

⊙ scissors for cutting sandpaper and string

⊙ screwdriver

⊙ rasp for smoothing a rough or splintered edge against the grain and for rounding corners on wood

⊙ 1-foot rule, yardstick

⊙ pencil

⊙ c-clamp

Storage and Care of Tools

A special wall-mounted tool board is essential for storing frequently used tools, while infrequently used tools can be stored in a cupboard. Paint the outline of each tool on the board so children can see where to put them away.

Saws should be professionally sharpened and oiled once or twice a year and wrapped in newspaper for long-term storage. Tools should be kept free from dust and rust; lightweight machine oil will remove any rust that forms.

Choosing and Using Woodworking Materials

Woods. The wood provided for young children in the woodworking area should be unfinished, smooth, and porous enough for children to pound or saw. Pine, balsa, poplar, and basswood are good, soft woods for children's use. Children work best with small pieces of wood of varying sizes, shapes, and thicknesses. Lumberyard scraps of doweling, molding, and mill ends offer endless possibilities when provided along with basic wood pieces.

Store wood in a container that allows visibility and accessibility to the child. Plastic vegetable bins work well for this.

Nails. Nails are supplied in pennyweights (dwt), which refers to the length of the nail. Common nail sizes are 2 dwt or 1″; 4 dwt or 1 ½″; 6 dwt or 2″; 8 dwt or 2½″; and 10 dwt or 3″. At first, most children have trouble pounding nails without bending them, so 1½″ nails with large heads are best. Store nails in small jars according to size to allow children to select them easily.

Glue. Glue can be used by children who have not mastered the skill of pounding nails well enough to fasten wood pieces together. A quick-drying, all-purpose glue can be used for this purpose. Glue can also be used to make wood sculptures, attach accessories, and strengthen joints.

Screws. Screws may be provided in the woodworking area but are often difficult for young children to handle. They can be made more manageable to children by making a guide hole with a nail first. Older children can work more easily with screws and screwdriver than young children. Provide both standard and Phillips-head screwdrivers with a variety of screw sizes.

Additional Materials for Woodworking

⊙ sandpaper in four weights: coarse, medium, fine, extra fine. Mount sandpaper on wooden blocks and use in a back-and-forth motion

⊙ brushes of medium and narrow widths

⊙ tempera paint for painting completed creations

⊙ accessories such as string; rubber bands; small pieces of rubber; scraps of leather; pieces of cloth and carpeting; bottle caps; pieces of Styrofoam; and metal gadgets like cuphooks, staples, paper clips, etc

THIS ONE'S for YOU!

Me Be Creative?... Artistic? But I Can't Even Draw!

Many teachers rely on ready-made art "recipes" for their early childhood art program because they feel they are not "creative" enough without them. An art recipe is comfortable for the teacher because he or she knows exactly what to expect; she or he knows what the product will look like. Materials can be organized ahead of time and remain neat and tidy. It is unfortunate for the child, however, because without any of their input the activity is not self-expressive or creative.

We want children to be able to think for themselves, to be able to make decisions, and to act on them. By providing a step-by-step art activity, we are not allowing young children to make decisions, nor are we teaching them to become independent.

A creative art opportunity allows the young child to begin choosing and seeking knowledge on his or her own, giving the child more and more confidence in his or her own abilities. Think about the art activities you offer children and see if they allow children this creative freedom.

Teachers often feel inadequate when it comes to art and may fall back on what they did in school as a child. Many of those activities were craft oriented, pattern determined, and teacher controlled.

Teachers are often not given enough training in the area of planning expressive art activities for children. Teacher preparation in this area is often minimal at best. This is why it's not fair to fault teachers who feel timid about letting children leap into art, when it is the teacher preparation programs that in many cases are lacking.

Many teachers feel that being creative is a talent that you either have or do not have. Research shows, however, that being creative, as well as being able to draw, are learnable skills. It is unfortunate for a child to hear a teacher say, "I can't draw," when the teacher really should say, "I never *learned* to draw." There is a big difference between these two remarks, and children are perceptive enough to notice it. If their teacher believes that artistic ability is an unteachable talent, then children will believe that. But if the teacher believes people can *learn* how to create with art materials, the children will believe that too (Szyba, 1999).

ADAPTATIONS FOR CHILDREN WITH SPECIAL NEEDS

Many of the assemblage activities in this chapter and in the collage activities in Chapter 13 involve a child's working with glue and paste. This type of activity may be challenging for certain children with special needs. The following are some suggestions for modifying the gluing and pasting processes for those children who find this type of activity challenging.

Developmental Delays

If the multistep process of gluing is too complicated for the child, make a collage or assemblage without glue by using contact paper or another type of sticky base. Turn the paper sticky side up and tape it into a cookie sheet or shirt box. The child only needs to place selected items onto the sticky surface to complete the activity. No glue or tape is needed.

The following are some additional suggestions on working with children with special needs:

- Try not to overwhelm the child with too many choices. Offer only one or two materials at a time.
- Help the child organize his or her space by providing containers for each type of collage/assemblage material.
- Provide the child with a large collage/assemblage base to compensate for less mature hand–eye coordination.
- Use a glue stick instead of white glue for children who have difficulty controlling the amount of glue to use in their work.

THIS ONE'S for YOU!

Using Recycled Materials in Three-Dimensional Activities

Recycled materials are perfect for three-dimensional art activities. They are free, readily available, and full of artistic possibilities. Recycled materials can be used in as many ways as you can imagine. Here are some possibilities to start you thinking about (and using) recycled materials for three-dimensional art activities.

PAPER BAGS

- Collect large paper bags with attached paper or plastic handles (at least one for each child); additional paper shopping bags to use as masks; an unbreakable mirror; a variety of materials such as juice cans, egg cartons, plastic-foam pieces, empty boxes, fabric scraps, and straws; scissors; glue; tape; crayons; and paint. Cut off the bottoms of the bags that have attached handles. Children can wear the bags as costumes by stepping into them and using the paper or plastic handles as shoulder straps. Arrange the collage and scrap materials on a table nearby so children can decorate their costumes with them.
- Make a class mascot. Provide children with two large paper shopping bags, colored yarn, and scrap materials that can be easily crumpled, including clean rags, newspaper, and pieces of cotton fabric. Invite the children to choose pieces of scrap materials, crumple them, and stuff them into the paper bags. To make the mascot's head, ask children to stuff the first bag halfway full, and then tape it closed. Children use markers, paint, or decorative materials to make a face. Invite them to decide together on special characteristics, such as what color yarn to glue on for hair. Encourage them to work together to make a mascot that represents the whole class.
- Suggest that children problem solve ways to create a body using the second shopping bag and remaining scrap materials. Children may work on this together for several days.
- Help the children attach the mascot's body to its head. Then the children can decide on a name for their mascot. Find the mascot a home in your classroom.

BOXES

- Moving things. Collect several medium-size appliance boxes that will hold one or two children. Share a story about vehicles—a train, a car, a dump truck, etc. Invite the children to use the boxes to make a vehicle themselves. Provide them with smocks, paintbrushes, and tempera paint and invite them to paint their vehicle. If they want to make a train, attach the boxes to one another with twine and place the train in your dramatic-play or outdoor area.
- Measuring. Invite the children to use the boxes for measuring, asking them to find out things like how many shoeboxes tall they are. Record their answers. Now, ask them to lie down on the floor and measure the length of their bodies using the smallest boxes. Encourage them to estimate how many boxes long they will be. Afterward, compare their estimation with the actual answer. How many boxes long or wide is the classroom?

PAPER TUBES

- Tube puppets. Invite children to make tube puppets to use in dramatic play. Provide the children with sturdy paper tubes similar to the length and weight of tubes used to hold foil or cellophane wrap. Set out a variety of materials including beady eyes, glue, yarn, felt, markers, scissors, oak tag paper, and small paper plates. They might base their puppets on favorite storybook characters.
- Tube bird binoculars. Tape together two toilet tissue rolls. Let the children decorate the rolls with crayons, markers and any other exciting "extras." Punch a hole on the outside of each of the tubes and string a ribbon or piece of yarn to make a strap for the binoculars. Then go outside and start bird watching!

(Continues)

THIS ONE'S for YOU! (Continued)

- Music makers. Use small paper tubes to make shakers for children to use during music and group-singing time. Invite children to decorate and individualize their shakers. Provide tempera paint, glue sticks, and collage materials. Enclose the bottom with oaktag secured with masking tape. Then the children may fill their shakers with sand, rice, or beans. Secure the other opening. Now, invite everyone to sing and play the shakers.
- Tube collages. Set up the art area with a variety of paper tubes, tape, glue, string, scissors, construction paper, and markers. Invite the class to make a tube collage using any or all of the materials provided.
- Counting the days. Collect small paper tubes (from paper tissue rolls) to use for this counting activity. Get a large spool of twine and invite a child to string on a paper tube each day of school. Each child can take a turn decorating the tube and writing the number for each day on it. Invite the class to predict how long their "tube necklace" will be. Record their prediction and then compare on the last day of school.

EGG CARTONS

- Use your imagination. What can you do with egg cartons? Provide the children with cardboard and Styrofoam egg cartons and a variety of construction materials including tape, glue, string, paper, scissors, feathers, buttons, markers, and paint. Invite them to use the materials to create their own works of art.
- Sand experimenting. Invite children to investigate the different ways they can use the cartons to manipulate sand. Give them a spray bottle filled with water so that they can moisten the sand. Can they use the egg cartons as a mold to create interesting shapes?
- Floating experiments. Give the children cardboard and Styrofoam egg cartons and invite them to make boats to use at the water table. Have them predict which type of egg carton will work best in water.
- Record their responses. Now have them conduct their experiment. Does the size of the carton affect how it floats? Can they cut up the cartons to make smaller boats? Will the cartons sink if they are filled with water?

Physical Impairments

For children with arm, hand, and finger control limitations, some of the following ideas may be useful:

- Stabilize the base of the collage/assemblage by taping it to the work surface to prevent slipping. A piece of nonskid shelving material or a placemat can also be used to stabilize the base of the assemblage.
- Use a 6-inch long 1- to 2-inch-wide dowel piece with a sponge attached to spread glue. It may be easier for a child with a weak or poor grasp to hold onto this dowel. Another alternative is to use a wide paintbrush for applying glue.
- Place glue in an aluminum pie plate that has been taped to the work surface. The pie plate is easier for a child with limited motor control to reach and use.

- Make certain all necessary materials are placed within the child's reaching distance.
- Minimize fatigue by reducing the number of steps of the collage/assemblage process.

Attention Deficit/Hyperactivity Disorder

Children with attention deficit/hyperactivity disorder (ADHD) frequently exhibit poor organizational skills. The following are some suggestions to assist a child with ADHD in collage/assemblage activities.

- Have an adult available to sit with the child and guide him or her through the activity, providing ample praise and frequent feedback at each step of the process.
- Do not place all the project materials out on the table. Too many materials will distract and confuse

children who are impulsive and easily distracted. Set out only the particular material needed for the next step of the activity. When that step is completed, set out the material for the next step, and so on.

⊙ Place each collage material in a separate container and place the child's collage/assemblage base in a shirt box or on a cookie sheet to help define the child's workspace.

Visual Impairments

Both children who are blind and children with low vision enjoy assemblages and collages. These children are able to use their heightened sense of touch to guide them through the process and then feel their finished product at the end. Here are some suggestions on facilitating their work with collage/assemblage:

⊙ Add yellow food coloring or yellow tempera paint to the glue so it is more easily visible on the collage surface. Use a contrasting dark blue paper for the collage base.

⊙ Add sand, sawdust, or other textures to the glue to enhance the tactile feedback.

⊙ Use a small squeeze bottle or a commercial glue stick instead of the dip-and-spread method to avoid lots of mess and spills.

⊙ Place glue in an aluminum pie plate to provide a larger target for dipping the gluing utensil. Place colored tape around the edge of the pie plate to emphasize its boundaries.

⊙ Mark the edges of the collage paper with a bright color paint, marker, or tape to help indicate the boundaries.

⊙ Line a shallow baking pan with a piece of nonskid shelving material and place the collage materials in the pan.

⊙ Guide the child's arm and show him or her where each material is located. Be sure to also say what you are doing and describe the position of each item. For example, you might say, "I am moving your hand to the right side of the pan, almost to the edge, to find the buttons" (Gould & Sullivan, 1999).

SUMMARY

Three-dimensional art refers to any art that has at least three sides. It is "in the round," which means one can look at it from many sides. Examples of three-dimensional art are modeling with clay and play dough, assemblage, cardboard construction, and other forms of sculpture.

Just as children have different drawing abilities at each age, so do they work with clay in different ways at each age. When young children first learn to use a three-dimensional material like clay, they go through much the same process as a child using crayons in the scribble stage. In work with both crayons and clay, children at this age have little control over their hands or the material. They enjoy the feel of the clay but do not have good control in working with it.

Older preschool children who can draw basic forms like circles or rectangles can also make clay into similar forms. Balls and boxes are examples of basic forms in clay. Children's muscle (motor) control helps them make these forms. Children in this age group can also put together basic forms in clay to make up figures. This is similar to making figures in the pictorial stage of two-dimensional media.

Children name their clay objects at about the same time that they name their drawings. Naming is an important form of communication in both two- and three-dimensional media.

A teacher needs to set up the room for the enjoyable use of three-dimensional materials by children. Proper tables, number of children, and care of materials are all points to keep in mind when planning for clay work.

Modeling refers to the manipulation and shaping of flexible materials. Modeling activities help children develop their sense of touch; their adaptation to change; their concepts of form and proportion; and, especially in older children, their sense of aesthetics.

Assemblage is a creative activity that involves placing a number of three-dimensional objects together to create a unified composition. Everyday materials found in the school or home environment are media for this type of activity. Cardboard is also a suitable material for construction activities for young children.

Woodworking, another three-dimensional activity, involves a range of activities from hammering nails to sanding, gluing, and painting. Woodworking experiences for young children contribute to their total development. These experiences must be planned so that appropriate, good-quality tools are provided for the children's use. Close supervision is required in woodworking. Assemblage activities may need to be adapted to meet the needs of children with special needs.

KEY TERMS

assemblage
modeling
paper pulp (papier-mâché)

random manipulation
three-dimensional art

LEARNING ACTIVITIES

EXERCISE 1

Goal: To experience how a child aged one and one-half to three years works with clay.
A. Use your hand opposite your writing hand.
B. Use a piece of real clay about the size of a large apple.
C. Squeeze the clay in one hand only.
D. Keep these points in mind:
  1. how it feels to lack good muscle (motor) control
  2. how hard it is to make an exact object
  3. how the clay feels in the hand

EXERCISE 2

Goal: To feel the differences in clay.
A. Prepare large balls of real clay, plasticene (oil-based) clay, and play dough.
B. Use the hand opposite the writing hand to squeeze and feel each of the three clay balls. (This should help you experience both the child's lack of muscle control and different materials.)
C. Consider the following points while working with each of the three balls of clay:
  1. Which is the easiest to squeeze?
  2. Which feels the best?
  3. Which is the most fun to use?
  4. Is the type most fun to use also the easiest to use?
D. Try the previous activity with children aged one and one-half to three years. Ask them these questions. Compare answers.

EXERCISE 3

Goal: To help you understand how children feel when they are given a model to copy.
A. Obtain and display small glass or porcelain figures. These could be decorative birds, glass dolls, or any other finished figure from a variety store or other source.
B. Provide all the students with small balls of clay. Have each student try to copy the model.
C. Look at and discuss the finished objects.
  1. How did it feel to copy such a difficult model?
  2. Was it a pleasant or frustrating experience?
  3. Did this copying exercise make you feel happy about working with clay? Did it make you like to copy?

4. How do you think children feel about trying to copy models the teacher sets up?
5. Why is it undesirable for a teacher to have children copy a model?

EXERCISE 4

Obtain some pictures of modern sculpture. (Henry Moore's are good examples.)
A. Show the pictures to the children before they work with clay.
B. See if there are any effects on their work in relation to the following:
  1. kinds of objects made
  2. new shapes made
  3. more or less clay work done
  4. change in the way objects are made
  5. change in the way child works with clay

EXERCISE 5

Read an exciting story to the children before they work with clay. For example, try M. Sendak's *Where the Wild Things Are* or Dr. Seuss' *To Think It Happened on Mulberry Street.*
A. Do not tell the children what to make.
B. See if their work with clay shows any influence from the story regarding the following:
  1. type of figures made
  2. size of figures made
  3. details of figures made

EXERCISE 6

To add variety to play dough activities, try one of these variations:
A. Work a drop of food flavoring and a drop of food coloring into your play dough recipe. Match scents with colors, such as mint flavoring with green and lemon flavoring with yellow.
B. Use a tasty mixture of peanut butter and powdered milk as play dough for another three-dimensional taste treat.
C. Make your play dough recipe slippery by adding a little vegetable oil.

ACTIVITIES FOR CHILDREN

WOODEN FRIENDS

You will need wooden clothespins, pipe cleaners, markers, popsicle sticks, felt scraps, glue, scissors, ribbon, sequins, beads, buttons, and yarn in various colors. The child uses the wooden clothespin for the body. Attach arms by twisting a pipe cleaner around the clothespin. When satisfied with the positioning of the pipe cleaner arms, glue them in place. Children may use markers to create the face. Discuss possibilities for using found materials for details. For example, popsicle sticks for skis, yarn for hair, ribbon for belts, etc. The little wooden friends come alive as children add clothes and other found materials for accessories.

Have children share thoughts and feelings about their wooden sculptures and the sculptures made by others. Ask them to comment on the likenesses and personalities of the figures and how accessories and details help convey personality and identity.

DOUGHY FRIENDS

For this activity you will need salt dough (see recipe in Appendix C), a photograph of best friends, paint, small objects, and yarn.

Work the salt dough while it is soft to be a size larger than your picture. Have the children work the dough with their hands or a rolling pin. Carefully press the picture into the soft dough. You can use a touch of glue behind the picture if you want. Gently press a small overlap of the dough around the edge of picture so it will be secure. Decorate the dough frame with objects by softly pressing them into the dough. Buttons, noodles, and little rocks make nice additions to the dough frame. Paint the dough frame with tempera paint if desired. Don't forget to make a small hole in the top of the frame before it dries so yarn can be run through it for hanging.

CLAY-COIL POTS

For this activity you will need potter's clay, a large plastic garbage bag, and tape. Split the garbage bag at the seams and tape it to the top of your work area.

Give each child a grapefruit-sized ball of potter's clay. Show the child how to make snakes by rolling out pieces of clay into coils. Make several coils or one very long coil. Roll a small ball of clay and flatten it into a round shape for the bottom of the pot. Moisten the edges of the round bottom piece with water.

Wrap the coils around the round bottom piece. Continue wrapping the coil around and around, putting coil upon coil. Moisten the pieces together as you coil. Let the pot dry before painting or decorating. You can also make free-form coil sculptures.

CREPE-PAPER CLAY

For this activity you will need crepe paper, 1 cup of flour, 1 cup of salt, a large container, and water. Place crepe paper in a large container and add enough water to cover the paper. Soak for about 1 hour until most of the water absorbs into the paper. Pour off excess water. You can save this colored water for dye in other projects. Add small amounts of flour and salt until mixture is clay-like. Mold and form shapes by hand with crepe paper clay. Let the forms dry before painting.

PIPE CLEANER SCULPTURE

For this activity you will need a flat sheet of Styrofoam, pipe cleaners of various lengths and widths, beads in various sizes, hole sizes and colors, and anything else with a hole in it (such as straws, pasta, etc.)

Lay out the materials on the table or work area. Show the children how the pipe cleaners can be stuck into the styrofoam. Then they can slide beads, straws, pasta, etc. onto the pipe cleaners.

BROWN BAG SURPRISE

For this activity you will need lunch-size brown paper bags, items such as paper tubes, sections of egg cartons, foil, cellophane, fabric, gift wrap, feathers, sequins, yarn, bubble wrap, paper plates, Styrofoam cups, stickers, glue sticks, child safety scissors, markers, and crayons.

Place different items into individual brown bags for each child. Vary the items in each child's bag to encourage different types of experiences.

Give each child a surprise bag full of art materials. The children can use the materials to create their own special art project. They can create whatever they want. It can be a flat collage or a three-dimensional assemblage.

When children have finished creating their artwork, ask them to write about it. They can write about how they made their work or what materials they used, or they can make up a story to accompany the work.

Encourage them to use invented spelling and to be creative. Assist those who need it with their writing.

Invite the children to share their work with the group. Encourage them to describe how they made their artwork. Find an area in the classroom to display the children's artwork and writing.

FOIL SCULPTURE

For this activity you will need aluminum foil, gummy tape, paintbrushes, liquid detergent, and tempera paint.

Crumple the foil into individual forms, shapes, or creations that when assembled will create a piece of sculpture. Join these forms together, if desired, with tape. Color can be added to the surface by painting with a drop or two of liquid detergent mixed in the tempera paint.

NATURAL OBJECT SCULPTURE

For this activity you will need natural materials (seeds, twigs, pinecones, seed pods, stones, driftwood, etc.), quick-drying glue, clear quick-drying spray, paint, construction paper, and felt.

Collect a number of natural objects of various sizes and colors. Arrange several of these items to create a small piece of sculpture. When satisfied with the creation, glue it together. Paint or colored paper can be added to enhance the design. Spray with clear spray to preserve the finish. (Spray with optimum ventilation, preferably outdoors.) Glue a piece of felt to the bottom to prevent scratching.

SPOOL SCULPTURE

For this activity you will need spools (a variety of sizes), assorted fabric pieces, glue, and anything that will serve to stimulate the children's imaginations as decorations.

Each of the spool sculptures is made differently according to the imagination of the artist. Basically, the procedure involves "dressing" the spool, which serves as a body. Materials are added for clothing and are glued onto the spool. If desired, a child may use the spool purely as a base; it does not have to be a figure to dress. Details can be made with drawing materials, and bits and pieces of yarn, ribbon, etc. can be glued on for interest.

BOX SCULPTURES

For this activity you will need boxes of different sizes and shapes, paste, tempera paint, brushes, construction paper, and scraps of fabric and trim.

Have children bring in an assortment of boxes. Be sure to include cereal boxes because they make great bases for box sculpture.

Use one box as a base. Glue smaller boxes on to make a sculpture design. Glue on cut construction paper details. Add fabric and trim scraps for more design details. Children may want to make a city of box sculpture buildings. They may choose to paint the sculpture. Boxes can become robots, imaginary animals, and anything else the children can imagine.

PAPER-TUBE SLIDING THINGS

For this activity you will need toilet-tissue or paper-towel tubes, crayons, yarn, construction paper, markers, tempera paint, paintbrushes, scissors, glue, and tape.

Cut the tubes into various sizes. Give each child at least five pieces. Have the children paint the tubes. The children may want to color the tube with markers or crayons instead of paint. Cut out a head and tongue. Decorate the pieces by drawing features with crayons or markers. Glue or tape the head and tongue to separate tube pieces. When decorating with paint, wait until the tube pieces are dry. Measure a piece of yarn long enough to extend through all pieces of tubes. String the yarn through the tubes, fastening it to the first and last tube pieces. String beads between the tubes for a colorful effect. Glue on such natural objects as acorns, leaves, and grasses for an interesting effect. Some children may need assistance fastening the yarn to the tubes.

MILK-CARTON CONSTRUCTION FUN

For this activity you will need milk, juice, or cream cartons (different sizes—all cleaned and dry!); white acrylic paint; gesso or white latex house paint; pencils; paintbrushes; tempera paint; and containers for water.

Discuss homes and neighborhoods with the children. Talk about the different styles of places to live: houses, apartments, condos, and so on. Talk about shapes and sizes and such details as windows, doors, roofs, and stairways.

Have the child cover the carton with white acrylic, gesso, or latex house paint. Let the paint dry thoroughly. Draw windows, doors, and so on onto the carton. Paint the carton (using tempera paint) to look like a house.

Children may want to make several houses for a neighborhood. They may even create a town/village from a favorite story.

IMAGINARY ANIMALS

For this activity you will need a collection of boxes of various sizes and shapes, paste, masking tape, stapler and staples, scraps of colored paper, fabric, trim, buttons, and yarn.

Talk about animals and their shapes, sizes, and colors. Give the children a collection of boxes of various sizes and shapes.

Children stack the boxes and rearrange them until they are satisfied with the arrangement. Shapes and sizes of boxes may suggest certain animals, such as an oatmeal box for an elephant or a long, narrow box for a giraffe's neck. Smaller boxes or towel rolls can be used for legs or a head. Fasten boxes together with glue, masking tape, or a stapler. Glue on details using scraps of colored paper, fabric, trim, buttons, or yarn.

Textured surfaces can be created by using corrugated paper or egg cartons for bodies of animals. Wood shavings, bark, or wrinkled-paper scraps can be glued to the boxes to create interesting textures. Exaggerated features help to create dramatic effects, such as large buttons for eyes, frayed string or rope for a mane or tail, or pieces of cloth for ears.

EGG-CARTON BUGGY THINGS

For this activity you will need egg cartons cut into single cups, pipe cleaners cut into small pieces, buttons, scraps of fabric and trim, crayons, and markers.

Discuss bugs, real and imaginary, with the children. Talk about colors, shapes, "feelers," legs, and textures. Talk about other creatures, real or imaginary.

Give each child one egg cup. Attach pieces of pipe cleaners for legs. Use buttons for eyes. Pipe cleaners can be used for "feelers." Details may be added with crayons or markers. Pieces of fabric or trim can be glued on for even more details.

String a thread through the top of the egg cup to hang the creations, or make a family of creatures. Tell stories about the creatures' adventures in the bug world. Make houses for the buggy creatures out of milk cartons or other recycled boxes. Decorate the houses with markers or crayons.

EGG-CARTON GARDENS

For this activity you will need tops from Styrofoam egg cartons, scissors, pipe cleaners, toothpicks, construction paper, crayons, markers, glue, glue brushes, glitter (optional), and twigs.

Give each child a top from a Styrofoam egg carton. Talk about flower gardens, real or imagined. ("Which kind of flowers can you see in your mind?" "Which kinds of flowers do you see in a garden?" "Think of colors and shapes.")

Children cut or tear the construction paper into flower shapes, or any shapes they want. Children decorate the flower and/or shapes with crayons and/or markers. Glitter can be applied to the shapes that have been brushed with glue. Insert a toothpick or pipe cleaner into the flower. Poke the flower into the Styrofoam egg carton top. Add twigs to fill the egg carton top as desired.

For variations: Make an egg-carton zoo. Fill the egg-carton top with paper animals. Create an egg-carton top filled with paper "people." Classmates, family members, and characters from a favorite storybook all make fun additions! Older children might enjoy creating a scene from a favorite story in the egg-carton top.

CONSTRUCTION-PAPER CHARACTERS

For this activity you will need construction paper, tape, scissors, crayons, markers, tempera paint, brushes, yarn, buttons, pieces of trim, and fabric scraps.

Talk about the people who are important in the child's life. Talk about those people's sizes, shapes, and other characteristics. Think about these things when making the construction-paper creations.

Form the body by rolling the paper into a tube and taping it on the ends. The tube is both the body and the head of the person. Cut-out feet from construction paper can be taped on the bottom of the tube. Glue on features made of pieces of construction paper. Glue on yarn or pieces of construction paper for hair. Add fabric or trim scraps for clothing details. Features can be drawn on with crayons, markers, or paint.

For variation: Make a family of construction-paper characters. Older children may want to make favorite characters from storybooks. Famous characters from history make good topics for older children.

CONSTRUCTION-PAPER BUILDINGS

For this activity you will need construction paper, crayons, markers, tape, stapler and staples, and markers.

Discuss types of buildings with the children, such as houses, barns, silos, and apartment buildings. Talk about the shapes, colors, and details on these buildings.

Give each child a supply of colored construction paper. Roll paper and tape on the ends for round shaped buildings. Fold paper for roofs. Tape four pieces of paper to make square or rectangular buildings. Add such details as windows and doors with crayons, markers, or paint.

For variation: Add cut-paper windows and doors, chimneys, and balconies. Make several buildings to create a city, small town, or farm. Store windows can have merchandise painted on, cut out and pasted on, or made and set behind cellophane windowpanes.

CUBE SCULPTURES

For this activity you will need boxes of sugar cubes, white craft glue, toothpicks, scrap pieces of fabric and trim, beads, buttons, and construction paper.

Give each child a good amount of sugar cubes. The child glues the sugar cubes together to make forms and shapes. Add details by gluing on buttons, pieces of trim, beads, and so on. Glue the cube sculpture to a construction paper base for display.

MARSHMALLOW SCULPTURES

For this activity you will need Styrofoam plates or trays, miniature and regular-sized marshmallows, toothpicks, gumdrops, pieces of vegetables, and grapes.

Cut up gumdrops, grapes, and vegetables into small pieces. Give each child a Styrofoam plate. Use one marshmallow as the base. Build a sculpture with other marshmallows and toothpicks. Add details with bits of gumdrops, grapes, and vegetable pieces.

For variation: Use colored marshmallows and regular white marshmallows. Make marshmallow animals, people, trees, flowers, and so on. Make marshmallow decorations for special occasions.

ROCK SCULPTURES

For this activity you will need: rocks of various sizes, glue, markers, paint, glue, and scraps of fabric and trim.

Go outside and collect the rocks for this activity. Talk with the children about the rocks—their colors, shapes, sizes, lines, textures, and other details. Ask them to think about what they would like to make with rocks.

Use one rock for a base. Glue on a rock for a head or simply for another part of the sculpture. Glue on other details with bits of trim and fabric. Draw on details with markers or paint.

For variation: Make a family of rock people. Make a zoo filled with rock animals. Make abstract sculptures out of rocks. Glue small pebbles to paper boxes for unusual gifts.

SOAP-BALL SCULPTURES

For this activity you will need a box of soap flakes, bowl, mixing spoon, water, and wax paper.

Pour the whole box of soap flakes into a large bowl. Add water to the soap flakes until the mixture is the consistency of paste. Working on a piece of wax paper, child rolls the mixture into balls. Put the balls together for designs or objects. Toothpicks help hold the soap balls together. Let the sculpture dry on a piece of wax paper.

STYROFOAM SCULPTURE

For this activity you will need Styrofoam of various sizes and shapes, such as sheets, broken parts of packaging materials, "peanuts," etc.; white glue; pieces of cardboard (optional); toothpicks; scraps of fabric; trim; ribbon; markers; tempera paint; and brushes.

Talk with the children about the collection of Styrofoam. Discuss size and shape of the pieces. Ask the children to think about what they would like to create with these pieces.

Use a piece of cardboard or sheet of Styrofoam as a base. Glue pieces of Styrofoam onto the base. Use toothpicks to add small pieces to the design. Continue gluing on pieces until satisfied with the design.

Use markers to draw details on the sculpture. Paint the sculpture with tempera paint. Glue on pieces of fabric, trim, and ribbon for interesting effects.

ACTIVITIES FOR OLDER CHILDREN (GRADES 4-5)

CREATING SOFT WIRE SCULPTURES

A. Have the students use three pipe cleaners to create a simple "skeleton" of a person.
B. Other pipe cleaners can be wrapped around the skeleton figure to suggest the form of muscles. Allow children to help one another.
C. After the students bend their sculptures into different poses, each pose is drawn on paper. The poses can be planned to create an action picture of a group of people. The poses might be planned and drawn to show a favorite sport, game, dance, or another activity such as a family watching television or on a picnic. Drawings of all the skeleton

figures should be made first. Then the students can draw in the details—clothes, faces, and the like.

D. Encourage students to draw the skeleton figures so they are about the same size as the wire sculpture. If the skeleton lines are carefully observed in each pose, their final drawings should be easy to complete and have interesting poses.

MEMORY BOXES–ASSEMBLAGE

Students in middle and upper elementary grades are often involved in collecting things that express their interests. Talk about what collecting means to them. How are the things we save and collect reflections of parts of ourselves? Introduce the idea of a memory box for presenting their personal memorabilia.

⊙ First, have the students prepare their memory boxes. They can paint the inside and outside of their boxes. Using a dark color, such as black or brown, works best because the objects of the assemblage will stand out more and the composition will be more unified.

⊙ After the boxes have dried, preferably overnight, the students will be able to compose their assemblages. Have them look through their memorabilia collections and select objects that they want to use. To avoid having the students glue in their objects before they have experimented with various compositions, do not pass out glue until everyone has had a chance to explore different combinations. The students should be advised to select objects with contrasting qualities in order to create interest and variety—objects with varying sizes, colors, shapes, and textures.

⊙ Remind the students that composition is the organization of parts into a unified whole. They should carefully consider the placement of each part of their assemblage to make a composition that is pleasing to them. Remind them that they should place objects so that they can be seen as the box stands upright or hangs on a wall; they should not compose the box to be viewed from above.

⊙ Have the students use white glue to attach all the parts of their assemblage. When the glue has dried overnight, set up a display of all the memory boxes.

⊙ Your students may be interested in shadow boxes. You may be able to find boxes with interior divisions, such as boxes used to package Christmas tree ornaments or various kinds of fruit, and use these interior divisions to create a shadow box display. A memory box with interior cardboard divisions (tiny interior shelves) can also be created by cutting and attaching strips of carefully

measured cardboard to the inside of the box. In this way, memorabilia items need not be glued down but only set on the cardboard "shelves."

MULTICULTURAL AWARENESS

Discuss examples of papier-mâché sculpture that students may have seen such as piñatas (Mexico) or large modeled heads or floats used in parades, puppets, and masks (Europe, the Americas, Asia). Ask the students to explain why papier-mâché is used as a medium for those art forms instead of other materials. (In many cultures, paper is inexpensive or is saved and recycled. The paste for papier-mâché can also be made easily from a variety of inexpensive "sticky" materials, such as flour and water.)

This is a good way to introduce and motivate students for a class papier-mâché project.

COMMUNITY AWARENESS

Have the students do research on the buildings within the block or area nearest to their homes. Have them focus on the materials that have been used and varied textures or patterns they see. Suggest they draw the materials, patterns, or textures on unlined index cards and place labels on the back of each card, naming the material. If they are unable to name the material, an adult may assist or the drawing can serve as a reference for library research. When the drawings are completed, have the class sort and help to display them in groups in relation to the type of materials (brick, concrete, etc.). Discuss the variety of drawing styles for each material as well as actual variations in how the materials are used (brick patterns, concrete that imitates the appearance of natural stone).

TROPHY SCULPTURES

For this activity you will need Styrofoam or wood block, pipe cleaners, glue, paper, markers, and small pieces of decorations.

This activity gives children the opportunity to create an original trophy and present it to someone they want to congratulate.

Ask the children to think of someone that they want to congratulate for something special and make them a personalized trophy. Use pipe cleaners to form the trophy person or object. Use small pieces of decoration to make the figure more fun. When satisfied with the figure, glue it to the piece of Styrofoam or wood block. Attach a label to the front of the block with the person's name and a message of congratulations. Be sure to have the children sign their work.

A trophy can be made from anything. Interesting things can be glued on a paper plate for one kind of a trophy. Some things to glue for a trophy are natural objects from outside, candy, or even magazine pictures and words.

POSITIVE AND NEGATIVE SPACE-HAND SCULPTURE

Discuss with the children the concept of positive and negative space. The space an object takes up is positive space. The "air" around it is negative space. When we create a painting, objects are positive space and are surrounded by negative space.

Have children trace their hands on a piece of cardboard. The cut-out hand is the positive space, and the cut piece of paper is the negative space. Use the cut-out cardboard hand as the base for the sculpture. Have the children try to figure out how to get the negative space to stand up (bend in half, bend bottom pieces to make a stand, use the cut out hand to support it.)

Cut out other hands from construction paper—you can use different "poses"—thumbs-up, peace sign, fist, etc. Add these to the base. Stress the idea of three-dimensional sculpturing.

EARLY AMERICAN WEAVING

Older children can experience the Native American and Colonial American art of weaving with this activity that uses a modern twist on a traditional craft. The simple instructions in this activity are for a woven belt or sash.

For this activity you will need five small beverage straws, four-ply yarn (solid color), four-ply yarn (variegated), thin wire, and masking tape.

To set up your loom, cut solid yarn into lengths three times the desired length of the finished product. You will need five of these—one for threading each straw.

Cut approximately 10 yards of variegated yarn and roll into a ball. Bend thin wire to form a "needle."

For each of the beverage straws, thread the wire "needle" with a length of solid yarn, pull the wire through the straw, and tape one end tightly to the straw.

After all straws have been threaded and taped, begin weaving. Weaving the belt:

⊙ Hold all five straws, with the taped ends up, in one hand.

⊙ Using the end of the ball of variegated yarn, begin weaving with an "under/over" pattern from the bottom of the straws (where you are holding them) to the top (taped edge). When you have woven to the top of the straws, carefully push the weaving down a few inches. DO NOT push all of the weaving off the straws.

⊙ Continue until you have reached a desired length, and tie off ends.

CHAPTER REVIEW

1. Define three-dimensional art and give two examples.
2. Choose the answer that best completes the following statements about three-dimensional activities and the child first learning to use clay.
   a. Children first learning to use clay
      (a) make basic forms with clay.
      (b) combine basic forms to make objects.
      (c) squeeze the clay in an uncontrolled way.
   b. Children using clay for the first time work with clay in a way similar to the way they draw in the
      (a) scribble stage.
      (b) basic forms stage.
      (c) pictorial stage.
   c. For children first learning to use clay the most important thing about working with clay is
      (a) what they can make with it.
      (b) how it feels.
      (c) how they can control it.

   d. The best kind of clay for children first learning to use clay is
      (a) potter's clay.
      (b) oil-based, plasticene.
      (c) ceramic, nonelastic clay.
3. Decide which answer best completes each statement about three-dimensional activities and the child who can draw basic forms.
   a. A child who can draw basic forms
      (a) cannot make similar forms in clay.
      (b) can make clay into similar forms.
      (c) combines these forms to make clay objects.
   b. Rolling clay to make balls is an example of
      (a) lack of motor control.
      (b) uncontrolled movement like scribbling.
      (c) a basic form in clay.
   c. Children can make basic forms in clay because they
      (a) can name their clay objects.

(b) now have better motor control.

(c) do not have enough motor control.

d. Some simple basic forms that children can make in clay are

(a) balls, boxes, and coils.

(b) flowers, houses, and animals.

(c) triangles, hexagons, and octagons.

4. Choose the answer that best completes each statement about three-dimensional activities and the child in the pictorial stage of drawing.

a. Most children like to make

(a) nothing in particular with clay.

(b) just balls and boxes with clay.

(c) definite things with clay.

b. When working with clay, a child in the pictorial stage can

(a) combine basic forms to make a definite object.

(b) make only basic forms in clay.

(c) make only uncontrolled hand movements with clay.

c. A simple combination of basic forms in a clay object is a

(a) house with four floors of clay and a four-part chimney.

(b) clay box.

(c) man made of a round ball head and a stick-type body.

d. When children in the pictorial stage name their drawings, they

(a) have no motor control.

(b) also name their clay objects.

(c) are not yet ready to name their clay objects.

e. When children name clay objects, it means they are in the related two-dimensional stage called the

(a) scribble stage.

(b) basic forms stage.

(c) pictorial stage.

f. A more complex combination of basic forms in clay is a

(a) man made with feet, fingers, hands, and arms.

(b) clay man with feet, fingers, hands, and arms.

(c) clay ball.

g. When a child makes a clay figure with many more details than another figure, it means

(a) nothing of any particular importance.

(b) that it is an important figure for the child.

(c) that it is a simple combination of basic forms.

h. When a clay object is made large, it means the object

(a) is a basic form.

(b) is not very important

(c) stands for something important.

5. Describe the right room set-up for clay work, in regard to

(a) table type.

(b) location of clay tables.

(c) number of children at table.

(d) amount of clay for each child.

(e) kind of storage container for clay.

6. List the types of modeling materials and tools appropriate for young children.

7. Discuss how modeling benefits young children.

8. List several suggestions to make working with modeling materials a successful experience for young children.

9. What is *assemblage?* Give examples of assemblage activities.

10. List the materials and tools needed for assemblage activities for young children.

11. List appropriate materials and tools for cardboard construction activities.

12. Discuss the value of woodworking in the early childhood art program.

13. List some specific equipment required for woodworking experiences for young children.

14. Describe the role a teacher must play in woodworking experiences for young children.

15. Discuss some ways to adapt assemblage/collage activities for children with special needs.

REFERENCES

Clemens, S. C. (1991, Jan.) Art in the classroom: Making every day special. *Young Children,* 4–11.

Gould, P., & Sullivan, M. (1999). *The inclusive early childhood classroom: Easy ways to adapt learning centers for all children*. Beltsville, MD: Gryphon House.

Szyba, C. (1999). Why do some teachers resist offering open-ended art activities for young children? *Young Children, 54*(1), 16–20.

ADDITIONAL READINGS

DeVries, R., Zan, B., Hildebrandt, R., Edmiaston, R., & Sales, C. (2003). *Developing constructivist early childhood curriculum: Practical principles and activities.* New York: Teachers College Press.

Helm, J., & Beneke, S. (Eds.). (2003). *The power of projects: Meeting contemporary challenges in early childhood classrooms—strategies and solutions.* New York: Teachers College Press.

Hohmann, M., & Weikart, D. P. (2002). *Educating young children: Active learning practices for preschool and child care programs.* 2nd ed. Ypsilanti, MI: High/Scope.

Mayesky, M. (2004). *Creative arts & activities: Clay, play dough & modeling materials.* Clifton Park, NY: Delmar.

Mayesky, M. (2004). *Creative arts & activities: Paper art.* Clifton Park, NY: Delmar.

National Research Council (2000). *Eager to learn: Educating our preschoolers.* Washington, DC: National Academy Press.

Peterson, S. (2003). *The craft and art of clay: A complete potter's handbook.* New York: Overlook Press.

Plomer, A. L. (2003). *Clay.* Milwaukee, WI: Gareth Stevens.

Rivera, H. H., Galarza, S. L., Entz, S., & Tharp, R. G. (2002). Technology and pedagogy in early childhood education: Guidance from cultural-historical-activity theory and developmentally appropriate instruction. *Information Technology in Childhood Education 1,* 173–196.

Wasserman, S. (2000). *Serious players in the primary classroom: Empowering children through active learning experiences.* 2nd ed. New York: Teachers College Press.

SOFTWARE FOR CHILDREN

Bob the Builder: Bob Builds a Park, 2003. Pre-K.

Clifford's Thinking Adventures, 2002. Pre-K.

Curious George Downtown Adventure, 2003. Pre-K.

Dora the Explorer, 2002. Pre-K.

Flash Action Colors, Shapes & More, 2003. Pre-K.

Thomas and Friends: Building the New Line, 2002. Pre-K.

Art Safari, 2003. Grades K–3.

Clue Finders 3rd Grade Adventures, 2003. Grades K–3.

Disney Princess Cinderella's Castle Designer, 2003. Grades K–3.

LEGO Creator Harry Potter and the Chamber of Secrets, 2002. Grades K–5.

LEGO Spybotics, 2002. Grades K–4.

Madeline Thinking Games Deluxe, 2003. Grades K–3.

Arthur Thinking Games, 2002. Grades 4–5.

Clue-Finders 5th Grade Adventures, 2003. Grades 4–5.

Dr. Brain Puzzleopolis, 2002. Grades 4–5.

FunCraftic Party Crafts, 2003. Grades 4–5.

Guess Who?, 2003. Grades 4–5.

I Spy Junior, 2002. Grades 4–5.

LEGO Chess, 2003. Grades 4–5.

HELPFUL WEB SITES

Art Interactive, http://www.hmsg.si.edu/
Click on Education. This site is presented by the Hirshhorn Museum and Sculpture Garden. Click on Art Interactive under the Education section for ideas on creating sculptures.

ArtSeek—Internet Art Resources, http://www.artseek.com/
Click on Arts Resources. Your source for over 150,000 affordable prints and posters from old masters to contemporary artists.

Yahoo Home: Arts: Education, http://dir.yahoo.com/Arts/Education/K_12
Yahoo search directory containing lists of sites with K–12 art activities. Categories include curriculum standards, drama, and lesson plans.

For additional creative activity resources, visit our Web site at http://www.EarlyChildEd.delmar.com.

PART TWO

Theory into Practice: Creative Activities for the Early Childhood Program

Infusing a creative approach into every area of early childhood curriculum is the focus of Part 2. Building and expanding on the theory presented in Part 1, the chapters in Part 2 cover several other areas of the early childhood curriculum in which a creative approach is appropriate. These curricular areas include dramatic play and puppetry, movement, music, language arts, science, math, food experiences, social studies, and health and safety. Also included in Part 2 are chapters on how to incorporate multicultural holidays in the early childhood curriculum. Chapters on the seasons are also included in Part 2 and contain a wealth of art activities, games, fingerplays, songs, and group projects.

All of the activities presented in Part 2 are based in developmental theory, yet are simple to reproduce and expand upon. All are presented in the hope that they will be adapted to children's individual needs, abilities, and interest levels. Information on adapting activities for children with special needs is included where appropriate throughout Part 2. They are designed in this way to be springboards to many learning experiences limited only by the child's and teacher's imagination and creativity.

Unlike simple manipulation of media, such as pounding clay and finger painting, the activities offered in this section generally require more skill on the part of the children and more instruction (at least initially) by the teacher. They tend to have a more definite focus and direction. In using these activities, there must be considerable latitude allowed for individual ideas to be expressed. These are valuable activities that provide opportunities for purposefulness and challenges to skills that children will appreciate. They also increase the variety of experiences available to young children in full-day centers.

In all chapters in Part 2 the teacher should *always* consider the developmental level of a child or a group of children before initiating any activity. Activities are included for children from preschool through grade 5. Appropriate age and/or grade levels are indicated on these activities.

Finally, while guidance of a child's activities is appropriate, *each child should be given the freedom to adapt these activities and the processes used to his or her own creative needs.* In other words, the approach should not be "What is it?" but "Tell me about what you've made." Most important, emphasis in all activities should be on the *process* and not the end product.

Rather than displaying a model or sample product at the beginning of an activity, have the children talk about their own ideas and plans for the activity. The beginning, middle, and end of every activity is *the child*—unique and singular in his or her own way.

SECTION 5

Creative Activities in Other Curricular Areas

REFLECTIVE QUESTIONS

After studying this section, you should be able to answer the following questions.

1. Do I use puppets as an instructional tool for encouraging creativity and dramatic play?

2. Have I included enough materials for puppet making for all the developmental levels, special needs, and multicultural backgrounds of my children?

3. Have I provided opportunities for young children to express themselves creatively in movement and music activities?

4. How will I modify my language arts activities so that they are appropriate for the multicultural children in my group?

5. At what levels of listening skills are the young children in my group? Do my lessons and activities meet these individual levels?

6. Have I presented language arts experiences that are appropriate to the children's current level of emerging literacy?

7. How can I be sure my classroom centers and activities are conducive to the young child's active science exploration?

8. Am I aware of the different levels of mathematic thinking present in my group of children?

9. Are my teaching practices reflective of the antibiased curriculum principles?

10. Have I planned food and nutrition experiences for young children so that they are developmentally appropriate? Do they help establish lifelong positive habits?

11. Do my room arrangement and instructional strategies emphasize appropriate health and safety practices for the young children in the group?

12. In what way can I improve the science experiences for young children in my program?

13. In considering my language arts curriculum, what are the areas I most need to improve? What positive steps can I take to implement these improvements?

14. In what ways are children verbalizing their mathematic thinking? Do I encourage this process by providing materials and activities that foster mathematical thinking?

15. As I evaluate my classroom's physical arrangement, how can I adjust it to better represent the curriculum areas of most importance to the young children who use it?

16. Does my current math and science curriculum provide an appropriate match to the developmental levels of the children in my group?

17. What are some specific ways I can be more creative (in my instructional strategies) in curriculum areas outside the arts curriculum?

18. How can I integrate art and creative activities into my entire curriculum?

19. In what way can I improve the range of language arts experiences so that the language arts are related to other curriculum areas?

20. Do my teaching and classroom practices emphasize respect for individual differences in language development? Individual differences in math and science understanding? Individual cultural differences?

21. In what way am I ensuring that young children grow in their understanding and respect for each other as unique and different individuals?

22. Have I planned to include parents and community members in my development of curriculum?

23. What is the relevance of my curriculum to young children's lives?

24. What role should young children play in planning the early childhood curriculum?

25. What skills do young children, who will live in the 21st century, need to learn in the early childhood curriculum?

26. Can I verbalize the rationale for each area of my curriculum and how it helps develop the creativity of young children?

Chapter 15

Dramatic Play and Puppetry

Objectives

After studying this chapter, you should be able to:

1. Give the objectives of dramatic play.
2. Discuss the importance of dramatic play to a young child's development.
3. Discuss the difference between dramatic play and creative dramatics.
4. Discuss appropriate ways to use puppets in the early childhood program.
5. Discuss ways to adapt dramatic activities for children with special needs.

A disturbing sight in some early childhood settings is a small group of children tensely acting out a play. The lines are memorized and said in a stilted, artificial manner. The children feel and look out of place in the costumes they are wearing. They may be excited, but many are also frightened—afraid of making a mistake or spoiling the show. Adults can be found looking on and making remarks like, "Isn't that cute?" Adult anxiety for the children is hidden by nervous laughter. An even more common response on the child's part is to say and do nothing, the safest way to avoid making a mistake in front of one's parents. This is not creative dramatics; it is a mistake. The error is made because the play is meant to please adults rather than children.

IMPORTANCE OF DRAMATIC PLAY

Dramatic play is an excellent means for developing the creativity and imagination of young children, who have instinctive ways of dealing with reality. They

need no written lines to memorize or structured behavior patterns to imitate to fantasize their world. What they do need is an interesting environment and freedom to experiment and be themselves.

One of the best ways children have to express themselves is through creative **dramatic play.** Here, they feel free to express their inner feelings. Often, teachers find out how children feel about themselves and others by listening to them as they carry out dramatic play. The pretending involved in such dramatic experiences, whether planned or totally spontaneous, is a necessary part of development. In the home center with dramatic kits and in other such activities, children can act out feelings that often cannot be expressed directly. For example, the child who is afraid of the doctor can express this fear by giving shots to dolls or stuffed animals in the home center. In a like manner, a child can act out with a friend a visit to the dentist. Thus, children can learn to deal with their anxieties as well as act out their fantasies through creative dramatic play.

Figure 15-1
One of the best ways children have to express themselves is through creative dramatic play.

Figure 15-2
For young children, dramatic play might involve toys and equipment or just the power of their imaginations.

Through the imitation and make-believe of dramatic play, children sort out what they understand and gain a measure of mastery and control over events they have witnessed or taken part in—making breakfast, going to work, taking care of baby, and going to the doctor. Dramatic play helps children enter and begin to make sense of the world of adults.

The Beginnings of Dramatic Play

The beginning of dramatic play is visible in the actions of children as young as one year, who put a comb to their hair, for example, and pull it along the side of their face, imitating the activity that has been performed on them with the same "prop." Given the right prop, the baby will imitate the behavior associated with that prop.

Figure 15-3
Children grow in self-confidence as they engage in dramatic play activities.

Teachers of young children encourage children's dramatic play by providing kits containing "props" for them to use. Dramatic play kits are created by assembling a variety of available everyday items into groups that have a common use or theme. Children select the props and use them in groups or alone to play roles or create dramatic play experiences. Just letting the children know about the use of these kits is often enough to get them started. Materials for these dramatic kits can be kept together in shoe boxes or other containers. Some common types of dramatic play kits are as follows:

Post Office and Mail Carrier
Index card file, stamp pads, stampers, crayons, pencils, Christmas seals, envelopes, hats, badges, mail satchel, supply of "resident" or other 3rd class mail

Firefighter
Hats, raincoats, badge, boots, short lengths of garden hose

Cooking
Pots, pans, eggbeaters, spoons, pitchers, flour sifter, metal or plastic bowls, salt and pepper shakers, aprons, measuring spoons and cups, egg timer

Cleaning
Small brooms, mops, feather duster, cakes of soap, sponges, bucket, toweling, plastic spray bottles, clothesline, clothespins, doll clothes to wash

Doctor
Tongue depressors, old stethoscope, satchel, bandages, cotton balls, uniforms

Beauty Salon
Small hand mirrors, plastic combs and brushes, cotton balls, towels, scarves, clip-on rollers, colored water in nail polish bottles, empty hairspray containers, wigs, play money, blowdryer

Grocery Store
Old cash register or adding machine, play money, paper pads, pencils or crayons, paper bags, empty food cartons, wax fruit, grocery boxes, cans with smooth edges

Plumber
Wrenches, sections of plastic pipes, tool kit, hats and shirts

Painter
Paint cans full of water, brushes of different sizes, drop cloth, painter's hat

Mechanic
Tire pump, tool kit, boxes to become "cars," shirt, hat

Entertainer
Records, cassette tapes, record player, cassette tape player, musical instruments, costumes

Many more dramatic play kits can be added to this list. It is important to encourage both boys and girls to assume a variety of roles. Imagination can also be used to transform regular classroom items into "new materials." Chairs can become trains, cars, boats, or houses. A table covered with a blanket or bedspread becomes a cave or special hiding place. Large cardboard cartons that children can decorate become houses, forts, fire stations, and telephone booths.

Figure 15-4
Dramatic play kits.

For example, if offered a cup, the baby drinks; a hat, the baby puts it on his head; or a pillow, the baby puts his head on it. Adults often describe this as pretend play, but it is more accurately pre-pretend play, because it involves only actions that are known to the child.

Actual dramatic play begins when a child uses a prop for something *other* than the activity for which he has seen it used by an adult. Thus, a hairbrush becomes a sailing boat; a wooden block, a hairbrush; or a stick, a bridge. This usually happens when the child is about two years old; that is the age when children seem to be capable of making an "as if" transformation of an object, a necessary prerequisite to pretend play involving objects, others, and themselves.

Development of Dramatic Play

As children grow and develop, so does their dramatic play. From simple imitative movement, children move on to more complex dramatic play.

It is important for teachers of young children to be very good observers and listeners, to see what children play with, to watch what they do with the materials, and to listen to what they say about the props and

THINK ABOUT IT...

Puppets, Puppets, Puppets— So Many Uses!

Did you ever notice what happens when children interact with puppets? They don't look at *your* face—they look at and talk to the puppet! The puppet becomes a character they can have a real conversation with.

Don't let your shyness or "stage fright" prevent you from taking out the puppets that may be collecting dust on the shelf and use them! You will be amazed at how many ways you can use puppets with young children. Here are a few ideas:

PUPPETS FOR TODDLERS

Put a puppet on your hand or finger and a small group of toddlers will gather in front of you. The magic of puppets helps toddlers increase their attention span. Children who would normally not last long in a group activity will be fascinated enough to sit down and stay awhile. Choose puppets children can interact with—shake their paw, tickle their ears, and give a kiss. And don't forget to have a puppet sing-a-long! You can make small finger puppets for the children to use on their fingers, too. Ideas for finger puppets are found later in this chapter.

PUPPETS FOR TIMES OF THE DAY

Use a special puppet to begin your morning meeting. Children like seeing the puppet every day, and this routine can also help them make transitions to and from the group. You can also use the puppet to welcome children, lead the hello song, or discuss the events of the day. It can also be used to share a recent experience that may be similar to one a child in the group has had. A puppet can also talk about feelings regarding a classroom situation that needs discussion. A large puppet that has an expressive face and moveable arms would be good in this situation.

PUPPETS FOR GROUP TIME

Here are some ideas for using puppets at group time.

- Use a puppet for teaching alphabet letters (i.e., a lamb puppet for the letter L). If focusing on a particular color, the puppet might wear the chosen color in a paper hat and a scarf.
- Make simple stick or finger puppets (see ideas later in this unit) representing characters from a favorite book. Do this, too, for story-songs such as "This Old Man" or "I Know an Old Lady." Children can use the puppets to play the different roles in the story or song.
- Use a puppet to introduce a story. When the story is finished, the puppet can discuss it with the children.
- Designate a special puppet, such as a Riddle Puppet, for asking children "What am I thinking?" or to play an I spy game. Children will know a riddle is coming whenever you bring out this puppet.

PUPPETS FOR TRANSITION TIMES

Use a puppet to announce cleanup or any other change in activity. The transition puppet might have a bell it rings or a drum it plays. Set aside a special puppet just for this role so that the children do not confuse it with others in the room. The puppet can also excuse children from group time with a song, riddle, or direction. "Anybody who is wearing BLUE can go wash their hands." Later in the year, children will enjoy taking turns using this puppet and providing the directions.

(Continues)

THINK ABOUT IT... (Continued)

PUPPETS AS PEACEMAKERS

A puppet can be an impartial negotiator. Try a puppet when an argument arises or a problem occurs in the classroom. Children can take their case to the puppet. Children are often more willing to listen and cooperate when they problem solve with an "impartial" puppet friend. You can even use homemade sock puppets set aside solely for this purpose to help children express their feelings. See information later in this chapter on how to make sock or glove puppets for this purpose.

PUPPETS AS SCHOOL TO HOME CONNECTIONS

Puppets, like dolls and stuffed animals, are wonderful for creating a home–school connection. Children can take the puppet—along with the puppet's overnight bag and journal—home for the weekend to visit with the family. Don't forget to pack the disposable camera so that children can record its adventures. This take-home puppet should be large enough that children can dress it up and play with it.

PUPPETS AS CLASSROOM FRIENDS

Introduce a new classroom family member to the class—a puppet! Children will delight in telling the puppet all about the rules and even give it a tour of the room after group time. This is especially effective with shy children. You may see them chatting away to the puppet in a way you have never seen or heard them before. A full-body puppet that looks like a stuffed animal is good for this activity because children will want to carry it around to the different centers in the room and sit next to it at snack time.

materials provided to them. It is equally important that the teacher becomes part of the play of the child, but—and this is essential—at the child's present developmental level. We all remember the relative who insisted that the Fisher Price garage could *only* be a garage, not a part of the fortress wall, and the legendary behavior of the father who gives the young child a gift of an electric train or racing car set and proceeds to insist that it be played with in terms of adult reality. In adult's play there is no flying cars one over the other to win and no make-believe drivers, only Grand Prix racers. No wonder the adult ends up playing by himself, while the child returns to playing with the racing car box. This way, he is allowed to pretend without adult guidance and limitations.

Many times creative dramatics begins with one child, and others soon join in. Playing store with a storekeeper and a number of customers is a form of creative dramatic play. Speaking on a toy telephone to a friend is another form. Puppet shows in which children use finger puppets and make up a story as they go along is still another form. Figure 15–4 contains suggestions on how to put together dramatic play kits to encourage children's creative dramatic play.

Dramatic play occurs daily in the lives of young children. It is one of the ways that children naturally learn. They constantly imitate the people, animals, and machines in their world. They enjoy re-creating the exciting experiences of their lives. Dramatic play is their way of understanding and dealing with the world.

Dramatic play is also an important medium for language development, as it encourages fluency in language. A child who is reluctant to speak in other situations is almost compelled to speak in order to be included in dramatic play. As play becomes elaborate, a child's language becomes more complex. When children talk with each other in a nondirective setting, such as the housekeeping center, it is possible for the flow and quality of language to develop. If others are to understand his or her role, a child needs to explain what he or she is doing so that friends will respond in appropriate ways. If the child is to understand what they are doing, he or she must listen.

When children become involved in complex make-believe, they need to listen and respond to each other. A child speaks convincingly to others when he or she wants them to change the nature of the play. If they still do not understand, he or she may try to find other ways to persuade them. When he or she needs to elaborate on his or her ideas, the child is likely to use a longer sequence of words and move from two words to more complex syntax.

As children play together they learn new words from each other. At their make-believe restaurant, Maria prepared tacos and Justin ordered fruitcake from the menu. Justin liked the sound of the new word, "tacos." He pretended he was eating one, even though he did not know what a "taco" was.

As children play, they repeat words and phrases they have learned and enjoy saying them. They name objects, talk about what they are doing, and plan as they go along. They begin to recognize the importance of planning and take time to formulate more detailed plans for their dramatizations.

DRAMATIC PLAY IN THE HOME (OR HOUSEKEEPING) CENTER

One of the best places for children to express themselves in creative, dramatic play is the housekeeping or home center. Here, in a child-sized version of the world, children are free and safe to express how they feel about themselves and others. While they carry out dramatic play in the housekeeping center, they can pretend to be many different kinds of people, "trying on," so to speak, many social roles. (Figure 15–7 presents a summary of basic home center experiences and equipment.)

The home (housekeeping) and creative dramatics center provides endless opportunities for the teacher, as a facilitator of learning, to broaden the children's horizons. The center can be decorated and rearranged to represent an area that pertains to a specific content. Possibilities include creating a home, hospital, post office, grocery store, and more. The change of seasons as well as certain holidays can be easily incorporated in this center. For example, during fall, a child's rake, sweaters, and pumpkins might be included in the center. During the winter months, mufflers, mittens, a

child's shovel, candles, candlesticks, and bells may be additions to the center. For spring, the teacher may add plastic or silk flowers and a variety of hats. The supplies in the housekeeping center should reflect the activities in the classroom and extend the skills being taught elsewhere in the room, as well as introduce new skills. Be sure to include clothing, dishes, and dolls that are familiar and represent each of the ethnic groups in your classroom.

It is important to emphasize a nonsexist approach in teaching, especially in the housekeeping area. For example, boys' dramatic play must be encouraged in an early childhood program as much as the girls' dramatic play. A good tactic to encourage boys' participation is to change the themes of the dramatic play corner to topics that interest some boys, such as garage, doctor, boat, etc. Include open-ended materials in the dramatic play areas such as blocks, flashlights, a rope, and small balls. An observant teacher, sensitive to both sexes' dramatic play and developing sex-role concepts, even gives cues that encourage *all* children to play in *all* centers.

Entering into the child's dramatic play is an important point of consideration here. The teacher should not be the leader or the organizer of the dramatic play

Figure 15-5

Dramatic play can occur in any center in the early childhood program.

Figure 15-6

Dramatic play allows children to "try on" adult roles in a safe environment.

and must try not to form premature conclusions or make assumptions for the child. The teacher observes and asks questions about what the child says and helps to draw out information from the child, maintaining the conversation on the theme provided by the child, but at a pace that allows the child to feel comfortable and pleased with the conversation. Use the Observation Sheet found in the Online Companion™ to assist you in observing the dramatic play of young children. The teacher also encourages children's play by providing props that extend the play but do not change the theme. In doing so, teachers provide for further dramatic play and thereby create a more effective basis from which thought processes and imagination can develop. Teachers help children with their thinking by making statements about their work—not evaluative statements, such as, "I like your cake," or assumptive ones, such as, "What a naughty cat, eating up all the meat!"—but statements of the obvious on which the child can expand, such as, "It's a bright yellow color!"

In the home center, dramatic experience often begins with one child, and others soon join in. In observing dramatic play in the home center with children of various ages, you can see definite age differences in their dramatic play. Younger children two to four years old generally are involved in such dramatic play for a much briefer period of time than children five years and older. Before the child is two years old, for example, he may say, "Nice baby," when he hugs a doll and then move on. After the age of two, the child's dramatic play may begin to combine several ideas, in contrast to the single-idea dramatization of the younger child. The older child may hold a doll and pretend to feed the "baby" a cookie. He or she may decide to put the baby to bed, covering the doll with a blanket because it is time for "baby to take a nap." This process of imitating what has been observed is called **modeling behavior.**

Instances of such modeling behavior in the home center and elsewhere are even more prevalent in older children. For example, a five-year-old child will feed

---

Activities in This Center Afford the Child Experiences in the Following:

- clarifying adult roles
- trying out social skills
- getting along with others
- sharing responsibilities
- making group decisions
- controlling impulsive behavior

- recognizing cause and effect
- developing positive attitudes about one's self and others
- enjoying the fantasy of the grownup world
- using oral language spontaneously
- practicing the use of symbols, which are subskills in reading
- learning social ease and confidence in his own strengths

Materials:*

Full-length mirror	Play dough	A variety of hats, dresses, shirts, ties, belts, scarves, shoes, pocketbooks, and jewelry
Stove	Doll bed, doll carriage, baby highchair	
Refrigerator		
Sink	Rocking chair	An old suitcase (for "trips")
Closet or rack of clothes	Empty cans, food boxes— multicultural foods	A nurse's cap (hypodermic needles—minus needles—pill bottles, a play thermometer)
Cooking/eating utensils		
Table and chairs	Mirror/hand mirror	
Tea set	Carriage	Play money
Telephone	Dolls/doll clothes-multicultural	An old briefcase
Stethoscope	Iron/ironing board	Dress-up gloves, rubber gloves, baseball gloves, garden gloves
Props for cleaning (broom, mop, dustpan, pail, sponge, rags, duster)	Puppets	

- Open-ended materials such as large sheets, scarves, and cardboard boxes.
- A "challenge box" of unusual items (tools, large beach ball, and funny glasses) to add new elements to their play. Challenge them: "What can you do with this?"
- Props from favorite stories to encourage retelling experiences.

*Add objects as needed for special emphasis.

Figure 15-7

Experiences and equipment in the home center.

THIS ONE'S for YOU!

Creative Dramatics in the Elementary Grades

While adults rely on reason and knowledge, children use play and imagination to explore and understand their world. It makes sense, then, for teachers to use these two resources—play and imagination—as a learning tool. Creative dramatics provides this venue, linking the world of play to the world of knowledge and reason.

Dramatic play is an accepted part of the preschool and kindergarten curricula. Yet, elementary teachers of young children often neglect this important learning tool for the elementary child.

Creative dramatics is a form of imaginative play that helps students learn and uses no written dialogue. This makes it different from performing a play. Actors in a play read or memorize lines written by somebody else. In creative dramatics, actors create their own words to convey meaning. Some examples of a creative dramatics experience would be the following:

- In a 3rd grade classroom, students using creative dramatics "become" metal containers, expanding with heat and contracting with cold. These expanding and contracting movements are put into a drama and eventually accompanied by a dance.
- In a 1st grade classroom, children become clouds releasing raindrops; shimmery rays of sunshine; and seeds that grow roots, sprout, and squeeze their faces through the dirt.
- A 4th grade teacher introduces a dramatic activity having individuals or small groups of students repeat the same line while portraying different qualities or characters. Say in a very mysterious way, "Are you going to wear the red hat to the fair?" Say in a very angry way, "Are you going to wear the red cap to the fair?" How might a mouse ask the same question? How might a spoiled rich kid ask the same question? The teacher repeats this using different lines, qualities, and characters. After five minutes, students are thinking creatively and are ready to move into a dramatic activity.
- In a 3rd grade class students are performing *The Three Billy Goats Gruff* with a twist. The teacher tells the actors before they begin that they can only use dog language. That is, they will have to do the whole drama using only barks, yips, and pants. This forces the children to convey meaning and develop characterization using only their faces and bodies, while watching and reacting to other actors.

In all of these examples, teachers are using creative dramatics to reinforce concepts in the curriculum. In the process, these teachers are creating an active learning experience that is fun, allowing the students to work together to achieve a common goal and allowing everyone to be successful.

This is the essence of creative dramatics. Creative dramatics is a form of imaginative play that helps elementary students learn in an active, enjoyable way.

the baby, discussing why milk was good for him or her, telling the baby it was nap time, and telling the baby that children must "be good" and listen to their parents. This dramatization is in marked contrast to that of the two year old.

Children involved in dramatic play in the housekeeping center also use materials from various parts of the room to support their play. For example, a child who needs some pretend money to put in a purse may decide to make some in the art area, or the child might go to the manipulative area to gather beads, chips, or even puzzle pieces to use as money.

Whether they are searching for materials or on their way to another related location, it is perfectly natural

and appropriate for children involved in dramatic play to move about the entire space as part of their play. Confining role players to one area or part of the room frustrates rather than supports their intentions. When their use of space and materials conflicts with other children's use of space and materials, the opportunity for group problem solving arises.

Dramatic play is a natural avenue for participation by children from diverse language and multicultural backgrounds. Children who are bilingual can participate easily in dramatic activities that call for nonverbal communication. The dramatic play area can also be a place where children learn the words for their play props. For example, nametags can be made for objects in the dramatic play center in both English and the children's native language.

Dramatic play also appeals to children's various learning styles or multiple intelligences. The body-smart learner gets obvious enjoyment from the active, physical movement involved in dramatic play. The child who is word smart enjoys the ongoing dialogue that is so naturally a part of the dramatic play experience. The child with a person-smart learning style thrives in dramatic activities involving the constant interaction with other children. The child with a picture-smart learning style enjoys creating the visual scenes that provide the background for dramatic play scenarios.

Remember also to provide outdoor materials and equipment for pretending and role play. With more space and fewer boundaries, outdoor dramatic play is often robust and highly mobile. Children will make use of anything available—wagons, tricycles, and other wheeled toys for cars, buses, trains, and boats; large packing boxes, boards, sheets, ropes, and tires for houses, stores, forts, and caves; and sand and sand utensils for cooking, eating, and building. They may also enjoy the addition of some "indoor" materials (hats, scarves, baby dolls, dishes, chalk) to their outdoor dramatic play.

Creative Dramatics in the Elementary Grades

Dramatic play is the free play of very young children in which they explore their universe, imitating the actions and traits of those around them. It is their earliest expression in dramatic form, but it is *not* the same as creative dramatics.

Dramatic play is fragmented, existing only for the moment. It may last for a few minutes or go on for some time. It even may be played repeatedly, but it is a repetition for the pure joy of doing. It has no clear beginning and no end and no development in the dramatic sense.

Creative drama refers to informal drama that is created by the participants. It goes beyond dramatic play in scope and intent. It may make use of a story with a beginning, a middle, and an end. It may, on the other hand, explore, develop, and express ideas and feelings through dramatic enactment. (See "This One's for You!" box in this chapter for examples of creative dramatic experiences.) It is, however, always improvised drama. Dialogue is created by the players, whether the content is taken from a well-known story or is an original plot. Lines are not written down or memorized. With each playing, the story becomes more detailed and better organized, but it remains extemporaneous

Figure 15-8

Puppets fascinate and involve children in a way that few other art forms can because they allow children to enter the world of fantasy and drama so easily.

and is at no time designed for an audience. Participants are guided by a leader rather than a director; the leader's goal is the optimal growth and development of the players.

The term *creative drama* is generally used to describe the improvised drama of children from age six and older. Creative drama offers elementary children the opportunity to develop their creativity and imagination. Few activities have greater potential for developing the imagination than creative dramatics.

Creative drama offers an opportunity for children with special needs to participate in a performing art. Because of its flexibility, drama can be a joyful and freeing adventure for groups of all ages. Special needs can be served by adjusting emphases and activities to fit the ability level of the children.

Through creative dramatics, the imagination can be stimulated and strengthened in elementary students. Figure 15–9 gives information on specific steps involved in setting up creative dramatic experiences for elementary children.

ADAPTATIONS FOR CHILDREN WITH SPECIAL NEEDS

The following suggestions are designed to help teachers include children with special needs in dramatic play. You may find these activities to be helpful.

The following guidelines should assist you in getting started on creative dramatics for elementary students:

⊙ **Provide a structure.** While pretending is very natural for children, improvising a short drama can be an abstract process. Children will need structure to guide their actions and dialogue during the initial stages. The teacher can provide this structure by modeling and demonstrating the basic story, as well as possible actions, dialogue, and characterizations. It is best to keep early dramas short and simple, using only two to four characters. Older students and those with experience in creative dramatics will need less structure.

⊙ **Encourage open-endedness.** Creative dramatics is spontaneous and changeable. Although it works best when teachers provide a beginning structure, this structure should be flexible and open-ended. As students become more comfortable with creative dramatics, they will begin to use ideas and experiences from their own lives to create unique variations on the original themes. Using a prepared script would prevent this kind of creativity and individualization. It is a good rule not to use written dialogue.

⊙ **Promote a safe environment.** Creativity is enhanced when the teacher creates a fun, safe environment. Closing the classroom door during the initial learning stages of creative dramatics can help to develop a sense of safety and community. A teacher who is willing to take creative risks by modeling and participating in creative dramatics encourages the children's participation. Positive, specific feedback that acknowledges actors and their efforts will put students at ease to continue acting creatively. Finally, a teacher should never force students to participate in creative dramatics; rather, she or he should always ask for volunteers.

⊙ **Provide feedback.** Students like to receive feedback, both formal and informal. Informal feedback is best when a teacher responds in a way that is appropriate to the dramatic experience (e.g., laughing at the comedic parts). Once a drama is over, the teacher can give more formal feedback by processing the experience with students, recognizing those things that were done well.

⊙ **Take your time.** Allow students to slowly become comfortable with creative dramatics. Remember, creative dramatics is meant to be an enjoyable learning experience. Make having fun your number one priority.

Figure 15-9
Steps to creative dramatics in elementary grades.

General Suggestions

⊙ Because the child should feel free to experiment and take risks, be careful not to make too many rules for the child's play. Enforce only those rules that are really needed for the child to play safely.

⊙ Let the child take the lead. This may involve some patient waiting for the child to choose something to do.

⊙ To encourage children to play together, define the space where children can play and keep it small. For example, position housekeeping toys around a small area rug and remind children that they need to stay on the rug while they are playing.

⊙ Children with attention deficits, autism, and developmental delays tend to flit from center to center. Children cannot fully benefit from the learning experiences in a center if they are there only a moment or two. Be firm and require that children initially spend at least five minutes in a center of their choice. Then gradually build on the amount of time the child can focus on dramatic play. If five minutes is impossible for the child, start with the amount of time the child can currently tolerate.

⊙ To help children put away dramatic play props and toys, label shelves with pictures as well as words.

⊙ Try to let the child play with other children as much as possible. The more often you interact with children, the less often children interact with their peers (Gould & Sullivan, 1999).

Developmental Delays

Adults may be tempted to intervene too much in the play of children with developmental delays. Children need an opportunity to play at their level of ability and to independently initiate play activities. If you need to intervene when the child is playing in a group, be as unobtrusive as possible. For example, you could simply sit down as part of the children's play and become a character or prop so that you could subtly make suggestions.

Other suggestions for working with children with developmental delays are to do the following:

- ⊙ Offer dramatic play materials that are familiar and part of the child's daily life experiences.
- ⊙ Encourage verbalization during play by asking questions and encouraging communication with other children.
- ⊙ Some children with developmental delays fatigue very easily. Make sure that the child has supportive seating.
- ⊙ The child who is not yet proficient at dramatic play may be able to carry out some kind of support role in the play, such as being the patient at a doctor's office. You can make this happen by having the appropriate props nearby or by verbally suggesting the role.
- ⊙ Bring out a few props at a time to avoid unnecessarily distracting the child.
- ⊙ Provide some dress-up clothes that are simple to get on and off and do not have tiny buttons or snaps. Large clothes are easier to get on and off.

Attention Deficit Hyperactivity Disorder and Behavioral Issues

Two traits—high activity levels and distractibility—may prevent children from participating in dramatic activities. These children are more able to focus on dramatic play that they have chosen and that is of personal interest. Novelty is very important. Adding a single novel toy to a play setting may be enough to refocus the child's attention. For example, if the child is playing in the home center and seems to be losing interest, add a doctor's kit with stethoscope and play syringe and cue the child to return to the play with a question such as, "Is the baby sick?"

Some additional suggestions on working with these children in dramatic activities are as follows:

- ⊙ Help children learn how to work out conflicts when playing with other children. The child may need adult help to verbalize what is bothering him or her rather than acting out aggressively (Allen & Schwartz 1992).
- ⊙ Make sure that there are clear behavioral consequences for inappropriate behavior. Carefully consider whether the rules you make are really necessary.

- ⊙ Exciting activities that are new or offer a lot of sensory input should be preceded and followed by calming activities. Involvement in dramatic play could be followed by quiet time sitting on a beanbag chair with a favorite toy.
- ⊙ If the child attempts to leave the center after a few moments of play, ask the child to stay and do one more thing. However, children should be allowed to leave play situations that are not productive.
- ⊙ Hyperactivity in and of itself does not get in the way of learning. If the child is focused on the play activity while actively moving about, there is no need to intervene. This is different from the child who cannot focus on the play or the other children and is darting aimlessly around the classroom. That child needs adult intervention to settle down to play.
- ⊙ Reduce distractions in the dramatic play center by hanging sheets or lengths of fabric from the ceiling to section off the center from the rest of the room. The dramatic play could also take place in a large box or under a table that has been draped with a sheet.
- ⊙ Set a timer to help the child stay in a play center. The timer provides an auditory cue for when the child can move to another center and gives the child a sense that his or her involvement in the center has a definite beginning and end.

Visual Impairments

Children with a vision impairment may have not had the opportunity to learn how to play by observing others. The child may also have had limited experience with exploring and manipulating objects. It is important that children with residual (limited vision) be encouraged to use their vision. Children who are blind should be encouraged to explore the sensory properties of objects.

- ⊙ Help the child explore the dramatic play area and to discuss what the objects are and what they are used for. Ask the other children in the center to explain the ongoing play to the child who is visually impaired (Monighan-Nourot, Scales, Van Hoorn, & Almy, 1987).
- ⊙ Intervene if the child is always assigned subordinate roles in play such as that of the baby or patient and suggest another role.
- ⊙ Encourage the child who is blind to develop social skills that will help interaction with other children. The child should learn to turn his or her face toward people when they are talking and to keep his or her head in midline (Gould & Sullivan, 1999).

PUPPETS

Puppets can be used for almost any of the dramatic experiences that have been described here. They offer the child two ways to express creativity: (1) the creative experience of making the puppet and (2) the imaginative experience of making the puppet come to life.

Puppets fascinate and involve children in a way that few other art forms can because they allow children to enter the world of fantasy and drama so easily. In this magic world, children are free to create whatever is needed right then in their lives.

Using Puppets

The use of puppets usually begins in the nursery or preschool, where they are invaluable when readily available for dramatic play. Teachers can teach fingerplays with simple finger puppets; hand puppets can act out familiar nursery rhymes. Music time is enhanced by a puppet leading the singing and other puppets joining in. The shy child who is reluctant to sing often will participate through a puppet. Puppets are also excellent for concept teaching and can help clarify abstract concepts and demonstrate concrete concepts. For instance, in the preschool the concepts of "above," "below," "behind," "in front of," and so on can be clearly shown with the puppet.

Puppetry, as a form of dramatic play, is a sure means of stimulating creative storytelling in younger children. Some teachers tape-record spontaneous puppet skits and, by writing them down, show the children how they have created a story.

In a room with a climate of flexibility and freedom, the children are bound to come up with countless

Figure 15-10
A hand puppet is one of the most basic puppet forms.

Figure 15-11
Some children enjoy wearing a mask for dramatic activities. Never force a child to cover his or her face if he or she doesn't want to do so, however.

other ideas for using their puppets, in addition to the following:

- Put together a puppet center—puppet materials, props, and theater—for children to use during the day.
- Recycle small plastic detergent bottles for a hand puppet rack. Bolt these small detergent bottles to scrap lumber and your puppets will have a "home." See Figure 15–13 for a diagram of this puppet rack.
- Consider having a specific puppet for each center area. This puppet could remind the class that it is music time, for instance, and be used to give directions and explain new concepts. If the puppet has trouble in an area, the children could teach it and straighten out its confusion. Through such dramatic experiences, self-confidence and skills are strengthened.
- Felt boards and puppets work well together. A puppet with hands can effectively help the adult or child put pieces on or take them off the felt board. One teacher who was teaching toddlers the parts of the face used a rather "stupid" puppet that kept making mistakes by putting the parts in the wrong place. The children had a lot of fun correcting it.
- In music experiences, teachers find that puppets help young children develop a feeling for rhythm and music interpretation by moving the puppets to the beat. They also encourage reluctant children to sing, since the puppet does the singing for the child. Puppets with moving mouths are most effective but not necessary.

- Social studies is a natural area for puppets; it presents countless opportunities to dramatize holiday ideas, represent particular ethnic customs, or portray the roles of various community helpers.
- Use puppets to help children voice feelings, such as fear; other activities can include using high- and low-pitched voices and making squeaking, growling, and chirping animal sounds.
- Provide opportunities for enactments of published or original stories.
- Encourage children to present original work. Young children may have difficulty manipulating puppets and saying words at the same time. Audiotape the story in advance so that the children can then focus on the puppets' actions.

These suggestions are simply intended to be idea starters. The use of puppets in the classroom is limited only by imagination—yours and the children's.

Kinds of Puppets

Some of the most common and easiest puppets to make are stick puppets, hand puppets, finger puppets, people puppets, wooden spoon puppets, mitten and sock puppets, paper plate puppets, play dough puppets, styrofoam ball puppets, vegetable (fruit) puppets, Ping-Pong ball puppets, and cylinder puppets. (See Appendix G for puppet patterns.)

Detergent Bottle Puppet Rack

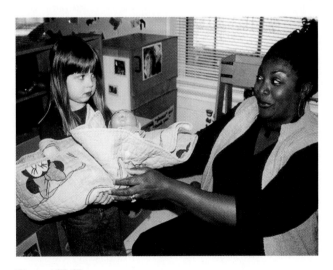

Figure 15-12

It is important that the teacher become part of the dramatic play of the child at the child's developmental level.

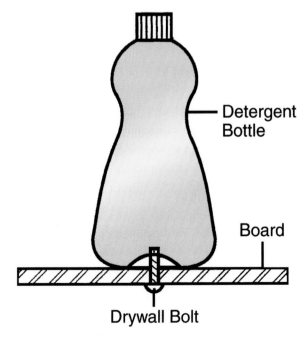

Detergent Bottle

Board

Drywall Bolt

Figure 15-13

Detergent bottle puppet rack.

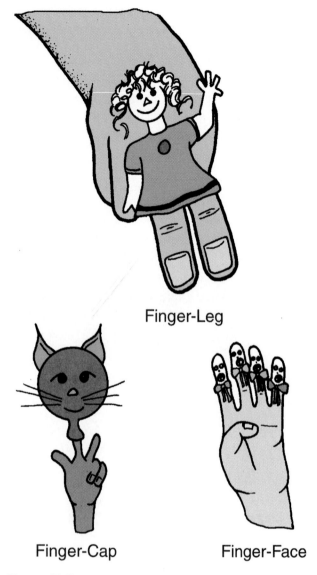

Finger-Leg

Finger-Cap   Finger-Face

Figure 15-14

There are many different kinds of finger puppets.

Stick puppets. The simplest of all puppets, stick puppets are controlled by a single stick (any slim, rigid support) that goes up inside the puppet or is attached to the back of it.

Stick puppets are fun and easy to make. The teacher can use sticks from the lumber yard, large twigs, pencils or wooden popsicle sticks. With this type of puppet, the child puts a bag or piece of cloth over the stick and stuffs the bag or cloth with wads of newspaper or cotton. The child then ties the top of the bag to the stick, making a head. A rubber band may be used instead of string to form a head.

The child can then paint the head or make a face with crayons or colored paper and paste. Scrap yarn, wood shavings, and buttons are also good materials for the puppet's face. Scrap pieces of fabric can be used to "dress" the puppet; wallpaper samples are an inexpensive material for puppets' clothes.

With the stick, the puppet is moved around the stage or turned from side to side. It has the advantage of being a good first puppet for preschoolers, since a stick can be attached to any little doll, toy animal, cutout figure, fruit, or vegetable, and the puppet is easy to operate.

Bag puppets. The common paper bag in any size makes a good **bag puppet** for young preschoolers. The bags are stuffed with wads of newspaper and tied, stapled, or glued shut. A body is made with a second bag stapled to the first, leaving room for the child's hand to slip in and work the puppet.

A face can be made with paint, crayons, or colored paper and paste. Odds and ends are fun to use for the face, too. Buttons make eyes; crumpled tissue, a nose; and yarn, hair. The search for the right odds and ends to make the puppet is as much fun as using the finished puppet later.

Hand puppets. Frequently called glove or mitten puppets, these are the most popular for young children. (See Appendix G for basic patterns for glove and mitten puppets.) There are many types of hand puppets, but most can be classified into two general groups: (1) those with moving mouths and (2) those with moving hands.

The first (with moving mouths) is any sort of hand covering—a handkerchief, sock, mitten, or paper bag—inside of which one's fingers open and shut, forming the mouth of the puppet. The second kind has a head and two hands and is operated by putting one or two fingers in the head and one in each hand. This kind of puppet can freely pick up objects and make hand motions, thus putting more realism into a performance.

Finger puppets. The three general types of **finger puppets** are the following (See Figure 15–14):

⊙ *Finger-leg.* Finger puppet in which two fingers (usually the index and middle fingers) serve as the puppet's legs.

⊙ *Finger-cap.* Finger puppet that slips over an individual finger.

⊙ *Finger-face.* Puppet made by drawing a face on a finger with a felt pen. Usually, one can perform with quite a few puppets of this type at one time. They are great for fingerplays!

Some advantages of finger puppets include the following:

⊙ They are easy to manipulate, even by a toddler.

⊙ They encourage small muscle action.

Figure 15-15
Garden glove puppets.

⊙ They are inexpensive to make.
⊙ One child alone can put on a performance with an "entire cast."
⊙ They maintain interest because they are always easy and quick to make.
⊙ They can be made in spare moments, since materials are small and mobile.

Wooden spoon puppets. You will need wooden spoons, yarn, string, material scraps, glue, and construction paper. Draw a face on the wooden spoon. Glue on yarn, string for hair, and scraps of material for clothing.

Two-faced (paper plate) puppets. Draw a face on the back of each paper plate. Add features with various types of materials. Insert a stick between the paper plates and glue it into place. Staple edges together.

Play dough puppets. Place a small amount of play dough onto a finger. Mold play dough into a face shape covering the finger. Add raisins, cereal, toothpicks, etc., for facial features and added emphasis.

Styrofoam ball puppets. Insert a stick into a styrofoam ball. Cover the styrofoam ball with fabric. Tie the fabric around the stick. Glue on buttons and felt scraps for facial features.

Ping-Pong ball puppets. Cut an X shape out of a ball. Place a piece of lightweight fabric on your finger. Cover the area of the ball with sturdy glue. Force the ball at the X onto the fabric on your finger. While the glue is drying, draw or paste a face onto the puppet.

Sock puppet. Pull the sock over your hand. Glue or paint facial features onto the toe of the sock or decorate as desired.

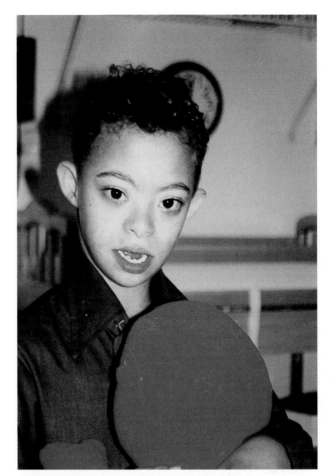

Figure 15-16
Dramatic play is different at various stages of development.

Finger puppets from gloves. Recycle stray gloves and use them for finger puppets. Recycle old rubber gloves, too, by drawing features on rubber glove fingers with marking pens. Glue pompoms on each finger for the "head" and glue on bits of cloth or felt for facial or character details. See Figure 15–15 for examples of garden glove puppets.

Old mitten puppets. A child can slip his or her hand into an old mitten and make the puppet "talk" by moving his or her thumb up and down against the four fingers.

Cardboard cylinder puppet. To make a **cardboard cylinder puppet**, place a cardboard cylinder from paper towels or toilet tissue over the fingers. Decorate with desired features. The cylinder could be used for the body, and a styrofoam ball or Ping-Pong ball could be placed on the top for the head. Decorate as desired.

People puppets. Also called **humanettes,** these are half-person and half-puppet. The easiest **people puppet** for children is a large paper sack put over the head. Holes are cut out for the eyes, and facial features and decorations are added with paint or paper and paste. The bags can be turned up slightly above the shoulder or cut away on the sides for arm holes. People puppets make a natural transition from puppetry to creative drama. Also, shy children generally feel more protected behind this kind of puppet than all the other types. Be sure not to force a child to use this type of puppet if he or she does not like his head covered!

More ideas for puppets are at the end of this chapter.

SUMMARY

Dramatic play is an excellent means for developing creativity and imagination in young children when it is related to the child's personal sense of reality without imposed adult standards. Dramatic play can be adapted so it is appropriate for children with special needs. Dramatic play kits are easy to make and help develop opportunities for creative play. The use of puppets provides opportunities for creative movement, dramatics, and language development. Creative dramatics refers to informal drama that is created by the participants. It goes beyond dramatic play in scope and intent. The term *creative dramatics* is generally used to describe the improvised drama of children from age six and older.

Other uses of puppets in the early childhood program include helping shy children express themselves, having children introduce themselves, and teaching new concepts in various areas. Types of puppets appropriate for use with young children are stick, finger, hand, people puppets (humanettes), vegetable, Ping-Pong ball, and styrofoam puppets.

KEY TERMS

bag puppet	finger puppets
cardboard cylinder puppet	humanettes
creative dramatics	modeling behavior
dramatic play	people puppet

LEARNING ACTIVITIES

A. Create two dramatic play kits not listed or suggested in this chapter.
   1. Try to make one that no one else might think of making.
   2. Compare with those of classmates.
B. Make up a play kit of "props" children might use in one of the following activities.
   1. playing mail carrier
   2. playing dentist
   3. playing airline pilot
   4. playing waitress/waiter
C. Make one of the types of puppets discussed in this chapter. Demonstrate its use to your classmates before you use it with children. Describe how you plan to use the puppet with children in the future.
D. If you had $200 to spend for drama equipment in setting up a new room in your first year of teaching, what would you buy and why? Itemize each purchase, and give at least three uses for each item. You may use a school supply catalog for assistance in your purchasing.

   Do this for a preschool class, a class in the kindergarten to grade 3 group, and in a class in the 4 to 5 grade range. Discuss the differences in each level and how it affected your purchases.

E. Field Work Assignment
   Observe in two early childhood rooms. Use the observation sheet found in the Online Guide. What roles did you observe children playing in dramatic activities? How do you think these roles are related to children's real-life experiences? Explain.

   Consult the teacher in each of the two rooms you observed to learn how information obtained through observing children's dramatic play is utilized (if at all) in guiding children or in making future plans. Give examples.

   In each of the rooms you observed, what limits were placed on children during dramatic play? How do you think these limits would change in an outdoor dramatic activity?

F. Make plans for bringing in new pieces of equipment and new props to help extend children's dramatic roles in each of the situations you observed. Bring them in, and then observe how children use these materials.

G. Visit an early childhood program. Interview the director, a head teacher, and a parent. Ask each how important they feel dramatic play is to their child(ren). Ask each to share their opinions about the last (or most currently produced) school program involving the child(ren). Compare the answers you received. Discuss the similarities and differences you found in these interviews.

H. Invite some children and adults to participate in creative dramatics together. See if you notice any differences in the ways they approach the activities. Adults should all have a chance to participate! You might also try this activity with students of different ages. See what you observe about their approaches.

ACTIVITIES FOR CHILDREN

PAPER CUP FINGER PUPPET

Give each child a paper cup. Explain how this cup will be their puppet's head. They can paint or use felt-tip markers to draw on the features. Yarn hair can be attached with glue. Paper ears or noses can be added. Cut two paper circles in the side of the cup to place fingers in the cup to work the puppet.

BODY/BOX PUPPET

Make a box puppet in which the child becomes the puppet. Each child will need a lightweight cardboard box (12″ × 24″ or 24″ × 30″). Often, the first body puppets may all be ponies and horses. If the children really love these puppets, you may later want to vary the construction and produce birds, airplanes, fish, or the like.

For each puppet, remove the bottom of the cardboard box. Center a hole in the top of the box. The child's torso should comfortably fit into this space. In the middle of each side, an inch or two down from the top, cut a rectangular hole. The child holds the puppet body up by the two handles. Staple the horse/pony head to the front of each body and horse tails (yarn or rope or crepe paper) to the end of each box. Have the children paint their body puppets, adding spots, saddles, blankets, manes, and faces. Once dry, the horse and pony puppets are put into action!

SHADOW PUPPETS

In this activity, children experiment with the effects that various light and puppet position have on shadows they make with their arms and hands. The children work in pairs to trace their shadows and create puppets with them.

Dim the lights and use flashlights to cast light on an open wall of chalkboard. Let the children play making hand puppets with their arms and hands on the open wall.

Working with a partner, children trace each other's shadow puppets onto oak tag or poster board with markers.

Children (or adult) cuts each traced hand shadow from the paper. Details are added to the hand shadow with crayons and markers.

Attach a craft or popsicle stick to the back of each shadow puppet with glue. Let the glue dry before using the puppet.

POP-UP PUPPETS

For this activity you will need poster board, crayons, glue, paintbrushes, scissors, markers, tempera paint, small box, craft (or popsicle) sticks.

Cut off sides of the box to make a puppet theater. Paint the box. On poster board, draw and color people and animals. Cut them out and glue each one to the top of a craft or popsicle stick.

Adult cuts slits into the bottom of the puppet theater so the puppet characters can pop up through the floor.

BALLOON PUPPETS

For this activity you will need balloons, markers, paste, pieces of yarn and trim, and masking tape.

Blow up the balloons—one for each child—or, if the children are able, let them blow up the balloons. Some children will need assistance. Tie the ends of the balloons.

Talk about how to handle the balloons so they will not break. Have extras on hand in case they do break.

Tape the balloon to the table. Use markers to make a face on the balloon. Glue yarn on top for hair. Add other pieces of fabric for clothing. Untape the balloon when finished decorating it and enjoy. Never use balloons with children ages three years and younger.

Use balloons of different shapes to create fanciful animals. Make a balloon body with other balloons taped to the head.

BOX PUPPETS

For this activity you will need small boxes (from pudding or gelatin), construction paper, paste, scissors, scrap pieces of fabric and trim, masking tape, markers, and crayons.

Give each child two small boxes. Tape the two boxes together, keeping the openings on both free. Cover the boxes with construction paper. The top box is the eye and top of the mouth. The bottom box is the bottom part of the mouth. Add bits of colored paper for eyes, a mouth, and other details. Add ears on the side of the boxes if desired. When all adhesives are dry, use and enjoy the puppet. To use the puppet, place four fingers in the top box and the thumb in the bottom box to work the mouth.

Variations: Use large boxes for big puppets. Be sure, however, that the boxes are small enough for little hands. Have fun making big tongues on the bottom box that will wag when the puppet talks. Add yarn hair that will be floppy and fun when the puppet moves.

ENVELOPE PUPPETS

For this activity you will need white envelopes, markers, scissors, and crayons.

Give each child a white envelope. Seal the envelope. Draw a face on the envelope lengthwise. Add facial details with markers and crayons. Cut off the short bottom edge of the envelope. Slip the puppet on the hand and use as a puppet.

POM-POM PUPPETS

For this activity you will need pom-poms of varying sizes and colors, popsicle or craft sticks, paste, hole punch, construction paper, scraps of fabric, yarn, and trim. Talk about the pom-poms. Discuss what kind of puppets could be made with them. Talk about colors, details, features, and so on.

Glue a large pom-pom to the stick. Glue on pieces of construction paper for features and details. Use smaller pom-poms for other details. Use a hole punch on colored construction paper. Glue on the colored circles from the hole punch, if desired. Add fabric strips to the stick for clothing. Glue on yarn for hair.

Variations: Make a group of pom-pom puppets for a group sing-a-long. Let the children choose the songs. Make animals for the song "Farmer in the Dell" and use them as you sing the song. Use cotton balls instead of pom-poms, but be aware that cotton balls are less stable decorations.

STUFFED-ANIMAL STICK PUPPETS

For this activity you will need popsicle sticks, twigs, pencils, small stuffed animals, yarn, or rubber bands.

Collect small stuffed animals. Attach a small stuffed animal to a stick or a pencil with a piece of string or rubber band. Dress the puppet with scraps of fabric and trim. Use this puppet like a stick puppet.

Variations: Attach small dolls to sticks to make puppets. Act out a fairy tale or a favorite story with the stuffed-animal stick puppets. Dress the stuffed animals with fabric, ribbon, and trim scraps.

ACTIVITIES FOR OLDER CHILDREN (GRADES 4–5)

AESTHETIC AWARENESS

Have students relate terms for movement in dance to terms that describe actual or implied motion in the visual arts. Examples include glide, dart, slide, pivot, hop, sway, and twirl. Have students create pantomimes or dances based on motions in nature such as a bird flying, a fish swimming, a leaf falling, etc. Have students invent vocal or instrumental sounds that seem to fit these motions, then orchestrate the sounds in different ways.

CREATIVE DRAMA EXERCISES

The following are some exercises to get elementary children started on creative dramatics. Refer to the guidelines presented in this chapter to help you use these activities.

- ⊙ Walk like the following: elephant, feather, grasshopper, cooked spaghetti, uncooked spaghetti, a very quiet mouse, or a very careful chicken.
- ⊙ Blow a bubble, catch it in the air, then set it down very carefully on the table.
- ⊙ Walk into the kitchen, take a jar of pickles out of the refrigerator, open the jar, and eat one. It is very sour.
- ⊙ Brush your teeth in the morning.
- ⊙ Prepare and eat ice cream with spinach on top.
- ⊙ Come into a room, look around, and hide in the closet.

- You are walking through a room when your foot gets stuck on some glue. You sit down to think and other parts of you get stuck, too.
- You are a mouse looking at some cheese on a mouse trap. Can you take if off?
- Lift something heavy, light, smelly, gooey, small, big, wiggly, or shaky.
- Tell a story without using any voice.
- Using only your face be angry, surprised, sleepy, hurt, afraid, funny, or silly or be someone who just heard a very loud noise.

NARRATIVE PANTOMIME

Explain that narrative pantomime is when someone tells a story while others use their faces and bodies to show the story. Have everyone find a personal space in the center of the room. Be sure there is room around each child so they do not bump into one another.

Give each child a card with an animal name on it. No one knows it but there are duplicates. Say "When I say 'start' everyone is to explore ways to show their animal in a variety of ways (e.g., shape, moves, size). Stay in your personal spot. At the 'freeze' signal everyone should stop. Start."

After the activity, discuss with the children their concentration, their unusual ideas, the focus, etc. Then, repeat the exercise in slow motion.

CHAPTER REVIEW

1. List the objectives of creative dramatics.
2. What are dramatic play kits? Give specific examples of some you would use in your classroom and what they would contain.
3. Discuss what you consider the early childhood teacher's role in children's dramatic play.
4. Do you feel that it is appropriate for the teacher to make special plans for children's dramatic play? Give examples in your explanation.
5. Discuss how to use puppets with young children.
6. Discuss the difference between dramatic play and creative dramatics.

REFERENCES

Allen, E., & Schwartz, I. (1992). *The exceptional child: Inclusion in early childhood education.* Clifton Park, NY: Delmar.

Gould, P., & Sullivan, J. (1999). *The inclusive early childhood classroom: Easy ways to adapt learning centers for all children.* Beltsville, MD: Gryphon House.

Monighan-Nourot, P., Scales, J., VanHoorn, J., & Almy, M. (1987). *Looking at children's play.* New York: Teachers College Press.

ADDITIONAL READINGS

Church, E. B. (2001, Oct.). Using puppets as language building partners. *Scholastic Early Childhood Today,* 45–46.

DeKroon, D., Kyte, C. S., & Johnson, C. J. (2002). Partner influences on the social pretend play of children with language impairments. *Language, Speech, and Hearing Services in Schools, 33*(4), 253–267.

Elias, C. L., & Berk, L. (2002). Self-regulation in young children: Is there a role for sociodramatic play? *Early Childhood Research Quarterly 17*(2), 216–238.

Esch, G., & Long, E. (2002). The fabulously fun finger puppet workshop. *Young Children 57*(1), 90–91.

Kolh, M. F. (1999). *Making make-believe: Fun props, costumes and creative play.* Beltsville, MD: Gryphon House.

Korat, O., Bahar, E., & Snapir, M. (2003). Sociodramatic play as an opportunity for literacy development: The teacher's role. *Reading Teacher, 56*(4), 386–393.

Mayesky, M. (2004). *Creative arts & activities: Puppets.* Clifton Park, NY: Delmar.

Texas Child Care Association (2002). Learning Centers—why and how. *Texas Child Care 25*(4), 30–42.

HELPFUL WEB SITES

Crayola, http://www.crayola.com

Sponsored by the Crayola Corporation, this site has hundreds of art activities arranged by age level as well as by theme.

ArtSeek—Internet Art Resources, http://www. artseek.com

This site is a source of over 150,000 prints and posters from the old masters to contemporary artists.

The Library-in-the-Sky—Lesson Plans, http://www. nwrel.org/

Type in "Lesson Plans" in Search Box.

Sponsored by the Northwest Regional Educational Laboratory, this site contains numerous resources for educators. Type in "lesson plans" in the search box for hundreds of lesson plans.

For additional creative activity resources, visit our Web site at http://www.EarlyChildEd. delmar.com.

Chapter 16

Creative Movement

Objectives

After studying this chapter, you should be able to:

1. Discuss the importance of creative movement activities for young children.
2. List creative movement activities that help children develop large and small muscles.
3. Discuss guidelines for providing creative movement activities for young children.
4. Discuss ways to adapt creative movement for children with special needs.

Young children learn by doing. They are immensely active and energetic. Movement activities are natural avenues for this energy.

Physical movement is the young child's first means of nonverbal communication. Closing his or her eyes, crying, shaking—a nonverbal infant very clearly communicates a need for attention! Physical movements provide one of the most important avenues through which a child forms impressions about himself or herself and his or her environment.

Anyone entering a preschool classroom cannot help but be aware of children's constant activity and movement. In fact, movement is valuable at any age to combat lethargy and spark an interest in our environment. We know that children's physical and motor development influences, and is influenced by, all other aspects of development: cognitive, language, social, and emotional. Even so, early childhood teachers too often believe that a child's motor skills will develop on their own. Therefore, they do not consciously plan for motor skill development as they do for other areas. This

chapter addresses the importance of motor skill development and provides some guidelines for adults working with young children.

Movement activities concern the whole child and not just physical fitness and recreation. Through **creative movement activities** a child is able to express his or her creative self in a very natural way.

THE IMPORTANCE OF MOVEMENT ACTIVITIES FOR YOUNG CHILDREN

To adults, the word "exercise" calls to mind ominous visions of doing calisthenics and other physically challenging actions. Yet to a child, physical exercise is one of the activities nearest and dearest to his heart.

This is because the young child is busy acquiring all sorts of large and small motor skills during the early years of life. The child's main learning strategy is through physical manipulation of his or her world. Movement activities, more than any other type of

Figure 16-1

Creative movement is movement that reflects the mood or inner state of a child.

children are free to express their own personalities in their own style. They do not have an example to follow or an adult to imitate. Creative movement can occur in any situation where children feel free and want to move their bodies. It can be done to poetry, music, rhythm, or even silence. By feeling a pulse, beat, idea, or emotion, children's bodies become instruments of expression. They are musical notes running along a keyboard or wheat waving in the wind. They are anything they want to be. Their movement is an expression of that being.

If creative movement is a regular part of the young child's curriculum, a number of objectives may be reached:

- relaxation and freedom in the use of the body
- experience in expressing space, time, and weight
- increased awareness of the world
- experience in creatively expressing feelings and ideas
- improvement of coordination and rhythmic interpretation

PLANNING CREATIVE MOVEMENT ACTIVITIES TO MEET YOUNG CHILDREN'S NEEDS

All movement activities best serve young children's needs when they address their current developmental levels. The following guidelines provide a framework to help teachers of young children be more effective in this important aspect of their work. (Appendix A presents a general measure of the *average* ages at which young children acquire physical skills.)

Guidelines for Early Childhood Teachers

When planning creative movement activities for children, teachers need to keep in mind the characteristics of each age group. Refer to Chapters 8–10 for characteristics of preschool children. Figure 16–2 summarizes the growth and development characteristics of children from kindergarten to grade 5.

As with any age group, preschoolers need to practice skills in order to learn them. Children of this age need many opportunities for practice. Several different activities should incorporate use of a particular skill, thus allowing for extended overall practice time and preventing children from getting bored. Teachers may want to prepare two or three movement activities, for example. Slight variations of an activity may be all that is necessary.

activity, offer children rich opportunities for the development of their total selves.

There is usually no planning or forethought on the part of children in creative movement. They forget about themselves and let the music's rhythm or an idea carry their bodies away. There is no pattern of movements to be practiced or perfected. Young children are free to move about in any mood the music or rhythm suggests to them.

Creative Movement

Creative movement is movement that reflects the mood or inner state of a child. In creative movement,

CHARACTERISTICS	NEEDS	TYPES OF EXPERIENCE
Kindergarten, Grades 1 and 2		
1. Spurt of growth of muscle mass	1. Vigorous exercise requiring use of large muscles	1. Running, chasing, fleeing type games; hanging, climbing, exercises
2. Gross movement skills becoming more refined	2. Exploration and variations of gross motor skills; chance to refine skills	2. Self-testing activities of all types; dance activities, movement tasks
3. Manipulative skills still unrefined but improving; will catch balls with body and arms more so than hands	3. Opportunities to manipulate large or medium-size objects; throw small balls	3. Ball-handling activities; work with beanbags, wands, hoops, progressing from large to smaller objects
4. Imaginative, imitative, curious	4. Opportunities for expression of ideas and use of body	4. Creative dance, story plays, creative stunt and floor work; exploration with all basic skills and small equipment
5. Very active, great deal of energy	5. Ample opportunities for vigorous play	5. Running, games, stunts, large apparatus like swings, jungle gym, slides
6. Short attention span	6. Activities that take short explanations and can be finished quickly	6. Simple games, simple class organization so activities can be changed quickly
7. Individualistic or egocentric	7. Experiences to learn to share or become interested in others	7. Much small group work, exploration of movement activities
Grades 3 and 4		
1. Gross motor patterns more refined and graceful	1. Use of skill for specific purposes	1. Introduce specific sport skills; expressive style skill utilized in dance; traditional dance steps
2. Hand–eye coordination improved; growth in manipulative skills	2. Opportunities to handle smaller objects; more importance placed on accuracy; throw at moving targets	2. Ball-handling activities, use of bats, paddles, target games
3. Sees need to practice skills for improvement of skill and to gain social status.	3. Guided practice sessions, self-testing problem situations	3. Drills, skill drill games, self-testing practice situations; task setting
4. Increased attention span	4. Activities with continuity; more complex rules and understandings	4. Organized games with more complex rules and strategy
5. More socially mature, interested in welfare of group	5. Make a contribution to large or small group, remain with one group for a longer period of time, help make and accept decisions with a group	5. Team activities, dance compositions with small groups
6. Greater sex differences in skills; some antagonism toward opposite sex (Gr. 4)	6. Ability grouping	6. Combative type stunts, folk dance; after-school activities, clubs

Figure 16-2

Summary chart of growth and development characteristics of children from Kindergarten to grade 5. *(Continues)*

CHARACTERISTICS	NEEDS	TYPES OF EXPERIENCE
Grade 5		
1. Coordination highly developed, keen interest in proficiency in skills	1. Need to learn more difficult skills; more coaching on refinement of skills; use of skills in games, routines and compositions	1. Lead-up games to sports in season; instruction and practice in sport skills; more advanced dance step patterns and folk dances; track and field; apparatus routines, intramurals
2. Greater sex differences in skills and interests; most prefer to play and compete with own sex	2. Separation of sexes in classes or within classes for some activities	2. Co-educational dance; swimming, gymnastics, recreational games; sexes separate in team sports and fitness activities; intramurals for each sex
3. Good skills and physique important to social acceptance	3. Instruction and practice sessions in skills, understanding of fitness elements	3. Fitness tests; developmental exercises; work with apparatus
4. Group spirit is high, allegiance to group is strong	4. Need to belong to a group with some stability; make rules, decisions, and abide by group decisions; longer term of membership on a squad or team	4. Team games, tournaments, group dance compositions, sport squads with student leaders, track and field meets
5. Social consciousness of need for rules and abiding by rules; can assume greater responsibility	5. Participate in setting rules, opportunities for squad captains or leaders	5. Student officials; plan and conduct tournaments in class and after school; students plan own strategy, line-ups, etc.
6. Flexibility decreases	6. To maintain flexibility within structural limitations	6. Stunts, tumbling, developmental exercises

Figure 16-2 (Continued)
Summary chart of growth and development characteristics of children from Kindergarten to grade 5.

Using Music and Poetry to Stimulate Creative Movement Activities

Let us now consider how music and poetry can encourage children's creative movement in the classroom.

Music. Listening to music is a natural way to introduce creative movement. Distinctive types of music or rhythm should be chosen for initial movement experiences. There are many ways and numerous books that can give teachers ideas on this topic. See the suggested additional readings at the end of this chapter for books on this topic.

In order to provide the music or rhythm for creative movement, only a few items may be necessary. A tape or CD player and some tapes or CDs, sticks, and bells may be more than enough.

Some basic concepts for the teacher to remember when using music for creative movement are as follows:

⊙ The teacher makes it clear that anything the children want to do is all right, as long as it does not harm them or others.

⊙ Children understand that they do not have to do anything anyone else does. They can do anything the music or an idea "tells" them to do.

⊙ The child is allowed to "copy" someone for a start if desired.

⊙ The children are encouraged to respect each other as different and able to move in different ways.

Figure 16-3

When planning creative movement activities for children, teachers need to keep in mind the characteristics of each age group.

Figure 16-4

One of the objectives of creative movement activities is the relaxation and freedom in the use of the body.

⊙ Encourage the children to experience freedom of movement, the relationship of movement to space, and the relationship of movement to others.

⊙ Children move in their personal space. This space can be explained by thinking of an imaginary circle or bubble around oneself.

The teacher may begin the experience by playing a CD or tape. Music that has a strong and easily recognized beat or rhythm is a good start. The children should not be told what to listen for. Let them listen first and then ask them to think about what the music is "saying" to them.

While the children are listening, the teacher may turn the music down a bit lower. The teacher might talk with each child about what the music is saying. Some of the children probably may already be moving to the music by this time, and the teacher may join in. The children may go anywhere in the room and do anything that the music "tells" them to do. For this

exercise, clapping, stomping, and even shouting are all possible and helpful. When appropriate, a quieter piece of music may be played to allow the children to rest and to give them a sense of contrast.

As children become involved in movement explorations, try to redirect, challenge, and stimulate their discoveries by suggestions such as, "Do what you are doing now in a slower way," "Try moving in a different direction or at a different level," or "Try the same thing you were doing but make it smoother or lighter."

Some creative movement activities with music can also be done with a partner. Some possibilities are the following:

◉ Face your partner and do a "mirror dance" with your hands and arms. Can you do a mirror dance with your feet and legs? How about with different facial expressions?

◉ Hold hands with your partner and slide, leap, gallop, etc., until you hear the signal; then find a new partner and continue to move to the music.

◉ Move the same way your partner moves until you hear the tambourine; then move in a different way.

◉ What interesting body shapes can you and your partner make? Can the two of you create an interesting design in the space you share? Practice until you and your partner can make three different designs to music.

This general approach can be adapted to movement with dolls and puppets; movement of specific parts of the body, such as hands, feet, or toes; and movement in different kinds of space or groups. The imaginations of the children and the teacher are the only limits.

Older children may begin to be a bit self-conscious and need other kinds of ways to encourage their creative movements. They often enjoy working in small groups for this reason. A small group activity involving mirror movements, copying, and shadowing movements is appropriate for older children. For example, working together in groups of three or more, children perform movements matching the leader of the group. The leader leads the group in a sequence of movements that the rest of the group copies as closely as possible. A second member takes over as leader, moving in a different sequence. Then, the third member leads the group in yet another sequence of movements. In this type of activity, the small group size helps students overcome the fear of the "whole class looking at me." It is also easier for children of this age to participate in a group when they know everyone else will be participating along with them in the activity. See the end of this chapter for more creative movement activities for older children.

Poetry and prose. For creative movement, poetry has rhythm as well as the power of language. It is not necessary to use rhyming verses at all times. In the beginning, poems that rhyme may help to start a feeling of pulse and rhythm. Poems should be chosen that fit

Figure 16-5

Outdoor play is another opportunity for creative movement.

Figure 16-6

Creative movement provides an opportunity for improved coordination.

the young child's level of appreciation. By adult standards, they may be quite simple. They are often short, vivid, lively descriptions of animals or motion, but children should not be limited to these, as there are many books and collections available with a wider variety. The local library is the best resource for this. The American Library Association Web site (http://www.ala.org) is another good source for poetry books.

A suggested beginning may be to ask the children to listen to a poem. After they have heard it, they may pick out their favorite characters in it. Discuss who these characters are and what they do. Read the poem a second time; suggest that the children act out their

characters as they listen to the poem. Anything goes—the children may hop like bunnies, fly like planes, or do whatever they feel. More suggestions are at the end of this chapter.

Encourage each child to move in his or her own way, and encourage as many variations as you see!

As readings continue, more complex poems may be selected, containing a series of movements or simple plots. The same general idea can also be carried through with prose.

As children become more comfortable in acting out poetry read aloud, they may become more sensitive to the less obvious actions or emotions described by the

THIS ONE'S for YOU!

More Possibilities: Suggested Movement Interpretations

The following are some suggested movement interpretations. Movement explorations and creative movement experiences can be used to interpret nearly every experience, thing, or phenomenon. This list can be expanded with endless possibilities.

1. Life cycle of butterfly
   a. caterpillar crawling
   b. caterpillar eating grass
   c. caterpillar hanging very still from branch or twig
   d. chrysalis hanging very still
   e. butterfly emerging from chrysalis
   f. butterfly drying its wings
   g. butterfly flying
2. Piece of cellophane or lightweight plastic
   a. item is put into teacher's hands without children seeing; children encouraged to guess what item might be, interpreting their guesses through movement.
   b. teacher's hands are opened, children watch plastic move, and then interpret what they see through movement.
   c. piece of plastic is used for movement exploration.
3. Shaving cream
   a. spurting from aerosol can
   b. foaming up
   c. spreading on face
   d. being used for shaving
4. Airplane sequence
   a. starting motor
   b. taking off
   c. flying

   d. arriving
   e. landing safely
5. Popcorn
   a. butter melting
   b. popping
   c. everyone ending in a ball shape on the floor, all "popped"
6. Water
   a. dripping
   b. flooding
   c. flowing in a fountain
   d. freezing
   e. melting
   f. spilling
   g. sprinkler
7. Laundry
   a. inside washing machine
   b. inside dryer
   c. being scrubbed on a washboard
   d. being pinned to clothesline
   e. drying in a breeze
8. Fishing
   a. casting out
   b. reeling in
   c. pretending to be a fish
   d. fly fishing
   e. pretending to be a hooked line
   f. frying and eating fish

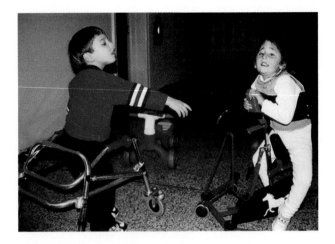

Figure 16-7
Experience in expressing space, time, and weight is one of the benefits of creative movement.

Figure 16-8
Movement activities contribute to the total physical, mental, social, and emotional growth and development of the child.

poetry. When stories or poems that have several characters and more complex interaction are read, the entire selection should first be read for listening only. Then it can be discussed to get some idea of the children's understanding and appreciation. If the children are interested, several readings may be necessary.

Older children are able to sustain their interest for a longer period of time and enjoy the procedure of listening, picking out roles, and acting out what is read. They also enjoy adding costumes and props to their creative movements.

Art and Creative Movement

Much of art is movement. Drawing, painting, and working with three-dimensional materials all involve movement. Lines and shapes are everywhere in art.

Creative movements can be planned so that they connect visual art with movement. The following are some suggestions to get you started.

Dance and art. Children can dance a painting or paint the dances they create. The kinesthetic pleasure of dance can motivate children to want to move, and this need to express themselves can extend to scribbles, drawing, painting, and modeling.

An example of how to help children connect dance with art is to show artwork with physical motion in it. (Degas' dancers are a natural choice.) Discuss how motion is shown in the work and why a particular step is "frozen" by the artist in the painting. Then let the children do the painting as a dance with movements. Then dance the painting as they think it would look before and after the artist "froze" the motions.

Creative movement and sound collages. Sounds of the body, city, nature, animals, machines, and children's names can all suggest movement. Brainstorm a category with students and then stretch it for movement possibilities. Encourage them to think of the shape, size, rhythm, energy, etc., of the words. Break into small groups and ask each group to make a collage of sounds and movements. Groups can then create a freeze-move-freeze dance and perform. This activity could be followed by a visual art collage around the same topics danced.

Dance a painting (older students). Display a print and ask students to brainstorm all the shapes, movements, and emotions they can see in it. Direct attention to the foreground, middle ground, and background of the painting in subjects such as landscapes, seascapes, and still life. Divide the children into small groups. Each group decides a way to dance the painting, using

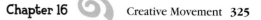

THINK ABOUT IT... Creative Movement for Transition Times

Whenever young children move from activity to activity (in transitional times), they often lose their focus and may even get a bit confused and disruptive. The following hints may help children move more easily from one activity to another.

- ◉ Pretend you are a train, with the teacher as the engine and each child a car in the train. Assign one child to be the caboose, to turn off the lights and close the door.

- ◉ Turn your jump rope into a dragon, worm, caterpillar, or other animal by attaching a head at one end of the rope and a tail at the other end. Have the children make the body and legs by holding onto the rope with one hand and walking down the hall and out to the playground.

- ◉ Imagine you are a tired puppy; yawn and stretch and roll on the floor. Then lie very still. (Suggested for the beginning of rest time.)

- ◉ Construct a "feel" box or bag or a "look" box or bag. Place an item in the bag or box that will suggest the next activity or topic for each child to feel or look at.

- ◉ To help children quiet down between activities, clap a rhythm for them to copy. Start by clapping loudly, then gradually clap more softly until your hands are resting in your lap.

- ◉ Pretend to be a bowl of gelatin and shake all over.

- ◉ Pretend to lock your lips and put the key in a pocket.

- ◉ Pretend to put on "magic" ears for listening.

- ◉ Pretend to walk in tiptoe boots, Indian moccasins, or elf shoes.

a beginning-middle-end structure. The goal is not to merely pantomime, but to stretch for ideas: What movements came *before* this moment in the art, *during, after?* What is just outside the subject matter (e.g., other people, movements)? After students prepare, take turns presenting. Background or mood music can be added.

Magic wand. Display a full-length portrait, such as a narrative scene from history with several figures in it. Let the children assume the figures' positions. When touched by a magic wand, they move in ways the figure might move. Remind the children to become conscious of how to bend and walk, the use of curved and straight lines, and positive and negative space. You can also add emotions: "Move as if you are in a hurry."

Artists that move. Set up a station with art books or assign students to locate art that includes movement (e.g., Matisse and Degas). Discuss how artists show movements through line, shape of body, and use of space.

Sculpture or architecture dances. Display pieces of sculpture or pictures of buildings or furniture. Ask about space, curves, and movements and how each might move if it came to life. Ask students to show the size, energy, and flow of these pieces with their bodies.

ADAPTING CREATIVE MOVEMENT ACTIVITIES FOR CHILDREN WITH SPECIAL NEEDS

Movement activities can be challenging for children with special needs. Because of physical disabilities, these children need encouragement to move. Large-motor activities are important for children with special needs because they help children gain in strength, endurance, and coordination. This section uses the term gross motor movements in place of creative movements.

During gross movement experiences, it is important not to do too much for children with special needs. They need the chance to figure out how to get their bodies to do what they want them to do, to problem solve, and to make choices. Whenever possible, gross motor movement should take place outside or in a large indoor area where there is ample space and children can move freely.

General Suggestions

- Follow large-muscle activities with quiet activities to help children to calm and focus on other learning experiences.
- Children will be more motivated and focused if the teacher is animated and energetic during movement activities.
- Integrate gross motor activities into the daily schedule as part of the curriculum, during transitions, and at cleanup time.
- You may need to modify your expectations for how long a child can do a gross motor activity. If the child has muscle weakness or attention problems, he or she might lack the endurance to sustain activities. Children with special needs do not need to participate in gross motor activities in the same way or as long as typically developing children. Partial participation is a valid form of involvement for some children (Sheldon, 1996). Build strength and endurance from the child's current level of skill.
- Encourage parents to send children to school in sneakers so that they can participate fully in gross motor activities.

Developmental Delays

Many children with special needs have low muscle tone and poor strength. Because of this, movement is difficult, so the child often doesn't move. This results in increased muscle weakness. It is important that the child is encouraged to have an active lifestyle in school and at home.

- Use exercise videos or tapes with a child who is developmentally delayed. In these videos the same movement and exercises are repeated, which gives the child an opportunity to practice and enables him or her to feel confident in his or her ability to keep up with the class.
- Encourage the child to participate in gross motor activities for gradually longer periods.
- Always demonstrate the activity first.
- Allow children to watch a role model engage in the activity before attempting it themselves.

- Familiarize yourself with gross motor developmental sequences. If the child's gross motor skills are at the two- or three-year level, she may be reluctant or unable to participate in gross motor activities that have been designed for typically developing four-year-old children.

Physical Impairments

Space in the room may be a problem if you have a child in the group who is physically impaired. The child might bring lots of equipment to school, such as a prone stander, a chair of some sort, and a wheelchair. Some children might have walkers or crutches. This child will also need space to maneuver between furniture.

- During movement activities in the classroom, it is fine to assist the child, but slow movements are best. Quick movements might increase muscle tightness.
- Avoid always giving the child physical assistance to move, and encourage the child to do what he or she can to move independently.
- The child with physical impairments who is walking may be able to do whatever the other children are doing but for a shorter time or shorter distance.
- Occasionally, the child with physical disabilities can play the role of "time keeper" or "music director" by turning the music on and off during a musical activity, but this should not be the child's only role. It is important that the child also be part of the movement activity.

Attention Deficit/Hyperactivity Disorder and Behavioral Issues

Movement activities can be calming for children with hyperactivity and behavioral difficulties but can on occasion be overstimulating and disorganizing. The large motor activities need to be structured with clear rules and expectations. Observe if the child is becoming overstimulated and redirect him or her to an activity where he or she can become calm and regroup (Gould & Sullivan, 1999).

- Teach children how to act in gross motor activities. Children need to be taught that there is no pushing, indoor voices should be used, and equipment must be shared on occasion. Instruction in these skills will have to be given frequently until the child has mastered them and can remember them even in the excitement of the activity.

- Notice and give praise when the child is following the rules during gross motor play (Rief, 1993).

- Some children who have ADHD are highly sensitive to being touched and may perceive an innocent bump from another child as being a push. To avoid this, make sure that the child has enough space in movement activities. Define the child's personal space during movement activities with hula hoops or rug squares.

- Make sure you have eye contact when giving instructions.

- Structure gross motor activities to eliminate waiting.

- Keep activities short. A child may be able to stick with ball activities for a few moments and then need to move on to some other kind of activity.

- If you aren't offering a choice, give clear directions rather than posing a question. Don't say, "Do you want to walk on the balance beam?" if you mean, "Walk on the balance beam" (Cook, Tessier, & Klein, 1992).

Visual Impairments

Studies have shown that children with visual impairments tend to have poor levels of physical fitness (Warren, 1994). These children will need lots of encouragement to move independently. When giving directions to the child who is visually impaired, be very clear and avoid vague words such as *this, that,* and *over there* (Mayfield, McCormick, & Cook, 1996). Be careful not to encourage anxieties by being overprotective of the child with visual impairments.

- Describe the movement experience or play equipment before involving the child. Let the child explore the equipment with his or her hands before attempting to use it.

- When giving directions to the child with visual impairments, use the child's name to get his or her attention and give him or her additional time to process directions and respond (Cook, Tessier, & Klein, 1992). Tell the child what will be happening next, especially before physically assisting him or her through a movement experience. Instead of just naming objects, describe them for the child (Mayfield, McCormick, & Cook, 1996).

SUMMARY

Young children learn by doing, and movement activities are a natural avenue for children's learning. Movement activities contribute to the total development—physical, mental, social, and emotional—of young children. Movement activity is as vital for children as are art and math, for in movement activities young children acquire skills, knowledge, and attitudes that help them discover and understand their body and their physical abilities and limitations.

Creative movement reflects the mood or inner state of an individual. Creative movement usually requires no planning or forethought on the part of children. They can forget about themselves and let the music's rhythm or an idea carry their bodies away. There is no exact pattern of movements to be practiced or perfected.

In planning creative movement activities for young children, the developmental level of each child is the starting point. The information provided in developmental skill charts (such as Appendix A) for young children can be used to get some idea of what to expect of children physically at different ages. Yet, the most important thing to remember is that the individual *child* is the measure, not any chart of developmental skills.

Poetry and music can be used to encourage children's creative movements. Listening to music is a natural way to introduce creative movement. Distinctive types of music with clear rhythmic patterns should be used for the initial creative movement experiences. Poetry also has rhythm as well as the power of language. Poems that rhyme are good to begin with, as they help children get the feel, pulse, and rhythm of the words. (There are rhythm poems at the end of this chapter, as well as in Chapter 18.) Fingerplays also provide many opportunities for creative movement activities. Whether movement activities occur with music, poetry, ropes, or hoops, they benefit young children by developing their relaxation, freedom of expression, and increased awareness of their own bodies.

Connections can be made between movement activities and art. Movement activities can be adapted for children with special needs.

KEY TERMS

creative movement
creative movement activities

LEARNING ACTIVITIES

A. Choose one of the action poems at the end of this unit. Use it to conduct a creative movement activity with a group of young children (or a group of your fellow classmates). Critique your experience. Cover these points:
1. Was the poem appropriate for the group? Why or why not?
2. What did you do (specifically) that worked well with the group?
3. What did not work and why?
4. How would you change your activity for future use? Be specific in your reply.

B. Observe a group of children involved in movement activities of any kind. Record evidence of each of the following situations:
1. A child discovers a new way to move.
2. A child uses small and/or large muscles in the activity.
3. A child discovers what other children are like as a result of the activity.

C. At the end of a long lesson (with children or your own classmates) try this movement activity to help you understand the importance of movement activity at all ages.

Toss around a small, soft ball for a few minutes, using these rules: You must be sitting in your seat, you cannot "whip" the ball at someone, and you may not throw it to someone who chooses not to play. The object is to see how many times you can catch the ball consecutively. This requires cooperation and encouragement. Everyone is given the chance to play, even if they aren't the world's best catchers. Encouraging one another leads to a higher count. See how high you can go with this one!

In the classroom, you can change the rule to correspond to your current lessons. For example, every student who catches the ball must name an adverb in language arts class, solve a problem in math, explain a date in history, or define a term in science. The purpose of movement is to wake up and revitalize students for their next learning experience.

D. Choose one of the movement interpretations in the "This One's for You" box. Act it out alone or with your fellow students. Then have a group of children act out the same movement. Describe the differences in their movements and your own (or fellow students'). What were the greatest differences? Try the same interpretive movement with different age groups of children and compare the results.

ACTIVITIES FOR CHILDREN

SHAPE AND MOVEMENT GAME

Cut out various shapes from construction paper. Have the children scattered around the room. When you hold up a triangle, they can only move their heads. When you hold up a circle, they move only legs. For a square, they move only shoulders. For a rectangle, they move only hips. For an oval, they move their entire bodies. Change shapes rapidly. Encourage children to be creative in their movements. Play music during this activity and it's even more fun.

SHOW ME MOVEMENTS

The children should be scattered around the room with adequate room between each child. Call out challenges such as the following:

Show me how small you can be (also how tall, wide, tall, thin, etc.)
Point to the farthest wall; touch it and return to your own place.
Point to the nearest wall; touch it and return to your own place.
Standing in your own place, make your feet move fast; slowly.
Show me how slowly you can walk.
Show me how fast you can walk.
Be a tree; wall; ball; river.

Guide the children toward looking at objects in the room and noticing where they are located. Have the children close their eyes and point to objects in the room that you call out (e.g., the door, chalkboard, window, wastebasket, floor, ceiling, playhouse area, wagons, teacher's desk, etc.).

SHADOW MOVEMENT ACTIVITIES

On a bright sunny day, go outside for a "shadow hunt." Encourage children to look for shadows made by your school building, playground equipment, bushes, and their own bodies. Talk about how large shadows, such as those from trees, make the cool, shady areas people enjoy on hot days.

On the inside, play a shadow game. Start by playing a cassette or CD. As the music plays, children dance or move in any way they choose, trying to avoid stepping on one another's shadows or letting shadows "step on" them.

Encourage children to watch the patterns their shadows make as they move. After a short time, stop the music and say, "Freeze." Children then stop moving and hold their positions until the music starts again. After you do this a few times, have a child operate the player. Let children take turns being in charge of the music.

For younger children, place a ball on the pavement of your outdoor play space on a sunny day. Invite children to take turns jumping on and off the shadow of the ball.

For older children, after trying their own creative movements, ask children to move in specific ways as they try to avoid one another's shadows. For example, ask children to move like mice approaching a piece of cheese, monkeys jumping from tree to tree, or lively kittens running after a ball of yarn.

Variation: Change the game to number freeze. Call out a set of numbers. Tell children that they need to freeze when they hear the number seven. Continue the game by encouraging children to freeze as you call out other specified numbers.

RUNNING MOVEMENTS

Before starting this activity, go outdoors and make a mental note of landmarks such as trees, the end of a sidewalk, a large bush—anything that can serve as a marker for a running path. Make sure that there are no sharp edges or items children might run into.

Take your group outside and gather together at a short distance from one of the markers you spotted earlier. Explain that you are going to make a running path together. Say, "Let's mark our path with these streamers. Come help me tie these markers on."

Together, walk around and tie a different color streamer onto each of the markers you've chosen. Then, step back and say, "Hey, let's all run over to that tree with the blue streamer. Come on and run with me!"

Let your enthusiasm and delight fill the mood of the activity as you encourage children to participate.

Catch your breath and call out, "Come on, let's run to the yellow streamer!"

Later, hand out streamers for children to carry as they run. Partners can share ends, and you can call out various ways to move—like a duck, like a robin, like a bear, etc.—as they run around the play space.

The fun in this activity is laughing and being silly together. In no way is this a race or a contest to see who can go the farthest or fastest.

"BECOME" ONE OF THE FOLLOWING

Let the children act out the features/characteristics of a bicycle, rake, hose, wheelbarrow, tire pump, beach ball, or any other familiar play objects the children come up with.

STOP AND GO

Children walk around doing whatever they want to with their arms and bodies. When the teacher says "stop," the children "freeze" and hold that position until the teacher says "go." Encourage children's movements of all kinds.

JUMP OVER THE RIVER

Two long sticks can serve as the banks of the river. Children jump from one bank to the other. The sticks can be moved further apart at times to make a wider river. Children can find ways to get from one side of the river to the other, like sliding, crawling, rolling, etc. Encourage any and all creative attempts to "cross."

LINE CHALLENGES

Use a tape or chalk to make a line on the floor and encourage the children to see how many things they can do: jump over the line, walk on the line, hop along the line, stand on the end of the line, stretch out on the line, slide on the line, tiptoe across the line, roll over the line, lie beside the line, run around the line, or skip round and round the line. Then have the children make up their own challenges.

JET PLANES

Encourage the children to use creative movements in becoming a jet plane. Pretend you are a jet plane. Use your body to show the jet: on the ground, in the air, climbing up into the clouds, nose diving, coming in for a landing, on the ground again. Take off again. This time, your jet is a stunt plane. It can write in the sky. It can make loops and turn upside-down. Now make a number 2. Make a 3. Now make a 5. Can you make an S? How about a P? Make the shape of a funny animal. How about a wiggly worm?

CAN YOU BE?

Ask the children to pretend their body is a huge tree. Show the tree in a big windstorm; losing its leaves in autumn; loaded with snow after a blizzard; in the summer when the sun is so hot.

CLASSICAL MUSIC AND MOVEMENT

Selected sections of the music of Saint-Saëns' *Carnival of the Animals* are excellent for encouraging the acting-out of various animal movements. The movements can include crawling, walking on all fours, jumping, and flying. Tell the children the title of the music and play it for them to enjoy. Encourage them to move their bodies like they think the animal in the music would be moving.

Another piece of music that is good for creative movements is Tschaikovsky's "Dance of the Little Swans" from *Swan Lake*. It's a natural for some fun tip-toeing!

For marching experiences, use Herbert's "March of the Toys" from *Babes in Toyland* or Grieg's "Norwegian Rustic March" from *Lyric Suite*.

For running movements, try Bizet's "The Ball" from *Children's Games*. Bizet's *Children's Games* also has a section entitled "Leap Frog," which is great for creative jumping movements. In the same composition, Bizet's "Cradle Song" encourages swaying and rocking movements. "The Swan" by Saint-Saens from *Carnival of the Animals* is also good for swaying and rocking movements.

Prokofiev's "Waltz on Ice" from *Children's Suite*, Tschaikovsky's "Waltz" from *The Sleeping Beauty*, and Khachaturian's "Waltz" from *Masquerade Suite* are all excellent pieces of music for waltzing and smooth gliding creative movements.

ROPE SKILLS

Lay out various lengths of rope in a straight line on the floor as if it were a tightrope. Challenge the children to try some of these skills. Can you do this while moving backward? Walk the "tightrope" with eyes shut. Jump from side to side across the rope without touching the rope. Hop from side to side without touching the rope. Lay your rope in the pattern of a circle. Get inside the circle, taking up as much space as possible, without hanging over the edges. Make up a design on your own. See if you can walk it. Can your friend? Can you walk your friend's design?

I CAN

Here is an action poem that leads to a lot of fun and movement.

Like a bunny I can hop
I can spin like a top.
I can reach way up high
And I almost touch the sky.
In a boat I row and row
Sometimes fast and sometimes slow.
Now a bouncing jumping jack
I pop up and then go back.
Then sway gently in the breeze
Like the little forest trees.
Make silly faces like a clown
And then I quietly settle down.

UNWINDING

Children pretend they are windup toys, such as dolls, dogs, monkeys, rabbits, or clowns. The teacher winds up the toys and the children begin moving at a brisk pace, getting slower and slower until they are completely "run down" and stop or collapse to the floor. The teacher or a child rewinds the toys and the sequence is repeated.

COLLAPSING

The teacher explains that "collapsing" means relaxing a body part or the whole body, allowing gravity to pull it down to earth. Children stand and stretch tall, then slowly collapse (relax) one part at a time, first the fingertips, then the wrists, elbows, arms, head and shoulders, and so on, until they are left collapsed on the floor.

RHYTHM POEMS

Repeat these as many times as needed, allowing the children to supply their own actions.
Little Birds

All the little birds
All asleep in their nest;
All the little birds
Are taking a rest.
They do not even twitter;
They do not even tweet.
Everything is quiet
All up and down the street.
Then came the mother bird
And tapped them on the head.

They opened up one little eye,
And this is what was said:
"Come, little birdies; it's time to learn to fly.
Come, little birdies; fly way up to the sky."
Fly, fly, oh, fly away, fly, fly, fly.
Fly, fly, oh, fly away, fly away so high.
Fly, fly, oh, fly away, birds can fly the best.
Fly, fly, oh, fly away—now fly back to your nest.

Flower Seeds

All the little flower seeds sleep in the ground,
Warm and snuggly and tucked in all around,
Sleeping, oh, so soundly the long winter through.
There really wasn't very much else for them to do.
There really wasn't very much else for them to do.
(Repeat preceding five lines.)
Now their eyes they opened and they peeked all
around.
And started to grow right up through the ground.
They grew so very slowly, but they grew straight
and tall.
And their leaves they unfolded and waved at us all.
And their leaves they unfolded and waved at us all.
Then the sun shone down and made the flower
smile.
And they swayed and swayed in the breeze for
awhile.
Until a big wind came and blew them all away.
And there were no more flowers that day.
And there were no more flowers that day.
Blow, blow, blow away, flowers. Blow, blow
away.

Worms Are Crawling

Worms are crawling, crawling, crawling.
Worms are crawling, crawling, all around
or:
Making tunnels in and out of the ground.
Wiggly, wiggly worms are squirming all around
Wiggly, squiggly, swiggly worms
Crawl in and out of the ground.
(This can be sung to "The Farmer in the Dell"
tune.)

Bobby Snake

Oh, Bobby Snake is crawling, crawling, crawling.
Oh, Bobby Snake is crawling, crawling right to
meeeee.
(Substitute the name of the child for meeeee)
Wiggly, wiggly, wiggly snake
Is crawling, crawling all around.
Slithery, slippery, flippery snake
Is crawling, crawling on the ground.

Turtle

(Tune: "Twinkle, Twinkle, Little Star")
Tur-tle, tur-tle, where are you?
Oh, you are so slow, slow, slow.

First one hand and then the other,
That's what makes you go, go, go.
Hide your winky little head,
And you cannot see, see, see.
Tur-tle, tur-tle, peek-a-boo!
Peek-a-boo at me, me, me.
(Repeat third and fourth lines.)

I Wiggle My Fingers

I can wiggle my fingers, I can wiggle my toes.
I can wiggle my shoulders, and I can wiggle my
nose.
Now no more wiggles are left for me.
So I will be as still as can be.

RELAXING EXERCISES

1. Pull back your shoulders, bend elbows and place
   Your fingers on shoulders, like chicken wings laced.
   Elbows outstretched, swing right one to front,
   As left one goes backwards, keep swinging
   and jump:
   And-a-one, and-a-two, and-a-three, and-a-four,
   And-a-five, and-a-six, and-a-now no more.
   Slump and relax, breathe deep and exhale,
   Now you are ready for the next thing in store.

2. Bring your head down to your knees,
   Let your arms swing freely, please.
   Swinging, swinging, back and forth,
   Arms lead upward—soaring forth,
   Upward, upward, toward the sky,
   Drawing head and body up high,
   Open hands and feel the rain,
   Now relax—Let's do it again. (Repeat)
   (Say same verse again.)
   That's the end.

3. Pick out a place and kneel right down,
   Close now your eyelids and without a frown,
   Let your head start to sway,
   Let it sway, where it may,
   Let it sway, let it sway,
   Let it sway many ways.
   Now open your eyes,
   And while you look around
   Rise to your feet,
   Moving head, shoulders, arms,
   And dance through the room
   Till the gong ends the charm.

4. Move around as soft as fluff,

    Till you hear the word, "Enough."

    Now move around as hard as nails,

    Firm as steel your body feels.

    Once again so soft and light,

    You move quite like a feather white.

Now stretch yourself like bands of rubber

Tight and strained, walk to another.

Now let go, relax and feel

All floppy, flopping, not quite real—

Maybe you're a Raggedy Ann,

Or, a Raggedy Andy walking man.

ACTIVITIES FOR OLDER CHILDREN (GRADES 4-5)

MOVEMENT, LINE, AND SHAPE

Artists use lines and shapes to send "wordless" messages or feelings to people. Present the students prints of several artists' work that exemplify such use of lines and shapes. Good examples for this would be works of Mondrian (for squares and rectangles), Georgia O'Keefe (for curvy, round shapes), and Salvador Dali (for clear lines of various shapes). Using the work of one or more of these (or other artists), the teacher asks the students to pick out some shapes from these works and convert themselves into the geometric figures used by the artists.

To make body sculptures, the teacher divides the class into small groups and asks them to pick a geometric shape in the artist's work and to make that shape with their bodies. Give them some rehearsal time. Children use their bodies to create the shape they see in the artist's work. Six children, for example, would be used to form a rectangle. They could do so by lying on the floor and connecting limbs so that four form the top and bottom and two form the sides. Larger versions of the shapes can be created by using more children to form each body sculpture. The groups show their body shape sculpture to the rest of the class and viewers identify the shape they see.

To build on this activity, divide the class into two groups. Each group is asked to prepare a body sculpture in which several shapes are linked. One for example, might have a triangle, a circle, and a square linked by connecting body parts. The other group has to identify the shapes present in the sculpture.

A further challenge would be to invite the children to invent new shapes and demonstrate them for the larger group. Together, have them come up with creative titles for their original inventions.

CLASSICAL MUSIC AND CREATIVE ACTIVITIES

Play Stravinsky's ballet *Firebird*. Discuss the story of King Kastchei, the Firebird, the Prince, and the Princess. The children might enjoy making masks for the hideous ogres found in the "Infernal Dance of King Kastchei." Students could act out the parts in the story, as well as narrate what happens in the ballet. Other students can be chosen to be either "low," "medium," or "high" creeping demons according to the dynamics of the music. When the theme isn't playing, the monsters can "freeze" until the theme comes back again. The children can make a class project of the performance with costumes and masks.

CREATIVE MOVEMENTS

Have the children use their bodies for the following activities:

⊙ Explore possible movements of body parts (i.e., bend, stretch, twist, turn, push, pull, swing, sway).

⊙ With a partner, facing each other, one moves and the other mirrors the movements. Move a body part. Keep that part moving as you transfer the movement to another part.

⊙ Working with a partner, do the same movement your partner does. Now do the same movement with another body part.

⊙ Create a dance with your partner using two different movements suggested by each person.

⊙ Begin a movement in one body part and gradually move the movement to adjoining body parts so that the movement begins with one body part and moves to others. Try moving in different ways.

⊙ Create a dance in which the movement flows from one dancer to another.

⊙ Explore moving different body parts in unison.

⊙ Move body parts in opposition.

⊙ Combine a movement. Create a dance combining unison (or opposition) movements of different body parts.

⊙ Put a piece of elastic around two body parts. Initiate a movement with one and have the attached part move with it.

- Initiate another movement and have the attached part resist the movement.
- Combine two or three movements initiated by the attached body parts moving in sequence or in resistance to the movement.
- Working with a partner, attach a piece of yarn loosely to a body part (not around your neck) and

to the same body part of your partner. One begins the movement with the attached body part following the movement. Try moving in different ways.
- Create a dance with each person initiating a movement in turn, which is followed by the attached body part of the partner.

CHAPTER REVIEW

1. List four points that teachers should remember when planning and carrying out creative movement activities for young children.
2. List some objectives of creative movement. On your list, indicate some activities you would use to accomplish each of these objectives.
3. How would you select music and poetry and fingerplays to use with young children in creative movement activities? What would be your criteria?
4. How would you use poetry or prose in creative movement activities?
5. Discuss how you can adapt movement activities for children with special needs.

REFERENCES

Cook, R. E., Tessier, A., & Klein, D. M. (1992). *Adapting early childhood curriculum for children with special needs*. (3rd ed.) New York: Merrill.

Gould, P., & Sullivan, J. (1999). *The inclusive early childhood classroom: Easy ways to adapt learning centers for all children*. Beltsville, MD: Gryphon House.

Mayfield, P., McCormick, K., & Cook, M. (1996). Adaptations for young children with visual impairments in regular settings. *Early Childhood Education Journal 23*(4): 231–233.

Rief, S. (1993). *How to reach and teach ADD/ADHD children*. West Nyack, NY: The Center for Applied Research in Education.

Sheldon, K. (1996). Can I play too? Adapting common classroom activities for young children with limited motor abilities. *Early Childhood Education Journal 24*(2), 115–120.

Warren, D. (1994). *Blindness and children*. Cambridge: Cambridge University Press.

ADDITIONAL READINGS

Carpenter, J. (2003). *Mix, match, and motivate: 108 activities for skills and fitness*. Champaign, IL: Human Kinetics.

Faurot, K. (2003). *Books in bloom: Creative patterns and props that bring stories to life*. Chicago: American Library Association.

Kogan, S. (2003). *Step by step: A complete movement education curriculum*. Champaign, IL: Human Kinetics.

Mueller, A. K. (2002, Dec.). Music and movement make natural partners. *Teaching Music, 56*–59.

Pangrazi, R. P. (2003). *Dynamic physical education for elementary school children*. Upper Saddle River, NJ: Benjamin-Cummings.

Pica, R. (2004). *Experiences in movement with music and activities: Birth to age 8*. Clifton Park, NY: Delmar.

Pica, R. (2003). *Your active child: How to boost physical, emotional and cognitive development through age-appropriate activities*. New York: McGraw-Hill.

Pica, R. (2003). *Teachable transitions: 190 activities to move from morning circle to the end of the day*. Beltsville, MD: Gryphon House.

Sanders, S. (2000). *Active for life: Developmentally appropriate movement programs for young children*. Washington, DC: NAEYC.

Shannon, G. (2000). *Frog legs: A picture book of action verse*. New York: Greenwillow.

Sherrill, C. (2003). *Adapted physical activity.* New York: McGraw-Hill.

Smith, K. L. (2002). Dancing in the forest: Narrative writing through dance. *Young Children* *57*(2), 90–94.

Torbeth, M., & Schneider, L. (2001). *Follow me too: A handbook of movement activities for three-to-five year olds.* Reading, MA: Addison-Wesley.

Weikart, P. S. (2003). *Round the cloth: Key experiences in movement for young children.* Ypsilanti, MI: High/Scope.

HELPFUL WEB SITES

Yahoo Home: Arts: Education, http://dir.yahoo. com/Arts/Education/K_12

Yahoo search directory containing a list of sites with K–12 art activities. Categories include curriculum standards, drama, and lesson plans.

Teaching Tips, http://www.teachingheart.net/ ultimate.html

This site includes free printables, lessons, lists of books, resources, and creative activity ideas.

For additional creative activity resources, visit our Web site at http://www.EarlyChildEd. delmar.com.

Chapter 17

Creative Music

Objectives

After studying this chapter, you should be able to:

1. Outline some basic goals for music activities for young children.
2. List guidelines for planning music activities for young children.

Lisa sang to herself in a sing-song way while drawing with crayons: "One purple, two purple, three purple, four purple." Next to her, William was humming the jingle for a fast-food restaurant advertisement and keeping rhythm with his coloring strokes.

Out on the playground, Drew chanted, "I-am-going-to-be-a-lawn-mo-wer." And as he slid down the slide, he made a sound like a lawn mower. Picking up his cue, Claire and Christy slid down after him, each on their stomach making motor-growling sounds.

Musical experiences like these are a common occurrence in a young child's life. Making up original chants and songs and moving rhythmically to musical beats are quite natural to a young child, for whom music is a favorite avenue for creative expression. In contrast, an adult finds it more difficult to be as spontaneous as children in the inclusion of music in everyday life. Consider how your peers would react to your chanting as you read this paragraph, "One paragraph, two paragraph, three to go—yeah, yeah, yeah." Unlike William's humming in our opening scenario, your musical monologue probably would not go unnoticed by your peers as they hummed to themselves!

This is the challenge in early childhood education—overcoming an "adult" approach to music so you can share musical experiences with young children in a way that preserves and encourages their innate spontaneous and open attitude. You are challenged in this chapter to put aside any self-consciousness and fears about your own musical talents and to try returning to the openness of a young child experiencing music. You don't need to know how to play a musical instrument or even be able to read music to plan and conduct creative music experiences for children.

If you feel shy about singing, you're not alone. We don't sing as much as we used to in this country because of the television and recording industries. We have gotten used to passively watching performers rather than making our own music and dances. Yet music is created so naturally and easily every day in many forms—by voice, by instruments, even by nature in the rhythm of the rain or the sound of a waterfall. Children are introduced very early to music through radio and television. Music sends commercial messages for everything from cars to breakfast food. Shoppers shop to piped-in classical music, meant to ease frazzled nerves and encourage purchasing. Sitting in a dentist's chair, the patient is treated to music designed to calm; soothe; and even more important, distract attention from the event at hand!

The child's world, too, is filled with music—even toys make musical sounds. Infants' windup musical teddy bears, crib mobiles, and go-to-sleep lullabies are just a few examples of early introductions to music. Young children respond quite naturally to music by rhythmic movement, and they also create their own

AGE	BEHAVIORAL CHARACTERISTICS	MUSIC EXPERIENCES
Newborn to 1 month	Responds to stimuli by moving entire body.	Quiet singing and rocking soothe the baby. Scary sounds avoided. Sound stimuli important.
1 to 4 months	Changes from hearing to listening. Turns head toward stimulus. Follows moving objects with eyes.	Same as for newborn.
4 to 8 months	Involved in purposeful activity. Reproduces interesting events. Develops hand–eye coordination.	Hits suspended bells again and again to reproduce the sound.
8 to 12 months	Anticipates events, shows intention. Knows that objects have functions. Imitates actions.	Hits drum or xylophone with stick. Claps hands to music. Hits instrument to produce a sound. Understands purpose of instrument.
12 to 18 months	Invents new actions. Uses trial and error to solve problems.	Experiments by hitting instrument in different ways with different objects.
18 to 24 months	Creates new actions through prior thought. Imitates actions after person leaves.	Continues music activity after adult stops. Listens to radio, dances to it.
2 years	Steps in place. Pats. Runs. Increases language. Has limited attention span. Attends to spoken words a few at a time. Develops independence, is very curious. Tendency to tire easily.	Enjoys action songs and moving to music. Can learn short, simple songs. Enjoys activities with short, simple directions. Many opportunities to experiment with instruments and sound. Likes record player because he can watch it turn. Opportunity for frequent rest breaks in strenuous rhythmic experiences. Avoid prolonged activities.
3 years	Jumps, runs, and walks to music. Has self-control. Attentive, has longer attention span. Uses more words. Compares two objects. Participates in planning. Initiative emerges.	Special music for special movements. Can wait for a turn. Longer songs or small group experiences can be planned. Experiments with sound comparisons. Suggests words for songs or additional activities. Can recognize several melodies and may have several favorites. Choices important along with an opportunity to try out own ideas.

Figure 17-1

Developmental characteristics and music experiences.

(Continues)

AGE	BEHAVIORAL CHARACTERISTICS	MUSIC EXPERIENCES
4 years	Has better motor control. Interested in rules. Plans ahead with adults. Likes to imagine.	May begin skipping. Rule songs and games appropriate. Can make suggestions for music activities. Adds words to songs. Creates songs on instruments. Makes dramatic movements. Likes to experiment with the piano. Likes to play records over and over. Can identify simple melodies.
5 to 6 years	Has good motor control. Likes to have rules. Vision not yet fully developed; eye movements slow; likely to have trouble seeing small print or making fine linear distinctions when music staff is not enlarged. Heart in stage of rapid growth.	Able to sit longer. Enjoys songs and dances with rules. Can follow specific rhythm patterns. May pick out tunes on the piano. Likes musical movies but may become restless. Strenuous activity periods should be brief.
7 to 8 years	Begins to read written symbols. Concerned with rules. Cooperation and competition. Logical thought processes emerge. Can compare more than two objects after first object removed (seriation). Thoroughly enjoys group play, but groups tend to be small. Boys and girls play together.	May be able to read words to songs. Rule dances and songs especially valued. Better able to tell reality from fantasy. Can compare three or more sounds or pitches. Likes duets and doing anything musical with a friend. May want to take piano or dancing lessons. Likes group activities including singing games, playing informal instruments, phrase games.
9 to 11 years	Has more developed language arts skills. Understands rules and strategies of games. Peer group assumes greater importance. Logical thought processes are present. Has more flexible thought. Enjoys play with peer group. Boys and girls prefer same-sex play. Begins to see other's opinions and ideas as unique.	Can read words to songs, can create original lyrics. Enjoys dances with varied steps and patterns. Begins to enjoy small group singing experiences, such as duets, trios, chorale. Can compare sounds, pitch, rhythms in music. Can understand elements of music such as tone, basic notations, styles, and forms of music. Introduce harmony and part singing for small groups. Provide duet singing experiences, all boy, all girl singing groups. Enjoys multicultural music and dance.

Figure 17-1 (Continued)
Developmental characteristics and music experiences.

musical patterns in original chants and songs as well as in unaccompanied rhythmic movements such as swinging, tapping, and even rocking in a chair. Activities that make up the natural beginnings of musical learning right in the home can be extended by the early childhood teacher to classroom music activities.

In an early childhood program, music of all kinds is appropriate. For example, the sounds of a slow Duke Ellington tune and a fast rhythmic portion of Stravinsky's *Rite of Spring* are equally appropriate for young children. Background music in the early childhood classroom can be as soft and soothing as Schubert's *Cradle Song* or Brahm's *Lullaby*. For a change of pace, and a more lively mood, classics such as *Tambourine* by Gretry or Bach's *Badinerie* can be used. Good music of all types has a place in all early childhood programs.

The valuable place of music in the early childhood classroom is obvious in the following special education teacher's journal entry.

I hurry into the school to get to my assigned first grade classroom. The children love, music, and I look forward to working with them. I crash nose-to-nose with a teaching assistant who works with the youngest children in the school district who have severe behavioral disabilities–the children in my assigned class. Many of them come to school with concerns that would make most of us stagger.

This is a particularly difficult Monday. The assistant quickly summarizes the turmoil. George has had a horrible weekend at home. Alexis has not taken her medication. Justin has spent the weekend away from the consistency of home with Mom and is in a spin as a result. Perhaps, I think, I can find a way to help.

In the classroom I find the teacher sitting in the rocking chair humming, rocking, and holding a child. Two other children are listening through headsets to Baroque music. Soft music comes from the CD player on the shelf. The music's power of relaxation fills the room. The teacher has found solutions on her own. It had been an overwhelming 90-minute beginning to the day, but now, with understanding and change of mood, the atmosphere is calm. The music speaks to the children's emotions. They can now leave their homeroom, go to their inclusive environments, and learn and play with their friends. Music has met the children's need for peace. It has elicited a sense of calm in all of them (Humpal & Wolf, p. 104, 2003).

As with other areas of the curriculum, **appropriate music activities** can be planned only if the teacher understands the developmental levels of the children involved. Although individual rates of development vary widely, the sequence of development follows a particular pattern. Figure 17–1 shows some important behavioral characteristics for each stage of development, along with their effect on a child's experiences with music. This material is based on the theories of Piaget (Wadsworth, 1979) and Erickson (1963) and the writings of Todd and Heffernan (1977). Figure 17–1 may be used as a guide for choosing from the musical activities for children listed at the end of this chapter.

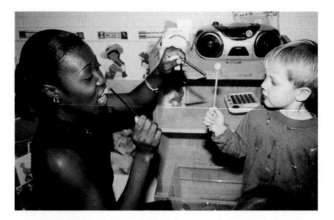

Figure 17-2

The challenge in early childhood education is to overcome an "adult" approach to music so you can joyfully share music with young children.

GOALS FOR YOUNG CHILDREN'S MUSIC EXPERIENCES

Music is a common and enjoyable occurrence in a young child's life. One of the main goals of musical activities for young children is to maintain this natural appreciation of musical experiences. Focusing and then building on this natural enjoyment of music will help you produce the most successful and joyous music program for young children. As in all early childhood activities, it is the *process* that teaches and enriches a young child and not the finished *product*.

Other goals of the early childhood music program include the following:

- numerous opportunities to sing a wide variety of songs
- frequent exposure to various forms of music with wide ranges of rhythms, tempos, and moods
- opportunities to hear and learn about music from different cultures and ethnic groups
- endless opportunities to express feelings and emotions in song, rhythm, and movement
- experience in playing simple instruments, moving to rhythms, and expressing emotions in motion during musical activities
- learning to identify some basic musical concepts and terms, such as loud and soft, fast and slow, and high and low

For older children, these goals also include the following:

- to have opportunities to sing in parts, in rounds, and in harmony

HOW TO PRESENT A SONG TO CHILDREN

The method you choose to present a song to children will depend on the mood and the nature of the song itself.

1. **Phrase-wise method.** Introduce the song with a brief story, discussion, or question. Sing one phrase and ask children to repeat. Then sing two phrases and so on.
2. **Whole-song method.** Present the whole song in a variety of ways, rhythmic moving, dancing, playing instruments, or dramatizing to make repetition interesting and meaningful.
3. **Combination of phrase-wise and whole-song method.** The teacher sings and presents the whole song, but asks the children to respond to the easiest part of it—with voices, hands, or an instrument.
4. **Teaching songs from recordings.** The whole-song method is used, responding to the music rhythmically, dramatically, and with instruments. The teacher can use his own voice to clarify the words after several playings.

   The songs in the "Activities for Children" section of this chapter are good choices for presenting songs to young children. You may, of course, have many other songs of your own to teach the children in your group. The songbooks listed in the Online Companion contain numerous other songs appropriate for young children.

Figure 17-3

How to present a song to children.

- to learn about a variety of major musical works such as operas, ballets, symphonies, concerts, and chamber music
- have listening experiences with instruments and tonal qualities of strings, woodwinds, brass, and percussion
- to recognize basic meter and rhythmic notation by sound

PLANNING MUSIC ACTIVITIES

The two keys to success in all your musical endeavors are **flexibility** and **acceptance.** You should be able to accept more than one kind of response to a music activity and adapt the activity accordingly. If, for example, the child in a planned clapping activity chooses to pat the rug or his leg, accept the response and imitate it as you continue the activity. In fact, the child may interpret your imitation of his response as a form of praise, thus making the enjoyment of what he is doing even greater. Or if the child is more interested in just listening to music than in dancing to it, accept that too. Try to catch him for your dancing activity at another time when he is in a dancing mood. In other words, take your cues from the children and build enjoyment and learning on what they already find enjoyable. Build, don't tear down, the joyful world music naturally creates for young children. The teacher in the following journal entry clearly knows how to build a joyful world of music for a child with special needs.

Five-year-old Sam uses a wheelchair. Due to a difficult birth, he has little motor development or control and no spoken language. He understands but can't speak.

Twice a week, I am the music teacher for 22 Kindergartners, including Sam. His level of participation is that of an observer, and at times I am not sure what he feels about our time together. The children accept his level of ability and when we put his wheelchair in the center of the circle for "Ring around the Rosy," his squeals of delight give it all away. He laughs and bobs his head back and forth, eyes sparkling all the while as we circle his chair, fall down, and bounce back up only to play the game one more time.

What did Sam gain from this musical experience? Pure joy! At first I felt I was slighting him. Wasn't there a way to make his experience more active and inclusive? We tried pushing the wheelchair in the circle, but Sam's response was not the same. He became withdrawn. The experience of sharing the joy from his pivotal center position evoked the most expression.

To onlookers Sam may appear passive, but all of us who know him well are aware of his participation. The music reaches him, as it does all of us, in his way and at his time and place. His squeals and screeches, sparkling eyes, and smiling face communicate his delight to everyone in the room (Humpal & Wolf, 2003, p. 103).

With these guidelines in mind and with an understanding of the developmental needs of children at different ages, a teacher may plan appropriate musical activities for young children. Let us now consider

THINK
ABOUT IT...
Music and Memory

According to a new study, children with music training had significantly better verbal memory than those without such training, and the longer the training, the better the verbal memory. The research, conducted at the Chinese University of Hong Kong, was published in an issue of the journal *Neuropsychology*.

Researchers studied 90 boys between the ages of 6 and 15. Half had musical training as members of their school's string orchestra program, plus lessons in playing classical music on Western instruments such as the flute or violin for one to five years. The other 45 students had no training.

Students with musical training recalled more words in a verbal memory test than did untrained students, and after a 30–minute delay, students with training also retained more words than the control group. No differences were found for visual memory.

In a follow-up study one year later, students who continued training and beginners who had just started learning to play both showed improvement in verbal learning and retention. But students who had stopped training three months after the first study failed to show any improvement, although they hadn't lost the verbal memory gains measured earlier.

"The present findings suggest that the experience of music training might improve the memory functioning that corresponds to neuroanatomical structures that might be modified by such training," said lead researcher Agnes Chan.

Although the study adds a large volume of research being done on music and the brain, it has also caused an intense amount of debate. Some experts criticized elements of the study's design and warned against misinterpretation of the results. Others cautioned that people should note that the differences between the groups were statistically significant but only modest.

One of the main criticisms is the "chicken or the egg" dilemma. "There is no way to tell whether students with better verbal memories are the ones that tend to study music, or whether students who study music develop better verbal memories," explains Evan Balaban, head of the Neurosciences Program at the City University of New York-College of Staten Island.

Added Robert Zatorre, professor at the Montreal Neurological Institute at McGill University: "The conclusion the authors are jumping to is that music causes improved memory is something we have to be extremely careful about."

Despite the controversy, most experts agreed that more work needs to be done. "The take-home message is that music training does have an effect on cognition," acknowledges Dr. Gottfried Schlaug, director of the Neuroimaging Laboratory and associate professor of neurology at Beth Israel Deaconess Medical Center and Harvard Medical School.

Experts caution against parents sending their children to music lessons just to make them smarter. "Despite all the media hype about Mozart and smarts, there's no evidence that listening to Mozart at any age makes anyone smarter," argues Sandra E. Trehub, professor of psychology at the University of Toronto.

"An unfortunate piece of this puzzle, in my view, is that our society sends parents the message that they should be playing music because it will help their infants with 'important' things like math or reading," says Jenny Saffran, University of Wisconsin-Madison associate professor of psychology. "This misses the point. Treating music as a means to non-musical educational ends, like making you smarter or helping your memory, dilutes what makes music special" (Choy, 2003).

some examples of specific musical experiences appropriate for young children.

> Life has been your art. You have set yourself to music. Your days are your sonnets. Oscar Wilde
>
> I can't listen to music too often. . . . It affects my nerves. Lenin
>
> Music was the first of the expressive subjects to take its place in the curriculum of the public schools. The fact that this could occur at a time when the value of a school subject in practical, everyday affairs was the criterion by which it was judged is evidence that music had become so strongly interwoven in community life that its utility could be taken for granted. Edward Bailey Birge

Musical Experiences

Infants and very young toddlers experience music by hearing it, by feeling it, and by experimenting with pitch and timbre as they vocalize. Adults can provide infants and toddlers music experiences daily while giving children caring, physical contact. Singing to children during changing and feeding times is a basic way to provide music experiences for very young children. If you still don't know how to begin, start at the opening of the day. Sing in your classroom as the children are arriving. In the mornings, to warm up your voice and the children's voices, hum a little bit.

Show children all the possibilities through song. Sing high, then low. Sing softly, then loudly. Change the words of a familiar song such as "Twinkle, Twinkle, Little Star." (See end of unit for suggestions on this.) Change the melody. Play with your song, just as you would take a ball and dribble, roll, or twirl it. There's certainly more than one way to play with a ball. The same is true for a song.

Playing music during periods of the day is another opportunity for a musical experience. Adults can further encourage the musical development of infants and toddlers by exposing them to a wide variety of vocal, instrumental, and environmental sounds. Simple things like talking about the sounds children hear on their walks outside, if they are loud sounds or soft, if they are near or far away, are basic beginning music experiences for very young children.

In the classroom, infants and toddlers need to hear all kinds of music. Adults need to talk about this music and how it expresses feelings. Rocking, patting, touching, and moving with the children to the beat, rhythm patterns, and melodic direction of the music are all appropriate musical experiences for infants and toddlers.

When children enter the preschool program, music continues to be an important part of their lives.

Listen to the sounds of young children playing in the housekeeping corner, on the playground, in the sandbox, and in the building block area—you will often hear young children in these everyday situations singing, humming, or chanting familiar songs. Songs and singing are a common occurrence in the everyday life of a young child. Therefore, teaching songs and singing are a natural part of the early childhood program. The way in which you teach songs and singing to young children reflects the same natural and enjoyable place music holds in a young child's life.

The following suggestions are intended to help you present songs and singing experiences in the early childhood program in a way that maintains the young child's natural musical interest.

- Choose songs that have a natural appeal for young children. Popular topics include the children themselves, family members, animals, seasons, toys, holidays, etc. Be sure to include songs for all ethnic and cultural groups represented in the class, as well as in the larger community group.

- Pay attention to the songs you choose. Select one in the right key (in other words, not too low, not too high) so the children can sing it. Sometimes it's not the song but the arrangement that is difficult. Be aware that some songs are not designed for the average singer (as anyone who has tried to belt out a rendition of "The Star Spangled Banner" can tell you.)

- Choose songs with a clear, strong melody. If the melody is easy to hear, it will be easier to remember.

- Try out all songs yourself first.

- Once you've chosen a song, learn it yourself—and learn it *well*. Nothing is less inspiring to eager songsters than a teacher who has to check notes while teaching a song.

- Based on the length of a song, you may want to teach it in sections, by verses, or even in short phrases. Often, a song's wording may be a bit tricky, and you may want to practice key words a bit more. Whatever method you choose, remember to be light on practice and heavy on praise. Don't make learning a song work; instead, give children lots of verbal encouragement during singing activities.

- Visual aids can help add to the pleasure of singing and song activities. Pictures of key characters in the song or a series of pictures of key song events,

THIS ONE'S for YOU!   ## Start the Music!

The National Association for Music Education (MENC), Texaco Foundation, National Association for the Education of Young Children, and the U.S. Department of Education developed Start the Music in 2000. This is a series of projects and events designed to help bring age-appropriate music education to every child in America. These organizations solicited the expertise of early childhood music educators, music therapists, education association administrators, early childhood educators, and health care providers to identify best practices for early childhood music education and to develop strategies to implement those practices.

Developmentally and individually appropriate musical experiences are guided by these beliefs (MENC, 1995):

⊙ All children have music potential.
—They bring their own unique interests and abilities to the music learning environment.
—They can develop critical thinking skills through musical ideas.
—They come to early childhood music experiences from diverse backgrounds.
—They should experience exemplary musical sounds, activities, and materials.
⊙ Young children should not be expected to meet *performance* goals.
—Their play is the work.
—They learn best in pleasant physical and social environments.
—They need diverse learning environments.
—They need effective adult models.

Start the Music recognizes the role adults play in assisting young children in their musical development. Families, caregivers, and teachers can all help children grow musically (Neely, Kenney, & Wolf, 2000, p. 1) by doing the following:

⊙ Immersing children in musical conversations while singing, speaking rhythmically, moving expressively, and playing musical instruments. By doing these things, we stimulate children's initial awareness of the beauty and the structure of musical sound.
⊙ Encouraging children's musical responses by smiling, nodding, and responding with expressive sounds and movements. Thus, we show children that music making is valuable and important.
⊙ Finding ways to encourage and motivate children's playful exploration, interpretation, and understanding of musical sound.

Start the Music recognizes that all children are individuals and that music experiences should be a part of *every* child's world.

add interest to song activities. For example, a flannel board with farm animals for "Farmer in the Dell" helps add interest to this old favorite song. Use puppets to accompany your teaching a song to children. If you're shy, this will help, as children can't help but focus on the puppet and not you!

⊙ Keep on hand a list of songs you have taught the children. They really enjoy singing old favorites, and it's easy to forget which songs they know. You may want to post the list with some associated picture words so that the children can choose their favorites.

⊙ Encourage *all* attempts at singing. Just as with other developmental skills, each child will perform at his or her own unique level. Thus, there is never any reason to compare children's singing or encourage children to compete with one another. If you've ever had the experience of hearing a group of children attempting to out-shout one another in a choral performance, you will know firsthand the results of encouraging competition between young children in singing.

⊙ In the first stages of teaching a song, use a record, tape, or CD. But be careful not to use them too often in the process of teaching songs to avoid causing a dependence on equipment over the human voice. You and the children can sing without them!

⊙ Add movements, gestures, and props when appropriate for the song and for the children. A too-heavy emphasis on gimmicks to teach a song is unnecessary if you have chosen a song that interests the children and is of an appropriate level of difficulty for them to learn. Added devices need to be thought of as "spices" and used as such: a few appropriately placed hand gestures in a song is like a dash of cinnamon in the applesauce. An entire routine of cute gestures and too many props adds too much "spice" to the recipe. Let preserving the integrity of both the song and the children be your guides in the use of all "extras" in teaching songs to young children.

⊙ Include the new song in other areas of the curriculum by playing the song softly during center time or rest periods.

⊙ Introduce new books related to the song's topic in the language-arts area.

⊙ Include art activities related to the song's topic throughout the week's activities.

⊙ Tape the children singing the song. Have the tape available in the listening center for the children to enjoy (with earphones or without). Play the tape during your next musical activity session. You may want to retape the next version—with rhythm instruments, with a "solo" performance by one of the children, or with any other new variation you and the children prefer.

⊙ Make rhythm instruments like the circle embroidery hoop, egg shaker, and small plastic bottle rattles (instructions provided in Appendix E) as an activity in the arts and crafts center. Have the children use these as a rhythmic accompaniment to the song.

⊙ Make "flutes" out of paper towel or tissue paper rolls. (Instructions provided in Appendix E.) Have the children decorate them with crayons, colored markers, and stickers, and use their "flutes" to "hum along" to the song.

Varying the Rhythm of the Program

Just as variety is the spice of life, variety provides the same spark for the early childhood music program. Although young children enjoy the stability that routine provides, it is important to vary these routines to prevent lessening their, and your own, interest in music. Consider how many people can't remember the words to our national anthem, even though they've heard it innumerable times: it has become so routine that people don't really *hear it* anymore. They've heard it so often, they don't actively listen to it anymore. The same thing can happen in your early childhood music program if you have too rigid a routine.

Figure 17-4

A basic early childhood music experience is using rhythm instruments.

Varying the rhythm of the music program helps hold children's interests and makes the experience enjoyable. Variety can be provided in your choice of music, your method of presentation, and your lesson planning.

Variety in choice of music. In choosing music for young children, your own interests as well as the children's can improve the variety of your music program. Children's music need not be exclusively from music resource books. In an early childhood classroom, music selections can include classical, jazz, rap, rock, Native American, South American, and African music, to name only a few. Young children are very interested in what's new and different and enjoy hearing popular music. In fact, most preschool children can name their favorite pop singers and their latest hits. Although music experiences should expose young children to a wide variety of musical styles, a music program including popular songs gives young children a familiar sound, a friendly starting point. Developmentally, it is appropriate to begin with the familiar, using it as a base for the introduction of new concepts to the child.

Variety in choice of music can also be provided by the families of the children. A teacher may find a rich source of musical variety by asking families to share the names of their favorite music or to share tapes, records, or CDs with the class for special activities. In preparing for special ethnic and cultural celebrations, for example, you might find families willing to share favorite holiday music with your group. Some parents may be willing to sing for the group or bring in special instruments for the children to see and hear. The key is to go beyond *your* likes and the dictates of curriculum guides into the children's lives, their parents' lives, and the community at large, where a variety of music awaits you and your group.

Variety in presentation. We've already discussed several basic methods of presenting a song. In addition to these basics, you need to consider other ways to add variety to your presentation of songs and musical experiences for young children.

⊙ Vary the time of day you have musical activities. Switch from afternoons to mornings and vice versa. Also, don't neglect the spontaneous inclusion of a song during the day. Mixing up a recipe together is an excellent time to vary your program by singing as you work with the children. Singing a song on a nature walk is another. Swinging and singing on the playground is fun. And who can refrain from a song ("The Wheels on the Bus" is an obvious example) on a bus trip? In essence, *plan* for the unexpected occasion to sing and have a mental repertoire of songs to sing with the children. Singing can make an ordinary event joyous, so start making a list of favorites for this very reason.

⊙ Vary your presentation by having the children choose the songs they want to sing and how they

Figure 17-5

Music is created so naturally and easily every day in many forms—by voice, by instruments, even by nature in the rhythm of the rain or the sound of a waterfall.

want to present them. Be sure to have available puppets, pictures, rhythm instruments, and audiovisual or other necessary equipment for their creative choices.

⊙ Play games with music. Musical chairs is only one of these games. Games can focus on voice recognition. For example, a child is challenged to guess who is humming the song or who sang the last verse. A "name that tune" game is also a way to vary the presentation of songs. Play, sing, or hum a few bars of a song for the children to guess. Charades, or acting out a song, is an appropriate musical game for older children.

Variety in lesson planning. The key to variety in lesson planning is *cross-curricular planning*. More specifically, music need not be planned for only one area of the curriculum. Music should cross all curricular areas, and this can be accomplished by specifically planning for it to do just that. Here are some suggestions for this specific planning:

⊙ When making lesson plans for the week, include music in at least two other curricular areas. For example, plan to play music during art activities, and note which selections you will use and on which day. Be sure to make a note to have the tape/CD ready and the tape/CD player set up for the days required. Then, plan to read a book at group time that relates to the new song(s) introduced that week. Plan to locate the book *early*.

⊙ Use music as your cue to adding new materials and props to the housekeeping and dramatic centers. For example, engineer hats, trains, and railroad signs are natural additions when you've planned to teach "I've Been Working on the Railroad" to the children. Putting the book *The Little Engine That Could* (Piper, 2002) in the book corner is another example of a music-inspired topic used in another curricular area.

⊙ Review past lesson plans to assist you in your future planning. We are creatures of habit and often tend to get in a rut when making lesson plans. Review past plans to see what kinds of music you have been introducing, the method of presentation, and curricular coverage. If a pattern is obvious, then you need a change! Make a conscious effort to find new types of music or methods of presentation, or plan a new schedule of times/days for music. If you are bored with the lessons and the planning of music lessons, the children will reflect this as well.

⊙ Use a variety of sources for music experiences for young children. See the book list in the Online

Companion for songbooks and other books on musical experiences for children.

Rhythm Activities

Rhythm is present from life's earliest moments, when a baby hears its mother's heartbeat. Infants continue to enjoy rhythms in many everyday situations, such as the soothing ticking beat of a windup swing or the soft sounds and smooth rhythms of a lullaby.

In an early childhood program, one of a child's earliest musical experiences is clapping and moving to rhythmic music. The addition of **rhythm instruments** is another traditional practice in early childhood music programs. Young children, who love movement and motion in general, are naturally drawn to the use of rhythm instruments. Listening first to the music for its

rhythmic pattern and then matching the beat with rhythm instruments is the most familiar method of introducing rhythm instruments. Having young children listen to the music and clap out the beat with their hands or tap it out with their feet is another appropriate, traditional rhythm activity.

A teacher can also help a child's development of rhythm by focusing on the natural movements of the child. For example, teachers can follow a child's natural walking or running tempo by accompanying her steps on the drum. This can quickly become a game as the child, realizing that his or her steps dictate the beat of the drum, walks faster and slower.

Following children's galloping and skipping with the drum can also illustrate through sound the asymmetrical nature of those rhythms. The drum can emphasize the accent when running children leap over an

THIS ONE'S for YOU!

Internet Sources for Music Experiences

The Internet is an excellent resource for information on early childhood music. Here are some Web sites that provide activities and ideas to expand and enliven your music program.

COMPOSE A TUNE! http://www.creatingmusic.com

Creating Music is a place where kids can compose music, experiment with tempo, or play with a musical sketchpad. There are games and puzzles, too.

LISTEN TO A TUBA! http://www.sfskids.org

What better place to learn about music than the San Francisco Symphony? At the SFS site, kids can learn about all the instruments of the orchestra and they can make their own synthesized music in the music lab.

NAME THAT TUNE! http://www.niehs.nih.gov/

Click on Kids' Pages. Are you a sing-along or karaoke fan? This Web site has the music and lyrics to hundreds of kids' songs, and there is also a fun "name that tune" game.

LISTEN TO FAMILIAR SOUNDS! http://www.playhouseradio.com

At PlayhouseRadio.com students can listen for free to hundreds of original children's songs. This site is teeming with hours of musical amusement—all with lyrics included. Extend the fun by visiting the Workshop to find how to make instruments that children can use to play along with the songs.

LISTEN TO SOME CLASSICAL MUSIC! http://www.classicalarchives.com/

Click on Music. With tens of thousands of full-length recordings, the Classical Archives is an important stop for students who are interested in classical music. Featured section contains a collection of MP3s by well-known orchestras and instrumental soloists. Visit the Archives to find biographies of thousands of composers, along with examples of their music.

object, or it can mark groups of beats (meter). Teachers can also mark the beat as children jump over a series of sticks laid out in parallel formation or pass a ball from hand to hand. Teachers provide a more fulfilling movement experience by fitting the external music source, such as a drumbeat, to the child's movement. Some teachers feel that percussion instruments such as drums are merely noisemakers. Drums, however, can be used for musical conversations as children ask each other questions using patterns, as they drum out the rhythm of their names as they count/drum out the syllables in their names, or as they simply explore the sound of a drum. The drum can be available for children's exploratory free play, for a guided experience with an adult at circle time, or for small-group interaction in a play center.

Whenever rhythm instruments are added, they should have a specific purpose. Instruments are not used just to make "noise," but rather to enhance the activity. Instruments should be in good condition. Be sure children know the proper use of rhythm instruments before beginning any activities. Try using simple signals for starting and stopping that don't require your shouting over the music. Holding up rhythm sticks in a crossed formation is a good visual "stop" signal. Holding the rhythm sticks straight up can be a visual "start" signal.

Using rhythm instruments, children learn to listen for a pattern of sounds in the music. In beginning rhythm activities, it's a good idea to choose music with a clear, easy-to-hear beat or rhythm. Marches and many types of ethnic music are excellent choices for this strong beat.

Some children may have difficulty hearing rhythms and/or reproducing them. This can be handled in the same way you would handle a reluctant singer. Specifically, never force the child to copy your pattern or to use a rhythm instrument or practice this activity. Your emphasis should be on the child's natural enjoyment of music. Whether he or she can reproduce a rhythm is not essential to his or her enjoyment of music. As many an adult can attest, not being able to sing on key or reproduce rhythms does not affect one's enjoyment of music.

Rhythm instruments may be made by the children as well as by the teacher. Using recycled materials, such as toweling rolls, pebbles, and spools, can be yet another creative outlet for young children. (See Appendix E for suggestions on how to create rhythm instruments from recycled materials.)

Music Experiences for Older Children

With children in the middle and upper elementary grades, teachers are able to offer a broader array of musical experiences for children. These activities are covered in detail in many of the books listed in the Online Companion.

One of the most basic experiences children of this age need to have is a broader experience with a variety of forms and styles of music. Students in this age group need to have even more listening experiences with the world's finest music including the classics, multicultural folk, and composed music. By the end of fifth grade, students should have been exposed to the main periods of music history and acquainted with composers and repertoire from each period. For these older children's listening experiences, the following are the periods of musical history and composers associated with each period:

- ⊙ Baroque—Bach, Handel, Corelli
- ⊙ Classic—Haydn, Mozart, Beethoven
- ⊙ Romantic—Weber, Schubert, Schumann, Mendelssohn, Chopin, Wagner, Liszt, Brahms, J. Strauss, Tchaikovsky, Moussorgsky, Saint-Saëns, MacDowell, Grieg
- ⊙ Post-Romantic and Impressionist—R. Strauss, Sibelius, Dukas, Debussy, Ravel, Respighi
- ⊙ Modern—Stavinsky, Bartók, Kodály, Prokofiev, Hindemith, Villa-Lobos, Copland, Thomson, Menotti, Bernstein
- ⊙ Light classic—Gershwin, Rodgers and Hammerstein, Gilbert and Sullivan, Irving Berlin
- ⊙ Jazz and popular—Miles Davis, Marselis, Basie, the Beatles, and Elvis
- ⊙ Ethnic and folk

Figure 17-6

Playing instruments can be a social experience.

The varied treatment that composers have given the musical elements has resulted in different styles of music. The labels that are given these styles are also applicable to art and literature. For example, music experiences in the Impressionist music of Debussy can be associated with Impressionist paintings of Mary Cassat. Art and music can both be enjoyed from the Impressionist style and time in history. The same is true for music of all periods.

Singing is an important classroom activity for children in the middle and upper elementary grades. Opportunities to sing in parts (harmony) or in rounds (like "Row, row, row your boat") are enjoy-

able musical experiences for children of this age. They are becoming more familiar with vocal ranges, female (soprano, mezzo-soprano, and alto) and male (tenor, baritone, and bass). They are able to sing simple melodies while reading a musical score. They are learning more about musical notation as well. For example, they can begin to recognize and understand what a whole note, half-note, and rest notations mean.

KEY TERMS

acceptance in teaching music
appropriate music activities
combination of phrase-wise and whole-song
     method
flexibility in teaching music
phrase-wise method
rhythm instruments
teaching songs from recordings
varying the rhythm of the music program
whole-song method

SUMMARY

Music is a common occurrence in a young child's life. Making up original chants and songs and moving rhythmically to musical beats are quite natural to a young child. Music is a natural avenue for a young child's creative expression. Appropriate musical experiences for young children must take into account the child's developmental level and need for self-expression. Careful planning is essential in providing successful learning experiences for children. In this planning, the teacher must consider many things. First, the teacher must plan for the developmental level of the group. Next, it is important to include activities from each area of music—singing, rhythm, instruments, movement, listening, and musical concepts such as loud and soft. It is equally important to be flexible and happy when presenting musical activities to children. You must enjoy yourself as much as the children. Presenting songs to children may be done by either the phrase-wise method, whole-song method, a combination of these, or teaching songs from recordings. Rhythm instruments may also be used with songs, and these instruments may be teacher- and child-made.

Older children can be introduced to an array of classical music styles. These can be related to art and literature of the same period. Children of this age group enjoy singing songs of varied styles and forms.

Figure 17-7

A teacher can encourage children's musical experiences by her own positive attitude.

LEARNING ACTIVITIES

A. Form a group of three or four children from your program, neighborhood, or local school. Spend at least 15 minutes with them singing songs they know and new ones you teach them. Following this session, write an anecdotal record for each child commenting on (a) participation in singing, (b) attitude, and (c) knowledge of songs. Compare and contrast the children and comment on the likenesses and differences you found in each anecdotal record.

B. Select from additional sources in the Online Companion an appropriate song for each of the following groups of children: four year olds, six year olds, and two year olds. Justify each choice using the criterion and information provided in this chapter. Do the same activity with a group of children in grades 4 to 5.

C. From your own childhood, recall several popular singing games and action songs that you have not found in this chapter. Tape each song along with clear directions on how to play the game or move to the song. Share the activities with your classmates.

D. Choose one of your own favorite songs (popular, rock, country). Teach it to your fellow classmates, using one of the methods discussed. Discuss your experience, including the following points: How well did your "class" learn by the method you chose? Did you feel comfortable using this method? Discuss how you would feel teaching a song you didn't especially like. Would it make any difference in your effectiveness?

E. Using a box of animal crackers and one of the suggested rhythm instruments (preferably a drum) or a hand-clapping accompaniment from your classmates, try the following creative/interpretive movement to rhythm activity:
   1. Take out one animal cracker and note what animal it is.
   2. "Become" that animal, acting it out by walking, hopping, sliding, etc.
   3. Have one (or several) of your classmates pick up your rhythm and beat or clap, accompanying your movement.
   4. See who can guess what animal you are. Whoever guesses correctly gets the next opportunity to "become an animal."

F. Using a concept song like "Round the Mulberry Bush" (describing a daily routine), make up several verses and accompanying motions. Share your song and actions with your classmates for comments and improvements. Tape your song to use later with a group of young children. Examples of other concept songs: "Old MacDonald Had a Farm," "If You're Happy and You Know It," and "The Wheels on the Bus."

G. Make a drum (tin coffee can with plastic lid, empty oatmeal carton with lid) for the following rhythm activity:
   1. Beat a rhythm on the drum for walking, running, skipping, and hopping movements.
   2. Beat out a pattern of rhythm and have your peers repeat it by clapping hands (or by using their own handmade drums!).
   3. Imitate a pattern clapped (or made on a drum) by one of your peers in the class.
   4. Sing a song (your own creation, if you like) to accompany a rhythm you make on your drum.

H. Begin a card file of songs for young children. Use your school library to locate songbooks for young children and choose at least two songs for each of the following categories:

Category	Sample Songs
emotions	"If You're Happy and You Know It"
actions	"Here We Go Looby Loo"
birthdays	
concepts	

I. Obtain a music supply catalog. Choose $150.00 worth of teaching materials. Explain why you chose each item, for what age group, and how you plan to use it.

J. Make a set of simple rhythm instruments as suggested in Appendix E. Use these instruments in a demonstration lesson on rhythm for your classmates.

K. Choose one of the composers from a particular period of music mentioned in this chapter. Get a CD or tape of one of the pieces referred to in this chapter. Make a lesson plan for either grade 3, grade 4, or grade 5 using this piece of music. Be sure to relate the music to art and language arts activities of the same period. Share your plan with your fellow students.

SONGS FOR CHILDREN

Note: These verses may be used alone or to a steady march tempo as accompaniment, such as "Turkey in the Straw." The value of these verses is in identification of body parts, counting, and creative activity.

Clap Your Hands

Clap your hands, count one, two, three;
Pull your ear, and slap your knee;
Stamp your feet, one, two, three, four;
Wiggle your fingers and touch the floor.

Raise your hands up to the skies;
Touch your nose, then touch your eyes;
Stamp your feet, one, two, three, four;
Wiggle your fingers and touch the floor.

Elbows out, now be a bird;
Touch your mouth without a word;
Softly clap and stamp your feet;
Tiptoe quietly and take your seat.

The Ants Go Marching One by One

The ants go marching one by one
Hurrah! Hurrah! (Repeat)
When the ants go marching one by one
The little one stops to suck his thumb
And they all go marching down to earth
—to get out of the rain—
Boom, boom, boom, boom, boom, boom, boom, boom!

The ants go marching two by two
Hurrah! Hurrah! (Repeat)
When the ants go marching two by two
The little one stops to tie his shoe
And they all go marching down to earth
—to get out of the rain—
Boom, boom, boom, boom, boom, boom, boom, boom!

The ants go marching three by three
Hurrah! Hurrah! (Repeat)
When the ants go marching three by three
The little one stops to climb a tree
And they all go marching down to earth
—to get out of the rain—
Boom, boom, boom, boom, boom, boom, boom, boom!

Verses:
The ants go marching four by four
The little one stops to shut the door.

The ants go marching five by five
The little one stops to kick a hive.

The ants go marching six by six
The little one stops to pick up some sticks.

Eight by eight—shut the gate.
Nine by nine—pick up a dime.
Ten by ten—shout THE END.

If You're Happy and You Know It

If you're happy and you know it
Clap your hands (Clap, clap). (Repeat)
If you're happy and you know it
Then your face will surely show it.
If you're happy and you know it
Clap your hands (Clap, clap).

If you're angry and you know it
Stamp your feet (Stamp, stamp). (Repeat)
If you're angry and you know it
Your face will surely show it.
If you're angry and you know it
Stamp your feet (Stamp, stamp).

If you're sad and you know it
Shed a tear (Sniff, sniff). (Repeat)
If you're sad and you know it
Your face will surely show it.
If you're sad and you know it
Shed a tear (Sniff, sniff).

If you're weary and you know it
Heave a sigh (Whee-you).
(Repeat refrains)

If you're joyous and you know it
Click your heels (Click, click).
(Repeat refrains)

ACTIVITIES FOR CHILDREN

MUSICAL LISTENING ACTIVITIES

The following are activities designed to help young children sharpen their musical listening skills. They are most successful when used as fun "musical challenges" for young children *and not as rote exercises*. Space them throughout your daily and weekly activity planning, not just in the music portion of your curriculum. The auditory and listening skills they develop are used in all curriculum areas.

A. *Listening for specific sounds and being able to tell what they are* (auditory discrimination).
   1. Have a child play a musical instrument such as a bell, tambourine, drum, triangle, or wood block. Another child closes his eyes and identifies the object played.
   2. A variation of the same game is to have two sounds played, and both are then identified. The number can gradually be increased to see how many can be identified at once.
   3. A child can go to the piano or some other instrument and hit a high or low note. The children can show with their hands, arms, or body whether the note is high or low.
   4. Listen for the sound of a bell, drum, etc., from some specific position in the room. The children close their eyes and identify where the sound came from. They might also identify the instrument and tell whether the tone was loud or soft.
   5. Children identify instruments by comparing two different tones, such as large and small horns, large and small bells, wood blocks, and play blocks.
B. *Listening for sounds of nature.* The children close their eyes and listen for the rain, leaves rustling, the wind, birds, hail, snow, etc.
C. *Listening for school sounds.* Children walking, people laughing, bells ringing, etc.
D. *Listening for outdoor sounds.* Whistles, trucks, cars, train, airplane, etc. Encourage children to use descriptive words for the sounds, such as, "It is like a bang, buzz, knock, or crash."

MUSICAL IMAGINATIONS

Ask your children to think of a small animal and a large animal. Then divide the group into two groups, having one group be the small animals and the other the large animals. When you play music with high notes, have the small animals move and dance. When you play low notes, have the large animal group move and dance.

SHARING PRERECORDED MUSIC

Try using the Suzuki method when introducing children to a musical classic such as "Peter and the Wolf." Before actually introducing the classic to the children, play the piece as background music for several weeks, during center time, for example. Then, when you tell the story of Peter and the Wolf, the children already will have learned to distinguish the various melodies in the piece and will be able to anticipate what comes next. Follow up with another few weeks of just listening to the piece. Using the Suzuki method, children will never forget the music they learned.

INSTRUMENT IDENTIFICATION GAME

Set up the music center with two chairs and tables separated by a divider. On one side of the divider, place several rhythm instruments on the table. On the other side, place pictures of the instruments. As the child on one side plays an instrument, the child on the other side holds up the picture of the identified instrument.

THE BLUE DANUBE WALTZ

Swinging and rocking are favorite movements of young children, and Strauss waltzes possess a compelling feeling of movement that even adults find hard to resist. Not only do children enjoy swinging their own bodies to Strauss waltzes, but they enjoy swinging with a doll or favorite stuffed animal or puppet. In modeling swinging movements, very young children may not be able to swing their arms in parallel motion because of an inability to cross the midline of the body. Thus, the teacher may need to model symmetrical arm movements. By three years of age some children will be able to swing arms in parallel action.

ANIMALS/INSECTS

Use the following classical musical selections for creative movements in acting out animals or insects. You may want to introduce the piece by giving its name and briefly discussing how this animal or insect would move.
- Griffes—"The White Peacock"
- Liadov—"Dance of the Mosquito"
- Rimsky-Korsakoff—"Flight of the Bumblebee"
- Saint-Saëns—"The Swan" from *Carnival of the Animals*
- Bizet—"Leap Frog" from *Children's Games*
- Debussy—"Golliwog's Cakewalk" from *The Children's Corner Suite*

"TWINKLE, TWINKLE, LITTLE STAR"–SINGING AND LANGUAGE SKILLS

One of the most enjoyable ways to develop language skills with young children is to invite them to write songs with you. Take a familiar tune, add an inviting topic (such as the children themselves), mix your own words into the tune, and sing! In the process, you are encouraging young children to use descriptive vocabulary and creative thinking skills. As you sing songs about each other, you are encouraging children to appreciate each other's similarities and differences.

Start this process by helping children create songs and cheers about one another. Use the tune for "Twinkle, Twinkle, Little Star" to create a song or cheer to celebrate the unique qualities of each child. Fill in the blanks in the song with each child's name, features, or favorite things.

My Own Cheer (Tune: "Twinkle, Twinkle, Little Star")
(Child's name), (Child's name),
she's so neat!
She loves (favorite food)
when she eats.
Her hair is (hair color)
and (hair style or length) too.
She's my friend
and so are YOU!
(Child's name), (Child's name),
he's so neat!
We always smile when we meet!

THIS IS WHAT I LEARNED TO DO (TUNE: "TWINKLE, TWINKLE, LITTLE STAR")

Try this group song/game to celebrate the special skills children have learned from family members.

This is What I've Learned to Do
This is what I've learned to do.
(Have child pantomime skill)
See if you can do it too.
This is what I've learned to do.
Now I pass it on to you!
This is what I've learned to do.
See if you can do it, too!

MULTICULTURAL GREETING–"GOOD MORNING TO YOU!" (TUNE: "LA CUCARACHA")

Add a multicultural flavor to your group-time greeting songs. Try singing them to the tunes of different styles of music. You can start this song with the tune of "La Cucaracha" and then try it to the tune of "When the Saints Go Marching In."

Good Morning to You
Good morning to you, good morning to you.
Let's all give a great big smile.
Good morning to you,
Good morning to you,
We can sit and stay awhile, cha-cha-cha.
Personalize the song by adding each child's name to the second verse: "Let's give Claire a big smile."

ACTIVITIES FOR OLDER CHILDREN (GRADES 4–5)

SING A PICTURE

Display a landscape, seascape, or cityscape and ask students to brainstorm all the sounds associated with different parts of the picture. Encourage them to think creatively about what "might be." Come to an agreement on a sound for five or six parts of the picture and then discuss the pitch, dynamics (areas that are louder or softer), and how many times the sound should be repeated. The teacher then points to each area, and students make the sounds, holding them or repeating them, as decided. Next, try harmonizing sounds or doing the sounds of the picture in round form.

Variation: Use prints with several people and break students into groups to find songs or create songs their characters would sing. Come back together and have each group present the songs of their characters.

FINDING MUSICAL ELEMENTS IN ART

Use a piece of art to ask students to find musical elements. For example, folk art and folk music can be compared. Find rhythm in art, texture, tempo, style aspects, and dynamics (areas that are louder or softer).

MEDIA SHOW AND SOUND COMPOSITIONS

Students prepare a sound and art presentation around a chosen topic—for example, friends, animals, feelings, weather, culture, or country. They may work in groups or pairs to find a piece of music to play as they present art on transparencies or on an easel as the song is played. Art could be student made or "found art." This also could be done as a computer slide show.

ILLUSTRATE A SONG

Each child chooses a favorite song to illustrate, or the whole class can do the same song to find all the ways one song could be interpreted. Students could create a group mural of a song, or songs can be cut apart, line-by-line, with children working on illustrating their part. By assembling all the art, the entire song is then depicted (e.g., "Home on the Range" will work).

MUSICAL MURAL

While teachers frequently provide background music during art activities, rarely do children have the chance to demonstrate their musical imaginations in a complete and satisfying way. Rather than treating the music as "wallpaper music" (i.e., present but not really a point of focus), this mural activity invites children to give shape to their thoughts and feelings associated with a piece of music. Whether they have visions of sugar plums or rap jive movements dancing in their heads, the teacher's task is to guide the children in developing their imagery into a story told through a mural.

Begin with a musical selection that is programmatic and concrete such as *Peter and the Wolf*. After discussing major episodes, assign children to particular scenes of the story to work on panels of the mural. Let the children flesh out details of the story through visual elements (colors, shape, perspective, and line). Draw their attention to musical aspects that help tell the story (volume, speed, instrumentation).

Next, children can progress to more abstract listening exercises connected to various content areas. The class, for example, could be divided into groups with each group painting a picture based upon *Pinocchio, Pocahontas, Sleeping Beauty*, or *The Nutcracker Suite* (language arts) or using other pieces of music such as *La Mer* (science), *The Blue Danube*, or *The Moldau* (social studies). The children can create the mural prior to learning the title and/or story of the music.

This exercise encourages active listening. Ask the children what story they hear in the music. Do they all hear similar stories? How does the story they have envisioned match the actual title of the piece? What do they think the composer had in mind? These are only some of the questions that can be used to help children compare/contrast while integrating concepts from several content areas.

ART HISTORY/AESTHETIC AWARENESS

Gather several musical selections from composers of the Impressionist Period listed in this chapter. Choose one or two to play for your class. Explain that the mu-

sic is from a period called "Impressionism" and that this was a movement in art as well. Obtain and display art prints of Impressionist painters such as Monet and Cassat. Briefly discuss Impressionism in art: Impressionism developed in France during the 1860s. The artists who worked in this style wished to portray the particular qualities of light and color at a moment of time during the day. They usually took their paints outdoors so they could see and study colors. The unusually light and bright colors in Impressionist paintings "shocked" many critics of the 1860s. Impressionist painters rarely used black or gray. For shadows they preferred deep violets, blues, and the like. They also preferred to use patches or dot-like areas of color rather than strong outlines. They wanted the eye to "blend" the colors by placing small dots of color next to each other, allowing the eyes to "blend" them together.

Students may want to paint in a similar manner to Impressionists to experiment with this technique. Of course, painting outdoors is the best way to experience this style!

MUSIC IN ART

An easy way of connecting music and art is to deal directly with both. Children do this when they listen to music and make pictures of what they hear or when they look at art and make music of what they see.

Many musicians have been inspired by art. Stephen Sondheim based an entire musical—*Sunday in the Park with George* (1984)—on a single painting, Georges Seurat's *A Sunday on La Grande Jatte* (1884).

Use the following suggested works of art to help elementary children "hear" art as music: Goya's *Boy on a Ram*, Lichtenstein's *Brushstroke with Spatter*, and Picasso's *The Old Guitarist*. Of course, you may use any other selections you feel are suitable for your particular group of children. The goal is to have them see, hear, and create music and art as a relationship between two art forms. An art museum is undoubtedly the best source for visual images, but good-quality reproductions of original art (available at art stores, museum shops or on the Internet) can serve as effective substitutes.

A teacher can begin by leading the children in an exploration of sound and movement. Ask the students, "How many ways can you move your hands?" "How many different sounds can you make with them?" "What kinds of sounds can you make with your mouth and voice?" "What sounds can you make with the classroom percussion instruments?"

These questions—and others like them—will establish a working repertoire and create a comfortable atmosphere for experimentation. Have the children describe the sounds in as much detail as they can. Let them tell you whether the sounds are loud, soft, long, short, high, low, smooth, rough, and so on. Invite them to elaborate on the things that they are reminded of by these sounds.

Such activities will invite the children to interpret as sound the trotting of the ram in Goya's *Boy on a Ram*. They will "hear" the tinkle of the ram's bell and the snap of the boy's riding crop. In Lichtenstein's *Brushstroke with Spatter* they will "hear" the bold splash and strokes superimposed over the regular precise dots. In Picasso's *The Old Guitarist* they will "hear" the mellow sounds from the old guitar.

Encourage the children to note size, shape, line, texture, color, repetition, emphasis, and contrast in the art prints. Suggest ways of interpreting all of these elements as sounds. They may propose playing the dots in Lichtenstein's piece in a regular rhythm on a woodblock throughout the entire composition. They may decide to play the spatter by striking and shaking a tambourine and the brushstrokes by stroking a guitar.

Another activity. Have students look at one of the works of art mentioned previously or other prints you have available. Ask them what they see. If they name things that can move or are depicted in motion, let them show the movement(s) with their hands. If they name things that make sounds, let them try to produce these sound(s) with their hands, mouths, voices, or an instrument. Repeat this procedure for all the things they see.

Once the children have finished the process of interpreting everything in art as sound, say to them, "Let's play this work of art." Find out which parts they think they should play alone, as solos, and which parts they want to play together, in chorus. Ask them in what order they think they should play the parts. Act as the composer/conductor for the first performance; then allow a series of students to take that role. Let the composer/conductor choose from the proposed sounds the ones that they want to use to represent each visual element. Allow them to conduct the piece more than once if necessary in order to achieve the effects they desire.

CHAPTER REVIEW

1. Discuss what you consider the greatest obstacles to overcome in order to be an effective music teacher. Relate these to your personal situation.

2. Describe some examples of how the child spontaneously approaches music. How early do children become involved in musical experiences? Who initiates these activities?

3. What are some basic ways to teach young children new songs? Give an example of each way from your own experience.

4. Discuss what you consider to be one of the most important teacher characteristics in a successful early childhood music program. Give additional characteristics you feel are also necessary.

5. How necessary is it to accompany the singing of young children? If you can't play the piano, how would you conduct a singing activity with young children?

6. How would you introduce a new song to young children? Use an example of a specific song.

7. What advice would you give a teacher who is afraid to teach music because she can't play an instrument and doesn't know anything about musical notation, theory, etc.? Be specific in your reply, giving suggested activities.

8. What would you do when instead of clapping the rhythm as directed, a child bounces up and down to the beat? How important is your handling of this situation?

REFERENCES

Choy, E. (2003). *Musical memory: Study links music training with improved verbal memory in children, but findings spark debate.* ABC News, Online: http://www.ABCNEWS.com.

Erickson, F. (1963). Childhood and society. New York: W.W. Norton.

Humpal, M. E., & Wolf, J. (2003, March). Music in the inclusive environment. *Young Children,* 103–107.

MENC (National Association for Music Education). (1995). *Pre-kindergarten music standards.* Reston, VA: MENC

Neely, L., Kenney, S., & Wolf, J. (2000). *Start the music strategies.* Reston, VA: MENC.

Piper, W. (2002). *The little engine that could.* Uhrichsville, OH: Barbour Publishing.

Piper, W. (1986). *The little engine that could.* New York: Platt & Munk.

Todd, V. E., & Heffernan, H. (1977). *Years before school: Guiding preschool children.* (3rd ed.). New York: Macmillan.

Wadsworth, B. (1979). *Piaget's theory of cognitive development.* (2nd ed.). New York: Longman.

ADDITIONAL READINGS

Dulabaum, G. (2003). *My teacher rides a Harley: Enhancing K–5 literacy through song writing.* Gainesville, FL: Maupin House.

Herr, J., & Larson, Y. R. (2003). *Creative resources for the early childhood classroom.* Clifton Park, NY: Delmar.

Hohman, C. (2002). *The High/Scope preschool key experiences: Essential elements of young children's learning.* Ypsilanti, MI: High/Scope.

Macintyre, C. (2003). *Jingle time: Rhymes and songs for early years.* London: David Fulton Publishers.

McDonald, D. T. (2002). *Music in our lives.* Washington, DC: NAEYC.

Nespeca, S. M., Hodgson, F. B., & Reeve, J. (2002). *Picture books plus: 100 extension activities in art, drama, music, math and science.* Chicago: American Library Association.

Shilling, W. A. (2002). Mathematics, music, and movement: Exploring concepts and connections. *Early Childhood Education Journal 29*(3), 179–184.

Swim, T., & Herr, J. (2002). *Making sounds, making music and other sounds.* Clifton Park, NJ: Delmar.

Tocalli-Beller, A. (2002). *Bilingual songs,* vol. 2. Cambridge, UK: Jordan Music Productions.

Young, P. G. (2003). Don't leave your students playing the blues. *Principal 82*(3), 20–22.

SOFTWARE FOR CHILDREN

Alice in Vivaldi's Four Seasons the Music Game, 2003. Grades K–6.

Animusic: A Computer Animation Video Album, 2002. Grades Pre-K–2.

Arthur's Preschool 2003 Edition, 2003. Ages 3–5.

Alfred's Essentials of Music Theory 21.0 Student Version, 2003. Grades 2–9.

Clifford's Musical Memory Game, 2002. Grades Pre-K–2.

Dolphin Don's Music School Version 3.2, 2002. Grades K–9.

Jumbo Music Ball, 2002. Ages 3–5.

Learn Through Music, 2003. Pre-K.

Mozart's Magic Flute The Music Game, 2003. Grades Pre-K–3.

Music Blocks Maestro, 2003. Grades Pre-K–6.

Music Studio Pixter, 2003. Grades K–6.

Pixter Music Studio, 2002. Grades K–3.

Tchaikovsky's Nutcracker The Music Game, 2002. Grades K–3.

HELPFUL WEB SITES

The Rock & Roll Hall of Fame for Teachers, http://www.rockhall.com/
Click on Enter, then on Programs.

PBS Jazz, http://www.pbs.org/jazz/kids/

The Classical Music Archives, http://www. classicalarchives.com/

Garden State Pops Youth Orchestra, http://www.gspyo.com/

Piano on the Net, http://www.pianonanny.com

San Francisco Symphony for Kids, http://www.sfskids.org

For additional creative activity resources, visit our Web site at http://www.EarlyChildEd. delmar.com.

Chapter 18

Creative Language Experiences

Objectives

After studying this chapter, you should be able to:

1. Discuss speaking and listening skills in young children.

2. Define "emerging literacy" and the various skills it involves.

3. Explain how to choose and use children's books for teaching young children.

4. List some guidelines to follow when reading to young children.

5. Discuss the importance of poetry for young children's language development.

6. Discuss the needs of bilingual/bicultural young children.

7. Discuss the anti-bias curriculum.

The following scene demonstrates the power of a young child's language, both verbal and nonverbal. It also demonstrates very clearly the fact that adults often assume they know exactly what young children are saying and respond to them on this basis. Yet, communicating can be a more complicated process than this, as the scene should emphasize.

On a warm, sunny, fall afternoon the store was filled with shoppers, many browsing the racks of women's sale-priced clothes. Among them were a grandmother and her daughter, who pushed a pretty toddler along in a stroller. The child wore a large patch over her right eye. Soon, she filled the air with pleading cries, "Off, off!" Her mother simply responded, "The doctor said you have to wear the patch, honey. We can't take it off." When the child continued to cry "Off, off!" in a plaintive voice, the grandmother took a more direct approach, saying, "Now, I'll have no more of that. You can't take the patch off." The little girl looked at her grandmother, then resumed her cries, "Off, off!" But this time, when she received no response from her cries, she tugged on the arm of her coat, saying, "Off, off!" She wanted her coat off, not her eye patch!

DEVELOPMENT OF LANGUAGE

Two points can be made from this scene: (1) we can never *underestimate* the ability of a young child to get her message across and (2) we should never *overestimate* our understanding of a young child's message. In this chapter we will explore these points and the many other facets of language development.

Language is part of a child's total development. As with physical growth, there is a definite developmental pattern to a child's use of language. There are four distinct skills involved in the development of language: speaking, listening (in the sense of comprehending or understanding speech), writing, and reading. Each of these, in turn, has its own pattern of development.

Ability in one language skill is not always directly related to competence in another. For example, many young children are far better speakers than listeners!

In the early childhood program, language experiences must take into consideration the developmental levels of children in each of these four distinct parts of language development. Emphasis in preschool programs, however, is *not* on teaching writing and reading. Developing skills that are *related* to reading and writing help prepare a child for more formal instruction in these skills in later years. While this chapter focuses on the development of language skills in the early years, activities and resources are provided for older children where appropriate. The reader is referred to the reading lists in the Online Companion for books on teaching reading to older children. Reading and writing skills will be handled as "emerging literacy" skills in this chapter. The term *reading readiness* is often used to describe these skills as well. However, the author prefers the term *emerging literacy* because it encompasses a broader range of prereading skills development.

DEVELOPMENT OF SPEECH

Speech is a form of language in which words or sounds are used to convey meanings. The ability to speak is not necessarily related to the ability to understand. For example, infants make many sounds as they practice vocalizing that probably do not mean nearly what eager adults like to read into them. Three-year-old children, as another example, can sing along, not missing a single word of popular songs on the radio, without really knowing what the words mean. Many children can sing the alphabet song and not know what letters really mean.

In the development of speech, there are differences among children in the age at which they begin to learn to speak and the rate with which they achieve competence. The overall developmental sequence with which speech is acquired, however, generally follows the basic sequence represented in Figure 18–1. Similar to the pattern of physical development (see Chapter 10), acquisition of speech develops from general to specific.

At first, the child's speech consists of sounds that are vague and difficult to understand. Yet even in these early stages of life (from birth to 36 months), very young children can communicate quite effectively with a minimum of vocabulary. See Appendix B for a summary of the basic characteristics of these early levels of speech development and some related activities for language development at each level.

Gradually the development of speech progresses to clear and distinct words that carry specific messages, which we call controlled verbal communication. Generally, by the age of three years, children are rapidly building their vocabularies. They continue to increase the number of words for the next few years.

DEVELOPMENT OF RULES OF SPEECH

As children learn to speak, they begin to put words together in patterns and gradually learn the grammatical rules of their language. They follow a sequence of language development, from sounds without meaning, to single words, to two-word sentences, to more complex structures. Jenny moves from saying, "Juice," to saying, "My juice," to saying, "Give Jenny apple juice." Children usually use nouns before pronouns, and "I" and "me" are often the first pronouns used.

Children usually learn the names of objects first and gradually make finer discriminations. They notice likenesses and differences. For Elise, all four-legged animals are dogs. Later she identifies dog, cat, cow, and horse and further refines her classification to little dog and big dog.

Concepts of time and space are difficult to comprehend. William cannot tell the difference between tomorrow and next week. He knows only that it is not now. After much practice and experience, children begin to recognize shades of meanings and become more precise and facile with language. Philip talks about his warm blue coat, and Alice knows that hers is bright blue because she has heard her mother describe it that way.

Children draw generalizations about how words come together to form sentences. Then they overgeneralize, not realizing that there are exceptions to rules. If "I cooked the egg" is a correct grammatical construction, then "I tooked the ball" seems equally correct to Claire. Instead of saying, "I forgot the picture," Sam is likely to tell his father that he "forgotted" the picture.

AGE	ABILITY
9 months and up	Begins to intentionally use words to communicate.
1 year	Imitates sounds.
	Responds to many words that are a part of experience: "Bye-bye," "Daddy," "Momma."
2 years	Should be able to follow simple commands without visual clues: "Johnny, get your hat." "Claire, bring me your ball."
	Uses a variety of everyday words heard in home and neighborhood: "Mommy," "Milk," "Ball," "Hat."
	Shows developing sentence sense by the way words are put together: "Go bye bye car." "Milk all gone."
3 years	Understands and uses words other than for naming; is able to fit simple verbs, pronouns, prepositions, and adjectives such as "go," "me," "in," "big" more and more into sentences.
4 years	Should be able to give a connected account of some recent experience.
	Should be able to carry out a sequence of two simple directions: "Bobby, find Susie and tell her dinner's ready."
5 years	Speech should be intelligible although some sounds may still be mispronounced.
	Can carry on a conversation if vocabulary is within his or her range.

Adapted from *Learning to Talk,* prepared by the U.S. National Institute of Neurological Disease and Stroke, National Institutes of Health, U.S. Department of Health, Education and Welfare. Washington, DC: U.S. Government Printing Office, 1969, pp. 22–24.

Figure 18-1

Child's development of language ability.

When Ella says, "I runned down the hill," she demonstrates an advanced stage of language development, using a grammar rule she discovered for herself. Children learn rules about past tense as they become familiar with the language. In a similar manner, they learn the rules about plurals. If the plural of house is houses, should not the plural of goose be gooses?

A child hears sounds all around. Adults, other children, radio, and television all provide aural stimulation. As children learn to speak, adults need to accept the language they produce. Whatever the nature of the sounds they make, they should be encouraged to talk and not be restrained by criticism or corrections. If the adults around them speak well, children usually begin to use words correctly, too. A child who has many verbal interactions with adults is likely to develop greater verbal proficiency and confidence in the use of words than one who has not had such experiences.

Literacy

All the information discussed to this point falls under the general term "literacy." **Literacy** in its most general sense is a mastery of language—speaking, listening, writing, and reading. Literacy learning, as discussed earlier, begins in infancy and continues through life. In helping children develop literacy, we must respect the language the child brings to school and use it as a base for language and literacy activities. To develop literacy we build on what the child already knows about oral language, reading, and writing. A child's literacy grows when we encourage children to see themselves as people who can enjoy exploring oral and written language.

Enhancing Language Development

A true mastery of language requires social interaction. A classroom in which children are given many opportunities to interact with others is one in which language development is fostered. A teacher can create an environment that fosters language development of young children by creating a child-centered classroom where young children are given many opportunities to pursue their own interests and trusted to know what it is they want and need to learn.

Language experiences during self-initiated play.
When children move freely to activities of their choice in self-initiated play in a child-centered environment, more language is used with greater richness of speech than when children are in classrooms where formal instruction dominates the program. When children discover they can satisfy needs by speaking, they gain confidence in their abilities to speak and begin to value language.

Interaction is an important part of communication. Children speak and listen as they play with clay, dough, paint, pegs, blocks, sand, and water. If they feel comfortable when they talk, they are more likely to experiment with language. In a housekeeping area, children talk to each other as they re-enact familiar roles. Formal or informal midday snack arrangements provide natural settings for conversations. Such activities as playing with blocks, pounding and rolling clay, and experimenting with magnets all offer children rich opportunities to speak, listen, and exchange ideas with others.

Language experiences in small-group activities. In small groups children are more likely to talk to each other and to the teacher and have less anxiety than when they are expected to respond in large groups.

Sharing time in an early childhood program is best when it involves a small group of three to five children. In a large group, it is necessary to limit each child's conversation so that several children have an opportunity to speak, and this limitation tends to discourage children from talking. A group of three to five is a more natural situation for young children.

Formal discussion periods are neither as interesting nor as meaningful as informal conversations in a small group. A child who takes a treasured item out of his pocket to share with two or three friends is probably enjoying a very personal experience. But when "Show and Tell" time is made into a daily ritual in which many children are expected to participate, the personal excitement may disappear for the speaker. The telling supersedes the sharing, and the personal reactions of peers are not part of the experience. When incorporated into a program at an appropriate time, "Show and Tell" can be valued by all as a sharing experience. When it is structured as a language lesson, its values are likely to be lost. Early childhood classrooms should reflect these and many other opportunities for young children's developing language skills. You may want to use the Observation Sheet, "Classroom Literacy Environment Survey" in the Online Companion to assist you in your classroom observations.

UNDERSTANDING BILINGUAL/ BICULTURAL YOUNG CHILDREN'S LANGUAGE DEVELOPMENT

Our schools are blessed with an ever growing multicultural population. This rich cultural mix is an exciting opportunity for children and teachers to learn about other cultures on a daily basis. Unfortunately, many young children from diverse developing nations are entering schools not fully prepared to receive them. The importance of including the needs of children who are bilingual/bicultural in the early childhood language program is obvious in our multicultural world.

The early childhood teacher plays a critical role in the lives of linguistically and culturally diverse young children. It is important to remember that children will not learn literacy skills in a language they do not yet speak. This is why it is so important to support the continuous development of the child's primary language while providing meaningful experiences with English. Consider using some of the following suggestions to help provide meaningful experiences in English to children from diverse language and multicultural backgrounds.

⊙ Bilingual children can participate easily in dance, art, and drama activities that call for nonverbal communication; the arts are universal languages used to communicate when words cannot or when words are inadequate for ideas and feelings.

⊙ Make connections to special cultural holidays, customs, people, and experiences in arts activities. Invite students to share their rich multiethnic backgrounds and use this as a basis for artistic creations. Invite parents as guests to share multicultural art forms.

⊙ Folk literature is a universal literary form, so it is one place to begin to integrate multicultural art. Many plot lines, like that of "Cinderella," have been found in hundreds of cultures and written in dozens of languages. Include stories from students' language and cultural heritages. Encourage students to share cultural stories from home, and use these for drama, dance, art, and music activities.

⊙ Drama, art, dance, or music based on children's literature can be a good vehicle for learning English vocabulary. Familiar songs in a language can be translated into English. Name tags or hats can be made for characters during drama (e.g., tags with *stepsister, mother, father, prince* in both English and the child's native language).

⊙ Give every child a small recipe box with empty index cards at the start of the year. Keep this "word box" nearby so that new words can be collected and used or referred to for children's writing activities. Make sure that each word is accompanied by a small, simple sketch representing that word.

⊙ Look around your classroom. How many words do you see? A print-rich classroom has meaningful words taped, glued, or written on objects and equipment in each learning center. These words can be written in both English and in the child's native language. To make labels, use any word processor with a large, clear font. Type out a list (in both languages), print it on regular paper, and

Figure 18-2

Pretend reading of favorite books is one activity familiar to many parents and teachers of young children.

tape the printed words on objects. Digital cameras are great for adding pictures to these labels.

The early childhood setting becomes a home-away-from-home, the first contact with nonfamily members, the first contact with culturally different people, and the first experience with nonnative speakers. A teacher's attitude and knowledge base is crucial in making the early childhood program accepting and appreciative of diversity (Duke, 2003).

The possibilities are endless for teachers of young children who, as role models, are in a unique position to establish the tone or "classroom climate" through decision making, collaboration, interactions, and activities. It is possible to offer the best teaching we can to all young children who are experiencing English as an

unfamiliar language. We can help these young children by doing the following:

- Accepting individual differences with regard to language-learning time frames. It's a myth to think that young children can learn a language quickly and easily. Avoid pressures to "rush" and "push out" children to join the mainstream classroom. Young children need time to acquire, explore, and experience second-language learning.

- Accepting children's attempts to communicate, because trial and error are a part of the second-language learning process. Negotiating meaning and collaborating in conversations are important. Children should be given opportunities to practice both native and newly established language skills. Adults should not dominate the conversations; rather, children should be listened to. Plan and incorporate opportunities for conversation within dramatic play, storytime, puppetry, peer interactions, social experiences, field trips, cooking, and other enriching activities.

- Maintaining an *additive* philosophy by recognizing that children need to acquire new language skills instead of replacing existing linguistic skills. Afford young children an opportunity to retain their native language and culture. Allow young learners ample social opportunities to practice emerging linguistic skills.

- Providing a stimulating, active, diverse linguistic environment with many opportunities for language use in meaningful social interactions. Avoid rigid or didactic grammatical approaches with young children. Children enjoy informal play experiences, dramatizations, puppetry, telephone conversations, participation in children's literature, and social interactions with peers.

- Incorporating culturally responsive experiences for all children. Valuing each child's home culture and incorporating meaningful, active participation will help children develop interpersonal skills and contribute to eventual academic and social success.

- Using informal observations to guide the planning of activities, interactions, and other conversations for speakers of other languages.

- Providing an accepting classroom climate that values culturally and linguistically diverse young children.

See Figure 18–3 for more suggestions.

The Anti-Bias Curriculum (ABC)

Creative teachers promote an **inclusive environment,** one that addresses both the daily life realities

DIFFERENTIATING INSTRUCTION FOR SECOND LANGUAGE LEARNERS

Here are some more strategies you can use to differentiate instruction for second language learners:

⊙ Establish a relaxed learning environment that encourages students to take risks and attempt to use both languages and emphasizes communication rather than language form. For example, correct students indirectly by restating their incorrect comments in correct form. If the child says "My notebook home," you say, "I understand, your notebook is at home."

⊙ Begin new lessons with reviews of relevant previously learned concepts, and show the relationships between previously learned concepts and new material.

⊙ Be consistent in your use of language, and use repetition to help students acquire the rhythm, pitch, volume, and tone of their new language.

⊙ Use gestures, facial expressions, voice changes, pantomimes, demonstrations, rephrasing, visuals, props, manipulatives, and other cues to provide a context that conveys the meaning of new terms and concepts.

⊙ Supplement oral instructions and descriptions with visual materials such as charts, maps, graphs, and pictures.

⊙ Make it easier for students to understand and respond by speaking clearly; pausing often; limiting the use of idiomatic expressions, slang, and pronouns; highlighting key words through increased volume and slight exaggeration; using rephrasing, simple vocabulary, and shorter sentences; and giving students enough time to respond.

⊙ Allow students to express their knowledge, understanding, and intended meaning nonverbally. For example, rather than asking a student to define a word or idea, ask the student to draw a picture showing it.

⊙ Encourage and show students how to use bilingual dictionaries and pictionaries.

⊙ Offer regular summaries of important content, and check students' understanding frequently. (Duke, 2003).

Figure 18-3

Differentiating Instruction for Second Language Learners.

of cultural diversity as well as the potentially biased attitudes and behaviors that are part of this reality. The early childhood teacher creating an inclusive environment plans the curriculum to address the cultural differences represented by the children in the group and in the society in general. This inclusive curriculum reflects a sensitivity to all cultural groups in all areas of the curriculum. Related inherently to the inclusive environment is the concept of an **anti-bias curriculum (ABC).** This concept developed by the NAEYC's ABC Task Force and Louise Derman-Sparks (Derman-Sparks ABC Task Force, 1989) is an excellent starting point for planning an inclusive, anti-bias curriculum. The Task Force's booklet, as well as other references at the end of this chapter, contain many excellent suggestions on ABC planning, working with parents, and suggested books and materials—all essential in preparing an inclusive environment for young children of all cultural groups.

The language arts curriculum is an excellent starting point for the ABC because there are hundreds of quality books for children representing a multitude of ethnic groups. Teachers of young children need to select literature that reflects the perspectives, experiences, and values of all ethnic and cultural groups. See Chapters 24–27 for more information on the ABC.

DEVELOPMENT OF LISTENING

Just exactly how a child learns to listen and understand language has been studied by many researchers and language experts. Some argue that language and thought grow somewhat independently, at least in the early stages of language development. This view does make sense when you consider the fact that young children are often able to learn words and phrases that have no meaning for them. (Remember how three year olds can sing popular songs yet do not understand the words.)

Listening is not a passive receiving of information. Good listening involves receiving and processing incoming information. Listening is more than simply hearing because good listeners filter out much of what they hear in order to concentrate on a message.

Children are not the only ones who should listen and teachers are not the only speakers. Rather, children *and* teachers need to be good listeners, and children should listen to one another as carefully as they do to adults.

Good listeners are *active.* They get involved with what they hear, both intellectually and emotionally. Active listeners give complete attention to what they hear. They are active in that they process the information, make pertinent comments, and ask relevant questions.

Young children may *act* as if they understand concepts at a level that they cannot yet express in words. Because young children think in simple, basic ways, they have difficulty comprehending adult language that is abstract or too complex. Abstraction is beyond the thinking capabilities of the young child in preschool and early elementary years. The teacher or child care worker who is not aware of these language limitations of young children can easily lose their attention. For example, a visiting firefighter who described the firehose as "a supplementary antiincendiary device" obviously was unaware of the language level of the audience and more accustomed to addressing adults! In the same manner, a teacher who directs a child pulling another's hair to "be nice" is too general and abstract in her directions. A more appropriate, direct, and less abstract request for a young child would be, "Don't pull Jane's hair."

Figure 18-4
Learning to listen is part of language development.

Physical conditions affecting the listener (deafness, hunger, fatigue, illness, and physical environment) can impair the listening process or influence the quality of listening.

The environmental climate or atmosphere in the early childhood program should motivate listening. The atmosphere needs to be one in which children are free to express their ideas; they should feel that their contributions will be accepted and respected.

EMERGING LITERACY

> From your parents you learn love and laughter and how to put one foot before the other. But when books are opened you discover you have wings. Helen Hayes

If reading is defined as the interpretation of symbols, it could be said that a child begins reading the day he or she is born. A baby gets excited when he or she sees her bottle. The baby stops crying when mother enters the room and smiles. The baby gurgles with pleasure when members of the family stop to play with him or her. He or she is responding to what *he or she* reads into the actions of others. These experiences precede understanding the printed word.

Not all children should be expected to learn to read in the same way, at the same rate, or at the same age. Children begin by reading pictures, taking great delight in recognizing objects with which they are familiar. As adults read to children, thereby exposing them to words in the books they read, children begin to understand that printed words say something.

THINK ABOUT IT... **They Are Listening . . . What Do They Hear?**

While walking along the sidewalk in front of his church, a minister heard the intoning of a prayer that nearly made his collar wilt. Apparently, his 5–year-old son and his playmates had found a dead robin. Feeling that proper burial should be performed, they had secured a small box and cotton lining, then dug a hole and made ready for the disposal of the deceased. The minister's son was chosen to say the appropriate prayers and with sonorous dignity intoned his version of what he thought his father always said: "Glory be unto the Faaaaather, and unto the Sonnnn . . . and into the hole he gooooooes."

What does the above scene tell you about young children's listening skills? About adults' use of words? Can you think of other similar stories from your own childhood?

THINK ABOUT IT...

Read-Alouds and Emergent Reading in the Early Childhood Classroom

Children who participate in read-aloud sessions and do their own emergent readings of favorite books grow as readers because they are engaged in authentic, natural literacy, not in instruction-focused tasks that break up reading into separate "skills." Practice in the natural activity of emergent reading is a good preparation for later, conventional reading.

By becoming aware of the benefits of linking emergent reading to read-aloud sessions and by arranging classroom space and time to promote these activities, teachers can maximize the benefits of reading aloud and emergent reading in early childhood classrooms in the following ways.

1. **Invite children to participate actively in read-aloud sessions.** Ask questions that require children to predict what will happen next and to link the story to their own experiences. As books become more familiar to the children, pause before familiar or repeated patterns and allow children to complete the reading. Give children opportunities to choose their favorite books to be read to the group.

2. **Provide frequent opportunities for young children to engage in book handling and emergent reading.** Although for many years many classrooms have featured daily book browsing time, there are still too many classrooms in which children look at books only as a transitional or optional activity with books available to children who have finished other "required" activities or who choose to look at books during "free-choice" times. As a result, children who have had less experience with books or who work slowly have little occasion for self-directed interaction with books. Teachers should instead establish daily "Serious Reading Time" when *all* children are expected to be involved with books in whatever manner is most comfortable for them—browsing through books, looking at pictures, emergently or conventionally reading.

3. **Read favorite books repeatedly to encourage emergent reading.** Follow through by making these books available for children to look at on their own or with other children and adults. Children are more likely to choose books and engage in emergent reading with books that are familiar to them. Set up the classroom so that familiar books are available and visible to children during independent time and free time. (More specific information on the book center is found later in this chapter.) Arrange for reading aloud to be done in or near the classroom book center so that children see the connection between hearing books read and reading them on their own and that books read by the teacher can be easily put in the library. Schedule time for children to independently read or look at books soon after the teacher has read to them, again highlighting the connection between the adult read-aloud and children's independent involvement with books.

4. **During read-aloud and independent-involvement times, teachers have opportunities to observe children's emerging literacy in real-life situations.** Become more aware of how children respond during read-aloud sessions (a tape recorder might be useful). Which of the children asked and answered questions? Which ones participated in reading by "chiming in" on familiar parts or by making predictions? How do children's questions and comments change over several readings of the same book? What kinds of questions and comments came from you, the teacher?

    By listening to children's emergent readings (live or taped), teachers can see how much book content and book language children incorporate. Do children use the distinctive language of books? Do they use literary formulae such as "once upon a time"? What sources of information do children use when they "read"? Do they use the pictures, the print, memory of the text and discussion, and their personal experiences?

5. **Educate parents about the ability of their child to "pretend read" books and to participate in reading through "completion reading."** Some parents worry that "pretend reading" will result in bad habits that will prevent children from learning to "really read." Reassure all of these parents that their children's reading-like behaviors, even though they may not involve attention to print, are a source of future reading success. Parents also need to understand that allowing children to participate in read-aloud sessions through joint reading and discussion can enrich the literacy experience for parents and children (Adapted from Elster, 1994).

Emergent Reading

Pretend reading of favorite books is an activity familiar to many parents and teachers of young children. During pretend reading—also called *emergent reading* (Sulzby, 1985) or *reenactment* (Holdaway, 1979)—children practice reading-like behaviors that build their confidence in themselves as readers.

Adults interested in emergent or pretend reading have long assumed that children imitate adult reading—that is, they pick up reading-like behaviors and story language after adults read aloud to them. We can see the beginnings of independent emergent reading when children participate in adult read-alouds by "reading along" with an adult reader—mumbling, echoing phrases, and completing sentences and phrases when the adult reader pauses.

During emergent reading children combine several information sources: the pictures and print in the book; input from adult listeners, as well as their own memory for having heard and discussed the book previously; their personal experiences; and their background knowledge about the world, language, and how stories sound. In emergent literacy programs, children enjoy and participate actively in reading experiences long before they are readers in the conventional sense of the word.

Both participation in read-aloud sessions and emergent reading give children opportunities to learn about the language and the meaning of reading in a natural setting. By giving children opportunities to interact with books, through read-alouds and emergent readings, teachers help children grow as competent and confident readers (Elster, 1994). The box, Think About It: Read-Alouds and Emergent Reading in the Classroom, presents more specific suggestions for emergent reading activities in the early childhood classroom.

Conventional reading involves total development—emotional, social, physical, and intellectual readiness. A child who has not yet acquired large-muscle control will not be able to develop more refined skills, such as matching shapes and recognizing patterns needed for reading. Some children are not interested or physically ready to read until they are six, seven, or even eight years of age. When children are forced to engage in reading activities before they are physically, intellectually, or emotionally ready, reading can become a burden. Vision, hearing, diet, and physical coordination are all factors to be considered. Eye-muscle development is necessary and cannot be rushed. Speaking skills are needed for success in reading. And motivation is a primary factor for success.

Figure 18-5
Picture books are one of the most popular forms of children's books.

PREWRITING SKILLS

Another skill that is part of a child's emerging literacy is writing. In the preschool and early childhood period, a child is developing the physical skills needed to write later on in school. It is not the goal to have young children "practice" letters and words in the early childhood language arts program. Instead, the goal is to provide young children with opportunities to practice the hand–eye coordination and small-muscle skills needed to be able to write.

For preschoolers, writing is a part of the total language experience, preceded by many fine motor control activities. Writing begins when children first become interested in making their own marks, and it continues to be a part of their everyday experiences. When children show an interest in writing, large pieces of paper are made available along with crayons, felt-tip pens, and pencils.

Figure 18-6

It is important to read favorite books often to encourage emergent reading.

Figure 18-7

Learning to identify shapes is necessary to learning the alphabet.

For preschoolers, reading and writing are closely related. Writing can be part of the language experience of children when children dictate stories for the teacher to write down.

Use children's artwork in conjunction with reading and writing. Besides making the obvious use of illustrations for stories, early readers can give titles to their work. Asking children if they would like to give their work a title reflects the teacher's valuing their work. Some children may want to give their work a title; others may not. Young children can also use photographs to tell stories that the teacher writes down. Preschool children might bring their baby pictures to school and then themselves be photographed by the teacher. Mount both pictures side by side, and then children can dictate descriptions of what they could do as babies and what they can do now that they are "big." Children can share the displayed individual books. A language experience approach such as this encourages literacy. Using cartoon boards and cartoon balloons enhances writing and reading motivation. Children can dictate or write captions in the balloons, stating what different characters in the strips are saying.

POETRY EXPERIENCES

Poetry is part of the magic that motivates children to love reading. The educational benefits of including poetry in the early childhood program are many. Exposure to poetry raises children's level of general language development and vocabulary development and whets their appetite for reading, too!

Some other benefits of including poetry on a regular basis in the early childhood program include the following:

⊙ Poetry's often playful approach to language helps children think about language forms as well as meaning. The predictable rhythms of Mother Goose rhymes naturally segment speech sounds and expose and highlight phonetic similarities and differences in a way that normal speech does not.

⊙ Children take pride in learning to recite short poems. Thus, poetry can be used to stimulate the development of memory, which will aid in future learning. Knowing poems enhances feelings of competence, which is important for young children. Young children who continually hear poetry read effectively and those who have the opportunity to join informally in reciting it will soon have

THIS ONE'S for YOU!

Mother Goose Is Back in Style

Mother Goose, it seems, really does matter. Buried in the nonsensical couplets chanted by generations of children is the link to understanding syllables and phonemes, the building blocks to literacy.

A slew of studies since the mid–1980s has shown that rhymes directly contribute to a child's vocabulary and understanding of language. To recognize that two words rhyme is to know something about the sounds that make up words. Learning to recognize the word "clean," for example, helps children learn new words like "lean" and "mean."

The better children are at detecting rhymes, the quicker and more successful is their reading progress—a relationship that holds true in dozens of studies despite children's IQs or social backgrounds. Research on children with reading difficulties has found that many struggling readers are strikingly insensitive to rhyme.

"When children rhyme, it really draws attention to the fact that words have parts," said Sally Shaywitz, a professor of pediatrics and a brain researcher at Yale University. "When most of us hear a word, we don't pay attention to the fact that even a simple word like *cat* has three sounds: kkkk/aaaa/tttt. When you rhyme the last part of a word, you are realizing a distinct part of the word and what the sound is. In order to read, you also have to appreciate that words are made up of different sounds. It's really the same ability. It's learning to break the code" (Farrell, 1999).

This deeper understanding of the power of rhymes has prompted a revival among reading experts for Mother Goose, that collection of English childhood rhymes, jingles, songs, and riddles that originated centuries ago.

It's why rhymes are dubbed "essential" for young children, ages three and four, in a joint statement for parents issued in 1999 by the National Association for the Education of Young Children and the International Reading Association.

What you have to do with Mother Goose is to lift the words off the pages of the book. Just reading a rhyme in a book with a child is not nearly as much fun as when you know the rhymes and use them as part of your daily life. You're diapering a child or riding in the car with your preschooler and doing "one, two, buckle my shoe." Then it's fun, it's alive. If you love it, your child will like it. If you read in a dull, boring way, your child won't relate to it. It's all in the presentation (Farrell, 1999).

But how much Mother Goose does anybody truly remember? A recent study by a Pennsylvania researcher suggests that nursery rhymes are part of a dying tradition, with few—if any—passed on to young children.

Beth Goldstone, an assistant professor of education at Beaver College in Glenside, PA, surveyed 150 preschoolers in a Philadelphia suburb and found that more than a third did not know *Jack Be Nimble, Hey Diddle Diddle,* or *Little Miss Muffet,* among others.

Kindergarten teachers often expect children to have that kind of background and too often the children don't. Mother Goose is one of the foundations of our language. She also plays a role in creating a community of knowledge. It's essential for children to hear those rhymes.

So Mother Goose is definitely back in style for young children!

---

quite a repertoire of memorized poetry without any effort. It is quite appropriate to expect three- and four-year-old children to happily chant finger plays, Mother Goose rhymes, and short poems such as those found at the end of this unit.

⊙ Fingerplays, or poems recited and accompanied by appropriate body movements, help develop co-ordination and muscle tone. Asking children to in-

vent their own movements helps them develop problem-solving abilities. Some of these poems also help in learning to name body parts ("Hokey Pokey," for example).

⊙ Acting out poetry can be a fun and beneficial drama and speech activity for children of all ages. By allowing children to organize and act out poems using props and costumes, the teacher encourages the development of creativity and positive self-concept as well as of language.

⊙ Children can be encouraged to illustrate favorite poems to display in the classroom or to take home, thus stimulating artistic expression and development while aiding language development. Using colored chalks, paint, markers, and crayons, many young artists will illustrate the mood of the poem more movingly than we ever could have imagined!

⊙ Smooth, natural transitions from one activity can be made through the use of carefully selected poems. The following poem, for example, is a perfect choice when the teacher wishes to move from an energetic activity to a quiet one like storytime or a group discussion.

> Touch your ears.
> Touch your eyes.
> Touch your nose.
> Now bend down and touch your toes.
> Wiggle your fingers.
> Turn around.
> Now bend down and touch the ground.
> Clap your hands—1, 2, 3.
> Now see how quiet you can be.
> (Janice Hayes Andrews)

Let poetry fill your and the children's days. Why not recite a verse while lining up to go to lunch? Memorize short poems to recite when waiting for stragglers to take their seats. Start the day with a poem; end the day with one as well. Create the job of poetry selector for the job chart. Poetry can rhyme or not, speak to deep emotions, or lift us with light language and witty wordplay.

Check out the Reading is Fundamental (http://www.rif.org) Web site for more tips on using poetry to build literary skills. You will find many ideas for incorporating poetry into the curriculum.

Selecting Appropriate Poems

Using poetry in the classroom will, of course, be much more valuable and enjoyable if the poem selection is made carefully with the children's interests and needs in mind. Not all children have the same needs. And by no means are all children at the same developmental level. Choose poetry that meets all developmental levels in the group.

Another important criterion for selecting poetry to present in any classroom is that the teacher should like it, too. It is not possible for a teacher to read a poem well or generate much enthusiasm for it if he or she does not enjoy it.

⊙ When selecting poems, think about what the children are likely to find appealing. From approximately three to six years old, young children like things that seem relevant to them. In order for something to be relevant to children, it must somehow relate to the world as they know it, if not directly to them. By selecting poetry about familiar objects, events, and feelings, the teacher takes a major step toward making poetry interesting and enjoyable for young children. Older children enjoy poetry that challenges their imagination and thinking skills.

⊙ Focus on popular topics. There are certain subjects that almost all young children enjoy. For this reason, these subjects are traditionally dealt with in most early childhood programs—self-awareness, the senses, the family, feelings, transportation, seasons, holidays, animals, plants, water, earth, sky. By selecting poems that deal with these subjects as they are being emphasized in class, you can capitalize on the interest generated by other classroom activities: science, social studies, music, and so on. Many children's poetry books classify poems according to these categories, making it easy to find appropriate poems. There are several good collections of children's poetry listed in the Online Companion for preschool, kindergarten, grade 3, and grade 4 to 5.

CHILDREN'S BOOKS

Children's books are a traditional part of the language arts program in most early childhood programs. These books must be chosen with care for young children's use. They must be right for the developmental level of the child. The pictures should be easily seen; the story easily understood by young listeners.

"ABC" or alphabet books for young children also must be chosen carefully. Very young children need simple, uncluttered alphabet books. Words should represent familiar, concrete objects, with "a" beginning "apple" rather than "atom."

First alphabet books typically pair initial sounds with words, and these associations should depict regular sounds. Pages that proclaim "K is for knife" or "G is for gnu" bewilder rather than educate. These key words should also have unambiguous names: "B is for bow-wow," in a book filled with objects rather than sounds, will confuse the child who identified the animal as a dog.

In addition, illustrations must be obvious and straightforward. Complications in naming lead to misunderstandings. One preschooler, upset because she had read an alphabet book incorrectly, sadly pointed out this problem: "I said 'R for rope' but the book meant 'S for snake.'" There are three additional features characteristic of good ABC books:

- ◉ Well-written ABC books focus on a central idea of concept and the alphabet sequence merely provides a story format. You should look for ABC books that follow a *limited* subject such as endangered species rather than a broad subject such as wild animals.

- ◉ The best ABC books provide thoughtful features such as bilevel text and addenda, with bilevel text appearing on the page in two font sizes for two reading skill levels. Younger listeners enjoy the illustrations and sometimes notice the letters of the alphabet or the larger print. Beginning readers may explore the accompanying text, which appears in smaller print size.

- ◉ Good-quality ABC publications invite the response or involvement of the children in the read-aloud experience, and they also provide teachers with a rich source of ideas for extended activities in the early childhood setting. ABC books can be starting points for group projects or individual activities (Rhoten & Lane, 2001).

Children interacting with their first texts are not reading in the traditional sense of relying solely on the printed word. Instead, as emergent readers, they depend on illustrations to create meaning. Consequently, in initial alphabet books, only one or two objects should appear on the page, acknowledging the young child's perceptual and spatial skills. There's plenty of time later on to hunt for hidden pictures, sort out numerous nouns, or locate obscure objects after letter-sound correspondence has been mastered.

See the "Think about it" box on page 368 for guidelines on what to look for in choosing books for children.

The Book Center

Create a place where children can explore the world of books. A library or book center is an important part of every early childhood classroom as well as elementary classrooms. As you use books during circle time, children will realize the "magic" of books, that they have good make-believe stories or are full of facts and have pretty pictures. Children will then want to explore those books on their own, so they need to have a well-organized place where they can go and read.

Think about the physical space first and be sure you find a place that is away from the more "active"

Figure 18-8
Forming letters may be appropriate for some young children in early childhood programs.

goings-on in the room, a place where the child can quietly explore books. Gather together a table, some chairs or soft cushions, and shelves for books, tapes, CDs, and magazines. When covering some units, you might want to create an unusual seating place, such as making an airplane out of a large box as you talk and read about types of transportation.

Take time to decorate the nearby bulletin boards or tops of shelves with book jackets, pictures, flowers, and special collections related to the books you have in the book center. If you choose to display the letters of the alphabet, be sure you do so in a developmentally appropriate manner. This means that they are as follows:

- ◉ Where children can see them. Alphabet displays way above children's heads are of little use. Letters need to be at eye level where children can examine them.

- ◉ Where children can refer to them as they work and play. When they are writing, children are far more likely to make use of letter guides that are close at hand. Teachers can apply alphabet strips to tabletops or laminate letter-writing guides that children can take off a shelf and bring with them to wherever they are writing.

- ◉ Where children can handle them. Children notice the shapes of letters when they do alphabet puzzles or use letter-shaped cookie cutters in damp sand or dough. Magnetic letters and alphabet

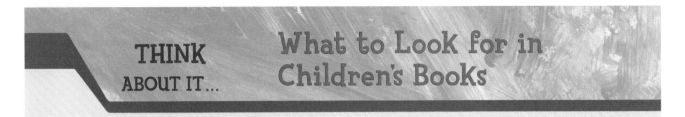

THINK ABOUT IT...

What to Look for in Children's Books

Children today live in an exciting media-driven time of television, video games, and computers. Yet, no medium can stir a child's imagination like the pages of a good book. There is an enormous selection of children's books available today. The following are some general guidelines on what to look for in choosing children's books from preschool through grade 5.

BABY BOOKS

There are four basic kinds of baby books.

1. board books that are made with sturdy cardboard pages that can be wiped clean
2. touch and feel books that have cloth, feathers, fur, and familiar "feely" things attached to them for little ones to discover
3. cloth books that are made of safe, washable material
4. bath books that are constructed of soft, durable plastic and can take a lot of abuse

What to look for:

⊙ simple text and art

⊙ repetition and bouncy rhymes

⊙ bright and familiar photos or artwork (there should be a connection between baby's surroundings and the book's pictures)

⊙ a sturdy book that can handle many spills

⊙ rounded corners for safety

⊙ a book the right size and shape for little hands

⊙ a book you will enjoy as well; baby will recognize your enjoyment

PRESCHOOL

Preschool books are on a higher level than baby books but on a slightly lower level than picture books. In addition to hardcover and paperback, preschool books come in a variety of novelty formats. Among them are

⊙ lift-the-flap books that have sturdy pages and flaps to lift that reveal hidden words or pictures

⊙ pop-up books that have paper-engineered pages that make pictures three dimensional

⊙ pull-tab books that have tabs to pull to change the pictures

Some books combine all of these features. These kinds of books are designed to be played with as much as to be read—yet another way to show that books are fun.

What to look for in preschool books:

⊙ a book that clearly covers the concept you are trying to teach

⊙ a book that helps develop the child's sense of humor

⊙ an easy and fun story line

⊙ clear and easy-to-read books

⊙ colorful, high-quality illustrations

⊙ illustrations that a child can connect with his or her own life and situation

PICTURE BOOKS

Picture books are one of the most popular forms of children's books and are appropriate for a wide range of ages and reading levels. Picture books have varying amounts of art and text (some are even wordless!).

(Continues)

THINK ABOUT IT... (Continued)

Some story lines are simple, while others are quite complex. Subjects can be beautiful, funny, moving, scary, or just plain silly. What is important is that you find a picture book the children in your life will relate to and enjoy.

What to look for:

- art or photography the child responds to
- story lines that elicit questions and discussions
- stories that develop the child's sense of humor
- stories that help with children's issues—such as sibling rivalry or going to school
- stories you enjoyed as a child and would like to share with children
- titles recommended by reviewers and award committees

EARLY READERS

These books are designed to supplement a child's reading program at school. As with picture books, early readers cover a wide variety of subjects. They are illustrated, though the emphasis is more on text than on illustrations. Early readers are targeted toward specific reading levels or by grade. As every child is different, you may wish to judge on your own which reading level is appropriate.

What to look for:

- a reading level that will challenge but will not intimidate the child
- clear text (the print size varies with reading levels)
- a topic that will stimulate further interest in reading
- favorite artists the child has enjoyed at an earlier level of reading
- nonfiction subjects the child enjoys, such as sports, history, fantasy, or adventure
- new subjects to introduce to the child, such as fantasy and folklore

FICTION

When we enter the world of fiction, we leave behind colorful pictures and favorite characters, and subject matter becomes more complicated. The early readers are the stepping stones to these more advanced works.

What to look for:

- books with a reading level that will challenge and stimulate
- books with a subject that interests the young reader; many children want to pick out their own books at this age
- some of the more popular and enduring titles are available in different editions (the trim size of the books may vary, and the cover art may vary as well, but almost without exception the text remains the same)
- some classic tales in abridged formats

---

blocks allow children to explore letter/sound connections, arrange and rearrange letters to form words, and become more aware of the sequences of sounds within words.

Place certain kinds of books on the shelves so that they are readily available at all times—Mother Goose books; poetry books; a children's simple encyclopedia (there are some two- and three-volume sets); "sense" books where children can touch, scratch, and smell as they look; some of the classic stories with which children are already familiar, such as *Goldilocks and the Three Bears, The Little Engine That Could, The Three Little Pigs,* and *The Cat in the Hat.* Books reflecting ethnic diversity should always be available for children's use. Books portraying ethnic diversity of children in the group as well as those not represented in the group need to be on the shelves.

Figure 18-9
Older children enjoy writing original stories.

As concepts—the alphabet, numbers, animals, families, and transportation—are introduced, provide a special bookshelf or display area where children can find books on those subjects and expand their knowledge about each concept.

You can begin to introduce the organization of a real library by color-coding the different types of books with a colored dot fastened to the bottom edge of each book. Then, use paper strips on the shelves so that children can replace the books where they belong just by matching the strip on the shelf with the mark on the book.

Help children determine what rules should be followed as they read in the book center; these should relate to behavior, care of books, and removal of books from the areas.

Encourage frequent use of the book center. This means that you need to change the displays and what books are available so that children will want to explore continually to see what is new. It's hard to be interested in a shabby collection of books casually tossed on a table in the corner of the room!

Involve the children in decorating the book center. They can help you change the display or make pictures for use on the library corner bulletin board. Then the book center will be a place where they feel they belong.

Just as important as *what* you read is *how* you read it to young children. The following section gives some guidelines for reading to young children in the best possible way.

Reading to Children

Reading to young children has a few very general requirements. For instance, it is best to work with children's short attention spans by choosing books that are not too long. Young children's visual discrimination also requires books that have pictures large enough for them to see. (Remember, the small muscles of the eyes are the last to develop to maturity.) A book with a story that is simple, yet interesting in its wording, is also good for young children.

Children in the middle to upper elementary levels still enjoy illustrated books, but the story is becoming equally as important to them. These children begin to enjoy fiction in which the subject matter becomes more complex. The variety of subjects available for use with older children reflects their expanding interests and personalities. Types of books of special interest to this age group are science fiction, fantasy, mystery, and tragedy as well as books on relationships, humorous tales, horror stories, and sports. Consider, the following suggestions to help you read stories to young children more effectively.

Guidelines for Story Groups.

1. Select a suitable spot—one that is quiet, away from distracting noises and activities. In the quiet corner, have books displayed at children's eye level. Have books already read out for children to look at and "re-read" themselves.

2. There is no law saying that reading aloud is always a large group activity. In fact, it is often very difficult to read to a large group of young children due to the fact that interest and attention span differences multiply as the group increases in size. Ideally, a small group of six to eight children is a more manageable and comfortable size for reading effectively to young children.

3. See that everyone is seated comfortably. Avoid crowding. Be sure that you as storyteller can see all the children's faces and that they can see yours. Rugs on the floor in a semicircle facing the teacher make a good seating arrangement. Sitting in chairs is uncomfortable for young children and causes a distraction if a child falls out of one.

4. If using a book, be sure to hold it so that all can see it. Do not hold the book in your lap. The best plan is to hold it out to one side up beside your cheek. This means that you must be able to read the story out of the side of your eye without turning the book toward you.

5. Be sure you like the story you read, otherwise you will put little enthusiasm into the telling of it.

6. Know your story well! If you do not, you will focus too much of your attention on the book. You must be free to notice the reactions of the children. Also, knowing the story well means that you will be able to tell it with appropriate enthusiasm, expression, and emphasis. Sounds are better made than read. For example, crow for "cock-a-doodle-do" and bark for "bow-wow" instead of just reading the words.

7. Read the story unhurriedly with an interesting, well-modulated voice. Read naturally—do not "talk down" to the children or have a special "story-telling" voice.

8. Do not comment so much throughout the story as you read it or point out so many things in the pictures that you break the thread of the story and spoil its effect.

9. Encourage comments and questions, but not to such a degree that it interrupts the flow of the story.

Practice reading a book to a group of children. Then go back to these guidelines to check to see if you used them effectively with children. It takes a good deal of practice to achieve mastery of the skill of story reading. If you make the experience a fun learning experience for yourself with the children, you are halfway there!

Reading to toddlers is an activity they truly enjoy. Here are a few guidelines for reading to this age group:

⊙ While you read to toddlers, follow the lines with your fingers. This helps toddlers who are learning that pages are read from top to bottom and from left to right and that pictures and printed words are related to each other.

⊙ Give toddlers a choice of books. Books at this age are good for memory development. As toddlers remember story lines, they begin to choose what they want to hear over and over again. Listening to preferred choices again and again increases a toddler's sense of self and security. Give toddlers several choices of books and you'll learn just which ones they love.

⊙ Choose interactive books. Some toddlers may have difficulty sitting still. Try to find books that encourage their participation by pushing moveable parts, uncovering a hidden character, making a figure pop up, or patting the bunny.

⊙ Use books that toddlers can carry. Toddlers like to possess books. Look for ones with handles or large plastic rings that toddlers can clutch and carry around as precious possessions.

⊙ Show your pleasure. As you settle down to read, let children know you enjoy books and reading together. After all, toddlers are great copycats. If

Figure 18-10
Children enjoy sharing ideas in language arts activities.

you are involved in a simple story, toddlers will get swept into the tale. As you encourage them to help turn pages, toddlers become truly involved with books for pleasure, for learning, and for life.

Storytelling

In today's modern world, storytelling has become a lost art. Despite a strong connection between storytelling and literacy, many teachers do not engage in storytelling to children. They may offer regular picture-book readings but neglect storytelling. Yet, the ancient art of storytelling is a vital way to inspire children's imaginations as well as language and listening skills. Storytelling *is not reading from a book to children*. In storytelling, the teacher weaves the story using his or her voice and expressions to compel the child's attention and interest.

Storytelling isn't limited to just one kind of story. When you develop your storytelling curriculum, be sure to include a good variety of these story types:

⊙ Fables—Short tales that have a moral and communicate a truth about life. The main characters in fables are often animals that act and think like humans.

⊙ Fairy tales—Stories that often feature fairies, elves, genies, pixies, leprechauns, and other make-believe characters.

⊙ Legends—Stories that revolve around incidents that are believed to have taken place in a particular culture's history.

⊙ Folk tales—Stories that come to us from many parts of the world. These stories reflect a particular country or people's flavor and preserve cultural traditions.

⊙ Poetry—Rhyming poetry, in particular Mother Goose rhymes, is a source of excellent storytelling for young children.

Tips for Storytelling.
Discover the right story to tell.

⊙ Look for stories that are age appropriate.

⊙ Find stories that you love.

⊙ Check picture books written for different age levels.

⊙ Collect stories from family, friends, and community.

⊙ Create your own stories.

Learn the story.

⊙ Read it several times.

⊙ Break it into a beginning, middle, and end.

Speak naturally.

⊙ Use your normal speaking voice.

⊙ Use sound effects, such as unusual voice and story sounds, sparingly.

Use simple, natural gestures.

⊙ Add gestures when they add to the story, but don't overuse them.

Polish the story.

⊙ Tell it, retell it, and retell it.

Once you have a story ready to tell to your satisfaction, the next step is to share it with the children:

⊙ Make eye contact with your listeners.

⊙ Introduce the story.

⊙ Tell the story looking directly into your listeners' eyes.

⊙ Encourage your listeners to interact with you.

⊙ Enjoy and work with your audience's enthusiasm.

A puppet is a natural prop to use when storytelling. Even a shy child will relate to a puppet. Puppets are also multisensory vehicles for storytelling. They create an art and language experience that children can understand. When you find a special puppet, give it a personality and a home, and you'll be amazed how children interact with it. Use it in your story and throughout your curriculum.

FLANNEL/STORY BOARDS

A flannel board or story board is another excellent addition to your storytelling. A story board can be used with any story. It can be held up or set up on an easel. By incorporating a storyboard in the telling of a story, children are encouraged to interact during your storytelling. Using a story board involves cooperation and interaction. Children can re-create the story as it unfolds by placing the characters on the story board in the order of their appearance. They can move them around, simulating the movements in the story. Putting the story up in sequence in this way builds a solid foundation on which to build future reading and writing skills.

Flannel board stories have a magical way of engaging children. They bring a rhyme, fairy tale, or story alive and immerse children in the emotions of the characters.

The tactile nature of the flannel board pieces invites children to "feel" each story component. And because the story is being "told" instead of read, there is more time to reflect on the behaviors and interactions of the characters.

Getting Started

To get started with flannel board stories, choose short stories children may know. This will not only invite their participation but also their willingness to delve into the deeper meanings of the stories. Fairy tales such as "The Little Red Hen," "Three Little Pigs," "Goldilocks and the Three Bears," and "Jack and the Beanstalk" all provide opportunities for children to empathize with the characters and their situations. Ask questions to get the conversation going: "How do you think the character feels in the beginning of the story?" "What problems arise?" "How would you feel if you were. . . . ?" Invite children to use the flannel board pieces to retell the story with their own words and feelings.

Longer stories can be used once children are familiar with the process. Traditional fairy tales such as "Hansel and Gretel" and "The Gingerbread Man" are good choices. A particularly good story for retelling is "Cinderella" because children can easily empathize with the main character.

Flannel Boards for Toddlers

With toddlers keep the pieces large and simple. It also doesn't hurt to make the pieces out of washable flannel that can be washed after the material has been lovingly "kissed!" Choose short and familiar nursery rhymes and songs that can be repeated over and over again. Good choices are "Hey Diddle Diddle," "Little Miss Muffet," and "The Itsy-Bitsy Spider." Don't worry if you don't get through the entire song or story. Initially, toddlers may just want to play with the pieces. Later they will be more interested in the story that goes with it.

Flannel Board Throughout the Day

For circle time, include a flannel weather doll that can be dressed with appropriate gear for the day's weather. At the end of the circle time, invite children to dress the doll for what they predict tomorrow's weather will be.

At the math center, use a poster board–size piece of flannel for a reusable graph. Divide the flannel into columns with boxes large enough for children to place small picture symbols, colors, and shapes. Children can also put a photo of themselves on a piece of felt and use it on the graph to "vote" for things.

At the listening center, put a tape recording of you and the children telling the flannel board stories in the center along with the flannel board and pieces for independent explorations.

A flannel/story board can be made by covering a piece of plywood or masonite cut to the desired size. Cover it with a piece of flannel as a backing with a piece of Velcro fabric on top. The children can use this story board to retell old and new favorite tales. Use Velcro fastening tape to affix storytelling characters to the story board.

You don't have to be an artist to make the story pieces. Besides drawing the story elements on felt, you can also cut or copy pictures from old books and magazines and glue them on felt pieces. Remember to use photographs of the children, too. These can be used on the flannel board to make up original stories.

When using Velcro, the soft side, or "loop" side of a piece of Velcro must meet the rougher side, or the "hook" side, of another piece of Velcro. Be sure when making puppets or props to use with a Velcro story board that the Velcro on the puppet will adhere to the Velcro on the story board. Self-adhesive hook Velcro can be cut into small pieces that you store until needed in a plastic bag. Self-adhesive Velcro can be placed on art foam, poster board, laminated materials, plastic, wood, felt, and fabric. It can also be applied to felt-board characters you already have so that you can re-use them with the Velcro boards. If Velcro pieces do not stick well, add a drop of quick-bonding glue and press in place. When taking down props that have been attached to a surface with Velcro, place your

Figure 18-11

Learning to identify words at sight–called "sight reading"–is part of learning to read.

thumb at the top of the item and gently pull down. (See end of chapter activities for more information on flannel boards.)

SUMMARY

Language is a part of the child's total development. Similar to physical growth, there is a definite pattern of development related to a child's growth of language, involving four distinct skills: speaking, listening, writing, and reading. Each of these four skills can develop at different rates in each individual child. This is why one child can be better at speaking than a peer who listens better than he or she speaks. A teacher of young children needs to understand each child's developmental level for each of these language skills in planning appropriate language arts experiences. For young children of non-English-language background, the early childhood teacher must create an environment that is accepting and appreciative of diversity. For non-English-speaking children, a teacher needs to accept individual differences with regard to language-learning time frames and give young children the time needed to acquire, explore, and experience second-language learning.

The ability to speak is not always directly related to the ability to understand. This is why young children can repeat words to a song without understanding what the words mean. Young children may also *act* as if they understand what is said when, in fact, they do not. The teacher or child care worker who is not aware of these language limitations of young children can easily lose their attention. This is because young children are really just learning how to listen.

Readiness for reading is termed "emerging literacy." This term refers to the time immediately before a child learns to read printed symbols as well as to the continuous development of prereading skills that begins at birth.

Prewriting skills are also considered a part of a child's emerging literacy. Learning to write involves fine motor skills and much hand–eye coordination. While actual writing practice is not appropriate in the early childhood program, activities that allow young children to practice these skills, such as painting, cutting, and working with clay, are practice writing skills.

Just as the child develops physically in a gradual process, reading skills also develop gradually. Early experiences at home and in the early childhood program can positively influence a child's reading readiness.

The use of children's books and poetry in the early childhood program helps develop young children's reading readiness. Children's books must be appropriate for the developmental level of the child. This means that the pictures must be easily seen and the story easily understood by the young listeners.

Older children enjoy illustrations in their books but the text is becoming equally important. Various kinds of fiction books are appropriate for middle and upper elementary children.

The way a teacher reads to young children is just as important as choosing the right books. Guidelines for reading to children as well as tips of storytelling are presented to assist teachers in these activities.

KEY TERMS

anti-bias curriculum (ABC)   literacy
inclusive environment   pretend reading

LEARNING ACTIVITIES

A. Observe an early childhood program and describe the language development of the children. Record at least three statements from the children to share with your classmates. Discuss your findings in class.

B. Visit a library and ask a librarian to recommend two good books for each of the following age levels: two year olds, three and four year olds, and five year olds. Compare each of the books on the following points:
   1. number of pages
   2. average number of sentences per page; average number of words per sentence
   3. theme of the book
   4. number of illustrations and size
   Discuss how the books were similar and different for each age group. If possible, bring your books into class. Share your ideas on them with your classmates.
   Make a second visit to the library and ask a librarian to recommend two good books for each of these levels: kindergarten to grade 3 and grades 4 to 5. Compare these books on the same points.

C. Give examples from your own experience with young children of the various language skills discussed in this chapter. For example, do you know any children who are better talkers than listeners? Better listeners?

D. Study the language development of a child three to six years of age and compare it to Figure 18–1. What similarities do you find? What differences do you find? You may wish to make comparisons with another child of approximately the same age.

E. Based on the information given in this chapter for selecting appropriate books, begin a story file with at least five excellent books for children three to six years of age. Make a card for each book. On the card, include the title of the book, author, illustrator, publisher, copyright date, age level the story is appropriate for, and a brief summary of the story.

F. Go to the drugstore or variety store and look over the inexpensive books offered there for children. Select and purchase a desirable and undesirable one and bring them to class. Be ready to explain their weak and strong points.

G. Observe groups of children at play to collect examples of their language. Group examples according to the ages of the children. What similarities and differences do you observe?

H. Observe in a classroom where young children have free-choice activities. Select three activities and, for five minutes during each activity, record children's language as they play. During which activity was there the most talking? Why do you think this was so? How would you change the activities to encourage more talking? Explain.

I. Use the Internet to research books for young children. (See the end of this chapter for additional Web sites.) Try these:
- ⊙ Reading Activities:
  http://www.storyarts.org
  http://www.seuss.org
  http://www.randomhouse.com/seussville
  http://www.mythweb.com
  http://www.planetozkids.com
- ⊙ Teacher Resources:
  http://www.goodcharacter.com
  http://www.makingbooks.com/kids
  http://www.reading.org (International Reading Association)
  http://www.cbcbooks.org (Children's Book Council)

Find books for preschool, kindergarten to grade 3, and grades 4 to 5. Share your experience with the Web sites and finding books in this way.

J. Explore the idea of concrete poems—poems in which the layout of the words depicts the concept of the poem. *A Poke in the I: A Collection of Concrete Poems* selected by Paul Janeczko (Candlewick, 2001) is a collection of visual poems. For example, "A Seeing Poem" by Robert Froman, is in the shape of a light bulb. For more concrete poems, look for *Outside the Lines: Poetry at Play* by Brad Burg (Putnam, 2002). Use these books to create some concrete poems yourself. Then motivate students to create their own concrete poems, too.

POEMS FOR YOUNG CHILDREN

ANIMALS

My Rabbits

My two white rabbits chase each other
With humping, bumping backs.
They go hopping, hopping
And their long ears
Go flopping, flopping
And they make faces
With their noses up and down.
Today I went inside their fence
To play rabbit with them
And in one corner under a loose bush
I saw something shivering in the leaves.
And I pushed
And I looked
And I found
There in a hole in the ground,
Three baby rabbits hidden away
And they made faces
With their noses up and down.

If You Find a Little Feather

If you find a little feather,
A little white feather,
A soft and tickly feather
    It's for you.
A feather is a letter
From a bird
And it says,
"Think of me,"
"do not forget me."

"Remember me always."
"Remember me at least until the little
    feather is lost."
So—if you find a little feather,
A little white feather,
A soft and tickly feather,
    It's for you.
Pick it up, and put it in your
    Pocket.

There Once Was a Puffin

Oh, there once was a puffin
Just the shape of a muffin
And he lived on an island
In the
    Bright
        Blue
            Sea!
He ate little fishes,
That were most delicious,
And he had them for supper
And he
    Had
        Them
            For tea.
But this poor little puffin,
He couldn't play nothin',
For he hadn't anybody
To
    Play
        With
            At all.

So he sat on his island,
And he cried for awhile, and
He felt very lonely,
And he felt
   Very small.
Then along came the fishes,
And they said, "If you wishes,
You can have us for playmates,
Instead
   Of
     For tea."
So they now play together
In all sorts of weather
And the puffin eats pancakes
Like you
   And
     Like me.

Caterpillar

A fuzzy, wuzzy caterpillar
On a summer day
Wriggled and wriggled and wriggled,
On his way.

He lifted up his head
To get a better view.
He wanted some nice green
Leaves to chew.

He wriggled and he wriggled
From his toes to his head
And he crawled about until
He found a comfy bed.

He curled up tight
In a warm little wrap
And settled himself
For a nice long nap.

He slept and he slept
And he slept until
One day he awoke
And broke from his shell.

He stretched and stretched
And he found he had wings!
He turned into a butterfly
Such a pretty-colored thing.

Oh, how happily
He flew away,
And he flew and he flew
In the sun all day.

Mice

I think mice
Are rather nice.
Their tails are long,
Their faces small.
They haven't any
Chins at all.
Their teeth are white,
They run about
The house at night.
They nibble things
They shouldn't touch
And no one seems
To like them much.
But I think mice
Are nice.

If I Were a Fish

I like to play in water
And if I were a fish,
I'd have water all around me
In a big glass dish.

My tail would make it splatter
'Til it splashed the sky,
And the mother fish would only say,
"No, don't get dry!"

Tiny Tim

I had a little turtle.
His name was Tiny Tim;
I put him in the bathtub
   To see if he could swim.
He drank up all the water;
He ate up all the soap;
And woke up in the morning
   With bubbles in his throat.

SEEDS AND PLANTS

Mister Carrot

Nice Mister Carrot
Makes curly hair,
His head grows underneath the ground—
And early in the morning
I find him in his bed
And give his feet a great big pull
And out comes his head!

The Apple

Within its polished universe,
The apple holds a star,
A secret constellation
To scatter near and far.

Let a knife discover
Where the five points hide.
Split the shining ruby
And find the star inside.

Seed

In the heart of a seed,
Buried deep so deep,
A dear little plant lay fast asleep.

"Wake," said the sunshine
"And creep to light."

"Wake," said the voice of raindrops bright.
The little plant heard
And rose to see
What the wonderful world
Outside might be.

Dandelions

On dandelions as yellow as gold,
What do you do all day?
I wait and wait in the tall green grass
Till the children come out to play.

Oh dandelion as yellow as gold,
What do you do all night?
I wait and wait in the tall green grass
Till my yellow hair turns white.

And what do the little children do
When they come out to play?
They pick me up in their hands
And blow my white hair away.

BIRTHDAYS

Five Years Old

Please, everybody look at me.
Today I'm five years old, you see.
After this, I won't be four,
Not ever, ever, anymore;
I won't be three, or two, or one,
For that was when I'd first begun.
Now I'll be five awhile, and then
I'll soon be something else again!

The Birthday Child

Everything's been different
All the day long.
Lovely things have happened,
Nothing has gone wrong.

Nobody has scolded me,
Everyone has smiled.
Isn't it delicious
To be a birthday child.

When I Was One

When I was one,
I had just begun.
When I was two,
I was nearly new.
When I was three,
I was hardly me.
When I was four,
I was not much more.
When I was five,
I was just alive.

But now I am six,
I'm as clever as clever
So I think I'll be six now
For ever and ever.

ACTION POEMS

A Swing Song

Up, down
Up and down,
Which is the way to London Town?
Where? Where?
Up in the air,
Close your eyes, and now you are
    There.

Swinging

Hold on tightly, up we go
Swinging high and swinging low.

See-Saw

See-saw Margery Daw,
Jack shall have a new master.
He shall have but a penny a day,
Because he won't work any faster.

The Ball

Bounce the ball and catch the ball
One, and two!
Bounce the ball and catch the ball,
And I throw it back to you.

Bounce the ball and catch the ball,
One, two, three!
Bounce the ball and catch the ball,
And toss it back to me.

Blocks

Blocks will build a tower tall,
Blocks will make a long, long wall,
Blocks will build a house or plane,

A truck, a tunnel, or a train.
Get the blocks, so we can see
What they'll build for you and me.

Soap Bubbles

Fill the pipe!
Gently blow;
Now you'll see
The bubbles grow!
Strong at first,
Then they burst,
Then they go to
Nothing, oh!

All Excited

I wondered and I wondered
When I could go to school.

They said I wasn't old enough
According to the rule.
I waited and I waited
I was patient as could be.
And now—I'm all excited
It's time for school for me!

The Train

My train runs on a track
Chug-a-chug, chug-a-chug
Slow at first, then faster,
Chug-a-chug, chug-a-chug,
Chug-a-chug-chug!

Round and round the wheels go
Just listen to the whistle blow,
Toot-toot-toot!
Chug-a-chug, chug-a-chug,
Toot-toot-toot!!

Toys

See the toys on my shelf?
I can count them by myself.
One, two, three, four, five.
Here's an airplane, zoom, zoom,
And a drum, boom, boom,
A ball that bounces up and down.
A top that spins round and round.
A telephone, so I can say,
"Come and play with me today."

Raggedy Ann

Raggedy Ann is my best friend
She's so relaxed, just see her bend.
First at the waist, then at the knee
Her arms are swinging, oh so free.
Her head rolls around like a rubber ball,
She hasn't any bones at all.
Raggedy Ann is stuffed with rags,
That's why her body wigs and wags.

The Cupboard

I know a little cupboard
With a teeny tiny key.
And there's a jar of lollipops
For me, me, me.

It has a little shelf, my dears,
As dark as dark can be,
And there's a dish of Banbury Cakes
For me, me, me.

I have a small flat grandmomma
With a very slippery knee,
And she's the keeper of the cupboard
With the key, key, key.

And when I'm very good, my dears,
As good as good can be,

There's Banbury Cakes, and lollipops
For me, me, me.

If I Were

If I were an owl,
At night I'd prowl.
If I were a bear,
At night I'd growl.
If I were a sheep,
At night I'd bleat.
But since I'm a child,
At night I sleep.

PERSONAL HYGIENE

New Shoes

I have new shoes in the fall time.
And new shoes in the spring.
Whenever I wear my new shoes
I always have to sing.

Shoe Lacing

Across and across the shoe we go,
Across and across, begin at the toe.
Criss and cross us over and then,
Through the hole, and across again!

Loose Tooth

I had a little tooth that wiggled
It wiggled quite a lot;
I never could be sure if it
Was coming out or not.

I pushed it with my tongue
To see if it would drop;
But there it stayed and wiggled
Until I thought I'd pop.

My auntie tied it with a string
And slammed the kitchen door!
And now I haven't got a tooth
That wiggles anymore.

But Then

A tooth fell out
And left a space
So big my tongue
Can touch my face.

And every time
I smile, I show
A space where something
Used to grow.

I miss my tooth,
As you can guess.
But then, I have to
Brush one less!

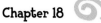

Washing

With soap and water,
I rub my hands;
With the bubbly suds,
I scrub my hands,
Rubbity, scrubbity scrub!

Rub my hands
And scrub my hands,
Til no more dirt is seen!
Rub and scrub;
Rub and scrub
And then my hands are clean!

Naughty Soap Song

Just when I'm ready to start
    On my ears,
That is the time that my
    Soap disappears,
It jumps from my fingers, and
    Slithers and slides
Down to the end of the tub
    Where it hides,
And acts in a most disobedient
    Way,
And that's why my soap's
    Growing thinner each day.

ACTIVITIES FOR CHILDREN

LANGUAGE ACTIVITIES

Name games. Playing with children's names can build a sensitivity to the sounds of language and the use of words.

⊙ The patterns and rhymes found in children's names can be explored. Begin by clapping the rhythm of children's names: Ste′pha′nie′, Rich′ard′, Al′li′son′. Children can use rhythm sticks, drums, or triangles to follow the beat of their names and find ways to jump, step, hop, or slide to the rhythm of their names. These activities will attune children to the sound of words.

⊙ Children's names can also be used to further understanding of the connection between the spoken and written word. Children's names are spoken and then written over cubbies, on paintings and artwork, and on other personal objects. Use lists of children's names whenever possible so the similarities and differences between names can be observed. You might list all of the children who have a birthday during each month or those voting to name the guinea pig Christina and those voting to name it Andrea. Other lists might name each child who has brown, black, or blonde hair.

Outdoor language experiences. Outdoor play materials can be used for language experiences. These can promote awareness of the printed word in young children. Tricycle paths can have traffic signs (commercial or teacher-made). The work bench can have rebus charts to describe something to build. Animal cages and insect containers can have rebus instructions for care. In addition, seed packages can be used to label

plants in the garden, graphs of plant growth can be created, and collections of nature objects can be gathered and labeled. Charts of pictures of safety rules can be on display.

Recycled materials for language experiences.

⊙ *Mail-order catalogs.* These are a comfortable hand size for young children and have more pictures and fewer words than regular magazines. Use them to find categories of colors, objects, beginning sounds, etc. Be sure to screen them first for any inappropriate pictures.

⊙ *Purse story.* Fill old pocketbooks with assorted items such as tickets, keys, lists, snacks, make-up, combs, and so on. Have the child examine the contents of the purse and tell about the owner. List the ideas. Draw pictures of how the owner of the purse might look. Tape stories about the owner.

⊙ *Original picture books.* Photograph events throughout the year and have the children use these pictures to tell stories. Place photos and children's stories in a self-sticking photo album to become a permanent part of the book corner.

⊙ For older children use catalogs for language arts activities. Discuss words used to describe materials. For example: find synonyms for "soft usable"; explain what "pre-shrunk jeans," "wash and wear," or "telescoping" mean; rewrite descriptions of items to give them another meaning.

BALL STORIES

This is a game that focuses on language skills as well as large and small motor skills. Have the children sit in a circle. It may be helpful to tape masking tape on the floor in a circle to help children in getting into a circle. Then, using a medium-sized, soft, ball (spongy Nerf balls available in most discount stores work well). Begin with a story-starter line such as, "Once upon a time there lived a frog," and then you toss the ball to a child in the circle. He says the next line to the story and then he tosses the ball to another child, who adds a line. The activity goes on until each child has had a chance to catch the ball and add a line to the story. The likely silliness of the story just enhances the experience by adding laughter and humor to your language arts program.

Because children have differently developing social skills and speech and language skills, do not expect each child to add a line to the story. Some may simply attempt to catch the ball and then toss it to another child. Some may want to add a word, a phrase, a partial sentence, or an idea. Others will be willing to add many lines to the story, depending on their language skills and their level of creativity.

FEELY BAG STORIES

Put a few toys, small stuffed animals, and dolls into a bag. Feel around inside the bag and pull out a toy. You might start the story by saying, "Once upon a time there was a . . . (little bear). He was happily walking along until, OOPS! He bumped into a . . ." At this point in the story, pass the bag to one of the children and ask him or her to pull out another toy and continue the story. After everyone has had a chance to pull out a toy and add to the story, use your toy to create a "happily ever after" ending.

RECYCLED TYPEWRITERS

Next time you see an obsolete typewriter at a yard sale, grab it for your language arts area. Children love pecking out their names, letter by letter, and then adding their own illustrations on the page. There is also a variety of durable "smart toys" (battery-operated tabletop toys such as LeapFrog) that provide tactile experiences with letters and sounds. If you have a computer, there are dozens of programs to choose from. See Software for Children at the end of this chapter for suggestions. As you would with other materials, test the software first to make sure there is a good match between the activity and the child. Most of the software listed offer activities that have multiple levels of difficulty and can be adapted to meet children's individual needs.

ACTIVITIES FOR MULTIPLE INTELLIGENCES

As we have learned earlier, all children have different learning styles or multiple intelligences. When working with young children in the language arts, try using some of the following activities to reach these various learning styles.

Body-Smart Activities

- Make letters with clay or paint, in sand or flour, and with the typewriter or on the computer.
- Use hand movements and body formations to show letters.
- Trace letters on the child's palm, and help the child trace sandpaper letters.
- Use jump rope chants with letters for exercise breaks.
- Play "Simon Says" with commands such as "Simon says write a B in the air."

Music-Smart Activities

- Use simple poems and rhythmic, repetitive stories.
- Use lyrics to simple songs to practice letters and reading.
- Sing the sounds.
- Use alphabet songs.
- Use tongue twisters to practice and isolate specific words.

Picture-Smart Activities

- Make pictures out of letters or groups of letters.
- Use different colors on bulletin boards to represent specific sounds.
- Draw "word pictures" to show the meaning of words. For example, *tall* would be written with tall letters, and *rain* would be written with drops around it.
- Have students draw a picture to represent the word and write the word inside the picture.

Number-Smart Activities

- Write sight words, numbered from 1 to 25, on a poster board. When students ask how to spell a word on the list, refer them to the appropriate number on the poster.
- Make dice with letters instead of dots on them.
- Use a flannel board with cloth letters or a metal board with magnetic letters. Show students how new words are formed by changing one letter (fine, dine, line).
- Locate letters numerically in the alphabet by creating a poster that shows letters ordered that way (A=1, B=2, etc.).

Word-Smart Activities

- Provide language experiences by writing down stories as children tell them to you.
- Use word flash cards.

⊙ Teach prereading skills—holding books, turning pages, and reading from left to right.
⊙ Use tracing activities.
⊙ Have students learn word families—words that are phonetically alike or sound similar.
⊙ Use echo reading. Students repeat what is read.

People-Smart Activities

⊙ Make reading a social event in the classroom.
⊙ Have students take turns reading letters, words, sentences, etc.
⊙ Have student partners read (or look at) a book together.
⊙ Have students teach younger children the alphabet and sight words.
⊙ Have reading parties at which students read individually and in small groups and listen to guest readers who are visiting the class.

Self Smart Activities

⊙ Provide a quiet, cozy reading corner.
⊙ Give students opportunities to read silently.
⊙ Provide books that have a high-interest value.
⊙ Keep special "Book Favorites" lists on a bulletin board where students can write their "All-Time Favorites."
⊙ Have students practice reading aloud to a stuffed animal.
⊙ Have students listen to a tape-recorded story and follow along in the book.

POETRY ACTIVITIES

Poem of the week. Use large newsprint to print the poem of your choice. Use illustrations. Try substituting pictures for words in the poem. Have them point to the pictures when you read the poem to them.

Cluster poems. Select a subject of interest to young children—animals, seasons, weather. Read several poems, each by a different poet. See if the children like one more than another. Have them talk about why. Draw or paint pictures of their favorite.

Rhyming nonsense. Although poetry does not have to rhyme to be effective, children do enjoy making their own rhymes. Allow them to create a poem using rhyming words of their choice. The words do not have to make sense. Write them on paper for the child.

Descriptive poem. Have the children select a subject that will be the title of the poem. Encourage them to give you two words that tell something about the

subject, for example, *cat*—furry, soft; *broccoli*—green, yucky.

LISTENING EXERCISES

Noisy story. The noisy story develops vocabulary and skill in sequencing of story events. It also permits pupils of varying levels to participate. Prepare a set of cards, each card having a noisy word on it such as PEEP, BANG, BUZZ, and ROAR. Give each child a card, considering individual readability levels. Select a leader to begin the noisy story, using the noisy word on his or her card. The other children take turns in adding to the story, using the words on their cards. The leader might start the story by saying, "Bill fed the baby chick and it went *peep*." The next child might add, "The baby chick was scared when the balloon went *bang*." The story would be completed when all the pupils have had a turn. Other groups of words could be used such as action words, animal words, people words, toy words, etc. The game could also expand to include writing the story, illustrating the story, acting the story out, and many other creative activities.

Who is that? Tape voices; radio and television are good sources, as well as people you know. Tape voices of people the children know: the custodian, the principal, other children. Tape singers, news announcers, political figures, comedians, cartoon characters, and movie stars. Play the voices back and have the children identify them.

Where is the bell? With the children seated in a circle, have one child leave the room. Give one of the children in the room a bell that is small enough to hide in one hand. Ask the child who left the room to come back in. When the child has returned, have all of the children stand and shake their hands above their heads. You may use more than one bell when the children become accustomed to the game. The player who is "it" will have three chances to locate the bell.

Are you listening? Fill eight margarine tubs (with plastic lids) with different materials: for example, two with flour, two with buttons, two with nails, two with pins. Have the children find the two that sound alike by shaking them.

Whose voice is it? Form a circle of several children. Blindfold one child or have him or her cover his or her eyes and have this child stand in the middle. Have the children regroup so that each will be in a different place in the circle. Then have each child make a simple statement such as, "I like to play games." The child in the center then points to one child and identifies this child or asks questions (up to three) that must be answered in a sentence. If the child who is "it" guesses correctly or fails to after three times, "it" returns to the circle and another child becomes "it."

MISCELLANEOUS ACTIVITIES

Flannel board tips. Flannel boards are excellent for language development activities. Consider the following hints when using a flannel board.

- ⊙ For easy-to-store flannel boards, purchase old fold-up gameboards at garage sales and cover them with flannel. The boards are sturdy and will stand up by themselves. Make several different backgrounds to use for favorite stories and activities.
- ⊙ If your room has a storage container on wheels, you can use it as a flannel board as well as a room divider by attaching flannel securely to the back with a staple gun.
- ⊙ A carpet sample or piece of indoor-outdoor carpeting can be used as a flannel board. Both are available at carpet stores and are relatively inexpensive.

- ⊙ When making a flannel board, slip a piece of wire screen between the flannel and the backing and use it with magnets.
- ⊙ Create flannel board shapes easily and inexpensively by making them out of paper towels. Thick, white, rather spongy towels work best. You can use felt markers to decorate the shapes, and the children will love playing with them.
- ⊙ Save used, sponge-type dryer fabric softener sheets to cut into pieces and use as backing for paper flannel board shapes.
- ⊙ Other materials that can be used for flannel board shapes or for backing are felt, flannel, flocked wallpaper, sandpaper, and fabric interfacing.

Tape that. Tape a story all of the children have read—but make some mistakes, changing words here and there. Have the children listen to the tape and pick out the errors.

I can read pictures. Gathering information from pictures is a useful skill. Have the children look at some pictures in a book. How much can they learn about the characters without reading any of the words? Do the words and pictures always agree? Could the children make up a different story to go with the pictures?

ACTIVITIES FOR OLDER CHILDREN (GRADES 4–5)

The following are some suggested activities to liven up the elementary language arts program. Use your knowledge of each child's reading level to choose those activities that are appropriate for your children.

Book Reports
The following are some fun ways to give book reports (sometimes a dreaded assignment).

- ⊙ Choose a friend who has read the same book; have a debate about it.
- ⊙ Illustrate a mural explaining the sequences of the book.
- ⊙ Simulate an interview about the book. Have a friend help you provide questions to ask about the book.
- ⊙ Act out or pantomime scenes from the book.
- ⊙ Make a time-line and enter on the time-line the sequence of events that occurred in the story.
- ⊙ Develop a brochure advertising the book.

- ⊙ Develop paper dolls that depict characters in the book and display the paper dolls as though they were giving the report.
- ⊙ Give the report in riddle form; have the class guess what book you are reporting on.
- ⊙ Make up comic strips depicting the story content.
- ⊙ Develop overhead transparencies that relate to the story. Present the report, using the overhead projector and transparencies.
- ⊙ Write the report as a newspaper article.
- ⊙ Develop the report as an advertisement for television.
- ⊙ If the story content lends itself to a real-life situation, report on the book as a happening in the present environment.
- ⊙ Develop some simple sketches that could be drawn on the chalkboard as you are giving the report.

Reversibles

Explain what reversible words are with examples (understand, stand under). Point out that while such turnabout words differ in meaning as they are reversed, the degree of difference is not the same in each case. Players are to write or tell sentences for six pairs of reversibles, trying to use them amusingly and effectively to show their differences. Here are some reversibles to begin the activity: understudy, study under; overcome, come over; indoors, doors in; outgoing, going out; overdone, done over; overturn, turn over; withhold, hold with; instill, still in. This can be modified to include illustrations of the reversibles, a spelling lesson, or working as partners to develop lists.

Start with a Poem

Read the following poem together and discuss what effect there would be on us if there were no stars. Students could make drawings of the night sky using dark-colored paper and white chalk.

> **The Stars**
> Like tiny diamond chips they shine,
> Suspended in the sky,
> Forever forming sparkling shapes,
> Beyond the clouds so high.
> But, if there were not there to view,
> How lonely nights would be,
> The sky would seem so empty, then,
> No twinkling stars to see.
> (Martin Shaw)

Invisible Milk Ink Writing

Milk makes a perfect invisible ink to use on cardboard or heavyweight papers such as cardstock or construction paper. Apply milk with a small paintbrush or cotton swab and then let it dry completely. To make the message appear, rub any type of dark powdery substance over the message and the powder will stick to the milk residue. Charcoal, chalk, or graphite from a pencil lead will all work. Try making hidden messages by letting one student write the message in milk and passing it to another student to "decode."

Word Game Day

Ask students to try their luck at a new "Word Game Day" at http://www.m-w.com/game. Children can try different puzzle formats, such as "Transform Brainstorm" that lets you change a word into another word, one letter at a time, using clues to the word's meaning.

Using the Dictionary

Have your class find pictures of things and their definitions in different languages at http://www.

pdictionary.com/. The children will have fun playing the games they find here with each other.

EFlash Cards

Visit the database at http://www.kidsnook.com and check out the multisensory eflashcards. Explain to the class that these eflashcards teach vocabulary by giving you a moving picture to connect to each printed term.

Contact the Experts

Contact real-world experts at http://www.askanexpert.com. This site can answer students' questions about specific subjects and help them learn the meaning of new words.

Poetry and Movement Activities

Theme dance. Any theme from a poem or book can be danced by first brainstorming all the ways to express the theme with body parts, movements, energy, and use of space and time. For example, the theme that courage comes out of fear can be danced in a frozen shape, movements, and frozen shape three-part dance planned and performed by small groups, who will each present a very different interpretation.

Key topic dance. Make a list of important words or topics in a poem or book. Brainstorm all the movements, shapes, levels, energy, etc., that could be used to convey the topic. Give small groups the choice of a topic or word to plan a dance or a series of creative movements to show it.

Character dance. Any character in a story or book can be explored through movement by considering all the ways a character might move. For example, how would Wilbur in *Charlotte's Web* move if he was happy? Hungry? Afraid? Tired? How is Wilbur's movement different from Charlotte's or Templeton's? How does body shape show something about a character?

Line by line. Read a poem to students first. Give each student or group a line from a poem. Then have them explore all the movement possibilities of the line (e.g., the rhythm of the words, the emotions expressed, the images). Encourage more than pantomiming. The poetry can then be danced line by line as a narrator reads, or groups can each plan to perform just one line.

Solutions

On separate paper strips, write these and other problems: lost my door key, scared to give my book report, came to school late, tore my jeans, etc. Post one of the problems on a bulletin board. Working in small groups, the children discuss how to respond to and/or solve the problem. Then, the groups present and defend their responses. Guide them in considering other responses and solutions.

Reading Pictures

Have students clip magazine photos that show feelings. Show one of the pictures to a group and have them brainstorm the feelings shown in the photo. Then they write what occurred just before the photo was snapped, the dialogue when the photo was taken, and a caption for the picture. For further activities, select photos and ask the students to remark on something happening in the picture. Photos of animals from *National Geographic* work well. Have students describe the weather and location. Next, ask them to tell what happened after the picture was taken, what will happen one day later, one week later.

Pantomime in language arts. Prior to the pantomime activity, design a homophone word list with the children. (Homophones are words that sound alike, but are spelled differently and have a different meaning.) Upon completing the list, the children form a circle. The teacher calls out a word and the children pantomime a meaning for that word. Then the homophone is called and the children show that meaning. Try using the following words in this exercise: ant/aunt; bear/bare; board/bored; buy/bye; clothes/close; eight/ate; flour/flower; grate/great; hear/here; knight/night; lends/lens; marry/merry; prints/prince; ring/wring; shoe/shoo; tow/toe; we/wee; yolk/yoke.

ACTIVITIES FOR MULTIPLE INTELLIGENCES

Learning sight words is an important reading skill. Planning sight word activities that are appropriate for children's multiple intelligences or learning styles can make learning sight words fun and challenging. Here are some ideas:

BODY-SMART ACTIVITIES

- **Sand letters.** Fill several shallow tubs with sand. Students can work in groups and take turns spelling each word in the sand. Once their teammates verify that a word is spelling correctly, they erase it.
- **Playground ball catch.** Using a Sharpie marking pen, write sight words all over each of several playground balls. Have students form groups of four and stand in a close circle. One student tosses a ball to another. The student who catches the ball reads the word closest to his or her right thumb. Younger students can read any word on the ball.
- **Sit up/sit down.** Tell students that you are going to be reading them a short story and that any time they hear one of the sight words, they should stand up. After all students are standing up, signal them to sit down. Do the same activity with the story projected on a screen as you read so that students can see the special word being read.
- **Body letters.** Choose several students at a time to come and spell out one of the sight words by forming their bodies into the shapes of its letters as best they can. Their classmates can guess the word.

MUSIC-SMART ACTIVITIES

- **Singing songs.** During singing time, take time to point out the sight words in song lyrics. You might also have students sing and spell the words in a familiar song.
- **Consonant-vowel spelling.** Have students spell each word out loud to a partner. Tell them to say consonant letters out loud and to whisper the vowels. This helps students become more aware of individual letters and memorize a rhythm as they are spelling. It can lead to a discussion of the patterns of vowels and consonants as they recognize that many words start with a vowel, others have a vowel in between, and still others end with a vowel.

PERSON-SMART ACTIVITIES

Group spelling. Ask several volunteers to come to the front of the classroom. Pronounce a sight word, and have members of the group spell the word, one letter per student. Once students understand the game, divide the class into groups of two or three and tell them to whisper the spelling of the word you say. Remind them that they are whispering so that other groups have to rely on their own knowledge to spell the words.

Buddy spell. Ask students to choose partners. Give each pair one set of alphabet tiles or cubes (or index cards with one letter on each card). One student says a word, and the other arranges the letters in the correct order. Once the word is correctly spelled, the students change places and continue until they've spelled all the words.

PICTURE-SMART ACTIVITIES

Word pictures. Have students write a sight word in large letters in the middle of a sheet of paper and then decorate the page with pictures and drawings.

Word search. Write a short story that includes sight words, and make a copy for each student. Have the students highlight or underline all of the sight words they can find.

Configuration clues. Have students write one word at a time on a sheet of paper. After each word is written, have them draw a box around it so they can see how the word looks (e.g., tall letters, short letters). Older students can draw individual boxes around each letter.

SELF-SMART ACTIVITIES

Study time. Give students a list of sight words to tape to their desk. Each day, give them a couple of minutes to study them.

Journal writing. Have students choose two words each day to copy into their personal journals. Ask them to write a sentence or illustrate a sentence that includes the word. Then relate the sentence to something they enjoy doing in their personal time.

WORD-SMART ACTIVITIES

Introducing words. On strips of butcher paper or word strips, write sight words one to a strip. Introduce students to a few words each week. Explain to students that they will be learning words that are used a lot. After introducing words to students, hang the strips in a wall pocket so students can see them throughout the day. Any time one of the words appears in a book or someone says it out loud, have students walk to the pocket chart and point to the word.

Student writing. Have students underline the sight words each time they use them in their writing assignments. Older students can keep a Special Word Dictionary where they write these words.

Paper-plate spelling. Write one letter on each of a number of paper plates and give each student several plates. Have students stand if they have a letter that appears in a word you say. If several students stand up at the same time, acknowledge all of them as you reinforce how the word is spelled.

LOGIC-SMART ACTIVITIES

Counting letters. To help students who need a mathematic connection to memorize the sight words, have them write each word, count its letters, and write the number of letters next to it. For example, students would write "the" and place a "3" next to it. An extension of this is to have students count the consonants and vowels. Students would write "the" and next to it write "C=2, V=1."

Categorizing words. Give groups of students each a set of index cards with one of the sight words written on each card. Ask them to work as a group to categorize words that might go together. After they are done, have each group explain its categories. For example, students may feel that all the three-letter words or all the words with *o* in them go together. For many students, categorizing similar words will help them memorize word families. This activity helps to build and strengthen sight word vocabulary as well as to increase students' awareness of phonetic similarities.

CHAPTER REVIEW

1. Describe ways by which children develop language skills. Explain the pattern of growth.
2. Discuss guidelines to follow when reading to young children.
3. Why can some children speak more easily than other children? Why are some children better listeners than others?
4. Why is it important for adults to speak with children at their level during their daily activities?

5. What are some things to consider when choosing books for young children? Why is it necessary to consider these things?

6. Much is said about being "ready" to read. What exactly does "emerging literacy" mean? How can a teacher help encourage this emerging literacy?

7. Why are teaching reading and writing not appropriate in the early childhood program? What is taught instead in these two areas?

8. Discuss how to work with bilingual/bicultural young children in language development.

REFERENCES

Burg, B. (2002). *Outside the lines: Poetry at play.* New York: Putnam.

Derman-Sparles, L., & ABC Task Force. (1989). Anti-bias curriculum: *Tools for empowering young children.* Washington, DC: NAEYC.

Duke, N. K.(2003, March). Reading to learn from the very beginning: Information Books in Early Education. *Young Children,* 14–20.

Elster, C. (1994, March). I guess they do listen: Young children's emergent readings after adult read-alouds. *Young Children,* 27–31.

Farrell, J. M. (1999, March 31). Literacy experts suggest dusting off Mother Goose. Knight Ridder Newspapers.

Holdaway, D. (1979). *The foundations of literacy.* Auckland, New Zealand: Ashton Scholastic.

Janeczko, P. (2001). *A poke in the I: A collection of concrete poems.* New York: Candlewick.

Rhoten, L., & Lane, M. (2001, Jan.). More than the ABC's: The new alphabet books. *Young Children,* 41–45.

Sulzby, E. (1985). Emergent reading of favorite storybooks: A developmental study. *Reading Research Quarterly, 20*(4), 458–481.

ADDITIONAL READINGS

Diller, D. (2003). *Literacy work stations: Making centers work.* Portland, ME: Stenhouse.

Duke, N. K., Bennett-Armistead, V. S., & Roberts, E. M. (Eds.). (2002). Incorporating informational texts in the primary grades. In *Comprehensive reading instruction across the grade levels,* Roller, C. (Ed.). 40–54. Newark, DE: International Reading Association.

Florian, D. (2003). *Teaching with the rib-tickling poetry of Douglas Florian.* New York: Scholastic.

Garan, E. M. (2002). *Resisting reading mandates: How to triumph with the truth.* Portsmouth, NH: Heinemann.

Kreplin, E., & Smith, B. M. (1995). *Figures and activities for ESL children.* Washington DC: Center for Applied Research in Education.

Lewis, S., & Tolla, J. (2003). Creating and using tactile experience books for young children with visual impairments. *Teaching Exceptional Children 35*(3), 22–28.

Lurie, A. (2003). *Boys and girls forever: Children's classics from Cinderella to Harry Potter.* New York: Penguin.

Miller, D. (2002). *Reading with meaning: Teaching comprehension in the primary grades.* Portland, ME: Stenhouse.

Neuman, S. B., & Dickinson, D. K. (Eds.) (2001). *Handbook of early literary research.* New York: Guilford.

Pinell, G. S., & Scharer, P. (2003). *Teaching for comprehension in reading: Grades K–2.* New York: Scholastic.

Roberts, L. C., & Hill, H. T. (2003, March).Using children's literature to debunk gender stereotypes. *Young Children,* 39–42.

Sadler, F. H. (2003). The itinerant special education teacher in the early childhood classroom. *Teaching Exceptional Children 35*(3), 8–15.

Seid, N. (2002, June). The 50 best children's books. *Parents Magazine,* 60.

Wasik, B. A. (2001, Jan.). Teaching the alphabet to young children. *Young Children,* 34–39.

Whaley, C. (2002, March). Meeting the diverse needs of children through storytelling. *Young Children,* 31–33.

Wilmes, D., & Wilmes, L. (2001). *Felt board stories.* New York: Building Blocks Press.

SOFTWARE FOR CHILDREN

Clicker 4, 2002. Ages 3 and up.
Clifford Reading, 2003. Ages 4–6.
Clifford Thinking Adventures, 2002. Ages 4–6.
Curious George Reading and Phonics, 2002. Ages 3–6.
Destination Reading, 2002. Ages 5–9.
I Spy Series, 2003. Ages 5–9.
LeapPad Pro, 2003. Ages 4 and up.
LeapZone Turbo Twist Spelling, 2002. Ages 6 and up.
LeapFrog's Leveled Reading Series, 2002. Ages 4–9.
My First LeapPad, 2003. Ages 3–6.
Reader Rabbit Learn to Read with Phonics for 1st and 2nd Grades, 2002.

Reader Rabbit Reading Builder EEV, 2003. Grades 1–3.
Reader Rabbit Preschool Sparkle Star Rescue!, 2003. Ages 3–5.
Reader Rabbit Toddler Deluxe, 2002. Ages 18 months–3 years.
Reading for Meaning Grades 3–8, 2002.
Reading Readiness K–1, 2003. Ages 4–6.
Scholastic Reading Counts!, 2002. Grades K–9.
The Literacy Center: Pre-K Edition, 2002. Ages 3–5.
Wizmo's Workshop: The Dragons of Frozzbokk, 2002. Ages 3–6.

HELPFUL WEB SITES

The Literacy Center, http://www.literacycenter.net
International Reading Association, http://www.reading.org
Children's Picture Book Database, http://www.lib.muohio.edu/pictbks
American Speech-Language-Hearing Association, http://www.asha.org

STORYTELLING WEB SITES

Creative Drama and Theatre Education Resource File, http://www.creativedrama.com
National Storytelling Festival, http://www.storytellingfestival.net
National Storytelling Network, http://www.storynet.org
Storytelling FAQ, http://www.lilliput.co.uk/faq.html.

For additional creative activity resources, visit our Web site at http://www.EarlyChildEd.delmar.com.

Chapter 19

Creative Science

Objectives

After studying this chapter, you should be able to:

1. State why science is important to the development of young children.
2. Name and describe three general kinds of science.
3. Discuss environmental education and its place in the early childhood program.
4. Discuss the discovery center and its importance in the early childhood program.

When considering creative activities, it is not possible to skip the area of science. This is because true science is a highly creative activity.

There are twenty young children in a classroom. Each has just been given a small box wrapped in brightly colored gift paper. There is a big ribbon around each box. There are some objects inside each box. Each child is trying to find out what is in a box without taking off the ribbon and paper.

Some children are shaking their gift boxes. Some are holding them up to their ears and listening very carefully. Others are squeezing them. A few are poking the boxes. The children are interested in finding out what is in their own wrapped-up box.

Is this a game? It may seem so, but it is not. It is a way in which children make creative discoveries. In many ways, it is also the way that scientists make creative discoveries. The little gift box is somewhat like the world in which the children live. The children study their own little "worlds" by shaking the box, smelling it, squeezing it, and looking at it. Each child makes some discoveries but cannot find out everything because the box cannot be unwrapped. The children may be able to make some good guesses after studying the boxes, however. Some things are open to the children's discovery; some things are not. Scientists are faced with the same problems. They, too, study the world. They, too, can observe some things and only guess about others.

SCIENCE AND THE YOUNG CHILD

For young children science is about trying to understand the world. Young children are natural scientists who observe the people, animals, and objects in their environment; conduct experiments; and report on their discoveries.

Science in early childhood is much broader than what you might at first consider it to be. Try to avoid thinking about science only in terms of activities devoted to "doing" science—such as growing plants or taking a nature walk.

Rather, view science as an ongoing part of the total curriculum, woven into daily activities and routines. Science education occurs naturally when Claire wonders why a cork floats and a penny sinks, when Mark questions why ice melts, when Scott observes he can hear his heart beating as he runs, and when Michelle wonders why the water she paints on the sidewalk disappears.

There are two things that both the child and the scientist do. They *investigate* (carefully study the world around them) to discover *knowledge* (find answers to questions or problems about that world). Science consists of two phases, or parts, that cannot be separated: investigation and knowledge.

Importance of Science

In dealing with young children, it has been found that investigating is much more important than the knowledge that comes from investigating. Young children need a lot of action, not a lot of facts. This does not mean that understanding the world is put aside completely for young children. It just means that learning *how to find* answers is considered more important than the answers themselves. However, investigation and knowledge are a team. They cannot be completely separated from one another. To provide the experiences children need to develop scientific creativity, teachers must understand the importance of science. They must help children investigate in order to find answers to questions about the world. How can a teacher do this?

Figure 19-1

Investigating a problem is science at its best.

There are three types of science experiences for young children: formal science, informal science, and incidental science. Each of these terms will be explained in detail later.

Science is important to young children in a number of ways. First, when children are actively involved in investigating their world, they are *learning by doing,* the most effective way for young children to learn.

Second, science activities help young children develop skills in using their senses. Use of these skills is not limited to science. These skills can be used every day throughout a person's lifetime.

Educators use the term *transfer of learning* to describe knowledge and skills that are gained in one area and used in many other areas. Science skills are particularly important because they are so highly transferable. Skills in seeing, feeling, and tasting are not limited to science even though they do represent the basic skills that are taught.

Third, science allows children yet another chance to exercise their creative abilities. Science allows young children a chance to play with ideas and materials in an open environment where there is freedom to explore without fear of being "wrong."

TYPES OF SCIENCE ACTIVITIES

There are three types of science experiences for young children: formal, informal, and incidental.

Formal Science

Formal science experiences are planned by the teacher to develop particular skills. An example would be planning for fine motor skill development by including pouring and measuring tools in the sand and water area. A teacher would plan to include a specific item, such as hanging a funnel low over the water table or attaching funnels to each end of a length of plastic tubing. These items would be included to serve a specific purpose—the development of fine motor skills. While many other learning experiences could occur due to their inclusion, they serve a specific developmental purpose.

Informal Science

Unlike formal science, **informal science** calls for little or no teacher involvement. Children work on their own, at their own rate, and only when they feel like it. They select the kinds of activities that interest them. They spend as much or as little time working at a given activity as they desire. It is when this sort of openness is available to children that creative potential begins to develop.

Most informal science activities occur in the discovery (science) center. The discovery center is an area in the early childhood classroom where children can participate in a variety of informal science activities that stimulate curiosity, exploration, and problem solving. In the discovery center young children develop many skills and concepts in their active exploration of such things as sand, water, magnets, and a multitude of other real-life objects. A more specific discussion of the discovery center follows later in this chapter.

Incidental Science

Incidental science cannot be planned. It sometimes does not take place once a week or even once a month. Just what is incidental science?

A city or town may be struck by a violent wind-

storm. Limbs of trees are knocked down; whole trees are uprooted. Great sheets of rain fall and streets become flooded. Children are scared by the great noise and wild lightning as the storm passes. Finally the storm is over.

Is this the time for an incidental science experience? Of course it is! This is the time for children who are interested to learn many things. They can study the roots of trees; they may have the chance to observe growth rings. They are able to examine tree bark. They can observe what happens to water as it drains from a flooded street. Some might want to talk about their feelings as the lightning flashed and the thunder crashed. Some may wish to create a painting about the experience.

A teacher cannot plan such an experience. A good teacher can, however, take advantage of such an opportunity by letting children explore and seek answers to questions. A teacher can encourage children to be more inquisitive and creative.

Figure 19-2

In science activities, children are free to explore, investigate, and experience the world around them.

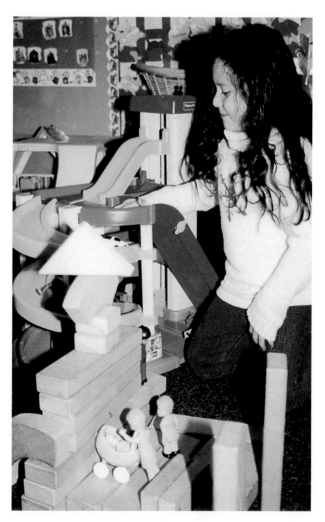

Figure 19-3

Working with blocks, children learn many science concepts such as balance, weight, and design.

Figure 19-4
Seeing how paint colors mix and merge is a science experience.

Figure 19-5
Science activities can include drawing pictures about nature and its many wonders.

National science education standards. In 1996 the National Research Council (NRC) defined standards for children at each grade level, from kindergarten through high school, in its document *National Science Education Standards* (NRC, 1996). All of these standards align with the National Association for the Education of Young People developmentally appropriate practice (Bredekamp & Copple, 1997). They reinforce the idea that children can best learn science when it is presented through "hands-on," meaningful, and relevant activities.

Hundreds of people cooperated in developing the standards, including teachers, parents, school administrators, curriculum developers, college faculty and administrators, scientists, engineers, and government officials. These standards present an outline of what students in kindergarten through grade 12 need to know, understand, and be able to do to be "scientifically literate" at each grade level. For more indepth information on these standards, visit the Web site www.nap.edu.

The Standards do not require a specific curriculum. Instead, they provide a broad outline of what science experiences students should have from kindergarten through grade 12. It is meant to be seen as a dynamic understanding that is always open to review and revision. A full listing of all these science teaching standards is not possible in this text due to their length and breadth. For our purposes, references will be made to specific activities and how they are appropriate for teaching certain science standards. The full text of the National Science Standards for teaching, professional

development, and assessment are found in the book, *National Science Education Standards* (1996).

ART AND SCIENCE

Aesthetics and Science

As we have learned earlier in this text, *aesthetics* means being sensitive to beauty in nature and art. Such sensitivity is fostered not by talking about beauty but by experiencing it in a variety of forms—the sign of snow on evergreen boughs, the smell of the earth after a spring rain, the sound of a bird singing overhead, and the feel of a kitten's fur or the moss on the side of a tree. It is easy to forget how amazing a pebble or a pinecone can be to a young child.

For the young child, the world of nature is an especially appropriate avenue for a sense of aesthetics. An early snowfall in winter may provide a child with his first remembered experience of snow. Seeing a rainbow in the sky may be something a three year old has never experienced before. Watching a butterfly move from flower to flower may provide a visual feast that a child has not yet come to take for granted.

Beauty is not just in what can be seen but is present, also, in what can be touched, felt, and listened to. Because the world of nature is so full of sights, sounds, and textures, it can serve as an incredibly rich and readily available resource for the development of aesthetics in young children.

Science and Art Materials/Activities

Children working with art materials make scientific observations, noting, for example, that water makes

Figure 19-6

In dealing with young children, investigating is much more important than the Knowledge that comes from investigating.

Figure 19-7

Sink and float experiments are always a popular science activity.

tempera paint thinner and that crayons become soft if left near the heat. Claire looks at her wet, drippy painting and says, "I wonder if I can blow it dry with my wind." Drew finds that his clay figure left on the windowsill overnight has "gotten all hardened up" because it is no longer wet.

Experimentation with art materials may lead to many other discoveries about cause and effect. Children notice that colors change as they are mixed and that the sponges used for printing absorb liquid. In contrast, other materials such as plastics are found to be nonabsorbent. Children using many materials observe differences between liquids and solids and see that other items such as wax crayons and oil paints resist water. In mixing paint from powder, children learn that some materials dissolve in water. The operations of simple machines can be understood through using tools such as scissors and hammers. The potential for developing science concepts is in the art materials and in the processes—ready to be discovered and applied. These experiences are consistent with the National Science Standard which states children should understand the properties of materials.

Animals link science and art. Young children's natural love of animals is a good place to begin when planning art activities that encourage science experiences. Children are intrigued with the study of animals. Studying animals is consistent with the National Science Standard, which endorses the study of animals and their environments. Yet, animals provide more than a science experience for children, as they stimulate children's artistic exploration. Young children, after touching, seeing, hearing, or smelling animals, will be stimulated to use art media for animal representations. Children with an emotional attachment to household or school pets will be additionally motivated to create visual images. Teachers create opportunities for guided learning about animals by providing art media and materials for children to use; engaging children in discussions about animals; and reading stories, showing pictures, and singing songs about animals.

Sometimes after a trip to a zoo or farm, children will be stimulated to visually express their ideas about animals. After the class trip to the zoo, four-year-old Scott painted an elephant immediately upon returning to school. "Look, elephants are so funny because they have a tail on both ends," he announced. The teacher accepted his work but, realizing his confusion, clarified the differences between a trunk and a tail. This example shows how art can serve as a vehicle for direct learning by helping children express their understandings. At the same time, the art responses give the teacher clues for further planning.

Learning about animals and pets can also take place as a result of spontaneous discovery and subsequent engagement in teacher-guided art activity. One day while his kindergarten class was out playing, Edmund found a grasshopper in the field. "Can we keep him?" he begged. By asking pointed questions and providing materials, the teacher guided the children's thinking about how best to keep the insect. She offered a clear plastic cup into which the children decided to put some moist earth and grass. Edmund decided to cover the cup with a piece of paper held on with a rubber band. "I'll make some air holes for air to go in," he responded in answer to a question by the teacher.

Although the insect was set free after one day, several children spent a good deal of time observing it. The teacher suggested that the magnifying glass could be used and guided the children by asking questions: "How does the grasshopper see?" "How are its eyes different from ours?" "Which legs seem to help him jump?" "How are they different from ours?" The detailed drawings of grasshoppers made the next day showed that the questions had motivated good observation. Edmund, whose personal attachment to the insect was the greatest, created five different representations of the insect.

Figure 19-8

Science is as basic as exploring the world of taste in trying new foods.

The following are some activities that expand further on the concept of animals/pets and art activities.

- ⊙ Encourage older children to draw, paint, or model representations of their pets doing something characteristic.
- ⊙ Suggest to children that they find pictures for collages showing animals that live in different places, move in various ways, or have different body coverings.
- ⊙ Provide opportunities for children to make their drawings, paintings, or cutout, pasted animals into booklets, murals, jigsaw puzzles, or puppets.
- ⊙ Offer a variety of boxes, trays, and found objects that children can use to make zoo cages or farm environments for toy animals or models they create.
- ⊙ Provide scraps of furry fabrics, yarns, and spotted and striped papers in different shapes for children to paste on a background and then add appendages for real or imaginary animals.
- ⊙ Make a variety of boxes, cardboard tubes, and other found objects available so children can create real or imaginary creatures.
- ⊙ Provide Styrofoam trays on which children can draw simple animal forms. Pierce the outline at regular intervals for the younger children to stitch. Older children can pierce through the trays themselves.
- ⊙ Transfer children's animal drawings onto felt or burlap. Cut out two duplicate shapes, stitch together, and fill with beans, seeds, or shredded nylon hose for use as toys to toss.

The following sections of this chapter provide ideas that may be used as the basis for planning both formal and informal science activities. These, of course, are meant to be starting points. Teachers will think of many more activities that suit their particular group interests and abilities.

THE DISCOVERY/SCIENCE CENTER

The discovery center should have things for the children to "do." It is not a center where children just look at objects. Most teachers use a sand and water table in the discovery center. Here various materials—rice, beans, cornmeal, sawdust, mud—can be placed in the table for children to explore, measure, and pour. Sand and water activities are usually informal science and open-ended—that is, children can freely explore and manipulate materials with no definite or specified purpose to the activity.

Another type of activity that usually is done in a discovery center is cooking. Recipes that children can prepare individually with a minimum of teacher supervision work well in the discovery center. There are many simple recipes that do not require cooking. See Chapter 21 for many examples of such simple recipes. If heating equipment is used, then an adult must be present to supervise and assist at all times.

The discovery center can house plants and animals for the children to observe. In addition to caring for them, the children can also record information about them, such as the amount of food given to the gerbil each day, the amount of water used for the plant, or the amount the plant has grown.

"Please touch!" is the implied invitation of an interesting, ever-changing discovery center. Many teachers begin the school year with noble intentions of welcoming nature finds and other objects of science interest that children bring from home. Perhaps they initiate the project attractively with a bird's nest propped in a small tree branch, some special rocks, and a recently shed snake skin. If the goal of a changing display is

Figure 19-9

The playground is full of science activity possibilities, such as learning about light and shadows.

forgotten, the old things will lose their meaning. Since there is little appeal in a dusty nest or a tattered snake skin, it is better to retire the too-familiar objects.

Discovery Walks

An easy way to keep the science discovery area new and exciting is to plan nature discovery walks as a regular part of your curriculum. The desire to collect things is a strong one in young children. A discovery walk can be a springboard to some memorable science experiences.

Give children shopping bags and take them on a mini field trip to a nearby playground or sidewalk. Ask them to collect anything interesting to add to their bag (keeping safety in mind, of course). You'll be amazed at what your young collectors find, including flattened bottle caps, blades of grass, and even an occasional penny.

Sorting and representing.   Ask children to unload their collections into a plastic tray or pan. Start sorting, comparing, classifying, and ordering. Have a sheet of paper and markers on hand so that they can trace and label their collections. If you have a computer, use a program such as Kidspiration to take this representation to another level using the program's rich library of stickers to represent each item. (For more information on Kidspiration software, see the Software for Children section). This program makes it easy to break the collection into groups, sorting by attribute such as floats/sinks, paper/no paper, and so on.

A closer look.   A magnifying glass is great for helping children examine their discoveries. Children can sort their collections by lines, textures, colors, or any other art element. For example, you can add magnetic strips to

THIS ONE'S for YOU!   # Why Is the Sky Blue?

In our day and time, children think up science questions ranging all the way from the traditional "Why is the sky blue?" to the complicated and controversial, "What is cloning and why do we do it?"

You don't have to have all the answers to these sometimes mind-boggling questions, but here are a few good places to look for the answers or just to keep yourself current in case one of those tough questions comes up:

http://www.nytimes.com/. Click on Science in the News listing. *The New York Times* "Science Times" section appears every Tuesday.

http://www.sciencenews.org. The Web site of the weekly newsmagazine *Science News.*

http://www.npr.org/. Click on Health & Science section. National Public Radio's "Talk of the Nation: Science Friday" broadcasts are archived online in audio files.

Figure 19-10

There are many excellent picture books about science concepts.

the backs of rocks and place them in categories (big/little, smooth/rough, shiny/dull, etc.) on a magnetic board.

Displaying objects in the discovery center.

When a child brings a collection of objects from home, provide a special place for this temporary display. For objects collected by the class, you can organize and store the displays in clear plastic boxes. This way, the displays can be easily rotated among children.

When you have popular items in your discovery center such as prisms or magnets, have duplicates on hand or use a sign-up system. Two to four children can sit on the floor and explore a collection out on a small carpet square or a bathmat. Four chairs set at a table invite four science investigators.

If you have access to a digital camera, snap a photo of each child's collection and print a large, one-page photo of each collection. Below the picture, write a short "I spy" description of a few items in the collection. For example write, "I spy an item that is round and has lines on it." This invites children's investigation and close observation.

You can also use interesting collections as table centerpieces for special occasions. If you have access to a video camera, you can make a video about the children's collecting and investigating process and share it with parents.

Discovery Centers–Set-Up

Try to locate the discovery center in an area that both invites children's participation yet controls distractions.

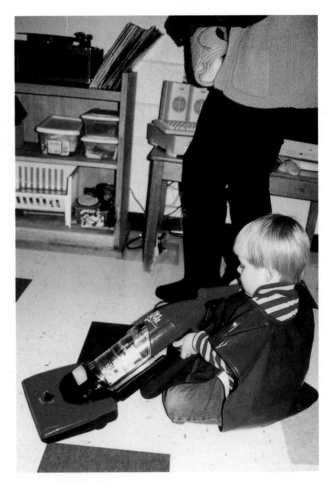

Figure 19-11

Learning about how things work is a basic science activity.

Varying the location to fit the requirements of the activity builds interest. Science is very popular on the days when it takes place under a blanket-covered table! Careful planning of space, materials, and time for science will allow children to work as safely, independently, and successfully as possible.

In preschool and kindergarten classrooms, and in elementary classrooms organized with learning centers, many science activities can be set up for independent use. Printed activity directions can be prepared to guide reading students. Tape-recorded guides can also be made to reduce the amount of direct supervision needed for small-group learning activities.

Discovery Centers–Younger Preschool Children

While the activities in this text were planned for children three years of age and older, many of the activities can be adapted for younger preschool children. Two year olds can enjoy simple sensory explorations such as feeling air as they move it with paper fans, spinning pinwheels, or swinging streamers on a breezy

Figure 19-12
Science is an ongoing part of the total early childhood curriculum.

day; feeling rock textures and weights; touching ice, then touching the water it melts into; watching, then moving like a goldfish; tasting raw fruits and vegetables that have grown from plants; listening to loud and soft sounds; or gazing through transparent color paddles to see surroundings in a new light.

Three year olds might be expected to engage in similar activities, taking in greater detail. They will be able to direct deeper attention to such things as exploring new dimensions with a magnifying glass. This group can enjoy some of the classifying experiences on a beginning level: sorting rocks from objects that are not rocks; things that float from those that do not float; and objects that are attracted by a magnet from objects that are not attracted.

In formal science activities, younger children need clearly defined steps to gain from science activities. For instance, the seeds in a planting experience should be large and easy to see. A fine, dark lettuce seed is hard to distinguish from a bit of dirt, and a child may not be sure of what he has actually done after planting it. A large, pale bean or pumpkin seed that is obviously different from the soil would be a better choice.

Very young children can be very easily sidetracked in their reasoning by what they observe. To keep the objective of an experience evident to them, avoid using materials with irrelevant, distracting details. For instance, if size comparisons are to be made with measuring cups, use cups of the same color and shape to help children focus on size. Younger children will still be exploring materials with their mouths as well as with their fingers. *Non-food materials must not be small enough to swallow.* Such foods as peanuts and popcorn should not be given to children too young to chew them well. As a matter of course, adults should closely supervise any activity for very young children.

Thoughtful questioning, careful listening to children's replies, and comments from the teacher guide formal science activities in the discovery center. Open-ended questions such as "What happens when you . . .?" help children focus their thinking. A question such as "Why do you suppose . . .?" allows the children to share their reasoning. Many of us use the pattern of stating the answers we hear from children in the form of a question. We may say, "So the cup of snow melted into a smaller amount of water, right? Isn't that what you found?" This style of questioning reduces children's need to discover answers for themselves, or tells them that the main discovery is to find out what the teacher wants them to say.

The discovery center is a place where many of the National Standards on Science can be taught. The most important aspect of the discovery center is that it is the place where children learn the creative thinking and problem-solving skills that are the foundation of the National Standards.

ENVIRONMENTAL EDUCATION

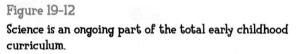

A four-year-old child stands at the sink gazing at the water pouring down over his fingers. After a while, he reaches for the soap and slowly turns the lathery bar over and over as the water flows in a column from faucet to drain. Finally, he rinses away the suds and turns from the sink. The waste basket is filled with slightly crumpled towels. For him, as for most of us, endless streams of clean water and inexhaustible supplies of convenience products are taken for granted.

Ecologists have varied estimates on how much time is left before we will have wasted natural resources and polluted the Earth to the point where we can no longer survive. Some fear the damage is already irreversible. Others believe that there is still time—provided a profound change in attitude and behavior occurs. For adults, it means finding new values. For children, it means growing up with an understanding of the environment and a desire to conserve and protect those things essential for continued life on this planet.

If children are to grow up in a world fit for human survival, the environment must be protected. Children should learn about nature from their earliest years. Nature is not the only part of a child's environment, however. Home, school, and neighborhood are all parts of the child's environment. In fact, everything that contributes to children's experiences—good or bad—is part of their environment. Can a child learn creativity by learning about the environment? Can a child learn to improve the environment? Can young children learn about ecology? The answer to these questions is "yes." Most of all, learning about these things can and must begin when a child is young.

Their environment is one of the most important influences in the lives of children. They need an environment full of love. They need an environment that provides for their other basic needs: water, food, clean air. Children need an environment that provides for their safety, that helps them grow intellectually, that they can understand and control.

In other words, children need to learn about their environment because their lives depend on that environment. This learning can be done in a very creative way. Activities that help children understand their environment can also help them become more creative thinkers.

Types of Environments

For the purposes of this chapter, the term **environment** refers to two things: man-made and natural things that children meet in their surroundings. Streets, houses, and schools are examples of man-made things in the environment. Trees, grass, and birds are parts of nature. Streetlights, cars, and buildings are man-made. Animals, clouds, and snow are natural things. Noise, light, and smells may be man-made or a part of nature.

Children have many environments in which they live. Home is one. It may be a pleasant part of a child's life or an unpleasant one. School is another environment that influences a child's life, and it, too, may be an enjoyable experience or an unpleasant one. The neighborhood environment may be friendly and safe, or it may be hostile and dangerous. There are also many people who are part of a child's environment: parents and neighbors, grocers and police officers, teachers and doctors. The people who make up the communities in which children live may make the children feel very good about their lives, or they may make the children feel unhappy.

In these environments, there are also natural things and natural happenings: grass, trees, and flowers; rain, wind, and earthquakes; cats, rats, and beetles. All these things are part of a child's environment. They all affect one another. Nature influences people; people influence nature.

Ecology

Ecology is the study of all elements of an environment, both living and nonliving, and the interrelation of these elements. The term comes from two Greek words: *ecos* meaning the "place to live" or "home," and *ology* meaning "study of."

If we stop to consider our work with young children, we have probably touched on the subject of ecology frequently. For example, we notice the changes in the weather and discuss how these affect plants, birds, animals, and ourselves. When we plant seeds, hatch eggs, or care for a pet, we notice those things that are necessary for life and growth—nourishment, light, heat, nurturing. We like to examine and observe many organisms,

Figure 19-13

Working with sand provides young children many science experiences.

but if we remove an insect from its home, we take care to restore it unharmed to its place after our observation is finished. Consequently, children learn that all life is precious, and no creature is more or less worthwhile than another.

Those of us in early childhood education are also old hands at recycling materials and using up discards. Bits of paper left over from cutting shapes find their way into the collage box instead of the wastebasket. Empty boxes evolve into constructions, large and small. The blank sides of printed sheets of paper are used for drawing. Old newspapers are used for many art projects. We all think twice before throwing anything away, and with a little encouragement children and their parents soon catch the saving habit.

By our example, we can teach other ways of living a more ecologically sound lifestyle. For example, using durable dishes for food service rather than disposable dishes is an ecologically sound practice. When food and beverages for snacks and meals come in bottles or cans, these containers should be cleaned and the cans flattened and deposited at a recycling center. The use of personal cloth towels instead of paper towels is another good ecological practice. To encourage parents to recycle, you might consider establishing a collection site at your school, perhaps making it a cooperative project run by the parents.

To truly grasp the concept of ecology, young children need opportunities to observe the total process rather than just a portion of it or only the finished product.

Help children understand the total process when you explain the need for conservation. Describing how the paper-making process begins with the cutting down of a tree in the forest and ends with the paper products that we use every day helps children understand why it is important that they use only one paper towel to dry their hands.

Incorporating the subject of ecology into the early childhood curriculum is endorsed in the *National Science Education Standards*. It is particularly relevant to the standard that states that children should develop an understanding of "types of resources" and "changes in environments" (National Research Council, 1996, p. 138).

These early experiences in ecology will provide students an eventual understanding and appreciation for their part in protecting the environment.

ENVIRONMENTAL ACTIVITIES IN SCHOOL

A child first learns about caring for the environment by caring for his most immediate environment, that is, home, school, playgrounds, and parks. In the early

childhood years, the teacher can use everyday experiences to point out to children the importance of caring for the environment.

Getting Started

Getting young children outdoors to touch and experience nature is the starting point for learning about ecology and the environment. Unfortunately, a visit to many early childhood classrooms reveals the obvious: indoor time and space are given far more priority than outdoor. Many early childhood programs allot only a short daily period of outdoor time for children's energy release and motor development. In the elementary grades, with state-mandated curriculum, it becomes even more difficult to find time to go outdoors to study and still cover all the required subjects and time requirements.

Increased time for outdoor learning experience can be worked into the daily routine without difficulty, however, at least in good weather. Music, movement, and art acquire new dimensions outside; there is often plenty of space for construction with large blocks, boxes, tires, and boards; and snack and lunch times

Figure 19-14

Guessing objects by feeling their shape and texture is a popular science activity.

become picnics. Best of all, the outdoors provides a natural setting, complete with props for dramatic play. Middle and upper elementary age students enjoy reading and working on projects outdoors. Small reading groups, project work, and other academic activities can often be done just as effectively in the outdoors. Just think how much you, as a student, enjoy reading outside on a sunny, pleasant day!

Even if the outdoor space is a concrete-covered square, children experience more of nature than they would inside. They know the warmth of the sun, the power of the wind, and the coolness of shade; they find plants that spring up in cracks and insects that crawl or fly; and they experience weather in its many forms.

Obviously, the more natural an environment, the better. Slightly unkempt spaces are more interesting to investigate than blacktop or grassy lawns. In many areas, the edges of property lines where the mower does not reach hold the greatest promise for exploration.

As stated in the National Standards on earth and science (Content Standard D), it is important that "all students develop an understanding of the properties of the earth" (National Research Council, 1996, p. 130). Young children are naturally interested in everything they see around them—soil, rocks, streams, rain, snow, clouds, and rainbows. During the first years of school, they should be encouraged to observe closely the objects and materials in their environment, note their properties, distinguish one from another, and develop their own explanations of how things become the way they are.

Figure 19-15

Older children enjoy keeping written records of their science experiments.

Teacher's Role

To be involved with nature, all you need are curiosity, joy of exploration, and a desire to discover firsthand the wonders of nature. Young children are naturals at this. Adults take a little longer. The teacher's most important role is sharing enthusiasm, curiosity, and wonder. Adults can best do this by using their legs—stopping and getting down to see what has caught a child's attention. Just the focusing of attention, perhaps with an expression of wonderment—"Look how pretty!" or "Great, you found something amazing!"—can encourage exploration and child-adult conversation. When we share our own ideas and feelings with a child, it encourages a child to explore his own feelings and perceptions. In middle and upper elementary grades, as children become more familiar with their world, the teacher guides them to observe changes, including cycle changes such as cycles of the moon, predictable trends such as growth and decay, and less consistent change, such as weather.

Art and Ecology

Art, music, dance, movement, and storytelling all provide opportunities for children to express their interests and discoveries developed through environmental education.

Setting up easels outdoors may inspire children to paint trees or their feelings about trees. Modeling clay outdoors may encourage children to create their own versions of natural objects in their outdoor play space. Use types of clouds to inspire soft sculptures: stratus, cumulus, etc. (See the recipes in the Appendices for play dough and other modeling material recipes). In movement activities, children may reflect the wiggle of caterpillars they observed on the playground. In music, the sounds of birds and crickets can be reflected with rhythm instruments or their own voices. They may dance the story of birds, flowers, and animals awakening to the springtime sun. Children's books are also excellent for further expanding a child's understanding and appreciation of the earth. (See lists in the

THIS ONE'S for YOU!

Art and Science—Working Together

Art is *not* just for art's sake. Consider how art assisted scientists in the following:

To determine how much Venice has sunk into its lagoon in the last few centuries, scientists have turned to the 18th century Venetian landscapes of Canaletto. By scrutinizing the paintings and comparing them with the same sites in present-day Venice, scientists found that the city has sunk more than two feet since 1727.

Can you think of any other ways art has assisted scientists today?

Online Companion for suggestions.) Children's science books are an excellent way to address the National Science Standard which states, "It is important for students to learn how to access information from books" (National Research Council, 1996, p. 45).

The preceding are all general ideas on how to incorporate environmental education and ecology into your early childhood program. The following are some more specific activities on environmental education and ecology for children of all ages.

⊙ When someone in the classroom breaks a toy or piece of equipment, use the opportunity to talk with them about the consequences—that no one can play with the toy or use the equipment until it is repaired; that if it cannot be repaired no one can ever use it again. Have the children discuss ways of preventing this problem.

⊙ Help children (and by your own example) use materials—paint, paper, crayons, etc.—conservatively by saving scraps, storing unused paint, completing a picture before starting another, and keeping pencils and crayons off the floor.

⊙ Encourage children to help care for and clean classroom furniture. Provide cleanup materials for washing off tables and chairs and cleaning up spills.

⊙ Before looking at books, discuss with the children the importance of caring for them. Suggestions might include: washing hands, turning pages at the corner, and putting them in a special place away from pets and younger brothers and sisters. Remind them of their disappointment over a missing page in a story.

⊙ Snack time offers an opportunity for children to learn to conserve. The same applies to older children at lunch time. Persuade them to take only what they will eat, to eat all they take, and to refuse what

they do not want. Each child should frequently have the opportunity to clean up after snack.

⊙ Before going on a class picnic, remind the children to pick up their trash in the park and let them discuss why this is important.

⊙ During the year encourage appreciation for the jobs of the school janitor and the garbage collector, etc. Have these helpers talk with the children about what they do and how the children can help make their job easier.

⊙ Avoid frightening children with threats about results of things they cannot control. (Example: What will happen when there is no clean air left?) Concentrate instead on the things they *can do,* such as keeping their own yards and school grounds neat, putting their own waste in proper receptacles, having a litter bag in the car, avoiding open burning, keeping pets clean, etc.

Pets in the Classroom

The best way for young children to learn about animals is to have them in the classroom. Through observing and caring for pets in the classroom, children can do the following:

⊙ grow in understanding the needs of animals for food and water, as well as safe, clean housing and attention.

⊙ grow in appreciation for the beauty, variety, and functional physical characteristics of animals, for example, the protective shell on a turtle, the webbed feet on a duckling, and the sharp teeth and claws on a hamster.

⊙ grow in the compassion for and humane treatment of animals.

⊙ obtain inspiration for many language experiences and creative activities.

Good classroom pets are (be sure no children have allergies to any of the pets) guinea pigs, rabbits, parakeets, white mice, hamsters, turtles, salamanders, gerbils, and goldfish.

Good short-time (an hour or so) classroom pets are chicks, ducklings, puppies, a setting hen, kittens, and turkey poults.

Children can help plan for the pet in advance by building the cage or preparing the terrarium or aquarium. The necessary food and water pans can be obtained, a food supply can be stored up, bedding can be prepared, and the handling of the pet can be discussed. Arrangements must be made for pet care during all holidays and vacation periods. A trip to a pet shop would be an excellent experience.

Children should help with the care of the pet once it is obtained, but in the final analysis the teacher is responsible for seeing that the pet is treated well. Children should learn that pets are not toys, that they have feelings, and that when provoked, some of them defend themselves by biting. Children should not be allowed to handle pets excessively or without supervision. It is cruel to let them "wrap pets up in blankets and take them for walks in a doll buggy" or to allow any other activity foreign to the pet's nature—and children should be helped to understand why. Neglected or mishandled pets give a negative message about responsibility and respect for life.

Besides caring for pets, some other activities that might be inspired by the presence of pets in the classroom are the following:

⊙ Discuss the way pets feel, how they look, the sounds they make, the way they move, the purpose of various parts of the body, the need for food, their homes, reproduction habits, etc.

⊙ Write experience charts about their care and characteristics.

⊙ Tell original stories based on the pet. Tape these stories.

⊙ Draw, paint, or model the pet out of clay.

⊙ Dramatize the pets' movements.

⊙ Take a trip to a pet shop or zoo.

⊙ Show pictures of animals. Have children tell which are tame and which are wild; which fly, hop, swim, etc.; and which live in water, on land, etc.

⊙ Tell animal stories, recite animal poems, and sing animal songs.

⊙ Older children can keep journals on their daily observations of the classroom pet. They can write stories with the pet as the main character.

OUTDOOR SCIENCE

Many activities work well inside the school. Others are more suited to the area outside the school building. All of the following activity suggestions are consistent with the *National Science Education Standards.* They apply most specifically to the Content Standard D on Earth Science. This standard is focused on the child's developing an understanding of: properties of earth materials, objects in the sky, and changes in earth and sky.

Beginning Activities

Children can learn many different things about nature by being outdoors. However, many young children come to school with limited direct experiences with natural environments. They may, thus, have little understanding and great fear about what may happen to them in their encounters with nature. They may fear the darkness of a wooded area. They may think that all bugs and insects bite or sting. In their minds, an earthworm may be a poisonous snake. Such children need a gradual exposure to the world of nature. They need to become familiar with the trees and bushes in the schoolyard before they feel comfortable hiking in the woods. They need to observe and care for classroom animals before they are asked to welcome a caterpillar crawling across their hand or feel the woolly head of a lamb while on a field trip to a farm.

Young children also need to realize that nature is all around them and that wildlife can be found anywhere. Some children seem to think that wildlife is somewhere very separate and far away from where they live. When asked where he might look to find wildlife, one little boy responded, "Africa." For such children, one of the most meaningful lessons would focus on becoming aware of and comfortable with wildlife in their immediate environment.

Ideas on how to begin with simple experiences include the following:

⊙ watching a bean seed sprout in the classroom before attempting to plant and tend a vegetable garden.

⊙ playing with snow in the texture table before making and crawling through tunnels of snow in the schoolyard.

⊙ watching birds and squirrels from a "window on nature" before suggesting that the children let a goat eat from their hands.

⊙ walking barefoot in puddles, then observing their footprints made on the sidewalk.

THIS ONE'S for YOU!
Art and Science Activities

Science is a natural springboard for art activities. Try some of the following activities to get children actively exploring the connection.

ART AND REALITY

Students can examine how a single object is shown realistically in many different ways by artists. For example, show five different pieces of art about an animal. Ask how each gives different information and feels different.

INVISIBLE ANIMALS

Examine water under a microscope or with hand lenses, and sketch living organisms. Emphasize close looking to capture specifics. Sketches can be enlarged into full paintings.

THREE-DIMENSIONAL HABITATS

Use boxes to create dioramas of an animal's habitat (land or water). Add clay sculptures, tempera paint, and found objects in construction.

SCIENTIFIC DRAWINGS

Examine the drawings of Beatrix Potter and Robert McCloskey, both of whom studied animals and plants carefully to render their images. Students can then choose to do a careful scientific drawing, focusing on important details. Use photos or actual plants for close looking.

COLOR SCIENCE

Each group of students needs a prism to investigate color. Paint or use crayons to record observations and discover colors.

GROWING THINGS

Use pantyhose feet to make living heads. Fill hose with a teaspoon of grass seed and then a mixture of soil and sawdust. Tie snugly with a string. Paint on face with fabric paint. Put head in a shallow dish and pour water over it. Place in a sunny area and watch the grass "hair" grow.

STEP INTO PAINTING

Have students think like scientists and tell or write their observations as they look at a piece of art (e.g., a landscape). Focus on how the painting might have been made and the content.

SPIDER WEB ANALYSIS

Slide a piece of black construction paper behind a spider web and bring it forward so that the web clings to the paper. Dust with flour or dusting powder. Spray with fixative or nonaerosol hair spray. Discuss the patterns of lines created by the web. Look closely to compare and contrast.

Figure 19-16

The discovery center is a place to try out ideas and "what ifs."

Introduce Nature-Related Materials into the Different Learning Centers

To the language-experience center, you can add books and pictures about nature. You can also add stuffed animals, animal puppets, and a variety of plant and animal flannel-board characters. Choose pictures and other representations of animals that are as realistic as possible versus those that have a cartoonlike appearance.

To add nature-related materials to the manipulative center, you might choose simple puzzles with nature themes (animals, plants, etc.) and shells or pebbles of different colors and sizes. You might also add pinecones, small pieces of bark, dry wood, and other objects found in or near the yard. Similar items could be introduced into the block center as well.

Materials from the outdoors also make wonderful additions to the art center. Dried leaves or small pieces of bark can be used for rubbings; seeds, shells, dry grasses, and feathers can be used for collages; and evergreen sprigs can be used as paintbrushes.

To the music or listening center, you might add audiotapes of sounds from nature (bird songs, ocean sounds, rainforest noises, etc.).

The dramatic play area, too, can be enriched with materials from the outdoors. Such materials include camping equipment, garden tools, and a picnic basket filled with a variety of picnic items.

Bird Feeders

Children can try to design bird feeders and build them in some way, or they can design the feeders and their parents can help them build the structures. Professionally built bird feeders can also be used.

Children can try to discover what kinds of food attract various kinds of birds. Where is the best place to put a bird feeder? When is the best time of year to watch for birds? What time of day is best for bird watching at a feeder?

Older children enjoy learning the names of the birds they see at the feeders. A book having colored illustrations of local birds can be a research source for this activity. They can keep records of which birds frequent certain feeders more than others, and speculate as to why this is the case. They can make graphs representing use of each feeder.

Cloud and Sky Watching

On a mild, partly sunny or cloudy day, children can learn much about their environment. They can lie on the ground and look up at the sky. They may see clouds of many shapes. Clouds may join together. The sun may disappear. It may get cool very suddenly. Birds may fly past.

The children may have many different feelings as they lie still and watch the sky. Questions may arise. How do clouds seem to move? What do they look like? Are there many colors in the clouds? What do clouds look like just before a storm? Ask the children if they can make up a story about the clouds. They may enjoy painting a picture about their cloud watching.

The Sounds of Nature

Walking in the woods or along a busy street can be made exciting by listening to the sounds. In the area next to a school, there are many sounds, too. When most of the children are indoors, one or two supervised children may want to go outside and just listen. They can take a cassette tape recorder along and record sounds, too. Play the tape and encourage children to move like the sounds make them feel.

How many different sounds can they hear? Can they hear sounds made by birds? By animals? What do the leaves in the trees sound like? How do trees without leaves sound? What other sounds can be heard? How do noises made by cars differ from noises made by trucks? How does a person feel if there is too much noise?

What Happens to Rain Water?

After a rainstorm, children can try to follow the paths taken by the water. Does all of the water flow into a sewer? Does some of it go into the ground? What happens in paved areas compared to grassy areas? What happens in dirt areas compared to grassy areas?

Older children can learn about erosion and the effects of it in their own parks and playgrounds. This can easily be done after a heavy rain storm on the

THINK ABOUT IT...

Scientists Tell All

Parents appear to be the biggest single positive factor in stimulating a childhood interest in science, according to a national survey of scientists released by Bayer Corporation and the National Science Foundation (Bayer Corporation & NSF) (1999). "The message to parents is clear: You don't have to be a science expert to help your children love the subject, or all learning for that matter," said Mae C. Jemison, former astronaut and Bayer Corporation's science literacy advocate for its Making Science Make Sense initiative. "You just need to encourage and support them as they pursue their interests." The Bayer/NSF survey, the Bayer Facts of Science Education IV: Scientists on Science for the 21st Century, polled more than 1,400 members of the American Association for the Advancement of Science. The survey asked them, among other things, to look back on their own educational and career experiences and forecast trends in science literacy and scientific advances in the new millenium.

More than half of the scientists said they first became interested in science during their elementary school years. Teachers were as influential as parents in sparking an interest in science. And, apart from formal science classes (82 percent), more than 80 percent of the scientists were influenced by science toys and equipment like chemistry sets and telescopes; 78 percent mentioned newspapers, magazines, and other media that covered science; 76 percent said science museum visits; and 69 percent felt that doing science experiments at home was influential.

While all scientists reported informal science activities like playing with science toys and doing experiments at home, these activities were more important for male scientists (85 percent and 71 percent, respectively), than for female scientists (60 percent and 55 percent).

"The fact that chemistry sets and microscopes had an effect on this many men makes perfect sense since they were probably given them as birthday presents," explained Jemison. "What we need to ask ourselves is 'What if more girls had access to and were encouraged to play with the same kinds of toys?'"

Few scientists (25 percent) believe science is given enough emphasis in elementary school, though 74 percent think it should be given the same priority as reading, writing, and arithmetic. In addition, most scientists (85 percent) say that, if asked, they would spend time in the classroom helping students learn and teachers to teach science (Bayer Corporation & NSF, 1999.).

playground or in a nearby park. Making mud pies and mud finger painting are great follow-up activities to these observations.

Animal Hiding Places

There may be a small hole in the ground or a sand hill in a crack on the playground. Thick grass or bushes serve as hiding places for animals. Under a large rock or near the foundation of the school there may be places for living things to hide.

Children seek answers to many questions about animals. Why do animals need hiding places? Can a child create a place where an animal will choose to hide? How many natural hiding places can be found? Can children create hiding places for themselves? How do they feel when they are in their hiding places? Can they move like an animal looking for a hiding place? Can they move like that animal as it goes into its hiding place?

If creativity is to be a part of activities such as these, decisions must be left to the children. Help from the teacher should not take the form of orders on what to do and what not to do. Advice is good; orders or carefully worded cookbook directions are not.

Plants in the Environment

Probably the best way to observe the magnificent color and variety to be found in plants is to visit the places where they can be seen firsthand. The school grounds are the closest source. Children can hunt with you for the tallest tree, the one with the roughest bark, and the ones with needles, pinecones, or smooth leaves. They can hunt for plants that are growing in cracks in the sidewalk, for plants that have been eaten by insects, and for seeds, berries, galls, and roots that are exposed.

Going beyond the schoolyard, trips can be made to the grocery store, supermarket, or farmers' market to examine firsthand the potatoes, carrots, onions,

Figure 19-17

The science curriculum at the middle and upper elementary level includes work in problem solving as well as in discovery.

eggplants, peas, cabbages, beets, and others. Vegetables represent great beauty in almost every color, shape, and size. If one of each kind could be brought back to the classroom, what a great opportunity for making comparisons they would offer!

The same kind of observations can be made with fruits, or with flowers at a greenhouse, shrubs at a nursery, or plants in an arboretum or small neighborhood garden or truck farm.

The plants can be looked at, cooked, taken apart, tasted, felt, counted, smelled, and weighed.

They could be compared for color, texture, juiciness, shape, kind of leaf, aroma, size, and outside covering.

They could be classified by the preceding characteristics as nuts, seeds, fruits, roots, leaves, stems, or vegetables, usually eaten raw or usually eaten cooked.

If trips are not possible, each child could be asked to bring one fruit, vegetable, or other plant to school, or the teacher could supply the necessary items from the school budget. Some other suggestions follow.

- Seed catalogs can be made available in the book center.

- Seeds can be planted in pots by the children, or better yet, if a small garden plot is available, they can be planted and cared for there. Seed dealers can advise you on types that germinate quickly and what care they need.

- Press a stick such as a tongue depressor down into the soil by the seed when it sprouts. Have each child mark the height of the sprout each week as it grows. The date and name of the plant can be put on the stick.

- If the seeds in some pots don't grow, dig them up to see what happened to them.

- Help the children build a model greenhouse in the block center, using planks, large blocks, and packing boxes. They can put their plants in the greenhouse, as well as small trowels, watering cans, a bag of potting soil, and experience charts.

- Plants can be started from seeds, cuttings, bulbs, roots, and tubers. Sweet potatoes, placed in glasses so that half the potato is under water, will produce roots and a luxuriant vine. (Try to find potatoes that aren't bruised.) Bulbs of all kinds can be started. Geraniums and philodendron will produce roots from cuttings placed in water and can then be potted. Pussy willow twigs will grow roots in water.

- Top gardens can be made by cutting off about an inch from the top of root vegetables, such as carrots. Place the cut end in water, and new leafy growth will shoot up.

- Seeds of various kinds can be broken or cut open and studied to observe the small plant inside. Then have a plant tasting party. Examples: Seeds—sunflowers; roots—carrots; stems—celery; leaves—lettuce; flowers—cauliflower.

- Seeds can be sprouted in such a way that their growth can be studied. A satisfactory way to do this is to cut up blotting paper or paper towels. Place a couple of layers in the bottom of a saucer, moistening the paper thoroughly. Drop six to ten radish seeds on the blotter. Smear a little Vaseline around the edge of the saucer and cover with a piece of window glass. Tiny white root hairs will develop.

- To see roots, stems, and leaves form, make a plastic bag greenhouse. Place folded paper towels inside a plastic, self-locking bag, then staple a line across about 2″ from the bottom. Children fill bags to just below the line of staples with water, then drop in seeds. Seal the bags and display on a bulletin board to observe growth and development.

Children will be able to see the roots, stems, and leaves form.

Water Play Experiences

No matter in what quantity or container water is available—in a pool or basin, in a puddle or cup—there are ways to take advantage of its learning potential! A wading pool or large basin lends itself to pouring, sprinkling, and mixing with water, while a cup or a puddle is ideal for floating tiny objects like foil boats or cork stoppers and for dissolving small quantities of sugar or drink mix. Whatever facilities can be provided, water is a marvelous science experience for young children.

Organizing the play space for water play is a matter of selecting and arranging suitable containers and appropriate equipment. A laundry tub or plastic wading pool can be placed outside with a bench or table nearby to hold objects. If water play is to take place inside, the floor covering must be water repellent, and a shelf can be used for equipment storage; a plastic tablecloth can be a weatherproof carpet and a small card table can substitute for the shelf. Plastic aprons are ideal for clothing protection, but garbage bags with neck and armholes cut serve well, too.

Objects that lead the child to science experiences might include the following:

⊙ sponges, corks, and light pieces of wood
⊙ funnels, strainers, colanders, plastic tubing, and siphons
⊙ spray containers, sprinkling cans, squeeze bottles, water guns, and rubber balls
⊙ plastic pitchers, margarine tubs, plastic cups, and yogurt containers
⊙ paintbrushes, paint rollers, and washcloths
⊙ spoons, dippers, plastic syringes, and plastic medicine droppers

Occasionally, bubble bath, cornstarch, food coloring, or other mixables can be added to vary the appearance and physical properties of the water.

Safety tips. Always have an adult with the children in any water play situation. Never leave a child unattended. Use only unbreakable materials for water play activities. Never use glass, ceramic, porcelain, pottery, china, or other breakable materials. Always gather materials ahead of time, so you do not have to leave the children unsupervised.

Develop water play rules with the children. Discuss and generate a list that is appropriate to your situation and revise them as needed. For example, you will need one set of rules when the children are playing at the water table and other rules for the outdoor pool.

Some ideas for rules might include:

⊙ no splashing
⊙ keep the water in the containers
⊙ mop up spills immediately

Specific activities for water play are included at the end of this chapter.

SUMMARY

In science activities children gain knowledge about the world around them by investigating that world. In science for young children, the emphasis is on investigating; the knowledge gained is less important. Science is important for children because it gives them all an opportunity to succeed.

Formal science activities are planned by the teacher to develop particular skills, such as fine motor skills or awareness of the five senses.

Informal science calls for little or no teacher involvement. Children work on their own and select the kind of activities that interest them.

Informal science activities are less structured than formal science activities. Creativity is, therefore, better served by informal than by formal science.

The National Science Education Standards present an outline of what students in grades K through 12 need to know, understand, and be able to do to be "scientifically literate." They provide a broad outline of what science experiences students should have from kindergarten through grade 12.

Ecology is the study of all elements in the environment, both living and nonliving, and how these elements are interrelated. The term comes from two Greek words: *ecos* meaning "place to live" or "home," and *ology* meaning "study of."

Children should begin to understand that all forces in the environment affect one another. Animals influence other animals. Plants affect animals. The climate has an effect on the environment. People can make the environment pleasant or very unpleasant.

Children should have experiences with both the natural and manmade environments. These experiences take place in the school building and in the play area around the school. They also take place in the community in which the children live. Playing with water is another excellent way for young children to experience the natural environment.

KEY TERMS

ecology
environment
formal science

incidental science
informal science

LEARNING ACTIVITIES

SCIENCE ACTIVITIES

1. Take a field trip around your home or your school. Walk within one square block of home or school. Identify all of the plant life in this area. How many trees, plants, shrubs, and weeds can you observe?

2. Create a file of resources in the community that could be used to foster children's concepts of their environment and the world around them.

3. Observe in a classroom where there is a living pet or pets. Record the children's conversations as they watch the pet. Discuss how much they have learned about the animal from direct observation. What did their questions/conversations tell you about their experiences with the pet? Be specific in your answers.

4. Using a pail of water, create a puddle on a playground in order to observe children's reactions as they approach it. Record the ways in which they play.

5. Plan a science table where children can be involved in making discoveries. List the objects you might include and describe the types of involvement each object might stimulate. Discuss your list with others in your class.

6. Visit a playground. List natural phenomena that seem to be of interest to children. As you observe children at play, describe behavior that indicates they do take an interest in these phenomena. Compare what interested you at the playground to what interested the children. Discuss the differences between your interests and those of the children.

7. Visit one (or more) of the Web sites listed in the Helpful Web Sites section of this chapter. Choose a science activity from the Web site and use it with children. Report on how successful the activity was with the children. Rate the Web site on the following: (1) ease of use, (2) quality of activities, and (3) developmental appropriateness.

MAKING OBSERVATIONS

The ability to make many accurate observations is an important skill for both children and adults. The following activity is designed to test your ability to make observations and use all of your senses (hearing, smelling, tasting, touching, and seeing).

A. Materials: A package of peppermint Life Savers, ruler, book of matches, small nail, sheet of sandpaper, glass of water, and waxed paper.

B. How many observations can be made about a package of peppermint Life Savers? Can as many as 40 observations be made? Try doing this with one or two partners, if possible. Do it for each of the items listed in part A.

C. List all the observations and write down the sense or senses that were used to make each observation (seeing, hearing, etc.).

FINDING OBJECTS FOR MAKING OBSERVATIONS

A. Find ten objects that can be used for making observations. Each object should provide opportunities for an observer to use all five senses. For instance, an ice cube can be one of the objects.

B. After finding the ten objects, try the following:
   1. Decide what other materials would help in making observations of this thing. A ruler or magnifying glass may be needed. Make a list of these materials.
   2. Collect all materials needed for observing each item and place them in small packages or boxes.
   3. Choose a partner. Make observations of three of the partner's objects using materials provided by the partner. Then let the partner try out your objects and materials.

DESCRIBING SHAPES

A. Draw three shapes on a piece of paper. The shapes should not be something everyone recognizes.

B. Choose a partner. Try to describe each of the shapes in such a way that the partner can draw pictures of them without seeing them. This is a difficult task.

FINDING MATERIALS

A. Visit rummage sales, farm auctions, store sales, and secondhand stores. Look for materials that could be used by children in science activities.

B. Make a list of things that can be bought, how much they cost, and where they can be purchased. Compare lists with two or more students.

C. Prepare a master list of these materials.

ACTIVITIES FOR CHILDREN

WATER PLAY ACTIVITIES

In all of the following activities, be sure that an adult is *always* present when children are playing with water.

SPRAY ART–MURAL MAKING

Collect spray mist bottles with trigger handles, squeeze bottles of food coloring, large white butcher block paper or a white sheet, scissors, tape, a large towel or plastic mat, and water.

Spread the towel or plastic mat on the floor. Cut a large square of butcher block paper. Tape the paper or the sheet to the table top or outside to a wall or fence. Fill the spray bottles with water. Squeeze 10–15 drops of food coloring into the spray bottles. Secure the top of the spray bottles. Prepare several spray bottles of water with different colors of food coloring mixture.

The child shakes the bottle, near the paper or sheet. Holding the spray bottle, the child sprays the colored water onto the paper to make a mural. When the children are finished spraying the colored water mural, the teacher removes the tape and dries the mural.

MISCELLANEOUS WATER PLAY IDEAS

⊙ Straws are great for blowing bubbles during water play. To prevent children from sucking up the soapy water by mistake, poke holes near the tops of the straws first.

⊙ Make soap bubbles last longer by adding a few tablespoons of sugar to the soapy water.

⊙ Add variety to the water play area by adding these items and activities:
   —Fill the water table with ice cubes and provide shakers of salt and lengths of string.
   —Punch a row of holes from the bottom to the top of a 2–liter plastic soda bottle.
   —Put salt in the water, then try to float and sink objects.
   —Put snow in place of water.
   —Put a large chunk of ice in the water table. Provide safety goggles, rubber mallets, and rock salt.
   —Provide lengths of plastic pipe, whole and also in sections cut in half lengthwise, to use as canals and ramps for rolling marbles, small toy cars, or blocks. Use the piping dry, then wet, and compare results.

   —Punch holes in the bottom of milk cartons to make sieves. Use a variety of sizes of cartons and vary the size of the holes.
   —Add foam or rubber alphabet letters and small fishnets to the play center. Name the letter you catch or catch the letters that make up your name.
   —Experiment with varying the amounts of water and air inside zippered sandwich storage bags in floating experiments.
   —Give children heavy aluminum foil to shape into boats.
   —Challenge children to create a boat from found objects, then move it from one end of the water to the other without using their hands.
   —Challenge children to make a bridge over a portion of the water, using scrap materials.

PUMP BOTTLE AND CHALK DESIGNS

Assemble these items: colored chalk, plastic pump bottles of different sizes.

Fill the plastic pump bottle with water. The child colors the sidewalk with colored chalk. The child presses the pump top and lets the water splatter over the chalk on the sidewalk, making a water design on the chalk. Use different-sized pump bottles, comparing the different water marks made by each bottle.

SPRAY ART–DESIGNER T-SHIRT

Assemble these materials: Spray mist bottle with trigger handle, food coloring, large white butcher block paper, scissors, tape, large towel or plastic mat, T-shirt.

Spread the towel or plastic mat outdoors, on the floor, or under a table. Place another towel or mat on the table. Tape a white T-shirt to the towel, mat, or to the towel on the table. Fill the plastic squeeze spray bottle with water. Squeeze 10–15 drops of food coloring into the plastic spray bottle and secure the top. Prepare several plastic spray bottles of water with different colors of food coloring. Shake the bottles.

The child shakes the bottle. Standing next to the table with the spray gun bottle in one hand, the child sprays the colored water onto the T-shirt. Add more food coloring if the color is too light. If you want to be sure of permanent color, use liquid dye instead of food coloring and water. When the child is finished with the design, remove the tape and hang the T-shirt to dry.

ROCKY ROAD TO KNOWLEDGE

Rocks, stones, and pebbles are not only interesting, abundant, and free for the taking, but they also provide a rich source of knowledge about matter and are a means of sharpening powers of observation, description, and classification.

A. Some of the things that can be done with rocks are:
1. sorting by size, color, texture, and surface.
2. identifying them by name.
3. taking a walk to see the many ways stone is used in buildings.
4. looking for fossils in limestone.
5. taking a field trip to hunt for interesting rocks.

B. Equipment that is useful in carrying out such a study includes scales of various types, magnifying glasses, and boxes (or egg cartons) for sorting.

EXPLORE THE POWERS OF THE SUN

Explore the power of sunlight—what it will pass through and what blocks it. Using different materials (clear glass, soda bottles of various colors, thin paper, construction paper), sort the items as to those sunlight can pass through and those it will not pass through. Talk about shadows, too.

INSECT CAGE

Cut openings in small plastic or cardboard cartons. Cover the opening with fine netting, taping it into place. Fine netting can also be taped over the top of any plastic container to provide a temporary home for insects. The children can observe insect life more easily if the insect cages are made from clear plastic containers.

A clean, empty, half-gallon milk carton also makes a good insect-viewer. Simply cut rectangular holes on two sides of the milk carton. Slip a nylon stocking over the carton and fasten at the top with a rubber band. Insects can be held inside for temporary viewing.

OBSERVING WORMS

Make an earthworm observatory with a large glass jar (a large peanut butter jar is good), worms, garden soil, and black construction paper.

Place a layer of small rocks or sand in the bottom of the jar so water will drain. Place 2 inches of moist soil and sand in the jar. Have children pick up worms and place them in the jar. Cover them with more soil. Keep the soil moist. Seal, using a lid with holes punched in it.

Wrap black construction paper around the jar. After 24 hours, remove the paper. The children should be able to see the worms tunneling through the soil.

Encourage children to talk about what interests them about worms.

GROW IT AGAIN!

Pineapple. Cut off the top and trim three rows of bottom leaves. Let dry for three days. Plant one inch deep in soil. Keep moist and sunny.

Carrot. Cut off the top and trim off all leaves. Place in a layer of pebbles in a flat dish. Keep well watered.

Onion. Find an onion that is already sprouted. Plant in soil. Keep watered and sunny.

SKY GAZER

Save the cardboard tubes from paper towel rolls. Punch two holes at one end of each tube and loop an 18-inch piece of yarn through them (make one for each child). Hang your telescope around your neck. Go outside on a nice, warm day and lie down on the grass. Using your telescope, look up into the sky. What do you see? Look some more. What else do you see? Tell each other.

BUILD A BIRD FEEDER

Treat a bird to lunch. Cut windows and doors into an empty milk carton or plastic soda bottle. Decorate it in such a way that birds will want to visit. Paste on colored pictures of big juicy worms! Glue on twigs, leaves, seeds, and other outdoor things with nontoxic glue. (Keep decorations to a minimum so as not to frighten the birds.) Tie it to a tree branch and fill it with birdseed. Watch and see how many birds and what kinds of birds use the feeder. Make pictures or paintings of birds that come to the feeder.

Pinecones can be used for another type of bird feeder. Spread sugarless peanut butter on pinecones and roll them in wild birdseed. Birds love peanut butter and it provides protein and oil for healthy feathers and bodies. Fasten the pinecones to the branches of a tree using floral wire.

ROCK HOUNDS

Young children love rocks! Encourage these "rock hounds" by the following activities:

⊙ Go on a collecting walk with the children. Give each child a paper bag and encourage everyone to look for rocks and pebbles of different sizes, shapes, and colors. Gather the children in a circle outside and look over the rock collection together. Have them work in small groups to study and experiment with the rocks.

⊙ Help children divide into groups outdoors. Give each group a mound of rocks and pebbles. Encourage children to use magnifying glasses to make close observations. Ask, "How are the rocks the same or different?"

⊙ Invite children to sort the rocks in any way they choose—by size, texture, shape, color, and so forth—onto paper plates. Once they are finished sorting, ask them to describe the rocks on each plate.

⊙ Make a chart describing the different ways children classified the rocks. Then invite them to count the rocks on each plate. Together, discuss which plate has the most and the least amount.

⊙ Ask children to arrange the pebbles from smallest to largest in an egg carton. Give out sheets of white paper and pencils, let children trace the smallest and largest pebbles, and compare their differences.

⊙ Let children use a pan balance to compare the weights of various rocks. Ask them to predict which rocks will be the heaviest or the lightest. Then, ask them to test their predictions.

⊙ After studying and experimenting with the rocks, create a rock museum. Display the rocks in your discovery center with signs describing the biggest, smallest, roughest, smoothest, heaviest, lightest, and so on.

⊙ Older children may use reference books to try to identify the different rocks in their collections.

⊙ Have a "rock'n roll" party! Take children to a grassy area outside. Ask them to curl their bodies in a ball as if they were rocks randomly strewn on the ground. Then, invite them to roll their bodies as if they were rocks rolling down a hill.

ACTIVITIES FOR OLDER CHILDREN (GRADES 4–5)

SOLAR SYSTEM–SCIENCE ACTIVITIES FOR MULTIPLE INTELLIGENCES

The following activities are designed to give children the chance to use their multiple intelligences to learn and truly understand the science concepts involved in a study of the solar system. After students have a foundation of knowledge about the solar system from classroom readings and discussions, the following activities can enrich and strengthen their learning.

Solar system model. Build a three-dimensional, scale model of the solar system (picture/logic smart).

Role-play activity. Choose a group of classmates to participate in a role-playing activity in which you are the sun and each of the other students is a plant. Write a script with the "planets" each saying something about themselves. Perform the skit for the class with everyone standing in the correct order holding signs to identify their part (word/picture/person smart).

Solar system tableau. Write a several-scene tableau that includes facts and information about the solar system. Choose a group of students to practice and perform the tableau (word/body/picture/person smart).

Solar system song. Create a song to teach younger students the order of the planets. The song should have a recurring rhythm and a chorus. Perform it for the class. Choose a primary class to perform it for (music/word smart).

Solar system report. Write a two- to three-page report about the solar system. Include three different references and one picture (word/picture smart).

Imaginary journal. Write an imaginary journal for a 10-day mission into space. You have been selected as the first student to go into space. Decide where within the solar system your mission goes, and keep a daily log explaining what you are seeing and learning. You'll need to research space missions and spacecraft before writing. They can find facts about space travel at the Smithsonian National Air and Space Museum Web site: http://www.nasm.si.edu/apollo/. Use your last entry to evaluate the entire mission. How successful was it? What would you do differently? How did it make you feel (word/person smart)?

Solar system math. Make a chart or graph to show the distance of each planet from the sun. Translate the actual distance into a smaller scale and draw the solar system to this scale (logic/picture smart).

Famous astronauts play. Research famous astronauts who have played a big role in the exploration of space. Write a short skit that tells interesting facts and information about these astronauts and their missions. Perform it for the class (word/person/body smart).

INTERVIEWING INVENTORS

Combine learning to use the library and making oral book reports with learning about inventions that have changed our lives. Before doing this activity, children should select one of the following inventors and read about that person and his/her invention.

Marie Curie—chemical processes, Geiger counter
Alexander Graham Bell—the telephone
Alice Chatham—the astronaut's helmet
Henry Ford—the automobile
The Wright Brothers—the airplane
Thomas Alva Edison—the electric light bulb, phonograph
Jonas Salk—polio vaccine
Rose O'Neill—the Kewpie doll
Rear Admiral Grace Murray Hopper—computer program compiler

Once the children know the inventor and the invention well enough to discuss them with classmates, pair the students. One child assumes the role of the inventor, and the other child assumes the role of the interviewer. Together, they develop and rehearse questions and responses for a radio or television talk show. These are then performed for the class. If the children are interested in switching roles, replay the activity, giving both students an opportunity to become the inventor that he or she has studied.

During the next phase, the children imagine that they are inventors. They are to develop a fictitious individual. They then create an autobiography for the inventor they imagine themselves to be and think of an invention for which they are famous. What have they invented? What does it do? After the children have had enough time to develop the character and to become familiar with the invention, use the interview format previously described.

Combine the two exercises by performing a television news show in which Bell, Ford, and other real inventors are interviewed. Between the interview segments, have the children perform commercials for the new devices that their imaginary inventors have developed.

TURTLES ARE SPECIAL

Science World Turtle Day has been established on May 23 around the world to protect turtles and tortoises as well as their habitats. Students can research these animals locally, through online zoos, or at http://www.tortoise.com. They can make dioramas of these animals' habitats or art projects showing the designs of their shells.

LETTERS FROM THE GARBAGE HEAP

To liven up lessons on recycling and decomposition, give small groups of students each a bag with clothespins, a diaper, an aluminum can, a cigarette butt, a rubber eraser, a banana peel, some wood, a plastic jug, a cotton sock, and an apple core. (Photographs or cut-out magazine pictures of the items also work well.) On a clothesline marked in increments with 2 through 4 weeks, 1 through 5 months, 1 year, 10 years, 25 years, 100 years, 500 years, and 1,000 years, ask each group to hang its trash, indicating how long they think each item will take to decompose. When groups have finished, reveal the actual times: apple, 2 through 4 weeks; banana and sock, 1 through 5 months; cigarette butt, 2 through 5 years; wood, 10 years; diaper, 25 years; plastic, 25 through 30 years; eraser, 50 through 80 years; can, 200 through 400 years. (A glass bottle takes 1,000 years to decompose!). After talking about how crowded a dump will get if we fill it with so many items that take years to decay, write down ways they can recycle to reduce the amount of things going to the dump.

MAKE A "GREEN MAP"

Send students on an Internet exploration to make their own "earth friendly" maps. At www.greenmap.com, students will learn that a Green Map is a map of a neighborhood, town, or city that focuses on "green," or ecologically-oriented sites. Green Maps also mark "toxic hot spots" and other polluted areas that need help. On this interactive Web site, students can view Green Maps of cities around the world such as New York and Copenhagen. Step-by-step instructions guide students in designing their own Green Maps, and a large collection of map icons is provided to mark sites such as gardens, recycling centers, and wildlife areas. Questions on the site ask students to draw conclusions about their mapmaking research and work.

ARTISTS' FLOWERS

Have art prints of flowers from at least two artists. Two good artists for this would be Van Gogh's *Sunflowers* and Georgia O'Keeffe's *Poppy*. Other floral works by these artists are also good, for example, Van Gogh's *Irises*. Of course, you may find many other artists whose paintings of flowers are appropriate for this activity.

The purpose of this activity is to see how two artists express their flowers in two contrasting ways.

Each artist has his or her own vision of representing them in art. Be sure to use art terms such as color, line, and shape when discussing these works.

Explain that the artist Georgia O'Keeffe created many paintings of flowers. She once said that she made the flowers large so people would really see the beauty of the colors, shapes, and edges. Explain that the poppy flower, like other flowers in O'Keeffe's paintings, seems to glow with life and energy. It is a close-up view of a flower in full bloom. Encourage students to make other observations about the painting.

Then lead them in a discussion of Van Gogh's *Sunflowers,* especially their texture. Guide them to describe the mood qualities in Van Gogh's painting. For example, the flowers are on the ground, no longer growing. Many of the seeds are gone, the stems are withered, the petals look shriveled and dry. Encourage other observations. Contrast and compare the two works, using the scientific analogy of a life cycle.

Emphasize the concept that artists in many times and places have created artworks about the same subject, such as flowers. Each artist creates his or her own picture in a special way (different, original style). Ask students to express opinions about which of these artworks they like to see, and discuss reasons for their preferences. Stress that students may like more than one kind or art and that everyone may not like the work.

ENDANGERED ANIMALS

Language arts

⊙ Students write a story in which the main character is an endangered animal who is trying to teach his family why the species is endangered.

⊙ Students debate in a small group about the issue of wild animals being captured and put in a zoo. Should they or shouldn't they?

⊙ Students write a short speech (2–4 minutes) about an animal topic that they feel strongly about. Topics might include how to take care of pets, endangered animals, or the similarities between animals and humans.

⊙ Students write a story in which they become an endangered animal lost in a large city. They write about how they feel being lost and endangered and what they would do in this situation.

⊙ Students choose an animal to observe for fifteen minutes. The time might be broken down into smaller segments if the animal is hard to observe. They write their observations and what they learned about the animal.

ART EXPERIENCES

⊙ Students make a clay model of an endangered carnivore and write a short paragraph telling key facts about the animal.

⊙ In pairs, students design an advertisement that could be published in a newspaper to promote the preservation of an endangered animal.

⊙ Students build a three-dimensional habitat model for an animal of their choice.

MOVEMENT

⊙ Students pretend that everyone is a different animal, then role-play how each animal might react to meeting the other.

⊙ Students perform a skit in which all of the characters are animals—some endangered and some not. The animals discuss the problems with being endangered.

⊙ Students invent a game called the Animal Game.

MUSIC

⊙ In a group, students make up an animal song and record it on a tape recorder.

⊙ Students write a poem or story about an animal and add animal sounds as they read it to other students.

HOW DOES WATER DISAPPEAR?

This is an initial experience with evaporation. You will need a sponge, chalkboard, water, and a heavy piece of cardboard.

1. Moisten the sponge.

2. Make a wide, damp streak on the blackboard.

3. Observe for several minutes. What happened?

4. Make two streaks about one yard apart.

5. Use the cardboard to fan one of the streaks.

6. Compare the time it took for each to disappear.

Students should learn from this activity that water is absorbed into the air by a process called evaporation. Increasing the amount of air moving over the water (fanning) increases the rate of evaporation. The amount of moisture the air already contains (humidity) will be a factor. Hints: If the sponge is just moist the results will be faster than if it is soaking wet. An alternate activity is to put a small amount of water (½ inch) in two small jars. Seal the lid of one and leave the other open. Observe for 24 hours.

Discuss the differences in water remaining in each jar.

SCIENCE: A DIFFERENT VIEW OF THINGS

Discuss the importance of imagination and observation in science. (Imagining that people might walk on the moon was the first and most important step in discovering how it might be done.)

Have the students collect unusual rocks, shells, dried seed pods, and other small objects. Glue several objects to the bottom of a clear plastic box. Challenge the students to draw the objects inside the box from each of the points they can see when looking straight through one side of the box. Provide square paper for the drawings.

Have the students create drawings from unusual or imagined vantage points, such as being in a hot air balloon, flying in an airplane, being inside of a mine or a cave, looking at things under water, or looking out the window of a rocket while it is being launched or is nearing a planet.

INSECTS

Contrast the way an artist and a scientist might study insects. Point out that scientists and artists are both very keen observers of nature. The artist is more likely to study insects to discover the beauty or the special lines, shapes, colors, etc. The scientist may look for the same features, but is more likely to want to explain their purpose—protection, reproduction, food gathering, etc. Encourage them to draw their own versions of insects, using either the artistic or scientific perspective.

AESTHETIC AWARENESS

Discuss texture as a property that we experience by sight as well as touch. Stress that scientists who wish to describe and classify living and non-living things carefully observe and often measure subtle differences in textures (as well as other properties) of objects. Provide magnifying glasses and a variety of textured materials for students to observe, touch, and describe. For example, fine white sand, salt, sugar, flour, baby powder, or varieties of rocks or paper.

SCIENCE BOOKS

Have students look through their science book or other books from the library to find information on nebulae and other bodies in space. Have students share some of their findings, including the illustrations. Then have students create a watercolor based on the theme of exploring space.

SCIENCE OUTDOORS

Take students outside to study the branching structures of trees. Guide them to see relationships between the branching structures in a leaf, among twigs that support leaves, larger branches, and the trunk. Have them identify other natural forms in which linear qualities are evident such as hair and fur, or shells with radial or spiraling edges. Have them draw representations of their observations.

SOIL

If you live in a region that has colorful clay soil, obtain samples that can be placed in clear plastic containers. Add water to each container so that the soil settles. Explain that some of the paint colors that artists use for neutral colors actually come from colored minerals (pigments in the earth). The finely ground minerals are mixed with oil or other liquids to create paint. Students can mix diluted white glue with the samples to create paint. Use paint on thick cardboard.

MAKING CRYSTALS

Making crystals is an amazing and fun science activity. To begin, carefully add 1 cup of very hot water to a mason jar for each child. Then have students help measure and add up to 2 cups of sugar to their water jars, ½ cup at a time, until no more dissolves. By doing this, students will be creating a saturated solution.

Have each student tie a string to a craft stick (or pencil) and a rust-proof paper clip, then suspend his or her clip just above the bottom of the jar. Cover jars with paper towels to keep dust out. As water evaporates, sugar crystals will form.

In a week or two, remove and dry the strings of crystals. Challenge students to find the edges, angles, and faces of the crystals.

Set up a crystal observation station with salt and sugar on sheets of black paper, a magnifying glass, and a flashlight. Students may notice some of the following characteristics of crystals:

⊙ Crystals have geometric shapes, such as cubes (salt), rectangles (sugar), diamonds, or pyramids.
⊙ Crystals have sharp, straight edges that meet to form angles.
⊙ Crystals are solids.
⊙ Crystal shapes range from simple to very complex.
⊙ Crystals break smoothly and cleanly at their weakest point.
⊙ Crystals' smooth sides are called *faces*.

CHAPTER REVIEW

1. What are the two phases of science? Which phase is more important for young children?
2. Choose the answer that best completes each statement about science.
   a. The teacher is most involved in planning for
      (a) formal science.
      (b) informal science.
      (c) incidental science.
   b. The teacher cannot plan for
      (a) formal science.
      (b) informal science.
      (c) incidental science.
   c. Observing skills are taught to children in
      (a) formal science.
      (b) informal science.
      (c) incidental science.
   d. Free investigation is used most often in
      (a) formal science.
      (b) informal science.
      (c) incidental science.
3. Define ecology and discuss its place in the early childhood program.
4. Discuss the discovery center and its importance in the early childhood program.

REFERENCES

Bayer Corporation & National Science Foundation (NSF). (1999). *The Bayer facts of science education IV: Scientists on science for the 21st century*. Pittsburgh, PA: Author.

Brede Kamp, S., and Copple, C. E. (1997). Developmentally appropriate practice in early childhood programs serving children from birth through age 8. Washington, D. C.: National Association for the Education of Young Children.

National Research Council. (1996). *National Science Education Standards*. Washington, DC: National Academy Press.

National Science Resource Center. (1996). *Science for all children: A guide to improving elementary science education in your district*. Washington, DC: National Academy Press.

ADDITIONAL READINGS

Barber, J., & Bergman, L. (2002). *Spark your child's success in math and science*. New York: Hall of Science.

Chalufour, I., & Worth, K. (2003). *Discovering nature*. St. Paul, MN: Redleaf Press.

Coates, D. (2003). *Challenges in primary science: Meeting the needs of able young scientists*. London: Taylor & Francis.

Danoff-Burg, J. (2002). Be a bee and other approaches to introducing young children to entomology. *Young Children 57*(5), 42–47.

Diffily, D. (2003). Creating a videotape about hurricanes: Experiences in project-based learning. *Young Children 8*(4), 76–81.

Fredericks, A. D. (2002). *Science fiction readers theatre*. New York: Simon & Schuster.

Koralek, D., & Colker, L. J. (2000). *Spotlight on young children and science*. Washington, DC: NAEYC.

McGinnis, J. (2002). Enriching the outdoor environment. *Young Children*. 57(3), 28–30.

Moore, J. E., Evans, J., Harber, C., Silverman, S. C., and Wolfe, L. (2002). *Science activities: English and Spanish*. New York: Evan-Moor.

National Science Teachers Association (2003). *Ten-minute field trips*. Washington DC: National Science Teachers Association.

Starbuck, S., Olthof, M., & Midden, K. (2002). *Hollyhocks and honeybees: Garden projects for young children*. St. Paul, MN: Redleaf.

Worth, K., & Grollman, S, (2003). *Worms, shadows and whirlpools: Science in the early childhood classroom*. Portsmouth, NH: Heinemann.

SOFTWARE FOR CHILDREN

Bundle of Bugs, 2002. Ages 3–6.
Carmen Sandiego's Think Quick Challenge, 2003.
Discovery Channel School's CD-ROM Science, 2002.
  Ages 8–12.
First Discovery of Nature—The Tree, 2002. Ages 4–7.
First Discovery of Nature—The Lady Bug, 2002.
  Ages 4–7.
Fisher-Price Rescue Heroes Tremor Troubles, 2002.
  Ages 4–8.
Fisher-Price Outdoor Adventures Ranger Trail, 2003.
  Ages 4–7.

JumpStart Animals, 2002. Grades Pre-K–6.
Kidspiration, 2003. Ages 5–9.
Learn about Life Science: Animals, 2002.
Pinball Science, 2003. Ages 9–14.
Sammy's Science, 2003.
Super Solvers Gizmos and Gadgets, 2003. Ages 7–12.
ThemeWeavers: Animals, 2003. Ages 3–7.
Thinking Science, 2003. Ages 6–8.
Tonka Construction Site, 2002. Ages 4 and up.

HELPFUL WEB SITES

http://www.ala.org/
  Type in "Parents Page" in Searchbox. Created by the
  Howard Hughes Medical Institute.
Ask Dr. Science, http://www.drscience.com
**San Francisco's Exploratorium, the Museum of
  Science, http://www.exploratorium.edu/**
Boston's Museum of Science, http://www.mos.org/

**National Science Teachers Association,
  http://www.nsta.org/**
PBS Science, http://www.pbs.org/
  Click on Teacher Source.
**American Association for the Advancement of Sci-
  ence, http://www.project2061.org**
**Discovery Channel, http://yucky.kids.discovery.
  com/**

For additional creative activity resources, visit our Web site at http://www.EarlyChildEd.
delmar.com.

Chapter 20

Creative Mathematics

Objectives

After studying this chapter, you should be able to:

1. Discuss the developmental pattern of learning mathematical ideas.
2. Discuss how mathematics learning occurs in learning centers in the early childhood classroom.
3. Define rote counting and rational counting.
4. Discuss classification and sorting.
5. Discuss comparing and ordering.
6. Describe the young child's understanding of shape and form.

Early childhood teachers face the challenging responsibility of opening young children's eyes to the world of mathematics. We may provide creative, stimulating, hands-on experiences that can initiate long-term positive feelings about mathematics, or we may provide a boring stream of workbook pages and dittos. In such a situation, where children are required to sit down, quiet down, and write it down, excitement about math may never have a chance to emerge. Math in the early childhood setting is not a sit-at-your-desk-with-paper-and-pencil activity. It is a part of a young child's active life.

Everything we know about young children tells us that early math experiences must be hands-on, filled with play and exploration. Young children's meanings and understandings of mathematical ideas take place in an action-based learning environment.

All young children need opportunities to explore their world and experience mathematics through their play. Early mathematical experiences include such basic events

as placing crackers in a toddler's hands while saying, "Here are two crackers—one, two," or when a three-year-old girl chooses how she wants her sandwich cut—into triangles, rectangles, or small squares. As a child arranges stuffed animals by size, a teacher might ask, "Which animal is the smallest?" or "Which is the largest?"

When children recognize a stop sign from the back, focusing on the octagonal shape rather than the red background and the word "STOP," adults have an opportunity to talk about different shapes in the environment. Teachers in any setting can help children look for mathematical connections and relationships, encourage their questions, and promote mathematical discussion about topics that interest children. The most powerful mathematics learning for a child is seldom acquired sitting down in a group lesson.

In this chapter, the emphasis is on this *active* exploration of mathematical concepts as a natural part of the early childhood program.

DEVELOPMENTAL PATTERN OF LEARNING MATHEMATICAL IDEAS

It is possible to look at the child's construction of mathematical concepts the same way we look at literacy development—as emergent. The idea that literacy learning begins the day that children are born is widely accepted in the early childhood field. Mathematical learning can be viewed in a similar way. Children begin to build the foundation for future mathematical concepts during the first few months of life.

Long before children formally use numbers, they are aware of them through daily experiences. For example, children become aware of sequences in events before they can talk about what is first, second, or third. At the age of two or three they know that one block on top of another is two blocks, and they know that if they add more they will have three, even though they may not know the words "two" and "three." When they lift objects, they experience lightness or heaviness. Cuddling up in their mother's lap, they feel themselves small and her big. They know all this by the reality of their experience through living and doing. Thus, children are able to tell differences in sizes of people, animals, and toys before they have any idea about measurement. They recognize, too, the difference between *one* and *many* and between *few* and *lots* before they acquire real number concepts. They develop a sense of time long before they can tell time by a clock. Their ideas of time grow out of hearing things like: "It's time for lunch." "It's time to go to bed." "We're going for a walk today." "We went to the park yesterday."

This pattern of early use of numbers is similar to the general-to-specific pattern of physical growth (see Part 1). In these early stages of mathematical thinking, the child has a general understanding of numbers that will gradually move toward a more specific understanding as the developmental process continues. Thus, a general understanding of time ("It's time for lunch") develops in a gradual process to a more *specific* understanding of time ("Twelve o'clock is lunch time"). The child gradually associates 12 o'clock with the time of day of lunch time. They learn with their senses, with their whole bodies. Their understandings become parts of themselves. Only after this has happened can they name these experiences. By the time they learn the words "big," "small," "light," "heavy," or the names of numbers, they will know by their own senses what these words mean.

Recognizing the importance of these early experiences in mathematics, the National Council of Teachers of Mathematics (NCTM) has developed a set of Principles and Standards for Children Pre-K–12 (1998). These

CONTENT

Five standards describe the mathematical content that students should be provided.
- ⊙ number and operation
- ⊙ patterns, functions, and algebra
- ⊙ geometry and spatial sense
- ⊙ measurement
- ⊙ data analysis, statistics, and probability

PROCESS

Five standards describe the mathematical processes through which students should acquire and use their mathematical knowledge.
- ⊙ problem solving
- ⊙ reasoning and proof
- ⊙ communication
- ⊙ connections
- ⊙ representation

SOCIETAL NEEDS FOR MATHEMATICS

- ⊙ *Mathematical literacy.* The underpinnings of everyday life are increasingly mathematical and technologic. Our students will live in a world where intelligent decisions often require quantitative understandings.
- ⊙ *Cultural literacy.* Mathematics is a great cultural and intellectual achievement of human kind, and our citizens should develop an appreciation and understanding of that achievement.
- ⊙ *Mathematics for the workplace.* Just as the level of mathematics needed for intelligent citizenship has increased dramatically, so too has the level of mathematical thinking and problem solving needed in the workplace increased.
- ⊙ *Mathematicians, scientists, engineers and other users of mathematics.* Equity and excellence both must be the object of school mathematics programs. By enfranchising more students, while maintaining high standards, there will be a larger number available to pursue these careers.

Figure 20-1

Overview of the National Council of Teachers of Mathematics National Standards for Grades Pre-K-12.

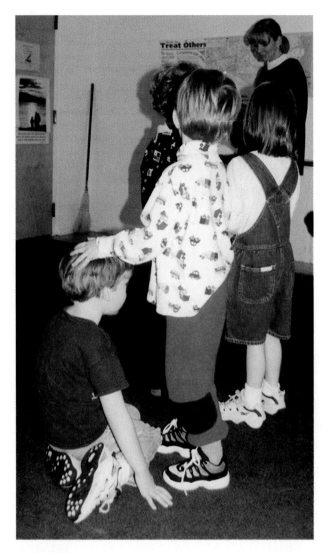

Figure 20-2
Playtime allows children many chances for counting with one-to-one correspondence.

Figure 20-3
Children learn about shapes and numbers in the block center.

standards propose mathematical content and processes students should know and be able to use as they progress through school. There are 10 standards, five content standards and five process standards that apply across the pre-K–12 grade span. (See Figure 20–1 for a summary of these standards.) Within each standard, a number of focus areas are identified to be emphasized at each grade level. Due to the length and amount of detail involved, it is not possible to present all of the information in this text. However, references to specific standards will be made where appropriate. The latest information on these national standards can be accessed at the National Council of Teachers of Mathematics Web site: http://www.standards-e.nctm.org. Let us now take a look at mathematics in action in the early childhood program.

MATHEMATICS IN THE MOVEMENT CENTER

As we observe in the movement center, we see children climbing over, ducking under, crawling through, and walking around several pieces of climbing equipment. Anthony approaches a ladder bridge suspended between two climbing frames and hesitates. He ducks under it, just clearing the ladder. He looks back to see what he did and repeats this action several times. "What would happen if you didn't duck?" asks the teacher. Anthony silently stands beside the ladder and indicates with his hand where he would hit his head (an example of measuring vertical distance by eye and comparing lengths). At the trampoline, Christopher counts as Justin jumps. "After 10 times, it's my turn," he tells Justin (an example of using a cardinal number to obtain access to classroom equipment). The rest of the children begin to count Justin's jumps. "I can jump highest because I am the tallest," comments Juliette (an example of explaining measurement between object and event). The children in line begin to measure themselves against each other (comparing length). When the teacher asks who jumped the highest today, the children all agree that it was Amanda. "Is she the tallest?" the teacher asks. "Well, tomorrow I'm going to jump the highest because it's my birthday," says Justin. "Amanda jumps in the middle," observes Juliette (showing she is thinking about location). "I'm going to try that tomorrow." These specific learning experiences in the movement center fall under the three National Mathematics content standards of number and operation, measurement, and spatial sense.

In the preceding scene, we see how moving their own bodies through space helps children learn these specific mathematical concepts.

Playtime will allow these children many chances to explore, extend, and refine their spatial discoveries. The children playing on the trampoline are learning to share power, space, things, and ideas as well as using counting for access and comparing their jumping skills by measuring in a nonthreatening way.

MATHEMATICS IN THE ART CENTER

Many incidental learnings related to mathematics occur during art activities. When materials are used for a particular process, children need to remember quantities and their order of use. Children can frequently be heard explaining a process to classmates by saying, "First you tear the strips, then you add the paste, next you stick them on the balloon." As art projects are planned, children learn to consider the number of items needed and

THIS ONE'S for YOU!
Using Children's Books to Teach Math

You will find that children's books can be used to launch many interesting math learning activities. There are many excellent sources of children's books for math (see the Online Companion). An example of using the book *The Very Hungry Caterpillar* by Eric Carle, which describes the life cycle of a caterpillar through the use of vibrant collage-like designs, will give you an idea of how to include books in math experiences.

Teaching Comparisons. Size comparison is the most obvious prenumber concept that can be drawn from this book. The caterpillar changes from a tiny egg laid on a leaf to a small, hungry caterpillar to a big brown cocoon and finally, to a large, beautiful butterfly. After reading the book, discuss the size relationships. Later, children can compare cutouts of these items and arrange them from largest to smallest.

Teaching Ordering. The prenumber skill of ordering can be related to both the days of the week and the life cycle. Ask children to tell the order of the days of the week or stages of the life cycle told in the book. Ordering the days of the week in this way can promote an interest in the calendar for daily record keeping of days gone by. The life cycle can be used in a game-like situation in which children order the pictures of the cycle. This can be made self-correcting by placing the numerals 1 through 4 on the back of the pictures.

One-to-One Correspondence. The fact that the caterpillar ate through a variety of foods one by one can be used to emphasize the one-to-one correspondence. A learning center follow-up could require children to match pom-pom caterpillars to plastic fruits to see if there is an equal match or if there are more caterpillars or fruit.

Rational Counting. Children can also be asked to rationally count the number of pieces of food the caterpillar ate in the story by counting the number of fruits and then the number of other foods eaten. They might also count the number of days of the week and the life cycle changes. A later concrete learning activity would be to have children count out pieces of fruit or other similar foods eaten by the caterpillar for their own particular snack time. Learning center games could involve the counting of food cutouts found in plastic containers.

Cardinal Number. Use the story to emphasize the prenumber skill of recognizing cardinal numbers. As the children look at the book, ask them, "How many things did the caterpillar eat on Saturday?" "How many on Monday?" Later, they can work with a learning center activity that involves counting holes made by the hungry caterpillar in card stock leaves to determine how many bites the caterpillar took. A self-correcting feature can be included by simply writing the answer on the backs of the leaves.

often the shapes that will be required. This experience relates directly to problem solving and measurement—two of the content standards in the national mathematical standards for children.

We hear, "My truck will have four wheels," and "I need a triangle shape of wood for the roof on my house." Children learn to decide how many as they draw and paint: how many eyes on the face, fingers on the hand, and buttons on the coat.

Differences and equivalences in number and size frequently concern children. Six-year-old Jonathan calls out, "I want 10 feathers on my peacock, and I have only nine." Brian, sitting next to him, responds, "I have more than you; I have 12 feathers."

Children also learn about one-to-one correspondence as materials are chosen and distributed to classmates. Four children need four scissors. Five paste cups need five lumps of paste. Three needles need three lengths of yarn, a direct hands-on experience with the standard of number and operation. The following scenario further demonstrates how art activities can be used to provide children practice in areas related to national mathematical standards.

Two children are making headbands using shape stamps to make designs on paper strips that will fit around their heads. "This is a skinny square," says Casper, referring to his rectangle stamp. Claire laughs and looks through the shape set. She picks up an oval shape, "This is a skinny circle!" The children laugh some more as they assign names to the other shapes (comparing shapes provides experience with the geometry and spatial sense standard). Soon they are finished and Casper holds the strip while Claire measures and cuts the correct length (measurement standard). On the first try, the strip is too short, and they come to the teacher with the problem. "How could you make it longer?" she asks. Claire thinks they can add some paper to one end of the strip (an example of extending length to make an object longer). Eventually the children make the headbands fit. When two different children approach the center later, Casper says, "You should cut the paper first to be sure it fits." One child takes this advice, but the other ignores him and begins to make designs on the paper strips.

The children in the preceding scenario had a prolonged opportunity to explore and talk about the characteristics of shapes. This was a fun, hands-on learning experience involving the mathematical concepts of shape, measurement, and problem solving.

MATHEMATICS AT THE WATER TABLE

Some of the greatest opportunities for integrating math in children's play occur at the water table. Constant "watery" sounds are heard as children fill containers with water and pour the water back and forth. "This won't hold all the water," Grace comments (an example of measuring volume). Elbert picks up a bottle and says, "This one is taller. It will hold the most." Grace disagrees, "This one might hold a lot because it's very fat all the way up." (She is comparing size and capacity of containers.) She suggests that they count how many cups each holds and begins to count, but Elbert just continues to pour water from one container to another. (He is comparing capacity by direct measure.) "This one holds 6 cups!" says Grace (an example of measurement). "How much does yours hold?" Elbert then begins to fill his bottle with water, using the cup and a funnel. Grace counts the cups and explains, "It's four and a little bit more—not the whole thing" (a real-life use of measurement—fractions).

In the preceding scene, play reveals a progression of mathematical thought. In this situation, the children's processing of their own experiences shows the way they grow in measurement thinking. They were not concerned with a particular goal or end as much as with the means to achieve it. They did not have a clear plan in mind, and their goals and ends were self-imposed and changed as the activity proceeded.

In addition to these spontaneous mathematical experiences, you can also plan activities at the water table to build children's mathematical concepts. For example, a teacher may construct a math puzzle with three empty plastic glasses. Pour water up to the brim on the first glass. Then fill the second glass halfway, and leave the third empty. Then ask the children to identify which glass is empty, which is full, and which one is *half-full.* Children generally understand the meaning of *full* and can identify the full glass of water. Most children will also understand the concepts of *empty* and *more,* but many children have trouble with *half* and *less.*

This experience at the water table may be continued in the manipulatives area by measuring cups of dried beans, buttons, or other materials to further explore the concepts of *full, empty, fewer,* and *less.* Through repeated interactions and dialogue, children learn some of the vocabulary and concepts that underlie mathematics such as equations, fractions, and the notion of zero. At the water table, these math concepts are experienced and learned by repeated activity, rather than sitting at a desk trying to do math worksheets.

MATHEMATICS IN THE HOME CENTER

Two children are rocking their dolls and sharing a book about a hospital adventure. Suddenly, Mary stops and says, "My doll is so sick. I have to call the doctor." She looks at a list posted near the telephone and dials (reading and using numbers). "His number is 555–1234" (ordering a sequence of single numbers). "Hello doctor? My baby is so sick. What should I do? Goodbye. My doctor says I have to give my baby eleventeen pills."

"Oh, well," says Meb. "My baby was so sicker the other day before today" (time sequence). "He had eleventy-seven pills" (using numbers from the teens to the over-twenty digits). The children continue to rock their babies and share the book.

These children are using play to translate their understanding of adult activities into their own actions. Mary understood how adults use numbers to make telephone calls. Play activity also involves intelligence. Mary used her understanding of the pattern of telephone numbers—three digits followed by four digits—to make her call. Her comment to Meb that her baby needed "eleventeen pills" showed her developing number sense; to Mary, teen numbers indicate a larger quantity of an item than single digits. Meb's comeback indicated that she, too, is developing a sense of numbers because she knew that numbers ending with "ty" are larger than numbers ending with "teen." Meb's verbal description of yesterday was understood by her friend and will be replaced later with the appropriate terms after more experiences with time. This scenario can also be related directly to the national standards in math. Two of the standards, "communication" in a mathematical sense and "connections" between mathematics and everyday life, were obvious in the children's play experience.

MATHEMATICS IN THE BLOCK CENTER

The block center is a perfect place for math experiences. Blocks are especially good for learning math because they are real-life examples of geometric shapes and solids. The block center is usually set up in preschool rooms, but it is just as important in the early elementary classroom. Figure 20–4 lists some suggested block materials to make this center as complete a learning place as possible.

To encourage rich and varied mathematical experiences in the block center, you need to carefully plan the appropriate equipment in this center. For example, the younger the children, the larger their first blocks should be. Smaller blocks can come later, when children feel the need to supplement larger blocks. If you give too many small blocks to the children early in the year and insist that they reshelve them neatly, the children may come to dislike blocks, defeating your purposes in having them at all. Aside from this, block building is a tremendously satisfying activity that nourishes minds, imaginations, and the development of mathematical concepts.

GOALS

Activities in this center afford the child experiences in

- ⊙ creating real and imaginary structures.
- ⊙ differentiating between sizes and shapes.
- ⊙ classifying according to size and shape.
- ⊙ selecting according to space.
- ⊙ conceptualizing about space, size, shape.
- ⊙ defining geometric shapes.
- ⊙ developing perceptive insight, hand–eye coordination, imagination, and directionality.

MATERIALS

Set of solid wooden unit blocks (approximately 200)
Wheel toys
Puppets (to use with puppet stage or theater)
Dolls (from housekeeping center)
Dress-up clothes, especially hats
Set of hollow blocks (varying in size)
Miscellaneous construction sets: Tinkertoys, Lego blocks, Lincoln Logs, Bristle-blocks, Connectos, etc.
Rubber animals (zoo, farm)
Small plastic/rubberpeople (family, farmer, policeman, etc.)
Planks, tiles
Old steering wheel
Packing crates, boxes, ropes
Traffic signs
Books related to building
Pulleys and ropes
Large quantities of "junk" construction materials, egg cartons, milk cartons, rods, spools, small rectangular boxes, etc.
Measuring tapes and unusual things to measure
Pan balance for exploring weight
Playing cards or cards with dots, numerals, or both

Figure 20-4
Suggestions for a block center.

If your block area is popular and children must wait for turns, make a waiting list—printed neatly for children to read—and set a timer. When you use a timer, children discover that turns are coming around in a fair way. You may also want to post stick-figure pictures indicating how many children can be in the area at one time.

A child building with blocks has many experiences related to math, such as classification (grouping by the same size, for example) and order (putting blocks in

Figure 20-5
Older children can practice math skills by using interactive math software.

order of largest to smallest). There are many other basic math ideas learned through block building, such as length, area, volume, number, and shape. Both small and large motor skills are also developed as children play with blocks.

Cleanup in the block center is another good chance to practice math skills. The following suggestions can help you make this cleanup a true learning experience.

⊙ Ask children to pick up all of the blocks that are curved.

⊙ Ask children to pick up blocks of three different lengths.

⊙ Ask children to pick up blocks according to size.

⊙ Ask children to pick up blocks similar to a specific block that the cleanup director names.*

⊙ Ask children to pick up blocks different from a specific block that cleanup director names.

⊙ Ask children to put away all of a particular shape or size block and ask how many of that block she or he used.

⊙ Ask children to stack all of the blocks that go in the lower left section of the blocks shelf. Then stack the lower middle shelf, etc.

⊙ Ask children to put away blocks in groups of twos, threes, fours, etc.

⊙ Ask children to put away one dozen long unit blocks.

⊙ Ask children to put away blocks according to size beginning with biggest or longest and ending with the smallest or shortest.

⊙ Select certain people to put away certain shapes, e.g., rectangles, cylinders.

⊙ Select certain people to collect blocks according to weight.

⊙ Have children put away a certain unit of blocks and all of the blocks that are a fraction of that unit block.

⊙ Use an assembly line to put away blocks. This encourages cooperation among the children.

⊙ Ask children to pick up a number of blocks that are greater or less than the number of blocks the cleanup director is holding (Hirsch, 2000).

MATHEMATICAL CONCEPTS: DEFINITIONS AND RELATED ACTIVITIES

In our preceding discussion many references were made to various mathematical concepts young children develop through everyday experiences in early childhood learning centers. This section provides a brief description of these basic mathematical concepts and suggests some related activities for development of these specific concepts.

Numbers

Children learn numbers by rote. A child often has no comprehension of what these abstract terms mean, but as a result of relevant experiences, he begins to attach meaning to numbers. Children talk about monetary values in their play, usually without any comprehension of what a dime or a quarter is. While playing store Irene glibly sold the apple for a dollar and later sold the coat and hat for ten cents.

Before the child is three years old, she often can count to ten in proper order. Such counting (called **rote counting**), however, may have little specific meaning for the child. The words may be only sounds to her, sounds

*The teacher need not always be the cleanup director. Children can make up ideas and take turns being director. Also, the teacher can make a list of block cleanup ideas and put it on the wall in the block corner.

THINK ABOUT IT...

Money . . . The Root of Much Mathematical Learning

Did you know that the dollar bill is printed on cotton, not regular paper? Or that piggy banks have nothing to do with pigs? The following fun Web sites will teach you and the children lots of interesting things about money. You can learn how money is made at the U.S. mint, find out how to start a coin collection, and practice making change. You'll even get a few tips on how to be a saver, not a spender!

COIN COLLECTING IS COOL

Visit the Smithsonian's site on kids and collecting to see some rare coins. Learn how to start and care for your own collection (http://www.si.edu/). Click on Smithsonian for Kids, then on Amazing Collections.

HOW COINS ARE MADE

Ever wonder how coins are made? At the U.S. Mint Web site, you can take a step-by-step tour of the minting process. At one point, new coins are actually put inside a washer and dryer to make them clean and shiny (http://www.usmint.gov/). Click on h.i.p. pocket change.

CARTOON CHARACTERS AND MONEY

Meet Dollar Bill, Mr. Money, and a whole bunch of other cartoon characters who will help you learn all about money, banks, saving, and more. Each character takes you on an adventure, and when you finish, you can take their money quiz to see how much you've learned (http://www.kidsbank.com/).

SAVING MONEY

Did you know that people used to save their money in kitchen jars made out of a clay called pygg? That's how the idea of piggy banks came into being. You can learn a lot of neat money trivia at this ThinkQuest site (http://library.thinkquest.org/). Click on Business & Industry, click on Money, click on Visit Site, then click on Banks.

MAKING CHANGE

Learning how to make change can be tricky. Play this fun piggy bank game, and you'll soon become an expert (http://www.funbrain.com/). Click on Math in Finding a Game by Subject Section, and type in "Making change" in the Keyword box.

repeated in a particular sequence like a familiar song. This rote counting is similar to the stage in the development of speech (see Chapter 18) when a child can repeat words without really understanding their meaning.

Quite different from and much more difficult than rote counting is understanding the numerals as they apply to a sequence of objects: that each numeral represents the position of an object in the sequence (button 1, button 2, button 3, and so on). Equally or more difficult to understand is the idea that the last number counted in a sequence of objects represents all the objects in the sequence, the total number of objects

counted. This is called **rational counting.** For example, in counting six buttons, the child must grasp the idea that six, the last number counted, tells her how many buttons she has—that she has six buttons *in all*.

Rational counting, a higher-level number understanding, develops slowly for most children. However, carefully structured activities that take one idea and present it to children one step at a time help them grow from a general to a more specific understanding of numbers.

Young children frequently hear counting—as steps are being climbed, objects are being stacked, foods are being distributed, fingerplays are being played, familiar

Figure 20-6

Number recognition puzzles are excellent for young children learning math.

nursery rhymes and songs are being enjoyed, and during many other activities. This repetition helps the child memorize the sequence and sounds of numbers, even before the meanings of these numbers are understood. Songs, fingerplays, and nursery rhymes using the fingers as counting objects should be common practice in early childhood programs to help young children practice the sounds and sequence of numbers.

True counting ability (rational counting) is not possible until the child understands one-to-one correspondence. In other words, to rote count (to say the number sequence) is one thing, but to count items correctly—one number per item—is more difficult. Very often when a young child is given a series of things to count, the child counts two numbers for one item or two items while saying only one number. Thus, as rote counting develops, teachers should also encourage the skills of **one-to-one correspondence.**

Having the child touch each object as she counts is one way to encourage one-to-one correspondence. Repeating this exercise in various experiences throughout the day reinforces the concept of one-to-one correspondence.

Young children should be asked to count only with number names that are meaningful to them, i.e., **cardinal numbers** (the numbers one, two, three, etc.). Young children just learning numbers often have difficulty in understanding the relationship between counting and number. For example, Claire may count, "One,

two books." Later, when asked to bring two books to the table, she may count, "one, two" and bring only the second book. **Ordinal number** refers to the *place* of an object in a series of numbers. The *second* book in the preceding example is an *ordinal* number. (The cardinal number is two.)

Classification and Sorting

Classification and sorting activities are the beginnings that help children perceive a variety of relationships among things in their world.

Classification. Putting together things that are alike or that belong together is one of the processes necessary for developing the concept of numbers. In order to classify, children must be able to observe an object for likenesses and differences, as well as for attributes associated with purpose, position, location, or some other factor. Children progress through the following stages as they develop the skill of classifying:

1. Sorting into graphic collections without a plan in mind. Children may put all of the blocks with a letter on them together and then, ending with a blue letter, continue by putting all blue blocks with the group. When the grouping is complete, they won't be able to tell you why the blocks belong together, only that they do.

2. Grouping with no apparent plan. When asked why all the things go together, children respond with some reason, but one not immediately clear to the adult: "Well, all these are like George's."

3. Sorting on the basis of some criterion. Children proceed to being able to sort a group of objects on the basis of one criterion. All of the green things or all of the round things go together, but not all of the green and round objects go together in a group.

4. Creating groupings on the basis of two or more properties, putting all of the green *and* round objects together in a group.

5. Sorting objects or events according to function, use, or on the basis of a negative concept, such as all of the things that are not used in the kitchen.

Before children can classify and sort, they need to understand concepts such a "belongingness," "put together," "alike," and "belong together." These concepts are acquired over time as children have varied hands-on experiences in the early childhood program.

Your role as a teacher is to help children gain these ideas through a variety of experiences with a wide variety of materials selected specifically for classifying and sorting activities. Activity suggestions for classifying and sorting are found at the end of this chapter.

Materials for children's classifying and sorting may be kept together on a shelf in the manipulative toy or game area of your room. Boxes or sorting trays (common plastic dishpans and muffin tins work well) are kept with the materials. Sorting trays can be constructed by either attaching a series of metal jar lids onto a board or piece of cardboard; mounting a number of clear plastic cups onto a board; dividing a board or tray into sections with colored pieces of tape; or by mounting small, clear plastic boxes onto a board. Egg cartons, plastic sewing boxes, tool boxes (such as those for storing nuts and bolts), and fishing boxes are also useful for sorting trays and stimulate children to use materials mathematically.

Comparing

The skill of **comparing** seems to come easily and naturally, especially when it is a personal comparison. "My shoes are newer than yours." "I've got the biggest." "My sister is little." "You've got more." When children build with blocks, they may be asked to make additional comparisons: "Which tower is the tallest?" "Pick up the heaviest blocks first." "Build something as

THIS ONE'S for YOU!
Recycled Math Materials

To add to your supply of math manipulatives, start saving bottle caps. You will find many uses for these recyclables. Here are a few suggestions.

BOTTLE CAP SIZES

Give each child a variety of bottle caps that vary in size. Ask them to organize the caps from smallest to largest. Then ask them to reverse the order and arrange them from largest to smallest.

BOTTLE CAP GROUPINGS

Collect a variety of bottle caps that vary in size, color, and texture. Invite a few children to sort the caps into like groups. Notice the different ways that children sort and classify caps. They may sort by size, shape, or color, or separate the plastic caps from the metal caps. Once they have completed their sorting, encourage them to describe their choice of groupings. Ask how many more are in one group than another? Is there any other way to group them?

BOTTLE CAP WEIGHTS

Provide children with a pan scale and a variety of bottle caps. Ask them to compare the weight of plastic and metal bottle caps. Which weighs more? Ask them to place a large bottle cap on one side of the scale. How many small caps are equal to the weight of the large cap? Are three large caps equal to the weight of three small caps? What would happen if I put 10 more with this group? Ten less?

BOTTLE CAP FILL AND COUNT

Fill a small clear plastic container with bottle caps. Ask the children to estimate how many bottle caps are in the container and record each child's estimate. Now ask them to count the number of bottle caps and compare their predictions. Then, give them another container, either smaller or larger, and ask them to estimate how many small bottle caps will fill the container. Invite children to count the caps as they fill it up.

BOTTLE CAP PAIRS

Collect enough bottle caps to have one pair of each. Mix them up and place them in a pile on the table. Give children time to explore the different bottle caps. Then invite one or two children to find the matching bottle caps. How many pairs of bottle caps did they find? What makes them similar/different from the other caps?

tall as this." Have children identify parts of their buildings using the vocabulary of comparison.

When different size and shape containers are used in sand and water play, children can make comparisons based on volume. In the early childhood program, these are informal and related to children's actual experiences. "How many blue cups of water will it take to fill this bucket?" "How many red?" "Which is the heaviest?" "This doesn't hold as much."

Stories and poems, often the folk tales children are already familiar with, offer other opportunities for informal comparisons. *The Three Billy Goats Gruff, Goldilocks and the Three Bears,* and others offer comparisons on the basis of differing attributes.

Throughout the preschool years, ask children to observe and note differences in the objects of their environment, to name them, and to discuss them with one another.

Ordering (Seriation)

Another mathematical idea that is a vital part of a complete number concept formation is the idea of **ordering (seriation).**

Ordering the environment into series begins when children are very young and continues throughout adult life. The child begins by perceiving opposite ends of a series:

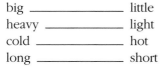

big _____ little
heavy _____ light
cold _____ hot
long _____ short

The intervention of an adult, suitable materials, and appropriate language lead to refinement of these early basic concepts. The comparison of the height of two children is beginning ordering, as is the comparison of two sets of things as more or less. Ordering sticks, blocks, or nesting cups in a sequence that leads gradually from the smallest to the biggest helps children see ordered size relations.

When children line up to go outdoors, they meet another idea of order: Juan stands in front of Claire, and Yvonne stands in back of Drew. They may use their understanding of sequence when they say, "I want to be first," or "Jimmy is last."

After listening to the story of *Goldilocks and the Three Bears,* their observations may become more refined as they discuss the story. The story contains big-little and one-to-one relationships, in addition to its many other enjoyable qualities.

The idea of ordering in size also appears naturally in other classroom areas. The teacher can make ordering a part of natural discussions in relation to the children's play and activities: sets of cans, bottles, and

books can also be used for practicing ordering of size. With younger children, only two objects are compared at first; this will be extended to three or more objects for older children.

Children enjoy ordering activities and do so spontaneously. Many table toys provide ordering experiences, as do ordinary objects like measuring spoons and cups.

Your role is to provide materials and sufficient time. When children find the existing materials too easy, you can awaken their interest by encouraging them to use the toys differently, by asking them questions, and by providing additional materials.

Ordering activities can include length (sticks), height (bottles), total size (bowls and shoes), weight (stones), color (from light to dark), and other endless possibilities. Suggestions for ordering activities are found at the end of this chapter.

Shape and Form

Young children need many experiences with shapes and making comparisons between shapes before they focus on naming shapes. Usually, it is enough to introduce one new shape at a time. As the new shape is understood, other shapes may be added, thus building new meanings on former learning.

In teaching young children about shape and form, it is important to include more shapes than the common geometric shapes of a circle, triangle, rectangle, and square. Since shapes aid in, or are sources of, identification, limiting instruction to the "basic shapes" excludes from the learning environment important aspects of recognition of shapes in general.

Yet familiar shapes must be taught before uncommon ones. Most of these unfamiliar shapes depend on previous shape identification and recognition. From the basis of understanding simple shapes, the child is able to build more complex structures.

As with the teaching of any ideas, shapes can be found throughout the child's environment. Words defining shapes should be used often. For example, everyday language should include such statements as: "That is a square box," rather than "That is square"; "The clock is round," rather than "This is round"; "Put the book on the square table," rather than "Put it over there." With these phrases, the object and its characteristic shape are made clear to the child. Later on, more characteristics, such as color, size, texture, and number may be added.

When unfamiliar shapes are introduced, a review of already familiar ones should precede the new introduction. Then the children's thinking can be stimulated with such questions as "How is this new shape the same as . . . ?" or "How is this new shape not the same as (or different from) . . . ?" Such comparisons reinforce and review shapes already learned.

MATHEMATICS: GRADES 3-5

Mathematics is a subject most students in grades 3 through 5 like. In fact, nearly three quarters of fourth graders report liking mathematics (Kenney & Silver, 1997). Students in grades 3 through 5 see mathematics as practical, are challenged with many new ideas, and believe that what they are learning is important. However, sometime between grades 4 and 8 students' interest in mathematics begins to wane. Although they continue to view mathematics as important, by grade 8 students are less likely to characterize it as interesting or to consider themselves good at math. (Kenney & Silver, 1997). It is crucial that the mathematics education in the upper elementary and early middle grades be challenging, relevant, and engaging for students.

The curriculum materials and instructional approaches a teacher uses help students connect mathematical ideas and provide a basis for making them meaningful. Because the amount of content in grades 3 through 5 expands greatly from that of the earlier grades, students need help in building connections and managing the many new concepts and procedures they are encountering. Students in grades 3 through 5 must also understand and bear responsibility for their learning. In math this means learning how to examine, ask questions, and consider different strategies—all with the goal of making sense of mathematical ideas and fitting them to other, related areas.

While the ten standards of the National Council of Mathematics Teachers apply to all grade levels, the instructional emphases for grades 3 through 5 build on those outlined for grades pre-K to 2 and extend well beyond them. Although number and operation continue to be cornerstones of the curriculum in grades 3 through 5, each of the content standards (number, data, measurement, algebra, and geometry) is essential for building student knowledge at this level. Several "big ideas" or central mathematical themes for this grade band are woven through these areas, including multiplication, equivalence, and the notion of unit.

Likewise, knowledge and use of mathematical processes should be deepened and expanded in these grades. Students in grades 3 through 5 are capable of sophisticated reasoning and should be challenged and supported in their learning.

In grades 3 through 5, extending understanding from whole numbers to fractions and decimals is a key dimension of the mathematics curriculum. Students need many and varied experiences in order to understand what fractions and decimals represent, how they

Figure 20-7

Learning geometric shapes is fun in the construction center.

are related to each other, and how they are different from whole numbers. Suggestions for fraction and decimal activities are found at the end of this chapter.

Calculators: Grades 3-5

The calculator and a variety of computer software should be considered legitimate tools for learning and doing math and should be available to students in grades 3 through 5. Teachers should create opportunities and make judgments about when and how these tools are used to support learning. As tools for doing math, students should use calculators and spreadsheets to carry out the procedures needed to solve problems. As a tool for learning mathematics, students in grades 3 through 5 should use graphing and geometry software and calculators to explore, experiment, verify, and visualize mathematical ideas. For example, students in grades 3 through 5 can explore geometric relationships using software to create, modify, and examine shapes. They can create graphs and consider how some presentations of data highlight or distort certain trends. They can use calculators to explore the relationship of decimals to whole numbers or of negative numbers to positive numbers. They should also have the opportunity

Figure 20-8

Children with an interpersonal learning style enjoy small group math activities.

to learn how to search the Internet to gather information and solve mathematical problems.

The calculator is an important tool in teaching mathematics in grades 3 through 5. However, calculators will not replace the need for quick recall of basic facts, a basic understanding of math concepts, or the ability to formulate and use strategies for computing. Rather, the calculator should support these goals by enhancing and stimulating student learning. As students solve problems involving many complex computations, the calculator should be used to perform calculations. The calculator serves as a tool for enabling the problem solver to focus on the big picture rather than become entangled in the calculating details. (See chapter end for some suggested activities for grades 3 through 5.)

SUMMARY

Long before a child formally uses numerals, he or she is aware of them through daily experiences. For example, a child becomes aware of sequences in events before he or she can talk about what is first, second, or third (ordinal numbers). The child recognizes, too, the difference between one and many and between few and lots before he or she acquires real number concepts. The pattern of early uses of number is similar to the general-to-specific pattern of physical growth. In these early stages of mathematical thinking, the child has a general understanding of numbers, which will gradually move toward a more specific understanding as the developmental process continues.

It is important that adults use number terms correctly in daily experiences with the child. Demonstrating their meaning in daily activities is just as important as using the right words. Mathematical concept learning is a natural part of daily activities in early childhood learning centers. In centers such as art, blocks, movement, water play, and language arts, young children are actively involved in using their emerging mathematical understandings.

Counting by rote (memory) is common for young children aged three and up. Counting with understanding (rational counting) does not occur until a child understands the one-to-one correspondence of number.

Classification, or putting together things that are alike or that belong together, is one of the processes necessary for developing the concept of number. In order to classify, children must be able to observe an object for likenesses and differences, as well as for other common factors.

Comparing is another mathematical process that is appropriate in the early childhood program. Children seem to make comparisons easily and naturally, especially when the comparisons involve them personally.

Another mathematical idea that is a vital part of a complete number concept is the idea of order. Putting things in a series or in order is a process that is appropriate for early mathematical experiences.

KEY TERMS

cardinal numbers
comparing
one-to-one correspondence
ordering (seriation)

ordinal number
rational counting
rote counting

LEARNING ACTIVITIES

A. Use one of the activities suggested in this chapter with a group of young children. Evaluate your experience. Share your evaluation with your classmates.

B. Make up some of your own activities for the mathematical concepts discussed in this chapter.

C. Choose at least two of the children's books listed in the Additional Readings in the Online Companion. Explain why you chose them and how you would plan to use them with young children. If possible, use them with a group of children and discuss your results.

D. Using a school supply catalog, choose three pieces of mathematical equipment appropriate for teaching each of the following: seriation, geometric shapes, size.

E. Imagine that as a teacher you have $150.00 to spend on mathematical equipment. Using a school supply catalog, spend this sum for your class of children. Explain how you spent your $150.00 as follows:
   1. developmental reason for choice
   2. purpose(s) for item

F. Choose one or two children from each of these age groups: three year olds, four year olds, five year olds. Assess each child's ability to count. Write up your results on each of the children in these age groups. Discuss what math activities would be developmentally appropriate for these children based on your findings.

G. Observe and talk with a preschool child, listening for comments and understanding related to numbers. If possible, ask the child such questions as "How old are you? What is your favorite number? How far can you count? Where do you see numbers?" Now make a comparison. Observe and preferably talk with a child between five and six years old and ask some of the same questions. You will want to ask more questions such as "Show me how you can add some things. Here are three pencils, and what will you have if you add two more pencils?" Challenge the child with number questions and problems. Now compare the differences in the two children you observed, keeping in mind the differences in their ages.

H. Log on to one of the math Web sites listed at the end of this chapter. Share your opinion of this as a resource with your fellow students. What was the most obvious plus of this resource? What was its greatest drawback? Will you plan to use this as a resource in the future? Why or why not?

I. Ask children in grades 3 through 5 their opinions on math. What percent of the children liked math? Ask them why they feel the way they do about math. Report on your results to the class.

J. Use the Math Observation Sheet in the Online Companion to observe in an early childhood classroom. Discuss the results of your observation with your fellow students. Did you observe any surprises? If yes, explain what they were.

ACTIVITIES FOR CHILDREN

Activities such as the following help children grasp the mathematical concept of counting.

⊙ In counting activities, have the child touch each object. Count only with number names meaningful to the child. Repeat this in various settings until touching or pointing to objects is no longer necessary. Provide for many manipulative counting experiences with beads, buttons, cookies, napkins, children, and chairs. Match beads to boxes, children to chairs. Determine the number of places, quantity of milk, silverware, napkins, and so on needed at the table.

⊙ Use buttons, bottle caps, or similar objects. The children practice counting *three* and putting *three* in a box and taking *three* (vary the number) out of a box. Then the child can use the buttons or bottle caps and glue them onto a piece of paper to make a picture if they like.

⊙ Bean Bag Toss: Have a large target and give each child a turn to try to get a specified number of bean bags into the hole. Have the child choose the specified number of bean bags and count them again as she throws.

BURIED TREASURE COUNT

Fill a clear plastic soda bottle ⅔ full with sand or rice. Drop in assorted small trinkets (beads, buttons, erasers, plastic insects, charms, jewels, etc.) Cover tightly, then secure the cover with masking tape. Let the children turn and shake the bottle and try to count how many treasures are buried in it. If someone counts correctly, remove the cap and add or take out some trinkets, then reseal the bottle.

NUMBERS AND SNACKS

Number concepts can be reinforced easily in everyday routines. Snack time is an excellent time for teaching about numbers. Once or twice a week, prepare snacks to reinforce mathematical concepts. Discuss the characteristic of each snack at service time. Then let the children eat while they learn from the special snack you have prepared.

A. Choose a number such as "four" and serve snack items in groups of four (four raisins, four carrot sticks, four banana slices, four crackers, etc.)

B. Choose a geometric shape such as a circle and serve round snack items (round crackers, cucumber slices, round cereal, carrot slices, banana slices, etc.)

CONCEPT OF NUMBER AND COUNTING

Cut face cards in half (make the cutting lines different on the separate cards so that only the two correct halves will fit together). Put the cards together as puzzles. Add these to the math center.

Place numerals from 1 to 10 around the room. Show the child a card with objects on it, and ask her to find the numeral that tells how many objects are on the card.

Make a number book by pasting the correct number of beans, pieces of macaroni, or colored squares next to written numerals.

Set up at the math center a numeral recognition and numeration activity such as "Counting Marbles."

Figure 20-9

Knowledge and use of mathematical processes should be deepened and expanded in grades 3 through 5.

Provide ten paper cups and label them with the numerals 1 through 10. Provide a box with lots of marbles. Place these on a table for a minimath center. Two children work together. One child examines the numeral printed on each cup and drops in the appropriate number of marbles. The child then gets her partner to check each cup and count the marbles to see if the correct amount was put in it. The marbles then go back into the box.

Math Experiences with Old Cassette Tapes. Few things are more interesting to a child than unraveling things. For this activity you will need one or more (ruined) cassette tapes; a trashcan; and a large, open area. Let the children discover what fun an old cassette tape can be. Smash the case open and pull on one end of the tape. Let the children unroll the tape into a large pile. Discuss how long they think the tape in the pile really is. Then pull the tape out as far as they can and count off how many paces long it is.

Wearing numbers. Purchase a supply of white paper hats—the kind restaurant workers wear—through a restaurant supply house. (Check with a restaurant manager to find out where to buy them locally.) Use these hats to reinforce number concepts.

Write a number on each hat. Have the children glue different sets of items that go with that number onto their hat. For example, three buttons on the hat with a "3" on it; four stickers on the hat with "4" on it; etc.

As a variation, make paper crown hats out of construction paper and have the children be Number Kings and Queens, using the same method as described previously.

Choose a geometric shape such as a triangle. Cut various colors and sizes of triangles out of construction paper. Children glue them onto their hats (or crowns) in any manner appealing to them.

Number books. Make a book for each child by stapling four sheets of white paper together with a colored construction paper cover. Title the cover according to a selected learning concept (Number Book, Matching Book, Shape Book, etc.). The children look through magazines and catalogs to find pictures that illustrate that learning concept. Then they tear out the pictures and glue them into their books.

Number books. Number the pages of each book from one to eight. The children glue pictures of one thing on page one, pictures of two things on page two, etc.

Shape books. Choose a geometric shape, such as a circle, and have the children glue pictures of circular things throughout their books. Or, label the pages of the books with different geometric shapes (circles, squares, triangles, etc.) and the children glue correspondingly shaped pictures onto the appropriate pages.

SIZE, SERIATION, AND ORDINAL NUMBERS

Ordering/seriation. Challenge the children with some of these activities.

- Find the shortest or longest block or tinker toy.
- Pick from three objects of differing heights the one that is shortest, and describe the remaining two objects.
- Describe how the objects in a series, arranged from shortest to longest, differ from one another.
- Collect nesting materials, such as a set of measuring spoons or measuring cups. Ask the child to arrange the objects in correct order so that they will properly "nest" together, one object fitting inside the other. Be sure to have the children set the objects on the table in order from smallest to largest after they have finished "nesting" them.
- Using three cans of different sizes and three bean bags in the three sizes, arrange the cans from smallest to largest in a row. Ask the child to line the bean bags up next to the cans, putting the smallest by the smallest, etc. Shuffle the cans and the bean bags. Let the child order the cans from smallest to largest this time and then match the bean bags to the cans.
- Cut out three fish. Make each fish large enough to totally conceal the next smaller fish when placed over it. Tell the children that the fish go in order, with the biggest fish first leading the others. Have them find the largest fish and then the fish that will follow. Check to see if the largest fish covers the fish that follows. For self-checking, the child places each fish on top of the next to see if the next fish is smaller. Variation: Order from the smallest fish to the largest fish.
- Materials such as buttons, gummed stars, lids, beads, feathers, and nails can be used as collage material or to seriate in order of size. Also, size comparisons between two or more of the objects can be made.
- Boxes or cans can be seriated or ordered from smallest to largest by placing them inside one another.
- Children can roll balls of various sizes from clay or play dough. They can then seriate these balls according to size.
- Make felt or cardboard cutouts in three or more sizes of different heights, for example, trees, houses, hats. Challenge the child to arrange them in a given order beginning with shortest or tallest. (Variation: Arrange trees in order of height.)
- To reinforce the use of the ordering words "first" and "last," have the children stand in line and identify the person who is first, the person who is last, and even the person in the middle (if possible).
- Cut out triangles of different sizes such as the same base length but different heights. Select a set of triangles that varies along one dimension. Lay them in front of the child in a mixed order, yet so that the child does not have to turn the triangles to discover the size variations. Have the child order them from smallest to largest (shortest to tallest) or largest to smallest.
- Show five blocks that have been ordered according to height. Arrange another set of blocks to match the first, third, and fifth blocks in the five-block pattern. Ask the child to put in the two remaining blocks so that both sets match. Repeat, using different blocks, such as second or fourth, etc.

Buttons and math activities. Ask parents to furnish buttons in all shapes and sizes. Use these for sorting by color and by size. Older children (four and five year olds) can even make graphs showing how many buttons of each color have been collected.

Make at least five different designs by gluing buttons to cards. Give children the same size cards and let them use buttons from the classroom supply to duplicate the designs on their cards.

MEASUREMENT

How big am I? Materials: boxes, cartons, tables, chairs, barrels, unit blocks, building blocks. Challenge the children with questions such as the following:

Can you build a building with blocks as high as you are tall?

Can you build something as high as your arm is long? As high as to the top of your leg? Waist? Shoulder?

Telling time. Use masking tape to make a large clock on the floor. Children move around in the 12 hour spaces by stretching arms to a person in the middle of the clock as a time is called by the teacher. Explore different times (recess time, lunch time) and ways to move around (fast, slow, hope, slide, skip).

Number shapes. Teacher calls out a signal and students make their bodies into shapes of numbers. They may need to work together to make some numbers. Challenge them to make these shapes combining with time, space, and force.

Measuring with our bodies. Write the word *measure* on a sheet of chart paper. Ask children to share what they know about measuring. What does it mean to measure something? What type of things do we measure? What do we use to measure? Why do we measure things? Record their comments on the chart paper.

Ask the children to use their bodies to measure different things. Ask children to estimate how many hands or arms something will be. Prepare another sheet of chart paper to record all the different things children will measure. Include their estimations and actual measurements.

Ask children to use their hands to find out how many "hands long" the tables are. Invite a few children to one of the tables. Ask them to first estimate, or guess, how many hands long the table will be. Record their estimate on chart paper. Then, ask them to line up their hands lengthwise on the table. Count and record the actual hand length of the table. Next, ask them to compare their estimation with their answer. Now, have them measure the width of the table. Estimate and then conduct the actual measurement. Are all of the classroom tables the same size?

Can they think of other ways to measure the tables with their bodies? How about how many hands high is the table from the floor? How many feet or bodies long are the tables? Encourage children to estimate and then compare their measurements.

Measuring shadows. Ask children to pair up to trace their shadows. Show them how one child in each pair can stand in the sun on a hard surface (or on a piece of paper if you're inside), while the other child uses chalk or a pencil to trace the shadow.

When children finish, ask them to trade places so everyone has a shadow tracing. Suggest that they write their names on their shadows.

Encourage children to think of ways to measure the shadows, then invite them to test out their ideas. Have a variety of measuring tools handy, such as yarn, string, and ribbon.

Help each pair measure their shadows using the material they chose. One child can hold the yarn or other material at the head of the shadow tracing while the other stretches it to the bottom. Then, help the children cut it so that each child will have a length of material that represents the length of his or her shadow.

Encourage children to predict whether their shadow lengths are longer, shorter, or the same as their own bodies, others' shadows, and other objects they see. Show them how to compare lengths of their materials against those objects to test their predictions.

For younger children: Take large sheets of kraft paper outdoors. Have children take turns lying on the paper. Trace and cut out the outlines of children's bodies. Later, bring paint cups and brushes outdoors and invite children to paint their paper "shadows."

For older children: Encourage children to hunt for outdoor objects (sticks, rocks, weeds) they can use as instruments to measure their shadows.

Variation: Ask children to try to change the shape of the shadows they see outdoors by moving the objects that create them. What happens to the shadow of a tricycle, a ball, a swing, when the object is moved in one way or another?

Math and science–honey bee measurement. On a single flight, a honeybee can visit more than 1,000 flowers, drinking nectar with its proboscis, a tongue that resembles a drinking straw. When its "honey stomach"—which holds only one-eyedropper's worth of nectar—is full, the bee deposits the nectar into hive cells.

Group children into "colonies" (small groups) for this activity. For each colony, place an eyedropper and cup of water at one end of the room and a plastic medicine cup (marked with teaspoon and tablespoon increments) across the room. To play, children take turns transferring water across the room to the medicine cups—one drop at a time! As the "bees" deposit their "honey" into the "hives," a recorder keeps count of the drops needed to produce the amounts of water, from 1 teaspoon to 2 tablespoons. When finished, explain that the drop count for each measurement equals the number of bee flights taken to produce that amount of honey. Tell children that each bee produces about ½ of a teaspoon of honey in its lifetime.

COMPARING

The following materials can be used to aid children in comparing.

- ⊙ String, ribbon, pencils, rulers, clay snakes, lines, or strips of paper. Ask children which is longest, longer, shortest, and shorter.
- ⊙ Buttons, dolls, cups, plastic animals, trees, boats. Have the children identify the biggest one or one bigger than another.
- ⊙ Containers and coffee cans filled with various materials and sealed, buckets or bags of items. Ask which is the heaviest or the lightest, which is heavier than another.
- ⊙ Toy cars, trucks, swings. Ask which is the fastest, slowest, which is faster than another?
- ⊙ Paper, cardboard, books, pieces of wood, food slices, cookies. Have children make or find one that is thick, thicker, thickest, or thinnest.

CLASSIFICATION AND SORTING

The following materials are helpful for classification and sorting activities.

⊙ Boxes of scrap materials—velvet squares, tweeds, and net cut into uniform sizes and shapes for feeling, sorting, and classifying according to texture.

⊙ A box or shelf of bells—cow bells, Christmas bells, decorative bells, sleighbells—all inviting children to sort and classify on any basis they decide, perhaps size, color, shape, or sound.

⊙ A box of various textured papers, cut into uniform shapes and sizes for the younger children and then into a variety of shapes for older children. Smooth papers, watercolor paper, textured papers, and others can be obtained from a local print shop.

⊙ Individual boxes of shells, beans, macaroni, seeds, beads, or rocks. Again, all should be large enough not to be put into the nose or ears.

⊙ Collections of nuts, nails, screws, and bolts to classify and sort according to shape, size, or function.

Sorting. Make two big loops with string on a table or on the floor. Have a set of round objects of several colors and a set of red objects of different shapes and sizes. Put a round object in one loop and a red object in the other loop. Have the children sort according to this rule. Then make the loops overlap.

Tell the children that only objects that are round and red can go in the middle loop. Have children re-sort the objects. Provide other sets of objects that lend themselves to this type of sorting and let the children determine the sorting rules.

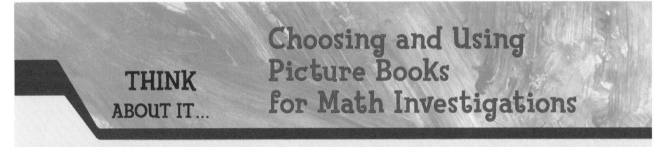

THINK
ABOUT IT...

Choosing and Using Picture Books for Math Investigations

Teachers and curriculum designers recognize the power of children's literature. In the past few years, children's literature has become an increasingly important component of mathematical curricula in early childhood programs. Good books provide a meaningful context for learning mathematical concepts. Stories spark children's curiosity about their world, serving as springboards for math investigations.

Children's literature needs to be thoughtfully used in the early elementary classroom. Teachers of young children must be able to decide when it is appropriate to use trade books, and they must select books of high quality. The following are some criteria for selecting children's books for math class.

1. Would I read this book to the children even if I weren't choosing it for a math lesson? This is an important question. Books should be used in the classroom because they are enjoyable, not because they teach a lesson. For a book to promote interest in reading as well as be appropriate for math class, it must be memorable, use natural language, have captivating images, and stand up to multiple readings.

2. Does the book stimulate curiosity and a sense of wonder? Are children inspired to do their own investigations? In the reading of these books, concepts that a teacher may be required to teach, such as proportion, measurement, weight, and shapes, become topics that children want to investigate on their own.

3. Is the book meaningful to the children? Can they make personal connections? The children should be able to identify with the characters in the book as having similar life experiences, doing activities children normally do.

4. Are the math connections natural? When math connections are embedded in a story, the reader not only enjoys the book but also is intrigued by the math concepts. Mathematical ways of thinking are emphasized; they are not facts presented in an authoritarian tone. As such, children have opportunities to question and pursue solutions (Thatcher, 2001).

Sorting beans. Materials needed are a bag with about 30 beans of three different kinds and three small containers, each labeled with a picture of one of the beans (or tape one of the beans onto the container). Explain to the children that there is a bag with three different kinds of beans in the math center. Display the beans and name them together. Show the children the three containers with labels on them.

Explain that they are going to sort the beans into the three containers when they are in the math center. They take the beans out of the bag one at a time and figure out which container it belongs in. When the child is finished (and you have checked the work), the child pours all the beans back into the bag for the next child.

Number quiz. Have the children make up and exchange riddles about "more" and "fewer." Examples: "I'm thinking of a number that is one more than the buttons on my shirt." "I'm thinking of a number that is one fewer than the windows in our room." Have the children make up and mentally solve riddles about same numbers. For example, "I am the same number as legs on a dog." "I am the same number as points on a triangle."

SHAPES

Shoe sorting. You will need 10 pairs of shoes of different sizes. To begin, put all the shoes in the middle of a circle. Ask the children to sort them into pairs (one-to-one correspondence) and then into groups of little, middle, and big. Of course, they'll need to try them on for size!

Shoe print patterns. Collect a variety of old shoes that have interesting patterns on the soles. Tape a large sheet of brown butcher paper across a table. Help children put smocks on and give them several colors of washable tempera paint and paintbrushes. Invite them to use one or several colors to paint the bottoms of the shoes. Then, encourage children to place the shoes on the paper to make a print. Ask them to describe the different types of patterns or shapes created by the shoes. How are they similar and how do they differ? Rinse the soles off with a wet cloth so it can be used again. Display the shoe prints in the classroom.

Shape matching game. For this activity you will need five or six colors of construction paper cut into shapes (circles, squares, triangles), one piece per child.

The children are seated in a circle. Each child places her shape marker in front of her. The teacher calls out one of the shapes, at which time all having that shape run around the circle in the same direction and back to their places. Different kind of movements can be used (skipping, galloping, walking, hopping, etc.). Variation: use colors instead of shapes. Make your color and shape cards into necklaces. Use numbered flash cards or addition/subtraction problems.

Shape crawl. For this activity you will need shapes cut out of cardboard. Spread the shapes around a space. Challenge the children to crawl through the shapes with questions such as the following:
- Can you crawl through without touching the sides?
- Can you crawl through using one arm and both feet?
- Can you crawl through using one foot and both hands?
- Can you crawl through with one arm and one leg?
- Can you crawl through on your back using arms and legs?

Shape identification game. You will need shapes of various sizes for this activity. Explain to the children that each shape has a movement that goes with it. Practice the moves with each shape. Have children in a scatter formation. When the teacher holds up a triangle, they can only move their heads. When the teacher holds up a circle, they move only legs. For a square, they move only shoulders. For a rectangle, only hips. For an oval, they move their entire bodies. Change shapes rapidly. This is fun to do with some lively music, too!

Shapes in art. For this activity you will need colored paper shapes (circles, square, rectangle, hexagon, oval, etc.), crayons, markers, scissors, and glue sticks.

Discuss the different shapes with the children. What does half a square (circle, etc.) look like? Try it and see. Discuss the idea of what is and is not a half, emphasizing equal amounts.

Pass out the paper shapes and invite children to experiment with folding the shapes into equal halves. Ask children to cut the shapes in half.

Brainstorm where the new "half" shapes might be found in the environment. Then invite children to use their two shape halves to create a picture by pasting the shapes and adding details to illustrate their use. Children may use the shape pictures to tell a story about the halves.

ACTIVITIES FOR OLDER CHILDREN (GRADES 4-5)

JUNK MAIL

Catalogs make fun lessons: Have the students find two items that total $11.98; add up all items on page 7; if you had $25.00 to spend for your friend's birthday, what would you select; figure shipping costs on a given item.

MULTIPLICATION ACTIVITIES

Memorizing the multiplication facts and understanding the concept of what these facts represent are a necessary foundation for further math learning and that can be particularly difficult for students. The following are some activities to help students develop this mathematical skill.

- ⊙ Multiplication art—Have each student select five multiplication equations that are especially hard to remember. Then ask students to draw a picture of the equation and the answer. Students can choose to draw a picture and put the equation and answer somewhere within the picture. For example, a drawing for 5×6 might consist of a boy who is wearing a shirt with the number 5 on it, standing in front of an apartment door with a 6 on it, talking to a woman who is celebrating her thirtieth birthday with a cake that has 30 written on it.

- ⊙ Multiplication building—For homework, have students choose two multiplication facts that are difficult for them. Then have them build three-dimensional creations that use those equations. For example, the equation $9 \times 6 = 54$ can be depicted by a model house with six rooms and nine objects in each room. Students should share their creations with the class without showing the equation. Students enjoy studying these models and figuring out the multiplication fact hidden within.

- ⊙ Multiplication baseball—Divide the class into two teams and designate a first, second, third, and home base in the room. For example, the pencil sharpener can be first base, the door can be second, and so on. One group stands at the front of the room (home base) while the other group is seated. One student from Team A is "at bat," while one student from Team B "pitches" a multiplication problem. The pitcher must know the answer to their team's problem or it's an automatic home run. After the problem is "pitched," the student at bat gives the answer and moves to first base. This continues until three students answer incorrectly at which time the teams trade places. To make the game more challenging, divide the multiplication problems into "singles" (easy), "doubles" (moderate), "triples" (difficult), and "home runs" (extremely difficult). Students at bat can choose which type of pitch they want. You can decide how many "innings" time will allow.

- ⊙ Musical activities—Some students who naturally learn and store information through music will enjoy memorizing their multiplication facts through songs and jingles. Don't be surprised if you hear these students singing a multiplication fact during math time. Ask students to work in pairs to create their own multiplication jingle using one multiplication pattern (5×0, 5×1, 5×2, etc.).

- ⊙ Multiplication talk show—Invite students to the "multiplication talk show," where they'll participate as the guest audience and/or the featured speakers. The show is moderated by Mickey Multiplication and the topic is "The Rough Life of Being a Multiplication Problem." Invite students to role-play multiplication problems after giving each number a personality. For example, Freddie Four may discuss how confused he gets when he has to play with Mr. Eight Snowman and that the last time they played a game, he caught Mr. Snowman cheating 32 times!

FRACTIONS AND MULTIPLE INTELLIGENCES

Some students experience a great deal of difficulty and frustration with the concept of fractions. Try some of these activities to reduce the fear of fractions and to help students understand what a fraction really is.

- ⊙ Fraction order—Order the following fractions from largest to smallest: $\frac{1}{10}$, $\frac{2}{8}$, $\frac{3}{4}$, $\frac{1}{15}$, $\frac{7}{8}$, and $\frac{5}{12}$; underneath each fraction, draw a picture to represent it (logic, word, picture smart).

- ⊙ Fraction story—Write a story about a fractional family. For example, the "Fourth" family has four members: $\frac{1}{4}$, $\frac{2}{4}$, $\frac{3}{4}$, and $\frac{4}{4}$. Give each member of the family a unique personality relating to its fraction (word, logic smart).

- ⊙ Fraction song—Make up a song to help students learn about fractions. You might want to use a familiar melody. Be sure the lyrics help students understand that fractions are used to break down a "whole" (music, word, logic smart).

- ⊙ Fraction P. E. game—Redesign a game you already play to include fractions. For example, in softball, every time a player scores, his team could score ⅔ of a point instead of one point (body smart).

⊙ The how-to fraction book—What problems did you have in learning fractions? Write a how-to book to help students with one of these problems. Include pictures, written explanations, and tips from your own experience (logic, word, picture, people smart).

⊙ Fraction skit—Write and perform a short skit that teaches students how to reduce fractions. You may want to use props to show that certain fractions are equal even if they look different (word, person, logic smart).

ART AND MATH

Emphasize how artists use their knowledge of measurement and geometric shapes and forms—in designing architecture, in planning beautifully proportioned vases, and many other aspects of art.

Discuss radial balance—in radial balance shapes and lines go out from a center. You see radial designs in many flowers and wheels. Have the students collect and display examples of radial balance and radial designs in human-made and natural forms. The examples might be actual objects or photos cut from old magazines and newspapers. Examples of radial balance include starfish, wheels, snowflakes, many flowers, and the like. After the students develop a display, teach them to use a compass and ruler to create precisely measured radial designs.

SHAPE AWARENESS

Discuss the difference between knowing that a shape is a circle cut from paper and the process of seeing the same shape from different angles or views. Demonstrate some of the positions from which a circle (cut from paper) can look like a wide ellipse, a narrow ellipse, and a straight line. Share art prints with them that show objects or people from different angles. Discuss how shapes are changed by angle of viewing. Encourage students to draw a familiar object from an unusual view to alter its shape and appearance.

100 DAYS OF SCHOOL ACTIVITIES

The 100th day of school is a good day to celebrate with some math activities. Here are a few ideas to challenge students while they're having fun.

1. Jump rope 100 times.

2. Build the tallest house of cards you can using 100 cards.

3. Flip a coin 100 times. Make a graph showing the number of heads and tails.

4. Roll a pair of dice 100 times. Create a chart showing how many times each number came up. Make a graph based on the chart.

5. Find someone who is at least 100 years old. Ask them what life was like when they were your age.

6. Find out which weighs more: 100 nickels or 100 quarters.

7. Have everyone in your class try to throw a tennis ball 100 yards. Measure each throw. Calculate the average throw.

8. Count by 100s to 10,000.

9. Recite multiplication facts up to 100 (10 × 10) with your eyes closed!

10. Guess how much 100 jelly beans weigh. Then weigh them and give a prize to the closest guess. Don't eat the jellybeans just yet.

11. Separate the 100 jellybeans by color. What percentage of the total is the most common color? What percentage of the total is the least common color? Don't eat the jelly beans yet!

12. Without using a calculator, figure out how many jellybeans each student would get if you divided 100 jellybeans equally among all students. Don't eat the jellybeans yet!

13. Blindfold a student and have him or her pass out the proper number of jelly beans. What is the probability that the first jellybean handed out will be the most common color? (Think about this one!). EAT THE JELLYBEANS!!

14. Measure the height of your classroom ceiling. How many classrooms that size could you fit into a structure that was 100 feet tall?

15. Measure the space required for a student's desk and the aisle around it. How big would your classroom need to be to hold 100 desks with the same spacing?

MATH IN EVERYDAY LIVES

(Based on NCTM Standard #4: Mathematical connections are made with everyday experiences both in and out of school.)

Have the students brainstorm a list of ways they use math at school. Have each student choose one item from the list and illustrate it. Then have the children bring in 10 ideas that demonstrate how they or their parents use math at home. Tally all the ideas of how math was used in their homes. Have students select one idea to illustrate. The drawings could be posted on a bulletin board with two sections: Math in School and Math at Home.

CHAPTER REVIEW

1. What is the developmental pattern in a young child's mathematical skills? Give examples and related activities in your reply.
2. What would you consider basic equipment and materials for a math center? Discuss the reasons for your choices.
3. How do learning centers assist a child's development of mathematical skills? Give examples in your reply.
4. What is rote counting? What is rational counting? How can you tell when a child is capable of either of these skills?
5. What does it mean to develop the skill of seriation? Give examples of activities that would help a child learn this skill.
6. How would you introduce shapes to a young child?
7. What are some ways to teach classification? Give specific activity examples in your reply.

REFERENCES

Hirsch, E. S. (Ed.). (2000). *The block book* (3rd ed.). Washington, DC: NAEYC.

Kenney, P. A., & Silver, E. A. (Eds.). (1997). *Results from the sixth mathematics assessment of the National Assessment of Educational Progress*. Reston, VA: National Council of Teachers of Mathematics, 36–38.

National Council of Teachers of Mathematics. (1998). *Principles and standards for mathematics grades pre-K–12*. Washington, DC: National Academy Press.

Thatcher, D. H. (2001, July) Reading in the math class: Selecting and using picture books for math investigations. *Young Children,* 20–26.

ADDITIONAL READINGS

Andresa, A. G. (2003). *Little kids—Powerful problem-solvers: Math stories from a kindergarten classroom*. Portsmouth, NH: Heinemann.

Baicker-McKee, C. (2002). *FussBusters*. Atlanta, GA: Peachtree.

Carruthers, E. (2003). *Children's mathematics: Making marks, making meaning*. London: Paul Chapman Publishing.

Clements, D. H. (2003). *Engaging young children in mathematics: Standards for pre-school and kindergarten mathematics education*. Mahway, NJ: Lawrence Erlbaum Associated.

Clements, D. H., Sarama, J., & DiBiase, A. M. (Eds). *Engaging young children in mathematics*. Mahway, NJ: Lawrence Erlbaum Associates.

Clements, D. H., & Sarama, J. (2003, Jan.–Feb.). Creative pathways to math. *Scholastic Early Childhood Today,* 37–40.

Clements, D. H., & Sarama, J. (2002). The role of technology in early childhood learning. *Teaching Children Mathematics 8,* 340–43.

Copley, J. (1999). *Mathematics in the early years*. Washington, DC: National Council of Teachers of Mathematics.

Crooks, L. (2003). *Connecting math with literature: Using children's literature as a springboard for teaching math concepts*. Huntington Beach, CA: Creative Teaching Press.

Meagher, S. (2003, Jan.). Not your typical math books. *Scholastic Teaching K–8,* 56–57.

Murray, A. (2001, July). Ideas for manipulative math for young children. *Young Children,* 28–33.

Seefeldt, C., & Setian, L.E. (2003). *Active experiences for active children: Mathematics*. Upper Saddle River, NJ: Prentice Hall.

Wise, B. (2001). *Whodunit math puzzles*. New York: Sterling.

Wrigley, T. (2003). *Schools of hope: A new agenda for school improvement*. Sterling, VA: Stylus Publishing.

SOFTWARE FOR CHILDREN

Clifford Thinking Adventure, 2001. Ages 4–6.
Disney Ready for Math with Pooh, 2002. Ages 3–6.
Flying Carpet: A Mathematical Journey, 2003.
Ages 8–12.
GeoSafari Knowledge Pads: Addition & Subtraction, Beginning Math, 2002. Ages 7–9.
Jump Start Study Helpers: Math Booster, 2003.
Ages 6–11.
LeapZone Turbo Twist Math, 2002. Ages 6 and up.
Math 1, 2002. Ages 5–6.
Math 3, 2003. Ages 6–8.
Math Blaster Ages 7–8, 2003.
Math Explorer: Shape and Size, 2002. Ages 9–16.
Math Missions K–2: The Race to Spectacle City Arcade, 2003. Ages 5–8.

Math Missions 3–5: The Amazing Arcade Adventure, 2003. Ages 8–10.
Mia: Just in Time! 2002. Ages 6–10.
Mighty Math Carnival Countdown! 2003. Ages 4–6.
Millie's Math House, 2003. Ages 4–6.
Mind Mania Math, 2003. Ages 7–12.
My First Math Adventure, 2003. Ages 3–5.
Ollo and the Sunny Valley Fair, 2002. Ages 3–6.
On-Track: Multiplication & Division, 2003. Ages 8–10.
Reader Rabbit Math 4–6, 2002.
Stuart Little: His Adventures in Numberland, 2002.
Ages 4–7.
Time, Money & Fractions, 2003. Ages 7–9.

HELPFUL WEB SITES

K–5 Math Challenges, http://auntymath.com
DuPage Children's Museum consists of math problems written as stories about Aunt Mathilda.
Math.com—The World of Math Online, http://www.math.com
This site has activities, games, homework help, practice, and Teacher and Parent sections.
KidsSource Online—Meet Professor Tobbs, http://www.kidsource.com/tobbs
This site has math activities for children ages 3 to 10.
Math in Daily Life, http://www.learner.org
Use the "Browse Teacher Resources" for topics of your choice. This site has everyday math activities with a teacher's guide from Annenberg/CPB. Explore probability, population growth, savings, and more.

U.S. Department of Education, http://www.ed.gov/
Click on Teachers, then click on One-Stop for Lesson Ideas. This site features an online booklet designed to help children enjoy math opportunities (such as a visit to the grocery store) with their parents.
National Council of Teachers of Mathematics Math Standards for Young Children, http://www. nctm.org
Check the directory of articles about the recent research on children's math learning, including this link for Standards for Grades Pre-K–2: http://www.standards.nctm.org/
Early Childhood Mathematics: Promoting Good Beginnings, http://www.naeyc.org/
Click on Public Policy, then click on NAEYC Position Statements. This is the NAEYC's position statement on Early Childhood Mathematics.

For additional creative activity resources, visit our Web site at http://www.EarlyChildEd. delmar.com.

Chapter 21

Creative Food Experiences

Objectives

After studying this chapter, you should be able to:

1. Describe four ways in which food activities develop children's skills.
2. List several ways to help make food experiences more creative.
3. Give an example of a creative food experience and the necessary steps involved.

Children learn best when they experience the world firsthand—by touch, taste, smell, sight, and hearing. If you wish to make the most of any food experience, children must be *directly* involved with real food and given as much responsibility as possible for growing, selecting, preparing, and eating the food.

Activities involving foods are included in most programs for young children. However, many of the food activities are under the complete direction of the teacher. The children sit and watch the teacher do the work. Sometimes the children are given spoons and told to stir a mixture or are allowed to pour liquids from one container to another. Sometimes they are given the job of listening for a timer to "ding." Rarely is the child allowed to decide what foods to use, how to use them, in what order to mix them, or for how long to stir things.

The use of foods in a classroom can be one of the most creative parts of the program. Foods are a part of each child's experience. Foods and cooking are interesting to children. All of their senses are used in food activities. They see the foods. They smell them, touch them, and taste them. The children can hear many kinds of foods boiling, popping, or frying. Other learning is enhanced by food activities, too. Art, science, and aesthetics are all related to cooking.

IMPORTANCE OF FOOD EXPERIENCES TO THE TOTAL PROGRAM

Concept Building

Food activities help children develop new concepts in many areas such as language arts, science, health and safety, and mathematics.

Children learn to describe things. Children experience many shapes, sizes, and colors. They see that some things start out in a round shape and become long and flat during the cooking process. Many foods change in size when they are heated; some change in texture and color. Foods come in many colors, and the colors sometimes change with mixing, heating, or

Figure 21-1

Food activities help children develop new concepts in many areas such as language arts and science.

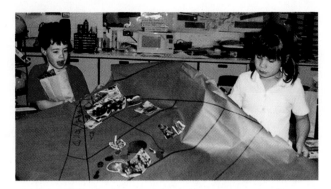

Figure 21-2

Cutting and pasting food pictures on a nutrition triangle help teach young children basic information on food and nutrition.

cold, warm, and cool are part of the food vocabulary. Children may learn the words "delicious" and "tasty." They learn a more complete meaning of terms like liquid and solid, freezing and boiling, smelly and odorless. When the words relate to direct experiences, the child's vocabulary grows.

The following scene is an example of how all these skills are developed in a simple food experience.

cooling. The child thus learns to name shapes, compare sizes, and describe colors.

Children learn about tastes. Children find out how heating or mixing changes taste. They learn that some things, such as salt or sugar, can change the taste of foods. They discover that some foods taste good when they are mixed together and that others do not. They also learn that a change in the outward appearance of some foods does not mean that the foods taste any different. Apple juice has the same flavor as a whole apple. Frozen orange pops taste like orange juice and a frozen banana tastes just like banana ice cream.

Children observe changes. As they did in science activities, children observe that foods change from liquids to solids and from solids to liquids. They also see steam (a gas) rising from liquids that are heated. They smell odors as foods change from solids to liquids to gases. They see how ingredients when mixed together form a new substance. In baking, this same substance changes even more.

Children learn to express themselves. Language develops as a result of food experiences. Words like bitter, sour, sweet, and salty have real meaning. Hot,

The making of pudding went over quite well, as do all food-oriented activities. My organization ahead of time helped it to be a pleasant and not too disorganized activity! We used instant pudding and it required a specified amount of milk to be added. This fact helped us discuss the number of cups of milk we would need, as well as the concept of milk and nutrition, etc. They poured out the milk, measuring the amounts, and all had a chance to use the hand rotary beater to beat the pudding. This was good small motor exercise for them all. They poured out the pudding (a bit messy!). Then we had to wait for five minutes for it to set, and this helped introduce the idea of time and where the clock's hands would be when five minutes went by. All these things were discussed in making the pudding, so I feel that it was a true learning experience for all. However, I'm sure the children enjoyed eating the pudding at the end of the learning experience the best!

Many concepts can be discussed in an informal situation such as this. I hope to use many more such situations when I assume my role as a teacher of young children. Learning under such a natural and relaxed atmosphere was a pleasure for both myself and the children (Author's Log).

Children learn about others. Food activities can be used throughout the curriculum to enhance children's learning. For example, a project on different breads from around the world can be used to teach about the diversity of people in the world and the many types of bread individuals eat. A literature table can be set up to include children's books (see Online Companion for suggestions). Children can make many types of breads from different cultures. Discussion can be held on how families and cultures use bread in celebrations and traditions. Children's literature provides many examples of how people in many different lands prepare and eat a wide variety of breads. Cooking activities can include tortillas, wontons, waffles, fry bread, challah, hoe cakes, bagels, pasta, hush puppies, latkes, and fortune cookies, to name just a few multicultural foods. Each of these foods can be used in connection with other projects to make a multicultural experience. (See Chapters 24–26 for more information on multicultural curriculum and activities.)

Skill Building

There are a number of skills that children can learn from working with foods. These skills can be developed during other parts of the program also, but working with food is an excellent way to build skills in fun activities.

Small-muscle coordination. Mixing foods and pouring liquids from one container to another are ways in which children develop coordination. The small muscles in the hands develop so that a child can hold a large spoon and help in the mixing process when using a recipe. The measuring, pouring, and mixing of foods all require the use of small muscles as well as hand–eye coordination. Thus, food activities provide excellent small-motor activities for young children.

Simple measuring skills. By using cups and spoons that have marks showing amounts, a child begins to understand measurements. The child is able to observe that a tablespoon is larger than a teaspoon and that a cup holds more than a tablespoon. The child can also begin to realize that by using too much flour, water, or salt, recipes don't turn out quite as well as if the correct amounts are used. The child begins to understand that the amount of each ingredient used makes a difference in the final product. This realization leads the child to look for ways to figure out amounts. This is when measuring tools are discovered. Older children can be challenged to make one-half of a recipe or double it.

Figure 21-3
Tasting is a fun part of a food activity.

This gives them a real-life opportunity to practice multiplication, fractions, and division skills.

Social skills. Food experiences are a natural avenue for social learning. Mixing, measuring, decorating, and eating all provide many opportunities for talking with others, exchanging ideas, sharing likes and dislikes, and learning about each other. You will find that in preparing food, children many times will talk more freely about themselves and their lives in the homey, routine nature of this type of activity.

In cooking, a child may need help in holding a pan steady while pouring something into it. He or she may need help in carrying ingredients or finding certain foods. Children with special needs enjoy cooking activities as much as other children. By using some of the ideas presented in earlier chapters on adapting equipment and space, teachers can provide children with special needs the opportunity to enjoy cooking activities

Figure 21-4
Learning to appreciate new kinds of foods is an important part of early childhood food activities.

Figure 21-5
Preparing food is a pleasant activity for young children.

at their individual levels. One child may need an "expert" opinion on how much lemon to squeeze into a drink. These things call for working together. As children work together, social skills develop in the natural give-and-take of group experiences.

Cooking activities provide children a chance to share information with each other about family recipes and food preferences. Learning about each other's cultural differences occurs naturally in cooking experiences.

Health and Safety

As children are involved in food experiences, they learn some basic information on routines and cautions about food and cooking necessary to good health and safety. This information is best learned in the process of working with food and not as a "lecture" type lesson.

For example, learning that cleanliness is important in all food preparation can be taught as children work with food. Both children and adults always wash their hands with soap and water before beginning and after ending any food experience. Aprons or other cover-

ups may also be necessary, especially if you are preparing foods that stain easily.

Children may need encouragement to keep fingers and utensils out of their mouths while preparing food. If they do lick fingers or spoons, simply and calmly ask the children to wash them before proceeding. This is a good opportunity to teach children about germs and how they are transmitted. Tasting is also a good opportunity to help children learn about how foods taste at various stages of preparation and to observe changes in texture. However, no products containing raw eggs should be eaten before being fully cooked. Raw eggs are a source of salmonella bacteria and can cause digestive problems.

Any cooking adventure involving heat, sharp knives, or operating appliances should be carefully supervised. Sharp knives are rarely needed, since plastic serrated knives will slice most produce and are much safer for even very young children. Children will need to be cautioned when observing food in the oven or on the range burner; utensil handles should be turned toward the center of the range at all times. Since electric burners don't always appear to be hot, children will need to learn how to identify when the burner is on, by recognizing the position of the switch or by reading "on," "off," "high," or "low," and by being made aware that the burner remains hot for a while even after it has been turned off. All of these are important health and safety lessons for young children in food experiences.

Finally, food allergies are very common among young children, and before planning any experience, you will need to know which children are allergic to specific foods. For example, in some schools no products with peanuts are used because of children's allergies. Some children may also have ethnic food restrictions that prohibit their eating certain foods as

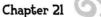

Figure 21-6
Encourage children to drink water instead of fruit drinks if they are thirsty.

well. Every adult participating in food activities, whether teacher, cook, parent, or community volunteer, must have this information. If fresh produce is to be used, adults must know what parts of plants are poisonous. Children should learn that these parts and any other wild plant must never be eaten.

Activities for Toddlers and Two- and Three-Year-Old Children

Even though food preparation activities are included in the early childhood program for children three years and up, adults are often inclined to think that children under the age of three would just make a mess. For example, many cooks in early childhood centers do not want to be bothered, and of course young children underfoot in a kitchen increase the risk of accidents and injuries. An alternative is to bring the foods and the appropriate utensils for cooking activities to the children's room. The term *cooking activities* in this instance includes all the steps necessary in the preparation and serving of foods, with or without the use of heat. The cooking-related activities that follow are

listed in progressive order, from the simple to the more involved. Many toddlers and two year olds are able to master many of these activities, and most three year olds are capable of mastering them all.

1. exploring cooking utensils (banging, nesting, putting away)
2. exploring cooking utensils with water (cups, bowls, beaters, spoons, funnels)
3. pouring dry ingredients (corn, rice)
4. pouring wet ingredients (water)
5. tasting fresh fruit and vegetables
6. comparing tastes, textures, colors of *fresh* fruits and vegetables
7. comparing tastes, textures, colors of *canned* vegetables and fruits
8. dipping raw fruits and vegetables in dip or sauce
9. scrubbing vegetables with brushes
10. breaking or tearing lettuce; breaking or snapping beans; shelling peas
11. stirring and mixing wet and dry ingredients
12. measuring wet and dry ingredients (use rubber band to mark desired amount on container or measuring cup)
13. placing toppings on pizza or snacks; decorating cookies or crackers that have been spread
14. spreading on bread or crackers
15. pouring milk or juices to drink
16. shaking (making butter from cream or coloring sugar or coconut)
17. rolling with both hands (peanut butter balls, pieces of dough for cookies)
18. juicing with a hand juicer
19. peeling hard-cooked eggs, fruits
20. cutting with dull knife (fruits, vegetables, cheese)
21. beating with fork or egg beater
22. grinding with hand grinder (apples or cranberries)
23. kneading bread dough
24. cleaning up

Curriculum Areas

Cooking does more than build physical, health and safety, and social skills. It is an ideal project for just about all of the curriculum areas. It involves reading, math, science, creative activities, opportunities for independent learning and following directions, and drawing and writing activities. Let's look briefly at these different areas.

Reading. For prekindergarten children, drawings with words and numbers can be used to help children understand the recipe. (See picture recipes in Figures 21–8, 21–9, and 21–10.) This is a good warm-up activity for reading in kindergarten or the primary grades. Older children can read the recipe, which itself is good practice. Many books, for both preschool and elementary age, talk about food and cooking. (See Online Companion for recommended books.) Display some of these books in your library area for the children to look at. If you find a book that applies to a specific cooking experience, read it to the group before beginning to cook.

In the language arts center, furnish a tape recorder for children's dictation of their real and imaginary recipes. Provide paper and art materials for later transcription into books.

Math. For most recipes, measuring instruments—cups, tablespoons, and teaspoons—are required. Measuring cups in specific colors are helpful in cooking activities for young children. For example, the blue cup is ¼ cup, the green is ½ cup, the yellow is ⅓ cup, and the red is 1 cup. The same method can be used with different colors for each measuring spoon. It's also helpful and interesting to have a food scale for measuring as well. Sequencing (measuring, mixing, and then baking), estimating, counting, adding, fractions, and discrimination of size and shape are all involved in cooking experiences.

Discuss each of these objects and activities as you go along, working with small groups so everyone gets a turn. Children learn better when they *do* than when they merely look and listen.

Older children can handle measuring and mixing ingredients on their own. You can challenge their math

Figure 21-7

Reading books about food is another way to help young children learn about nutrition.

Figure 21-8

Picture recipe for applesauce (recipe at end of chapter).

skills by asking them to measure the ingredients for one-half of the recipe you're going to use. Or they can figure out how to double or triple the recipe for a larger group.

Science.   Cooking develops sensory skills. It involves physical and chemical changes, the use of simple machines, and predicting the outcome of a cooking experiment. For example, when making cookies, place all the ingredients on the table and give everyone a chance to smell, touch, and taste each one. Then mix the ingredients with spoons, forks, or eggbeaters. Ask the children about shape and texture as you mix. Ask them to predict the outcome of your cooking experience. Then, after baking, compare your predictions with the results.

Older children can suggest ways to alter the recipe to make it turn out in different ways. They enjoy experimenting with different spices to give their recipes a new and special flavor. It's fun to use spices from different cultural groups, too.

Science center.   Provide open-ended activities for cooking explorations. For instance, try a taste test of all the different ways apples are used in cooking and eating: apple juice, cider, sauce, butter, dried, even apple cider vinegar. Or compare the appearance, taste, and texture of red, green, and yellow apples. You can also explore bananas. Brainstorm a list of how many different ways you can cook or eat them. What can you do with a frozen banana? Make ice cream! (Put chunks of frozen banana in a blender with just a hint of milk, blend until thick, and eat immediately.) How do bananas taste when they're sliced in circles? Try it and see. Try drying fruit and vegetables in the sun for tasty, healthful snacks (see recipes at chapter's end.)

Creative activities.   Almost all recipes can be extended, modified, changed, or given an unexpected twist. Use your imagination, and, more important, get the *children* to use theirs! Use a soft pretzel recipe (recipe at end of chapter) to make animals or three-dimensional sculptures instead of the traditional pret-

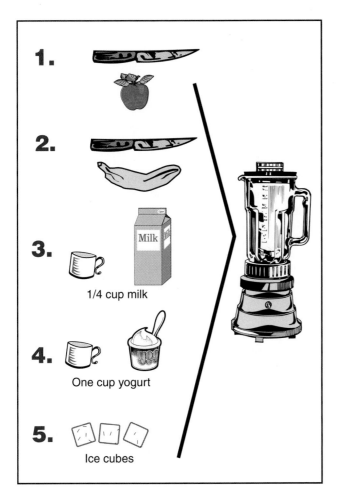

Figure 21-9

Picture recipe for banana apple icy (recipe at end of chapter).

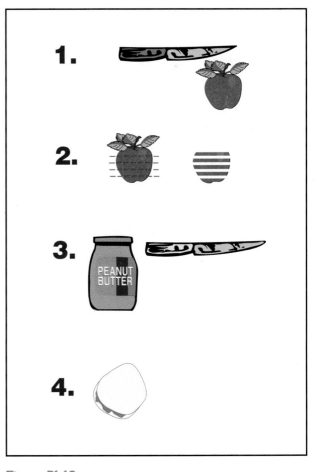

Figure 21-10

Picture recipe for apple sandwich (recipe at end of chapter.)

THIS ONE'S for YOU!

Fun French Toast Facts

Here are some interesting facts about this common breakfast food:

⊙ French toast was created by medieval European cooks who needed to use every bit of food they could find to feed their families. They knew day-old bread could be revived when moistened and heated. They also added eggs for additional moisture and protein.

⊙ Medieval recipes for French toast suggest this meal was also enjoyed by the wealthy. These recipes used white bread (the very finest, most expensive bread available at the time) with the crusts cut off—something a person of meager means would be unlikely to do.

⊙ Recipes for French toast can also be traced to Ancient Roman times. One of the original French names for this is *le pain a la Romaine* or Roman bread. Apicius, Roman culinary expert born 25 B.C., wrote: "Another sweet dish: Break fine white bread, crust removed, into rather large pieces which soak in milk and beaten eggs. Fry in oil, cover with honey and serve." (*Apicius Cookery and Dining in Imperial Rome,* edited and translated by Joseph Dommers Vehling, recipe 296.)

⊙ According to the *Encyclopedia of American Food and Drink,* French toast does have its origins in France, where it is known as "amerite" or "pain perdu" (lost bread).

⊙ The phrase "French toast" first appeared in print in the *Encyclopedia of American Food and Drink* in 1871.

---

zel shape. Add food coloring to the coating mixture (in the recipe) and paint your animals or sculptures before baking.

Drawing and writing. Have the children dictate stories, anecdotes from home, and highlights of their experiences cooking in your classroom. Involve parents and other volunteers in this activity. Those children who wish to can tell and draw about the day's cooking activity. Older children can keep personal journals of their cooking experiences. They may want to select certain favorite recipes and make up their own cookbooks.

GUIDELINES FOR CREATIVE FOOD ACTIVITIES

The following are some guidelines to use to ensure that food experiences for young children are planned to enhance their creativity.

1. *Activities should be open-ended.* If all children must follow the same directions at the same time, they will not have a chance to be creative. In fact, just the opposite will happen. The children will conform and do what the teacher tells them to do. Teachers who want to help children be creative must let the

children create their own directions and work at their own pace.

2. *Activities should be challenging, but not too difficult for the children.* If food activities are too hard, children will give up. If they are too easy, the children will not be challenged. It is important to start with easy things. It is also important to increase the possibilities, so children will do more challenging things as they go on.

3. *Activities should be varied.* Children get bored if they do the same thing day after day. Variety is needed. Children should work with foods they know. They should also work with new foods they have not seen or tasted before. Some activities should be very short. Others should take a longer time to finish. In some activities, children may use just one type of food. In others, they may mix in several ingredients.

4. *The process is more important than the product.* Emphasis should not be placed on what the children create, but on how they have done it. If only the final product is considered, then many children will fail. Things do not always taste good—especially when children create new recipes. But if children are rewarded for the way they create, then what they have created does not seem so important.

THINK ABOUT IT... Internet Experiences and Cooking

Children in the early and middle elementary levels can explore many food ideas on the Internet. For example, they can learn when the ice cream cone was patented at http://www.abcteach.com/. Click on Theme Units, then on Fun/Kids, and then on Ice Cream.

They can learn a multitude of facts about apples and Johnny Appleseed at http://www.educationworld.com/. Type in "apples" in the Search box.

Chocolate Day is another fun food concept children will learn about at http://www.theteacherscorner.net/. Under Thematic Units, click on Unit Index, then click on Chocolate. In fact, you can make chocolate the topic of many more Internet experiences for children. Here are some more ideas:

- Visit http://www.cocoapro.com with your class to learn about Xocolatl and to unlock the secrets of this beverage once reserved for Aztec warriors and nobility. Students can view videos on the history of chocolate and more.

- Discover the different kinds of chocolate candy the Mars company makes when you and your students visit http://www.mars.com/. What other products does Mars make? Why do you think they make such a variety of foods?

- Teach your students about *cacao*—the source of chocolate—when you visit "The Sweet Science of Chocolate" at http://www.exploratorium.edu. Type "chocolate" in the Search box. Kids can find out about chocolate's importance to early Americans.

- Find out with your class what the Ms stand for in M&M's candy by going to http://goodbyemag.com/. Under 1999, click on July–August, then click on Forrest Mars, Candy Man. You can also click on Vernon: Global M&M's. Why did these two men create M&M's in the first place? How has their product changed over the years?

- Take a video tour of a chocolate factory with your class and follow a chocolate bean until it becomes part of a chocolate bar when you visit Exploratorium magazine at http://www.exploratorium.edu/. Type "chocolate" in Search box.

- Visit http://virtualchocolate.com/ and have your students send virtual postcards of "chocolatey" greetings to friends. They can also read chocolate quotes, download chocolate pictures for their computer screens, and write their own chocolate quote or comment.

---

5. *Inexpensive materials and small amounts should be used.* No child should feel badly if a recipe does not work. If ingredients are inexpensive, there is less chance that children will be made to feel discouraged because something they made did not taste very good.

6. *Activities should be carried out in a variety of places.* Food activities do not have to be limited to the indoors. They can also be done outside the classroom. They work well on the school grounds or in a nearby woods. *Note:* An important restriction for outdoor cooking is for the teacher to see and inspect all food before it is used. Poison mushrooms and berries are sometimes gathered by children. These foods must be avoided.

GETTING STARTED

Planning

Careful planning is crucial to successful food experiences. All ingredients (in sufficient quantities) need to be purchased, utensils assembled, and objectives for the activity established.

Children's abilities should be matched to the food experience so that the adult does not carry out the preparation while the children watch. Depending on the complexity of the recipe, the number of children, whether children with special needs are part of the group, and the time available, it may at times be necessary for the adult to complete some tasks or to use prepared foods. Keep in mind, however, that the more the adult does, the less the children learn. The extra time children take learning is well spent.

Objectives for the children's learning will help focus the activity for the adults involved. Do you want children to successfully cut celery into finger-sized strips? Is your objective to have the children sample a variety of food textures and discuss the differences? Will children try less familiar foods? Is your goal to facilitate cooperative work in a small group?

Common goals for food experiences for young children include strengthening their manipulative skills, expanding their knowledge about nutrition, and trying new foods. You will want to develop your own objectives for each recipe you choose based on your knowledge about the children in the group.

Goals for very young or inexperienced children will be different from those for more advanced food preparers. Initially, try to plan food preparation activities that involve only one or two skills and a limited number of ingredients. Squeezing orange juice involves one ingredient and two skills, squeezing and pouring. Washing vegetables or fruits (in a basin to conserve water, rather than under running water) and possibly then cutting them into convenient pieces is also a good beginning activity. For children who are just becoming competent in balancing, pouring, or cutting, these tasks are a real challenge. The following list will help you prepare for successful food experiences.

1. Work out ahead of time a sequence of steps for the activity.

2. Plan a series of activities that are gradually more complex.

3. Encourage the children to talk about what they are doing.

4. Relate the activity to home experiences.

5. Give the names for new foods, processes, and equipment used.

6. When appropriate, involve the children in getting supplies for the activities.

7. Encourage discussion of what has been done. Allow a good amount of time for tasting and touching.

8. Use follow-up activities to reinforce the learning. (See Figure 21–11).

INTEGRATED FOOD UNITS– ELEMENTARY LEVEL

Too often in the elementary school teachers plan food activities as "special events" or simply as an add-on to other curriculum areas. Few teachers attempt to integrate food activities into the elementary curriculum. Yet, it is quite possible to develop units based on food and food groups and to integrate learning activities from all areas of the curriculum. The following are two examples of integrated food units for the elementary school level. These units will get you started on developing many of your own integrated food units.

Potato Unit

This unit begins with the reading of Tomie de Paola's book *Jamie O'Rourke and the Big Potato* (1992). (Or you could also use McDonald's *The Potato Man,* 1996.) After reading the book to the group, make it available for them to read on their own for at least a week. Use the book as a basis for student's research on the history of the potato and about Ireland. Have the children write factual reports on these topics. They can then be compiled into a class "Potato Book."

Use a 10-lb. bag of potatoes as a source of math experiences. Challenge the children to estimate the number of potatoes in the bag. Then help them sequence their estimations in numerical order (ascending or descending). Then have them actually count the potatoes. Discuss their estimates and compare the actual number of potatoes to these estimates. Have them make up a summary graph showing the range of numbers between the estimates and actual number of potatoes. Then give each child a potato and have them count its eyes, estimate then measure the circumference, and graph the results. Then, using a balance scale, have the children weigh each potato. Discuss with the children the nutritional value of potatoes as you make dishes using recipes from the children's families.

Vegetable Soup

Two books that are good to read at the beginning of this unit are *Growing Vegetable Soup* by L. Ehlert (1990) and *Neighborhood Soup* by J. Nelson (1990). These books can be used as the basis for several related activities, such as a plant- and vegetable-growing activity. During the plant activity, children can plant seeds and observe their growth. Children can also keep written records of plant growth under a variety of conditions, including without light and without water.

Have the children use seed catalogues and real vegetables to examine the edible parts of various plants. Then, have them taste a variety of vegetables—raw and cooked—and compare the nutritional value of each. Then, use the raw vegetables in the art center for making vegetable prints.

Have the children work cooperatively to make the neighborhood soup. Then discuss the creation of new soups. Have the children brainstorm ingredients for their original soups and also create labels for their own soup cans. Have them work together to present a play based on the *Neighborhood Soup* story. Preparations can include making props and promotional posters.

USING FOOD IN SCIENCE ACTIVITIES

- plant an outdoor or indoor garden
- have a tasting party
- arrange unusual foods on a science table
- place carrot, beet, or pineapple tops in a shallow bowl of crushed stones or pebbles covered with water, allow it to sprout
- cut off the top third of a sweet potato and put it in water; allow sprouts to vine at the top; hold the potato part way out of the water
- examine a coconut, then break it open
- examine and cut a fresh pineapple
- taste baby foods
- place seed catalogs on the reading shelf
- make a food dictionary
- draw pictures of your favorite foods from each food group; make a meal: draw a picture of a plate and cup and fill them with your foods to make a nutritious meal; make sure you label each food

CREATIVE ART ACTIVITIES WITH FOOD

- fruit-colored play dough
- potato printing
- broken eggshells on paintings
- child-made food books
  Foods I Like
  Fruits I Like
  Foods My Daddy (or Mommy, Sister, etc.) Likes
- a class mural made of pictures of foods
- creating flannelboard pictures (have foods cut from flannel for child to arrange on a flannel or story board)
- food pictures cut from newspaper or magazine advertisements to paste on colored paper
- have children paste pictures of foods on a chart with areas for fruits and vegetables, breads, milk, and meats
- make picture charts of favorite recipes

TABLE ACTIVITIES–FOOD EXPERIENCES

- sewing cards with food pictures
- dishpans of beans with funnels, measuring cups
- food scale with beans for weighing
- balance for weighing

FIELD TRIPS–FOOD EXPERIENCES

- grocery store
- vegetable garden
- fruit orchard
- school kitchen
- bakery
- restaurant
- pizza parlor
- ice cream store
- fruit and vegetable stand
- bottling company
- dairy
- canning factory
- hatchery
- cornfield, strawberry or melon patch
- kitchen of one of the children's family

GAMES FOR COOKING EXPERIENCES

- Can You Remember? (display foods on a tray; cover; try to remember where each is)
- How Many? (different foods, etc.)
- Which? (foods that can be eaten raw, foods that are yellow, etc.)
- Grouping (those that are yellow, those that are eaten for breakfast, etc.)
- Touch and Tell (place food in a bag; have child feel and try to identify)
- Smell and Tell (have child close eyes and try to identify food by smelling)
- Guess What? (describe the characteristics of food; children try to identify)

Figure 21-11

Follow-up activities to reinforce learning.

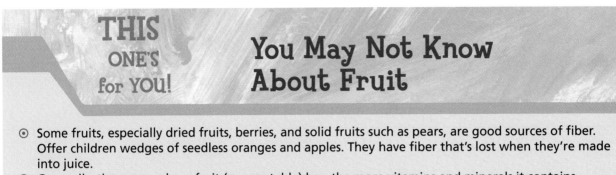

THIS ONE'S for YOU!   You May Not Know About Fruit

- Some fruits, especially dried fruits, berries, and solid fruits such as pears, are good sources of fiber. Offer children wedges of seedless oranges and apples. They have fiber that's lost when they're made into juice.
- Generally, the more color a fruit (or vegetable) has, the more vitamins and minerals it contains.
- For toddlers, avoid fruits with seeds. Pay special attention as toddlers eat dried or frozen fruits and cut firm fruits to be sure they don't choke on the hard bits of food.
- Bananas and avocados are favorites of young children because the fruits' textures are appealing. Both are rich in potassium and other minerals.
- Products marked "juice" must contain 100 percent juice. "Drinks," "ades," "punches," "cocktails," and other beverages may be little more than fruit-flavored sugar water.
- Giving a child juice made from concentrate is a good way to provide fluoride if your water supply is fluoridated.
- Encourage plain water for thirst. Juice is a food and children will fill up on it and not eat other foods. The American Academy of Pediatrics recommends 4 to 6 ounces of juice per day (AAP, 2001).

THINK ABOUT IT...   The First Sandwich!

November 3 is the birthday of the Earl of Sandwich. More than 200 years ago there was a man named John Montagu. He lived in England in the town of Sandwich and besides being called *Mister* Montague, he had another title: he was called an Earl. His full name was Mr. John Montagu, the fourth Earl of Sandwich.

John Montagu loved to play card games. He loved to bet money that he could beat everybody else in the game. One time, they say, he played cards all day and all night and again all day. He didn't even stop to sleep or eat. When he finally got hungry he asked the cook to put a piece of meat between two slices of bread—that way he could eat without having to use a fork or spoon! The cook did as John asked and then as a joke, he called the food a SANDWICH! So now you know how we got our very first sandwich!

Ask the children about their favorite sandwich. Keep track of their answers because these can give insight into their eating habits and nutritional needs. Ask them: "Do you like mayonnaise on your sandwiches? Lettuce? Cream cheese?" "What is your favorite jelly?" (Do you know the difference between jelly and jam? Jelly is made from the juice of the fruit and it's clear. Jam has crushed fruit right in it.) "What kind of meat sandwich do you like best?" "What is your favorite bread?" (A sandwich is more bread than anything else, so it's important to have a good bread on your sandwich. A brown bread is the best because it gives your body more natural vitamins and minerals than a white bread does.)

Let their answers to these questions guide you in selecting recipes for them. Make some homemade peanut butter, homemade bread, or homemade jelly. (See end of chapter for recipes.)

REDUCING SUGAR IN CHILDREN'S DIETS

Research on the human infant shows that even infants prefer sweet over bitter or sour taste (Ausubel, 1980). This preference posed no problem when early human diets consisted of natural fruit and vegetable sources of sweetness. However, when refined sugar came into our diets, the total amount of sugar consumed increased dramatically. Soft drinks are the leading source of added sugar in the diet of American children (Blasi, 2003). A long-term research study examined soda consumption and its effect on children's body weight. The study

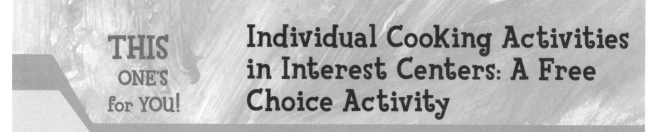

Individual Cooking Activities in Interest Centers: A Free Choice Activity

It's John's turn to "cook" during free choice activity time. First, he washes his hands; second, he puts on a white paper chef's hat; and third, he begins cutting fruit into bite-sized pieces with a plastic knife. He is following a picture recipe and will eventually put the fruit on a skewer to make a fruit kabob for his snack to be eaten later with his classmates. And, he made his snack all by himself! Independent snack preparation can easily be set up in the classroom with some basic equipment and recipes designed for individual portions.

Ideas and recipes to help you get started cooking independently in your classroom follow.

Cut off one of the end flaps of a sturdy cardboard box and cut the box apart at the side seam so it will stand up using the other end flaps as supports. This will be your instruction "board." Cover the entire box with colorful contact papers. The box can be set up on a table to designate your snack and work area. Sequential picture recipes can be clipped to each section of the box/board. For example, the pictures in sequence would indicate to (1) wash hands, (2) cut fruit into pieces, (3) put fruit on skewer, and (4) place on paper plate with name on plate. Basic equipment for your snack activity center would include measuring cups, small bowls, tongue depressors, small wire whisks, five-ounce paper cups, plastic serrated knives, electric skillet, blender, and paper chef's hats. AN ELECTRIC APPLIANCE IS OPERATED BY ADULTS ONLY.

After you've designated your snack area and gathered your equipment, you're ready to begin with the recipes that follow. Before each child actually begins the snack preparation, gather the children in a group, tell them briefly about the recipe, and remind them of any specific directions. For example, a direction might be that each child may cut up only one slice of melon. While one or two children are working in the snack area, the teacher always needs to be available for assistance as the children need it.

PEANUT BUTTER PUDDING FOR ONE

You'll need: 2 tablespoons dry milk; 2 tablespoons instant vanilla pudding mix; $\frac{1}{3}$ cup water; 1 tablespoon fresh peanut butter (no sugar added)

What to do: 1. Using a tongue depressor for leveling dry ingredients, measure dry milk and pudding mix in 5-ounce paper cup. 2. Add water and stir using a small whisk, $1\frac{1}{2}$ minutes. 3. Add peanut butter and whisk until smooth. 4. Chill.

LETTUCE WRAP-AROUNDS

You'll need: lettuce leaves; any combination of luncheon meats or cheese slices, or spreads such as cream cheese, peanut butter, or egg salad

What to do: 1. Lay lettuce leaf flat on cutting board. 2. Place meat and/or cheese slice on lettuce leaf. 3. Add a spread or other filler and roll up the combination securing with a toothpick. These may be eaten rolled up or can be cut into bite-sized pieces with a serrated knife.

BANANA SHAKE BAG

You'll need: $\frac{1}{4}$ cup chopped peanuts; 1 banana

What to do: 1. After peeling banana, cut in 1-inch chunks. 2. Place peanuts in a plastic baggie. 3. Put a few banana chunks at a time in the bag and shake. Serve bananas on paper plates.

PINEAPPLE MIX-UP

You'll need: $\frac{1}{4}$ cup plus 1 tablespoon instant nonfat dry milk; $\frac{1}{2}$ cup pineapple juice, chilled; $\frac{1}{2}$ cup cracked ice

What to do: 1. For cracked ice, wrap some ice cubes in a towel and pound with a hammer. 2. Combine all ingredients in a blender and blend on high 30 seconds until thick and foamy.

Watch the food disappear at snack time because the children love these activities. Don't forget the paper chef's hats (available at a party store) or you can make your own hats! The hats make the children feel even more special, like "professional" chefs.

THINK ABOUT IT... Eating Better at Lunchtime

Teachers are always looking for ways to help students choose healthful foods and actually finish eating them. One way is to try sitting with them at lunch. A number of studies note that lunchtime is an opportune time to build a sense of community, foster social skills, and help improve children's eating habits.

"More schools need to take advantage of extending the learning during lunch," says Vincent L. Ferrandino, executive director of the National Association of Elementary School Principals (NAESP).

According to a study by the Columbus (Ohio) Children's Hospital, when teachers spend lunchtime with their students, the children actually eat more nutritious foods, finish the food, and eventually develop better eating habits (Cooper, 2003).

The research study, led by dietitian Kristina Houser, found that in one class, students whose teacher sat with them at lunch drank all their milk and ate about 20 percent more of their food. The teacher encouraged the students to eat fruits and vegetables and to try new foods (Cooper, 2003).

Another study of lunchtime activities, by Karen Evans Stout of Lehigh University, found that creative activities to build community, such as allowing children to go to the library to hear read-alouds while eating their lunch, can do wonders for building bonds. That can also transfer to helping students re-examine their eating habits, once teachers have developed a relationship with the students (Cooper, 2003).

At Dorothy C. Goodwin Elementary School in Storrs, Connecticut, school staff turned the cafeteria into a literary experience, with themes from library books and matching food. For Chinese New Year there were Chinese foods and books about Chinese culture.

The more time students have to socialize, relax with their food, and interact with teachers, the greater the chance teachers have to extend learning to books and to nutrition.

found that for each additional daily serving of a sugar-sweetened soft drink, the incidence of obesity was significantly increased. Researchers also discovered that the odds of becoming obese increased 1.6 times for each additional glass of sugar-sweetened soft drink consumed above the daily average (Gortmaker, 2001).

Although we do not know what proportion of all of this sugar is consumed by children, we do know many parents and teachers are trying to limit children's sugar consumption for two main reasons: the danger of tooth decay and a diet with too many empty calories.

Tooth decay. If teeth are not brushed frequently, sugars can cause tooth decay—dental caries or what are more commonly called "cavities." One way to avoid dental caries is to avoid foods that are high in sugar. However, some of the foods that are most likely to cause cavities (because they are high in fruit sugar or fructose) are very nutritious. Another sugar, lactose, is contained in milk. Obviously, it would not be appropriate to eliminate all sugar-containing foods. A more preferable goal is to eliminate those foods that are high in sugars and low in nutritional value.

Empty calories and the prevention of obesity. Nutritionists and pediatricians concur that infantile and childhood obesity should be prevented. Not all overweight children are destined to become overweight adults. Conversely, not all overweight adults were overweight children. However, one study (2001/02) showed that if a child is overweight at age six, his or her likelihood of adult obesity is more than 50 percent (Axmaker 2001/02). Obesity is considered the number one health risk for children in the United States. The number of children who are overweight has doubled in the last two or three decades; currently, one child in five is overweight (Torgan, 2002).

The best plan to prevent obesity in children is to balance their caloric intake with the number of calories they expend through exercise. Children who are overweight may also have a tendency to overeat, so they may need to reduce their consumption of empty calories as well as the size of their portions.

The best way to reduce obesity is to limit empty calories—foods high in fat or sugar but low in protein, vitamins, and/or minerals. Sugar is not the only source of empty calories. High-fat and/or high-salt snacks

Figure 21-12

Playdough is a fun, three-dimensional material.

should also be eliminated. Good choices then for snacks and meals will include vegetables, fruits, and protein-rich items.

Because young children have a limited capacity for food intake and because for many 22 percent of their caloric intake comes from snacks, it is important that empty calories be avoided. Snacks, as well as meals, must center around foods that contribute to children's need for a balanced diet.

How to limit children's sugar intake. There are four primary ways to limit children's sugar intake: (1) avoid obvious sources of high-sugar foods, (2) avoid "hidden" sugars, (3) find alternative sources of sweetness or reduce the amount of sugar, and (4) find other ways to celebrate special events without serving foods high in sugar.

Avoid high-sugar foods. The term **sugar** is generally used to refer to "sucrose," which is refined sugar from sugar cane or beets. The most common form of sucrose is white, granulated table sugar. This type of sugar is an ingredient in cakes, cookies, doughnuts, pies, candy, and soft drinks. One obvious way to reduce sugar intake is to reduce the intake of these types of foods. Another method is to use one half or less of the sugar called for in a recipe.

Other common forms of sugar are fructose, dextrose, lactose, and maltose. Read the list of ingredients on prepared foods and watch for words ending with "ose," which indicates that some form of sugar is present. These different forms of sugar have varying degrees of sweetness. For example, "lactose" (milk sugar) is the least sweet per unit. Fructose is nearly twice as sweet as sucrose, and invert sugar is about 30 percent sweeter than sucrose. All, however, provide basically empty calories.

Avoid hidden sugars. Most parents and teachers are aware that foods like candy, cake, and soft drinks contain sugar and are low in nutritional value. Very few people are aware, however, that sugar is also present in catsup, peanut butter, luncheon meats, hot dogs, pork and beans, nondairy creamer, fruit-flavored yogurt, and canned vegetables. Although these foods do contain nutrients, the addition of sugar is usually unnecessary. Use foods that contain no sugar.

Find alternative sources of sweetness. Snacks and desserts of unsweetened foods can be emphasized at home and school. Examples include unsalted popcorn, cheese, vegetables with dip, and no-sugar-added peanut butter on apples and celery.

Fresh fruits and vegetables should be given priority. When you must use canned fruits, look for fruits canned in their own juices or in the juices of other fruits. Avoid fruits canned in heavy syrup and accept those canned in light syrup only if fresh or water-packed fruits are not available.

ACTIVITY AND OBESITY

Although genetics and sugar intake play a role in obesity, they alone cannot account for the huge increase in obesity rates over the past few decades. Eating too much and moving around too little are two other major causes of obesity. Most experts agree that watching excessive amounts of television is a significant risk factor associated with obesity; almost half of children ages eight to 16 years watch three to five hours of television daily (Torgan, 2002). Children who are the most overweight watch the most television and eat too many snacks with a high fat content (Axmaker, 2001/02). Television viewing, video games, and surfing the Internet often take the place of physical activity for

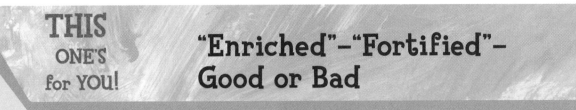

THIS ONE'S for YOU!

"Enriched"–"Fortified"– Good or Bad

Don't worry about giving young children some foods, such as white bread and sandwich buns, which say *enriched* or *fortified* on the label. Enrichment replaces some of the nutrients lost during processing and fortification adds others. Some people say that white flour and products made with white flour are not nutritious. This is not true. It's just that whole grains are a bit better because they have more of some vitamins, minerals, and fiber. All starches are valuable sources of vitamins, minerals, and calories for young children. Even the youngest child needs at least four servings from the starch group each day. It's best to offer a variety of selections from the list rather than four or more portions of the same starch.

WHOLE-GRAIN STARCH CHOICES

barley	oatmeal	whole-grain wafers
brown rice	pumpernickel	whole-grain Melba toast
bulgar	rye bread	wheat germ
corn tortilla	Rykrisp	whole-wheat pasta
millet	whole-grain breads	
oat bran	whole-grain cereals	

BEST ENRICHED/FORTIFIED STARCH CHOICES

bagel, bialy	cornbread or corn muffins	raisin bread
bread sticks	matzo	rusks
cereals (ready-to eat, not too sweet)	melba toast	spaghetti
cooked cereals (all kinds)	noodles	
	pasta	

OTHER STARCH CHOICES

English muffin	graham crackers	muffins (unenriched)
flour tortilla	french bread (unenriched)	oatmeal cookies
hard rolls	italian bread (unenriched)	pasta salad
biscuits	white bread (enriched)	pretzels
bread stuffing	white rice	rice cakes
fruit/nut bread	Zwieback	

many children. The trance-like state associated with these activities can slow children's metabolism so much that they resemble children at complete rest (Murate, 2001/02).

Recommendations to Reduce the Risk of Obesity

The American Academy of Family Physicians offers the following tips on preventing childhood obesity:

- ⊙ Respect the child's appetite: children do not need to finish every drink or clean off their plates.
- ⊙ Avoid pre-prepared and sugared foods when possible.

- ⊙ Keep a limited amount of high-calorie foods at home.
- ⊙ Provide healthful meals, with 30 percent or fewer of the calories derived from fat.
- ⊙ Provide ample fiber in the child's diet.
- ⊙ Skim milk may safely replace whole milk when the child is two years of age.
- ⊙ Do not provide food for comfort or as a reward.
- ⊙ Do not offer sweets in exchange for a finished meal.
- ⊙ Limit television viewing.
- ⊙ Encourage active play.
- ⊙ Establish regular family activities such as walks, ball games, and other outdoor activities (Moran, 1999).

SUMMARY

Foods can be used in activities that help children become more creative in their approach to the world, as they learn new information and skills. They develop knowledge about names of shapes and colors; tastes; changes in shape, size, color, and taste; and new words. Food activities also help young children develop skills in hand–eye and small-muscle coordination, simple measuring, and socialization.

In order to ensure that food experiences for young children are planned to enhance their creativity, they must include the following basic guidelines. They must (1) be open-ended; (2) be challenging, but not too hard for three to five year olds; (3) be varied, giving children choices; (4) emphasize the doing, not the end product; (5) involve inexpensive materials; and (6) not be dangerous to children.

Food activities work best in a small group. It is important that children be allowed to make decisions for themselves about what foods to use and how to use them. Adults responsible for the diets of young children must limit sugar consumption by avoiding obvious sources of sucrose and hidden sugars. Using natural sources of sweetness, reducing the focus on sweets, and finding other types of sweets for young children are all essential ways to reduce sugar in children's diets. Childhood obesity has become a major health problem in the United States. Some causes of childhood obesity are genetic, but sugar intake and lack of physical activity play a large role.

KEY TERM

sugar

LEARNING ACTIVITIES

A. Try testing the sense of taste of some fellow students by making "creative juice."
  1. Materials and ingredients:
     blender
     common vegetables: cucumber, carrots, tomatoes, cabbage, celery, green pepper, and parsley
     salt
     sugar
     lemon juice
  2. Begin with any two vegetables. Add one-half cup of cold water or crushed ice and blend. A pinch of salt and sugar and a small amount of lemon juice will improve the flavor. Taste a small amount.
  3. Add a third vegetable to the mixture. Taste. Keep track of the vegetables and amounts used. Continue to add vegetables, one at a time. Try to make:
     a. a tasty vegetable juice.
     b. a juice whose vegetables no one can identify.
     c. a mystery juice.
B. Observe a group of children experiencing a type of food for the first time—perhaps eggplant, squash, or rutabaga!
  1. What kinds of expressions do they make when they taste the food?

  2. How do they react when they find out what the food was that they tasted?
  3. What can be said to make a child more willing to taste new foods?
C. Experiment with the sense of taste.
  1. Each person who tastes a food in this experiment must wear a blindfold or cover his or her eyes.
  2. Use small slices of baking apples or potatoes and a freshly sliced onion or garlic.
  3. Hold the onion under the blindfolded person's nose. Slip a small piece of apple or potato into the person's mouth. Have the person chew up the food and tell what it was.
D. With a group of children, try out at least one of the food experiences listed in this chapter. Evaluate the experience. Would you use this recipe again? Would you organize the experience in the same way next time? If not, what changes would you make?
E. Develop your own additional food-related activities. Develop an integrated unit on food for an elementary grade level. Share this unit with your fellow classmates for their input.
F. Keep a food diary for at least one week. Summarize your findings on your eating habits. Compare your eating habits with the recommended food pyramid in your summary.

ACTIVITIES FOR CHILDREN

CURRICULUM IDEAS

Music/movement. Play Hot Potato! Invite the children to sit in a circle. Play recorded music as the children pass a real potato around the circle. When the music stops, the child with the potato leaves the circle. Each child who leaves the circle gets a turn to start and stop the music.

Math—crunching numbers. Use graham crackers when introducing mixed numbers. Have students demonstrate on napkins and then on the overhead what $1\frac{3}{4}$ looks like. Use the crackers to add and/or subtract at each table as someone is doing it on the overhead projector, first with crackers and then without. Challenge the students to find another way to illustrate what mixed numbers look like.

Social studies. A trip to a local restaurant, pizzeria, or bakery can provide children with a wonderful opportunity to learn about how a favorite food is prepared. Invite children to prepare a list of questions they would like to ask during their visit. Consider taking along a portable tape recorder and camera to record the steps of the recipe the children are learning about. Children can then make the recipe at school. They can write a story about their experiences using the photos as their inspiration.

Pretend play. Wash empty yogurt containers and lids and frozen juice containers and place in the dramatic play area. Provide the children with plastic spoons, bowls, and plastic fruit or small colored blocks to represent the fruits. Encourage the children to use the snack props as they incorporate dolls and their classmates in dramatic play.

Math. Children wash their hands. Then, give children a bowl filled with crackers in a variety of shapes: goldfish, oyster, square, and oval. Place paper plates for each type of cracker on the table. Ask children to work together to sort the crackers onto each plate. Now children can pass the plates around and choose crackers to eat with their soup.

After a food activity, make a bar graph that lists all the recipes you've used in your class. Indicate the names of the children who liked each one. Which recipe did most children prefer? Which recipe was least preferred? Brainstorm with the children how they could change the recipes to make them even better.

Literature and art. Read *Pretzel* by Margaret Rey (1997) to the children. Make real pretzels with the recipe for soft pretzels found at the end of this chapter. Provide them with materials to create drawings about their pretzel-making experience. Record their dictations and encourage them to create their own pretzel book. Children can continue making pretend pretzels with play dough or clay or by twisting brown butcher paper.

GET SOUPED UP

Did you know that January is National Soup Month? This frosty winter month (in many places in the United States) is the perfect time to enjoy steaming mugs or bowls of the children's favorite soup while sharing books like Lois Ehlert's *Growing Vegetable Soup* (Harcourt, 1990), in which soup begins as seeds in vivid collage illustrations; *Stone Soup* by Ann McGovern (Scholastic, 1987), in which a young man tricks an old woman into cooking a pot of soup just for him; and Stewart Murphy's math storybook *Seaweed Soup* (HarperCollins, 2001), in which a turtle must count out the correct number of place settings for guests who have stopped by to partake of the soup of the title.

LEARNING FROM LABELS

Have students collect wrappers from several candy bars. Help them examine and compare the prices; nutritional components; and percentages of fat, carbohydrates, protein, and sugar in each. What conclusions can they make?

SUN RECIPES

Sun tea. The youngest of children will enjoy preparing large bottles of water with suitable herb teabags (apple cinnamon or mandarin orange spice are good choices) suspended inside and setting these out in the sunshine "to brew." From time to time check the coloring of your tea and bring it inside when it has steeped to suit your taste. Serve your sun tea warm or ice cold and sip it together outside.

Sundried fruits and vegetables. Older children will be able to pare and slice apples, apricots, peaches, carrots, zucchini, and celery. Use a large blunt-nosed needle and heavy thread to pierce and string each piece.

Leave air spaces between the pieces. Do not dry in direct sunlight because it may make apricots bitter.

Fruits dried in this way will keep for months and are wonderful for snacks, either with plain yogurt or by themselves. The vegetables can also be stored until some chilly autumn day when the children toss them into chicken broth for a warming soup snack.

APPLE EXPERIENCES

Count the seeds. Before you cut an apple, have the children try to guess how many seeds will be inside. Cut open the apple and count them. How close were they? Write down the children's guesses and how many seeds that were in the apple. The next day repeat the process. Compare your results. Were there more, less, or the same amount of seeds in the two apples?

Different apples. Next time you go to the grocery store on a field trip with the children, point out all the different kinds of apples. Tell the children their names. Buy a few different kinds and when you get back to school, let the children try them. Ask them how each one tastes. Ask them how each one is different.

Apple sequencing. Gather three to five different-sized apples. Set them on a table and ask a child to arrange the apples according to size. For younger children, you can just start with two apples and ask which is the smallest.

Apple hide and seek. Have all the children cover their eyes while you "hide" an apple in the room. (It should be placed in plain view.) Tell the children to find the apple but not to touch it. Once they spot it they should sit back down in their spot. The first one to sit down again will get to hide the apple.

Apple hide and seek #2. Play the game the same as the previous game, except hide the apple. Then tell the children individually whether they are "hot" or "cold" in relation to the apple. Allow the other children to have a chance to hide the apple, and tell children whether they are "hot or cold." It may be a good idea to discuss the meaning of hot and cold before you play this game.

Apples in the basket. You need apples and a small laundry or bushel basket. Ask the child to place five apples in the basket. Count with the child as they place the apples in the basket. How many apples will fit in the basket? Have the child guess how many will fit, and then see how many it takes to fill the basket. You can also tape numbers onto the bottom of the baskets, and have the child place the appropriate number of apples into each basket.

Apple chart. Prepare sliced apples for lunch using red and yellow apples. Ask each child which color apple they ate. Allow them to mark the column on a graph that corresponds to their answer.

FOOD RIDDLES

Children's listening and thinking skills will improve as they identify foods by guessing the answer to riddles.

Children sit in a small group of four to five people. The adult reads the entire riddle before children respond. You can write the following riddles on index cards to read to the children.

Sample riddles:

1. I'm in the dairy group. I'm white. People drink me out of a glass, cup, or carton. You put me on cereal. What am I? (milk).

2. I'm in the vegetable group. I'm long, orange, and crunchy when eaten raw. What am I? (carrot).

3. I'm in the fruit group. I'm round, shiny, and smooth to touch. I'm crunchy to bite into. I grow on a tree. What am I? (apple).

4. I'm in the meat group. I'm flat and round in shape. I often come on a bun. Sometimes people put catsup on me. What am I? (hamburger).

5. I'm in the bread and cereal group. I come in a loaf. You can slice me to make sandwiches. I smell good right after I'm baked. What am I? (bread).

6. I'm a member of the meat and poultry group. I have an oval shape. I come from a chicken. You can fry me, scramble me, or boil me. Inside I am yellow and white. What am I? (egg).

7. I'm a member of the fruit group. I'm tiny, brown, and wrinkled. I used to be a grape. You can eat me in a cereal, in cookies, or just by myself. I'm sweet but not a junk food. What am I? (raisin).

Children who are familiar with the game enjoy making up their own food riddles. Riddle games could be played concentrating on only one food group, ethnic foods, etc.

FRUIT FEAST

For this activity you will need small plastic bowls, a large spoon, several plastic knives, a large knife (for an adult), paper or plastic plates, chart paper, and markers.

Send a note home to inform families that, as a way to learn about one another, the children are requested to bring in their favorite fruit. On the day that the activity is planned, have several extra pieces of fruit handy just in case some children forget to bring their own.

Invite everyone to bring their piece of fruit to the meeting area. Write the question, "What is your favorite fruit?" on the top of a sheet of chart paper. Then, go around the circle and invite everyone to show what they brought. Record the children's responses, review their comments, and engage them in a discussion about the fruit that they brought in. How many children like the same fruit? Are there any fruits that they have never seen before?

Ask children to place their fruit in the middle of the circle. How are the fruits similar? How are they different? Ask them to touch and smell the fruits. Create another chart to record their observations.

Explain that they will use their fruit to make a fruit salad bar for their snack. Divide them into two small groups, each led by an adult. Begin by washing hands and reviewing cooking safety rules. Invite children to help wash, peel, and cut the fruits with plastic knives. Ask an adult to cut the harder fruits first and give the pieces to the children so that they can safely cut them and then place the different fruits into individual bowls.

Give each child a bowl and invite them to make their own fruit salad. Before they eat, invite children to name the different fruits they have chosen.

Remember that many young children may not be enthusiastic about trying new foods, and some may have an aversion to specific types of food textures. Offer everyone the opportunity to participate and to touch and smell the different types of fruit. Do not require them to eat fruit if they do not want to.

ORIGINAL RECIPES

Ask each child to dictate a recipe to you that is made in his home. Write it down *exactly* as he tells you (mistakes and funny parts, too). Put the recipes together in a little booklet for parents. It will be a treasure to save and enjoy for years to come.

GREAT GRAPES

Give young children the opportunity to make choices and be creative by concocting their own snacks using only one harvest food—grapes! Set out an assortment of red, purple, and green grapes. Discuss the many grape products we eat or drink (jelly, juice, etc.). Suggest that children brainstorm new ways to prepare and eat grape snacks.

Here are a few suggestions for great grape snacks. A grape cookbook, with each recipe signed by the cook, would be a wonderful follow-up activity. Sugar-free and reduced-sugar recipes are designated by the smiley face symbol.

Frozen grapes. Place washed grapes on a cookie sheet with spaces between each one. Cut them in half to avoid choking. Freeze. When frozen, place in a plastic bag. Eat frozen.

Grapes to raisins. Wash and dry a large bunch of green grapes. Place in a basket in a warm sunny spot for four to seven days. You will then have raisins!

Grape fruit cocktail. Slice grapes in half with plastic knives. Add sliced grapes to a can of fruit cocktail. Add fresh fruit chunks as desired.

Grape surprises
A. Ingredients:
   ½ cup peanut butter
   ½ cup nonfat dry milk powder
   2 tablespoons honey
   grapes
B. Procedure:
   1. Mix peanut butter, milk powder, and honey until a soft, non-sticky "dough" is formed.
   2. Knead dough, then press out pieces into 2-inch circles.
   3. Place a grape in the center. Wrap dough around grape and seal well.
   4. Variation: Place grapes inside cream cheese balls, then roll in chopped nuts.

Grapes and yogurt
A. Ingredients:
   small bunch of grapes
   1 cup yogurt or sour cream
B. Procedure: Slice grapes with plastic knife and add to yogurt (or sour cream).

RECIPES FOR COOKING EXPERIENCES

Soft pretzels
A. Ingredients:
   1½ cups warm water
   3 cups flour
   1 pkg. yeast
   1 tablespoon sugar
   1 teaspoon salt
   1 tablespoon vegetable oil
B. Procedure:
   1. Mix together all the ingredients.
   2. Add small amounts of flour until mixture does not stick to your hand.
   3. Roll out 12 small balls of dough to make snakes or worms.
   4. Loop ends together to make a pretzel knot.

5. Coat with a mixture of one egg yolk and two tablespoons of water.
6. Sprinkle a few pieces of salt on each pretzel.
7. Place on a slightly greased cookie sheet.
8. Bake at 425°F for 10–12 minutes.

Applesauce. Picture recipe in Figure 21–8.
A. Ingredients:
   4 to 6 medium apples
   ¼ cup sugar
   ½ stick cinnamon (or 1–2 whole cloves, if desired)
B. Procedure (if food mill is not used):
   1. Peel and core the apples.
   2. Cut apples into quarters, and place in pot.
   3. Add a small amount of water (about 1 inch).
   4. Cover the pot and cook slowly (simmer), until apples are tender. The cooked apples can then be mashed with a fork, beaten with a beater, or put through a strainer.
   5. Add sugar to taste (about ½ cup to 4 apples), and continue cooking until sugar dissolves.
   6. Add ½ stick of cinnamon (or 1 to 2 cloves) if desired.
      Note: If a food mill is used, it is not necessary to peel and core the apples. After the apples are cooked, they are put through the food mill. Children enjoy turning the handle and watching the sauce come dripping out of the holes.
Variation:
   7. For fun, add a few cinnamon candies. What happens to the color of the applesauce? Is the flavor changed? Be sure to add them while the applesauce is still hot.

Banana apple icy. Picture recipe in Figure 21–9.
A. Ingredients:
   1 apple
   1 banana
   ¼ cup milk
   1 cup plain yogurt
   3 ice cubes
B. Procedure:
   1. Peel and core 1 yellow apple.
   2. Cut it into small cubes.
   3. Peel and slice 1 banana.
   4. Put these in a blender with the milk and yogurt.
   5. Add 3 ice cubes.
   6. Blend until smooth.
   7. Makes enough for 2 small glasses.

Apple sandwich. Picture recipe in Figure 21–10.
A. Ingredients:
   1 apple
   peanut butter

B. Procedure:
   1. Peel and core an apple.
   2. Cut it crosswise into slices.
   3. Spread peanut butter on one apple slice and top with another apple slice.

Fruit soup
A. Ingredients:
   honeydew and/or cantaloupe melon
   1 banana
   1 plum
   kiwifruit
   grapes and other fruits
   1 cup of orange juice
   1 scoop of frozen yogurt.
B. Procedure:
   1. Scoop balls from melons with a melon baller. (Kids love doing this.) Use a honeydew melon or cantaloupe or some of each.
   2. Cut up banana with a butter knife.
   3. Add the orange juice for the base of the soup and put in a blender.
   4. Add banana pieces and whirl on high for 30 seconds.
   5. Pour soup into 3 or 4 bowls—or into 8–10 small cups.
   6. Add cut-up fruit to each and then top it off with a scoop of frozen yogurt.

Beautiful bagels
Use bagels as your "easel." Take ½ of a bagel, and let the child spread it with cream cheese. Have available a variety of sliced vegetables such as carrots, cucumbers, bean sprouts, cherry tomatoes, green or red bell peppers, and black olives. Children can decorate their snack to their own "taste" both artistically and health-wise.

Stuffed baked apples
A. Ingredients:
   4 tart apples
   ¼ cup crunchy breakfast cereal
   ¼ cup chopped walnuts
   ¼ teaspoon cinnamon
   1 cup raisins
   2 tablespoons honey
B. Procedure:
   1. Core apples.
   2. Combine ingredients and spoon equal amounts into each apple cavity.
   3. Place apples in shallow baking dish and add ¼ cup of water.
   4. Bake uncovered for 40 minutes at 300°F.

Banana breakfast split

A. Ingredients:

1 banana, sliced lengthwise

½ cup cottage cheese

1 tablespoon wheat germ

1 tablespoon raisins

1 tablespoon chopped nuts

B. Procedure:

1. Place banana slices in a bowl.
2. Put scoops of cottage cheese on top.
3. Sprinkle with wheat germ, raisins, and nuts. Makes one serving.

Pear bunnies

A. Ingredients:

ripe pear, cut in half lengthwise

1 lettuce leaf

1 teaspoon cottage cheese

1 red cherry

raisins

almond slivers

B. Procedure:

Place pear half on lettuce half, rounded side up. Decorate, using cottage cheese for "cottontail," cherry for nose, raisins for eyes, and almond slivers for ears.

Fruit leather.

This recipe reinforces the concept that fruits like apricots, peaches, raspberries, apples, etc., can be changed and used in new ways.

A. Ingredients:

1 quart or 2 pounds of fresh fruit

sugar

cinnamon

plastic wrapping paper

B. Procedure:

1. Help children break open, peel, and seed or pit fruit.
2. Puree prepared fruit in blender until smooth.
3. Add 2 tablespoons sugar and ½ teaspoon cinnamon to each 2 cups of puree.
4. Pour mixture onto sheet of plastic wrap that has been placed on a large cookie sheet. Spread mixture thinly and evenly.
5. Cover mixture with a screen or a piece of cheesecloth and place in the sun until completely dry—about one or two days. It can then be eaten or rolled and stored.

Peanutty pudding

A. Ingredients:

1 package regular pudding

2 cups milk

peanut butter

B. Procedure:

1. Prepare pudding as directed on package. (You may choose to use the sugar-free type.)
2. Pour cooked pudding into individual bowls.
3. While still warm, stir in 1 tablespoon peanut butter to each bowl.

Fruit Kabobs

A. Ingredients:

1 cup vanilla or lemon yogurt (low fat, low-sugar variety)

2 cups fresh or canned fruit (chunk-style)

pretzel sticks

B. Procedure:

1. Thread fruit chunks onto pretzel sticks. Talk about how colors and sizes look next to each other.
2. Dip each end piece into the yogurt before eating, or spoon yogurt over the entire kabob.

Strawberry yogurt shake

A. Ingredients:

½ cup frozen unsweetened strawberries, thawed

2 tablespoons frozen orange juice concentrate, thawed

½ cup banana (optional)

1 cup vanilla or lemon yogurt

B. Procedure:

1. Puree strawberries in blender.
2. Add remaining ingredients to blender and mix until frothy.
3. For holidays or special occasions, stick straws through colorful paper shapes and serve with shakes. Makes two servings, ¾ cup each.

Peanut butter banana smoothie

A. Ingredients:

1 cup vanilla yogurt

1 to 2 tablespoons peanut butter

1 banana

B. Procedure:

1. Combine all ingredients in blender.
2. Whip for 30 to 60 seconds or until smooth.
3. Serve in custard cup or small bowl to eat with a spoon, or pour into cups to drink.

Broccoli trees and snow

A. Ingredients:

¾ cup small curd cottage cheese

½ cup plain yogurt

¼ cup fresh minced parsley

1 bunch broccoli

B. Procedure:

1. Mix cottage cheese and yogurt in blender until smooth.

2. Add parsley and refrigerate until cool.
3. Cut broccoli into "dippers." (Cucumbers, zucchini, celery, carrots, radishes, and green peppers make good "dippers," too.)
4. Dip vegetables into yogurt mix and enjoy.

Fruit sun

A. Ingredients:
grapefruit, sections
muskmelon, balls
cherries
raisins

B. Procedure:
1. Arrange grapefruit sections in a ring around muskmelon balls.
2. Cherries and raisins may be used to make a face.
3. Amounts depend on the number to be served; ½-cup servings are appropriate.

Pigs in a blanket

A. Ingredients:
frankfurters
bread slices
American cheese
butter
mustard

B. Procedure:
1. Spread butter on bread.
2. Place bread slices on ungreased baking sheet and top each with a slice of cheese.
3. Place frankfurters diagonally on cheese.
4. Fold bread over to form triangle. Brush with butter.
5. Set broiler at 550°F.
6. Broil about 2 minutes.

Meatballs

A. Ingredients:
1 pound hamburger
1 cup bread crumbs
1 or 2 eggs
¾ teaspoon salt
⅛ teaspoon pepper
¼ cup milk

B. Procedure:
1. Mix ingredients well.
2. Shape into small balls.
3. Brown until cooked through in electric skillet.

Carrot and raisin salad

A. Ingredients:
3 cups shredded carrots (teacher to prepare)
¾ cup raisins

juice of one lemon
3 tablespoons sugar
dash of salt

B. Procedure:
1. Mix ingredients thoroughly.
2. Serve immediately.

Banana bake

A. Ingredients:
1 banana, peeled
butter, melted

B. Procedure:
1. Place peeled banana in shallow baking dish and brush with melted butter.
2. Bake in moderate oven (375°F) for 10–15 minutes (until tender).
3. Serve hot as a vegetable.
4. Yield: 1 serving.

French toast

A. Ingredients:
8 slices bread
4 eggs
¼ tablespoon salt
2 cups milk

B. Procedure:
1. Beat eggs slightly. Add salt and milk.
2. Dip slices of bread in egg mixture and fry in electric skillet.
3. Serve hot with jelly, honey, or syrup.

Carob-nut snack

A. Ingredients:
1 cup dry-roasted unsalted peanuts
1 cup unsweetened carob chips
1 cup unsweetened dried banana chips
1 cup unsweetened cereal

B. Procedure:
Children can take turns shaking ingredients in a plastic container with lid to mix. Serve in small cups, or carry in plastic bags on field trips. Can be stored in container for several weeks.

No-bake brownies

A. Ingredients:
1 cup fresh peanut butter (no sugar added)
1 cup nonfat dry milk
¼ cup soy protein powder (plain, no dextrose or other sugar substitutes)
1 teaspoon vanilla
2 tablespoons carob powder (or cocoa if you don't mind the caffeine)
½ cup fructose
¾ cup water

½ cup raisins (optional)

coconut or chopped nuts (optional)

B. Procedure:

1. Mix peanut butter, dry milk, carob (or cocoa), fructose, and vanilla with mixer or pastry blender.
2. Add water, a little at a time, mixing after each addition. At first it may seem too wet, but the water will be absorbed.
3. Add raisins. Add more water if needed.
4. Press mixture into 8″ × 8″ pan sprayed with nonstick coating.
5. Sprinkle coconut or chopped nuts on top.
6. Cut into squares. Refrigerate unused portion.

Chow mein crunchies

A. Ingredients:

1 package chocolate chips (or 1 package butter-scotch chips)

1 can chow mein noodles

1 cup salted peanuts

B. Procedure:

1. Melt chocolate chips in a double boiler or in a saucepan over very low heat.
2. Add chow mein noodles and salted peanuts.
3. Stir until the noodles are coated with chocolate mixture.
4. Drop by spoonfuls on waxed paper.
5. Place in refrigerator until cool.

Cottage cheese cookies

A. Ingredients:

¼ cup butter

½ cup sugar

½ cup cottage cheese

1 teaspoon vanilla

1 cup flour

½ teaspoon salt

1 teaspoon baking powder

B. Materials: fork, cookie sheet

C. Procedure:

1. Mix butter and sugar.
2. Add cottage cheese and vanilla.
3. Add flour, salt, and baking powder.
4. Stir. Smooth into balls.
5. Put on greased cookie sheet. Flatten with fork. Bake at 375°F for 10–15 minutes.

Peanut butter balls

A. Ingredients:

½ cup fresh peanut butter

1 tablespoon jelly

½ cup dry milk powder

1 cup bran or corn flakes

⅓ cup bran or corn flakes (crushed)

B. Procedure:

1. Mix the peanut butter and jelly in bowl.
2. Stir in milk powder and 1 cup bran or corn flakes. Mix well.
3. With your hands, roll the mix into small balls. Roll the balls in the crushed flakes.

Peanut butter apple rolls

A. Ingredients:

1 8-ounce can refrigerated crescent rolls

2 tablespoons fresh peanut butter

1 apple, peeled and finely chopped

B. Procedure:

1. Separate dough into 8 triangles.
2. Spread a thick layer of peanut butter on each triangle.
3. Top with 1 tablespoon of apple.
4. Start at the shortest side of each triangle and roll to other side. Place on cookie sheet.
5. Bake at 350°F for 10–15 minutes.

Peanut grahams

A. Ingredients:

graham crackers

fresh peanut butter

one or more of the following toppings—nuts, sunflower seeds, raisins, chocolate chips, sliced bananas, sliced apples

B. Procedure:

1. Break each graham cracker in half.
2. Spread some peanut butter on one half.
3. Place your favorite topping on the peanut butter.
4. Spread some peanut butter on the other graham cracker half.
5. Press the two halves together to make a sandwich.

Peanut logs

A. Ingredients:

1 cup creamy peanut butter

1 cup honey

1 cup instant nonfat dry milk

1 cup raisins

1 cup graham cracker crumbs

B. Procedure:

1. Blend peanut butter, honey, and dry milk.
2. Add raisins and mix well.
3. Stir in graham cracker crumbs.
4. Roll teaspoonfuls of mixture on waxed paper to shape into logs.
5. Refrigerate one hour. Makes about 50.

Nutty swiss cheese spread

A. Ingredients:

2 cups Swiss cheese, shredded

½ cup fresh peanut butter
½ cup sour cream
¼ cup raisins
B. Procedure:
1. Mix all ingredients well.
2. Use spread on bread or crackers.

Graham cracker bananas

A. Ingredients:
4 bananas
¼ cup evaporated milk
½ cup graham cracker crumbs
¼ cup butter or margarine, melted
B. Procedure:
1. Peel bananas and cut in half lengthwise.
2. Roll bananas in milk, then roll in graham cracker crumbs.
3. Place in greased baking dish. Pour melted butter over top.
4. Bake at 450°F for 10 minutes.

Broiled bananas

1 banana (unpeeled)
1 tablespoon plain lowfat yogurt
Make a small slit in the banana skin. Place un-skinned banana slit-side up on a piece of aluminum foil. Broil for 5–10 minutes, until softened. Open skin to expose banana. Serve with a dollop of yogurt. Most children like bananas, so this recipe should be a hit. In this recipe, the banana is eaten with a spoon and the skin becomes the dish.

Frozen banana coins

An excellent use for a very ripe banana. Peel bananas. Freeze bananas on a tray. Place frozen banana in a freezer bag or freezer container. Return to freezer until ready to use. To serve, remove banana from freezer and slice into ¼″ pieces. Serve immediately, or pieces will become soggy. Yield: ½ banana per serving.

Frozen banana pop

Cut banana in half horizontally. Carefully push one popsicle stick into each banana half. Freeze. Serve directly from freezer.

Popcorn mix. For children older than three years of age.

A. Ingredients:
2 cups plain popped popcorn
¼ cup quartered dried apricots
¼ cup raisins
¼ cup peanuts
Mix all ingredients together. Store in a tightly covered container. Yield: 2¾ cups.

Rice pudding

A. Ingredients:
4 tablespoons uncooked rice
4 cups milk
1 tablespoon butter
3 tablespoons sugar (optional)
½ teaspoon vanilla extract
nutmeg
B. Procedure:
1. Combine all ingredients except nutmeg in buttered casserole.
2. Sprinkle nutmeg on top.
3. Bake at 300°F for 1½ hours.

Baked popcorn treat

A. Ingredients:
½ cup butter
½ cup brown sugar
3 quarts popped corn
1 cup peanuts
B. Procedure:
1. Mix butter and sugar until fluffy.
2. Combine corn and peanuts. Stir into butter-sugar mixture.
3. Place in baking dish and bake at 350°F for 8 minutes. Pour into bowl and serve.

Crunchy fruit munch

A. Ingredients:
3 quarts popped popcorn
2 cups natural cereal with raisins
¾ cup dried apricots, chopped
¼ teaspoon salt
⅓ cup butter or margarine
¼ cup honey
B. Procedure:
1. Preheat oven to 300°F. Combine first four ingredients in large baking pan; set aside.
2. In small saucepan, combine butter or margarine and honey. Cook over low heat until butter or margarine is melted.
3. Pour over popcorn mixture, tossing lightly until well coated.
4. Place in oven. Bake 30 minutes, stirring occasionally. Makes 3 quarts.
5. Store in tightly covered container up to 2 weeks.

Popcorn with peanut butter

A. Ingredients:
2 quarts popped popcorn
1 tablespoon fresh peanut butter (creamy or chunky)
2 tablespoons butter or margarine

B. Procedure:
1. In small saucepan, melt butter or margarine and peanut butter until smooth.
2. Pour over popped corn and mix well.

Popcorn cheese snacks

A. Ingredients
2 quarts popped popcorn
½ cup butter or margarine
½ cup grated American or Parmesan cheese— or both
½ teaspoon salt
B. Procedure:
1. Spread freshly popped popcorn in a flat pan; keep hot and crisp in oven.
2. Melt butter and grated cheese and add salt.
3. Pour mixture over popcorn. Stir until every kernel is cheese flavored.

Turtle pancakes

A. Ingredients:
pancake or biscuit mix
⅓ cup nonfat dry milk
2 cups milk
B. Procedure:
1. Follow package directions. (For extra nutrition, add ⅓ cup nonfat milk to the standard recipe calling for 2 cups milk.)
2. The batter should be in a bowl rather than in a pitcher; the child puts the batter on the griddle by spoonfuls, sometimes deliberately dribbling for effect.
3. A turtle is made by adding four tiny pancakes (the legs) around the perimeter of one round pancake about 3 inches in diameter.

Homemade peanut butter. Bring to school a large bag of peanuts in the shell. Let the children help you shell the peanuts. Put a cupful of peanuts into a blender. Add 1 tablespoon of peanut oil to blend the peanuts to the consistency children like.

Homemade jelly: a quick version. Defrost a 12–ounce can of frozen grape juice concentrate. Dissolve a package of unflavored gelatin into the juice. Pour this mixture into a pan and bring to a boil, stirring to dissolve the gelatin. Remove from heat and allow to cool. Pour the mixture into a wide-mouthed jar and refrigerate.

Homemade quick whole-wheat bread. Soften 3 tablespoons dry active yeast in 3½ to 4½ cups warm water and milk (half-milk, half-water) in a large bowl. Add 2 tablespoons honey, 2 teaspoons salt, ½ cup nutri-

tional yeast (available at health food stores), and 8 cups of whole wheat flour.

Blend well. Dough should be slippery and glutenous yet stiff enough to cling to the spoon. It shouldn't flatten out and there should be no liquid showing in the bowl. Add more (or less) flour to achieve this texture.

Fill oiled bread pans ⅔ full. Let dough rise 15 minutes (while you are cleaning up) at 85 to 90°F, until it increases in height by 25%.

Bake at 400°F for 15 minutes. Turn down oven to 350°F and continue baking for 20 minutes more—or until it is golden brown.

Fruit smoothies. You'll need ½ cup plain yogurt, ½ cup orange juice, ¾ cup fresh fruit (strawberries, blueberries, raspberries, bananas or a combination), 1 tablespoon honey, and ½ cup ice.

Place all ingredients in a blender. Blend for about 2 minutes or until mixture is smooth. Pour into cups and enjoy. Serves 2.

CALCIUM-RICH RECIPES

Did you know that three out of four Americans don't get the calcium they need? Remind the children to eat 3-a-day . . . three servings of calcium-rich milk, cheese, or yogurt every day. To make it easier, here are some calcium-rich recipes for young children.

Polka dot milk. Fill circular ice trays with chocolate and strawberry-flavored milk. Drop the festive frozen milk cubes into a glass of plain milk for fun, tasty "polka dots."

Lunch in a crunch. Mix the child's favorite cereal with yogurt for a creamy and crunchy lunch.

'Nilla banana ice. Create a smooth, delicious drink by blending together 1 cup of low-fat milk, banana slices, ice, and a few drops of vanilla.

Cool cuts. Cookie cutters aren't just for cookies. Use them to cut out fun shapes from cheese slices or grilled cheese sandwiches to liven up lunches.

Festive fruity flavored milk. Mix 1 cup fat-free, skim, or 1% low-fat milk and 2 tablespoons apricot, blackberry, raspberry or strawberry fruit syrup. For each cup of milk, stir in 2 tablespoons fruit syrup. Try experimenting with different flavors of fruit syrups until you find one that provides the perfectly pleasing color to your milk. Fruit syrups are available in natural and artificially flavored varieties and are usually found in the section with pancake mixes.

Finger lickin' good yogurt. Give kids a yogurt "palette." With a plate and two to three "colors" (flavors) of yogurt—try blueberry, strawberry, and banana—kids can paint on a graham cracker canvas and eat their great-tasting masterpiece.

Perfect cheese picks. Pair cheese with other healthy foods that will satisfy even the pickiest eaters. Wrap a slice of turkey around mild Mozzarella string cheese or slices of tangy Cheddar around apple wedges.

ONE-STEP COOKBOOK

These are one-process recipes. They require some preparation but the actual recipe uses one method that demonstrates what happens when food is prepared in that manner.

Carrot curls. For this activity, you will need carrots, a vegetable peeler, and ice water. Show the children how to use a vegetable peeler safely. When peeling carrots, the peeler should be pushed down and away from the body, rather than towards the body or face.

Help children peel off the outside skin of the carrot, then make additional carrot peels. Place peels in ice water in the refrigerator until they curl. Use the carrot curls for a snack.

Apples with cheese. Halve and core apples. Fill hollowed center with smooth cheese spread. Chill for 2 to 3 hours before serving.

Yogurt and cereal parfait. In a tall glass, layer lemon, vanilla, or fruit-flavored yogurt with a favorite breakfast cereal.

Banana breakfast bites. Peel bananas and cut into bite-sized pieces. Dip each piece in yogurt, then drop into a plastic bag filled with wheat germ. Shake to coat. Serve as finger food.

Fruit cubes. Make frozen cubes with fruit juice, placing a small piece of fruit in each cube before it freezes. Add a popsicle stick to each cube to make individual fruit treats on a stick.

Banana on ice. This is a tasty, low-calorie treat—only about 85 calories per banana. Simply peel a banana and wrap it in plastic wrap. Place it in the freezer for several hours or until hard. (Don't leave it in the freezer too long.) Eat frozen. It tastes exactly like banana ice cream.

Smiling sandwich. Spread peanut butter on a rice or corn cake. Use two raisins for eyes and a banana or apple slice for a smiling mouth.

Ants on a log. Fill celery sticks with peanut butter, cream cheese, or pimento cheese. Use raisins or nuts as the "ants."

Apple bake. Place a cored apple in a dish with a small amount of water. Cover with foil (for oven) or cover loosely with plastic wrap (for microwave) and bake at 350°F for 20 minutes (oven) or on HIGH for 5 minutes (microwave). Add a sprinkle of cinnamon if desired.

Juice freeze. Fill a 6-ounce paper cup with sugar-free fruit juice, cover with plastic wrap, and push a plastic spoon through center of wrap. Freeze. Tear away cup to eat.

Dried banana chunks. Slice bananas into ¾-inch thick slices. If desired, roll in chopped nuts. Place on baking sheet in 150°F oven with oven door open about 2 inches. Dry until shriveled, or about 12 hours.

ACTIVITIES FOR OLDER CHILDREN (GRADES 4-5)

FRUIT SCIENCE

On a table, place three or four different varieties of apples. In front of each kind, place a label with the name of it. The children read the names and describe and compare the varieties. Give the children thin slices of the varieties to name, taste, and compare. Then, have them research facts about apples: uses and food value, growth and environment, etc. Make a special dessert or salad using the apples. The children taste, describe, and enjoy.

EGGS

Read *Green Eggs and Ham* by Dr. Seuss (1976). Have the class try to state the moral of the story as succinctly as possible. The moral might be stated: "You never know if you'll like a new food until you try it" or "Try it, you'll like it." Make your own green eggs and ham.

Discuss with your students purchasing environmentally sound egg cartons. Molded pulp cartons are generally made from 100% recycled paper. That makes these a better choice than polystyrene egg cartons. Polystyrene is not recycled, nor is it biodegradable.

Have students use their imaginations by drawing and coloring a picture of a food. Encourage students to color the picture so that the food looks interesting or fun to them. Students may wish to write a paragraph to go with their pictures.

FOOD FROM ANIMALS AND PLANTS

Have students draw or cut out pictures to make a farm scene of plants and animals we eat. Then ask them to add some plants and animals we do not eat.

Ask students to think about the grocery store. Are products from plants and animals sold together in one department or are they in separate departments? Students should distinguish produce departments from meat/deli and dairy departments. Aisles in the middle of the stores are often combinations of plant and animal products.

Polyvinyl chloride (PVC) is a huge contributor to environmental pollution. Supermarkets package their meat, fish, and poultry in polystyrene trays and then wrap them in PVC wrap. But the deli counter will cut meat and wrap it in freezer wrap or molded pulp trays, which are better. Have students offer suggestions for alternative ways to buy and package meat.

FOOD AND THE MEDIA

The last week of April is National Library Week. Challenge your students to read a book about foods or food groups.

Provide newspapers and magazines with food advertisements. Ask the students to cut out the ads and put them into food groups. Use food advertisements and have the students "stop and think." (See the rhyme in the next paragraph.) Evaluate foods by having students respond to a series of questions related to the food groups.

Make a poster or bulletin board with the "Eating Advice" rhyme—"Before eating, keep repeating, stop and think, will this help me grow?" Refer to this rhyme throughout any nutrition activities.

FOOD GROUPS

Ask students to generate a list of typical foods eaten at breakfast. Then write one breakfast menu. Count the number of servings from the bread, fruit, vegetable, meat, and milk groups. Knowing how many servings of each food group is recommended for a day, have the students subtract the breakfast servings to determine the food to eat the rest of the day.

After lunch, have students determine how many servings from each food group have been consumed. How many servings need to be consumed at supper in order to meet food requirements?

CHAPTER REVIEW

1. Name several ways in which food activities help children learn information.
2. Name several skills that develop from activities with foods.
3. Decide which of the following statements are true:
   a. Teachers should give detailed directions to children during food activities.
   b. Children should work at their own pace.
   c. Food activities must be very easy so that no child feels challenged.
   d. Food activities should be varied.
   e. Children should work with new kinds of foods—things they have never tasted before.
   f. The end product is all that counts in food activities.
   g. Foods used in food activities should be inexpensive, if possible.
   h. Children must be warned never to throw foods away.
   i. Food activities should always be done in a kitchen.
   j. Food activities can sometimes be done in groups.
4. Decide which of the following statements are true or false:
   a. Research shows that human infants must learn to prefer sweet over sour.
   b. The average American consumes about 104 pounds of sugar per year.
   c. To avoid cavities, it is essential to eliminate all fructose from the diet.
   d. To avoid cavities, children should brush within 50 minutes after eating.
   e. The best way to reduce obesity is to limit empty calories.

f. Empty calories are foods that are low in calories but high in protein.

g. Hidden sugars are found in things like catsup, hotdogs, pork and beans, and canned vegetables.

h. The most common form of sucrose is milk sugar or lactose.

i. Approximately 12 percent of a young child's caloric intake comes from snacks.

j. The major cause of childhood obesity is inherited genes.

REFERENCES

American Academy of Pediatrics (2001). News Release: AAP Warns Parents and Pediatricians that Fruit Juice is Not Always the Healthiest Choice. Online: http://www.aap.org/advocacy/archives/mayjuice.htm.

Ausubel, D. P. (1980). Enhancing the acquisition of knowledge. *National Society for the Study of Education Yearbook,* 1979 (Part 1), 227–250. Chicago: National Society for the Study of Education.

Axmaker, L. (2001/02). *Childhood obesity should be taken seriously.* Retrieved from Vanderbilt University, HEALTH Plus, Health and Wellness Web site. Online: http://vanderbiltowc.comdh.content.asp?10=8.

Blasi, M. J. (2003). A burger and fries: The increasing dilemma of childhood obesity. *Childhood Education,* Annual Theme Issue, 321–322.

Cooper, T. (2003, March). More fruits and veggies at lunchtime. *Scholastic Instructor,* News and Trends, p. 17.

de Paola, T. (1992). *Jamie O'Rourke and the big potato.* New York: Scholastic.

Ehlert, L. (1990). *Growing vegetable soup.* New York: Harcourt Brace.

Gortmaker, S. (2001). *Increased consumption of soda promotes childhood obesity.* Retrieved from Harvard School of Public Health Web site. Online: http://www.researchmatters.Harvard.edustory.php?article_ID=21.

McDonald, M. (1996). *The potato man.* Chicago: Children's Press.

McGovern, A. (1987). *Stone soup.* New York: Scholastic.

Moran, R. (1999). *Evaluation and treatment of childhood obesity.* American Academy of Family Physicians, February 15. Online: http://www.aafp.org/aft/990215ap/861.html.

Murate, T. (2002). *Video creativity.* Berkeley, CA: APress

Murphy, S. (2001). *Seaweed soup.* New York: HarperCollins.

Nelson, J. (1990). *Neighborhood soup.* New York: Modern Curriculum Books.

Rey, M. (1997). *Pretzel.* Boston: Houghton Mifflin.

Seuss, D. (1976). *Green eggs and ham.* New York: RandomHouse.

Torgan, C. (2002). *Childhood obesity on the rise.* Online: http://www.nih.gov/news/WordonHealth/jun2002/childhoodobesity.htm.

Vehling, J.D. (1977). *Apicius, cookery and dining in Imperial Rome.* New York: Dover Publishing.

ADDITIONAL READINGS

Cook, D. F. (2003). *Kids multicultural cookbook: Food and fun around the world,* Vol. 10. Charlotte, VT: Williamson Publishing.

Book, R. E., Tessier, A., & Klein, M. D. (2003). *Adapting early childhood curricula for children in inclusive settings.* Upper Saddle River, NJ: Prentice Hall.

Cunningham, M. (1995). *Cooking with children: Fifteen lessons for children, age 7 and up, who really want to learn to cook.* New York: Random House.

Hodgman, A. (1999). *One bite won't kill you: More than 200 recipes to tempt even the pickiest kids on earth: And the rest of the family, too.* Boston: Houghton Mifflin.

Kohl, M. F., & Potter, J. (2001). *Snackactivities: 50 edible activities for parents and young children.* Beltsville, MD: Gryphon House.

Lagasse, E. (2003). *Emeril's there's a chef in my soup! Recipes for the kid in everyone.* New York: HarperCollins.

Oliver, J. (2003). *Jamie's kitchen: A cooking course for everyone.* New York: Hyperion.

Rose, R. (1999). *Cooking for kids.* New York: Robert Rose, Inc.

Spears, J. A. (2003). Cooking with kids. *Texas Child Care* 24(2), 24–31.

Thompson, C. A. (2003). *Overcoming childhood obesity.* Boulder, CO: Bull Publishing.

Whittington, J. (2003). *50 ways to take the junk out of junk food: Quick and healthy treats to make with kids.* Guilford, CT: Globe Pequot Press.

SOFTWARE FOR CHILDREN

Arthur's Adventures with the Picky Eater Living Book, 2002. Ages 3–7.

Learning Center 1st Grade Jump Start 1st Grade, 2003.

My Disney Kitchen, 2003. Ages 3–6.

Ozzie's World, 2003. Ages 3–6.

Pajama Sam You Are What You Eat From Your Head to Your Feet, 2002. Ages 3–8.

Piglet's Big Game, 2003. Ages 3–6.

The Mammoth Food Dig, 2002.

HELPFUL WEB SITES

Nutrition and Environmental Resources, http://www.TeachFree.com

Current nutrition and environmental education for K through grade 12 includes teaching kits, student masters for classroom instruction, and more than a dozen hot links. Sponsored by the National Cattlemen's Beef Association.

Fast Food Facts, http://www.olen.com/food

This Web site allows users to search the nutritional analysis of favorite fast foods.

Nutrition and Weight Management, http://www.caloriecontrol.org

Calorie Control Council's Web site provides timely information on low-calorie and reduced-fat foods and beverages, weight management, physical activity, and healthy eating including recipes.

Shape Up America, http://www.shapeup.com

This organization has a new support center on the Internet to assist consumers in individualized weight management. Developed in consultation with experts in behavior modification, nutrition, and physical activity, the center provides weight control help on a 24–hour basis.

U.S. Dept. of Agriculture, http://www.usda.gov/

U.S.D.A. has developed a Food Guide Pyramid for young children. This pyramid provides educational messages that focus on children's food preferences and nutrition requirements. The key point of the pyramid is to eat a variety of foods. An accompanying booklet, "Tips for Using the Food Guide Pyramid for Young Children 2–6 Years Old," is available for teachers and parents at their Web site.

National Dairy Council, http://www.dairyinfo.com

Food and Nutrition Information Education Resources Center, http://www.nalusda.gov/

Click on Services/Programs.

For additional creative activity resources, visit our Web site at http://www.EarlyChildEd.delmar.com.

Chapter 22

Creative Social Studies

Objectives

After studying this chapter, you should be able to:

1. Describe some of the first things a young child learns about himself or herself in a social sense.

2. Discuss how to use appropriate activities involving a child's name, voice, and personal appearance.

3. Discuss the importance of teaching about peace in the early childhood program.

4. Discuss personal celebrations.

5. Discuss ways to include information on community workers in social studies learning experiences.

6. Describe some points to remember in planning field trips for young children.

As we begin this chapter on social studies, consider these two examples of young children in social situations.

SITUATION 1

Kim is waiting at home for her son Billy, who is playing next door. When he arrives 20 minutes later than scheduled, she asks what happened. "Well, Mom," he begins in a grown-up fashion, "Claire's doll broke and I wanted to help her."

"I didn't know you knew how to fix dolls" is his mother's somewhat surprised reaction.

"Oh no, Mom. I <u>don't</u> know how. I just stayed to help her cry."

SITUATION 2

Greg and Marc are building together with blocks. Marc gets angry because Greg takes a block from him. They fight. The teacher intervenes and talks with Marc about using words instead of fists. She tells him to try talking to Greg instead of hitting him—to tell Greg what was making him angry. Finally, believing she has made her point, she asks Marc, "Now, what would you like to do?" Marc answers without hesitation, "Hit him!" And he does!

These incidents, while a bit amusing to the adults involved, both demonstrate the funny, unpredictable nature of young children in social settings. They also illustrate clearly the fact that learning to be part of a social group is not something that is natural or inborn in human beings. Young children, like those mentioned, often react in a socially unpredictable way by their very spontaneous reactions to life. Yet, young children can be very sensitive to the feelings of others, even though they are direct and uninhibited in many situations. The fact is that learning about oneself, about others, and how to act with others is a long process.

Social studies is the study of human beings in their environment and of the concepts, skills, and attitudes that are needed in order to become social beings. Both the content and the processes of social studies can be integrated into activities in which even very young children can participate. As boys and girls reenact the roles of adults known to them, as they build houses, farms, airports, stores, and parks that they have seen, or dramatize past experiences that have special meaning for them, they learn the content of social studies. As children become aware of community services such as fire and police protection or library and post office facilities, they incorporate them into their play.

Social studies are an important part of a child's education; they help the child understand the complex world in which he or she lives and enable him or her to be productive and happy within society's framework. Socially, children in the early childhood years are just coming into touch with their own feelings. Some children are so young they are just learning the names for these feelings and barely beginning to understand their meanings. Others are dealing with emotional changes as they make the transition from preschool to elementary school. Still others are moving from early to middle childhood and experiencing the many emotional adjustments this entails. Guiding young children in their developing understanding of their own and others' emotions is a highly sensitive, challenging part of the teacher's job. Adults are most instrumental in helping young children deal with their feelings and those of others. To do this, adults must be able to deal with their own feelings, too.

Consider your own emotions for a moment and your own early childhood experiences. Think about all the changes you've come through to get you to the point you are now in your life. Change is inevitable in both your life and the lives of young children.

How do *you* feel about change? Do you look forward to the future, or do you hold onto the past? Do you accept or fight change? Does your view of the life cycle include both an appreciation for what has been and excitement about what might be?

Your personal approach to change has a direct effect on your relationship with young children. If you are

1. Culture
2. Time, Continuity, and Change
3. People, Places, and Environments
4. Individual Development and Identity
5. Individuals, Groups, and Institutions
6. Power, Authority, and Governance
7. Production, Distribution, and Consumption
8. Science, Technology, and Society
9. Global Connections
10. Civic Ideals and Practices

Figure 22-1

The ten thematic strands of social studies.

open to change yourself, you won't shy away from their concerns about growth and development or their questions about death and aging. Your attitude toward change is conveyed in a healthy acceptance of your own life and all the changes, emotions, and challenges it brings. With this approach, teaching young children social studies concepts will be a joy for you and the children.

National Council for the Social Studies–National Standards

A fresh era of thought about teaching social studies began in 1994 when the National Council for the Social Studies (NCSS) identified **ten thematic strands of social studies** in which all children (K–12) should have learning experiences. These ten themes were developed from a definition that described the social studies as "the integrated study of the social studies and humanities to promote civic competence" (NCSS, 1994, p. 3).

The themes point to a fundamental knowledge drawn from many subjects and most heavily from these social sciences: anthropology, archaeology, economics, geography, history, law, philosophy, political science, psychology, religion, and sociology. The first seven thematic strands are social science discipline oriented and the remaining three are meant to be multidisciplinary.

Each of the themes derives meaning from one or more of these subjects. The ten strands are listed in Figure 22–1. The ten themes are meant to serve as a framework for social studies curriculum planning. This chapter will discuss several of these themes as they relate to our discussion of the social studies curriculum. The reader is referred to the reading list in the Online Companion for resources with more detailed, in-depth coverage of these ten social studies thematic strands and their application in the curriculum.

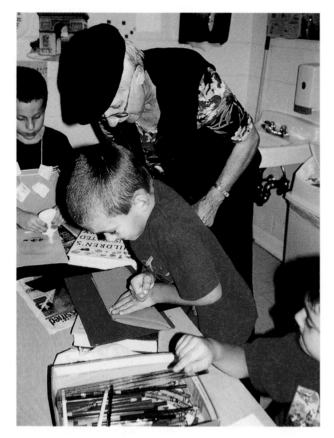

Figure 22-2

Young children learn how to function as a member of a group in the early childhood program.

Let us now look at general social characteristics of children at various age levels in the early childhood program.

Social Characteristics

While it is impossible to predict with any certainty the developmental pattern of any individual, there are general characteristics common to age groups. It is helpful to have some general idea of what type of social characteristics to expect at various age levels. The following is a summary of age-level social characteristics.

Preschool and Kindergarten. Socially at this age level, friendships are usually limited to one or two "best" friends, but these may change frequently. Play groups are not too well organized and tend to change often. Although quarrels are frequent, they tend to be of short duration. There is great pleasure in dramatic play and beginning awareness of sex roles.

Emotional development is at a volatile stage—emotions are expressed freely and outbursts of anger are common. A vivid imagination frequently leads to grossly exaggerated fears. Competition for adult affection breeds jealousy. Mentally, students are developing rapidly in the acquisition of language. They enjoy talking to each other and in front of groups. Imagination and fantasy are at their peak.

Primary grades (6-9 years). Although friendship patterns are still likely to be characterized by "best friends," greater selectivity is now evident in the choice of friends. Games are more organized, but there is great emphasis on "rules." Quarrels are still frequent as are physical aggression, competition, and boasting. Although the difference in interests of boys and girls becomes more pronounced at this age, there is great variation in behavior from one classroom to another because of influences exerted by teachers.

Emotionally, children become very sensitive during this period. Criticism, ridicule, and failure can be devastating. Despite their own sensitivity, they are quick to hurt others. Generally, students are eager to please the teacher and want to do well in school, for which reasons they require frequent praise.

Eagerness to learn is common to this age group. Learning occurs primarily through concrete manipulation of materials. Eagerness to talk is still evident and there is much experimentation with language—including obscene language. Concepts of reciprocity, fairness, and right and wrong develop during this period.

Elementary grades (9-12 years). Peer groups begin to replace adults as sources of behavior standards and the recognition of achievement. Interests become more sharply different between the sexes—frequently resulting in "battles" between them for recognition and achievement, as well as the exchange of insults. Team games become more popular, along with class spirit. Crushes and hero worship are common.

This is the period when the conflict between adults and the group code begins to emerge. Instead of a rigid following of rules, youngsters at this age begin to understand the need for exceptions. Frequently they set very high standards for themselves—sometimes unreal standards—hence feelings of frustration are common. While the desire for independence grows, the need for adult support is still strong—therefore unpredictable behavior often results. Children at this age can behave in a very "grown-up" way one minute and revert to more "childish" behavior the next. Curiosity still remains strong at this age. Children frequently become "collectors" during this age.

With these social developmental characteristics in mind, let us now look at how the early childhood program can include both developmental levels and the social studies themes/standards.

LEARNING ABOUT ONE'S WORLD

A child's universe begins with himself or herself, extends to his or her family, and then to the larger community. The development of a child's self-concept, awareness of self, is the important beginning point in social studies for young children.

To know oneself in a social sense involves learning such things as one's name, one's ethnic background, one's family grouping, and occupations in one's family. In the early childhood years learning about oneself is at a basic level—that is, young children are learning about how their lives fit into the larger social group.

Children learn about where they live—in a house, an apartment, or a condominium—and how it is like and unlike the residences of their peers. They learn the similarities and differences among families in form, style of living, and values.

Those who work with young children from preschool through the early and later elementary years can help them discover and appreciate their own uniqueness by beginning with a positive acceptance of each child.

In the early childhood years, young children need opportunities to *live* important experiences, to learn in an *active* way.

The following sections contain suggestions for including the thematic strands of social studies in the curriculum.

INDIVIDUAL DEVELOPMENT AND IDENTITY (THEMATIC STRAND #4)

Self-Awareness—How Do I Look?

A positive awareness and acceptance of one's own appearance is part of the social aspect of learning "Who am I?" In the room, for example, a full-length mirror in a safe, but clearly visible, place at child-level is one way for children to see themselves and each other. Some children have few opportunities to see their reflections because mirrors in their homes are too high. Providing an unbreakable hand mirror in the room is another way to encourage children to see themselves. Magnifying makeup mirrors also produce interesting reactions from the children when they see their enlarged images.

The following suggested activities are designed to develop a young child's awareness and appreciation of the uniqueness of his or her physical appearance.

- ⊙ Use an unbreakable mirror to bring out the idea that we are more alike than different. Discuss color, size, and shape of eyes, hair, nose, mouth, ears, etc. Children may draw pictures of their faces. Pictures are cut out, mounted on a low board, and labeled.

- ⊙ Supply children with pictures of people with missing body parts. The children describe what part is missing.

- ⊙ Put flannelboard cutouts of a boy and girl on the flannelboard. The teacher deliberately places body parts in the wrong area, such as an arm in the leg's place. Have children be detectives to discover what is wrong and place parts in the right location.

- ⊙ Play the game "Policeman, Where Is My Child?" One child is the policeman, another the mother. Mother describes the physical appearance of her missing child (dress, hair, eyes). All the children become involved as they look at themselves to see if they're being described. The policeman tries to guess which child in the room belongs to the mother.

- ⊙ In the art center keep available an array of found materials for making dress-up accessories such as jewelry, hats, or masks.

- ⊙ Trace the shape of children's bodies as they lie down on large sheets of paper. Children can dress these life-sized figures with fabric, felt, yarn, buttons, beads, and any other found materials that interest them.

- ⊙ Offer finger paint or water-based ink for making handprints and footprints.

- ⊙ Provide plaster of Paris for making molds of hands.

- ⊙ Encourage older children to draw self-portraits.

- ⊙ Make shadow silhouettes of older children. In direct sunlight, have the child stand on a sheet of paper large enough to contain an outline of his shadow. Draw around his or her shadow on paper. Compare drawings of shadows made in the morning, at noon, and later in the day.

Additional activities are at the end of this chapter.

Learning Names

One of the first social learnings a young child has is to learn to recognize his or her own name. In the early childhood program, this recognition is further developed by teachers' and peers' recognition of this name. This basic learning is directly related to a child's individual identity.

Make it a point to concentrate on individual names of children. Avoid using names such as "honey," "sweetie," and "sugar." Instead use the child's first name, and alternately use the child's first and last name. This will further develop children's

Figure 22-3

Many young children in the early childhood program are dealing with emotional changes as they make the transition from preschool to elementary school.

self-knowledge as well as help them appreciate their own uniqueness. It also helps children learn each others' full names. The following strategies are suggested in your work with young children to help focus on the individual uniqueness of each child.

Strategies for Focusing on Each Child's Uniqueness

⊙ Write a child's name on his or her work in the upper left-hand corner to teach the left to right sequence. While writing the child's name, say it. This provides an auditory and visual model.

⊙ At transition times call the child by name to go to another activity or to tell the teacher which activity he wants to go to. "Johnny Jones, you may ride the tricycle today. Sally Smith, you may clean off the table."

⊙ Instruct the children to go tell another child something. "Jim, please tell Mary it is time to come inside." Here the child is not only hearing his name, he is beginning to be able to say the other child's name and a sentence as he follows the teacher's direction.

⊙ When the children are in a group for a story, the teacher can go around and say each child's name. This can then progress to letting the other children,

as a group, say the child's name as the teacher places his or her hand in front of the child.

⊙ Encourage children to draw, paint, or model themselves and their families in personally meaningful ways: Me and My Best Friend; I Am Playing with My Favorite Toy; I Am Helping at My House; My Family at Dinner Time; My Family Went to . . . ; My Wish. These renditions can be used for cooperative murals, booklets, and jigsaw puzzles.

⊙ Provide a variety of media and found materials in the art center for children to make puppets of themselves or their families. Additional activities are at the end of this chapter.

Concentrating on the child's voice, which is as individual as each child's name, is another good way to help develop young children's awareness of self identity. Here are some suggestions on how to *actively* involve young children in learning that they each have a unique voice.

⊙ Compile a tape of all the members of the class. Discuss how each person has a different voice tone. Children speak into the tape recorder, listen to the voices, and guess whose they are.

⊙ Record children telling their favorite stories *(Goldilocks and the Three Bears, Three Billy Goats Gruff, Little Red Riding Hood),* emphasizing voice inflections for the different characters.

⊙ Play the game "Who Am I?" One child is in the center of the circle and is "it." "It" tries to guess who says "Who Am I?" The speaker disguises his or her voice after the children have mastered the game with their natural voices.

⊙ Have the children feel objects of various textures. Another day, discuss voices using familiar comparisons. "Is your voice grating? High? Low? Soft? Hard? Scratching?" Have a box or chart of textured objects for the children to feel, such as steel wool, corrugated metal, silk, velvet, cotton puffs, wool, or a small mirror.

Additional activities are at the end of this chapter.

People, Places, and Environments: The Block Center

Learning about people, places, and environments is the third social studies theme in the national standards. The block center is an excellent place for learning about the community and neighborhood. Play models of various members of the family and people from various races, ethnic groups, industries, and professions, as well as small wheel toys with the blocks, all encourage true social play in the block center.

When children play together in the block corner, they learn to share, communicate, and resolve conflicts. Children see that cleanup is easier when they cooperate with one another. Building with blocks builds friendships, too, as children create structures together and role-play events from daily life or their imaginations. Dramatic play using blocks also helps young children work through important emotional issues. Because there is no right or wrong way to play, building with blocks helps boost a child's self-esteem. Knocking down block structures helps children feel powerful and in control.

Here are some ways to encourage block play for all children.

⊙ Locate the block and housekeeping areas side by side, so children can combine activities.

Figure 22-4

Being able to be independent and function as a member of a group is an important social goal.

⊙ Provide props and accessories that appeal to girls as well as boys. Include tools, transportation toys, and uniformed block figures as well as accessories, like scarves, fabric pieces, and carpet samples. Be sure to include bits of colored paper, pencils, crayons, and markers. Family block and animal figures are also appealing to both boys and girls. Be sure to include family block figures of various ethnic groups, and representations of children with special needs.

⊙ Intervene when you observe gender bias—if you hear Sam and Anthony telling Mary she can't play with them because they're building a firehouse and girls can't be firemen, let children know that in your room everyone can play with everything that's available. You might introduce the term "firefighter," instead of "fireman," or read books about adults having careers traditionally held by the opposite sex.

⊙ Decorate the block-corner walls. Hang pictures, photos, posters, and blueprints of buildings, bridges, towers, and roadways. If children enjoy drawing their own pictures of construction sites, hang those up, too. Include pictures of men, women, and children of all races doing a variety of jobs to let children know that blocks and construction are for everyone.

⊙ Include puppets, rocks, flashlights, pulleys, string, and other interesting extras.

⊙ Include toy vehicles of all varieties, such as cars, trucks, airplanes, helicopters, fire engines, ambulances, buses, taxis, boats, etc.

PEOPLE IN THE COMMUNITY (THEMATIC STRAND #2)

Because a child does not exist in isolation, he or she is dependent upon people in the community. Many people provide services for him or her—the police, the bus driver, and the baker, for example. As a child meets people in the community, he or she learns about the many roles people play and tests some of these roles in dramatic play. The child takes a tool kit and goes to fix the telephone. He or she becomes involved in relationships in which adults play varied roles and people depend upon each other. He or she passes a firehouse in the neighborhood and sees where the firefighters are stationed. The child goes to the garage with his or her mother and sees the mechanic fix their car. He or she goes to the post office with a family member and mails a letter to Grandmother. Children learn, through everyday experiences such as these, that others help them and they help others.

A good place to begin a discussion about understanding others in the child's world then is to learn about people in the child's most immediate environment. This includes the people who serve the school and community. There are many people in the child's immediate environment. It is important to emphasize the importance of all of these individuals. Each member helps to make the whole community where we live and go to school what it is; all jobs are important. The following activities are designed to help develop the idea of the importance of community workers.

Community workers

⊙ Find out when the garbage is collected at the school. Be there when the truck comes. Talk to the workers about their job, the service they perform, the truck and its operation and care, and possibly how citizens can help get the garbage ready for the collector. Don't overlook the fact that these helpers are also people with personal lives. Children can learn to understand that the men and women in our labor force also have spouses, children, hobbies, pets, and so on, just like the rest of us.

⊙ Follow the preceding procedure for postal workers, grocery store clerks, mechanics, painters, laundry workers, bus drivers, cooks in the cafeteria, and custodians.

⊙ Follow the preceding procedure for professional and semiprofessional workers—secretary, principal, nurse, music teacher, librarian, and others. Such activity should follow careful planning with the children as well as with the people you may visit. Preparing the adults beforehand for the kind of questions they can expect will give them a chance to organize their thinking. Discussing courteous and safe behavior with the children is also important. If the people you talk to can be persuaded to visit the classroom informally, the experience will be all the more effective.

⊙ Be a worker. Learn about the world of work by visiting workplaces in the neighborhood. Then children may enjoy acting out what they observed. Costumes for this can be simple, with only a hat, a mask, or an object to carry suggesting the characterization. Some children may want to bring an

Figure 22-5
With older children, the peer group becomes more important to the child socially.

Figure 22-6
Early friendships develop in the early childhood program.

Figure 22-7

Children grow in self-confidence as they learn new skills in the early childhood program.

Figure 22-8

Working together can be a social learning experience.

article of clothing to serve as a costume. Playing the role of adults may take the form of a parade, a guessing game, pantomime, or play. Such experiences help broaden the child's understanding of life in the local community.

Excursions into the community. Every school is located in a community. You can safely assume that every community has members who care about the well-being of its children and who possess talents, hobbies, and resources that can enrich children's learning experiences.

An excursion into the community may help young children gain new information and clarify other information and can enhance and extend children's experiences. After one trip around the block, a group of five-year-old children built a block barber shop and kept up their dramatic play as barbers for several days. Even the teacher sat in a chair as the children pretended to cut hair using their fingers as scissors.

Often the comment is heard, "Why take children to a fruit and vegetable store when they shop there

every week with their parents?" A visit to a store with a teacher and a group of peers is a very different experience from the same trip with mother. When a teacher takes a group to a store, the purpose of the trip is to give the children a specific experience. The event focuses on them and their purposes. When children go to a store with their families, ordinarily they are hurried along and the child's experience is not the major consideration of the trip. Thus, because the purposes are different on a school excursion, the experience is different.

Any planned excursion should be either an outgrowth of children's experiences or meet a specific need. A teacher helped a group of children order carrot and radish seeds from a catalog for the school garden. Then they took a trip to the corner mailbox, a meaningful excursion because they were carrying an important letter.

Within the same group of children, needs will differ. For instance, a teacher taking four children to the zoo found that for three of them the short bus trip back and forth was the exciting part of the trip because they had never been on a bus before. For the other child, the bus ride was an everyday event, and the giraffe was the highlight of the trip. When a teacher took two children to a department store to buy burlap for a bulletin board, the ride on the escalator was the event most remembered.

Planning for trips. A teacher needs to do a good bit of planning for a trip. The purpose of a trip is to provide children with firsthand experiences. A child should not only be able to see, hear, and smell, but he or she should be able to touch and taste as well. A teacher also needs to know the children and their special interests and concerns.

You should not consider any trips until you are certain that you know the children well enough to anticipate any potential disruptive behavior. In many classrooms, some children may become overstimulated by the interruption of their daily routines.

You will need to familiarize yourself with the community in which the school is situated before planning excursions—become familiar with street signs and working people who come and go from the school, shops, business establishments, buildings, and service. Talk with people in the community. As you plan, try to anticipate the children's reactions, remembering that you are planning for *young* children. This means that you will need to keep in mind these basic guidelines in planning all excursions.

- ⊙ Keep it simple.
- ⊙ Discuss, read about, and organize play around the places to be visited in advance.
- ⊙ Encourage close observations while on the outing.
- ⊙ Give small amounts of information if children are interested.
- ⊙ Provide time, materials, and enthusiasm for follow-up plans and projects.

Celebrations (Thematic Strand #1)

Celebrations are part of a child's life. A child becomes more sensitive about his or her own feelings and of the feelings of others when he or she rejoices with them in celebration. Through celebrations, a child in his or her own way can be part of a group and acknowledge a special day or event.

Birthdays are special events for the child, and they should be treated according to individual needs. All the children in the room need not join a birthday celebration. Sometimes they will, but often only a small group joins a child in honoring his or her birthday. In many schools, parents are invited for the occasion. The parents' presence at the party is welcome, but if parents are unable to attend, this should not be allowed to detract from the celebration. Many parties given in honor of a child's birthday are overstimulating. For some children, a large crowd of people and too much confusion are upsetting. Young children are happy with small recognitions; a child counts the candles on the cake and then blows them out—a very exciting event for him or her.

Children are the living messages we send to a time we will not see.–Jewish proverb

Figure 22-9

A supportive teacher helps a learn about the world around them.

Personal celebrations. In the life of any child, there are events that deserve celebrations. When a teacher observes that a child, through his or her glee or sadness, is moved by a situation, the experience is worth emphasizing with a small but **personal celebration.** For example, a boy ties his shoes by himself for the first time. For many children, this is a very special event. The teacher may take time to say, "Great! You did it," or "Show me how you did it!" or "How does it feel to do it all by yourself?" You might want to share a new accomplishment of your own at a time like this. "I just learned how to download my photos onto my computer all by myself!" Share good feelings with children, and a child begins to learn that feelings are important and worth celebrating. When a child ties his or her shoes, the teacher's knowing glance the next day reaffirms the child's positive feelings about himself or herself.

TEACHING YOUNG CHILDREN ABOUT PEACE

Preventing conflicts is the work of politics; establishing peace is the work of education. –Maria Montessori

This quote very simply outlines a very complicated mission for early childhood teachers—teaching about peace. More than 15 years ago (1991), the National Association for the Education of Young Children, challenged early childhood teachers to teach peace,

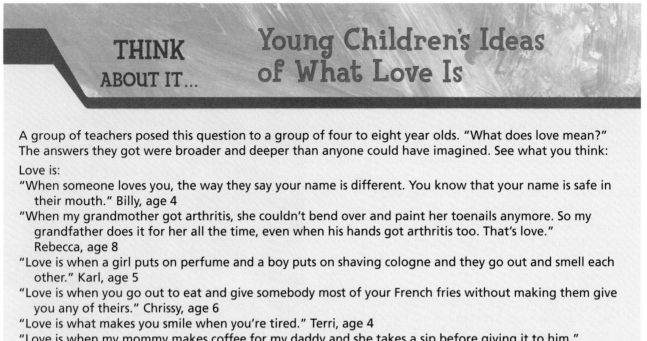

THINK ABOUT IT...   **Young Children's Ideas of What Love Is**

A group of teachers posed this question to a group of four to eight year olds. "What does love mean?" The answers they got were broader and deeper than anyone could have imagined. See what you think:

Love is:

"When someone loves you, the way they say your name is different. You know that your name is safe in their mouth." Billy, age 4

"When my grandmother got arthritis, she couldn't bend over and paint her toenails anymore. So my grandfather does it for her all the time, even when his hands got arthritis too. That's love." Rebecca, age 8

"Love is when a girl puts on perfume and a boy puts on shaving cologne and they go out and smell each other." Karl, age 5

"Love is when you go out to eat and give somebody most of your French fries without making them give you any of theirs." Chrissy, age 6

"Love is what makes you smile when you're tired." Terri, age 4

"Love is when my mommy makes coffee for my daddy and she takes a sip before giving it to him." Danny, age 7

"Love is what's in the room with you at Christmas if you stop opening presents and listen." Bobby, age 7

"During my piano recital, I was on a stage and I was scared. I looked at all the people watching me and saw my daddy waving and smiling. He was the only one doing that. I wasn't scared anymore." Cindy, age 8

"Love is when Mommy sees Daddy smelly and sweaty and still says he is handsomer than Robert Redford." Chris, age 7

"Love is when your puppy licks your face even after you left him alone all day." Mary Ann, age 4

"I know my older sister loves me because she gives me all her old clothes and has to go out and buy new ones." Lauren, age 4

"You really shouldn't say 'I love you' unless you mean it. But if you mean it, you should say it a lot . . . People forget." Jessica, age 6

reminding us that of all the lessons we hope to teach young children, the ability to act *in peace* is one of the most important. This continues to be critical in light of the increasing violence in our country, as well as in our schools.

This is a complicated idea—**teaching peace**—for many reasons. First, many adults don't understand the meaning of peace. For purposes of our discussion, peace is defined as a "state of tranquility or quiet; a freedom from civil disturbance, a state of security or order within a community provided for by law or custom" (Bernat, 1993, p. 36). Peace is not the absence of conflict, but rather the evidence of resolving differences in a positive way. Another reason peace is such a difficult topic to teach is that it's obvious that most adults have not been able to maintain peace in their own world. Finally, we certainly must ask a basic question—how can we teach young children about peace in a world so filled with strife and conflict?

Figure 22-10

Drawing about experiences on field trips is a popular social studies art project.

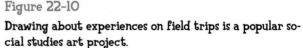

THIS ONE'S for YOU!   Virtual Field Trips

The Internet is a powerful tool for learning about the world. Older students will enjoy the following virtual field trips and other social studies–related Web field trips.

VISIT THE WHITE HOUSE

On this Web page you can take a tour of the First Lady's garden, read current press releases, and access information about other government agencies (http://www.whitehouse.gov).

AFRICA

Michigan State University is the home of Exploring Africa: Africa in the Classroom (http://exploringafrica. matrix.msu.edu/). CNN's Student News Bureau provides news and discussion activities about Africa (http://cnnstudentnews.cnn.com), including a visit to the Nelson Mandela Peace Village. The Peace Corps Coverdell World Wise Schools site features lesson plans for studying Africa's water issues (http://www. peacecorps.gov/). Click on Kids in the Resources for Section, then click on Explore the World.

LATIN AMERICA

The University of New Mexico's Latin American Institute offers two resources on Latin America: The Latin America Data Base (http://ladb.unm.edu), and an outreach program, Resources for Teaching about the Americas (http://ladb.unm.edu/), which includes resources for art, literature, social studies, and science and math units that include Latin America.

ASIA

The Asia Society has a wide range of resources for K through 12 teachers and students (http://www. AskAsia.org). Asia for Educators (http://afe.easia.columbia.edu) has materials on China, Japan, Korea, and Southeast Asia, including primary source texts and multimedia modules. The National Clearinghouse for U.S.–Japan Studies at Indiana University (http://www.indiana.edu, click on K–12 Education) provides information about Japan for K through 12 students, teachers, specialists, and curriculum developers. Australia's Asia Education Foundation features curriculum materials on Asia (http://www.curriculum.edu.au/accessasia).

MIDDLE EAST

The Outreach Program at the Center for Middle Eastern Studies at the University of Texas at Austin (http://menic.utexas.edu/) has developed numerous resources for K through 12 educators and students, including an exploratory language unit for Arabic for the middle school grades, and links to online lesson plans, curriculum guides, and education sites.

Many early childhood experts have written about this challenge of teaching young children about peace. To sum up the core idea of these writings, peace begins with a basic attitude, made up of trust, respect, and consideration toward everyone. When the attitudes of trust, respect, and consideration are present in the environment, it is a safe place for people to be themselves. In a safe environment, people have a sense that it is acceptable to be unique; it is acceptable

to disagree; and it is *expected* that disputes are settled without hurting one another. Every interaction in a safe environment reflects consideration and respect for individual differences (Bernat, 1993; NAEYC, 1991).

We can choose to create an environment that teaches children how to live peacefully with one another. In every action we have with another person, we can cause hurt or not. It is our choice. It is the responsibility of a teacher to realize that this choice exists and to teach children about their choices. If we realize this, we will choose carefully. Teachers can be "conduits of peace" when they help children make positive and supportive connections with others. Maria Montessori taught us long ago to create peaceful environments where children can make choices within the context of clear limits and a sense of order. When she required children to walk *around* someone else's mat, she was teaching a simple lesson about respecting others.

If we respect one another, we will not choose to harm each other. In turn, we must help young children understand their choices. For example, an increase in rowdiness results in an increase of people getting hurt. Children must learn to make choices about their style of play, and they must learn that they share responsibility for the results of their actions. They also need to learn that they can choose to stop upsetting behavior in the future, to slow the pace before someone gets hurt.

One expert in teaching peace, Valerie Bernat, suggests that this process of teaching young children about their choices begins with the implementation of two simple rules.

- ☉ Don't hurt anybody.
- ☉ Use words to settle problems (Bernat, 1993, p. 36).

Don't hurt anybody.   This is a simple rule—on the surface. Yet, just think of how many ways there are to hurt other people. Physical blows hurt. But so do

Figure 22-11
Young children can learn about different jobs adults have in social studies activities.

Figure 22-12
A child learns to relate to adults other than his or her parents in the early childhood program.

unkind words, gestures, teasing, and exclusion. All of these are harmful and can interfere with a child's ability to learn in general, as well as learning how to act in peace.

Use words. Disagreements are a natural part of life, and they will occur in the lives of young children. The key to peaceful settlement is to maintain harmony in stressful situations. It is sometimes difficult for a child to take a deep breath and clearly express the feelings of the moment. At stressful times, times of conflict or disagreements, it is important for the teacher to be with the children—but to show, not to tell. Steady the children in whatever way you can. Holding them closely in your arms or on your lap often helps a child gain focus in a stressful situation. Help the child express herself. But don't put words in the child's mouth. And make sure that children in a conflict listen to one another. Asking them to repeat, or retell, what each has said to the other is one way to see if they are listening to each other.

A Teacher's Role

It is not necessary (or possible) for you to find solutions for every child's problems. You need only create an atmosphere in which children can work out their own solutions. It is the teacher's job to give children the tools they need to define and settle differences. Teaching children how to use words to express themselves instead of actions to express emotions is one of the most important of these tools.

Childhood classrooms are very special places, and they must be focused on the child. In these classrooms, there are many different personalities, different needs, different styles of behavior, and different ethnic and family backgrounds. Common to all these groups is the need to feel safe. Only on this basis can we begin to build a framework of trust and respect. It is within such a framework that each child has a chance to grow and learn. It is in the preschool class that the teaching of peace must begin. If young children do not learn it from us, will they learn it at all?

Social Studies for Older Children

The main focus of this chapter has been on social studies for children in the early years. Now let us briefly consider social studies for older children. As we have seen, children in the middle and upper elementary levels are capable of more flexible thought. Social studies activities are an excellent avenue for exploring the personal and social changes this age group is experiencing. For example, the social studies standard's theme of Individual Development and Identity can provide the basis for many learning opportunities in areas such

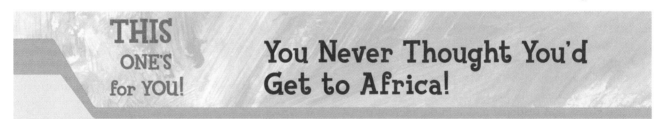

THIS ONE'S for YOU! **You Never Thought You'd Get to Africa!**

Want to visit a really amazing place? The place is the grassy lands of Eastern Africa called the Serengeti. It is home to some incredible animals. Here are some links to sites that will help you and the children learn about this amazing place.

⊙ At http://www.serengeti.org, the official site of the Serengeti National Park, you can start your journey in the photo gallery. The pictures of the land, the animals, and the people are amazing. Click on Discover Serengeti to begin.

⊙ A new tree frog has been discovered on the Serengeti plains. At http://www.calacademy.org/ you can read about how a young boy made this important find. Click on Research, then on Herpetology, then on African frogs.

⊙ Want to know more about the people who live in the Serengeti? Go to http://www.maasai.com/ to see pictures and read an article about the Maasai, one of the tribes that lives in this area.

⊙ Lions live in the Serengeti, and there's a big research project there to help us learn more about the "King of the Beasts." At http://lionresearch.org/, you can find answers to frequently asked questions on the Serengeti lions. Click on "Enter," then on FAQ.

⊙ For more fantastic photos, visit http://www.jao.com/. Click on Pictures I took in Africa. Here you'll view 16 pictures of lions, giraffes, antelope, and more.

Excerpted from "Let's Visit the Serengeti", Sept./Oct. 2002, Children's Software and New Media Review, p. 33.

Figure 22-13

Paper weaving is an art activity that teaches children about the art of different cultures.

as peer pressure, conformity, personal identity, self-concept, and social expectations, to name a few.

The social studies theme of Power, Authority, and Governance is an excellent base for developing learning experiences for students about their own individual rights and responsibilities in the increasingly complex social world of which they are part. For example, students can be asked to develop hypothetical communities in which certain students play different power and authority roles. They can role-play enforcing rules when someone breaks one. They can also begin to study power and authority in their local community.

Using the NCSS theme of Culture and Cultural Diversity as a curriculum base, teachers can develop experiences to provide students an in-depth study of the specific aspects of particular cultures in similar and different places, times, conditions, and contexts. Teachers can encourage students to consider the direct and indirect connections between the assumptions, beliefs,

and values of a culture. Teachers can help students analyze ways that a people's cultural ideas and actions influence its members. Through such study, students can begin to consider the impact traditions have on a person's thoughts and actions within any particular social group.

Basing learning activities on the ten social study themes will provide students at this age level many opportunities to explore their complex and changing social world. More activity ideas are found at the end of this chapter.

SUMMARY

Knowing how to be part of a social group is not natural or inborn in human beings. Learning about oneself and others and how to act with others is a long learning process. Social studies are an important part of a child's learning; they help the child understand the complex world in which he or she lives and enable him or her to be productive and happy within a social framework. The social studies of the preschool child must focus on the experiences of the child in his or her immediate environment. In 1994, the NCSS developed ten thematic strands in which all children (K–12) should have learning experiences.

Learning about oneself in a social sense includes learning one's name, one's ethnic background, and such things as family grouping and occupations in one's family. In the early childhood program, learning about oneself is at a basic level—that is, young children learn how their lives fit into the larger social group.

Those who work with young children from preschool through the entire period of early childhood can help them discover and appreciate their own uniqueness by beginning with a positive acceptance of each child.

Teaching young children about peace begins with a basic attitude of trust, respect, and consideration toward everyone. Two basic rules make up the basis of teaching about peace: (1) don't hurt anybody and (2) use words.

KEY TERMS

personal celebration
teaching peace
ten thematic strands of social studies

LEARNING ACTIVITIES

A. List specific ways to enhance a child's understanding of self, other than those in this chapter.

B. There are many activities and experiences appropriate for teaching children concepts of self and other people. Think of at least three ideas other than those in this chapter.

C. Prepare a unit plan on one of the following: family, self, or a specific community worker such as a firefighter. For your unit plan, include a section titled "Children's Books" and include stories and other appropriate language arts activities.

D. Child Study:

1. Select three children of different ages (e.g., three, five, and nine years) and ask each separately to describe things like what fathers do, what the children can or cannot do when they grow up, or what happens when they are afraid. Do not contribute your own opinions until you are sure the children have said all they would like to about the matter.

2. What changes in ideas do you notice as you listen to children of different ages? Did any of the children have a definite misunderstanding about some aspect of the issue you discussed? If so, how did you respond? How should parents respond when this happens?

3. Observe a dispute between children in an early childhood setting. Record how it was settled. Then compare this method of settlement with the information presented in this chapter on teaching about peace. How did the real-life settlement compare? Did it help the children involved learn about peace? Why or why not?

4. Interview an experienced first, second, or third grade teacher. Present that teacher with each of the situations that follow. Then ask her or him to answer the questions for the situation. Write the answers down and compare them. Discuss similarities and differences in the replies.

    Situation 1: Clay ignores his fellow students most of the time. When his teacher tells the class it is time for finger painting, he grabs as many paint jars as he can. When asked to share these paints, he refuses.

    Question 1: In your years as a teacher, have you had children who have behaved like this? Why do you think they do it? What need or needs underlie their behavior?

    Question 2: As a general rule, what would you say is the best way to respond to this kind of behavior? Why?

    Question 3: What is the worst way to respond? Why?

    Situation 2: Anton is a clown. If he's not making faces, he's telling jokes—and he's always disrupting the class. The other children laugh at him, but they don't seem to like him. In the schoolyard, he's generally alone.

    Ask the same questions here as in Situation 1.

ACTIVITIES FOR CHILDREN

SUGGESTIONS FOR EXCURSIONS APPROPRIATE FOR YOUNG CHILDREN

Supermarket. As eager as young children are, they have a limited attention span, so do not try to do too much. Make several trips to the supermarket, each with a different focus. Watch the goods being delivered. Watch the boxes being unpacked and merchandise being stamped. Look at all the different kinds of machines in the store.

Produce department. What are some things displayed on special cardboard or wrapped in individual papers? Why are some things displayed on crushed ice or refrigerated? See if you and the children can name the fruits and vegetables.

Dairy department. What kinds of things are sold here? Why are they kept cold? Where do the various products come from?

Meat department. Watch the butcher cut and package meat. Why is the meat kept cold? Is it cold in the back, too? See how many varieties of meat you can name.

Bakery department. Compare the ovens with ovens at home and the size of the flour sacks with the sacks that you buy. Notice the quantities of baked goods and the process of baking. What kinds of clothes do the bakers wear? Why?

Shoe repair shop. Watch the person make repairs. Try to give the person something that needs fixing. What kinds of machines do they have? What kinds of materials do they use? Try to get some scraps to take back for making collages.

Dry-cleaning shop. What kinds of smells are in the air there? What kind of machine is used for ironing? How does the cleaner know which clothes are yours?

Pet store. What kinds of pets does this store have? Are there any unusual ones? What do the various pets eat? What kinds of houses do they provide for the various pets?

Florist's shop. Visiting this shop is an especially good activity on a cold winter's day when everything outside is barren and bleak. A walk through the greenhouse may bring many questions to mind: Why are the flowers growing inside the greenhouse and not outdoors? What kinds of plants are there? What kinds of smells are there? How does the florist keep cut flowers from dying? Buy a plant and learn how to take care of it. The workroom, where bouquets, baskets of flowers, and corsages are assembled, will be of interest to children.

The police officer and crossing guard. Within walking distance of your school there is probably an intersection or a school where a police officer or crossing guard is on duty. Watch what he or she does. How does he or she tell the vehicles and pedestrians to go? To stop? The children enjoy talking to the officer and getting a good look at his or her uniform. The police station is of interest to the children, too; perhaps the desk sergeant on duty will spend a few minutes visiting with the children. (You will plan this in advance, of course.) He may show the child the inside of a police car, show them the radio, and give the children a short safety speech.

Mail delivery. Make arrangements to meet your own letter carrier at your mailbox and then at the nearest pick-up box on the corner to watch him or her gather the mail. Buy a stamp and mail a letter at the post office. Children are not usually allowed in the back of most post offices, but they can see a good deal if they look through the window of the parcel-post counter. Watch the packages being weighed and mailed.

Bus driver (conductor). Sit near the driver of the bus. Watch what he or she does. Look at the uniform.

Fire station. Some fire departments have open-house days. If yours does not, make an appointment for a visit ahead of time. Do not insist that the children get on the equipment, even if invited to do so. Climbing on an engine can be a frightening experience for some young children. Usually the child is invited to try on a firefighter's hat, watch a firefighter slide down the pole, and inspect the engine. Find out how the fire alarm works, where the different firefighters stand on the truck, and what each of them does at a fire. Later look at fire hydrants and fire escapes in buildings. Point out fire doors and fire extinguishers or sprinklers in various buildings.

Library. Take the children to the children's section of the library. Let them browse. Show them that all the books have letters or letters and numbers written on the bindings. Why? Perhaps your library has a storybook time that you can attend. How does the librarian know which book you take out? Take out some books so the children can see the procedure.

Sanitation workers. Be aware of the sanitation workers, street sweepers, or snowplow drivers in action and how they are dressed. Why do they wear gloves?

Construction site. What kind of building is going up? What are the girders for? What kinds of machines can you see? What do they do? How do the workers dress? Why?

Repair site. Observe a surface or underground repair site. What is being fixed? What equipment is in use? How are the workers dressed? Why? What is under the street or sidewalk? Where did the rocks and soil come from? Try to explain to the children that the site of the city was once countryside.

Printing plant or newspaper plant. Call ahead of time and find out if tours are available and when the presses are operating. Remember to bring some paper remnants back for the children's artwork.

SELF-AWARENESS ACTIVITIES

All about me
- From magazines, children can cut pictures that they like or that remind them of themselves.
- Make a puzzle of each child's name, using both first and last names.

◉ Make up "Guess Who" riddles describing individual children. Suggest clues that reflect the child's positive characteristics.

◉ Make a set of flash cards or similar cards with pictures of community workers. The children could be encouraged to bring pictures of their parents at their jobs or wearing clothing appropriate for that job. An additional game could be collecting pictures of tools or items related to various jobs and having the children sort them.

◉ Interviews with community helpers could be taped on a recorder if the workers cannot visit the classroom. Children will be especially proud to hear their parents tell about their professions and jobs.

◉ Encourage children to cut or tear out and paste magazine pictures that show people or families of different ages or cultures having fun or working together.

◉ Keep a supply of pictures of people available for very young children to paste into books. Older children might wish to mount the pictures as a mural on a background they have prepared with other media.

How do I look?

◉ Discuss differences in sex. Ask: "Do girls look different from boys? How? Dresses? Hair? What else? Do men look different from ladies? How? Do they sound different?" If a child brings out the difference in sex organs, accept it very matter-of-factly.

◉ Take snapshots of the children, alone or in groups, and mount them on a bulletin board or in a scrapbook with the names of the children printed beneath the pictures. These pictures are an excellent starting point for a discussion about how we all have the same body parts, even though we all look different. In this and other such activities, the teacher can bring out that we are more alike than different. Natural points in such a discussion are color, size, and shape of eyes, hair, nose, mouth, etc.

◉ On a more personal level, try the following self-study activity to see how you look to the children you work with.

Self-study: How children see you. Select one or two children who are at least four years old. Seat them individually at a table with paper and crayons (or felt-tip pens) and ask them to draw a picture of you. Encourage them to take their time and include as much as they want. When they are finished give them another sheet of paper and ask them to draw a self-portrait.

When both pictures are completed cut them out and paste them side by side. First look at each child's drawing of you. What features appear to be most important to the children? Did they overlook any important characteristics, such as a beard, long hair, or glasses? Compare the drawing of you with the self-portrait. How are they similar? How are they different? Is there more detail in your picture or in the self-portrait? Is one bigger than the other? Is there a difference in emotional expression? Do these drawings reveal anything about how these children view themselves and you?

TECHNOLOGY AND SOCIAL STUDIES

Thanks to technology, we have some powerful new tools that can help us document and tell children's personal stories. Computers, camcorders, tape recorders, and digital cameras are steadily gaining acceptance by more teachers on a regular basis. The following activities use this technology to teach some social studies concepts.

OUR BABY BOOK

Give each child one page or screen, and invite families to send in baby pictures and information about their child as a baby. These can be scanned into the computer onto the child's page. Children's voices can be recorded as they talk about what they thought their lives were like when they were babies. Children's drawings, voices, and family photographs can be included in the project.

MY BOOK

With the help of an adult, invite each child to create his or her own e-book about himself or herself, using software such as HyperStudio. Each page or screen can include unique family traditions. Children's drawings can be scanned and their voices can be recorded as they share their favorite stories. If you do not have access to a software program such as HyperStudio, ask children to create their drawings on white construction paper and describe their drawings and print their dictations on accompanying pages. Display children's books in the book area where they can be easily shared.

STAR OF THE WEEK

Designate a special week for each child. During the special week, invite family members to visit the classroom and talk about their family's heritage. As they share special items, document the event with a digital camera. The teacher, child, and family then together create a HyperStudio project about the child or Star of the Week. If a digital camera is not available, you can take pictures with any standard camera and sequence the pictures on construction paper pages to create a Star of the Week memory book for each child.

FAMILY RECIPES

Collect family recipes on paper, and then type them into any word processor or use HyperStudio or PowerPoint. The pages can be printed and sent home to each family.

FAMILY HAPPENINGS

Take digital pictures or video of children's family dances, rituals, or songs. Using software like iMovie or PowerPoint, create a special video for any family night or parent/teacher conference.

ALL ABOUT US

This activity centers on the children's heads and faces. Ask them to describe everything that they all have on their heads and faces. Record their responses on chart paper.

Prepare separate sheets of chart paper for each part of the head and face (nose, eyes, ears, mouth, and hair). Tell children that each day they will focus on a different part and discuss their differences and their similarities.

Invite children to begin each investigation by discussing how they all use each body part and how they are all similar, such as, "We all use our eyes to see." Record their responses. Ask children to spend time looking at each of their classmates' specific facial features. How are their eyes similar or different? Notice how lips have different shapes. Do ears all look the same? Record children's observations on each chart.

Have the children work together to summarize what they learned about their facial features. Ask

them to think about why it is special to look different. What would happen if everyone looked the same?

Provide children with a variety of art materials to create a self-portrait. Include flesh-tone markers, crayons, and paper. Encourage them to use a mirror to observe their facial features and to notice the details of their faces. Ask children to describe why they are special. Record their words on a sheet of paper and attach it beneath each self-portrait.

PEACE PUPPETS

Create puppets that encourage children to talk about feelings and solve problems in peaceful ways.

Ask the children to think about all the different ways people feel and all the different ways they feel, too: happy, sad, angry, cranky, excited, and so on.

Talk about how the same person can feel many different ways at many different times. Explain that they are going to make puppets and that they can decide whether their puppet will represent one feeling (and which one) or many feelings.

Provide children with a variety of materials to design their puppets: socks, paper bags, fabric, pompoms, yarn, felt. (See Chapter 15 for puppet making ideas). Ask children to name their puppets and help them label each one with the feeling or feelings they choose.

Invite the children to share their finished puppets with the group. Talk about how these puppets can be used to help people talk about and sort out feelings. For instance, if someone is feeling lonely or afraid, the appropriate puppet(s) can be brought out. If there's an argument, children might enlist the help of a puppet or two to listen to the problem and help them come up with solutions. Work together to decorate the box in which the puppets will be stored. Ask children to suggest a name for the special box—Peace Place, Puppet's Place, or the like.

PLAYING WITH PEACE PUPPETS

The children can be seated in a circle. One child can wear one of the newly made puppets on his or her hand. Whisper to the child sitting closest to you to create a facial expression that shows a particular emotion. You might ask the child to show sadness, anger, or happiness. The child wearing the puppet will try to "read" the child's facial expression and talk as the puppet about that feeling. "I feel sad because I wanted to go to the store last night and my mom said we couldn't go." Continue the activity until each child in the group has had a chance to show an emotion or express an emotion as the puppet.

ACTIVITIES FOR OLDER CHILDREN (GRADES 4-5)

GEOGRAPHY ON THE INTERNET

Students can learn geography at http://www.maps.com where they can see all different kinds of maps and play geography games that teach and test their knowledge of place names around the world.

Your home state. On a map of the United States, have students find their state. Ask them what states border on the state in which they live and have them locate the state capital. How far are they from the state capital and our country's capital?

World Religion Day. January 20 is World Religion Day. This might be a good time to introduce the novel *A Stone in my Hand* by Cathryn Clinton (Candlewick, 2002). It is the story of a young girl whose father has gone into the Gaza Strip for work and has not returned. It shows the everyday life and struggles of a Palestinian family as tension mounted in 1988. This book will open the door to better understanding as you discuss current affairs in the Middle East.

Heroes all around. Introduce your students to the book *The hero's trail: A guide to a heroic life* by T. A. Barron (Penguin Putnam, 2002). This book shares profiles of heroic young people and inspires readers to realize that anyone can be a hero. While reading the book together or out loud, challenge your students to find stories of everyday heroes in the newspaper and in news magazines they can bring to class to share.

NATIONAL TREASURES

Divide the class into groups. Have each group research a National Park (there are 53 to choose from). Begin online at http://www.nps.gov/parks.html; from there, each group can link to their individual selection. Prepare presentations including maps, posters, tourist attractions, history, etc.

The Taj Mahal. Although not everyone has had the opportunity to visit, many people have heard about India's Taj Mahal. Have students see and read about this monument:

http://www.taj-mahal.net
http://www.greatbuildings.com/, Type in Taj Mahal in the Name of Building box.
http://www.galenfrysinger.com/, Click on Asia, then on India.

What does the Taj Mahal look like? How would you describe its style? Which decorative features did you see? What is the purpose of this building?

The Roman Colosseum. People have gathered at the Roman Colosseum throughout history. See what it looks like today:

http://www.the-colosseum.net/
http://www.greatbuildings.com/, Type in Roman Colosseum in Name of Building box.

What was the original function of this structure? How has it been used throughout history? Does the Colosseum look different now compared to when it was created? What shapes were used in designing it? Can you think of any modern structures that could have been influenced by the Colosseum?

ART AND SOCIAL STUDIES

Update art. Do a modern-day version of an artist's work, one that reflects the current time rather than the time in which it was created. Change the background or dress of portraits.

Class flags. Examine the flags and symbols of countries. Discuss how and why they use the colors, shapes, designs, materials, and lines that they do. Divide into groups to create a class flag to represent what's important about the class. Make fabric, paper, paint, and collage materials available for the design.

Famous people sculptures. Students choose a person they wish to study who has made a significant contribution to history (explorer, president, artist, musician, activist). Brainstorm what students would like to know. They then find details about how the person looked, moved, talked, and dressed and what she or he ate, valued, achieved, etc. Students then construct sculptures from papier mâché or make a puppet (See Chapter 15 for puppet making ideas). Students use sculptures or puppets to role play and do a presentation to the class. Allow time for questions.

HISTORY MAKERS–SOCIAL STUDIES THEME: CONTINUITY AND CHANGE

On the classroom calendar, mark and label the birthdays of Betsy Ross (January 1) and Martin Luther King, Jr. (January 15). Half of the class researches Betsy Ross. The other half researches Dr. King. The

Ross group presents a research fact, and the King group presents a finding for a similar or the same category (e.g., birthplace). Continue the activity until no further similarities can be found.

FREEDOM–SOCIAL STUDIES THEME: CONTINUITY AND CHANGE

Call attention to the anniversary of the Emancipation Proclamation (January 1st). Guide the children in considering and finding meanings of *emancipation* and *proclamation*. Help them research the historical actions and decisions associated with the Emancipation Proclamation. Probe for and emphasize reasons the proclamation was needed.

TELEPHONE BOOK RESEARCH–SOCIAL STUDIES THEME: CULTURE AND CULTURAL IDENTITY

The telephone book can be used as a reference for learning about the local community.

Study the Yellow Pages; what names are predominant and what might they tell you about early settlers in the area? You might divide the class into groups to consider sources of people's last names—occupation, animal names, colors, where they live. Get information on local industries from the Yellow Pages. Watch for unusual advertising wording; identify state, city, county resources. Seek out information on such things as zip codes, history of the area, location of streets.

REGIONAL CRAFTS–SOCIAL STUDIES THEME: CULTURE AND CONTINUITY

Provide reference materials showing crafts created in your area in the last 100 years. Lead a discussion about how these objects are both functional and beautiful.

Have small groups of students each choose one craft that they find especially appealing. Encourage each group to choose a different craft. Ask them to list questions about the craft such as the following.

1. How was this (basket) made?

2. How long have people been making these (wooden boxes) by hand?

3. Do people still make these (silver buttons) today?

4. What tools were needed to create the (lace on this apron)?

Then have students do research to find the answers to their questions. Suggest that they interview craftspeople in addition to using nonfiction books, encyclopedias, and multimedia sources. Have students report their findings about the craft to the class.

TIE-DYED SQUARES–SOCIAL STUDIES THEME: CULTURE AND CONTINUITY

Tell students that they will create a type of fiber art called tie-dyeing. Explain that this art form originated in China between A.D. 617 and 906. Tie-dyed fabrics created at that time were worn mainly by the nobility and priests. You will need: art smocks, 10–inch squares of muslin (at least one per student), acrylic or tempera paint, containers for water-paint mixture, string, safety scissors, and rubber gloves.

Prepare several tubs of dye by mixing tempera paints or acrylic paints with water. Next, provide fabric squares and string. Then have students put on rubber gloves and do the following:

⊙ Place the cloth on a flat surface.
⊙ Use their fingertips to gather a clump of material.
⊙ Tie the clump by tightly wrapping string around it.
⊙ Repeat until several clumps have been created.
⊙ Submerge cloth in dye for about 20 minutes.
⊙ Remove cloth and untie or cut away string.
⊙ Dry cloth on a flat surface.

OBELISKS–EGYPT AND WASHINGTON, DC: SOCIAL STUDIES THEME: CULTURE & CONTINUITY

Display a picture of the Washington Monument. Explain that the structure was designed by an architect named Robert Mills and that he based his design on a type of ancient Egyptian structure called an obelisk.

Have students work with partners or in small groups to create a chart comparing the Washington Monument with an example of an Egyptian obelisk. (Students may want to research one of the obelisks called Cleopatra's Needle, for example.) A sample chart is shown here. Students may want to use the categories listed or ones they create.

	Washington Monument	Egyptian Obelisk
Height		
Weight		
Date completed		
Designer		
Today's location		
Other information		

TIME CONTINUITY AND CHANGE STANDARD–ACTIVITIES FOR MULTIPLE INTELLIGENCES

Using the theme of time, the following activities are designed for various multiple intelligences.

Time theme. Construct a sundial. Explain to the class how sundials were used, and give them a brief history of the sundial. (Spatial/Bodily-Kinesthetic)

Music feelings. Listen to several pieces of music that have different rhythms and speeds. Have students write a short paper on how slow music makes you feel compared to fast music. Make sure to identify the songs and their singers or composers. (Musical/Intrapersonal)

Be on time! Prepare a five-minute oral report on the importance of being on time. Give students a list of reasons why you feel being on time is important. (Verbal-Linguistic/Interpersonal)

Seasonal fashions. Have students design a report to show how the seasons influence the clothes we wear. Include as many types of media as you can in the report. (Visual/Spatial/Word Smart)

Family research. Ask students to talk to their parents about what it was like for them to be a child of the same age they are. Look through family albums for photographs. Scan them into the computer. Have them write a brief report about their parents growing up and how it made the students feel to learn about them during that time in their lives. (Verbal-Linguistic/Intrapersonal)

Dance. Students learn a dance such as the waltz or the swing that were popular in the past and still enjoyed today. Demonstrate the dance for the class, and tell them about the history of the dance. (Bodily-Kinesthetic/Interpersonal)

Time line. Students make a timeline for a period of history that you've recently studied, marking the important and interesting events. Add pictures and colors to make it even more interesting. (Spatial/Math-Logic)

Family scrapbook. Students research their family history and create a family tree. See how far back they can trace their family members and where they came from. Use the family tree to start a family scrapbook. Add funny stories or interesting facts about family members as well as pictures, letters, and drawings. (Intrapersonal/Interpersonal/Spatial/Verbal-Linguistic)

CHAPTER REVIEW

1. Discuss art activities appropriate for the following units: community helpers, self-awareness, learning one's name.
2. What areas of the curriculum (e.g., art, music, language arts) would you use to help children learn their own and others' names in various ways? Give some examples of activities you would use in each of these areas.
3. Relate incidents similar to the opening scenes in this chapter, demonstrating young children's level of social awareness. Explain why you think the children acted the way they did. Explain how an adult (or older child) would react in the same situation.
4. What community/school "helpers" would you invite to your room to aid children's understanding of their community? What would you have these visitors talk about; bring with them to class; and do with the children (if anything)?
5. What are some ways the block area can be used to teach social studies ideas?
6. What are the two basic rules for beginning to teach young children about peace?
7. List the ten themes of the National Council for the Social Studies standards for grades K through 12.

REFERENCES

Bernat, V. (1993, March). Teaching peace. *Young Children, 36–39.*

National Association for the Education of Young Children. (1991). Guidelines for appropriate curriculum content and assessment programs serving children ages 3–8. *Young Children, 46*(3), 21–38.

National Council for the Social Studies (NCSS). (1994). *Expectations of excellence: Curriculum standards for social studies.* Washington, DC: Academy Press.

ADDITIONAL READINGS

Chicola, N. A. (2002). *Creating caring communities with books kids love*. Golden, CO: Fulcrum Publishing.

Gartrell, D. (2002). *The power of guidance: Teaching social-emotional skills in early childhood classrooms*. Clifton Park, NY: Delmar.

Greenberg, P. (2002). *Character development: Encouraging self-esteem and self-discipline in infants, toddlers and two-year-olds*. Washington, DC: NAEYC.

Greenman, J. (2000). *What happened to the world? Helping children cope in turbulent times*. New York: Bright Horizons.

Haas, M. E., & Laughlin, M. A. (1997). *Meeting the standards: Social Studies readings for K–6 educators*. Washington, DC: National Council for the Social Studies.

Hyson, M. (2003). *The emotional development of young children: Building an emotion-centered curriculum*. Washington, DC: NAEYC.

Katz, L. G., & McClellan, D. E. (2002). *Fostering children's social competence: The teacher's role*. Washington, DC: NAEYC.

Levin, D. E. (2003). *Teaching young children in violent times*. (2nd ed.). Washington, DC: NAEYC.

Levin, D. E. (2001). *Remote control childhood? Combating the hazards of media culture*. Washington, DC: NAEYC.

Partin, R. L. (2002). *Social studies: Teacher's book of lists*. New York: John Wiley and Sons.

Riley, S. (2001). *How to generate values in young children: Integrity, honesty, individuality, self-confidence and wisdom*. Washington, DC: NAEYC.

Savage, T. V. (2003). *Effective teaching in elementary social studies*. Upper Saddle River, NJ: Prentice Hall.

Stone, J. G. (2002). *Building classroom community: The early childhood teacher's role*. Washington, DC: NAEYC.

Warren, R. M. (2001). *Caring: Supporting children's growth*. Washington, DC: NAEYC.

Zarillo, J. (2003). *Teaching elementary social studies: Principles and applications*. Upper Saddle River, NJ: Prentice Hall.

SOFTWARE FOR CHILDREN

Blast! Software Family Tree, 2003. Ages 5 and up.

Carmen Sandiego World Treasures of Knowledge, 2002. Ages 8–12.

Discovery Channel School's CD-ROM Science and Social Studies Collection, 2002. Ages 8–12.

Explorer II Globe, 2002. Ages 8 and up.

Furreal Friends, 2002. Ages 6 and up.

Furreal Friends Go Go My Walking Pup, 2003. Ages 4–8.

Jump Start Explorers, 2002. Ages 5–8.

Liberty's Kids CD-ROM: The Real Adventures of the American Revolution, 2002. Ages 8–12.

National Geographic Kids Homework Help, 2003. Ages 6 and up.

Neighborhood MapMachine 2.0, 2003. Grades 1–5.

The Little Raven and Friends: The Tricycle Story, 2002. Ages 3–9.

Thomas and Friends: Building the New Line, 2002. Ages 3–5.

USA Explorer, 2002. Ages 5–9.

HELPFUL WEB SITES

http://www.socialstudies.org/
Click on Notable Social Studies Books. List of notable trade books in social studies. Annual list compiled as a joint project of the National Council of Social Studies and the Children's Book Council.

http://startsomething.target.com
Target and the Tiger Woods Foundation have teamed up in a free online program that will help kids ages eight to 17 to pursue their interests and reach their goals.

The 50 States, http://www.teachersfirst.com/
Type "States" in Keyword box. Extensive elementary resource on the 50 states; a single-stop resource for state projects of various sorts.

Labor Day Lessons, http://www.classbrain.com/
Click on Projects & Reports.

Citizenship Day, http://www.patriotism.org/
Click on Directory of Holidays.

Grandparents' Day, http://www.grandparents-day. com

For additional creative activity resources, visit our Web site at http://www.EarlyChildEd. delmar.com

Chapter 23

Creative Health and Safety Experiences

Objectives

After studying this chapter, you should be able to:

1. Discuss the basic health practices in the early childhood program.
2. Discuss the appropriate way to work with young children in health and safety matters.
3. Discuss traffic safety, fire safety, and poison safety in the early childhood curriculum.

Health is a physical state in the here and now. Safety is also a present state. Young children don't think in terms of the distant future. It's the *now* that interests them, not a talk on how a bad health or safety habit can hurt a person in the future.

Preaching, lecturing, and rote learning of health facts are all ineffective techniques in the early childhood classroom. What should be stressed is a positive, fun, but most of all *natural* approach to health and safety in the classroom. Above all else, good lifestyle habits are often *caught* rather than taught. Whether it's the food choices they make or the physical activities they're involved in, young children often model their behaviors after adults.

HEALTH AND SAFETY IN THE EARLY YEARS

Good health and safety practices need to be modeled by adults as much as they are included in actual lesson plans. Emphasis in this chapter will be on presenting basic concepts of health and safety in simple classroom activities that do not require special equipment or curriculum guides. Common sense and daily experiences form the basis of these activities.

In the area of health and safety, your actions surely speak louder than words. For example, your own shining hair, clean body, neat clothing, and fresh smell "tell" children so much more about personal hygiene and good health practices than any lesson plan. Your providing *and* eating healthy snacks along with the children sends a clear message about the importance of eating healthful foods. Along with this emphasis on modeling behaviors, this chapter contains some basic health and safety ideas and tips on how to use them in classroom activities.

HEALTH PRACTICES

Good health is often not appreciated until the later years in life, when one doesn't always have it. It is important in the early years of life, when we least appreciate health, to learn practices that will extend our health long past the early years.

Good health practices include simple ones such as brushing one's teeth and hair, bathing regularly, and having a general interest in cleanliness. Getting enough sleep and good food are also basic to good health at all ages. All these ideas and tasks are usually first taught at home and are then reinforced in the classroom. However, some young children may learn these health basics at school first because of various home situations. Teaching young children about good health practices can be done in many ways, but informal talks and simple activities work best with young children just learning to really care for themselves physically. With older children you can plan more in-depth activities and units to investigate various health and safety topics of interest to the children. (See chapter end for activity suggestions.)

Unlike for you and other adults, daily personal hygiene tasks are not yet routine for children. For instance, when a six-year-old boy gets up and ready for school, he often may forget to brush his teeth or comb his hair. He doesn't automatically do these tasks but has to "remember" them every morning. Often, a young child may forget to brush his or her teeth. His or her peers may forget as well. Thus, the child suffers no great social embarrassment. In this situation an adult's gentle (confidential) reminder can help prod the memory of a forgetful child. Yet in no way should learning personal hygiene be a cause for shame or negative comments.

TOPICS	GRADE 3	GRADE 4	GRADE 5
Mental Health	Thinking clearly; getting along with others; stress; healthful self-concept; criteria for responsible decisions	Being special; strengths and weaknesses, attitudes; good mental health; stress	Healthy behavior; communication-definition; expressing feelings; emotions—definition; stress management; effects of television on health; definition of health and wellness; using refusal skills
Family and Social Health	Getting along with family and friends; family, friends, and your health	A friend-definition; choosing friends, family and friends, peer pressure	Focus on the health of others; sharing feelings and feedback; decision making; adoption; responsible parenting
Drugs	Uses of medicine: kinds of medicine; safe use of medicine; caffeine; alcohol; tobacco; marijuana	Making decisions about drinking and smoking; a history of alcohol and tobacco; peer pressure, advertising methods; laws; marijuana; depressants, stimulants, psychedelics, and inhalants; cocaine and crack	Drugs; uses and effects; prescription and over-the-counter drugs; chemicals in cigarette smoke; effects of smoking and alcohol; illegal drugs and their effects; chemical dependence; problem of crack, marijuana
Personal Health	Being in good health; proper dental care; being well-groomed; proper medical care; caring for nails; good posture	School health services; community health services; dental health products and services; care of teeth	Using seat belts for safety; using power mowers safely; health professionals; health careers; consumer protection
Safety and First Aid	Safety at home; safety at play; first aid for minor injuries; bicycle safety	Joint damage and fractures; muscle injuries; fire safety; safety from animals and strangers; recreational safety; first aid for insect stings and reactions from poisonous plants; bicycle safety	Bicycle safety; poisoning and preventive action; first aid for poisoning; safety around harmful vapors

Figure 23-1

Health curriculum topics, grades 3 through 5.

The health curriculum for older children in middle and upper grade levels focuses on health issues that encompass more than personal health issues. Figure 23–1 outlines some of the basic health topics generally covered in grades 3 to 5. You will probably have more topics you will want to add to this list.

Positive Approach to Health and Hygiene

In any health or personal hygiene matter, emphasis must be on the *positive* view of self. In all health and hygiene tasks that young children learn in the early childhood program, the teacher needs first of all to model good health and hygiene practices. There also must be planned space and time to practice these tasks.

A large mirror at children's eye level, a sink easily reached and operated by young children, and soap in a form that children can handle easily—these are but a few examples of arrangements and equipment that help children "practice" good personal hygiene. To be sure that children always have soap available for hand-washing, place a bar of soap in a old knee-high nylon stocking. Tie the stocking to the faucet of the sink. This prevents the soap both from landing on the floor and leaving a soapy mess in the soap dish.

The routines of dressing, washing, eating, and resting will take up a great deal of time when working with young children. In fact, you will sometimes think of yourself as a caregiver and not a teacher. Yet, these everyday activities are both essential for good health and equally essential for *teaching* about health. By simply *talking* about these routines as you are doing them you are *teaching* children about important health concepts. All of these daily routines serve as the basis for teaching children concepts of body functions and parts, as well as the habits of caring for themselves.

Each program will have routines for body care. If you're working with children under age five, it's probably mandated that child-sized toilets, sinks, and mirrors be available. If these are not, arrange for the use of platforms or small sturdy benches or stools so children will be able to reach sinks, get their own toothbrush, and turn on faucets for themselves.

Washing hands before and after using the toilet and before eating, as well as washing hands and brushing teeth after eating, are routines that should be established and followed at all age levels.

Another part of daily hygiene involves the quality of the classroom environment. Not only is personal hygiene important, but the learning environment itself needs to be clean and attractive. Children need to be actively involved in keeping their classroom orderly. A clean and orderly room also mirrors the importance of good hygiene practices.

In your classroom check to see if you have the following:
( ) storage shelves and cupboards: low, open shelf space accessible to children and cupboard space for storing supplies. Most shelf space should be movable to permit rearranging the room.
( ) a peg rack or cubbies for children's coats.
( ) screen dividers or other means to create specific play areas and to provide picture display space.
( ) enough wastebaskets, preferably of plastic or other washable material.
( ) dust brush, dustpan, whisk broom, sponges, small mop, and plastic pail.
( ) paper or cloth towels.
( ) small bars of soap for washing hands, toothbrush containers.
( ) a bulletin board for emergency numbers, first-aid procedures.
( ) file cards and box of parents' home and work telephone numbers, child's doctor, and other authorized adults responsible for child.
( ) a fix-it box: a carton in which to put things that need attention. (Be sure that they are fixed!)
( ) adequate space for storing items that are not being used as well as expendable items, such as paper and paints.
( ) at least one drawer/cabinet with a child-proof latch for storing potentially dangerous material.

Figure 23-2

Checklist of equipment for keeping space clean and in order.

Figure 23–2 contains a checklist of equipment for keeping a space clean and in order. When using this checklist, remember that even the smallest child can pick up and put away a toy after playing with it.

The child's involvement in room maintenance helps his or her growing sense of responsibility, while it also helps keep the play area uncluttered and pleasant looking. It is much easier to teach children about health and hygiene when the classroom reflects a concern for cleanliness.

EARLY CHILDHOOD HEALTH CONCERNS

Prevention

While a teacher can often do very little to prevent the *illnesses* children bring to school, he or she *is* in a position to do a great deal about preventing *injuries* at

AGE	CHARACTERISTICS	ACCIDENT HAZARDS	MEASURES FOR PREVENTION
2–3 years	Fascinated by fire; moves about constantly; tries to do things alone; imitates Runs and is lightning fast; impatient with restraint	Traffic Transportation	Keep child away from streets and driveways with strong fence and firm discipline. Teach rules and dangers of traffic. Demonstrate safety; use seat belts, etc. Maintain vehicles including safety equipment and mechanical condition of brakes, suspension, tires, etc.
3–6 years	Explores the neighborhood, climbs, rides tricycles; likes and plays rough games	Tools/equipment Water Play areas Toys Burns Poisoning	Store dangerous knives, sharp scissors, and garden equipment out of reach. Teach safe use of tools and kitchen equipment; careful supervision when using. Use guards on fans. Even shallow wading pools are unsafe unless carefully supervised. Guard against children involving themselves in play beyond physical capabilities (climbing up something, unable to come down). Large sturdy toys without sharp edges or small removable parts are safest. Provide close supervision when equipment with small parts in use. Identify safety rules for pedestrians, passengers, and cyclists. Use guards for radiators, hot pipes, and other hot surfaces. Temperature of water not to exceed 120°F. Minimize and properly store all combustible material. Store all medicines and poisons in locked cabinet. Store cleaning products out of reach. Store kerosene or gasoline in metal cans and out of reach. Screen windows to protect against insect bites, food contamination. Use proper sanitation procedures in all food preparation. Never use lead-based paint.
7–11 years	Growing independence; Peer group grows in importance, can understand other's opinions, has a larger view of the world outside the classroom.	Cycling, pedestrian, sports accidents Losing flexibility Negative feelings can lead to physical fights Spending time at home alone Minor injuries as normal part of more outside and group activities	Encourage use of proper safety equipment such as bike helmets, knee pads for skating; rules of the road Provide physical exercise and activities on a regular basis. Teach ways to resolve conflicts in nonviolent ways. Provide information on ways to ensure safety when home alone. Describe first-aid procedures for treating minor injuries. Describe ways to respond to serious injuries.

List specific policies of your center or school for prevention of accidents. It is recommended that the staff review their "minute-by-minute" accident prevention policies periodically in order to evaluate what changes are needed and to include changes in listed guidelines for substitutes and volunteers. The accident log should be consulted in such an evaluation. The same applies to the classroom teacher: Consistent accident prevention policies should be followed as well as reviewed on a regular basis.

Based on information provided by the American Academy of Pediatrics. (1999). *Standards for Day Care Centers.*

Figure 23-3

Accident prevention.

Figure 23-4

By doing simple, everyday tasks, a child learns independence, as well as how to take care of himself or herself.

school. Figure 23–3 presents some basic ideas about accident prevention for children from two to eleven years of age.

When it becomes necessary to deal with injury or illness, it is important to remember that a teacher is neither the child's doctor nor parent. Other than providing simple first aid and large doses of comfort, the teacher's primary responsibility is to notify the parent according to instructions on the child's emergency card. The teacher can also make the child comfortable until someone who is responsible arrives to take over. A school nurse may be available in some schools to handle a child's injury or illness.

Fortunately, real medical crises are rare, considering the number of hours and the number of children involved in routine school days. The crisis is far more likely to rest in the psychological effect on the staff, the child, and the parent.

Another area of prevention concerns poisonous plants. Knowing which plants are poisonous, a teacher can avoid an accident involving a child eating a poisonous plant. Figure 23–5 lists several common plants and which parts, if any, are toxic. It also lists treatment for a child who may have eaten part of a poisonous plant. There is a new National Poison Hotline that makes information more readily available for teachers,

parents, and other caregivers. For the first time ever, people can call one national number to be connected with local poison treatment and prevention experts: 800–222–1222. This national hotline was created by Congress and is administered by the American Association of Poison Control Centers to ensure that life-saving help is available around the clock. For more information, or if you'd like to request posters and stickers for your classroom that feature the toll-free hotline, check out http://www.1–800–222–1222.info.

SAFETY EDUCATION

Accidents are the leading cause of death for children under age 14. Thus, the importance of providing children with an environment prepared for their experimentation and exploration cannot be understated. Accidents most frequently occur to children who have had little opportunity to explore, to find out for themselves, or to experience minor scrapes and bumps—children who feel no responsibility for their own safety.

When children do not have a safe environment in which to practice or the opportunity to face challenges, they're more likely to be involved in some type of accident. They have no idea of the consequences and no experience in making decisions or judging hazards.

A safe environment is not only free from hazards, but contains the presence of a diligent, observing, and supervising adult. Even though you have safety checked the play yard and playroom prior to the time the children arrive, you should be continually alert for potential hazards. As children play you must reinforce safety rules that have been decided by you and the children. You might even post them as a reminder. But you will have to keep on reminding young children, in a positive yet firm way, as they play: "Ride your bike here." "Climb the tree with your hands free." "Remove the truck from under the swings." Being prepared means looking over both your indoor and outdoor play areas for all potentially dangerous areas. For example, if swing seats are too slippery, cover them with a coat of paint to which you have added some fine sand. The sand will give just enough traction, yet it won't scratch the children. Or, cover swing seats with pieces of foam rubber to prevent slipping.

For any other potential emergencies, you, other adults who work with you, and the children all need to practice a prepared emergency plan.

Being prepared is a must. The plan should be written and posted. Decide who will stay with the children, what the children will do, and what the other

COMMON NAME	BOTANICAL NAME	TOXIC PART	TREATMENT CODE
African Violet	*Saintpaulia ionantha*	Probably none**	A, B
Azalea	*Rhododendron*	All parts	A
Begonia	*Begonia spp.**	Probably none**	A, B
Buttercup	*Ranunculus spp.*	All parts	A, C
Castor Bean	*Rincinus communis*	Chew seeds, leaves	A
Christmas Kalanchoe (or Flaming Katy)	*Kalanchoe bloss Feldiana "compacta"*	Probably none**	A
Christmas Pepper	*Capsicum annum*	Fruit—causes burns	C
Daffodil	*Narcissus spp.*	All parts, especially bulb	A
Dandelion	*Taraxacum officinale*	Probably none**	A, B
Dogwood	*Cornus florida*	Probably none**	A, B
Dumbcane	*Dieffenbachia spp.*	Leaves	A, C
English Ivy	*Hedera helix*	Leaves, berries	A
Hemlock	*Conium maculatum*	All parts, especially seed	A
Holly	*Ilex*	All parts, especially berries	A
Hyacinth	*Hyacinthus orientalis*	Bulb	A
Hydrangea	*Hydrangea arborescens*	Leaves and buds	A
Impatiens	*Impatiens spp.*	Probably none**	A
Jack-in-the-Pulpit	*Arisaema triphyllum*	Roots (in quantity)	A, C
Jerusalem Cherry	*Solanum pseudocapsicum*	Leaves, unripe berry, possibly unripe fruit	A
Jimson Weed	*Datura stramonium*	All parts	A
Lily-of-the-Valley	*Convallaria majalis*	All parts	A
Mayapple	*Podophyllum peltatum*	All parts, except ripe fruit	A
Mistletoe	*Phoradendron spp.*	All parts, especially berries	A
Mockorange	*Philadelphus spp.*	Probably none**	A, B
Mountain Laurel	*Kalmia latifolia*	All parts	A
Nightshades	*Solanum dulcamara, S. nigrum*	All parts	A
Philodendron	*Philodendron spp.*	All parts	A, C
Pokeweed	*Phytolacca americana*	Berries, leaves if cooked improperly	A
Poinsettia	*Euphorbia pulcherrima*	Sap in plant	A
Pothos	*Scindapsus aureus*	All parts	A, C
Privet	*Ligustrum vulgare*	Berries, leaves	A
Pyracantha	*Pyracantha coccinea lalandi*	Probably none**	A, B
Rhododendron	*Rhododendron maximum*	All parts	A
Rose	*Rosa spp.*	Probably none**	A, B
Wandering Jew	*Tradescantia fluminensis*	Probably none**	A, B
Water Hemlock	*Cicuta masculata*	All parts, especially roots	A
Wild Strawberry	*Fragaria vesea*	Probably none**	A, B
Yew	*Taxus spp.*	All parts	A

*spp. includes all species of the plant
**No known toxic reaction; individual children may have allergic reactions.
Treatment Codes:
A. Call the local poison information center to report ingestion and verify plant. Post this number near the phone.
B. No treatment necessary.
C. Give milk immediately and then call the local poison center.

Based on information provided by the American Academy of Pediatrics in "Standards for Day Care Centers," 1999.

Figure 23-5

Poisonous plants and treatment for their ingestion.

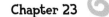

THINK ABOUT IT...

The STARBRIGHT Foundation

The STARBRIGHT Foundation is dedicated to the development of projects that empower seriously ill children. STARBRIGHT's goal is to help these children combat the medical and emotional challenges they face on a daily basis. The Foundation's projects educate and entertain, but they also address the issues that accompany illness—the pain, fear, loneliness, and depression that can be as devastating as the condition itself.

STARBRIGHT brings together key people from technology, medicine, and entertainment to design products and services that will make a difference in the lives of children with diseases such as cancer, diabetes, asthma, and kidney disease. In addition to the three CDs listed here, their projects include STARBRIGHT World, a private online community connecting more than 30,000 children living with chronic and serious illness. Kids can chat, e-mail, read bulletin boards, find friends, learn about health care condition, surf Web sites, and play games—all in an environment just for them. STARBRIGHT World can be accessed by registered users from homes and 97 children's hospitals across North America. Another STARBRIGHT project, Hospital Pals, uses Actimate's Interactive Barney along with a video to help young children prepare for radiation treatments. In the video, kids see the Barney doll receiving the same treatments they will receive, which helps them feel more secure about what will happen.

Clearly, STARBRIGHT's goals are worthy of praise, but so is their dedication to quality. Their CDs are well done, especially the program dealing with Asthma. Better yet, the programs are distributed free to any child with the condition. The Asthma software is so compelling that even kids with no direct connection to the disease enjoy playing the game over and over again. Visit http://www.starbright.org for more information.

STARBRIGHT Asthma CD-ROM, Quest for the Code (ages 7 and up)
STARBRIGHT, Life Adventure Series: Diabetes, CD-ROM (ages 5–13)
STARBRIGHT, Explorer Series: Living with Kidney Disease (ages 10–15)

adults will do. Teach children how to use the phone. Have them practice dialing the emergency number, and teach those age two or under how to obtain the operator should the need arise. Even very young children can find the "0" for operator, especially if a red dot is painted over the number.

Think ahead. Who will transport an injured or ill child to the doctor or hospital? Have parents record the numbers of their preferred doctor and hospital, but inform them that in an emergency you may call the health facility nearest to the school. Written permission from the parent needs to be on file, giving the teacher permission to take the child for any emergency medical care.

Decide about the precautions required for special needs children. Who will stay with the child with a visual or hearing impairment, or how will you handle the child in a wheelchair if you need to evacuate the building?

Keep a first-aid kit ready, freshened periodically and within easy access in the room and the play yard. The kit should include the following:

- a box of assorted adhesive bandages
- a box of 3″ sterile gauze squares
- sterile gauze bandages, both 2″ and 1″ sizes
- a roll of 1″-wide adhesive tape
- absorbent cotton
- antibacterial spray
- petroleum jelly
- cloth or absorbent sanitary pads for application of pressure

For occasional bumped foreheads and cut lips, keep on hand some form of cold pack in the freezer. An easy-to-hold, dripless cold pack can be made by half-filling a small plastic vitamin bottle with water and putting it in the freezer. Or keep a wet sponge or washcloth in the freezer to use as a cold pack; they're easier for little hands to hold than an ice cube.

At least one permanent staff person should be trained in first aid and cardiopulmonary resuscitation (CPR). Your local Red Cross or other health agency offers free courses in accident preparedness and first aid. This training needs to be updated annually.

All children should have a feeling of being responsible both for their own and the group's safety. Plan to include content from the guidelines of traffic, fire, and poison safety in your curriculum, since

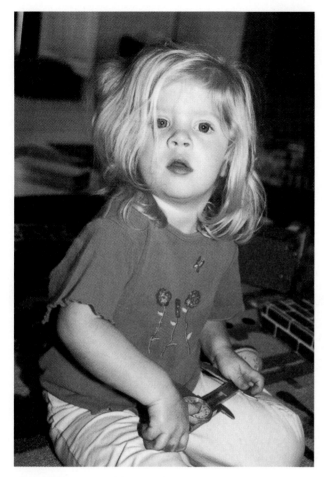

Figure 23-6
In any health matter, emphasis must be on the positive view of self.

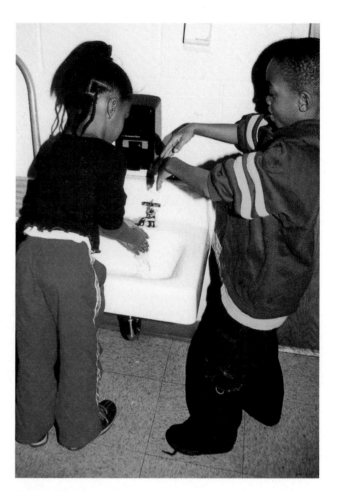

Figure 23-7
Young children learn good health habits in the early childhood program.

these are the three leading causes of injury and death among children.

Traffic Safety

You share in the responsibility of helping children learn to cope in traffic. Real experiences are the best way to teach young children about traffic.

The most common cause of traffic accidents involving young children is darting out in front of cars. Children, intent on their play or crossing the street to join a friend, dart into traffic midblock. Most of these accidents happen on residential streets. The goals of traffic safety, therefore, should address the midblock or "dart-out" accident and include these points.

- Stop before entering any street.
- Listen and look for traffic before crossing the street.
- Walk across residential streets cautiously.
- Be able to interpret traffic signs and signals correctly.

Stop before entering any street. For children under age five, or those who have not yet learned traffic safety, the first lesson should be on stopping before entering any street. Two year old children begin by going outdoors and identifying the different surfaces of the school and play yard and stopping every time the surface changes. Next, children are taken to a quiet, residential street or on a walk around the block and are asked to identify places where the surfaces change, stopping at each place.

The curb is another place to stop since the surface changes here. Learning and practicing stopping in this way establishes the habit of stopping before entering a street. Parents should also be involved in practicing this habit.

Listen and look for traffic. Once children learn to stop at the curb, they must learn to look and listen for traffic before crossing the street. With adequate adult supervision, take the children on a field trip to learn these precautions. Children under age five are confused

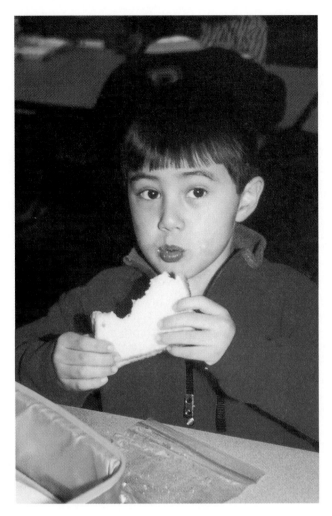

Figure 23-8
A balanced diet is a major part of good health.

as to whether traffic is traveling toward or away from them. They'll need to practice observing traffic and identifying direction as well as the speed at which cars are traveling.

Crossing a residential street. Construct a pretend street with crosswalks and corners, using masking tape or chalk on the play yard surface. Have children use their tricycles or other vehicles to role-play pedestrians and drivers. Using this street, children practice crossing. They are first reminded to stop when the surface of the yard changes and the street begins and to listen and look for oncoming traffic. Additional practice can be structured using a tabletop street with toy cars and people.

With trained and adequate adult supervision, take a group of children to a corner and practice crossing the street. Emphasize to the children that they should *never* run across the street. Running to cross is another major cause of traffic deaths. Children, who are

generally less coordinated than adults, trip and fall in front of oncoming traffic. Teach children to walk with deliberate speed as they cross. Ask them to focus on the task of crossing, not playing, thinking about anything else, or running.

Interpreting traffic signals and signs correctly.
Instead of easing the task, traffic signals and signs make crossing streets more difficult for children. Often children cross midblock in order to avoid the signs and signals that they do not understand.

Children need to be taught the meaning of the lights and signals found at intersections. First, they need to learn that red is used to symbolize danger and means "stop." Use red on objects that may be hazardous in the room and play yard. Ask children where red flags should be placed.

Play "follow-the-leader" games, with children stopping whenever a leader holds up a red flag. Once children understand the meaning of red, play the same games using green and yellow flags. Practice crossing a pretend playground street, following the signals given by one of the children with others role-playing pedestrians and drivers.

Do not attempt to practice crossing streets at an intersection without the aid of a police officer and other well-prepared and trained adults. Police officers can take small groups of children to the intersection to explain the traffic signal lights and to practice crossing with them. Children should be at least five years of age before exposure to this activity.

Protecting children in traffic is the role and responsibility of teachers, parents, and the community alike. All adults and older children will serve as models and thus should practice traffic safety themselves at all times.

Fire Safety

Project Burn Prevention, funded by the U.S. Consumer Product Safety Commission, is a program designed to provide schools with fire prevention information. It conducts a nationwide campaign on preventing injury from burns to children. The program instructs children on what to do in case of a fire. Some goals for fire safety include the following:

⊙ teaching children to approach fire with caution and respect.

⊙ involving children in practice fire drills.

⊙ teaching young children to "drop and roll" should they be involved in a fire.

⊙ teaching young children where the fire extinguisher is and how to use it, as well as how to call the fire department.

THIS ONE'S for YOU!

Breakfast and Academic, Psychosocial Performance

A study by researchers from the Massachusetts General Hospital (MGH) and other institutions lends support to the traditional beliefs about the importance of a good breakfast. The report in the journal, *Archives of Pediatric and Adolescent Medicine,* finds that children who increase their participation in school breakfast programs tend to show improvement on a wide range of measures of social and academic functioning.

Conducted in public schools in Philadelphia and Baltimore, the study found that increased school breakfast participation correlated with less tardiness and absence; higher math grades; and reductions in problems such as depression, anxiety, and hyperactivity. The researchers also found that students were more likely to participate in school breakfast programs when the meals were offered free to all students, compared with programs that provided free meals to low-income children while others paid for their breakfasts.

"What your mom told you is true, eating a good breakfast really does make a difference," says J. Michael Murphy, EdD, the study's first author and a member of the MGH Child Psychiatry Service. "What we find particularly exciting is that this is a relatively simple intervention that can significantly improve children's academic performance and psychological well-being. Now the challenge is to ensure that each child actually gets a good breakfast, either at home or at school."

This study is the latest in a series conducted by Murphy and Ronald Kleinman, MD, MGH chief of pediatric gastroenterology, that examines the impact of undernutrition in low-income children. "While we don't usually see children who are really starving in this country, we know that a significant number of children experience hunger because their families cannot provide sufficient, nutritious food," Kleinman says. The researchers gathered data on elementary and middle school students in three inner-city public schools: one in Philadelphia and two in Baltimore. Prior to the study's outset, all three schools offered breakfast according to a conventional payment system: free, reduced-price, or full-price meals depending on family income. Before a program of universally free school breakfasts was instituted, the researchers conducted interviews with students who enrolled in the study group and their parents to assess levels of depression, anxiety, and other psychosocial problems using standard questionnaires and checklists. They also determined levels of school breakfast participation for the study-group students and for the schools as a whole via information recorded by the school cafeteria staff members in the week before the universally free program was instituted.

Approximately four months after the universally free program went into effect, study-group students and their parents were reinterviewed. Cafeteria staff once more recorded whether students took a school breakfast during a week near the end of the term. In addition, the participating schools provided information regarding the study-group students' school attendance and their grades in math and three other subject areas during the semesters before and after the universally free program was instituted.

Almost half of the study-group students increased their participation in the school breakfast program when it was offered without charge. Those students who increased school-breakfast participation had significantly greater increases in math grades and significantly greater decreases in absence and tardiness during the four-month study period than did students whose school-breakfast participation remained the same or decreased. They also showed greater improvement in student-reported levels of depression and anxiety and, for the Baltimore students, reduced levels of hyperactivity, as reported by teachers. Changes in reported behavioral problems from the parental interviews were not statistically significant. No significant changes were seen in nonmath grades.

"This is the first time anyone has looked at the psychological and academic impact of school breakfast over an extended period of time," Kleinman says. "Other studies have looked at what happens when well-nourished children miss one breakfast. But all of us miss a meal from time to time and generally do fine. This series of studies shows that those children who are consistently hungry are most likely to do poorly in school and in other aspects of their lives" (*Science Daily,* 2000).

THIS ONE'S for YOU!

Sleep on It-An Important Academic Skill

You may find the following research interesting for yourself and the children you are working with.

School kids may be cutting back on sleep to finish ever mounting piles of homework, but it could be a self-defeating strategy. Harvard Medical School researchers have found that people who stay up all night after learning and practicing a new task show little improvement in their performance. The study also suggests that no amount of sleep on the following two nights can make up for the toll taken by the initial all-nighter.

"Our research shows that you need sleep that first night if you want to improve on a task," says Robert Stickgold, Harvard Medical School assistant professor of psychiatry at the Massachusetts Mental Health Center.

The study, which appeared in the journal *Nature Neuroscience,* adds a critical piece to a growing body of work by Stickgold and others showing that sleep is necessary for learning. See http://www.med.harvard. edu/ublications/Focus/Oct27_2000/index.html.

Previously, Stickgold and his colleagues found that people who learned a particular task did not improve their performance when tested later the same day but did improve after a night of sleep.

To see whether the night of sleep actually caused the improvement, Stickgold trained 24 subjects in the same visual discrimination task, which consisted of identifying the orientation of three diagonal bars flashed for a sixtieth of a second on the lower left quadrant of a computer screen full of horizontal stripes. Half of the subjects went to sleep that night and the other half were kept awake until the second night of the study. Both groups were allowed to sleep on the second and third nights. On the fourth day, both groups were tested on the visual discrimination task. Those who slept the first night identified the correct orientation of the diagonal bars much more rapidly than they had the first day. The other group showed no improvement, despite the two nights of catch-up sleep.

"We think that getting that first night's sleep starts the process of memory consolidation," says Stickgold. "It seems that memories normally wash out of the brain unless some process nails them down. My suspicion is that sleep is one of those things that does the nailing down" (*Science Daily,* 2000).

This is some good information to keep in mind at final exam time!

Figure 23-9

Children need sufficient rest, including naps during the day, to be healthy.

Invite a firefighter to the classroom to introduce the children to fire safety practices. The firefighter can teach children the habit of dropping and rolling should they, or their clothing, catch on fire. They can also demonstrate precautions to take when using fire or heat. Follow this demonstration with a lesson on respect for fire. Even if it's only the candles on a birthday cake, teach them to keep a bucket of sand and water nearby whenever handling fire. You don't have to frighten the children; just teach them the potential dangers of fire.

While the firefighter is visiting, show the children where the fire extinguishers are and how they are used. Have them practice dialing the number to reach the fire department, and hold a fire drill. Ask yourself these questions.

⊙ Do I have a written plan for a fire drill?

⊙ Do I conduct monthly drills based on the plan?

Figure 23-10
Routine health practices are learned and practiced in the early childhood program.

Figure 23-11
Playing outdoors is an integral part of a healthy day.

Figure 23-12
Adults help children learn safe practices by word and example.

- ⊙ Have I had the plan reviewed by the fire department?
- ⊙ Have I held a meeting with the other staff to discuss the plan?
- ⊙ Does everyone know where the fire extinguisher is and how to operate it?
- ⊙ Have I practiced fire drills during nap and meal-times?
- ⊙ Do I have an assembly location outside of the building?
- ⊙ What method do I have for accounting for the children once outside?
- ⊙ Have I held fire drills with different exits blocked?

Poison Safety

Thousands of children each year are victims of accidental poisoning. The development of the poison control centers has helped to eliminate many cases of accidental poisoning. Yet children in an early childhood setting are just as susceptible to poisonings as children in a home setting. In the school, it becomes your responsibility to protect children from possible poisoning accidents. Your responsibility is to teach the children these important safety facts.

- ⊙ Take medications only from adult family members, parents, physicians, or health personnel.
- ⊙ Understand that some things are to eat, while others are not.

Using food for art confuses young children on this point. Food is to eat; other substances—berries found on the playground, art materials, toys, leaves, flowers—are not for eating. Older children are more able to understand the use of food if it is included in art activities. For example, an older child is able to understand that a potato long past its peak of freshness can

THINK ABOUT IT...

Sneezing Through History

It happens everywhere, on the street, shopping, at the movies. You sneeze and people around you, perfect strangers, feel a compulsion to say, "God bless you!" or simply "Bless you!" If you have been schooled in polite behavior you will respond, "Thank you." You can't escape it. "Gesundheit!" say Germans. "Yarhamak Allah," say Arabs. "Tihei mauri ora," say Polynesians of the South Pacific (Renner, 1998).

Where did this street theater of social etiquette come from? The beginning of the practice is lost in the mist of prehistory.

"It comes from the idea that you are sneezing out your soul," said Moira Smith, librarian at the Folklore Institute at Indiana University in Bloomington. "In primitive belief, the soul has flights," she said. "You could be alive one minute and dead the next if you weren't careful about the soul flying off."

"There are a lot of ancient beliefs in general about a separable soul. It could separate for a brief period of time. When you dream, your soul is out of your body so it can't 'get back in if you're sneezing,'" she said. Even yawning posed a danger.

Smith pointed out that the idea of invoking divine protection in a sneeze was documented by the Roman naturalist, Pliny the Elder. Pliny wrote in his Natural History in 77 A.D.: "Why is it that we salute a person when he sneezes, an observation which Tiberius Caesar, they say, the most unsociable of men, as we all know, used to exact, when riding in his chariot even?"

A more up-to-date variation on the theme of the dangers of sneezing has been the notion that the heart stops when you sneeze—and everybody knows what happens when the heart stops. In case you were wondering, the heart does not stop when you sneeze.

"It does not stop whatsoever," said Dr. Jose Missri, chief of cardiology and chairman of medicine at St. Francis Hospital and Medical Center in Hartford, CT.

Professor Robert V. Blystone, who teaches biology at Trinity University in San Antonio, sees a common thread running through concern about sneezing. "In a world without antibiotics, a sneeze could mean the start of an illness which could kill," he said. "There were no magic bullets to take care of the aftereffects of the early warning system called a sneeze" (Renner, 1998).

be recycled by carving it into a useful printing tool rather than discarding it as inedible.

When you work with children under age five, you must supervise them carefully, preventing them from putting anything into their mouths. You can't expect babies not to put things into their mouths, as this is their way of learning about their world. However, you are responsible for observing the children, freeing the environment from poisonous substances, and removing nonfood objects that do find their way into the children's mouths. (See Figure 23–5 for a list of poisonous plants and materials. Also see Chapter 12 for list of unsafe art supplies.)

Check your room and outdoor play area for all poisonous substances, and remove all that you find. Note which cleaning supplies and other toxic materials are stored in a place that children might encounter accidentally. If you serve meals, be certain that food items are stored separately from nonfood items. There have

been tragic mistakes by hurried cooks or teachers who confused a bag of flour with a cleaning product.

Keep the number of your nearest poison control center posted by the phone, or use the National Poison Control phone number, 800–222–1222 to obtain help.

SUMMARY

Health and safety are physical states of being in the here and now. Young children don't think in terms of the far-distant future. It's *now* that interests them, not a lecture on how a bad health or safety habit can hurt a person in the future. Preaching, lecturing, and rote learning of health and safety information are all ineffective techniques in the early childhood health program. Instead, a positive, fun, but most of all *natural* approach to health and safety in the classroom should be emphasized.

Good health practices include brushing one's teeth and hair, bathing regularly, and having a general interest in cleanliness. Getting enough sleep and good food are also basic to good health at all ages.

In all health or personal hygiene matters, emphasis should be on the positive view of the child. Even more important, the teacher must model good health and hygiene himself or herself.

Other areas that need to be included in the early childhood curriculum are traffic safety, fire safety, and poison safety. When teaching concepts in these areas, young children need real, concrete experiences instead of more abstract lessons.

A teacher is in a position to do a great deal about preventing injuries at school for both young children and children in grades 3 to 5. Knowing what to expect from children six years of age and younger helps a teacher prevent accidents. Knowing which plants are poisonous can also be an excellent preventive measure in the early childhood classroom.

LEARNING ACTIVITIES

A. Interview children to find out what they know about the traffic system. Ask them what traffic lights mean and where, how, and why they should cross streets. Design a lesson to promote traffic safety based on their responses.

B. With the children, demonstrate their growth from birth weight to present weight by stacking hardwood blocks on a bathroom scale to equal the two weights for each child. Children may want to enter the following information in books they make up called *ALL ABOUT ME.* When I was a baby, I weighed as much as ———— blocks; now I weigh as much as ———— blocks. Each child can feel good about her present state of growth when compared with past growth.

C. Log on to one of the Web sites listed in the Helpful Web sites on page 511. Choose one of the activities in the Web site to use with a group of children. Plan a lesson around this activity. Share your plans with your fellow students for their input.

D. Design several safety-related activities of your own. Use them with a small group of children. Evaluate your experience. Share the results of your activity in class.

E. Assemble a list of local resources you could invite into the class to speak on health and safety issues. Make enough copies of your list to share with each of your classmates.

F. Choose one of the children's books listed in the Online Companion. Plan a lesson around this book. Be sure to include the following in your plans: age/grade level, name of book, health topic to be taught, and related activities in addition to the book.

ACTIVITIES FOR CHILDREN

DENTAL HEALTH ACTIVITIES

Brushing teeth fun. Cut the bottoms off large plastic soda bottles and turn them upside down—they look like teeth! Secure ten together—use a hole punch to make holes and twist ties to hold them together. Spray them with shaving cream and give the children toothbrushes to brush the teeth clean. You might consider doing this activity in your sensory table or in a large shallow tub on the floor to control the mess.

Staining teeth–A science activity. You will need two hard-boiled eggs and dark cola. To show the children how easily teeth can stain, place one egg in a jar of water and one egg in a jar of cola. The next day, remove the eggs and compare their colors. Talk about how different they look and why. Then use a toothbrush and toothpaste to brush away the stain from the cola-tinted egg. If possible, give each child a turn (you may need to soak several more eggs.)

Variation: Locate some small white ceramic tiles from construction sites, tile stores, parents who are remodeling, etc. Provide children with a variety of food products to smear on the tiles such as jelly, ketchup, syrup, peanut butter, etc. Have children brush the tile "tooth" with toothbrushes and real toothpaste. Which tile is stained? Talk about why.

Dental art activities. Try some of these art activities to reinforce dental health ideas:

- Paint with toothbrushes.
- Finger paint with toothpaste (the gel kind works the best).
- Make a tooth necklace using white clay and dental floss.
- Design a new toothpaste brand and tube.
- Draw pictures of what you think the tooth fairy looks like.

MISCELLANEOUS DENTAL ACTIVITIES

Apple smiles. You will need apples, miniature marshmallows, and peanut butter for this activity. Cut apple into wedges. Give each child two apple wedges and spread peanut butter on one side. Stick mini marshmallows on the peanut butter on one of the apple wedges. Put the other apple wedge on top (peanut butter sticking to the marshmallows). The apples are lips and the marshmallows are teeth.

What brushing does. Boil an egg in water with a tea bag. The tea bag will stain the egg brown. You can then give the children a toothbrush and toothpaste and let them brush the egg. The stains will disappear as they brush. Explain to them that this is what brushing does to their teeth.

How to brush your teeth. Show the children how to properly brush their teeth. Obtain packets with a toothbrush, red tablets, and toothpaste from a local dentist. Then allow the children to chew the red tablets. Have them brush their teeth and then look in a mirror and see what they missed. The red spots will show the parts they missed.

Toothpaste taste test. Get as many different kinds of toothpaste as you can. Have all of the children taste them. Graph which ones are the most favorite and the least favorite.

HEALTH

Hand washing check. Have children wash their hands. Then take small pieces of cotton dipped in rubbing alcohol. Rub the back of each child's hand with the moistened cotton. Look at the dirt on the cotton and

discuss what it means. Even when you think you've washed your hands, there still may be dirt present.

Our health helpers. When the children arrive at school in the morning, give them name tags that resemble little Red Cross badges. Then have them explore the different areas you have set up in the room.

- Collection of books about community helpers in the book center
- Housekeeping area with hospital arrangement (bandages, small pillows, adhesive bandages, empty spray cans, gauze, syringes, and tape)
- Art area—constructing nurses' or doctors' hats from available materials
- Dentist's office, complete with magazines, reception desk, telephone, office chair, teeth models, white shirts, cloth to go over patients, tongue depressors

This activity enables children to examine tools used by medical helpers and to experience some role playing.

Colds and germs

Equipment: Atomizer from an empty perfume bottle or sprayer from window cleaning fluid.
Procedure: Discuss colds with the children. Some questions to ask: "Have you ever had a bad cold? Did you go to the doctor or get medicine to take? Were you allowed to go to school or play with friends when you had a fever? Why not?" Explain that people can give someone else their cold or other sickness just by being around them. The germs they have can be carried in the air or on their hands.

Let the children spray water into the air and watch how it disappears. Explain that in coughing we can easily spray germs we cannot see onto others.

Say to the children: "Sometimes we have to be by ourselves when we are sick so that others will not get sick, too." Point out that if they cough or sneeze, they should cover their mouth and nose and use a handkerchief.

Another way to "spread germs." When talking about how germs are spread and the importance of hand washing, use flour to illustrate how germs get on everything. Dip your tissue in flour and pretend to sneeze. Watch the flour-germs fly. Then touch things with the tissue, leaving germs on everything.

Is it safe?

Equipment: Pictures cut from magazines or drawn freehand that show both safe and unsafe situations—untied shoelaces, child near stove, spilled paint, etc.

Procedure: Initiate a discussion with the children, reviewing things they've learned about safety. Review safety ideas for the classroom, home, and personal safety. Then introduce the "Is It Safe?" guessing game. Hold up a picture and have them tell if it shows a safe situation or an unsafe situation. Continue showing pictures, discussing each, and emphasizing *why* each situation is safe or unsafe.

HYGIENE

⊙ To clean stuffed toys, rub or shake them in a bag half filled with cornmeal. Let the toys stand for a while before brushing them off.

⊙ When game cards get sticky from too much handling, shake them in a bag filled with talcum or baby powder.

⊙ To remove felt marker ink from skin, try rubbing on toothpaste, then rinsing with water. Repeat the process until the ink disappears.

HELPING CHILDREN DRESS THEMSELVES

⊙ When boots won't go over a child's shoes, use a plastic bread bag (or any other plastic bag) over the shoes first; boots slip over the shoes easily.

⊙ When young children are learning to button up their own coats and sweaters, have them start at the bottom. They'll be more likely to get all the buttons in the right buttonholes this way.

⊙ When zippers stick, rub them with a lead pencil to get them gliding smoothly again. Or, rub the zipper with petroleum jelly or spray it with WD40 (an aerosol lubricant), being careful not to get it on the fabric.

⊙ Use old leg warmers or old socks with the toes cut off for extra warmth for children playing in the snow. When dressing to play in the snow, slip the legwarmers or toeless socks over their arms after pulling on their snowsuits and mittens. The legwarmers (or socks) prevent snow from getting between mittens and sleeves and keeps wrists warm and toasty.

HEALTH AND SAFETY COMMUNICATIONS FOR PARENTS

Whenever you have important information on health and safety practices (or any other area of the program for that matter), place it on a Parent Bulletin Board by the entrance of your room to ensure greater visibility.

Important notices and letters for parents often fall off cubby shelves and are lost. To solve this problem, use a shoebag to make an attractive parent "mailbox." Label each pocket in the shoebag with a parent's name and have mothers or fathers check daily for their "mail."

ACTIVITIES FOR OLDER CHILDREN (GRADES 4-5)

Health and safety education serves as a place in the curriculum where students focus on personal health issues, health issues of others, and environmental issues. A variety of exciting strategies is available to assist you in teaching health and safety to middle and upper elementary students. The more varied your approach, the more stimulating your classroom will be. The following strategies for health and safety instruction can be used to enhance your curriculum with this age group.

CARTOONS

Students can draw and label their own health and safety cartoons, or they can collect cartoons that depict healthful and unhealthful practices. Share and describe these cartoons. Example: Mental Health: There is a saying, "Laughter is the best medicine." Have students find a cartoon that helps them laugh at themselves.

CASE HISTORIES

A case history is a short description of an event or happening. It can be used to illustrate a point. Students may also be asked to write or react to a case history to evaluate learning. Example: Nutrition: Develop a case history about someone who has poor eating habits—skips breakfast or heavily salts food. Ask students to read the case history and identify the poor eating habits.

COMMERCIALS

Students can write and act out commercials that promote positive health behaviors. Example: Mental Health: Have students write and act out a commercial about ways a person can help cope with depression. These commercials could be videotaped to show to other classes.

COMMUNITY RESOURCES

Arrange field trips to community resource agencies. Community resources include the local health department, lung association, heart association, life insurance company, mental health center, pharmacy, and crisis centers. Example: Safety and First Aid: Visit a water treatment facility. Discuss how this facility works to keep water safe to drink.

CURRENT EVENTS NEWSLETTER

Students can research current events on a local, national, or world level and write short articles to include in a "Health Happenings" newsletter. Example: Diseases and Disorders. Have students learn which communicable diseases are currently most prevalent in their community or in their country. Write short articles describing the cause, symptoms, transmission, and treatment of those diseases. Describe health habits that may reduce the incidence of the disease.

DEBATE

Students, individually or in organized teams, can research a health issue or topic to formulate a detailed, well-documented viewpoint to use in a debate. Example: Diseases: Select students to form pro and con teams to debate, "Should students who are carriers of the AIDS virus be permitted to attend school with other children?"

DIARY OF EVENTS

Students can record daily happenings in a diary to learn more about their health and behaviors. Be careful to tell students that it is not necessary to share what they have learned about themselves. Example: Exercise and Fitness: Have students write down their daily physical activities for one week. Also ask them to describe their feelings after each activity. What did they learn about their behaviors?

MATH FOR HEALTH

Incorporate running and/or brisk walking to reinforce math concepts while enjoying a healthy activity. Whether you run or walk as a class, tell students to set a goal at the beginning of the year of how many miles or laps around the schoolyard they will complete each week. Have students keep a calendar to record their laps or miles as they try to reach that goal. Then have them use those calendars to add their total laps; convert the laps to miles; get the class total for the week; and average their daily, weekly, and monthly totals. You can even use brisk walking or running to teach the metric system, converting meters into miles.

HEALTHY BODY SALAD

This is a great activity to teach young children about how healthy eating benefits the heart and mind. You can do it to celebrate a great week of student work or as the culmination of a unit about Mr. Amazing Heart/Body. Tell students you will have a "heart-friendly party" with healthy foods that are fun to prepare and tasty to eat. Ask children to bring in a healthy ingredient to make a salad, such as green-leaf lettuce (rather than iceberg, which has low nutritional value), carrots, black olives, low-fat cheese, or fat-free dressing. As each child adds his or her ingredient into a large bowl, describe how the ingredient is a heart-smart food. Then toss the salad and enjoy! For added fun, serve angel food cake with fresh strawberries.

POISON PREVENTION

Take time to discuss poisons with your class. Contact the nearest poison control center for Mr. Yuck stickers for students to take home and put on the bottles under the sink. Also talk about dangers that exist from plants as well as those dangers inherent in taking someone else's medicine. Other ideas can be found at http://www.ppsinc.org.

SAFETY SIGNALS

Plan with children how they might determine whether red traffic lights really are longer than green lights. Determine the best way to set up the study, then choose an intersection and provide stopwatches. Have students make a hypothesis and then set out to prove it.

READING LABELS

Collect ingredient labels from several different food items. Explain to the students that they must be listed in descending order of quantity in the specific item. Then provide them with a list of minimum daily requirements for various vitamins and minerals (available at http://www.fda.gov.). Challenge the students to check the requirements against the labels from their favorite foods. Will that cause them to make different nutritional choices?

MOVING FOOD CHAIN

When students incorporate movement into a unit about the food chain, they're more likely to remember what they've learned. To help them, have students choose a plant that is a producer—either a fruit or vegetable—that they will act out during an imaginary growing period. Tell students not to reveal their choice; they must remain silent. Then have them make their bodies as low to the ground as they can, as if they were simulating the shape of a plant that has yet to grow. Tell students they will grow based on the sound and rhythms of a hand drum. Then play the drum very softly when they are seedlings in the ground, somewhat loudly when they are half way to maturation, and very loudly when they are fully mature and ready to be harvested. Walk around and gently tap each student to signal that they can reveal what plant they have grown into. You might also ask students to tell what they know about the plant or describe its nutritional value.

INTERVIEWS

Students can interview someone in the community. Students should be prepared with a list of questions before the interview takes place. The information can be shared with the class. Example: Mental Health: Have each student interview someone who works in the area of mental health. They might select a psychiatrist, psychologist, psychiatric nurse, social worker, or health educator.

JINGLES

Students can make up jingles to describe health products or practices, or they can analyze jingles that are used on television or radio commercials. Example: Consumer and Personal Health: Have each student share a favorite jingle with the class. Why does the jingle appeal to them?

MURAL

A mural can be made by having students write or paste pictures on long sheets of paper. The mural can illustrate events that have happened over a long period of time. Example: Diseases and Disorders: Have students trace the history of major epidemics of communicable diseases and make a mural that shows (1) disease outbreaks—tuberculosis, plague; (2) disease breakthroughs—penicillin, Bacille Calmette-Guerin (BCG) vaccine; and (3) important people in their health fields. Place these happenings with their dates on the mural.

PHOTOGRAPHY

When appropriate, encourage students to take photographs and write a description of what they see. This strategy can be used on a field trip to highlight what the students have learned. Example: Safety & First Aid: Students can take pictures of safety hazards in their community. Describe ways to remedy these hazards.

POSTERS

Posters are available from many health organizations as well as from local health departments. Posters, such as "Thank You for Not Smoking" from the American Cancer Society (http://www.cancer.org), can be displayed in the classroom to reinforce learning. Students can make their own posters to use in the classroom or to display in the community. Example: Drugs: Have students make a poster that discourages smoking or drug use.

SKITS

Through skits, students can explore different issues that they might experience in real life. The teacher can design the roles for specific situations. Example: Consumer and Personal Health: Devise a skit in which a quack sells a health food. Use as many persuasive techniques as possible to sell the product.

CHAPTER REVIEW

1. In teaching young children about health, what is the best approach and teaching strategy to use? Describe activities you would plan to use in teaching young children about health.

2. What do you feel are some of the most basic health and other types of information you should have on hand for each child in case of emergency? Explain.

3. Discuss several ways you can prevent accidents with children six years old and younger.

4. What are some safety hazards for children ages 7 to 11?

5. What are some other areas of the curriculum in which to include health and safety ideas? Give specific examples of activities.

6. How would you teach young children about fire, traffic, and poison safety in concrete ways? Give specific examples in your reply.

REFERENCES

American Academy of Pediatrics. (1999). *Standards for day care centers.* Evanston, IL: AAP.

Renner, G. (1998, Sept. 25). Sneezing through history. *The Hartford Courant,* C–8.

Science Daily, Massachusetts General Hospital, Nov. 21, 2000. "School Breakfast Participation leads to academic, psychosocial improvements. Online: http://sciencedaily.com/releases/1998/09/980919115732.

Science Daily, Harvard Medical School, "New Reason to 'Sleep on it': Study shows importance of sleep to memory consolidation and task performance." Online: http://www.sciencedaily.com/releases/2000/11/001122075125.htm.

ADDITIONAL READINGS

American Academy of Sports Medicine (2003). *Physical fitness assessment guidelines.* Philadelphia, PA: Lippincott Williams & Wilkins.

Aronson, S. S. (2003). *Model child care health policies.* Washington, DC: NAEYC.

Aronson, S. S. (Ed.). (2003). *Healthy young children: A manual for programs.* Washington, DC: NAEYC.

Greene, B. (2004). *Keep the connection: Choices for a better and healthier life.* New York: Hyperion.

Hardman, A. (2004). *Physical activity and health: An evidence-based assessment.* New York/London: Routledge.

Holmes, E. (2004). *This thing called you.* New York: Putnam.

Howley, C. T. (2003). *Health fitness instructor's handbook.* Champaign, IL: Human Kinetics Publishers.

Pruitt, B. E. (2003). *Decisions for healthy living.* Upper Saddle River, NJ: Pearson Education.

Reicheler, G. (2003). *Active wellness: Feel good for life.* New York: Avery.

Robertson, C. (2003). *Safety, nutrition, and health in early education.* Clifton Park, NY: Delmar.

Rominger, L. (2004). *Kid friendly food allergy cookbook.* Gloucester, MA: Rockport Books.

Rossol, M. (2001). *The artist's complete health and safety guide.* New York: Allworth Press.

Sapontzis, S. F. (2004). *Food for thought.* New York: Prometheus Books.

Sullivan, K. (2004). *The parents' guide to natural health care for children: How to raise happy, healthy children from birth to 15.* Boston, MA: Shambhala Publications.

SOFTWARE FOR CHILDREN

F.D.N.Y. American Hero Firefighter, 2002. Ages 8 and up.

Fisher Price Rescue Heroes Hurricane Havoc, 2003. Ages 4–7.

Fisher Price Kindergarten Ready for Kindergarten, 2003. Ages 4–5.

Health Beats Feelings and Worries, 2002. Ages 7–13.

Health Beats Keeping Healthy, 2002. Ages 7–13.

Health Beats Body Parts, 2002. Ages 7–13.

Health Beats Growing and Developing, 2002. Ages 7–13.

Health Beats Aches and Pains, 2002. Ages 7–13.

Putt-Putt Enters the Race, 2003. Ages 3–8.

Switches-on Schoolhouse Health, 2002. Ages 6–12.

Tonka Firefighter, 2003. Ages 4–7.

Youthealth Inner Explorers Series One, 2002. Ages 5–10.

HELPFUL WEB SITES

Sparky's World, http://www.sparky.org
This site provides health and fire safety information and ideas. The appropriate age range is from 6 years and up.

Safety City, http://www.nhtsa.dot.gov/kids
This site provides information on traffic safety, health, accident prevention, to name just a few topics available. Children ages 7 to 12 will enjoy this site.

Otto Club, http://www.ottoclub.org

This site, presented by the AAA Traffic Safety Department, provides health and traffic safety information and activities for preschoolers through grade 5.

Bright Futures, http://www.brightfutures.org

Bright Futures is a national initiative dedicated to promoting and improving the health of the United States' children. The Bright Futures Web site offers information on children's health and development in a new and practical format. There's something for everyone interested in the well-being of children. Some materials in Spanish are also available on the site, as well as links to the organizations that support Bright Futures and other useful sites for professionals and families.

Deaf World, http://www.deafworld.org/

This Web site is the meeting place for the global deaf community. It offers links to numerous services and organizations around the world.

American Dental Association, http://www.ada.org

This Web site provides information for children, parents, and teachers on good dental health.

Environmental Protection Agency, Public Information, http://www.epa.gov

This Web site provides information and services on teaching about the environment. This information is especially designed for classroom use.

Environlink Library, http://www.envirolink.org/

This Web site provides links to hundreds of worldwide organizations devoted to protecting the environment.

All of the following sites have great ideas and information for teachers to use in health and safety activities for children.

National Safety Council, http://www.nsc.org
Parents Resource for Drug Education,
  http://www.prideusa.org
Food & Drug Administration, http://www.fda.gov
Consumer Information Center,
  http://www.pueblo.gsa.gov
Consumer Product Safety Commission,
  http://www.cpsc.gov/

The following Web sites are good sources for information on diseases, prevention, and control.

American Cancer Society, http://www.cancer.org
American Heart Association, http://www.amhrt.org
Centers for Disease Control & Prevention,
  http://www.cdc.gov
Juvenile Diabetes Foundation, http://www.jdf.org/

These sites are good sources for information on emotional and mental health.

National Institute of Mental Health,
  http://www.nimh.nih.gov/
National Mental Health Association,
  http://www.nmha.org

For additional creative activity resources, visit our Web site at http://www.EarlyChildEd. delmar.com.

Creative Celebrations: Holidays in the Early Childhood Curriculum

REFLECTIVE QUESTIONS

After studying this section, you should be able to answer the following questions.

1. Have I thought through my personal feelings on holidays and their place in the classroom?
2. What are my plans for including celebrations in my early childhood teaching practice?
3. How can I be sure my classroom and activities are nonbiased and reflect the culture in my school and community?
4. Have I thought and worked through with my colleagues and parents the holidays we feel are important in our curriculum?
5. Have I reflected on my own feelings about the religious aspects of holidays?
6. Do I have a good idea of how to develop a holiday policy for my early childhood classroom practice?
7. Do I know how to implement the basic steps to developing a holiday policy?
8. How will I assess the effectiveness of my holiday policy?
9. Have I thought through what I feel should be the goals of my holiday policy?
10. What are some basic markers of a quality, multicultural, anti-bias program?
11. Do I have a good idea of how to decide which holidays need only discussion and which are to be celebrated?
12. Am I using a developmentally appropriate approach to holiday celebrations in my work with children?
13. Am I including holidays in the curriculum in ways that fit the normal routine and do not overstimulate children?
14. Am I including process-oriented, open-ended, creative activities as part of my holiday curriculum?
15. Have I reviewed my holiday curriculum to be sure that there are no stereotyped presentations of holidays or holidays that might frighten children?
16. Have I included all of the families and cultural groups necessary in the holiday curriculum planning?

The early childhood classroom has changed dramatically over the past ten years and will continue to do so. In 25 of the largest cities in the United States, at least one-half of the students are from linguistically and culturally diverse groups, and Hispanics are the fastest-growing population in the country (Smith & Luckasson, 2002). The growing diversity of the student groups in our classrooms provide teachers an exciting opportunity to help children understand and appreciate their own and other children's unique, cultural differences. Because of the great diversity of cultures represented in early childhood classrooms today, this section is designed to be a guide to assist you in creating your *own* unique and group-specific anti-bias celebrations. This approach is taken in the hope that holidays will be a meaningful, nonstereotypical part of your curriculum.

In the following pages, you will find many suggestions and ideas for addressing what many teachers call the "holiday question." Yet, this section will not do the work involved in finding the appropriate anti-bias approach to celebrations in your school setting. You will need to do the work it takes in getting to know each of the children in your group and the special cultural differences each represents. From this assessment you will be able to decide which celebrations are most appropriate for your own group.

Each of the chapters in Section 6 is designed to encourage critical thinking about celebrations and how to include them in the curriculum in an anti-biased, multicultural way. You will *not* find lists of holiday activities for children at the end of each chapter. Instead, you will find numerous references to Web sites, which in turn provide a multitude of suggestions for multicultural art activities, fine art from many cultures, children's books, history, and much more. You are encouraged to apply the ideas in these chapters to design your creative holiday activities for your own unique situation. A list of Web sites containing reviews and listings of the latest books about multicultural holidays is included at the end of Chapter 26. It is the author's hope that in these resources you will have access to the most current information on children's multicultural and holiday books as possible.

Section 6 is divided into the following chapters:

Chapter 24
The Place of Celebrations in the Curriculum
Chapter 25
Including Celebrations in the Curriculum
Chapter 26
Developmentally Appropriate Celebrations

The Place of Celebrations in the Curriculum

Objectives

After studying this chapter, you should be able to:

1. State the ABC Task Force's position on the place of holidays in the curriculum.

2. Explain how children learn best about other cultures.

3. List at least three reasons why it is important to include holiday celebrations in the curriculum.

4. Discuss ways to approach the religious aspects of holidays in working with young children.

Holidays and celebrations have been a traditional part of the early childhood program. Holidays represent special times in the lives of families, communities, and cultures. Yet, there is a prevalent misconception that an anti-bias approach means the elimination of all holiday celebrations from the early childhood curriculum. The ABC Task Force's book, *Anti-Bias Curriculum: Tools for Empowering Children* (Derman-Sparks, 1989) is often used as a reference for this approach. However, Louise Derman-Sparks, one of the authors of the ABC Task Force report, asserts that their report "does *not* say that people should stop all holiday activities in their educational program." (Bisson, 1997, xiii). Instead, the ABC Task Force raised questions about how we have used holidays in the past and how we have presented and involved children in holiday activities.

The primary message of the ABC Task Force's chapter on holidays is to encourage early childhood educators to rethink and make changes necessary in their practice with regard to celebrations or holidays.

MEANING OF HOLIDAYS

Holidays hold deep meaning for many people. They represent a whole complex of experiences, feelings, connections, and memories of families and friends. Some holiday memories are warm and positive; some are not. Some of us can't wait for holidays, some of us want to "run away from home" at the thought of yet another holiday season. So, asking people to rethink their approach to using holidays in the curriculum is a more complex task than appears on the surface.

517

CELEBRATIONS AND HOLIDAYS— THE OLD WAY

Many curriculum guides are organized around holidays. If these are commercial curriculum guides, when we use them with children, we're often at the risk of providing activities that are meaningless to the children we teach. This is because the activities do not come from the children's own experiences, interests, or questions. In addition, relying on holiday-based curriculum guides can mean neglecting other important and meaningful activities for children.

Teachers know that it is important and essential to celebrate cultural diversity in the classroom, and we often seek out holiday celebrations to do this. Celebrations of holidays from different cultures has become a popular way for teaching about culture and diversity. This may seem to be a logical approach, since celebrations of holidays already play an important part in the curriculum in many programs. Yet, when celebrations become the main or only way to teach about cultural diversity, teachers do a great injustice to children's education. Culture is not taught through a simple, single focus such as a holiday activity. Children learn about their culture every day of their lives, in daily living, in daily activities, and in daily interactions with others. They learn about other cultures over *time,* by getting to know the people of a culture and how they live their daily lives. Since celebrations of holidays are special times of the year, regular routines are *not* practiced at that particular time, and children won't learn about the usual, everyday living of a cultural group by only learning about their celebrations of holidays. The result is a "tourist curriculum" and not an anti-bias curriculum (Derman-Sparks, 1989). Just like a tourist, the children "visit" a culture, participate in a few isolated activities as one might do on a vacation in another country, then return home to "regular classroom life" (Derman-Sparks, 1989).

This discussion may lead you back to the beginning of this chapter and the idea that a "no holiday" approach may be the best. Yet, leaving celebrations completely out of children's classroom experiences can have a negative effect, especially for those children whose special holiday celebration is never reflected in stores, in television programs, in movies, in greeting cards, or in the general public. Also, if you don't include celebrations in your program, you are leaving out an important part of families' lives.

Celebrations of holidays can help teach children to respect diversity and demonstrate in the classroom that different beliefs are good. Celebrations can also serve to connect children's lives at home and school. They also provide another way for children and teachers to

- ⊙ To promote connections among children, families, and staff
- ⊙ To learn about important events in the lives of all children and families in the program
- ⊙ To support and validate the experiences of children, their families, and staff in the program
- ⊙ To reinforce connection to cultural roots
- ⊙ To celebrate both similarities and differences in children's lives
- ⊙ To stretch children's awareness and empathy
- ⊙ To teach children critical thinking about bias
- ⊙ To teach activism (Bisson,1997)

Figure 24-1

Summary of reasons for including holiday celebrations in the early childhood program.

get to know each other on another level. By developing a curriculum that reflects the diverse celebrations of the children in your group, it provides an opportunity for a child to feel special. (Figure 24–1 summarizes these reasons for including holiday celebrations in the curriculum.)

Celebrations create memories. As a sign over the portal of one of the Reggio Emilia schools said, "We are Friends When We Have Memories Together" (Scharmann, 1999, p. 26).

Celebrations should never *take over* the curriculum; the day-to-day routine has great significance for young children and shouldn't be continually interrupted by special events—either those loved by the adults in the program or those selected in the name of multiculturalism. The same is true for older children. Letting holidays take over the curriculum distracts rather than adds to the focus on the multicultural curriculum. Overexcitement and lack of attention are just two effects of an overemphasis on holidays for older children.

The challenge is to select a few holiday celebrations to explore in depth during the school year and let the others go, as far as your program is concerned. Chapter 25 presents ways to help you make the decision on which holidays you will incorporate into your program.

CELEBRATIONS—FEELINGS AND BELIEFS

A culture's celebrations often have religious roots, and religious beliefs and differences have been a major source of conflict throughout history. One of your most challenging and important jobs will be to handle

Figure 24-2
Celebrations are good occasions for special art projects.

Figure 24-3
Young children learn about other cultures in day-to-day experiences, not single events.

religion in ways that respect families' beliefs without going against our constitutional guarantee of the separation of church and state. Just as much of a challenge will be to handle religious celebrations by not trivializing them by losing the essence of their meaning or focusing on their commercial representations. (Chapter 26 will help you deal with the issue of stereotypes.)

Religion is a part of culture and has a strong impact on the way many people see the world and live their lives. Yet, just as it is important to put aside your personal feelings about celebrations in general, you need to be able to separate from your work with children your own religious beliefs and any biases that you might have about other beliefs. Supporting and respecting children's and families' beliefs doesn't necessarily mean you agree with them, but such support is essential in helping each child in his or her social–emotional development. To be able to provide this support, you must understand your own feelings and beliefs about religion. Honestly explore your feelings about religion yourself and with colleagues, your supervisor, or other adults. Don't be surprised if you react personally to matters of religion. It's easy to become sensitive or defensive if a practice you believe in is challenged or omitted from the curriculum. In this regard, consider the various feelings that arose when an early childhood staff chose to celebrate "el Día de los Muertos" (The Day of the Dead, a holiday originating in Mexico) instead of Halloween at their center.

The Day of the Dead honors the ancestors, inviting back their souls to be among us for a time of family reunion. It is both a celebration of love and a frank acknowledgment of the reality of death. The celebration of el Día de los Muertos was seen as appropriate by staff of our school.

The primary teachers saw the celebration as age-appropriate for their six- to eight-year-olds.

Other adults with strong religious values reacted differently. In the primary class, one boy's mother wouldn't let him participate in making sugar skulls, an activity that offended her Christian views. The staff arranged for the child to visit kindergarten during this activity. He accepted his mother's limits, although he was concerned about being left out of something fun.

Another parent who was Christian, reacting to the skeletons Manuel had hung outdoors and to the use of the word "altar," called other parents to try to organize a protest. "It's Satanism," she insisted. "Did you read the explanation of el Día de los Muertos that the teachers wrote?" she was asked. "No I saw enough to know that it's Satanism," she replied. Finally, asking, "Am I the only one with this issue?" she withdrew her child from the school (Neubert & Jones, 1998).

Reprinted with permission from the National Association for the Education of Young Children.

Obviously, celebrations can sometimes cause disagreements. These disagreements, small and large, that exist among us are part of our learning to live together as a diverse group. Yet, the airing of genuine differences among people is a source of continuing growth and learning for both children and adults.

Doing things (including celebrations) the way "we've always done them" can be educationally unsound in a diverse and ever-changing world. In the 21st century, many choices will be available to our children. Making intelligent choices requires information as well as a values base. In the previous example, "I don't want to learn about it" was the reaction of one

Figure 24-4

Holiday celebrations should never interrupt important routine activities like playing with sand and water.

THINK ABOUT IT... History of Holiday Symbols

During the early decades of the 20th century, art activities based on immigrant crafts, folk traditions, and ethnic holidays flourished for all ages and all groups. School children adopted ethnic symbols as their own. These various holiday symbols—turkeys, bats, reindeer, bunnies, black cats, holly, shamrocks, pumpkins, and hearts to name a few—continue to be seen in holiday art projects today. They have become so commercialized and so stereotyped that few of us know anything about their original meaning.

Although children learn how to make these symbols, their cultural meanings are rarely, if ever, explored. If their origins and traditions were explored in depth, some would most certainly be banned from the classroom. For example, few teachers are aware that when young children dance around a maypole, they are paying tribute to the reproductive powers of males. Of course, this, like the origin of the Easter Bunny as an ancient fertility symbol, can be ignored.

Opportunities for art expressions associated with holidays can be significant learning experiences if they have meaningful objectives, inspiring art examples, clear criteria for their use, and a place in the overall curriculum.

For children of all ages and in all seasons of the year, the making of art of any kind is not just about how to use materials, but more importantly, why it is worth their time to do it.

Here are some ideas to help you focus on multicultural art forms rather than stereotyped holiday symbols:

⊙ Any country or culture can be studied through its art forms. Assemble prints, pictures, and artifacts and then discuss the details and patterns.

⊙ Ask about what the figures are doing and why.

⊙ Students can research the background of pieces of art (media, techniques) and then experiment with these. Emphasize the values that are portrayed in each art form by asking, "What does this show about the people?"

⊙ Each child may enjoy making a personal collection of art from different cultures and ethnic groups using magazines, advertisements, and postcards.

⊙ See Web sites in the Online Companion for multicultural art from many countries.

Figure 24-5

Meaningful activities for young children come from the child's own experiences, interests, and questions.

parent from a strong religious faith. In contrast, "I want to know about things," was the reaction of a teacher from a similar faith background. While affirming her own values, she took professional responsibility for learning more in order to be helpful to children. She was able to recognize and appreciate the fact that different cultures celebrate events in different ways (Neubert & Jones, 1998).

Celebrations, then, will force you to try new things. Trying new things requires us to stretch, to gather new information, to experience the disequilibrium that many developmental experts insist is essential to cognitive and social development.

As one teacher concluded from our el Día de los Muertos example, "Good curriculum is significant; it raises issues to be grappled with by adults and children alike. Multicultural curriculum isn't just nice, it's about genuine differences among people and the biases accompanying those differences as well as about the commonalties we share" (Neubert & Jones, 1998, p. 9).

SUMMARY

Holidays have been a traditional part of the early childhood program. Holidays represent special times in the lives of families, communities, and cultures. While the ABC Task Force raised questions about how

THIS ONE'S for YOU!   Reflecting Diversity in Art

Children grow to like what is comfortable and familiar and may shrink from the unusual. If they are to become accepting of differing forms of beauty, they need immersion in all its variations. For example, a classroom should contain art of many styles showing people of different ages, races, ethnic backgrounds, sexes, and skin colors. It is important for children to see art from different places and time periods—images of people going about life in ways that may be unusual to the children and yet show how basic needs for food, clothing, shelter, knowledge, love, and beauty are universal.

Respect for diverse peoples can be encouraged by displaying works in which individuals are portrayed in dignified contemporary situations, not just historical garb. We must take care not to demean groups: to just show Native Americans half-naked, wearing skins and feathers, is inaccurate, to say the least. Avoid commercial cutouts; cute cardboard pin-ups; coloring books; and patterns of ethnic groups and races *only* in historical traditional clothing, which suggests they are less advanced and still live this way (think how silly it would be to show Americans in Pilgrim outfits as a "typical" American image).

Original art and a variety of types of art show children there are many possibilities. Sculpture, fine art prints, postcard prints, and art books are ways to show authentic cultural images. Most schools and public libraries have children's literature containing art in every style and media, and students can be invited to bring artifacts from home (pottery, quilts, photographs, etc.) that may be stunning sources of aesthetic stimulation and family heritage. We can cultivate the aesthetic by planning quiet times to pass around objects for close examination.

we have used holidays in the past, their primary message is to encourage early childhood educators to rethink and make changes necessary in their practice of holidays.

The early childhood curriculum should not be organized around holidays. This practice can result in neglecting other important and meaningful activities for children. Centering the curriculum around holidays can also cause you to run the risk of providing activities that are meaningless to young children.

Using holidays as the only means of introducing young children to other cultures can cause children to have an inappropriate view of cultures. Culture is not taught through a single focus such as a holiday activity, but in daily living, in daily activities, and in daily interactions with others.

The challenge to early childhood educators is to select a few appropriate holiday celebrations to explore in depth in a developmentally appropriate manner during the school year and let the others go.

A culture's celebrations often have religious roots. One of your most challenging and important jobs will be to handle religion in a way that respects families' beliefs without going against our constitutional guarantee of the separation of church and state.

Views on holidays can differ among individuals and can sometimes cause disagreements. These disagreements are part of our learning to live together as a diverse group. Airing of genuine differences among people is a source of continuing growth and learning for both children and adults.

Using an anti-biased, multicultural approach to celebrations will force you to try new things. Trying new things requires us to stretch, to gather new information, and to experience the disequilibrium that is essential to cognitive and social development.

LEARNING ACTIVITIES

A. Everyone has had experiences with holiday celebrations. Spend at least five minutes going back over the years of your holiday celebrations. Then write down your thoughts in response to these questions:
   1. What is your earliest recollection of a holiday?
   2. Use one adjective to describe this first holiday memory.
   3. What is one of your happiest holiday memories? Your saddest? Your most disappointing?
   4. Did your memories contain any religious connections to holidays?
   5. Think back to your family holiday celebrations. When (if ever) did you understand the religious significance of the holiday?
   6. Did you have childhood friends who celebrated different holidays than you celebrated? If so, did you understand why and/or what these holidays were? Did you participate in their holiday celebrations?

After answering these questions, summarize your holiday experiences according to what was presented in this chapter. For example, were your experiences multicultural? Anti-biased? Do your background and experiences with holidays relate to the experiences of the children in your group today? More specifically, do you feel that you can relate to the children in your current early childhood classroom with your own background on holidays?

B. After completing item A., list your plans to address the problem/issues raised by that item. Example: Problem—My background on holidays is all Protestant Caucasian middle class with no experience with other religions, cultures, or classes. My current teaching situation is with a multiethnic, multicultural group with several Eastern and Hindu religions represented. Plan—To learn about the Eastern religions and cultural groups represented in my group of children and to learn about their holidays and cultures. Source of information—Parents, community, children, colleagues, supervisors.

C. Did you ever experience a "tourist curriculum" in your childhood years? If so, relate your experience to the class. What could have been done differently to prevent this? Be specific in your answer.

D. Pretend that you can eliminate one holiday from *ever* existing. What holiday would it be and why? Compare your answers to your classmates'. Is there a consensus on this? If there is, what does this tell you about this particular holiday? About holidays in general?

E. Since you cannot totally eliminate the holiday noted in D., what can you do to make it a more acceptable, pleasant holiday for yourself? Does your new approach to this holiday make it more appropriate for young children? Why or why not?

CHAPTER REVIEW

1. You are asked by your supervising teacher to cover Mexican cultures with the children in your group. She suggests a food activity of making tortillas for lunch during May. Then she wants you to have an art activity of making maracas for the music corner. Are these appropriate activities for introducing Mexican culture to young children? Why or why not?

2. Using the same situation as in the first question, describe how you would correct the situation. Include in your answer your activities, your overall approach, and your curriculum ideas.

3. Why are curriculum guides that are designed around holidays not appropriate for the early childhood program?

4. What is the ABC Task Force's position on holidays in the early childhood curriculum?

5. What is a "tourist curriculum?" Why is it not an anti-bias curriculum?

6. How do young children learn about different cultures?

7. Why are holidays not an appropriate way to learn about cultures?

8. Why is it not appropriate to completely eliminate holidays from the early childhood curriculum?

9. Explain why celebrations should never take over the curriculum.

10. Is it possible to eliminate religion from holiday celebrations? Why or why not?

11. Disagreements sometimes arise in the early childhood program about holiday celebrations. Are these destructive to the early childhood program? Why or why not?

REFERENCES

Bisson, J. (1997). *Celebrate! An anti-bias guide to enjoying holidays in early childhood education programs.* St. Paul, MN: Redleaf.

Derman-Sparks, L., & ABC Task Force. (1989). *Anti-bias curriculum: Tools for empowering young children.* Washington, DC: NAEYC.

Neubert, K., & Jones, E. (1998). Creating a culturally relevant holiday curriculum: A negotiation. *Young Children, 53*(5), 14–19.

Scharmann, M. W. (1999). We are friends when we share memories together. *Young Children, 53*(2), 26–29.

Smith, D. D., & Luckasson, R. (2002). *Introduction to special education.* (2nd ed.) Needham Heights, MA: Allyn Bacon.

ADDITIONAL READINGS

Banks, J. A. (2002). *An introduction to multicultural education.* (3rd ed.) Boston: Allyn & Bacon.

Barrera, I., & Corso, R. M. (2003) *Skilled dialogue: Strategies for responding to cultural diversity in early childhood.* Baltimore, MD: Paul H. Brookes.

Copple, C. (2003). *A world of difference: Readings on teaching young children in a diverse society.* Washington, DC: NAEYC.

deMarquez, T. J. (2002, Nov.). Creating world peace: One classroom at a time. *Young Children,* 90–94.

Fassler, R. (2003). *Room for talk: Teaching and learning in a multilingual kindergarten.* New York: Teachers College Press.

Jones, G. W., & Moomaw, S. (2002). *Lessons from Turtle Creek: Native curriculum in early childhood classrooms.* St. Paul, MN: Redleaf.

Kaiser, B., & Rasminsky, J. S. (2003, July). Opening the culture door. *Young Children,* 53–56.

Levin, D. E., & Lobo, B. (2000). Learning about the world through play. *Scholastic Early Childhood Today, 15*(3), 56–59.

Rettig, M. A. (2002). Cultural diversity and play from an ecological perspective. *Children and Schools, 24*(3), 189–199.

Tiedt, P. L., & Tiedt, I. M. (2002). *Multicultural teaching: A handbook of activities, information and resources.* (6th ed.) Boston, MA: Allyn & Bacon.

HELPFUL WEB SITES

Anti-Defamation League, http://www.adl.org
Peace Gallery: Pictures from Around the World,
   http://www.peacegallery.org
Precious Children, http://www.pbs.org
Educators for Social Responsibility, http://www.
   esrnational.org
Southern Poverty Law Center, http://www.
   tolerance.org

For additional creative activity resources, visit our Web site at http://www.EarlyChildEd.
delmar.com.

Chapter 25

Including Celebrations in the Curriculum

Objectives

After studying this chapter, you should be able to:

1. Discuss the importance of developing a holiday policy.
2. List the three steps involved in developing a holiday policy.
3. Discuss how to formulate goals of a holiday policy.
4. Discuss how to establish the curriculum specifics related to the goals.
5. Explain how to assess the effectiveness of your holiday policy.

Now that the importance of celebrations has been established in the early childhood curriculum, this chapter explores the ways to go about including celebrations in the curriculum in an appropriate, anti-biased way.

DEVELOPING A POLICY FOR CELEBRATIONS

The first step to including holiday celebrations in the curriculum is to develop a **holiday policy.** Formulating a holiday policy at the same time you shape your new approach to holidays will help you make your decisions easier in the future. A holiday policy is a guide for everyone involved in your program to help them choose, implement, and evaluate celebration activities. Developing a holiday policy involves much critical

thought guided by questions such as, What universal values does the holiday represent? What cultural tradition? Is it developmentally appropriate in terms of children's ability to understand? Does the holiday promote stereotypes? Will children learn all about it outside of your school?

Using questions such as these, you are able to formulate a holiday policy appropriate for your particular situation. A holiday policy developed by a program in a culturally diverse metropolitan school would include holiday practices quite different than a school in a rural, small town with a largely homogenous population. In both cases, however, a holiday policy would guide their decision, *not* a commercial curriculum guide and *not* the general public.

Your holiday policy must be clear, specific to your situation, and flexible. If you are a classroom teacher, it may be applicable to your individual room only. Directors or supervisors may develop holiday policies to guide an entire program.

Once you put your policy in place, you will always have it to refer to, to help guide your decisions as different situations arise. The time you put into developing a holiday policy will pay off in time saved by not having to decide how to handle each holiday as it comes up throughout the year. An established holiday celebration policy can also be used to communicate your holiday approach to new staff and families as they enter the program. It is important to remember that improving and changing the policy is an on-going responsibility of those in the early childhood program. For instance, as a new ethnic group is included in your school, their input in the holiday policy would be important.

Developing a holiday celebration policy involves time and effort. Your policy will naturally evolve and change as you experience successes and failures in your classroom with each passing holiday. But more than that, it is vital that you involve all those who will be affected by the policy in its development. This means all teachers, assistants, and parents and guardians of the children in the group need to be included in formulating your policy on celebrations. If you don't have everyone's participation, you run the risk of not having them "buy into" the policy. When this happens, the teachers or family members involved may say that they understand and agree with the policy, but then may withhold their support and cooperation (Bisson, 1997).

Some teachers or directors have developed holiday policies or made decisions about how to handle holidays that work well for them without consulting with families and co-workers. This solo approach is sometimes easier than organizing a group effort and working with others. Some teachers feel that they have more knowledge about child development and working with children than families and therefore think some decisions are better made by them and not parents. While these may be valid reasons for bypassing a group approach, this solo approach misses out on opportunities as well. One of the most valuable outcomes of bringing educators and families together to think about goals for holidays is the thoughtful discussions that ensue.

Getting together and thinking through the issue of holidays provides an opportunity for community building between teachers and families. It is a wonderful chance for people to get to know one another, hear each other's points of view, practice respectful listening, and learn about different values and practices. Families deserve to be involved in curriculum decisions, particularly decisions about how holidays—which are so individual, personal, and important—will be handled. Given the chance, most families jump at the chance to be heard and to participate in the decision-making process.

As a final note, be sure you present your basic ground rules before the group begins to work on a policy. For example, if you know that you will not allow violent or stereotypical costumes or decorations at Halloween, say so. If you cannot allow religious activities in your program, make sure everyone knows this before talking about Easter, Rosh Hashanah, Ramadan, or other religious holidays.

BASIC STEPS TO A HOLIDAY POLICY

The following are three basic steps to formulating your holiday celebration policy: establishing goals, designing specific activities to meet your goals, and assessing your outcomes.

Step One—Establishing Goals

While each group will have its own individual set of goals, the following list may help you get started formulating your goals.

⊙ Write down what you want to accomplish by including celebration activities in the program. (Example: To validate children's and families' holiday experiences and traditions; to build a sense of community; to provide accurate information about holidays in a developmentally appropriate way; to provide a break in the routine, etc.)

⊙ Be sure that these goals relate to the children and families in your group (that is, include holidays in the curriculum in a way that reflects the ethnic mix in the group).

⊙ Be sure that these goals relate to your overall program and anti-bias curriculum goals.

⊙ Decide what place holidays will have in your program. (Fit the holidays *into* the curriculum and *not the curriculum around the holidays*.)

Figure 25–1 is an example of one program's holiday policy goals. Once you have established your goals for including celebrations in your curriculum, you are ready to establish the specifics of your holiday policy, the second step.

Step Two—Establish Specifics of Your Holiday Policy

In this step you move beyond your broad, basic goals and set down the specifics of your holiday policy. These specifics are drawn directly from your broad, basic goals. At this point, you will want to consider the following points.

⊙ Determine how much total curriculum time will be spent on holidays.

⊙ Decide how many holidays you will include each year.

⊙ Calculate how much time will be spent on each holiday.

⊙ Determine just exactly how you will include holiday celebrations in the curriculum. (Do we want to have a party for each holiday? Read a story and talk about each holiday?)

⊙ Make sure that all activities are developmentally appropriate to the children in the group. (See Chapter 26 for more information on this.)

⊙ Make sure that all activities are culturally sensitive and nonstereotypical.

⊙ Make plans to involve families in holiday activities.

Figure 25–2 is an example of how one center fit holidays into the curriculum to meet their goals.

There are some special considerations that also may be a part of formulating your holiday policy. These special considerations have to do with religious issues,

---

GOALS FOR INCLUDING HOLIDAYS IN THE CURRICULUM

⊙ To understand, respect, and validate the diverse needs of children and families

⊙ To understand that holiday celebrations are only one aspect of cultural diversity

⊙ To develop a self-awareness of culture and the role it plays in beliefs, attitudes, and expectations

⊙ To encourage critical thinking about bias and unfairness

⊙ To provide accurate information about holidays in a developmentally appropriate manner

⊙ To work as a team with families and other community members to design developmentally appropriate holiday activities that meet the needs of individual children but also reflect the diversity of the group

⊙ To develop a classroom environment that reflects diversity of cultures and their celebrations in the selection of books and other learning materials

⊙ To involve parents in decision making at the school to ensure that holidays are culturally sensitive and reflect the culture of children and families

⊙ To teach children to respect and value holiday celebrations and traditions from diverse cultures

Figure 25-1

Sample goals.

SEPTEMBER

⊙ Whole class cooperative adventures
⊙ Labor Day
⊙ 16th—Mexican Independence Day
⊙ Cooperative math activities
⊙ Harvest festivals from around the world
⊙ Study of seasons, plants, life cycle
⊙ Autumnal Equinox
⊙ Students interview each other, do each other's portraits, start class meetings and group art projects
⊙ School and community walks
⊙ Writing (or taping) daily journals
⊙ Drawing about visions for ideal classroom/ideal school

OCTOBER

⊙ Visit local museum for exhibits for Day of the Dead
⊙ Painting neighborhood shop windows with harvest, Halloween, and Day of the Dead themes (at request of owners)
⊙ Columbus arrival from perspective of Native Americans
⊙ Sukkot—Jewish holiday of harvest

NOVEMBER

⊙ Thanksgiving from many perspectives
⊙ Festival of Light (Diwali, Hanukkah, Solstice, Christmas)
⊙ Connect to science curriculum on light and shadow
⊙ Neighborhood projects to show thanks to our neighbors
⊙ Art projects on light and shadow

Figure 25-2

Sample curriculum including holidays–grade 3.

Figure 25-3
Formulating a holiday policy will help you shape your approach to holidays in the future.

Figure 25-4
A holiday policy will help you decide which activities are appropriate for celebrations.

which are often part of holiday celebrations. Some of these considerations are as follows:

- Consider your individual circumstances to determine if it is appropriate to include holidays with a strong religious component. For instance, while recognizing a diverse group of holidays validates children and their families, bringing religious leaders into a public school setting is not appropriate.
- Decide if you will talk about the religious component and, if so, in what way.
- Will teachers initiate the conversation on the religious aspects or will it be discussed only if the children bring it up?
- Use holiday activities as a way of enhancing respect for religions and traditions different from one's own, but stress common themes as well. (See Chapter 26 for ideas on this.)
- Have a plan for working with children and families who don't celebrate a specific holiday or any holidays.

- Be sure in making any plans that no child is excluded and all children have choices to participate or choose alternative activities.

Step Three—Assessment

As in all experiences in the early childhood program, you will learn by experience how adequate your holiday policy is for the children and families in your program. It helps to think of your holiday policy as a journey and not a destination. As you implement your holiday activities into the curriculum, you need to be constantly assessing. You need to be assessing their developmental appropriateness. You need to be assessing if they are culturally sensitive and nonstereotypical. You need to be assessing their effectiveness in being a true anti-bias approach to different cultures and not a "tourist curriculum."

Figure 25-5

Developing a holiday policy helps you in planning appropriate activities for young children.

Figure 25-6

Reading a book about a holiday can often be enough for young children.

In addition to your ongoing self-assessment, it is also important to get input from families about their perception on the success of the celebrations. Keep notes on the daily success or failure of your holiday activities. Get input from other teachers and assistants who were involved in the celebration activities. You may also want to get input from older children (such as those children in grades 3 to 5) as to their feelings about your holiday activities. With younger children, their reactions are generally more obvious and "out in the open." Then, use all of this assessment information to improve, redesign, and fine tune future celebrations in your curriculum.

Holiday celebration policies will be as individual as each program and the families, children, and teachers in it. The crucial point is that the policy is thoughtful and reflective of the group.

If early childhood teachers plan holidays to reflect the cultural make-up of their individual groups, not every school would choose to celebrate the same holidays such as Halloween or Christmas. The "cookie-cutter" holiday approach, driven by holiday curriculum books, wouldn't exist in a program truly representative of our diversity as a country. Chapter 26 gives further insight into benefiting young children by including celebrations in the curriculum in a developmentally appropriate manner.

SUMMARY

The first step to including holidays in the curriculum is to develop a holiday policy. Formulating a holiday policy at the same time you shape your new approach

to holidays will help you make your decisions easier in the future. A holiday policy is a guide for everyone involved in your program to help them choose, implement, and evaluate holiday activities.

Your holiday policy must be clear, specific to your situation, and flexible. It is vital that you involve all those who will be affected by the policy in its development.

Getting together and thinking through the issue of holidays provides an opportunity for community building between teachers and families. It is a wonderful opportunity for people to get to know one another, hear each other's points of view, practice respectful listening, and learn about different values and practices.

Be sure to present your basic ground rules before the group begins to work on a policy. For example, if you know that you will not allow violent or stereotypical costumes or decorations at Halloween, make this a ground rule.

The three basic steps to a holiday policy are (1) establishing goals; (2) establishing the specifics of your holiday policy based on these goals; and (3) assessing your policy.

Establishing goals involves listing what you want to accomplish by including celebrations in the program. Be sure that these goals relate to the children and families in your group.

Establishing the specifics of your holiday policy involves considering the following points: The amount of time you will spend on holidays, the number of holidays you will have each year, and the way you will include holiday celebrations in the curriculum.

There are special considerations that also may be a part of formulating your holiday policy. These special

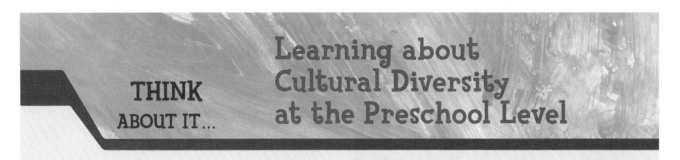

THINK ABOUT IT...

Learning about Cultural Diversity at the Preschool Level

Interest in cultural diversity usually focuses on ethnic differences. Cultural diversity is much more than ethnicity, however. People have different views about and experiences with living, working, and playing together in a community. With young children, an awareness of cultural diversity needs to be thought of in broader terms to include differences in gender, language, religion, social class, and presence or absence of disability.

Differences make the classroom—the whole community—a vibrant and interesting place to live. The curriculum, which begins with children's own experiences, can gradually help children understand, accept, and celebrate the diversity of people through play on a daily basis. By age three, children have an awareness of differences in language, skin color, or customs. By age four, children become aware of differences associated with handicaps. This awareness depends somewhat on how obvious the difference is. Even in the early childhood years, however, children are developing attitudes toward other racial groups.

With an understanding of the developmental sequence through which children become aware of differences, adults can better teach children about diversity. For preschoolers, the initial focus should be on increasing their knowledge about similarities and differences among children. This knowledge can be revealed through awareness of different foods, family structures, celebrations, and cultural traditions. All adults need to model support and understanding of cultural diversity.

A preschooler's primary means of learning is through play. Play across cultures often involves the use of toys. Toys and other things that children play with reflect culture and provide insight into the norms and values of a society—hence, the importance of "Show and Tell." Because toys and playthings have an important influence on the play of young children, adults need to make sure that the toys available are appropriate and reflect cultural diversity. Adults should evaluate the toys and make sure that they are varied and span different developmental areas. Toys also should be examined to be sure that they are accessible and do not reflect a cultural bias (Rettig, 2002).

Explore your classroom for diversity. Use story tapes made by adults to create a multiple-language library. Create a class "Book About Us." Invite children to create drawings and paintings to illustrate their class books. Have children create a classroom mural depicting their family members. Display posters and photographs in the art center and around the room. Take snapshots of objects around the room. Ask families to share music from their countries of origin. Play recorded music from a variety of countries and cultures. Introduce children to the different breads we enjoy from other countries. Talk with children about their family members and the traditions they enjoy together at home.

Play is a most natural way of promoting cultural awareness among young children. Throughout history and across cultures, play is a means by which societies communicate cultural values to children, both directly and indirectly. Helping young children gain an understanding of themselves and others should be an integral part of school programs and should involve all school personnel.

considerations have to do with religious issues, which are often part of holiday celebrations.

The third step in developing a holiday policy is assessment. As you implement your holiday activities into the curriculum, you need to be constantly assessing.

In addition to your ongoing self-assessment, it is also important to get input from families about their perception of the success of the celebrations. It also helps to get input from other teachers and assistants who were involved in the activities. Then, use all of this assessment information to improve, redesign, and fine tune holidays in your curriculum.

KEY TERM

holiday policy

LEARNING ACTIVITIES

A. You are a teacher in a large, inner-city, multicultural program. Write at least three goals that you have formulated for your holiday policy. Give your rationale for each goal. Next, choose another contrasting type of center (you make up the specifics) and write at least three goals that you have formulated for your holiday policy. Compare and contrast the goals for these two centers.

B. Role play this situation with fellow students: You are a teacher in a large, multicultural, urban school. You have been asked by your center director to be in charge of the Christmas holiday program for the school. Respond to this request. Include in your dialogue with the director: (1) reasons for and/or against the program; (2) your school's goals for this (and any other) holiday celebration; and (3) the role of assessment in your plans for this holiday celebration.

C. Use the same situation from B. and role play another conversation with the program director. In this scenario, you have decided to celebrate a different holiday than Christmas. What holiday would you celebrate instead of Christmas? In your dialogue, give the director your rationale for choosing this holiday. Give a brief summary of what activities you are planning. Explain how these activities are consistent with the goals of this school's holiday policy.

D. In your program, one of the goals of your holiday policy is to validate children's and families' holiday experiences and traditions. Using this goal, write a letter to parents sharing with the families what curriculum specifics you have planned for a particular holiday(s).

E. During a conference, a parent tells you that her child is afraid to come to school since you have started discussing El Día de los Muertos. How would you respond to this parent? How would you examine your current activities with regard to this parent's concern? What role does developmental level play in this situation? After examining the activities in your holiday curriculum, what changes do you anticipate you would have to make, if any?

F. Write a holiday activity assessment survey for the families of children in your room or field work setting. What questions would you include? Explain

how you would use this survey information in future planning.

G. Obtain a copy of an early childhood curriculum guide. Evaluate it for these points.
⊙ number of holidays included
⊙ number of activities included for each holiday
⊙ amount of time estimated to be spent on each holiday
⊙ developmental appropriateness of holiday activities
⊙ inclusion of anti-bias, nonstereotypical holidays and activities.
Discuss your evaluation of the curriculum guide. Based on your evaluation, would you use this curriculum guide? Why or why not?

H. In your program, you have several children whose religion does not allow any holiday celebrations. Write out some specific curriculum activities for these particular children during the time the group is involved in holiday activities. Include in your activities age of child(ren), type of activity, and why it is developmentally appropriate for this age group.

I. Visit two contrasting early childhood programs (preferably at holiday time). For example, visit one small suburban center and a large, federally funded urban center. Compare and contrast the holiday activities you observed in each setting. If it is not a holiday time, review activity plans from a holiday already past. Can you see in these activities the evidence of a holiday policy? Why or why not? Do the activities reflect the ethnic and cultural make-up of the group? Be specific in your reply. Are the activities developmentally appropriate? Explain why or why not.

J. Obtain an early childhood program supply catalogue. Review it for the following: supplies for holiday activities; children's books on holidays; holiday activity books/curriculum guides; different ethnic groups represented in toys, such as puppets, dolls, or housekeeping corner supplies. Is there an emphasis on any particular holiday(s)? If so, which one(s) did you find? Did you find any supplies, books, toys, etc. that you would buy for your own use in your work with children? Explain which ones and why you would purchase them.

THIS ONE'S for YOU!   Respecting Other Cultures

The values, beliefs, and behaviors of the many Spanish-speaking groups in the United States may differ from group to group and from those of the larger society. When a family or child expresses a preference that does not pose an ethical dilemma, accept and support the preference.

For example, you may notice that a child from a Hispanic culture in which children are taught to be respectful and obedient to adults does not initiate or participate in interactions with the teacher beyond giving the information the teacher requests. Allow the child to find what works best for him or her within the classroom environment. Over time, the child who is supported in the classroom will gradually adjust to classroom behaviors in ways that meet his or her needs.

Here is another example. In some cultures, children are taught that particular behaviors or activities are masculine or feminine—that is, that certain things are done only by males or by females. A child so socialized may choose not to participate (or the family may discourage the child from participating) in activities that are typically associated with the other sex, such as dramatic play with aprons and dolls or climbing on the jungle gym. If a child verbalizes or shows a desire not to participate, that desire should be respected. Of course, the child should not be allowed to express this opinion in a way that negatively affects the feelings or perceptions of other children.

CHAPTER REVIEW

1. What is the first step to including celebrations in the curriculum?
2. What is a holiday policy?
3. What are some advantages of having a holiday policy?
4. Who should be involved in formulating a holiday policy?
5. Why is the solo approach to formulating a holiday policy sometimes ineffective?
6. What are some advantages of working together as a group on formulating a holiday policy?
7. What are ground rules in formulation of a holiday policy?
8. What are three basic steps to formulating a holiday policy?
9. List some things to consider when developing goals for your holiday policy.
10. What are some specifics to consider in formulating your holiday policy?
11. What are some special considerations that may be a part of formulating your holiday policy?
12. Why is assessment important in formulating a holiday policy?
13. Which individuals should be included in your holiday policy assessment?
14. Why should families be included in holiday activity/curriculum decisions?
15. Will a holiday policy be the same year to year? Explain why or why not.

REFERENCES

Bisson, J. (1997). *Celebrate: An anti-bias guide to enjoying holidays in early childhood programs.* St. Paul, MN: Redleaf Press.

Rettig, M. A. (2002). Cultural diversity and play from an ecological perspective. *Children and Schools, 24*(3), 189–199.

ADDITIONAL READING

Jones, E., & Nimmo, J. (1994). *Emergent curriculum.* Washington, DC: NAEYC.

Levin, D. E., & Lobo, B. (2000). Learning about the world through play. *Scholastic Early Childhood Today, 15*(3), 56–69.

Luenn, N. (1998). *A gift for Abuelita.* Flagstaff, AZ: Northland.

Pike, G., & Selby, D. (2000). *In the global classroom 2.* Toronto, Canada: Pippin Publishing.

Smith, D. D., & Luckasson, R. (2002). *Introduction to special education.* (2nd ed.) Needham Heights, MA: Allyn & Bacon.

HELPFUL WEB SITES

Teacher's Guide to Holidays, http://teacher.scholastic.com/lessonrepro/k_2theme/ tguidedec00.htm

Kathy Schrock's Guide for Educators, http://school. discovery.com
Type in "holiday" in Search Box.

Teachers.net, http://www.teachers.net
Click on Lessons, then click on "Search Lessons."

For additional creative activity resources, visit our Web site at http://www.EarlyChildEd. delmar.com.

Chapter 26

Developmentally Appropriate Celebrations

Objectives

After studying this chapter, you should be able to:

1. Describe the markers of a quality, multicultural, anti-bias curriculum.

2. Explain how to include holidays in the curriculum in a way that is developmentally appropriate.

3. Discuss the place of holidays in the curriculum with regard to the normal routine.

4. Describe how holiday activities can be process-oriented and open-ended.

5. Explain how mainstream holidays can be adjusted to fit developmentally appropriate practice.

6. Choose appropriate, nonbiased children's books for use in holiday celebrations.

7. Use appropriate Internet sources for children's books and activities.

When asked the question "What does a multicultural classroom look like?" one educator replied, "Instead of considering it a *melting pot* where cultures are blended and assembled, a better analogy is a *salad bowl,* where uniquely individual ingredients are necessary and distinct (Madrazo, Jr., 1999, p. 6). Incorporating celebrations into the early childhood curriculum is much like this "salad bowl" approach. In blending holidays into a developmentally appropriate curriculum, each child's uniqueness is a necessary and distinct ingredient to the holiday curriculum. Individual uniqueness is not lost but savored when celebrating holidays in a developmentally appropriate way. Figure 26–1 presents the basic

characteristics of a quality, multicultural, anti-bias curriculum in which holiday celebrations are incorporated.

The same anti-bias, developmentally appropriate approach is the main ingredient for successful holiday activities in the curriculum. It involves understanding developmentally appropriate practice and planning activities that meet developmental needs. It is as simple as that!

Yet when it comes to holidays, it's all too easy to lose sight of all we know about early childhood development and practice and fall into a "holiday trap." For example, early childhood teachers know that a three year old's concept of time is very basic and generally tied to familiar, real events, such as the next time she wakes up in the morning or what comes next on the day's schedule. However, it is not uncommon for teachers of three-year-old children to introduce units about the first story of Thanksgiving, an event that happened hundreds of years ago. This is obviously far too complex a concept for three year old children to grasp. It is a meaningless event to a three year old child. In the same way, many teachers work hard all year to provide creative art activities that are open-ended and process-oriented. Yet, these same teachers can be found encouraging children to paint a red, heart-shaped cutout at Valentine's Day, to glue cotton balls on a bunny shape at Easter, or to make hand prints on tie shapes for a Father's Day present. The creative *process* is lost in creating *products* that often have little meaning to young children.

If you find yourself somewhere in this description, consider taking some time to review the abundance of material about the cognitive stages of young children that is available to you as an early childhood educator. (References are found in Chapters 8 through 10). NAEYC's publication, *Developmentally Appropriate Practices–Revised* is another important resource (Bredekamp & Copple, 1997). Reflect on the information you already have from this text or refer to the sources in Chapters 8 through 10 for new information to guide you.

When considering incorporating holiday activities for young children in the curriculum, be sure to consider the following:

- Very young children learn through actions and need concrete, hands-on experiences.

The following markers, defined by Louise Derman-Sparks (1999), describe a program well on the way to a quality, multicultural, anti-bias education.

- The *daily* curriculum incorporates children's *daily* life experiences.
- The staff adapt curriculum and teacher–child interaction to meet cultural as well as individual and developmental needs of their children.
- Knowledge from parents or family care-givers about their home cultures is incorporated into the curriculum.
- Both the curriculum and daily classroom life incorporate diversity and justice issues related to gender, disabilities, socioeconomic status, and the many ways of being a family, as well as issues related to ethnicity and culture.
- A variety of strategies are used by staff to involve parents actively and regularly in the program.
- Children are encouraged to develop critical thinking and tools for resisting prejudice and unfair behavior directed at themselves or others.
- The cultural diversity and language of the children and families, as well as in the community, are reflected in the program.
- There is a continuous examination by staff of their practice and the influences of their cultural backgrounds to help each other uncover and change biases and hurtful (even if unintentional) behaviors (Derman-Sparks, 1999, p. 43).

Figure 26-1

Check your curriculum for anti-bias quality markers. (Printed with permission of the National Association for the Education of Young Children.)

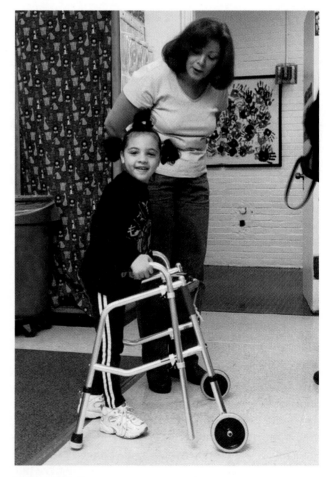

Figure 26-2

A nonbiased curriculum includes children with special needs.

◉ Young children are egocentric and believe that everyone shares their thoughts and experiences: "Everyone is like me."

◉ Older children can begin to understand more abstract concepts.

Many theorists feel there is a developmental shift for children around the ages of 5 to 7 years, when children begin to have a wider and more flexible understanding of different people and different rituals. Because their minds can handle a little bit more abstract thinking, teachers are able to introduce concepts that are more complex than in the preschool and kindergarten years. For example, fourth graders can talk about people in other countries, what they wear for celebrations, and what they wear on a normal day. Older children are able to compare and contrast the practices of people in other countries with what they do in their own houses. Four year olds, however, do not have the same ability to think abstractly and reason in the same way as fourth graders. Without direct experience with the lives of people who live in other countries (or in other ways), pre-school children are not able to comprehend who these people are or how their lives are similar to or different from their own. These children need concrete, first-hand experiences in order to learn and understand.

ACHIEVING DEVELOPMENTALLY APPROPRIATE HOLIDAY CELEBRATIONS IN THE CURRICULUM

An early childhood curriculum with developmentally appropriate celebrations will *not* necessarily include routine celebrations of all national holidays such as Thanksgiving, Christmas, Easter, or Mother's Day. These holidays represent the cultural/religious way of life and view of history of a large part of the population in the U.S.—*but not all of it*. Many people do *not* consider these holidays central to their cultural or religious

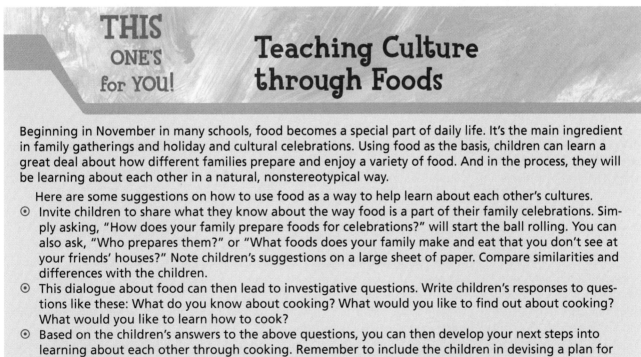

THIS ONE'S for YOU!

Teaching Culture through Foods

Beginning in November in many schools, food becomes a special part of daily life. It's the main ingredient in family gatherings and holiday and cultural celebrations. Using food as the basis, children can learn a great deal about how different families prepare and enjoy a variety of food. And in the process, they will be learning about each other in a natural, nonstereotypical way.

Here are some suggestions on how to use food as a way to help learn about each other's cultures.

◉ Invite children to share what they know about the way food is a part of their family celebrations. Simply asking, "How does your family prepare foods for celebrations?" will start the ball rolling. You can also ask, "Who prepares them?" or "What foods does your family make and eat that you don't see at your friends' houses?" Note children's suggestions on a large sheet of paper. Compare similarities and differences with the children.

◉ This dialogue about food can then lead to investigative questions. Write children's responses to questions like these: What do you know about cooking? What would you like to find out about cooking? What would you like to learn how to cook?

◉ Based on the children's answers to the above questions, you can then develop your next steps into learning about each other through cooking. Remember to include the children in devising a plan for how to explore answers to their questions and how they want to learn about cooking.

◉ Invite families and friends to share their favorite cultural celebration food with the class. Be sure the adults let the children participate in the preparation. Encourage children to ask questions and taste new things.

◉ A culminating event can be something large like a class-created Cultural Foods Smorgasbord to share with the families or something smaller like writing and drawing a Class Cookbook. You might even decide to have a bake sale and give the money earned to a charity of the children's choice.

Food is a natural favorite of children. Learning about each other through preparation and enjoyment of food together is natural, fun, and delicious!

THIS ONE'S for YOU!

Using Dance as a Means of Understanding and Expressing Culture for Older Children

"Sometimes dancing and music can describe a true image of the customs of a country better than words in a newspaper." Gene Kelly

All art forms are vehicles for conveying the ideas and values of their creators; they are means of coming to understand other cultures. Dance is no exception. Multicultural units are particularly appropriate contexts for using dance to help students feel sensations created by particular dance forms (e.g., hip hop, tap, jazz, ballroom, country line, jitterbug, mazurka). Students can also view dances and then analyze them for the messages they give about what is important to the dancers and the culture represented. Through dance investigations, historical events can be understood from an entirely different point of view. For example, Native American ghost dancers in the 19th century created dances to celebrate the return of the lands taken by the U.S. government. The dancers tried to conjure up the powers of their ancestors and created such a fervor among tribes that the government eventually forbade the dance!

Combine dance with multicultural music for another way to introduce children to other cultures. Integrate the music and dance of each culture and time period studied by analyzing how songs are historical records of how people felt, thought, and acted. Find out the significance of songs and how music even influenced history by studying France's "La Marseillaise" or the Mexican-American workers' "De Colores." Possibilities abound: Native American music, Irish jigs, music of the Civil Rights movement, tribal mountain music, western cowboy tunes, patriotic songs, and African tribal music. Students can come to understand how music helps create identity and explore a people's values and passions expressed in a song.

group's way of life. For example, not all groups would agree with the view of history as expressed in the traditional Thanksgiving story. Many families do not fit into the one-gift-for-Mother's-Day category. We will discuss a bit later in this chapter how to make these celebrations (if you choose to include them) more developmentally appropriate for children.

Too many holidays that occur too often and overwhelm children with food, decorations, and music are a problem in many programs. These activities are exciting but can be too exciting, overstimulating children and neglecting their everyday developmental needs for familiar, predictable routines. The following are some basic strategies for including holidays that address the developmental needs of children.

Discussing Rather Than Celebrating

Not every holiday activity has to mean a party. Instead, it may be more appropriate to hold a circle time discussion or read books about a holiday, or even to have family members visit to talk about how they celebrate at home.

For example, in one program in which many families celebrate Chinese New Year, children and their families set the tone of the celebration. One child brought in a Chinese calendar and another brought in a book about Chinese New Year. A third child brought in some Lei See (red envelopes with lucky money inside, traditionally given out on Chinese New Year). Several families brought in different paper lions similar to the ones they would see at the Lion Dance in Chinatown. The teacher talked about the holiday these families would be celebrating. Then the class shared the paper lion one child brought, while the child described how she was afraid of the huge lion head that the dancers carried during last year's parade and how she wouldn't be afraid this year. Then the teacher read the book about Chinese New Year. The discussion ended with one child distributing the Lei See to the children. No additional activities were planned. The children did ask to have the children's book read to them again on several occasions (Bisson, 1997).

This low-key, developmentally appropriate approach works especially well when there is a holiday that attracts the children's attention, but is not developmentally

Figure 26-4

Teachers also enjoy simple celebrations in the early childhood program.

Figure 26-3

Schedule holiday activities to fit regular routines. Have parents visit at snack time to share this short time together.

appropriate to cover with young children. By way of example, children who attend a program housed in a public school may notice pictures of George Washington and Lincoln on bulletin boards. They may ask about these men. It is, of course, appropriate and necessary to answer children's questions directly and simply about what Presidents Day is all about. However, because these men who lived long ago don't have particular relevance in their own lives, young children will not understand much about them. Therefore, it's not appropriate to explain the holiday in great detail or plan activities around this day.

Schedule Holidays to Fit Regular Routines

Introduce activities that allow you to follow your normal routines as much as possible. Holiday activities that last for more than a day or two or that include a lot of sugary snacks, large parties where families visit and stay too long, or coaching children to memorize songs for a program can all be too much for young children (and their teachers, too!). Instead of these developmentally inappropriate activities, design holiday celebrations to fit developmentally appropriate practice. For example, set up holiday art or decorating activities during regular free choice or activity time. Have families visit for a short meal at the regular lunch time so children still have time to rest. Learn songs together as you normally would. Then invite families to *participate* in a sing-along instead of a pressure-filled performance by the children. Throughout your holiday activities, observe children to make sure they do not become overstimulated by too many people, activities, or food.

Do Not Make Holidays the Center of Your Curriculum

It is important to reiterate that it is best not to make any holiday the entire focus of your curriculum for an extended time. In some programs, for example, teachers turn December into one long holiday activity. This approach overstimulates children and also leaves out a lot of other wonderful activities and curriculum themes that are meaningful for children. Also, children who don't celebrate holidays in December feel left out for a very long time.

Avoid Holidays that May Frighten Children

At Halloween it is very common for young children to be frightened by masks and people in costumes. This is due in part to the difficulty young children have in telling the difference between reality and fantasy. In a similar way, children might be afraid of the lion's head carried by dancers in the Lion Dance performed at Chinese New Year. And we all know how many children are frightened of a "real" Santa Claus. In your planning, look for ways to avoid the scary aspects of these rituals and still create opportunities for fun. For example, instead of having children come to school wearing their costumes and masks, provide a wide variety of dress-up clothing and materials for mask-making in the centers. Introduce a smaller model of the lion carried in Chinese New Year dances instead of a full-sized version.

Concentrate on Process-Oriented, Open-Ended, Creative Activities

Holiday-related projects that allow for individual process and creativity provide a good balance for more hectic activities and large social gatherings so prevalent at holiday times. The two- and three-dimensional activities in Chapters 13 and 14 provide many options for activities during the holidays. Water play, digging in sand, and making and modeling clay are activities that are always calming and appropriate for holidays. If you wish, you can make them more festive by adding holiday-related colors to sand or water in the sensory table or spices to play dough.

For creative art projects, combine holiday and non-holiday possibilities that allow children to create anything they choose. For example, if you are setting out tissue paper and pipe cleaners so children can make paper flowers for Cinco de Mayo, include other materials such as fabric scraps, different types of paper, and glue for other activities children may prefer such as collage making. Add plastic bottles filled with liquid starch along with the tissue paper and children would have the option to make "stained-glass" creations.

To meet children's developmental needs, you will want to have a variety of creative activities available every day that address all areas of development, including language, math, science, small and large motor skills, creative, cognitive, and social development. But instead of trying to fit all of these into a holiday theme, consider making one or two of the activities holiday-related. The remaining ones can focus on other topics that are relevant and interesting to children at the same time, such as changing seasons, new babies, or growing things.

Altering Holidays to Fit Developmentally Appropriate Practice

As early childhood educators we can use what we know about development to create an environment that is appropriate for young children. We can use developmental theory to help us choose books, toys, and all the materials in the program so that they are nurturing for young children. In this same proactive way, we can change our approach to holidays so they are developmentally appropriate for young children.

You can pick and choose aspects of a holiday to focus on without losing the essence or meaning of the holiday. This can be useful in making activities developmentally appropriate, as well as emphasizing the most meaningful parts of holidays, and avoiding commercialism and materialism.

Sometimes a new angle on a holiday is all that's needed to make it more suitable for an early childhood curriculum. To get you started thinking along these lines, the following are three examples of changing the focus of a holiday to make it more developmentally appropriate.

Thanksgiving–A developmental approach. Thanksgiving is a difficult holiday to present to young children for several reasons. First, it recognizes an event that happened hundreds of years ago, too long ago for young children to grasp. Second, it relays, most often in a one-

THINK ABOUT IT... Music Expresses Culture

"Without music life would be an error." Nietzsche

So important is music to cultures that the act of music making is considered a gift—a gift of beauty through sound. West African cultures view music this way, and in American culture it is a high tribute to have a song written especially for you. Music reveals cultural values, is used to celebrate triumphs, helps in the grieving process, expresses fears, gives hope, sustains traditions, and is integral to religion. Recorded history is replete with songs and music that tell stories of heroes, passions, and wars. For example, in our country it is impossible to think of the Civil Rights movement without recalling the songs of marchers or not to associate World War II with Glenn Miller's big-band sound. At a time in history, each tribe or cultural group had a unique musical identity. Today, diverse kinds of music represent the human family. In the United States we have become culturally diverse in our musical tastes and embrace every genre and style from folk to classical, rock and roll to rap. Blues? Jazz? All are readily available at the local mall. Teachers who share the wondrous varieties of music and celebrate the unique music of cultures and ethnic groups are showing children that diversity is something to be respected and treasured.

sided manner, a part of history that has more than one side. Third, it often reinforces misinformation and negative stereotypes about Native Americans (Bisson, 1997).

You can make this holiday more meaningful for young children and at the same time avoid its inappropriate aspects by focusing on the more general concepts of harvest and thankfulness, rather than the historical aspects. These two themes are more appropriate and easier for young children to understand. This is because they are more concrete concepts young children can see and experience in everyday life.

Teachers can introduce activities about foods and where they come from. Discussions can follow about which food(s) are the children's favorites and all the things they are most thankful for. These concepts can also be included in science, math, and creative and language arts activities. The main theme of this holiday is that people in all cultures and countries celebrate and are thankful for the food they have to eat. They are also thankful for family, friends, and a safe place to live.

Valentine's Day–A developmental approach.

This holiday has become very commercial, which is unfortunate because there are some wonderful themes in this holiday that are meaningful to young children, such as friendship and caring. Valentine's Day can be modified by focusing on appreciation of others in an Appreciation Day. This approach avoids the commercial nature of Valentine's Day while keeping the caring essence of the holiday. An Appreciation Day can show appreciation to any and everybody in the school community who help make children's days easier. This could include people such as secretaries, the director/principal, janitor, cook, and others. Small-group discussions with the children about how lucky they are to

have these special people can be held for several weeks. A day or so before the Appreciation Day (which happens on or around February 14), the children can make and deliver invitations, inviting all of these people to come to their room for muffins and juice. A group of children and adults can bake the muffins for the party and set them out on the table in time for the guests to enjoy.

Mother's and Father's Day–A developmental approach.

Young children naturally enjoy making things. Making gifts for mothers or fathers is a natural extension of this. However, considering the diversity in the kinds of families in our society, traditional ways of celebrating these days may no longer be appropriate for many children. Encouraging children to make gifts for mothers on Mother's Day can be very hurtful for a child whose only parent is a father. Similarly, putting out materials for children to make Father's Day gifts doesn't work for a child who has two moms and no dad. A better approach to this celebration is to have a Family Day instead. A Family Day allows children from any family configuration to be included. In your art area have materials available so children who want to can make gifts or cards for anyone in their family. No

Figure 26-6
Not every holiday has to mean a party. Dancing to the music is an everyday, simple approach to a celebration.

Figure 26-5
Children may enjoy writing invitations to parents, inviting them to their celebrations.

Figure 26-7
Older children enjoy creating special art objects for holiday celebrations.

child in this situation would be required to participate if they did not feel like doing so. Of course, making gifts for special people doesn't have to be on one or two designated days. Have materials available throughout the year in your art center so children who feel like making a gift for a parent, caregiver, or other special individual can do so whenever the mood moves them.

Connect Unfamiliar Holidays to Familiar Ones

Throughout the early childhood curriculum, children need adults to make connections for them as they learn and grow. As educators we do this when we present new ideas in the curriculum by helping children associate them with more familiar, already-grasped ideas. Just as teachers design curriculum on present learning, new cultural celebrations can be introduced by associating them with those already familiar to young children. One way to make the connection for children is to focus on the underlying themes that many holidays have in common, such as festivals of light or liberation (Bisson, 1997). Children are able to identify more successfully with a holiday and the people who celebrate it when the new celebration has a theme they can understand.

Consider the following examples of related themes to aid you in planning developmentally appropriate celebrations for young children.

- Celebration of Lights: Christmas, Hanukkah, Kwanzaa, Santa Lucia Day (Swedish Light Festival), Diwali (Hindu festival of lights)
- New Year: American New Year's Day, Rosh Hashanah (Jewish New Year), Chinese New Year, Shogatsu (3-day Japanese New Year's celebration), Hmong New Yea, Tet (Vietnamese New Year). This is just a sampling, as almost all cultures celebrate the New Year.
- Harvest: Thanksgiving, Kwanzaa (African American harvest celebration), Sukkot (Jewish harvest festival), Makahiki (Hawaiian harvest)
- Freedom: Fourth of July, Mexican Independence Day, Passover, Hanukkah, Cinco de Mayo, Juneteenth (the 19th of June, 1865, the day slaves in Texas learned of their freedom), Martin Luther King, Jr.'s birthday.
- Death: Día de los Muertos (Mexican Day of the Dead), Kwanzaa, All Souls Day, Memorial Day
- Spring/New Growth: Easter, Semana Criolla (Creole Week—Holy Week); Burning of Judas (Mexican holiday before Easter), Carnaval (Brazilian holiday in late February); Tet Nhat (Vietnamese Springtime holiday with unicorn as a symbol); Ch'ing Ming—Chinese Springtime celebration of trees, Kalpa Vruksha—Indian festival of tree planting; Setsu Bun—Japanese holiday on February 3rd is a bean-throwing festival; Tu B'Shvat—Jewish celebration of New Year of Trees marking the beginning of Spring; Apoo—Ghana's Spring Festival, celebrated during the Spring equinox; Thailand's Songkran—National Spring Festival when the new moon appears in the April sky; Zimbabwe's Whitsunday, a Springtime festival celebrated on the seventh Sunday after Easter.

DEVELOPMENTALLY APPROPRIATE HOLIDAY CELEBRATIONS-BALANCE IN THE CURRICULUM

The key to successfully using all of the preceding information on developmentally appropriate celebrations is to maintain a *balance* in your approach to holidays. Maintaining a balance means that activities about a holiday should never be the child's *first* introduction to or *last* experience with a cultural group. Children must first have an understanding of who people are and how they live their *daily* lives so they can build a context on which to really understand a celebration. Without this

THINK ABOUT IT... Stereotypes

Stereotypes are damaging to the people stereotyped and to every child who will grow up with false information. Many of our national holidays reflect common examples of stereotypes. Think about the following points and check off any that apply to your classroom.

_____ Children who aren't Native Americans wear "Indian" costumes for a holiday celebration or at any time. Dressing up to be "Indians" is offensive.

_____ Senior women are portrayed as green-faced, wart-nosed evil beings in Halloween decorations.

_____ The color black is portrayed as bad and evil through black cats, black bats, and black witches' costumes for Halloween celebrations.

_____ Native Americans are portrayed as half-naked, uncivilized, grunting individuals in the Thanksgiving story.

_____ The story of Columbus reflects only the European perspective, ignoring the fact that thousands of Native Americans were already in America at the time of the "discovery."

_____ The Thanksgiving story is told from the European perspective, leaving out the story of Native Americans.

_____ Pilgrims are portrayed in an overly simplistic fashion with large-buckled shoes, high black hats, and starched white collars, missing the realities of their dress and customs at that time in history.

You will have other stereotypes to add to this list that may be specific to your own experiences.

context, information about a holiday may be too different from their own experience and too difficult to understand. As a result, children may form stereotypes about the "strange" people who celebrate this "different" holiday (Bisson, 1997). Establishing a multicultural approach in the classroom year round helps children learn to appreciate similarities and differences in different cultures everyday. Use the Multicultural Observation Sheet in the Online Companion to help guide you in assessing your early childhood classroom to see if it reflects this multicultural approach.

In all holiday experiences, focus on the feelings people have when they celebrate their special holiday or engage in a family tradition. Feelings are real for young children. Feelings are something they can connect to and identify with, especially if it's a feeling they've had before. In all developmentally appropriate holiday activities, it is important *not* to extract external "bits and pieces" of a holiday (such as food or dress) without the feeling component.

Just as important to the success of these celebrations is doing your research. If you take the time to really research the celebration, you will not run the risk of implementing activities from other culture's holidays inappropriately. Doing your research will avoid giving children any misinformation or perpetuating stereotypes. If you are unsure of any aspect of a culture's holiday, ask the people in that community for information. A

Figure 26-8

Be sure that holiday celebrations don't get in the way of the important routine activities for young children.

visit to the communities of people who celebrate the holiday can provide you with a great deal of information. Of course, you can use the library and cultural centers for further information as well. The concluding section of this chapter contains lists of Web site resources for children's books and activities for multicultural teaching and developmentally appropriate celebrations.

RESOURCES FOR CELEBRATIONS

Children's Books

There are many excellent educational Web sites that provide lists of children's books reviewed by teachers, parents, librarians, and other professionals. In these Web sites, children's books have been selected on the following criteria: (1) they contain accurate, sensitive, and reflective presentations of people from many ethnic and cultural groups; 2) they are free of stereotypes; and (3) they are good children's literature. Most of these books are set in the present time. But if the story does happen some years ago, the pictures and experiences are familiar enough so that children are able to relate to them.

When choosing from the recommended books in these Web sites, you will want to choose books that reflect the celebrations of holidays that the children, families, and staff in your school celebrate and how they celebrate them. The books should also help meet your holiday goals and follow your holiday policy.

INTERNET SOURCES FOR CHILDREN'S BOOKS

The following are some suggestions on Web sites that feature bibliographies of children's books on multicultural holidays. These are meant as starting points; you will find links to many other sites as you use these sites listed.

The International Children's Digital Library

This Web-based library (http://www.icdelbooks.org) will give children, parents, and teachers a place to read children's books from around the world. It has nearly 200 titles representing 45 different cultures.

The Children's Literature Web Guide

This is an excellent place to begin your search because it has links to other sites specifically devoted to children's literature. It also has discussion boards and quick reference lists of award-winning and best-selling books for children. You'll also find links to other resources for parents, teachers, and even writers and illustrators. Their address is http://www.acs.ucalgary.ca/~dkbrown/.

"On-Lion" for Kids

This is a Web site put together by the New York Public Library. Its name was inspired by the two great stone lions that guard the library system's flagship building. This site offers a whole range of choices, including recommended reading lists built around different celebrations of the year (such as Hispanic Heritage Month, Thanksgiving, and Kwanzaa). You will also find information on authors, titles, and favorite characters as well as links to science and technology Web sites. The address is http://www.nypl.org/. Click on "On-Lion" for kids under the Online Resources section.

The New Mexico State University Library

This is a children's literature "gopher" site. It isn't much to look at—a gopher site can be accessed by most Web browsers, but unlike a Web site, it doesn't usually contain pictures or images. However, the information in this "gopher" site is invaluable for anyone interested in children's literature. You can access back issues of book reviews from selected children's literature journals and find digitized versions of some of the classic texts in children's fiction. These full-length versions of texts can be printed out to be read to children, chapter by chapter. The address is http://lib.nmsu.edu/.

Fairrosa Cyber Library

This is an online collection of articles, book reviews, archives of discussion group posts, information about authors, and electronic texts of classic children's books. The site is oriented toward parents and teachers, not children. This is a very comprehensive site. The address is http://www.fairrosa.info.

Youth Division of the Internet Public Library

This site is organized by the Dewey decimal system, so children can use this site to start to learn how to find other books even as they explore the different resources and links on this simple but excellent site. At its heart, it's a directory of links to other Web sites, many of them book-related, but the descriptions are so child-friendly, they will love to use this site. The address is http://www.ipl.org/youth/.

Don't forget to check with your local and national professional groups for their Web sites. You will find up-to-date information on developmentally appropriate materials and practice from these sites.

The Barnes and Noble Web Site

Here you will find a section titled "The Reader's Catalog." This section provides recommendations for both adult and children's books on holidays and many other topics. This catalog of more than 40,000 books has been compiled by the editors and friends of the *New York Review of Books*. You can browse in a number of categories or search for a specific title. You can search by age group and by subject as well. The address is http://www.barnesandnoble.com.

Enjoy the process of searching for just the right literature for your special group of children. The joy of seeing children's faces when they can really relate to the book you are reading to them is reward enough for the time it takes to search out appropriate literature. Only you can know which of the following resources are appropriate for your unique situation.

Boulder Public Library

http://www.boulder.lib.co.us/, Click on Kids & Young Adults.

This site has a section of Multicultural Books for Children and Young Adults.

East Carolina University

http://coe.ecu.edu/Diversity/childrenslit.htm.

Visit this site for a good list of books for children titled Children's Multicultural Page—Children's Books.

Children's Book Council

http://www.cbcbooks.org.

This is a nonprofit trade organization dedicated to encouraging literacy and the use and enjoyment of children's books.

International Reading Association

http://www.reading.org/choices.

This site lists teacher's and children's choices for best books for each year arranged by categories. On the 15th of each month, they list the "Hot Off the Press" books that they anticipate to be best sellers.

The Kid's Page of Makingbooks.com

http://www.makingbooks.com/kids.

This site shows kids how to get started on making handmade books. There is an interesting illustrated

account of "Books Around the World" and a bibliography of related books.

Teacher's First-Reading Lists

http://www.teachersfirst.com/, Click on Books & Reading.

This site offers hundreds of titles recommended by teachers and librarians for students of all ages.

How to Choose the Best Multicultural Books–Instructor Magazine

http://teacher.scholastic.com/, Click on Lesson Plans, then "Browse Our Lessons, and click on Social Studies.

In this Web site, you find an article that leads to 50 great books, plus advice from top educators, writers, and illustrators on how to spot literature that transcends stereotypes.

Awesome Library

http://www.awesomelibrary.org.

This site organizes the Web with 23,000 carefully reviewed resources including the top 5 percent in education.

USING THE INTERNET FOR RESOURCES

The Internet is a vast place to search for information on multicultural holidays. The following sites are provided to help you get started on your venture into cyberspace in search of resources for multicultural holiday materials. Of course, the list is not all inclusive; it represents a beginning point for your search. You will discover many more Internet resources as you explore on your own.

Web Sites for Multicultural Teaching Resources

http://www.nameorg.org. This site has resources for teachers on places to find K through 12 books, lesson plans, and excellent professional sites. The Web site is sponsored by a member of the board of NAME (the National Association for Multicultural Education).

Magic Tales of Mexico. http://www.g-world.org/, Click on Park Map, then click on Magic Tales of Mexico. This site is useful for finding folk tales about Mexico. The great thing about this site is that you're actually reading content developed in the source country.

Native Americans. http://www.teachersfirst.com/share/states/. If you'd like to examine the Native Americans who were indigenous to your own area, try this site. It includes all 50 states and includes a discussion of the native populations that lived in the area, how they got there, and what happened to them.

Native American Crafts. http://www.teachersfirst.com/summer/nativecrafts.htm. This is a collection of simple activities that replicate some of the toys and crafts that Native American children might have taught their European counterparts.

Thanksgiving. http://www.teachersfirst.com/lessons/thanksg.htm. If you're an elementary teacher, you will enjoy this site, which includes many "what was it really like?" resources and some additional cultural links. There are several resources here that attempt to sort out the myths about the Pilgrims and Native Americans from the realities of 17th century life.

Teacher's Guide to Holidays: Pre-K-Grade 2. http://teacher.scholastic.com/, Click on Lessons, then click on Social Studies in the Browse Our Lessons Section. This site presents a theme unit complete with activities and resources that are all designed to meet national standards for English/Language Arts as stated by the International Reading Association and the National Council of Teachers of English.

Native American Art and Culture. http://www.teachersfirst.com/archives/. This site presents excerpts from the Smithsonian collections featuring Native American art.

Native American Culture. http://www.teachersfirst.com/, Click on Keyword Search, then type in "Native Americans" in the Search by Title box. This site has links to many Web sites that feature Native Americans and local history, art, literature, ecology, and other subject areas.

Cinco de Mayo. http://www.teachersfirst.com/cinco.htm. This site features a collection of resources that will enable any school to learn about Cinco de Mayo and to celebrate the day. It includes activities and recipes for traditional foods.

Cinco de Mayo Webquest (Grades 2-3). http://www.teachersfirst.com/webquest.htm. This Web site covers the subject areas of social studies, art, language arts, and music. Students will learn about the history of Cinco de Mayo and the Hispanic culture on this Webquest. In groups of four, they work through seven different activities that involve Web research. Activities range from answering questions to making a piñata to sampling Mariachi music. A list of books on Cinco de Mayo is also included.

Origami. http://www.origami.as. This site provides clear instructions and elegant models in the traditional Japanese art of paper folding from Joseph Wu in Japan. Contains links to many other origami sites, including "How to Make an Origami Crane."

Oriland. http://www.oriland.com. This extensive site offers an origami world to explore, an opportunity to design cities with folded paper models, basic techniques and tips, and a studio with clear directions for folding more than 70 forms, as well as poetry and games.

Travel to Oriland. http://library.thinkquest.org. Type in "Oriland" in the Search the Library box. Join the fold and journey to Oriland, a vast world of origami people, forests, and castles created by a Thinkquest team from Russia.

Japanese Cookbook for Kids. http://jin.jcic.or.jp/. Click on Web Japan, then type in Kids Cooking in the Search box. This site offers not only an explanation of what Japanese food is like, but also gives recipes for dishes popular among Japanese school children.

Faith Ringgold–African-American Woman Artist. http://www.faithringgold.com and http://www.guggenheimcollection.org/. Click on Artist then click on Ringgold, Faith. Faith Ringgold has been an artist for many years working in several media. Visit these sites to see what materials the artist has worked in; what issues she finds important in her life; and the people, places, and things she has seen.

Mariko Mori–Japanese Artist. http://www.mcachicago.org/MCA/exhibit/past/Mori/, http://www.thedreamexperience.homestead.com/, and http://www.krayner.freeserve.co.uk/mariko.htm. These sites features Mariko Mori, a Japanese artist who presents unique imagery in photography and video.

FINE ART SITES

World Art Treasures–J. E. Berger Foundation

http://www.bergerfoundation.ch/.

This site features art of China, Japan, India, Laos, Cambodia, Thailand, Myanmar, Burma, and Egypt.

African Art

http://www.lib.virginia.edu/. Click on Fine Arts, then click on Art on Online Resources, then click on Databases, then click on African-American Artists Bio-Biographical.

This site features a discussion of elements of African art.

African Odyssey Interactive

http://artsedge.kennedy-center.org/. This site presents art, music, dance, and more from the Kennedy Center.

Guide to Asian Art on the Internet

http://www.artindex.com/, Click on Japan Gallery.

Images of Power and Identity

http://www.si.edu/, Click on Museums, then click on National Museum of African Art.

From the Smithsonian Museum, this site presents an online exhibit of African visual arts by country. Information about each country is also included.

Art of South and Southeast Asia: A Resource for Educators

http://www.metmuseum.org/, Click Enter, then click on Permanent Collections, then click on Arts of Africa, Oceania, and the Americas.

The Metropolitan Museum of Art site includes summaries of the history and art of South and Southeast Asia, Internet-based resources, lesson plans, and bibliographies for teachers and students.

Native Americans at Princeton

http://www.princetonartmuseum.org/, Click on Collections, then click on Curator's Choice.

Native American art links.

World Wide Art Gallery

http://www.theartgallery.com.au/kidsart.html. See examples of art done by children from around the world, and connect to links of art activities and information about art and art history around the world.

MISCELLANEOUS SITES

Native American Day

http://www.holidayinsights.com.

Hispanic Heritage Month

http://www.factmonster.com, Type "Hispanic Heritage Month" in the Search box.

Citizenship Day

http://www.patriotism.org/citizenship.

SUMMARY

Understanding developmentally appropriate practice and applying this knowledge to planning holiday activities are key to successful holiday activities in the curriculum. Yet, many times teachers fall into a "holiday trap" and lose sight of what they know about child development and practice.

An early childhood curriculum with developmentally appropriate holidays will not necessarily include routine celebrations of all national holidays such as Thanksgiving, Christmas, Easter, or Mother's Day.

Not every holiday has to mean a party. Instead, it may be more appropriate to read a book about a holiday, to discuss it at circle time, or even to have family members in to talk about how they celebrate at home.

Schedule holiday activities in a way that allows you to follow your normal routine as much as possible.

Other ways to approach holidays in a developmentally appropriate practice include avoiding holidays that frighten children; de-centering holidays in the curriculum; and concentrating on process-oriented, open-ended creative activities.

The focus of holidays can be altered so that they are more developmentally appropriate for young children. You can pick and choose aspects of a holiday to focus on without losing the meaning of a holiday.

Just as teachers design curriculum on present learning, new cultural celebrations can be introduced by associating them with those already familiar to young children. One way to make the connection for children is to focus on the underlying themes that many holidays have in common, such as festivals of light or liberation.

Maintaining a balance in your approach to including holidays in the curriculum is most important. Maintaining a balance means that activities about a holiday should never be the child's first introduction to or last experience with a cultural group.

LEARNING ACTIVITIES

A. Choose a standard, national holiday—for example, Thanksgiving. List the various groups involved in this holiday (e.g., Native American men, women, and children, Pilgrim men, women, and children). What would each group's feelings be about this event? Would each group be "thankful"? Why or why not? What does this tell you about this "mainstream" holiday? How appropriate is this holiday for young children? Be sure to use your knowledge of development in your answer.

B. Continue the approach to holidays in A. This time, focus on Columbus Day. What would the point of view on this holiday be for Native Americans, Italian Americans, and Jewish people? After reflecting on the views of all of these people, what effect (if any) does this exercise have on your using Columbus Day in your curriculum? Why is it necessary to work through these issues for ourselves, with our colleagues, and with the families and communities where we live and work?

C. A visitor from space lands on earth on October 31st. What would this visitor think about us? What would our view of senior women seem to be in this visitor's eyes? What would our use of the color black reflect to our visitor? Describe how you could change this visitor's perception on his October 31st visit.

D. Out of context (as in C.), Halloween reveals little about our strengths and struggles as people. This is like using only holidays to teach children about other cultures. With this in mind, choose a "mainstream" holiday. Make a lesson plan for this holiday that would help children get a better picture of this particular holiday and the cultures involved in it. Include in your lesson plan: age(s) of children, ethnic and cultural make-up of group, goals, related developmentally appropriate activities, and resources and individual/groups you would involve in your plan.

E. Your program has a high population of a particular ethnic group (you can choose which group). The parents of the children in this group want to eliminate all holiday celebrations not related to their ethnic group. Write out what you would say to these parents, using information from this chapter and Chapter 24. Have your colleagues critique your reply. Rewrite your reply to include these comments, if applicable.

F. Using the Internet Sources for Children's Books section in this chapter, do an online search for non-biased, multicultural holiday activities for children. Print out your search results. Share your results with the class. Evaluate these activities for stereotypes, bias, and developmental appropriateness.

G. Choose one of the holiday-related themes in this chapter. Write a lesson plan for a group of four-year-old children using this theme. Include in your plan: goals, developmentally appropriate related activities, resources, and individual/groups to be involved in your planning. Share your plan with your colleagues for their input.

H. Using the same theme as G., design a lesson plan for a group of fourth graders. Include the same items in your plan. Share your plan with your colleagues for their input.

I. Discuss the differences in the lesson plans in G. for four year olds and in H. for fourth graders. What are the main differences in these two lesson plans? What are the similarities (if any) in these plans?

J. Your group of children are currently very interested in plants and animals. They are at present fascinated by their ant farm and measuring their growing seedlings. Your supervisor reminds you it's time to begin making Christmas hand-prints as gifts for parents. Does it make sense to stop your curriculum and focus on a holiday in this manner? Why or why not? Explain how you could incorporate aspects of a holiday into your curriculum without disturbing the balance in your curriculum. Include specific activities for the art, block, housekeeping, book, and music centers. Be sure to specify the age of the children in your group, ethnic and cultural group, and type of center.

K. Use an actual center for this activity, or go back to your own early childhood memories. Evaluate holiday art activities at this center. Evaluate the materials for appropriateness in celebrating this holiday. Who really did the art work? Were the holiday activities too hard for the children to complete themselves? Did they all look the same? Did the holiday activities help develop children's creativity and use of materials or did they reflect an adult's idea of holiday decorations?

L. Using the activities you listed in K., redesign those activities that were stereotypical, developmentally inappropriate, and biased. If applicable, describe how you would achieve a better balance in the curriculum for this group of children.

CHAPTER REVIEW

1. Why is the celebration of Thanksgiving developmentally inappropriate for young children, especially three to five year olds?
2. What are the basic developmental characteristics of young children that need to be considered when incorporating holidays in the curriculum?
3. What is the developmental shift that occurs around the ages of five to seven years and how does this relate to planning holiday activities?
4. Why do many developmentally appropriate early childhood programs *not* include all national holidays?
5. When would it be more appropriate to discuss a holiday than to celebrate it?
6. Why is it important *not* to make holidays the center of your curriculum?
7. How can you alter holiday celebrations to fit developmentally appropriate practice?
8. How can you make Thanksgiving more meaningful for young children?
9. How can you alter Valentine's Day to make it more meaningful for young children?
10. How can you alter Father's and Mother's Day to make them more meaningful for young children?
11. How can you connect unfamiliar holidays to familiar ones for young children?
12. Why should your curriculum include developmentally appropriate holiday activities in the room as well in the curriculum year round?
13. Why is it important to maintain balance in your approach to holidays in the curriculum?
14. Why is it important to concentrate on process-oriented, open-ended creative activities for children?
15. What is the main ingredient for successful holiday activities in the curriculum?

REFERENCES

Bisson, J. (1997). *Celebrate! An anti-bias guide to enjoying holidays in early childhood programs*. St. Paul, MN: Redleaf.

Bredekamp, S., & Copple, C. (Eds.). (1997). *Developmentally appropriate practice in early childhood programs*. (Rev. ed.). Washington, DC: NAEYC.

Derman-Sparks, L. (1999). Markers of multicultural/anti-bias education. *Young Children, 54*(5), 43.

Madrazo, G. M., Jr. (1999, Feb.). So, how does a multicultural classroom look? Sound? *Science and Children, 7*(2), 6–7.

ADDITIONAL READINGS

Banks, J. A., & Banks, C. A. M. (Eds.). (2003). *Multicultural education: Issues and perspectives*. New York: John Wiley & Sons.

Clayton, J. G. (2003). *One classroom, many words: Teaching and learning in the cross-cultural classroom*. Portsmouth, NH: Heinemann.

Dilg, M. (2003). *Thriving in the multicultural classroom: Principles and practices of effective teaching*. New York: Teachers College Press.

Ellermeyer, D., & Chick, K. A. (2003). *Multicultural American history through children's literature*. Westport, CT: Libraries Unlimited.

Ferro, M. (2003). *The use and abuse of history: Or how the past is taught to children*. New York: Routledge.

Fassler, R. (2003). *Room for talk: Teaching and Learning in a multilingual kindergarten*. New York: Teachers College Press.

Grant, C. A., & Sleeter, C. E. (2003). *Turning on learning: Five approaches for multicultural teaching plans for race, class, gender and disability*. (3rd ed.). New York: John Wiley & Sons.

Richardson, T. R., & Johanningmeier, J. (2003). *Race, ethnicity, and education: What is taught in school*. Westport, CT: Greenwood Publishing.

Tileston, D. E. W. (2003). *What every teacher should know about diverse learners*. Thousand Oaks, CA: SAGE Publications.

Tyack, D. (2003). *Seeking common ground: Public schools in a diverse society*. Cambridge, MA: Harvard University Press.

Waxman, H. C., Tharp, R. G., & Holberg, R. S. (Eds.). (2003). *Observational research in U.S. classrooms: New approaches for understanding cultural and linguistic diversity*. London: Cambridge University Press.

For additional creative activity resources, visit our Web site at http://www.EarlyChildEd.delmar.com.

SECTION 7

Seasons

After studying this section, you should be able to answer the following questions.

1. How do my classroom art activities reflect the aesthetic qualities of the seasons?

2. Am I planning activities that encourage children's aesthetic sensibilities to the seasons?

3. Am I planning developmentally appropriate activities that enrich children's aesthetic appreciation of the seasons?

4. Do I build on children's natural affinity to the wonder of the world around them by regularly planning time for outdoor activities?

5. Have I planned specific activities for each season of the year that emphasize the unique differences in each season?

6. How do children react to the seasonal aesthetic experiences I plan for them? Do they appear motivated and involved?

7. Am I planning a wide variety of seasonal activities including all areas of the curriculum as well as two- and three-dimensional activities?

8. Have I evaluated my seasonal aesthetic activities and materials for their developmental appropriateness and effectiveness?

9. Am I keeping the joy of wonder in the world around me in my own approach to the seasons?

10. How will I modify my lessons and activities so they reflect a sensitivity to the beauty and uniqueness of each season?

Chapter 27

Seasons: Aesthetic Awareness

Objectives

After studying this chapter, you should be able to:

1. Discuss the young child's aesthetic awareness of the seasons.
2. Describe ways to enhance children's aesthetic awareness in the seasons of the year.
3. Discuss how teachers can encourage children's aesthetic awareness in the early childhood program.

The unfolding beauty of the seasons is not lost on very young children. Toddlers squat down to touch and really look at fallen leaves. For them, it's not enough to look—they love to roll and tumble and crush the leaves. Bugs crawling in the grass are closely examined by young eyes. Flowers are full of little children's noses, when they bury their faces in them to smell the flower's scent. The beauty of nature is very much a part of very young children's lives. As you read this, you can probably go back in your memory to times when you were closer to the earth. Perhaps you can remember a time when you turned over rocks to see the squirmy things underneath or when you played with "roly poly" bugs in the dirt. These times are now just memories for many adults.

But as the years go by, a child's world gets fuller and fuller with new learning experiences. Books, toys, television, and computers compete with nature to fill a young child's world. Their closeness with nature lessens and lessens.

The purpose of this chapter, "Seasons: Aesthetic Awareness," is to preserve, encourage, and enrich the child's appreciation of the beauty of nature—his or her aesthetic awareness—through an appreciation and awareness of the seasons of the year. The term "aesthetic awareness" is meant to be a unifying strategy for looking at all of the seasons. All of the seasons are covered in this one chapter in this context of aesthetics instead of separately by seasons. The focus on the aesthetics of the seasons is an attempt to direct your focus to the beauty of each season and away from stereotyped, "cute" seasonal activities found in many curriculum activity books.

"Aesthetics," as we learned in Chapter 3, refers to an appreciation for beauty and a feeling of wonder. Aesthetic awareness involves being aware of and appreciating the beauty in the changing seasons. Appreciation for the special, unique beauty specific to each season is the goal of this chapter.

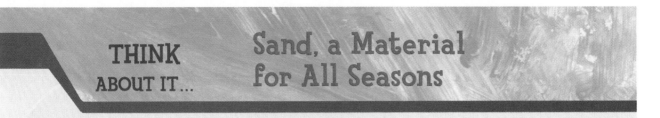

Sand, a Material for All Seasons

Sand is a material full of creative and aesthetic potential. Children love playing with it at the sand table as well as at the beach. Sand is also an excellent source of many other learning experiences.

For example, ask the children the following questions about sand:

- What is sand? (Sand is broken-down pieces of bigger rocks.)
- How is sand made? (When a big rock is worked on by the wind, rain, and the cold, it begins to break down and little pieces fall off. These pieces get worked on by wind or water and they get smaller. The pieces of rock are now sand.)
- Where can you find sand? (You can find sand any place where rocks have been out in the weather. A good place to find sand is at a beach. There the water has beaten off pieces of rock and rubbed them back and forth, wearing them down. The wind has blown the sand pieces, making them smaller and smoother. Dry streambeds are also good places to find sand. Did you know that some big deserts are really dry seabeds?)
- Why is sand good? (Some plants, like the cacti and the watermelon, only grow in sand. Part of your house is made of sand; when you mix sand with cement and water it makes mortar, a thick paste that holds bricks and stones together. If the sand and cement and water are poured out in big spaces, you get concrete. Floors, sidewalks, bridges, and walls can all be made from concrete. The windows in your house and school are made from sand—melted sand makes glass! Sand is also used to keep our water pure, to make sandpaper, and to fill sandboxes. That's why sand is good.)

Now, try these activities for some indoor fun with sand.

STRAINING SAND

Use some different grades of wire mesh and screening to let the children sift sand. Strain the sand through a coarse screen first. Have them examine each successive sifting. Let them use a magnifying glass to really study the sand grains. (Why do some sand grains have ragged edges, and why are other bits of sand smooth? The jagged grains of sand are made from harder rocks than the smooth sand came from.)

DRIPPING SAND

Fill a big coffee can with a soupy mixture of sand and water. Have the children dip small frozen juice containers into the mixture and take out some of this mixture to slowly drip down into a cardboard box. Let the children experiment with this procedure, holding the juice can higher, then lower and varying the thickness of the sand–water mixture. Tall sand mountains, sand castles, and sand stalagmites can be created, and the high sides of the box should help keep the floor clean.

SHAKING SAND

Put a big spoonful of mixed grains of sand into a large jar of water. Screw on the lid. Let a child shake up the contents. Then set the jar on the table so everyone can watch what happens. Ask: "Why do the biggest pieces of sand go to the bottom of the jar first? (They are the heaviest, so they fall to the bottom the fastest.) Why do some pieces of sand float? (They are probably little bits of wood or plants or sand that have little air holes.) Notice how as the water clears, the last sand sorts itself out by size: the heaviest sediment falls first and tinier pieces of sand, the silt, finally float down to rest on the very top of the sand.

SORTING SAND

Obtain some sand that has a lot of black grains in it. Spread the sand out on a big sheet of paper on a table. Let the children run a magnet back and forth through the sand. The black sand grains that stick to the magnet are a black iron oxide called magnetite.

(Continues)

THINK ABOUT IT... (Continued)

Now take all the magnetite and place it on a piece of lightweight cardboard. Tell the children that they can make that black sand move around without touching or blowing on it. Can they guess how? Put the magnet up against the underside of the cardboard and move it around. The black sand follows the magnet. Let the children try it. Finally place the magnet flat under a sheet of paper. Gather up the magnetite and sprinkle it on top of the paper. Watch how the magnetite is attracted to the two ends of the magnet so that it makes an outline of the magnet on the paper.

SAND PAINTING

Sift clean white sand and divide it into several small bowls. Into each bowl mix a different ingredient from the following list: dry mustard, paprika, blue clothes detergent, and instant coffee. You might find other coloring agents in your kitchen. Add water and a little white glue to each bowl and then let the children make sand paintings.

SAND PRINTMAKING

Apply white glue liberally to the veined underside of a leaf or fern. Then press the leaf onto a sheet of colored paper, and lift it off again. Sprinkle the glue leaf print on the colored paper with fine white sand and your sand print will appear.

As in all other chapters in this text, you are encouraged to adapt the ideas found here to suit your own special group of children. You will not find separate activities for children or student learning activity sections at the end of this chapter since activities are the main focus of the chapter itself. The same is true for all other chapter end sections. You will find suggested books for children in the Online Companion. These lists are not intended to be all inclusive, but to be a starting point for seasonal books for children. You will find hundreds of appropriate children's books listed on-line at the Web sites mentioned in Chapter 18. You will also find that your school and public libraries are excellent sources for children's books on the seasons.

THE AESTHETICS OF AUTUMN

Autumn is nature's last fling of the year. The landscape is brilliant with raw and muted colors ranging from bright yellow to red-orange to red and from red-brown to red-violet.

> "Anyone who keeps the ability to see beauty never grows old."–Kafka

AUTUMN EXPERIENCES FOR CHILDREN

The fall is a great time for children to explore the outdoors, learn about seasonal transitions, and develop a variety of cognitive skills. Nature-related experiences can foster a child's emerging sense of wonder, and the early years of life are the best time to begin providing direct, on-going interactions with the natural world. There's no need to venture to far-away national parks to explore nature. In fact, young children learn best when they are in an environment that is familiar and comfortable. Focus on the foliage, animals, and insects in your own backyard, the playground, or local park before venturing into heavily wooded areas. Keeping safety concerns in mind, adults should allow children to touch, feel, and smell while they explore the environment.

The young child is naturally sensitive to the wonders and beauty of nature: the colors and rhythm of leaves whirled by autumn winds, the texture of dried seeds and weeds, the form and color in the harvest. There are a number of things a teacher can do to enlarge children's understanding of their world and to encourage them to learn to look, feel, and think.

⊙ Begin a collection of objects from nature for classroom use. Encourage closer observation of design in nature.

⊙ Take children on walking trips to discover and observe the colors, shapes, and textures in trees, plants, clouds, buildings, and vehicles. Individual observation can be shared with others at group time.

The children draw and paint the beauty of nature as they each see it, using their own feelings and ideas. Their growing visual awareness is gradually reflected in picture making, as they mature in the ability to interpret their environment. Some topics for drawing and painting are as follows:

- Leaves in Autumn
- Birds Flying South
- A Rainy Day in Fall
- The Fall Harvest
- Raking Fall Leaves
- My Neighborhood in Autumn
- An Autumn Collage

The traditional beginning of school in the fall of the year is an excellent time for increasing awareness of the world around us. It starts the year off with practice in observation skills.

- Children can be encouraged to be more aware of their environment in only a few minutes. Discuss the fact that leaves will change color and watch together to see when it happens. Make a game of finding the largest, smallest, and most unusually colored leaf. Focus on an evergreen or pine and talk about the needles and pinecones and the fact that they stay green and don't drop off. Talk about people needing jackets and animals growing winter coats.

- Collect leaves of different sizes and shapes. Show the children that one side is smooth and one side is rough. Have them put the rough side up and a piece of paper over it. Take a small crayon turned on its side and rub over the paper. The outline of the leaf will show through. It's fun to change colors. This can be used on any object with texture.

- Fall is also the time when apples are harvested. There are almost 10,000 varieties grown in the world. A fun experiment to do with the children is to buy one of several kinds in the grocery store. See how many ways they are alike and different. Say their names. Taste a piece of each one. If you cut two pieces from each one, can the children find the ones that taste the same or different?

Fall Colors and Leaves

The beautiful color change of leaves that occurs in the temperate eastern portions of large continents—the northeastern United States, China, Japan, and a small area of southwestern Europe—might serve as a hands-on study of colors. Throughout the world and in every season, the leaves of conifers (cone-bearing trees, also called evergreens) provide comparisons and contrasts of greens: light green, dark green, yellow green, blue green, or blackish green. To study different shades of green, lay out leaves for comparison and classification with an accompanying tempera paint or watercolor mixing activity.

Collections of leaves can be preserved for future study by pressing them between the pages of an old telephone book or a big dictionary, then encasing them in clear Contact paper or laminating them.

Leaves can be duplicated with rubbings or printed by painting a leaf with tempera paint, transferring the leaf to paper, then pressing on it. But an awe-inspiring leaf print is made by applying block-printing ink with a brayer (ink roller) to both sides of the leaf, then placing the inked leaf between a folded sheet of paper and rubbing it thoroughly. Two different and beautiful versions of nature appear, and the child who has done the inking, folding, and rubbing is the artist of this marvelous creation!

First Day of Fall

Read the story of *Frederick* by Leo Lionni about mice getting ready for the long winter ahead. Take a fall stroll. Collect beautiful colored leaves as you walk.

Figure 27-1

It's easy to tell when a child is happy in his or her environment.

When you return, glue the leaves onto a small paper bag. Put the bag in a safe place. Next time you go walking, take the bag along and collect more fall items to use in the fall activities that follow.

Leaves and Learning Concepts

Math concepts can be introduced with a leaf collection. The children may sort assorted leaves by color, shape, size, edges, or texture. Feeling the leaves will reveal a variety of surfaces, both top and underside. For example, American elm leaves have a sandpapery top surface, while white poplar leaves feel like velvet on the underside. Other leaves may feel smooth, bumpy, or sticky. Beech leaves are reputed to feel like new money! Children can match textures with samples of known objects, such as pine needles with toothpicks, white poplar with velvet, American elm with sandpaper, or holly with satin ribbon. Leaves can be matched, arranged from smallest to largest, or patterned in a series (e.g., one

Figure 27-2

Young children are in touch with their senses, including their aesthetic sense.

oak, one maple, one oak, one maple; or one oak, two maples, one oak, two maples).

Don't forget the sense of smell! Sassafras, black walnut, and pine have identifiable odors, as do many herbaceous plants such as yarrow, lavender, wild onion, garlic, mustard, creeping charlie (ground ivy), and all of the herbs. To add fun to a sensory experience, rake leaves into a pile and let the children jump in, lie down, and smell!

A craft project making a monocular or binoculars out of toilet-paper tubes—one tube or two joined together, with attached strings so the binoculars can be worn, and decorated according to available materials and whim—will be popular. The binoculars may be used to help children focus their attention on finding the darkest, lightest, or yellowest green in the landscape.

Weed Brushes

On a nice day, take the children on a walk collecting Queen Anne's lace, wild oats, goldenrod, grass, etc. The next day let each child dip these items into different colors of tempera paint and use them as paintbrushes, using either one or several different colors. If the children do not want to paint with their "weed" brushes, they can simply dip their weeds in colors, leave them to dry, and take them home in a plastic bag. These dried, colored weeds make a pretty fall arrangement.

Center of Interest Autumn Collage

The children may enjoy making an arrangement with objects of nature that can be pasted easily to a flat background such as a shallow box or box lid. Sheets of heavy construction paper or cardboard are also suitable. A variety of objects (different textures, shapes, and colors) create interesting designs.

Begin the collage by placing the most important object on the background. Then arrange the other objects around it so that it remains the center of interest. A collection of autumn collages makes an attractive classroom display.

Fall Leaves Banner

This fall leaf activity can be both an art and math learning experience. For this activity you will need a collection of fall leaves the children have collected. If you don't have a fall season in your area of the country, fall-colored leaves can be found at craft stores.

Have the children sort and classify similar leaves into piles. Talk about which piles have the most or least and how the leaves are similar and different.

Show the children how to brush tempera paint on the veined (back) sides of the leaves and gently press them onto a 1 to 2 yard piece of plain or light-colored muslin or cotton cloth.

Children can create leaf print patterns by alternating two different leaves and colors in a row across the fabric. Provide gel markers for the children (or you) to add their names to the cloth. Other decorations can also be added with markers.

When the cloth is dry, apply iron on hem tape around the edges to frame the banner. This banner can be hung from the ceiling or on a wall. It can also be used as a welcome sign on the classroom door. Another use is as a colorful tablecloth.

Repeated Forms Autumn Collage

Another nature collage can be made using seeds, pods, and other things scattered on the ground and left by the wind.

- Children may classify the objects as large, small, round, straight, rough, smooth, hard, soft.
- An egg carton is a good receptacle for small objects.
- The objects may be arranged into a pattern of repeating forms, using contrasting shapes, textures, and colors. A group display tells the story of nature's materials.

Fall Designs

After collecting a variety of natural objects from their fall walks, some children may want to arrange them in bouquets. Provide children a variety of containers such as tin cans, old vases, or paper cups. They will also need sand, marbles, pebbles, clay, play dough, or salt clay to make a base to hold their natural bouquets. Children place objects randomly in the base until they are satisfied with their arrangement. The more objects available, the more interesting the arrangements will be. They are nice fall decorations for the housekeeping center, as well as a centerpiece for fall snack time.

Fall Group Mural (Cut/Torn Paper)

A group mural using cut or torn paper is another form of picture making in which each child can participate and make a contribution. It generally works best with children five years old and up. Cut or torn paper is a flexible technique that encourages the child to arrange and rearrange pieces on a background, grouping and overlapping them as desired.

Discuss with the children possible topics for the group mural. Each child decides what she will make,

expressing their own ideas. A variety of papers may be used, such as different colors of construction paper, foil, tissue paper, wallpaper, and colored magazine pages. After children are satisfied with their creations, they glue the pieces on the background.

Fall Walk Photographs

Take photographs during a fall walk. A digital camera, a regular camera, or even a disposable camera all work equally well for this activity. Try to take pictures that show a sequence of events. Back in the classroom, arrange the photographs on display in sequence. Have the children think of captions for the pictures, then the story of the event, following the sequence shown in the pictures. Children who are not yet writing can dictate their captions and story to the teacher. They can also dictate their stories on a tape recorder to enjoy at a later time.

Fall Collections Display

In your outdoor walks, encourage the children to collect fall items that appeal to them. They may enjoy collecting items such as leaves, acorns, small pinecones, twigs, etc. These items can be displayed in box lids, on pieces of cardboard, or on paper plates. If children prefer, these items can be glued onto the base for a more permanent arrangement.

Fall Wreath

A fall wreath may be made by cutting out the middle of a paper plate. The child may want to paint the rim a fall color. Once the paint has dried, the child can glue his special fall objects onto the paper plate's rim to create a fall wreath.

If you live in an area where your seasons don't change, you can obtain supplies from the crafts store or use fall-colored items such as buttons, beads, and small pebbles. (Do not use these small items with children under 3 years or age.)

Fall Nature Experiences

Capitalize on children's natural interest in animals by doing some of the following fall nature activities:

- Children can make bird feeders with pinecones. Simply tie a string to the wide part of the pinecone; roll the cone in peanut butter, shake it in a bag or birdseed, and hang the cone onto a branch outside. Talk with the children about the birds as they come to feed from the cone.

- Sit outside and watch the busy squirrels as they collect food for the winter. Discuss what other animals do to prepare for cold weather.

- Observe the birds flying overhead as they migrate south for winter months. Talk about how far they must fly, about where they might sleep at night, and where they find food on their journey. Children might want to act out the birds' movements to music. They may also enjoy representing the birds' journey using crayons, markers, or paint.

Falling Leaves

In this activity, children explore nature's cycles as they recreate the path of a leaf. Use music with a slow, floating quality. ("The Autumn" from *The Four Seasons* by Antonio Vivaldi or *Canon in D* by Pachebel are two good choices). You will also need real or construction paper autumn leaves and a photograph or picture of an autumn tree.

Talk with the children about how autumn affects the leaves in the trees—how they change colors and then fall. Suggest that they move the way a leaf twists and floats as it falls. Invite a few children to demonstrate some of these motions with their hands—for instance, reaching up high and slowly swaying down using both hands as if they were floating to the floor.

- Create a "woods in fall" atmosphere by bringing in colorful leaves (or cutting them out of paper). Hold each one up, then let it drop while children brainstorm words to describe its path. Write their words on a large piece of chart paper.

- Ask children to lift up their hands and copy the path of a floating, tumbling, twirling leaf. You may want to use some of their words from the previously mentioned chart. Then choose a space for them to recreate the path of a leaf with their bodies. Indicate the path by posting or drawing a picture of a tree at one end of the room and placing a leaf (for the leaf pile) at the other end.

- Group children at the "tree" end of the room. Tell them that in their playing falling leaves they should start with their hands reaching up high into the tree branches to show they are still attached to the tree, and then spin, sway, and float all the way to the designated leaf pile. Suggest that they start on tiptoe and gradually get lower and lower, crouching as they drift and twirl, until they are gently rolling along the floor toward the leaf pile.

- Put on the music and send the leaves on their way, one by one, with a tap for each. When all children have reached the leaf pile, ask them to relax and listen to the music. Repeat the activity, tapping each resting leaf when it's time to walk slowly back to the tree area and attach to the branches to begin again.

- Children also learn by watching each other. Have half the group watch the other half travel the leaf pathway. Add interest by asking the leaves to freeze their positions. Then ask the audience to notice and comment on the leaf shapes and places in their fall. Switch groups and repeat. Encourage the children to try out any new movements they observed.

AUTUMN EXPERIENCES FOR OLDER CHILDREN

An appreciation of the fall season is probably even more important for middle and upper elementary age students, since they are even further removed from the early years' sense of wonder. In addition to the activities already covered, you may wish to approach this changing season with more complex artistic activities. Here are a few suggestions.

Textures

Provide students with a variety of leaves, long grasses, and other natural objects. You might want them to bring in similar natural objects as well. Have them

Figure 27-3

Writing a poem about the falling leaves is a fun fall activity.

AUTUMN

1. Harvest time
2. Food
   Eating and life
   Storing for winter (people and animals)
   Cooking and preparing
3. Seeds
4. Changes in plants and animals
   Caring for plants for winter
   Falling leaves
   Changing colors
5. Animals preparing for winter
   Birds leaving
   Nests
   Changes in fur
   Caterpillars
6. Cooler weather days
   Effect on clothing we wear
   Frost

WINTER

1. Cold weather
   Melting and freezing
   Ice, snow, sleet, fog
   Clothing necessary
2. Animals
   Resting and shelter/protection
   Pets that need care
   Bird feeding
3. Plants
   Need for warmth and light
   Freezing/resting outside
   Winter bulbs and flowers
4. Heat and light
   Short days and darkness
   Awareness of moon and stars
   Warmth of sun on some days
   How buildings are heated
   Drying and evaporation
5. Light and color
   Bubbles
   Prisms
   Flashlights
   Lenses
6. Electricity
   Clinging elements of static electricity
   Used for heat and light
   Helps us with our work

SPRING

1. Weather
   Rain, fog, hail, wind
   Lightning, thunder
   Thawing
   Warm sun
   Effect on clothing we wear
2. Animals
   Baby animals
   Growth
   Changes in trees and plants
   Flowers and buds
3. Water, sand, and mud
   Evaporation
   Absorption
   Flow and forces of water
   Mixing, dissolving, combining
4. Smells
   Damp things
   Flowers
5. Machines and their uses
   People working after the winter
   Construction (streets and buildings)
   Tree-trimming and spraying
   Tools used on lawns, gardens, fields
   Weights and balance
   Aids to moving things

SUMMER

1. Weather
   Hot sun, shade, breezes
   Heat, rain, thunder, hail
   Effects on body (light clothing, resting, need
   for water, perspiration)
2. Animals
   Providing food, water, shade
   Discovery of worms, insects, spiders (how they
   live)
   Growth of baby animals born in spring
3. Plants
   Growth
   Need for sun, water, some shade
   Development and ripening of foods
   Preparing fresh fruits and vegetables
4. Machines
   Heavy machinery
   Construction
   Concepts of levers, wheels, pulleys
   Continued use of sand, mud, water

Figure 27-4
Seasonal themes.

make rubbings using white crayon or oil pastel and black paper. Suggest that students do a repeated rubbing of the item until the entire paper is covered. Discuss the results as a record of textures that can be viewed as artwork as well as a display for science. Students might want to research the types of grass and leaves they used in this activity.

Fall Textures

Have the students make and illustrate vocabulary cards for words that describe fall textures. Have them arrange the items by tactile sense (e.g., rough, soft, smooth). Encourage them to use these terms appropriately in storytelling and in other activities.

Mystery Textures

Tell students they will make a mystery texture bag. Provide small paper bags for each student. Have them secretly collect items that have varied textures of fall or any season. These are the mystery items that others will be guessing. Working in pairs, students exchange bags and try to guess what the mystery objects are by feeling the textures.

See Figure 27–4 for more seasonal themes.

Lines, Patterns, Textures

Have students bring in a large leaf. Place viewfinders over one part of the leaf and observe lines, patterns, and textures. Have students create a large drawing of the small section of the leaf seen in the viewfinder.

Varieties of Colors

Have students look selectively for varieties of red in leaves and bring them to class. Have them describe the differences using terms such as light, dark, shiny, or dull. Focus on other visual elements in the same way. For example, ask students who are wearing rough textures to stand and point them out. Develop an awareness of terms to describe textures such as bumpy, prickly and silky.

Weather Diaries

Have students keep a weather diary with drawings that portray the weather as it occurs at the same time each day for five days. The time might be lunch or recess. At the end of five days, have students work in small groups to compare and contrast the different interpretations. The total group can choose drawings that best represent the weather for each day. The drawings might be put into a booklet entitled "The Weather Diary of Grade Four." Present the booklet to the school library.

New Colors

Ask students to think about colors they have *never* seen in fall flowers or leaves. Have them create a fall drawing or painting using these colors. Discuss the mood or feeling of these artworks with each student.

Photographers' Vision

Bring in books with fall photographs by Ansel Adams, Paul Weston, Alfred Steiglitz, Margaret Bourke-White, and other well-known photographers. Have the students discuss the subject matter portrayed by these photographers. Discuss why each may have chosen his or her subject and how the images were planned. Does it look like the fall where you live? What are the similarities? The differences?

Fall Memory Book

Children in the primary grades can create a "fall memory book" with pressed leaves, pictures, and writings about fall activities and specific events they have enjoyed. Wrap the book in paper and put it away until it's almost spring. When they open it again and look at the leaves and read their writings, they will be able to remember fall and can compare the differences in seasonal colors.

Pumpkin Writing Prompts

One of fall's most common vegetables is the pumpkin. You can use pumpkins to encourage children's writing and thinking skills with some of the following writing "prompts" (ideas to get children started):

- Finish the following sentence: "If people grew like pumpkin plants, pretty soon . . ."
- To grow, a pumpkin needs soil, water, air, and sunshine. What do you need to grow? Write about the things that your body needs to make you healthy and strong.
- A pumpkin is a *producer*. It uses air, water, and sunshine to grow. Other animals depend on the pumpkin plant. Write about an animal that uses a pumpkin for energy, and describe where the energy from the pumpkin goes.
- Cut the pumpkin. Have students look at the skin, pulp, and seeds, and then answer, "How is the pumpkin like planet Earth?"

Autumn Reflections

By observing the landscape, students can explore the natural forms and colors seen in trees and the pattern of reflections in water. For this activity you will need 12″ × 18″ pieces of white paper, pencils, watercolor paint, and brushes.

Let the children practice learning how to paint thin lines using only the tip of the brush. Talk about the kind of scene they want to make and what details to include such as wildlife, buildings, people, plants, etc.

Have the students fold their paper in half. The crease represents the shoreline of a river, lake, or pond. Let the children lightly sketch the scene they want.

Explain that reflections in nature are always the mirror image of the scene above. Show examples of photos from calendars and the like.

Demonstrate how to paint the mirror image of a scene reflected in the surface of the water. Paint a little bit of a tree, and then fold it. Paint a little more, then fold it again. By folding the paper, it makes a mirror image on the bottom half of the paper.

Demonstrate how to paint a tree by starting with a large letter "Y" for the trunk, then medium-sized "Ys" for branches and very small "Ys" for twigs.

Encourage students to practice making a variety of lines with the tip of the brush on a scrap piece of paper. Discuss autumn colors and the importance of color choices.

THE AESTHETICS OF WINTER

"In the depths of winter I finally learned there was in me an invincible summer."–Albert Camus

Young children greet winter with delight. In many areas of the country it means ice-skating and sledding, rolling snowballs to make a snowman, sliding on the ice, jumping in snowdrifts, and catching snowflakes on warm mittens. In other areas, it means colder weather and shorter days, even though there is no snow. The idea of snow in winter, however, is traditional even in parts of the country where it never snows!

Winter offers many stimulating subjects for aesthetic experiences. Children can experiment with paints to depict the bright colors of winter clothing and the active lines seen in outdoor sports. The delicate textures can be created by painting with bits of sponge, crushed paper, or old toothbrushes. White chalk also works well for winter pictures. It may be used alone, on colored paper, or in combination with crayon. Some topics for picture making are as follows:

- ⊙ Playing in the Snow
- ⊙ Our Street in Winter
- ⊙ Feeding the Birds
- ⊙ Riding on My Sled
- ⊙ We Play Safely in Winter
- ⊙ Ice-Skating with My Friends
- ⊙ Building a Snowman
- ⊙ Dressing for Winter Weather

Some other suggestions for experiences that encourage a child's aesthetic sense are as follows:

- ⊙ walking around the block to see how homes look in the winter
- ⊙ observing and studying plants in winter (encourage children to discover for themselves which plants stay the same all year)
- ⊙ observing melting of icicles and snow as temperatures warm or as they are placed over heat
- ⊙ observing snowflakes with a magnifying glass
- ⊙ discussing animals in the winter
- ⊙ observing water placed outside, with discussion of temperature as it relates to freezing and liquids and to formation of snowflakes
- ⊙ discussing migration of some birds before winter
- ⊙ observing birds at a bird feeder
- ⊙ recognizing the differences between birds seen at the bird feeder

For another aesthetic experience, after a walk in the wintery weather, children may enjoy creating their own three-dimensional scenes of winter. All you need is a surface covered with white, either a sheet or white roll of (freezer) paper. Discuss what they saw on their walk and what they may want to create. Provide a supply of cardboard boxes as well as paint, markers, bits of cloth, and ribbon. Natural objects like twigs, pinecones, and leaves are interesting additional materials. This could be an ongoing project that children can add to or change over the course of several days.

WINTER EXPERIENCES FOR CHILDREN

Soapy Sculpture Dough

Add this soap dough mixture to your modeling materials in the winter time. It is white and very pliable and easy for children to manipulate. To make the soapy mixture, pour a box of soap flakes into a large container. Add water slowly until the mixture is the consistency of paste. Invite the children to mix it with you. Then have the children form grapefruit-sized balls with a lump of the mixture. Provide enough of these balls so each child has his own modeling "soap." You may want to supply toothpicks, pipe cleaners, buttons, and sequins for the children to decorate their soap dough creations.

Outdoor Artwork–Snow Designs

Save the squeeze bottles that dishwashing detergent comes in. Rinse thoroughly. Fill with colored water. Let the children "draw" bright designs by squirting the colored water on the snow.

Finger Painting with Ice Cubes

For this variation of finger painting, use regular finger paint and glossy paper, but do not wet the paper as you normally would to prepare for finger painting. Give each child an ice cube with which to spread and dilute the paint while making designs on the paper.

Winter Observations

- ⊙ Find an outdoor plant that changes dramatically with the seasons—perhaps with flowers, leaves, and/or fruit. With children, observe it about once a week. If possible, measure its growth. Record bud sizes, bark color, and other changes. Use rich words to describe the scene.

- ⊙ At seasonal intervals, ask children to make their own creative representations of the plant. Save these in their portfolios to document not only the change in seasons but also their progress in drawing and writing.

- ⊙ Ask the children what they notice about the plant their group has adopted. With crayons, draw the plant the way it looks today. Include details and colors. Create texture with heavy layers of crayon.

- ⊙ Label the drawing with the child's name and date. Ask if they can see dew on leaves or ice crystals on branches. Decorate the drawing with glitter and glue.

- ⊙ On the back of the picture, write about the plant. A teacher can write this for children unable to write for themselves. What season is it? How is the plant changing? What do you think will happen next?

- ⊙ For a variation, draw outdoors so children can look directly at the plant.

- ☝ Adopt a tree, plant, or shrub. How can the children help care for it?

⊙ At the end of the year, display the four seasons as depicted by each child.

Winter Dramatizations

Dramatizations can be stimulated by phenomena in our everyday world. Encourage the children to pretend (by acting with their body movements) to be any of the following:

- ⊙ leaves waving in a gentle wind, a heavy wind, and then eventually flying through the air
- ⊙ snow falling softly, being made into a snowman, and then melting
- ⊙ an ice cream cone or icicle melting in the sun
- ⊙ rain trickling down, running into a swift stream, the sun coming out, and a rainbow appearing
- ⊙ an icy hill that is hard to walk up
- ⊙ a thick fog to find one's way through
- ⊙ creative movements relating to jobs in winter, such as shoveling snow
- ⊙ creative movements depicting a snowman as it melts
- ⊙ creative movements of winter sports and activities—ice-skating, throwing snowballs, etc.
- ⊙ creative movements depicting birds flying around the bird feeder, eating seeds, flying in the air

You and the children may think of others.

Observing the Moon

Read the book *Wait Till the Moon is Full* by Margaret Wise Brown (HarperCollins, 1989). Moon facts are

Figure 27-5

Fall art activities include drawing pictures and writing poems about the changes in nature.

THIS ONE'S for YOU!   Backpacks!

As you explore the changing seasons on your nature walks with the children, provide each child a backpack to hold treasures collected along the way. You can use storebought backpacks, or do the following activity for child-made backpacks.

To make a backpack, you will need large empty detergent boxes, construction paper, scissors, crayons, and markers. Cut off the top of the detergent box. Punch holes to string heavy soft yarn through the box for straps. (See Figure 27–6). Paste a piece of construction paper on the front of the box so the child can decorate it. Have the children color and decorate their backpack with markers, crayons, glued-on bits of cloth, paper, etc. Loop the straps over the child's arms to hold the pack on.

BACKPACK IDEAS

Children enjoy backpacks. You can incorporate them throughout the day in the following activities:
- Create a *Writing Backpack* filled with pads of paper on clipboards and colored pencils for children to carry off to a private place to write.
- Pack a *Snack Backpack* for taking snacks outdoors. Fill the bag with napkins, a tablecloth, and finger foods.
- Stuff a backpack full of *Puzzles and Quiet Games* for children to take to a private place for quiet gatherings together.
- Put together a *Take-Home Backpack* filled with this year's favorite toys, games, and books for children to share with their family.

NATURE STUDY BACKPACK

Pack your bag with some of the items listed to inspire children to explore nature all around them. Start by inviting children to look around the area and describe what they see, smell, feel, and hear. Then pass out materials for free exploration. Blow a whistle when you want to bring children back to a gathering place and share their findings. Exploration items: unbreakable magnifiers, paper towel tube "spy glasses," and pads of paper and crayons.

ART BACKPACK

There is so much excitement when art materials are taken outdoors. Introduce a material (see following list) and a technique on a table or blanket and then give children time to explore the area. Materials: drawing paper and flat crayons for nature rubbings; chalk for sidewalk and wall drawings; a collection of boxes with fasteners, rope, and glue for making a group sculpture, and paintbrushes and containers of water to paint everything in sight!

Printed with permission from *Scholastic Early Childhood Today,* May 2002, "Backpack Activities throughout the Day," E. B. Church, p. 52.

woven into this story about a young raccoon that must wait for the full moon before he can go out at night.

Read this story aloud on the first day of a new moon. Explain that from one new moon to the next is the time it takes the moon to make one revolution around the earth. Then have students make a calendar grid on a sheet of large chart paper and mark the current date with "New Moon." Tell the children that each day one person will take the moon calendar home (in a poster tube). The child should go outside with an adult or to a window to observe the moon and add a drawing of how the moon looks that night. Save a brief moment in your morning routing for the moon report. You can show children daily images of the moon on the Internet at http://kids.msfc.nasa.gov/Earth/Moon. Click on Current Moon Phase.

Bird Feeders

Winter is a wonderful time for feeding the birds. Young children are able to understand how important

Figure 27-6

Backpack from recycled detergent box.

food is and that birds can't always get to food they need if snow covers the ground. Even in areas where it does not snow, young children can see the bare trees, brown grass, and lack of flowers, which are all food sources for the birds. In areas where winters are very mild, children can simply help the birds more easily find food by making bird feeders. Bird feeders are easy to make and provide many learning opportunities for young children.

Hang them up near windows where children are able to observe the birds enjoying their food. Young children are keen observers of nature and will enjoy the variety of birds their feeders attract.

As winter goes on, children enjoy the daily ritual of feeding the birds and possibly putting out some water when it is freezing. Other bird feeding ideas include the following:

⊙ Under supervision, even quite young children can manage to thread peanuts in shells onto a string with a large dull-tipped rug needle. Be aware of children who may be allergic to peanuts when using this activity. Hang up these "necklaces" for the birds.

⊙ Children can also make "bird pudding" from stale bits of bread, raisins, bird seed, and bacon rind, moistened with water and put out for the birds. Put the pudding out as is or put it into half a co-conut shell. A small hole drilled into the coconut shell will enable you to hang it up where it can swing freely as birds land to feed.

WINTER EXPERIENCES FOR OLDER CHILDREN

Winter is an excellent time to focus attention on the designs of nature. Trees without leaves are more interesting to study for design and line patterns. The light and shadow in the winter is different than in other months. Animals have different coats in the winter. There are different colors and kinds of birds seen in the winter. The following ideas are more suggestions on using the aesthetics of winter for art activities.

Skeletons

Artists learn to see and sketch things in two ways. One way is to look for geometric shapes. The other is to look for lines that show the "skeleton" or hidden structure of an object. Bare trees in winter are perfect to study as "skeletons" for shape and drawing activities. Take a few trips outside with sketchbooks and observe the barren trees for shapes and designs. Remind the children to look at them as if they were "skeletons." This shape is hidden when the leaves are on the tree. Help students find geometric shapes in these "skeletons." Use words like "circle," "oval," and "ellipse" to describe shapes of trees. Encourage the children to sketch what they see. Discuss any geometric shapes they see in terms of how the shapes all combine into one design—the tree itself.

Light Sources

Set up an environment with a light source and several geometric forms. Have the students develop some experiments that will allow them to move the light source or the forms a measured distance from each other. Have them observe and draw the changes in the length and the shapes of the cast shadows when they move the light source or the objects.

Winter Landscape

Have the students create a collage of a winter landscape using rubbings made with oil pastels or crayons. To make a rubbing, place 6″ × 9″ newsprint on a textured surface. Use the flat edge of an unwrapped oil pastel or crayon to rub the paper. Hold the paper so it does not move. For complex textural effects, place a completed rubbing over a second surface and rub it with a second color. After the rubbings are cut and pasted down, have students add other textures and details based on a winter concept.

Winter Awareness

Ask students to look for examples of unusual shapes and colors in the winter environment (sunsets, changing colors and shapes of clouds, puddles of water with reflections). Have students use the wet-into-wet technique (painting on a wet piece of paper) to create paintings of the sky with soft fuzzy clouds of different shapes. Note possibilities for pictures of stormy skies, sunsets, etc.

Animals in Winter

Have the students go to the library and select an illustrated book about animals in winter. They should choose the book because they like the style of the illustrations. Have them share their choices and explain features of the illustrator's style. Compare and contrast the styles, emphasizing the special qualities of each. Encourage students to invent descriptive style names such as scientific or realistic, fantasy or imagination, or cartoon-like.

Science Research

Have students work in small groups with science books. Have them do research on topics such as glow-in-the-dark animal life (firefly, glowworm, electric eel) and glow-in-the-dark visual effects (reflective surfaces on roads, fluorescent colors seen under special liquids). Have them share their research with the class. Encourage them to draw, paint, or model the research in original creations.

Winter Moonlight

Read the story *Happy Birthday, Moon* by Frank Asch. As the story is read, show the illustrations. At the end of the story, discuss with students how the illustrator has shown moonlight in the various scenes in the book. Have the students describe their own memories of how things look at night when the moon is full. Encourage imaginative recall about shadows and special differences in seasons (snow) or weather (rain). Have the students draw a picture using the book as a starting point. They may also want to write a story or poem to go with their work.

Beating the Winter Blues

Have the students read *Blueberries for Sal* by Robert McCloskey. Pour a can of blueberries into a jar. Ask students how many ways they can estimate the number of blueberries contained in the jar. Then let them count the berries in different ways. For example, one group may count them by grouping them in tens and recording the number. Another group of students may want to put them into groups of three and try counting them this way. This group could then produce a multiplication statement showing the total.

⊙ Have the students create a bulletin board that is a guessing game. Have each student make an illustration that shows the nursery rhyme, poem, or song that includes the word "blue." Post the illustration on the board. Provide an answer list for those wishing to guess the title and check their guess.

⊙ Bake blueberry muffins with the students to enjoy while listening to *Blueberries for Sal*.

⊙ Read several different books that incorporate the blue theme to the students (*Ol' Blue* by Mark Taylor; *The Blue Whale* by Donna Grosvenor; *Blue Lobster* by Carol Carrick). After each reading, discuss fiction and nonfiction genres, main ideas, facts learned, ideas, ideals or lessons taught, and an appreciation of literature developed.

⊙ Using a map of the United States, have the students locate Maine, the setting of *Blueberries for Sal*. Explain the climate and why blueberries grow there.

⊙ Identify this region as part of the northeastern region of the United States. You may want to incorporate dictionaries, encyclopedias, atlases, and Internet sites to illustrate these concepts.

The Color Wheel

Winter is good time to learn about colors, especially if there may be a lack of them in nature in your area of the country.

Explain to the children that the color wheel is a chart that shows how colors are related and sorted to make it easier for an artist to mix the right colors for paint. Refer to Figure 27–16 when explaining the color wheel to the children.

Primary colors are blue, red, and yellow and cannot be made by mixing other colors together.

Secondary colors are orange, purple, and green and are made by mixing two primary colors from either side of the color wheel.

Tertiary colors are made by mixing a primary and a secondary color together. Like purple and blue, green and yellow, or blue and green.

Complementary colors are opposite from each other on the color wheel and they contrast because they do not have any colors in common. Green is made by mixing yellow and blue, so it will complement red.

Analogous colors on the color wheel are right next to each other and have a color in common—for example, blue, blue/green, and green all contain blue. Red, orange, and yellow are analogous because red and yellow make orange.

Cool colors are made mostly of green, blue, and purple and they remind you of cool things and make you feel cooler.

Warm colors are made mostly of red, orange, and yellow and they remind you of warm things and make you feel warm.

Local colors are realistic colors because they appear in nature, such as green grass, blue sky, brown earth, etc.

Earth colors are not seen on most color wheels. Black, grays, whites, browns, beiges, and tans are earth colors and can be made by mixing all three primaries together with some black or white.

Artists use colors to create moods, show contrast and create depth in artwork. Let the children experiment with mixing colors, using complementary colors, and any other color combinations they are interested in using.

Figure 27-7

Animals in nature inspire children in their artwork.

THE AESTHETICS OF SPRING

The gradual coming of spring brings many signs of beauty, such as the color and texture of flowers in the sunlight and the pattern of delicate leaves against the sky. Children can share their experiences during informal discussions and they can bring in objects of nature for closer observation. Objects may a include bouquet of dandelions, a piece of moss, some pussy willows, or a budding tree branch. These discoveries motivate children to learn by stimulating their curiosity about the world around them and arousing new interests and ideas.

Young children enjoy the rainy and windy days of spring. They learn more about wind and rain if they have a chance to taste, feel, and walk in it. They can then discuss, question, and accept the elements more easily and add to their knowledge of nature.

> "It is not the language of painters but the language of nature which one should listen to, the feeling for the things themselves, for reality, is more important than the feeling for pictures."
> –Vincent Van Gogh

SPRING EXPERIENCES FOR CHILDREN

Spring is a time of growth and changes. The world springs into colorful growth. People shed heavy winter clothes for sneakers and head for the outdoors to play.

The following spring activity suggestions will help young children experience nature up close.

To help young children experience rain try the following:

- Take a group of children for a walk in a light rain. Wear boots, raincoats, and hats.
- Take a walk after a heavy rain; feel the drops as they fall from trees; explore the puddles.
- Let two children at a time use an umbrella and take a walk in the yard.
- Use a porch or other shelter for unlimited chances to hold hands, tongues, or containers out in the rain.
- Collect rain in clean containers for tasting; use for washing hands and face; try it with soap; blow bubbles. For tasting, put a plastic cup or glass for each child in a cake pan or such to keep from being blown over.
- Listen for the sound of rain. Is it sprinkling? A heavy rain? A blowing rain?

⊙ Listen to the sound as rain hits different surfaces: windowpane, roof, outside shelter, ground, puddle of water.

⊙ Have four and five year olds experiment with rain hitting various surfaces; put out inverted tin pan, pan of water, pan of dirt, paper sack.

⊙ Note the smell of fresh rain.

⊙ Watch what happens as the rain hits the windowpane or a puddle of water.

⊙ Watch what happens as a rain begins—as it hits dry ground, the sidewalk, leaves on a tree.

⊙ What is different about the sky, clouds, and sun? Older children may visually compare the color of clouds, sun, and sun rays on various days.

⊙ For children who walk to school: What was different about coming to school—puddles, sidewalks, cars splashing, etc.?

⊙ For children who ride to school: What was different about driving to school—windshield wipers, lights on, driving slowly, slippery streets?

⊙ What was needed to go out in the rain: umbrella, newspaper, boots, raincoat?

⊙ Is there a rainbow?

⊙ On a hot, sunny day let older children experiment with a sprinkler or hose to make a rainbow.

To experience the wind try the following:

⊙ Make a simple kite of paper with 3 feet of string attached securely (put end of string through pinhole, knot end, and secure with tape); let each child experiment with his or her own kite.

⊙ Tie crepe paper streamers to a stick to let the wind blow and to run with. Older children can experiment with streamers tied in a stationary place and watch which way the wind blows streamers from day to day.

⊙ Use scarves for dancing outside.

⊙ Use toy sailboats in a large pan or tub of water to see how they move in the wind.

⊙ Listen for the sounds of wind through the trees and around buildings.

Wind Words

Read *The Wind* by Robert Louis Stevenson. Create a windy day with an electric fan. Or take the children outside on a windy day. Have them close their eyes and feel the wind in their faces and at their backs. Hold up a strip of tissue and watch its movements. Encourage the children to call out words that describe how the wind feels to them and how it moves.

Figure 27-8
Even very young children can enjoy the unfolding beauty of the seasons.

Spring Aesthetics–Science

The natural changes in the world in the spring are wonderful topics for aesthetic experiences. The following science activities will help children focus on the exciting things happening in the world around them in the spring.

⊙ Plant an outdoor garden or plant seeds in small flower pots for windowsill observation of the growing process.

⊙ Plant seeds—vegetable or flower—in the classroom.

⊙ Observe the stages of growth of a plant, such as a fruit tree, during the spring.

⊙ Watch seeds such as beans and alfalfa sprouts and eat them.

⊙ Study and observe kinds of flowers—note colors, shapes, smells, and growth patterns.

⊙ Study and observe animal babies—their names, the sounds they make, what they eat, whether they are dependent on their mother.

⊙ Study birds and what they do in the spring.

Garden Signs

Gather a group of seed packets for children to study for ideas about designs and growing information. Make sure seed packets are empty if children still put nonfood items in their mouths. You may want to tour a garden store to see gardens or flowerbeds with signs.

To make garden signs, each child will need a piece of 8½″ × 11″ construction paper cut in half lengthwise. The child can cut this himself or herself or an adult can help if necessary. Fold this piece in the middle to make a seed packet. Place the open side down.

Ask the children to think how their plant will look when it is grown. Will it have flowers? Fruit? Leaves to eat? Look at pictures of flowers or food for ideas.

Children fill one side of their sign with a picture of the plant or its produce using crayons or markers. This is the front of the garden sign.

On the other side of the sign, write the child's name. List care instructions such as "water twice a week." Write down what the *child* considers to be care instructions, avoiding adult corrections.

Open your sign and lightly cover the inside with glue. Place a craft or popsicle stick at the bottom with most of it sticking out. Fold the sign and press to seal. Let it dry overnight.

The signs can be used to plant an imaginary garden or a real one! Find out which plants thrive in your climate. Grow foods children can eat, such as leaf lettuce. Visit farmer's markets and groceries regularly to see the wide variety of fruits and vegetables. Find out which are grown locally. Taste new items each time.

Spring windows. Flowers can bloom as often and as long as you like by decorating your windows with children's flower creations.

Be sure windows are securely closed and locked before decorating them. Flowers can be painted onto the window with thick tempera paint or markers. Or you may want to use Crayola Window FX Washable markers. To begin, children draw the outline of their flowers directly onto the windows using a black crayon. Then they can fill in the outlines with thick tempera paint and a paintbrush or markers. As new spring flowers bloom outdoors, they can also be added to the window display. When animals appear they too can be added to the drawing for an ever-evolving window masterpiece.

Children can even anticipate spring's arrival by including robins or dandelions in their window displays before they appear in nature.

Plant press. Collect nonpoisonous fallen leaves and flowers such as dandelions or clover. Only with permission, pick flowers from gardens.

To make a plant press: On top of a piece of corrugated cardboard, layer two or three paper towels. Spread out leaves or flowers flat on the paper towels. Place several sheets of newspaper on top of this stack. Write the child's name with markers on the top.

Put heavy books or bricks on top of the plant press. Dry overnight. Change the newspaper each day until the plant is dry.

Use the dried leaves and flowers to make a collage by arranging the dried plants on colorful construction paper in a design. Cut pieces of construction paper may be glued on for added designs. Add more decorative details with markers or crayons.

Variations: Let children predict what they think will happen to the color and shape of plants as they dry. Measure sizes. Draw before and after pictures.

Feast on dried foods. Make fruit leather, dried fruit, or jerky. Taste raisins, dried plums, and apricots. Mix up dried milk. Make gelatin or pudding.

Study plants such as milkweed and dandelions. Make dazzling bouquets with dried flowers.

Dandelions

In spring dandelions are everywhere, and children not only notice them but touch them, note their color, count them, and pick them.

Dandelions seed early, rapidly, and in great quantity. They grow fast and recover from damage quickly and powerfully! So children may pick them, dig them up, and tear them apart. Respect for nature is an important aspect of learning about the environment, but exceptions to rules exist in every field of study. Weeds are exceptions because of their hands-on study value for young children.

Ask the children if they ever noticed that dandelions let out a milky juice when picked? Or that the stem is hollow? Rub the flower on paper to obtain a yellow pigment, or create a "duplicate" dandelion by rubbing flower, stem, leaves, and soil on the paper. How fast do the dandelions in a lawn grow after being cut? Try watching and measuring. How deep do the roots of a dandelion go? Why not dig up some dandelions and compare which is the longest?

Early French explorers named this weed "dent-de-lion," mispronounced by the English as "dandelion." The original means "tooth of the lion" and refers to the leaves. Can you see and feel "teeth" on the leaves? If you cut several leaves from the plant and superimpose one upon another, you will recognize the diversity of shapes.

Aesthetic Observations–Flowers

Children notice the first arrivals of flowers in spring. They are keen observers of nature, not yet oblivious to its ever-changing beauty. They may enjoy making their own creative versions of spring flowers.

Figure 27-9
The beauty of nature inspires young children's writing.

Figure 27-10
Young children are very aware of the sights and sounds of nature.

Suitable papers for flower making include newsprint, construction paper, tissue paper, foil, cellophane, and gift wrap. Other materials are also useful, such as paper cupcake liners, small frozen pie tins, paper cups, toweling tubes, and egg cartons. Also provide pipe cleaners, toothpicks, wire, straws, and popsicle sticks. If children want to put their flower creations in containers, have on hand small discarded flower pots, egg cartons, and paper cups.

Spring Murals

After a walk in the rain, a dance in the wind, or another spring experience, plan a group mural. After coming inside, discuss what was seen, heard, tasted, and felt. Discuss with the children things that can be included in a group mural. Each child decides what they will make for the mural. Then, the children create individual works, representing their personal experiences. These pictures and designs can be glued onto one large sheet of paper.

Spring Painting Ideas

Windswept. This activity is fun outside, but can also be done indoors. The child uses a spoon to put a dab of several colors of tempera paint onto a piece of construction paper. For interesting effects, have bright, primary colors, as well as white tempera paint, available. The child uses a small piece of cardboard to push, pull, turn, and twist the paint all over the paper. Blowing by the child (and the wind) will also create a unique, windswept appearance.

Blow painting. Provide the child a small amount of watery tempera paint in a container and a plastic spoon. The child puts a small puddle of the watery tempera paint onto a piece of paper (copy paper works well). Using a straw, the child blows the paint in any way or direction. Ask how it looks when he blows gently? Hard? When the wind blows it?

Shaving cream painting. Children enjoy playing with foamy shaving cream any time of the year. In the spring, add some dry tempera paint to the shaving cream. Children can mix the paint up with the foam on a cookie sheet, on the tabletop, or on a piece of shiny finger paint paper. They may simply want to experience the wonderful sensation of playing with the shaving cream. Some may want to draw with it. The object is, however, to enjoy the sensations of touch, sight, and smell.

Figure 27-11
Being in the outdoors is an aesthetic and fun experience for young children.

Kites

What is better on a windy spring day than kite flying? To make a kite, begin with a piece of 12″ × 18″ construction paper, or use newsprint if a larger size is desired. The child makes a design or drawing. After the design is made in crayon or paint, the paper can be folded and stapled with all corners toward the center in a diamond shape. Strips of masking tape may be criss-crossed on the back for reinforcement and a string may be fastened in the center. A tail can be added using several bow ties of cloth or paper tied to a length of string. Smaller kites make colorful room decorations when used on bulletin boards or strung across open areas.

A Rainbow in Your Room

Make a rainbow in the classroom. All that is needed is a glass of water and a sunny day. (Be sure to use a clear glass. The wider the mouth, the better.) When the glass is placed in sunlight, there should be a rainbow

where the shadow would fall. What is made is a simple prism, which can be used in lessons about the color spectrum. Point out to the children that a rainbow forms outdoors when drops of water in the air act as prisms.

Spring Signs

Discuss the look, feel, sound, and smell of spring and the other seasons as they happen. How do the children know that it is spring in their neighborhood? By the green grass and pussy willows? Mud? Reruns on television? Different clothes? Baseball? Divide the bulletin board into four areas: "My Eyes See Spring," "I Feel Spring," "I Hear Spring," "My Nose Knows It Is Spring." Have the children draw pictures to illustrate each theme.

SPRING EXPERIENCES FOR OLDER CHILDREN

Spring Sketches

Have students take a sketchbook home and draw five to ten small patches of different textures that they find in nature. Under each patch, have students write down the name of the material from which the sketch was made (a tree, a rock, a piece of a leaf, etc.). Have the students use their sketches to create a colored and enlarged version of these textures on a 9″ piece of paper. Display and discuss the drawings.

Patterns in Nature

Discuss regular and irregular patterns seen in plants, animals, and other natural forms in the spring. Some irregular patterns are found in the camouflage of animals. Structural patterns tend to be regular, as seen in shells, leaf veins, and many plants.

Visual Elements

The visual elements in patterns can be mathematically varied in size, shape, position, and in the intervals of spacing between them. Computers provide an excellent way for students to explore the logic of making patterns.

Forms of Letters

Have students create letter forms by printing them with objects. Almost all letters of the alphabet can be created from straight lines (edge of tongue depressor or cardboard), circles (bottle caps or spools), and half circles (rubber washers cut in half). Students can also use this printing technique to illustrate an original poem.

Group Objects

Have four or five students work in a group, using the objects from the above activity (cardboard, bottle caps, spools, and rubber washers cut in half). They will share their printing objects to make a picture. Brainstorm creative ways to use the objects they have (e.g., repeated circles become animal shapes, edges of cardboard become repeated blades of grass, etc.) Display these pictorial prints so that others in the room can see them.

Georgia O'Keeffe's The Mountain, New Mexico

Obtain an art print of this work. It is an excellent example of a landscape and varieties of warm and cool colors. If this print is not available, any other landscape with warm and cool colors will suffice.

Briefly review the concept that colors are an important way to express moods and feelings in art. Point out that many color words help people to tell about feelings. Examples include feeling blue, green with envy, or red or purple with rage.

Explain that artists often refer to these color qualities as warm or cool. These terms can mean that a color is used to show warm things (a fire) or cool

things (a lake). More often, the artist also remembers that colors help to express feelings.

Explain that the warm colors in this painting show the red earth of mountains in New Mexico, but they also help to express the artist's warm feelings about the land. Georgia O'Keeffe thought that forms and colors of the desert and nearby mountains were beautiful. Guide students to see the delicate shading and rhythmic curves that fill the whole painting. Discuss how the painting makes them feel about the place depicted.

As a follow-up activity, have students create a picture of a landscape on a planet no one has seen. Have them use warm or cool colors to show and express the feelings of the people.

Color Awareness

Have students cut out several geometric shapes from gray paper and glue them onto a background of the same color. Display the work. Discuss how the shapes are "lost" when viewed from a distance. Have the students use a pencil to add value changes or textures to

Figure 27-12

Teachers enjoy the beauty of nature along with the children.

Figure 27-13

The colors in the world around them inspire children in their artwork.

"reveal" each shape. Discourage outlining of the shapes. Display and discuss the revised drawings. Go outside and observe the leaves in the trees. How do the leaves blend into one another? Is this the same as the gray shapes on the gray paper? Why is this so?

Shadows

Use the tree drawings made earlier in this chapter. Explain that shadows are created by a definite source of light such as the sun. Students need not draw a sun to show the source of sun in their drawings. Instead, they can simply decide if shadows will be on the left or right side of the tree in their drawings. (The implied light source is on the opposite side.)

Encourage students to be inventive with lines and shading so that textures of trees, bark, and leaves show up in their drawings. Point out that clumps of leaves will have shading on the same side as the shadows on the tree trunk.

While the students work, help them to concentrate on the "logic" of shading. You might have students look out a window if shadows are prominent. Or you might pause several times and illuminate objects in the room so that students can see shadows. Most students can produce inventive shading.

I'm Into Spring!

Make large individual cards with the letters S, P, R, I, N, G. Have a student hold up the corresponding letter as the poem is read. Put these letters on a bulletin board and have the children illustrate them in any way they choose. Next, ask the children to write a rhyming acrostic about spring together. For example:

I'm **S**winging in the sunshine,
I'm **P**rancing in a shower,
I'm **R**unning with a dragon kite,
I'm **I**magining I'm a flower.
I'm **N**ature-hunting ladybugs,
I'm **G**rowing things to eat.
I'm singing in the springtime
With my guests who TWEET TWEET TWEET.

See-Through Masterpieces

Show students pictures of stained glass windows. Ask them to make a colorful patterned picture on white paper. Next, have them color in all the parts of the pattern with a variety of colors of crayons. Then submerge the paper in cooking oil. Remove and pat excess oil on a paper towel. Tape the dried piece to the window and let the light shine through.

THE AESTHETICS OF SUMMER

Summer is a time for growing. Young children are very aware of the ever-new earth around them. See with the children the many features of the summer:

⊙ the tiny world of ants
⊙ the large and tiny wildflowers
⊙ the colors and shapes of the clouds
⊙ the rainbow after a summer shower
⊙ the ladybug crawling up a flower stem

Experience with the children all these things and many more during the summer. Talk with the children about them. This will help them develop and extend their aesthetic appreciation of the world in the summertime.

Summer is an excellent time for being aware of nature, since both children and adults spend much more time outside. Summer is the time when children learn to appreciate, love, and care for their environment by observing adults. When adults handle tree buds, flowers, or insects gently and with respect, children begin to comprehend the value of nature. Short, simple directives such as, "If it's attached, please leave it attached," or "We need to leave nature the way we found it," and if it is alive, "Let's be scientists and observe," can be understood by even a very young child and will be followed if the adult models them.

Observing insects is fun! Children find their bizarre, unique behavior fascinating. They are common in just about every environment and are easy to find. Stay near one spot and usually they allow you to get quite close. One method of finding insects is to go to an area where there is a variety of plants, such as a field, woods, or garden, and sit in one place for several minutes. Look closely at the plants around you. Soon you will see insects crawling on leaves, flying about, or even landing on you.

Observe their social behavior, the interactions between individuals of the same species. It usually involves some form of communication. For example, ants may touch antennae, and fireflies may "light up" to attract mates.

Observe their hunting behavior. Some insects are active hunters like the robber fly, which darts out from perches to catch other insects in midair. But insects can be passive hunters. They wait, usually camouflaged, for their next meal.

Observe, if you can, the camouflaged insects. They may be disguised as a twig, green leaf, dead leaf, or thorn. Poke and pick around in lawn grass. There's a lot of life down there!

Observe how insects defend themselves. They are breakfast, lunch, and dinner to a lot of creatures and many of them have developed some interesting ways to protect themselves from being eaten. Some have coats or armor; others have weapons such as the hairs on caterpillars, which are like needles with an irritating chemical. Of course, there are the well-known stingers that bees and wasps use as their defenses. Grasshoppers jump out of harm's way.

Even when insects are not present, evidence of their activity can nearly always be found. You may find anthills, beehives, egg cases, and holes in leaves. Close examination of fallen leaves might reveal that various insects made quite different holes. Some insects eat out nice, neat little holes; other take big, irregular chomps; and still others, like picky eaters, eat only the soft, tasty tissue, leaving the veins.

SUMMER EXPERIENCES FOR CHILDREN

> "The big artist . . . Keeps an eye on nature and steals her tools." Thomas Eakins

Sponge Creations

Pieces of cut-up sponges provide young children another opportunity for creating. Provide them with full-sized rectangular sponges and smaller pieces cut into shapes such as a circle, square, oval, triangle, etc. These can be glued together to create "floatable" creations for use in the tub or wading pool.

Children's Outdoor Art Show

What could be more fun on a summer day than an outdoor art show? In addition to displaying the children's work on tables, walls, and portable easels, include some of these ideas:

- ◉ pictures drawn with colored chalk on the sidewalk
- ◉ colorful string or yarn woven in a fence
- ◉ large sculptures created with giant discards
- ◉ pictures hung from a line with clothespins
- ◉ areas where children can draw or paint while their art show is in progress

Fun with Shadows, Clouds, and Rainbows

Capitalize on sunny summer days. Help the children make and play with shadows made with their hands, objects, and moving things. Look at clouds long and often. Find shapes that look like the beginning of a story. Then tell it. Then look for another cloud figure that gives you an idea for how to continue the story.

Use the garden hose or a gentle sprinkler to make rainbows on the next sunny day. Experiment with stopping and starting the rainbows. Can the children figure out why they are able to do this?

Bring a few crystals to school. Twirl them in the sunlight. Ask, "Do you know why crystals can make little rainbows?" Explain that sunlight looks clear and yet it has all colors in it. The lines of light that come down from the sun are called rays. When the sun's rays hit the many sides of the crystal, the rays bend and show all the colors that there are. We usually don't see all the colors because the sun's rays usually just hit flat sides. But because a crystal (and a prism) have more than one flat side, they break up the sun's rays and make them show all the colors there are in sunlight. Invite children to use the colors of the rainbow in their drawings and/or designs. They might enjoy making a cut paper collage using the colors of the rainbow they have seen with the crystal.

Tie-Dye

Materials:
    large pan of warm water
    marbles
    rubber bands
    pieces of old sheets, undershirts, or cloth squares to
       use as a scarf
    liquid dye

Fill a large pot one-third full of warm water. Add the liquid dye and stir. The brightness of the color will depend on how much dye you add. Show children how to tie-dye by placing marbles inside the cloth and fastening them with a rubber band. (Adults may need to tighten the rubber bands.) Tie several marbles into the cloth at different places, then quickly dip the cloth in the dye. Remove the rubber bands and show the children that the area under the rubber band is not dyed. It's best to do this activity outdoors to avoid spilling the dye on the carpet or furniture.

Bubble Painting

Enhance your summer art program with bubble painting. Make bubble solution by pouring ⅔ cup of liquid detergent into a gallon container. Add 1 tablespoon food coloring and enough water to fill the container; let the solution sit for a few hours before using. Put in clear jars or glasses, and add liquid food coloring or tempera in primary colors. Form secondary colors by mixing. Experiment with further color mixtures. Compare the bubbles you can make with these colored solutions to bubbles made with plain solution. Make an

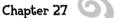

Figure 27-14

Aesthetics refers to an appreciation for beauty and a feeling of wonder.

interesting spatter design by blowing the colored bubbles over absorbent paper.

Sponge Printing

Another use for cut-up sponge pieces is in printing activities. Include these pieces of sponge, cut into varied shapes, in your printing supplies. For summer printing, include bright colors of tempera paint along with the sponge pieces. Be sure to include yellow and white tempera paints for those who are inspired to print "dandelion-like" designs.

Additional Art Experiences

Some other ideas include the following:

- ⊙ painting with weeds for brushes
- ⊙ blot painting with white paint to represent clouds on gray or blue paper to represent the sky
- ⊙ flowers made out of nut cups, using pipe cleaners for stems; stems placed in clay base in paper cup
- ⊙ sponge painting of sunrise or sunset
- ⊙ collage of summer—sand, shells, rocks, pebbles, grass
- ⊙ painting rocks
- ⊙ child-made hats decorated for a summer outdoor parade
- ⊙ painting with water outside
- ⊙ having an art show of the children's work

Summer Science Awareness

In summer the world of nature abounds with opportunities for aesthetic awareness. Some of these opportunities are to do the following:

- ⊙ study and observe shadows
- ⊙ study, observe, and grow seeds and plants
- ⊙ study and observe ants, caterpillars, spiders
- ⊙ study the life cycle of a frog
- ⊙ study and observe flowers, clouds, and sunlight and its effect on growing plants

Poison Ivy Movement Activity

Discuss what poison ivy is. Ask the children if any of them have had a rash from poison ivy. Talk about how it feels. This discussion leads naturally to this activity.

Define a small area in which the children can move freely. Ask the children to move around in this space without touching anyone with any part of their bodies. If they do touch someone, they will get "poison ivy" and must move to the side and swing their arms up and down, side to side, or hop on one leg as it "heals." Call out instructions for the children to change direction, pace, and type of movement.

Falling Rain Dance

For this activity you will need long pieces of materials, such as colorful scarves, and recorded instrumental music.

Play instrumental music that changes tempo often, fast to slow and back again. Tell the children they're going to pretend to be raindrops falling to the ground. Dance together moving your bodies to the music—move slowly when the music is slow, faster as the tempo picks up. When the music stops, they can all fall down into puddles.

Next, give children scarves. Have fun holding the scarves and moving to the music. Try tying the scarves to children's clothing or wrists. Then continue your rain dance with added drama.

Remember to dance with the children and share *your* enthusiasm. Choose a variety of types of music. Don't tell children how to move, just set a mood and allow them to move as they feel like moving.

For younger children be sure to have a well-defined area for their movement. This will help to keep them safe and refrain from getting "carried away with the music" and bumping into other children.

For older children you can play a wide variety of music with varying tempos. Talk with them about how the different types of music make them feel. Then, give children the opportunity to demonstrate these feelings by moving independently or in small groups.

For another variation, divide the children into two groups. Provide rhythm band instruments for one group and scarves for the other. Go outdoors and invite children to play the instruments while the group of children with scarves dances to their original tunes.

On a rainy day, draw children's attention to the weather. Look through the window together. Ask questions such as, "What is happening outside today?" "What is making the puddles?" Then put on your coats, hats, and boots; grab your umbrellas; and go for a short rainy day walk. Help children notice the rain and the wind. Together, look at rain fall onto leaves, the grass, and into puddles.

Go outdoors on a sunny day and ask children if they can move like raindrops. Can they drip-drop into puddles? Can they drop onto leaves? How would a raindrop move in the wind?

Recite this poem as they move:

> All the rain is falling down,
> Falling, falling to the ground,
> The wind goes swish right through the air,
> And blows the rain 'round everywhere.

All of these activities can also be done indoors. Just be sure you have a clear area so the children can move freely about.

Summer Excursions

To help increase children's aesthetic appreciation of summer, plan for some trips outside the classroom. Trip ideas include the following:

- a beach or swimming pool for wading and water experiences
- a picnic for enjoying food and nature
- a backyard garden for planting, caring for, and enjoying plants
- the zoo to enjoy the patterns, designs, and variety in the animal kingdom
- an outdoor walk to see summer beauty all around

After a Zoo Trip–Continued Awareness

All the excitement and beauty of a zoo trip can be continued in the classroom after the trip. Here are some ways to extend the children's aesthetic awareness of the zoo trip in some classroom activities.

- Sort through the photos you took and encourage the children to help put them in order, tell stories about them, and put their drawings and words together with the photos to make an "experience story," mural, or class book.

- Over the next few days, continue to read zoo animal books and reexamine the posters, records, or films you used before your trip. Children love repetition and will now have real experiences to relate to these materials.

- Be sure to allow lots of opportunities for follow-up activities in all areas of the curriculum. Make zoo animal–shaped cookies for snacks, do creative movement activities about animals, have a paper-bag animal parade, and record children's accounts of the trip. Set up the dramatic play area as a "petting zoo," with stuffed animals or paper-bag animal costumes or even as the bus you rode to the zoo, and encourage the children to make thank you cards to give to parents who accompanied them on the trip.

Fun Dandelions

When you and the children are out on a summer nature walk, pick dandelions. Encourage the awareness of them by trying these activities.

- Using your thumbnail, slit the sides of dandelion stems down the ends. Dip the stems in water to make "curls" and wear them tucked over your ears.
- Hold a dandelion in your fist and use your thumb to flip off the flower head. (Save the flowers to make a "floating garden" in a bowl of water.)
- Start a dandelion chain by slitting the stem of one dandelion and pulling the stem of another dandelion through the slit. Continue the process until you have a long chain.
- Blow seeds from the dandelion tops. Talk about how they look, feel, and fly.
- Encourage children to think of other fun things they can do with their dandelions.

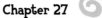

Bubble Experiments

For this activity you will need a plastic dishpan, ingredients for bubble-blowing solution (½ cup water, ¼ cup liquid detergent, 1 tsp. sugar, food coloring [optional]), commercial bubble pipe and solution (optional), toilet paper tubes, sieves, straws, and pipe cleaners.

Take the children outside and talk about blowing bubbles. Try sparking children's curiosity by blowing some bubbles from a commercial bubble pipe. Explain that each child will get a chance to experiment with different ways to blow bubbles.

Put out the dishpan of bubble solution along with a variety of bubble-blowing objects such as toilet paper tubes and sieves. Invite children to experiment with these objects.

Using straws, help children construct their own bubble blowers. For each child, make slits in one end of a straw and help the child bend the slits back. Invite each child to dip that end of the straw into the solution and blow bubbles.

Pass out the pipe cleaners and help children create wands to dip in the solution. Encourage them to create different shapes with their pipe cleaners, and to wave the wands through the air.

While children blow bubbles with the straws and pipe cleaners, ask, "What size bubbles does each one of the blowers make? How many bubbles come out at a time? One? More than one?" Talk about which blowers your children thought worked best.

For younger children you may want to offer several commercial bubble blowers, which tend to be sturdier and easier for small hands to manage.

For older children, encourage experimenting with ways to strengthen the bubbles they make. Ask, "Which bubbles seem stronger, the big or small bubbles?" "Which seem to last longer?"

Be sure to have extra bubble solution on hand in case of accidental spills. You can store any leftover solution in a jar for the next day.

As a follow-up to this activity, invite children to move as if pretending to be bubbles floating through the air. When you say, "Pop!" encourage children to jump up to represent popping bubbles.

SUMMER EXPERIENCES FOR OLDER CHILDREN

Picturebooks as Inspiration

Read the story *Bringing the Rain to Kapiti Plain* by Verna Aardema (1981), but do not show the illustrations to the students. Discuss parts of the story that refer to the rain. Reread these passages. Have the students illustrate the coming of the rain. Remind them to use different kinds of lines to depict wind and rainy weather (wavy lines, slanting lines, etc.). Display their artwork. Reread the story showing the illustrations. Have students compare their work and the work of the author/illustrator.

Storytelling and Art

Discuss the importance of storytelling and artwork for communicating ideas. In many cultures, artwork is used to illustrate stories (Inuit rawhide cutouts, Polish stencil prints, Nigerian relief wood carvings, American cartoons, etc.). Then read selected passages from the book *Meet Matisse* by Nelly Munthe (1983). Discuss selected illustrations with the students, and how Matisse—and all artists—are constantly faced with making choices about what to include in an artwork and what to leave out.

Class Mural

As a follow-up to the previous activity, have everyone help create a class mural. This will give them an opportunity to experience artistic decisions on what to include and what to leave out. Select a story or theme (circus, summer fun, transportation, etc.). Have students cut a variety of shapes—large and small—related to the theme. Smaller shapes should be about as large as one of their hands. Add crayon details to the shapes, then paste them onto the mural paper. Paste the largest shapes first. Mural making may take two or three class periods. During this experience, have the children discuss what is important to include and what could be left out of their mural. Reinforce that this is an artistic decision.

Banners as Artistic Expression

Have students make banners for the school. Discuss and list things that make your school a positive and special place. Assign each student one positive attribute of the school. Have them draw and cut out an appropriate symbol for this attribute and paste it onto a large piece of paper placed on the floor. Remind students that the banner will be displayed vertically, and to place their work accordingly. Present the banners to the principal and ask if they can be displayed in the hall or cafeteria for everyone to see.

Increase students' multicultural awareness by sharing with them the background of banners. Banners of varied kinds have been created to identify groups to others, and often to remind people of their own

Figure 27-15

Being outside in the beauty of nature can't help but encourage a child's creativity.

history. For example, the Dahomey tribe in western Africa has made applique banners for over 200 years. The banners' most important function is to tell the history of the tribe. Brightly colored images are sewn onto a black or gold background to tell of heroic deeds. Once, only Dahomey kings could possess the history banners, but now they are copied and made for tourists to buy.

Aesthetic Awareness–Light

On a sunny day, direct a beam of light through a prism onto a white piece of paper. Have students take turns describing the colors. With white paper and crayons, have them record the colors using yellow and green to achieve a yellow-green, red, and purple to achieve a red-purple, and so on. Guide them to see that these colors are similar to a color wheel.

Color Wheel Chart

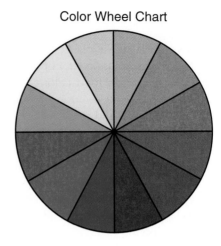

Figure 27-16

Color wheel chart.

Stained Glass–Awareness of Light

Find a book illustrating stained-glass windows in Medieval cathedrals in Europe such as Chartres and Notre Dame. Discuss how the windows were made, their purposes (teaching people and inspiring them to pray), and what meanings they may have for people today. Then tie this into a more modern day glassmaker, Louis Comfort Tiffany. Tiffany was the son of the founder of Tiffany and Co., a New York company specializing in making jewelry and metal crafts. Louis was trained as a painter, but became best known as the developer of stained-glass windows, lamps, and vases for homes in the United States. He experimented with new ways to color glass and shape it into sculptural forms as well as windows with qualities of paintings. Imitations of his work are often seen in restaurants and stores. Students may enjoy drawing or painting their own versions of summer-inspired stained-glass creations.

Aesthetic Awareness–Van Gogh's Irises

Obtain an art print of this work by Van Gogh. Discuss with children the repetition of the triangular shapes of the iris leaves and the shapes of flowers. Ask if the shapes are exactly alike (they aren't). Discuss how Van Gogh changed the shapes a little each time. These variations help us see differences in each plant. They also add more interest to a work of art. Have students identify comparable variations in the colors of the flowers and leaves. Some children may enjoy creating their own summer flowers using these subtle variations to add interest to their work.

Optical Illusions—A Different Way of Seeing

Ask the students to find library books that have optical illusions. These books are usually in the science or art section of a library. Have the students look for examples of optical illusions based on positive and negative shapes or "hidden figures." Have the students select one of their favorite examples and try to create an original artwork based on the illusion.

Appreciation of Still Life

Early Dutch still life painters liked to paint things that appealed to the five senses (sight, sound, smell, taste, and touch). Have students cut pictures from magazines that represent the five senses (e.g., a beautiful scene [not a still life item], a musical instrument, a rose, a cake, and a fuzzy toy) and arrange the cutouts in a photo-collage still life.

Summer Collage

Have students make a collage of summer from magazine pictures. Encourage them to choose large, brightly colored images that will overlap and cover the entire paper. Photocopy the collages and mount each next to the original work. Compare and contrast the original colored collage to the photocopy, noting how dominant shapes may show more readily in black and white. Have students discuss which image they prefer and why.

ADDITIONAL READINGS

Art, H. W. (2003). *Woodswalk: Peepers, pikas, and exploding puff balls! What you'll see, hear, and smell when exploring the woods.* North Adams, MA: Storey Books.

Chalfour, I., & Worth, K. (2003). *Discovering nature with children.* St. Paul, MN: Redleaf Press.

Low, M. (2003). *Creek stompin' and gettin' into nature: Environmental activities that foster youth development.* Martinsville, IN: American Camping Association.

Piper, P. (Ed.). (2003). *Father Nature: Fathers as guides to the natural world.* Iowa City, IA: University of Iowa Press.

Wood, A. J. (2003). *Beetles and bugs: A nature trail book.* San Diego, CA: Silver Dolphin Books.

Worth, K. (2003). *Worms, shadows and whirlpools: Science in early childhood education.* Portsmouth, NH: Heinemann.

HELPFUL WEB SITES

http://www.teachersfirst.com/storm.html
Dozens of units on hurricanes presented on this Teachers First website.

http://www.sanford-artedventures.com/
Click on the "Teach Art" icon for dozens of ideas for seasons of the year.

http://www.crayola.com
This Web site is presented by the Crayola Company. It has hundreds of activities for the seasons of the year.

http://www.artseek.com
This is an excellent source for prints and posters of artists from the Old Masters to Contemporary art.

www.kidsdomain.com
Click on "Holiday Fun" for a wealth of activities for the seasons of the year.

http://earthday.wilderness.org/
Click on "Find what you need in our Teacher's Lounge" for excellent resources on teaching about nature and the seasons.

For additional creative activity resources, visit our Web site at http://www.EarlyChildEd.delmar.com.

Gross and Fine Motor Skills*

BY TWO YEARS

Gross Motor

- walks forward (average age 12 months)
- walks backward (average age 15 months)
- walks upstairs with help (average age 17 months)
- moves self from sitting to standing (average age 18 months)
- seats self in small chair (average age 18 months)
- uses rocking horse or rocking chair with aid (average age 18 months)

Fine Motor

- builds tower of two blocks (average age 15 months)
- builds tower of three or four blocks (average age 19 months)
- places pellet in bottle (average age 15 months)
- places blocks in cup (average age 15 months)
- places four rings on peg or large pegs in pegboard (average age 18 months)
- imitates vertical line stroke (average age 20 months)
- turns pages of book, two or three at a time (average age 21 months)

BY TWO AND ONE-HALF YEARS

Gross Motor

- kicks ball forward (average age 20 months)
- jumps in place (average age 23 months)
- runs (stiffly) (average age 2 years)
- hurls small ball overhand, one hand, without direction (average age 22 months)
- pedals tricycle (average age 2 years)

Fine Motor

- builds tower of six cube blocks (average age 23 months)
- imitates circular motion with crayon, after demonstration (average age 2 years)
- turns pages of book, one at a time (average age 2 years)

BY THREE YEARS

Gross Motor

- walks up and down stairs without adult help, but not alternating feet (average age 22 months)
- walks four steps on tiptoe (average age 2¼ years)

---

*90% of children at specific age level will have acquired skill.
Adapted from Gesell, A., Ilg, F. L., Ames, L. B., & Rodell, J. L. (1974). *Infant and child in the culture of today: The guidance of development in home and nursery school.* New York: Harper and Row.

- jumps from bottom step (average age 2 years)
- walks backward 10 feet (average age 28 months)
- broad jumps 24–34 inches (average age 2½ years)
- balances on one foot one second (average age 2½ years)

Fine Motor

- imitates vertical line from demonstration (average age 22 months)
- imitates vertical or horizontal line (average age 2½ years)
- imitates V stroke from demonstration (average age 2½ years)
- strings four beads in two minutes (average age 2½ years)
- folds paper (average age 2½ years)
- builds tower of seven or eight cubes (average age 2¼ years)

BY THREE AND ONE-HALF YEARS

Gross Motor

- walks on tiptoe 10 feet (average age 3 years)
- balances on one foot five seconds (average age 3¼ years)

Fine Motor

- imitates bridge of three blocks from demonstration (average age 3 years)
- copies circle from picture model (average age 3 years)
- imitates cross from demonstration (average age 3 years)
- closes fist, wiggles thumb (average age 35 months)
- picks longer of two lines (average age 3 years)

BY FOUR YEARS

Gross Motor

- hops, preferred foot (average age 3½ years)
- walks up stairs, one foot on each step, holding rail (average age 3½ years)
- walks downstairs, one step per tread (average age 3½ years)
- throws ball with direction (average age 3½ years)

- balances on toes (average age 3½ years)
- jumps over rope 8 inches high (average age 3½ years)
- swings on swing independently (average age 3½ years)
- jumps from height of 12 inches (average age 3½ years)
- holds standing balance, one foot advanced; eyes closed, 15 seconds (one of two tries by 4 years)

Fine Motor

- buttons up clothing (average age 3 years)
- cuts with scissors (average age 3¾ years)
- touches point of nose with eyes closed (by age 4, two of three tries)
- puts 20 coins in a box, separately (by age 4, one of two tries)

BY FOUR AND ONE-HALF YEARS

Gross Motor

- balances standing on one foot, five seconds (average age 3¼ years)
- does forward somersault with aid (average age 3½ years)
- catches ball in arms, two of three tries (average age 4)
- catches bounced ball (average age 4 years)
- heel to toe walk (average age 3¾ years)
- jumps from height of 2½ feet (average age 4 years)

Fine Motor

- copies cross from picture model (average age 3¾ years)
- draws a person, three parts (average age 4 years)
- copies square from demonstration (average age 4 years)

BY FIVE YEARS

Gross Motor

- balances on one foot for 10 seconds (average age 4½ years)
- hops on nonpreferred foot (average age 4½ years)

- bounces ball two times successively with one hand (average age 4½ years)
- catches large bounced ball, two of three tries (average age 4 years)
- somersaults forward without aid (average age 4¾ years)
- balances on tiptoes for 10 seconds, one of three tries (by age 5 years)
- jumps over cord at knee height, feet together, one of three tries (average age 4½ years)
- walks heel to toe (average age 4¾ years)
- walks heel to toe, backward (average age 4¾ years)
- walks 2″ × 4″ balance beam, 3″ off floor, without falling (average age 4½ years)

Fine Motor

- builds pyramid of six blocks after demonstration (average age 4½ years)
- clenches and bares teeth (by age 5 years)
- draws diamond after demonstration (average age 4½ years)
- copies square from picture model (average age 4¾ years)
- ties any knot that holds with lace (average age 5 years)

Language Development Objectives and Activities for Infants and Toddlers

LEVEL	OBJECTIVE	ACTIVITY
Birth to 1 month	1. To develop intimacy and awareness of communication based on personal contact. 2. To introduce the concept of oral communication. 3. To introduce verbal communication. 4. To stimulate interest in the process of talking.	1. Whisper into the child's ear. 2. Coo at the child. 3. Talk to the child. 4. Let the child explore your mouth with his or her hands as you talk.
1 to 3 months	1. To develop oral communication. 2. To develop auditory acuity. 3. To develop the concept that different people sound different. 4. To develop the concept of oral and musical communication of feelings.	1. Imitate the sounds the child makes. 2. Talk to the child in different tones. 3. Encourage others to talk and coo to the child. 4. Sing songs of different mood, rhythms, and tempos.
3 to 6 months	1. To develop the concept of positive use of verbal communication. 2. To stimulate excitement about words. 3. To develop the concept that words and music can be linked. 4. To develop the ability to name things and events.	1. Reward the child with words. 2. Talk expressively to the child. 3. Sing or chant to the child. 4. Describe daily rituals to the child as you carry them out.
6 to 9 months	1. To develop use of words and reinforce intimacy.	1. Talk constantly to the child and explain processes such as feeding, bathing, and changing clothes.

LEVEL	OBJECTIVE	ACTIVITY
	2. To develop the concept that things have names.	2. Name toys for the child as the child plays, foods and utensils as the child eats, etc.
	3. To develop the concept that there is joy in the written word.	3. Read aloud to the child, enthusiastically.
	4. To develop the concept that language is used to describe.	4. Describe sounds to the child as they are heard.
9 to 12 months	1. To develop the concept that body parts have names.	1. Name parts of the body and encourage the child to point to them.
	2. To reinforce the concept that things have names.	2. Describe and name things seen on a walk or an automobile trip.
	3. To stimulate rhythm and interest in words.	3. Repeat simple songs, rhymes, and fingerplays.
	4. To stimulate experimentation with sounds and words.	4. Respond to sounds the child makes, and encourage the child to imitate sounds.
12 to 18 months	1. To develop the ability to label things and follow directions.	1. Link up various objects and, naming one, ask the child to get it.
	2. To expand vocabulary and lay the foundation for later production of sentences.	2. Act out verbs ("sit," "jump," "run," "smile," etc.)
	3. To reinforce the concept of names and the ability to recognize names and sounds.	3. Use animal picture books and posters of animals.
	4. To encourage verbal communication.	4. Let the child talk on a real telephone.
	5. To reinforce the concept of labels and increase vocabulary.	5. Describe things at home or outside on a walk or an automobile trip.
18 to 24 months	1. To stimulate imitation and verbalization.	1. Tape-record the child and others familiar to the child, and play the tapes back for the child.
	2. To improve the ability to name objects.	2. On a walk around the home or neighborhood with the child, point out and name familiar objects.
	3. To encourage repetition, sequencing, and rhythm.	3. Play counting games, sing songs, and tell and retell familiar stories.
	4. To develop auditory acuity, passive vocabulary, and the concept of language constancy.	4. With the child, listen to the same recording of a story or song over and over.
	5. To stimulate verbalization, selectivity, and—eventually—descriptive language.	5. Cut out of magazines and mount on stiff cardboard: pictures of foods, clothing, appliances, etc. Have the child identify them as you show them. Use memorable descriptions: "orange, buttery carrots," "the shiny blue car."
	6. To stimulate conversation.	6. With the child, prepare and eat a make-believe meal.
24 to 36 months	1. To practice descriptive language and build vocabulary.	1. Keep a box of scraps of materials and small objects. Have the child select objects, using words to describe them ("fuzzy," "big," "red," etc.).

LEVEL	OBJECTIVE	ACTIVITY
	2. To encourage verbalization, repetition, comprehension, and speaking in sentences.	2. Ask the child: "Show me the floor," ". . . the door," etc. When the child points, say "Here's the floor," etc., and encourage the child to imitate you.
	3. To develop the concept of written symbols.	3. Label the child's possessions. Use the child's name repeatedly: "Mike's bed," "Mike's toy chest."
	4. To encourage specific and descriptive language.	4. Ask "Which one?" when the child gives a single-word description, and expand on the child's language (e.g., Child: "Cookie." You: "Yes, this is a ginger cookie.").
	5. To increase understanding of the relation between spoken and written language, and to stimulate the use of both.	5. Call to the child's attention familiar brand names or identifying symbols on products, buildings, and so on.

Appendix C

Basic Program Equipment and Materials for an Early Childhood Center

INDOOR EQUIPMENT

The early childhood room should be arranged into well-planned areas of interest, such as the housekeeping and doll corner, block building, etc. This encourages children to play in small groups throughout the playroom, engaging in activities of their special interest, rather than attempting to play in one large group.

The early childhood center must provide selections of indoor play equipment from all the following areas of interest. Selection should be of sufficient quantities so that children can participate in a wide range of activities. Many pieces of equipment can be homemade. Consider the age and developmental levels of the children when making selections.

Playroom Furnishings

- ⊙ tables—seat four to six children (18″ high for three-year-olds, 20″–22″ high for four- and five-year-olds)
- ⊙ chairs—10″ high for three-year-olds, 12″–14″ high for four- and five-year-olds
- ⊙ open shelves—26″ high, 12″ deep, 12″ between shelves
- ⊙ lockers—12″ wide, 12″ deep, 32″–36″ high

HouseKeeping or Doll Corner

Item	Number Recommended for 10 Children
Dolls	3
Doll Clothes	Variety
Doll bed—should be large enough for a child to get into, bedding	1
Doll high chair	1
Small table, four chairs	1 set
Tea party dishes	6-piece set with tray
Stove—child size, approximately 24″ high, 23″ long, 12″ wide	1
Sink—child size, approximately 24″ high, 23″ long, 12″ wide	1
Refrigerator—child size, approximately 28″ high, 23″ long, 12″ wide	1
Pots and pans, empty food cartons, measuring cups, spoons, etc.	Variety
Mop, broom, dustpan	1
Ironing board and iron	1
Clothespins and clothesline	1
Toy telephones	2

Dress-up box—men's and women's hats, neckties, pocketbooks, shoes, old dresses, scarves, jewelry, etc.	Variety
Mirror	1

Art Supplies

Item	Number Recommended for 10 Children
Newsprint paper 18″ × 24″	1 ream
Colored paper—variety	3 packages
Large crayons	10 boxes
Tempera paint—red, yellow, blue, black, white	1 can each
Long-handled paintbrushes— making a stroke from ½ ″ to 1″ wide	10–12
Easels	1
Finger paint paper—glazed paper such as shelf, freezer, or butcher's paper	1 roll
Paste	1 quart
Blunt scissors	10
Collage—collection of bits of colored paper, cut-up gift wrappings, ribbons, cotton, string, scraps of fabric, etc., for pasting	Variety
Magazines for cutting and pasting	Variety
Clay—play dough, homemade dough clay	50 pounds
Cookie cutters, rolling pins	Variety
Smocks or aprons to protect children's clothes	10

Finger paint recipes*

1. *Starch and Soap Finger Paint*

1 cup starch

1½ cups boiling water

½ cup soap flakes (not soap powder)

1 tablespoon glycerine (optional, makes it smoother)

Method: Mix starch with enough water to make smooth paste. Add boiling water and cook until glossy. Stir in soap flakes while mixture is warm. When cool, add glycerine and coloring (powder paint, poster paint, or vegetable coloring).

*Interesting smells can be obtained by adding different food flavorings (mint, cloves) or talcum powder to finger paint if desired.

2. *Flour and Salt Finger Paint, Cooked*

2 cups flour   3 cups cold water

2 teaspoons salt   2 cups hot water

Method: Add salt to flour, then pour in cold water gradually and beat mixture with egg beater until it is smooth. Add hot water and boil until it becomes glossy. Beat until smooth, then mix in coloring.

3. *Flour and Salt Finger Paint, Uncooked*

1 cup flour   1 cup water

1½ teaspoons salt

Method: Combine flour and salt, add water. This has a grainy quality unlike the other finger paints, providing a different sensory experience.

4. *Argo Starch Finger Paint*

½ cup boiling water   6 tablespoons cold

2 tablespoons Argo starch   water

Method: Dissolve starch in cold water in cup. Add this mixture to boiling water, stirring constantly. Heat until it becomes glossy. Add color.

5. *Wheat Flour Finger Paint*

3 parts water   1 part wheat flour

Method: Stir flour into water, add food coloring. (Wheat flour can be bought at low cost in wallpaper stores or department stores.)

6. *Tempera Finger Paint*

dry tempera paint   ½ cup liquid starch or

                                        ½ cup liquid dish-

                                        washing detergent

Method: Mix the tempera paint with the starch or detergent, adding starch gradually until desired thickness is reached. Paint extender can also be added to dry tempera paint.

7. *Easy Finger Painting*

clear liquid detergent

dry tempera paint

Method: Mark off sections on a table with masking tape the size of the paper to be used (newsprint works fine). Squirt liquid detergent on this section and add about 1 teaspoon of dry paint. After the picture has been made, lay the paper on the finger paint and rub. Lift off carefully.

8. *Cold Cream Finger Paint*

Dry tempera paint can be mixed with most brands of cold cream. This is good for a first experience with a child reluctant to use colored paint with his fingers.

Paste recipes

1. *Bookmaker Paste*

1 teaspoon flour   1 heaping teaspoon

2 teaspoons salt   oil of cloves

¼ teaspoon powdered alum   1 pint cold water

Method: Mix dry ingredients with water slowly, stirring out lumps. Slow fire; cook over double boiler until it thickens.

2. *Hobby Craft Paste*

   ¾ cup water   ½ cup Argo starch
   2 tablespoons light Karo   ¾ cup water
   syrup   ¼ teaspoon oil of
   1 teaspoon white vinegar   wintergreen

   Method: Combine first ¾ cup water, corn syrup, and vinegar in a medium-sized saucepan; bring to a full boil. Stir cornstarch into second ¾ cup water until smooth. Remove boiling mixture from heat. Slowly pour in cornstarch-water mixture, stirring constantly until smooth. If lumps form, smooth them out with back of spoon against side of saucepan. Stir in oil of wintergreen. May be used immediately but will set to paste consistency in 24 hours. Store in covered jar. Keeps two months. Makes about 2½ cups.

3. *Flour Paste*

   Mix together: ¼ cup flour
                     cold water—enough to make
                        creamy mixture

   Method: Boil over slow heat for 5 minutes, stirring constantly. Cool. Add cold water to thin if necessary. Add a few drops of oil of peppermint or oil of wintergreen.

4. *Co-op Paste*

   1 cup sugar   1 cup flour
   1 tablespoon powdered   1 quart water
   alum   oil of cloves

   Method: Mix and cook in double boiler until thick. Remove from heat and add 30 drops of oil of cloves. This mixture fills a juice container (8–10 oz.) about ¾ full. Needs no refrigeration.

Recipes for Dough and Other Plastic Materials

1. *Cooked Dough*

   ½ cup flour   2 cups boiling water
   ½ cup cornstarch (blend   ½ cup salt
   with cold water)

   Method: Add salt to boiling water. Combine flour with cornstarch and water. Pour hot mixture into cold. Put over hot water and cook until glossy. Cool overnight. Knead in flour until right consistency, adding color with flour.

2. *Cooked Dough*

   4 tablespoons cornstarch   ½ cup boiling water
   ½ cup salt

   Method: Mix cornstarch and salt. Add color if desired. Pour on boiling water, stir until soft and smooth.

Place over fire until it forms a soft ball. In using, if it sticks to fingers, dust hands with cornstarch.

3. *Sawdust and Wheat Flour*

   4 parts sawdust   1 part wheat flour

   Method: Make paste of wheat flour and water. Add sawdust. Presents interesting sensory appeal.

4. *Uncooked Play Dough*

   3 cups flour   1 cup water
   ¼ cup salt   1 tablespoon oil
   coloring

   Method: Mix flour with salt; add water with coloring and oil gradually. Add more water if too stiff, add more flour if too sticky. Let the children help with the mixing and measuring. Keep dough stored in plastic bags or a covered container.

5. *Salt Dough*

   1 cup salt   ¾ cup cold water
   ½ cup cornstarch

   Method: Combine all ingredients in a double boiler placed over medium heat. Stir the mixture constantly; in about two to three minutes it should become so thick that it follows the spoon in mixing it. When the consistency is similar to bread dough, place on wax paper or aluminum foil to cool. When dough is cool enough to handle, knead for several minutes. It is then ready to use. To store for up to several days, wrap in wax paper or place in plastic bags.

6. *Ornamental Clay* (Suitable for Dried Objects)

   1 cup cornstarch   1¼ cups water
   2 cups baking soda

   Method: Cook ingredients together until thickened, either in double boiler or over direct heat—*stir constantly*. When it is cool enough, turn it out and let children knead dough and make it into whatever they wish. If used for ornaments, make hole for hanging ornament while dough is still moist.

7. *Baker's Dough* (Suitable for Dried Objects)

   4 cups flour   1 to 1½ cups water
   1 cup salt

   Method: Mix ingredients to make a dough easy to handle. Knead, and shape as desired. Bake at 350° for 50 to 60 minutes. Material will brown slightly, but baking at lower temperatures is not as successful.

Block Building Area

Item	Number Recommended for 10 Children
Unit blocks—purchased or homemade (directions are available)	276 pieces, 11 shapes

Large, lightweight blocks	Variety
Small wooden or rubber animals and people	Variety
Small trucks, airplanes, cars, and boats	12
Medium airplanes	3
Medium boats	2
Medium-sized trucks—12″ to 24″	3

Music Corner

⊙ record player, tape player, CD player
⊙ suitable records, tapes, and CDs
⊙ rhythm instruments
⊙ dress-up scarves for dancing

Manipulative Toys

Item	Number Recommended for 10 Children
Wooden inlay puzzles—approximately 5 to 20 pieces	6
Color cone	1
Nested blocks	1
Pegboards—variety of shapes and sizes	1
Large spools and beads for stringing	2 sets
Toys that have parts that fit into one another	2
Lotto games	2
Dominoes	1

Books and Stories (20–30 Books)

A carefully selected book collection for the various age levels should include the following categories.

⊙ transportation, birds and animals, family life
⊙ community helpers, science, nonsense rhymes
⊙ Mother Goose rhymes, poems, and stories
⊙ homemade picture books
⊙ collection of pictures classified by subject
⊙ library books to enrich the collection

Nature Study and Science

⊙ aquarium or fish bowls
⊙ plastic materials
⊙ magnifying glass, prism, magnet, thermometers
⊙ growing indoor plants, garden plot

⊙ additional material such as stones, leaves, acorns, birds' nests, caterpillars, worms, tadpoles, etc.

Woodworking Center

Basic woodworking operations are as follows:
⊙ sanding
⊙ gluing
⊙ hammering
⊙ holding (with a vise or clamp)
⊙ fastening (with screws)
⊙ drilling
⊙ sawing

Materials for a woodworking center include the following:
⊙ sturdy workbench (or table)
⊙ woodworking tools: broad-headed nails ¾″ to 1½″ long, a C-clamp or vise (to hold wood), flat-headed hammer weighing about 12 ounces for beginning woodworking experiences, later a claw hammer may be added, 14″ saw with ten teeth to the inch
⊙ soft white pine lumber scraps (it is difficult to drive nails into hardwood; plywood is not suitable either). Packing boxes of soft pine can be disassembled and used for hammering work.

Sand Play

In an outdoor area, sand should be confined so it does not get scattered over the rest of the playground. The area should be large enough so several children can move about in it without crowding each other. A 10″ to 12″ ledge around a sandbox can serve as a boundary and at the same time provide children with a working surface or a seat. If sand is about 6″ to 8″ below the top of the ledge, it is less likely to spill onto the playground. Sand should be about 18″ deep so children can dig or make tunnels. Four or five inches of gravel on the bottom of the sandbox provides drainage.

Basic equipment: Ordinary plastic or metal kitchen utensils—cups, spoons, pails, shovels, sifters, funnels, scoops, bowls.

Water Play

Water play can be either an indoor or an outdoor activity, depending upon the climate. Clear plastic water basins can be used for water play. When they are on a stand with wheels, they can be moved easily to any area of a room. When these plastic containers are

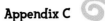

used, children have the advantage of being able to see through the sides and the bottom. If a table stands on a carpeted floor, a plastic runner can be used to protect the carpet, and spillage will not be a serious housekeeping problem.

Materials: Clear tubing, sponges, strainers, funnels, corks, pitchers, and measuring cups. For added interest, rotary beaters, spoons, small bowls, plastic basters, and straws.

OUTDOOR EQUIPMENT

The outdoor play equipment should be grouped according to use. For example, plan for both active and quiet play; allow for free areas for use of wheel toys. The following is a list of suggested basic outdoor play equipment for the early childhood program.

- climbing structure(s)
- large and small packing boxes
- slide
- swings with canvas seats
- wagons and wheelbarrows
- pedal toys—tricycles, cars, etc.
- sandbox with spoons, shovels, pails, etc.
- balls
- a variety of salvage material, such as rubber tires, tire tubes, lengths of garden hose, ropes, and cardboard boxes, to enrich the play

Many activities, such as housekeeping play and art activities, at times can be transferred to the outdoor area.

Use the following checklist to evaluate your playground setup.

- There are clear pathways and enough space between areas so that traffic flows well and equipment does not obstruct the movement of children.
- Space and equipment are organized so that children are readily visible and easily supervised by adults.
- Different types of activity areas are separated. (Tricycle paths are separate from swings, sand box is separate from the climbing area.)
- Open space is available for active play.
- There is some space for quiet play.
- Dramatic play can be set up outdoors, as space is available.
- Art activities can be set up outdoors.
- A portion of the play area is covered for use in wet weather.
- A storage area is available for play equipment.
- A drinking fountain is available.
- The area has readily accessible restrooms.

Appendix D

Room and Yard Organization, Exhibitions, and Displays

ROOM AND YARD ORGANIZATION*

Large Cardboard Cartons

Puppet theaters, post offices, and stores are easily constructed by slicing or sawing out a rectangular portion in the top half of the front section of a large carton. When folded to the inside, the flap can be cut back to the desired width for a stage or shelf. The flap is supported by a dowel or a length of heavy cord strung from one side of the box to the other. Leftover latex wall paint is ideal for painting these large structures. This type of paint conceals advertising, does not smear when dry, and can be washed off a brush or child's hands with water. Use old postage stamps, greeting cards, and envelopes if this is to be a post office. Paper tickets, signs, money (bottle tops, etc.) can be used if the structure is to be a theater.

Cable Spools

Empty cable spools are fun additions to the outside play area. Two or three spools may be secured one on top of another with a plumber's pipe inserted through the center of each; a second pipe can be sunk in concrete close enough to the structure to be used as a firefighter's pole. A rope ladder attached to the top spool adds to the climbing challenge.

Cardboard Boxes

To create a table easel from a large cardboard box, measure one side the equivalent length of the bottom and mark. Cut diagonally across from this mark to the bottom corner on both sides. This produces a sturdy cardboard triangle that serves as a table easel once two slits have been made for clothespin clips at the top. The children themselves will be able to remove or replace newsprint for paintings.

The same triangular arrangement covered with a piece of flannel makes a nontipping flannel board for children's and teacher's use. A show box containing flannel board figures may be stored beneath the triangle for the child's convenience. It can be used for retelling stories or reworking number experiences in small groups or as a solitary, self-selected activity.

Wooden Crates

Wooden crates are durable and good for school use. At a minimal cost, these crates may be transformed into a stove, sink, sofa, work bench, or locker arrangement. To form a solid front, it is necessary only to tap the wooden slats loose, add a few additional slats, and replace side by side. To create a stove, individual pie tins

---

*These suggestions are taken from Jean W. Quill's *A World of Materials,* Washington, DC: National Association for the Education of Young Children, 1969.

can be turned upside down to simulate gas burners. These are especially effective when painted black to look like "grating." Painted bottle tops add stove controls. A spool set on top of a scrap of wood and painted silver makes a faucet; the entire "sink" may cost little more than the price of the required pan. Many leftover aluminum foil pans are suitable for this purpose. The ends of cantaloupe crates make sturdy frames for children's drawings or trays for the doll corner or science table.

Wooden and Plastic Soft-Drink and Milk Crates

These crates, sometimes available at a small charge, are excellent substitutes for commercial hollow blocks. Paint them bright colors with latex paint. A set of casters on one crate can produce a durable wagon for hauling friends or blocks. Set the casters far enough in to allow stacking at those times when the crates are not in use. They also make excellent "cubby holes" for storage.

Boats

At the beginning or end of the boating season, some rowboats may be destroyed or abandoned as no longer seaworthy. These boats are often donated by marina managers to a school or playground, if transportation is provided by the school. When stored safely, these boats can be made into useful playground equipment.

Recycled Tires

Used tires, hung either horizontally or vertically, make excellent swings. Inflated tubes can be rolled from place to place, bounced on, and used for various movement games.

Ice Cream Containers

A circular, spatter-paint screen may be created from the three-gallon containers discarded by ice cream stores or restaurants. Cut the bottom from one of these containers, leaving only a narrow edge to which the edges of a circular piece of screen may be glued. A matching narrow circle, cut from another piece of cardboard, placed over the first and glued down, will secure the screen. A paint-dipped toothbrush is scraped across the screen; any object placed beneath will leave a design on the paper on which it is resting. The carton should be cut down to leave approximately one quarter of its original length; this gives a satisfactory height for spatter painting.

Ice cream containers can also be converted to wastebaskets, space helmets, and diver's masks. To make the latter, simply remove an area from an upside-down carton large enough for the child's face to appear. Allow the child to paint in a choice of colors. Ice cream containers can also be used as storage space, when bolted together.

Sawdust

Sawdust is available from the lumber mill for use in making sawdust clay. Simply mix a small amount of wallpaper paste in water and add sawdust until a pliable consistency has been reached. This clay hardens over a period of time.

EXHIBITIONS AND DISPLAYS

It is stimulating and educational for children to see their work displayed. Whether the purpose of the exhibit is to introduce new ideas and information, to stimulate interest in a single lesson, to show the children's work, or to provide an overview of their work, the subject of the exhibition should be directly related to the children's interest. Exhibits should be changed often to be of educational and decorative value.

Labels

⊙ Make large, bold letters that can be easily read.
⊙ Keep titles brief. Descriptive material should be in smaller letters.
⊙ Label children's work with their names as a means of creating pride through recognition of their work.
⊙ Vary the material in making letters. In addition to paper letters, labels can be made of paint, ink, crayon, chalk, cloth, fancy papers, string, rope, yarn, and other three-dimensional materials.

Color

⊙ Choose a basic color scheme related to the visual material displayed. Seasonal colors can be used, such as warm colors for fall (yellow, orange, red), cool colors for winter (blue, blue-green, gray), and light and cool colors for spring (colors with yellow in the mixture, such as yellow-orange).
⊙ Use colors for mounting that are more subdued than the materials mounted. This may be accomplished by using lighter, darker, or grayer colors.
⊙ Select a bright color for accent, as in bands or other pleasing arrangements on the larger areas of gray, lighter, or darker colors.

- Create a contrast to emphasize or attract attention. Intense color makes a visual impact, such as orange against black.
- Use both light and dark color values.
- Create color patterns that lead the eye from area to area.

Balance

Balance can be achieved formally or informally. To create formal balance, the largest piece of work may be placed in the center with similar shapes on either side. Informal balance is more interesting, subtle, and compelling. Material may be grouped in blocks of different sizes, colors, or shapes, and still be balanced. Margins of the bulletin board should be wider at the bottom.

Unity

Unity in design is the quality that holds the arrangement together in harmony.

- Ideas can be unified with background paper, lettering, strips of construction paper, yarn, or ribbon.
- Repetition of similar sizes, shapes, colors, or lines can help to create harmony.
- Shapes can be arranged to lead the eye from one part of the board to another.
- One large unusual background shape helps unify the design.
- Avoid cluttering the display; items placed at all angles destroy the unity.

Variety

Variety in arrangement prevents monotony. Use interesting combinations of color, form, line, and texture.

Emphasis

Emphasis is the main idea or center of interest. This can be achieved by using larger letters, a brighter color, a larger picture, an unusual shape, texture, or a three-dimensional object. Other material should be grouped into subordinate areas.

Line

Line is used to draw the eye to a specific area, suggest direction, action, and movement, and to hold the display together. Use thick or thin lines; solid, dotted, or dashed lines. Diagonal lines are used to show action; zigzag lines suggest excitement; and slow-moving curves are restful. Lines may be painted, cut from paper, or formed with string, yarn, ribbon, or tape.

Texture

Texture may be created with a variety of materials.

- paper and cardboard—textured wallpaper, sandpaper, metallic foil, egg containers, corrugated cardboard
- fabrics—netting, flannel, burlap, fur, felt, carpet remnants, assorted felt scraps
- miscellaneous—chicken wire, metal screen, sheet cork

Three-Dimensional Effects

- Pull letters or objects out to the head of the pin.
- Staple a shallow box to the board as a shelf to hold lightweight three-dimensional items.
- Mount a picture on a box lid and fasten it to the board.
- Use shallow boxes as buildings, animals, and people.
- Pleat a strip of paper in an accordion fold with pictures attached.
- Use paper sculpture—strips of paper can be twisted, curled, folded, rolled, fringed, perforated, or torn. Puppets, animals, birds, flowers, people, abstract forms, and masks can also be made.
- Use three-dimensional materials in displays—Styrofoam, egg cartons, paper plates, paper cups, soda straws, cupcake cups, paper lace, toweling tubes, and other discarded materials.
- Use objects from nature—branches, shells, bark, driftwood, feathers.

Background Materials

- display paper, tissue paper, burlap, corrugated cardboard, construction paper
- egg carton separators, blotters, textured wallpaper, shelf paper

Display Boards for Two-Dimensional Work

- standard cork boards or sheet of plywood to which cork tiles have been glued
- builder's wallboard with wood strip nailed to the top with hooks for hanging
- thick cardboard that will hold pins
- a pasteboard box open for standing on a table or the floor, depending on size

- a folding screen made from an old crate or packing box
- wide strips of binding tape attached along a blank wall; pin pictures to tape
- wire stretched across an empty space with pictures attached to it

MORE ON BULLETIN BOARDS-KINDERGARTEN AND ELEMENTARY LEVEL

The most immediate evidence of an art program is the display of children's artwork. A teacher's creative approach to display is an extension of the art program in the physical environment. Bulletin boards are the most frequent form of display. Consider the following fairy tale.

> Once upon a time there was a carpenter who was building a classroom. When he was on the very top of his ladder, a hammer fell and crashed into the wall, making a very large hole. The carpenter did not know what to do since he had no materials left to repair the wall. Suddenly he had an idea! He found a 4' x 8' slab of cork and hung it over the hole. Then he tacked wood strips around the edges and said, "I am well pleased." He named his creation "Bulletin Board."

The dictionary defines a bulletin board as "a board on which bulletins and other notices are posted." Teachers often have other definitions for this term: (1) a surface that must be covered before the first day of school and before parents' night; (2) a board that is always three inches wider than the paper just cut for it; and (3) a rectangle that has a width never sufficient for the number of letters needed to be pinned across it.

Whatever your definition, a bulletin board is much more than a board on which notices are posted. It is a visual extension of a learning experience, a visual form of motivation, and a reflection of a curriculum area. Because bulletin boards are a visual phenomenon, teachers should be concerned about their content and appearance.

Thirty spelling papers or fifteen identical paper pumpkins hanging up like someone's laundry do not constitute a good bulletin board. Mimeographed pictures, commercial cardboard turkeys, and corrugated cardboard trim are *not* visually appealing and certainly are not reflections of the children whose interest you are trying to catch.

A display designed for the eye is also designed for the mind. Children are very much attuned to symbols. Television commercials, billboards, posters, and cereal boxes attest to the impact of images. Bulletin boards should attract constructive attention. Stereotypical smiley faces and dog-eared paper letters with a thousand pin holes will not do it. Ideas and paper fade. Stereotyped versions of an upcoming holiday do absolutely nothing for children's art development.

For an early childhood teacher, one of the best solutions is to display the children's artwork. Art is a visual extension of the child and her own unique ideas and expression. It is the result of the child's own experience and serves as a motivation for others and the child herself. Any subject can be the theme for an effective bulletin board, but one rule of thumb is that all boards should be student oriented and entice student participation. Boards that ask questions, have games to play, or have objects to be handled can be fun *and* valuable learning experiences.

Eye-catching photographs (of the children, if possible) and short stories, poems, and cartoons are exercises for both the eye and mind. Whatever the mode, the key is visual impact. In order for a bulletin board to be a learning experience, it first must get the child's attention. Bright colors, bold design, legible, catchy, succinct phraseology, and relevant themes are vital to bulletin boards by, for, and about the children.

Try some of these suggestions for improving your bulletin boards.

- Take advantage of interest in the World Series, Olympics, or other big sports events for a variety of projects. Find bulletin board space for newspaper clippings, pictures of heroes and heroines, and posting of scores and relative standings. Have the children write reports or draw pictures of games in which they are interested. Make up graphs with scores for each team. Vary these activities according to the level of the children's interest and abilities.
- If you have a bulletin board too big to cope with, cut it down to size by covering it with wallpaper samples, outlining each sample with black construction paper in a kind of giant patchwork quilt effect. Each child can use one of these squares as a personal bulletin board. Or you could use each of the squares to depict a different aspect of one main theme: holiday symbols, kinds of animals, favorite people, etc.
- Be sure all your bulletin boards and other kinds of displays are at the children's eye level.
- When your classroom closet is awash with caps and mittens, why not bring their splashy colors and designs into the open with a self-portrait mural for

a bulletin board? On a strip of butcher paper, draw a circle for each child. Have the students add features to turn these circles into self-portraits. Two lines looping down from each face become instant arms. Finally, have each child draw her own hat and mittens on the heads and hands. Encourage the young artists to copy the actual styles, colors, and designs of their own apparel as exactly as possible. This mural not only makes a colorful bulletin board, but also helps you easily identify the owners of any stray clothing.

Display Areas for Three-Dimensional Work

- Use tops of cupboard or built-in shelves.
- Build shelves with boards supported by bricks, used permanently or temporarily.
- Attach a shelf of wood or particleboard underneath a bulletin board.

- Dioramas are especially useful where exhibit space is limited.
- A card table can be used for temporary exhibits, then folded up when not in use.
- If obtainable, a small showcase is valuable for displaying museum-type objects.
- Cardboard boxes fastened to bulletin boards make a display place for lightweight objects.
- Use driftwood as an interesting display for weaving and jewelry.
- Puppet display rods can be made with a board and some dowel sticks.
- Mobiles are attractive display devices. Coat hangers can also be used.
- Cover cardboard boxes and use them as bases for displaying art objects.
- Use a pegboard with brackets.

Appendix E

Recycled Materials

Creative teachers find that art possibilities abound everywhere, including a new look at old, discarded materials. For example, in the following teaching suggestions, one kind of discarded item—gallon milk containers—provides a wealth of storage, display, and equipment possibilities.

TEACHING SUGGESTIONS: EMPTY CONTAINERS FULL OF PROMISE

When that plastic gallon milk container is out of milk, it is full of potential for classroom implements you can make yourself. Scoops, funnels, sorting trays, display or storage containers, and carrying baskets are just waiting to be cut out.

Outline the area you wish to cut with a felt-tip marker and use a sharp knife or a small pencil-type

soldering iron to do the cutting. (If you use the iron, be sure to work in a ventilated area and avoid the fumes.)

The containers are so readily available you can afford to experiment with a few to find just the shapes you are after. Here are directions for some basic cuts to get you started.

⊙ Scoop—Cut away the handle and part of the side below it. The container's handle instantly becomes the scoop's handle, while the section below becomes the scoop itself.

⊙ Sorting trays—Cut off the bottom or the entire side opposite the handle to make trays of varying depths. These are perfect for sorting small objects, such as pebbles or shells, or for examining small amounts of sand or soil.

⊙ Funnel—Cut the handle a few centimeters from the top. Then cut around the base of the handle to make the funnel's body from the curved section of the jug. The top of the handle becomes the spout. For a larger funnel, just cut the bottom from the container and use the top as the spout.

⊙ Carrying basket—Cut away the upper portion of the side opposite the handle. The children then carry the jug by the handle and use it to transport all kinds of items.

⊙ Display or storage container—Cut the bottom off the jug just below the handle. You'll end up with a square container about 3" deep, perfect for displaying or storing the specimens that students collect on their outings.

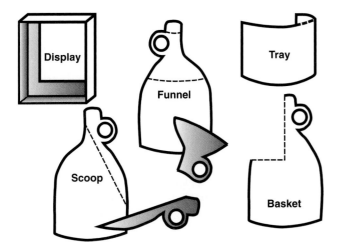

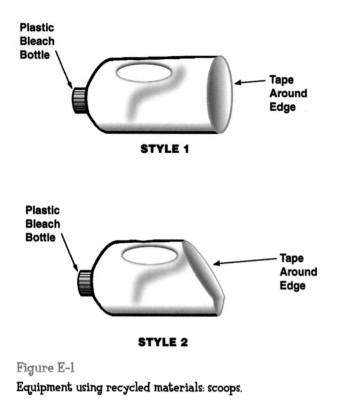

Figure E-1

Equipment using recycled materials: scoops.

Figure E-2

Plastic scoop and yarn ball.

EQUIPMENT FOR MOVEMENT ACTIVITIES FROM RECYCLED MATERIALS

A valuable addition to the movement program in the early childhood classroom is equipment made from recycled materials. For example, empty plastic gallon milk jugs can be used as safe game goals, pins for indoor/outdoor bowling games, or cut out for scoops (see Figures E–1 and E–2) to toss yarn or other light balls in classroom movement activities.

Old pantyhose can be used to make light child-sized rackets for great hand-eye coordination practice in racket games. These rackets are especially good for young children as they are light enough to handle and yet sturdy enough to hit a yarn, Nerf, or plastic ball.

Using recycled materials has an obvious cost benefit in addition to demonstrating the importance of conservation to young children. Young children can possibly use these same materials at home for their own play experiences.

Even better, you can enlist parent participation and involvement in the program by asking parents to donate recycled materials to make movement equipment. Perhaps parents and children together could even get involved at home in making some of the equipment for the class's use, such as yarn balls or pantyhose rackets.

OTHER IDEAS FOR RECYCLING MATERIALS

Just as recycled materials were used for making movement equipment in Chapter 16, these same "discards"

PLEASE SAVE . . .

- yarn and ribbon scraps
- large empty spools
- shirt cardboards
- leftover wallpaper
- men's shirts—we will turn them into smocks
- juice cans with smooth edges
- plastic squeeze bottles
- bits of fabric, trim
- buttons, old jewelry

THEY WILL BE USED BY YOUR CREATIVE CHILD(REN) IN THE EARLY CHILDHOOD PROGRAM.

can be valuable art materials. Both conservation and creativity can be practiced in ways like these:

- Be a scavenger. (But remember that the word is "scavenger," not beggar or receiver of junk goods.)
- Begin your scavenger hunt by making a list of the equipment and supplies that you feel you might find in your community at little or no cost.
- Search for your treasures in attics, basements, garages, thrift or Goodwill Industry stores, and at garage sales.
- Ask parents to contribute to the needs of creative children, or send a "want ad" home being specific about what you need. Your ad may read something like the ad in the box on page 600.
- Check with wallpaper and carpet dealers. Wallpaper dealers will sometimes give you their old sample books, and carpet dealers will often sell their sample swatches for a very small sum. These carpet swatches are useful as sit-upons, as rugs for houses the children build, as colorful mats under items on display, and as working mats for use under table toys.
- Trim the bristles from 1"-wide house painting brushes to about 1" in length and use these in place of more expensive easel brushes.
- Gather paper from a variety of sources:

Be a bag grabber. Collect plain paper bags. Cut them open and use them for painting, crayoning, etc.

Save old newspapers for easel painting. Bright tempera (water color) paint on a newsprint background makes a very attractive and interesting work of art.

Check with your community or local newspaper office. They may donate or sell newsprint or old newspapers to you at a minimal cost.

Other materials listed in Figure E–3 can be valuable in the art center.

Sandbox Toys from the Kitchen

From the cupboard—use plastic storage containers such as scoops, molds, or buckets. Foam cups are good scoops or molds. A plastic flowerpot with drainage holes can be a sifter.

Cut an egg carton into individual egg cups for molds.

Make an egg-carton sifter by cutting the lid off an egg carton and cutting the egg cup section in half the short way. In the bottom of each cup, poke a hole. The holes may be the same size or of varying sizes.

The following materials can be valuable instructional tools in the art program as well as in other curriculum areas.

1. Empty plastic containers—detergent bottles, bleach bottles, old plastic containers. These can be used for constructing scoops, storing art materials, etc.
2. Buttons—all colors and sizes. These are excellent for collages, assemblages, as well as sorting, counting, matching, etc.
3. Egg shells. These can be washed, dried, and colored with food coloring for art projects.
4. Coffee or shortening can lids and cans themselves. These can be covered with adhesive paper and used for the storage of art supplies, games, and manipulatives materials.
5. Magazines with colorful pictures. These are excellent for making collages, murals, and posters.
6. Scraps of fabric—felt, silk, cotton, oil cloth, etc. These can be used to make "fabric boards" with the name of each fabric written under a small swatch attached to the board, as well as for collages, puppets, etc.
7. Yarn scraps. These can be used for separating buttons into sets; also for art activities.
8. Styrofoam scraps.
9. Scraps of lace, rick rack, or decorative trim.
10. Bottles with sprinkler tops. Excellent for water play and for mixing water as children finger paint.
11. Wallpaper books of discontinued patterns.
12. Paper doilies.
13. Discarded wrapping paper.
14. Paint color cards from paint/hardware stores.
15. Old paintbrushes.
16. Old jewelry and beads.
17. Old muffin tins. These are effective for sorting small objects and mixing paint.
18. Tongue depressors or ice cream sticks. Counters for math, good for art construction projects, stick puppets, etc.
19. Wooden clothespins. For making "people," for construction projects, for hanging up paintings to dry.

Figure E-3

Beautiful junk list.

Musical Instruments from Recycled Materials

Recycling Egg Cartons for Tambourines. Young children can make a simple tambourine from egg cartons and bottle caps. Simply put a few bottle caps in each egg carton, tape the carton closed, and you have an instrument that players can shake or hit. Children will love playing it both in rhythm and creative movement activities.

Recycling Nuts and Bolts for Rattles. For an unusual set of musical instruments, assemble an assortment of large nuts, bolts, and washers. Young children will get excellent practice in fine finger movements when they create musical rattles out of these. All you have to do is place several washers on each bolt and loosely turn the nut onto the bolt. Place these inside empty, metal adhesive bandage boxes, tape shut, and use as interesting sound instruments (rattles).

Making Music with Bottles. Gather a collection of bottles with both small and large mouths, soft drink bottles, ketchup bottles, quart canning jars, mayonnaise jars, etc.

Show the children how different sounds can be made with different-sized bottles by blowing across the various openings. Have them listen for high and low sounds. Stand the bottles on a table and gently tap them with a spoon. The children can explore different sounds the bottles make by blowing across them and by tapping them with a spoon.

Rhythm Instruments from Recycled Materials. The following are suggestions for simple rhythm instruments the children can make to use in their musical experiences. Creating rhythm instruments from found objects gives young children another opportunity for self-expression. They receive satisfaction and pleasure from beating rhythmic sounds and keeping time to music with instruments they have created.

Materials:

paper plates	plastic egg-shaped
empty spools	containers
pebbles	small plastic bottles
nails	sticks
toweling rolls	old Christmas bells
embroidery hoops	bottle caps
small boxes or cartons	peas or corn
dried beans	wire

Bottle cap shaker. Remove plastic from inside bottle caps. Punch a hole in the center of the bottle cap. String bottle caps on a string and attach to a package handle. Paint if desired.

Spool shaker. Paint designs on a large spool. Force four pipe cleaners through the center of the spool. Attach a Christmas bell to the end of each cleaner by bending.

Plate shaker. Decorate two paper plates with crayons or paint. Put pebbles, dried corn, peas, or beans between them and staple or sew the plates together with bright yarn or string. Bend wire to form a handle, and fit the ends inside.

Box shaker. Place small pebbles, beans, or seeds in a small box or empty clean milk carton to make a shaker. It can be used with or without a handle. Decorate as desired.

Flute. Use a paper towel or tissue paper roll. With a pencil, punch three or four holes (about one inch apart) in the cardboard tube. Cover one end of the roll with a piece of waxed paper, as described later in the instructions for the Hummer. Hum a tune in the open end, moving your fingers over the holes.

Sandpaper blocks. Paint two small wooden blocks. Place a strip of sandpaper on the surface, allowing an overlap on each end for fastening with thumbtacks. Sandpaper may replace carpet on old eraser blocks. Rub together to make a sound.

Clappers. Nail bottle caps to a painted eraser block.

Cymbals. Decorate two lids from tin cans. Fasten a small spool or block of wood on for a handle.

Tambourine. Punch holes in bottle caps and tie them together with thin wire, pipe cleaners, or string. Punch a hole in a paper or tinfoil plate and tie on the bottle caps.

Hummer. Decorate a tube from a waxed paper or paper toweling roll. Fasten a piece of waxed paper over one end of the tube. Humming through the waxed paper is fun. Be sure to change the paper after each use.

Circle shakers. Stretch two layers of plastic cloth with uncooked rice or tapioca between them over one half of an embroidery hoop. Fasten with the other half of the hoop to make a circle shaker. (When making any shaker-type toys, be sure that the small objects used are sealed securely inside. Small objects like beans, peas, and rice can pose a serious choking risk to young children.)

Egg shakers. Fill plastic egg-shaped containers (either panty hose containers or plastic Easter eggs) with dried beans. Tape the halves together and use them as maracas.

Bottle shakers. Collect empty small plastic bottles. Fill with rice, beans, or nuts until half full. Seal bottles that don't have childproof lids with tape. These are excellent shakers for tiny hands.

Drums. Glue lids on salt containers, cereal boxes, or ice cream boxes and decorate with paint to use as drums. Older children may make drums from restaurant-size tin cans with canvas or heavy paper stretched and laced to cover the ends.

Kazoo. Use a piece of waxed paper over a clean comb. Play by pressing your lips against the paper and humming.

Gong. Use an old license plate (the older the better). Strike with a mallet to play. Describe the sounds.

Jingle instrument. Use a set of metal measuring spoons. Play by slapping them into your hand.

Wrist or ankle bells. Lace two or three bells through a shoestring. Tie to wrist or ankle. Move to shake your bells.

Rubber Band Box. Another addition to rhythm instruments is a rubber band box. Gather together one cigar box (or similar-sized and weight box), five rubber bands of several lengths and thicknesses, and 10 brass fasteners.

Punch five holes, 1½″ apart in each end of the box. Attach a rubber band to a brass fastener, push through one of the holes, and open the fastener on the inside of the box to hold it down. Stretch the rubber band tight to the other end of the box and attach it in the same way. Attach the rest of the rubber bands. To use: The rubber band box can be held, placed on a table, or placed on the floor. Encourage the children to pluck the rubber bands with their fingers or strum the bands with their thumbs. They can experiment with sounds and beats: high-low, fast-slow, and loud-soft.

Sound Box. Another rhythm instrument is the sandpaper sound box. Gather together four pieces of sandpaper (of various grades from fine to coarse), glue, scissors, and a dowel (½″ × 6″ long). Glue the top and bottom of the box closed. Allow enough time for it to dry completely. Cut the sandpaper to fit all sides of the box. Glue the sandpaper strips to the box. To use: Rub the dowel on the sandpaper. While the children are using the sound boxes, you can introduce such musical concepts as loud-soft and fast-slow. The dowels can also be used alone in a rhythm band or in a parade. Extend this activity by having the children make their own sound boxes if they are interested.

Appendix F

Criteria for Selecting Play Equipment for Young Children

1. *A young child's playthings should be as free of detail as possible.*
   A child needs freedom to express himself by creating his own childlike world; too much detail hampers him. Blocks are the best example of "unstructured" toys. Blocks, construction sets, and other unstructured toys and equipment such as clay, sand, and paints allow the imagination free rein and are basic playthings.

2. *A good plaything should stimulate children to do things for themselves.*
   Equipment that makes the child a spectator, such as a mechanical duck, may entertain for the moment but has little or no play value. The equipment provided for play should encourage children to explore and create or offer the opportunity for dramatic play.

3. *Young children need large, easily manipulated playthings.*
   Toys too small can be a source of frustration because the child's muscular coordination is not yet developed enough to handle the smaller forms and shapes. A child's muscles develop through play. A child needs equipment for climbing and balancing.

4. *The material from which a plaything is made has an important role in the play of the young child.*
   Warmth and pleasurable touch are significant to a child. The most satisfactory materials have been established as wood and cloth.

5. *The durability of the plaything is of utmost importance.*
   Play materials must be sturdy. Children hate to see their toys break. Axles and wheels must be strong to support a child's weight. Some materials break so readily that they prove to be very expensive.

6. *The toy must "work."*
   What frustration when a door or drawer won't shut, wheels get stuck, or figures won't stand up. Be sure parts move correctly and that maintenance will be easy.

7. *The construction of a plaything should be simple enough for a child to comprehend.*
   This strengthens his understanding and experience of the world around him. The mechanics, too, should be visible and easily grasped. Small children will take them apart to see how they tick.

8. *A plaything should encourage cooperative play.*
   As we seek to teach children to work and play together, we should supply the environment that stimulates such play.

9. *The total usefulness of the plaything must be considered in comparing price.*
   Will it last several children through several stages of their playing lives?

What are some good toys and play materials for young children? Most suggestions for younger children are also appropriate for older children.

All ages are approximate.

SENSORY MATERIALS	ACTIVE PLAY EQUIPMENT	CONSTRUCTION MATERIALS	MANIPULATIVE TOYS	DOLLS AND DRAMATIC PLAY	BOOKS AND RECORDINGS	ART MATERIALS
2 Year Olds and Young 3 Year Olds						
Water and sand toys: cups, shovels Modeling dough Sound-matching games Bells, wood block, triangle, drum Texture matching games, feel box	Low climber Canvas swing Low slide Wagon, cart, or wheelbarrow Large rubber balls Low 3–wheeled, steerable vehicle with pedals	Unit blocks and accessories: animals, people, simple wood cars and trucks Interlocking construction set with large pieces Wood train and track set Hammer (13 oz. steel shanked), soft wood, roofing nails, nailing block	Wooden puzzles with 4–20 large pieces Pegboards Big beads or spools to string Sewing cards Stacking toys Picture lotto, picture dominoes	Washable dolls with a few clothes Doll bed Child-sized table and chairs Dishes, pots, and pans Dress-up clothes: hats, shoes, shirts Hand puppets Shopping cart	Clear picture books, stories, and poems about things children know CDs or tapes of classical music, folk music, or children's songs	Wide-tip watercolor markers Large sheets of paper, easel Finger or tempera paint, ½″ brushes Blunt-nose scissors White glue
Older 3 and 4 Year Olds						
Water toys: measuring cups, egg beaters Sand toys: muffin tins, vehicles Xylophone, maracas, tambourine Potter's clay	Bicycle Roller skates Climbing structure Rope or tire swing Plastic bats and balls Various sizes rubber balls Balance board Planks, boxes, old tires Bowling pins, ring toss, bean bags and target	More unit blocks, shapes, and accessories Table blocks Realistic model vehicles Construction set with smaller pieces Woodworking bench, saw, sandpaper, nails	Puzzles, pegboard, small beads to string Parquetry blocks Small objects to sort Marbles Magnifying glass Simple card or board games Flannel board with pictures, letters Sturdy letters and numbers	Dolls and accessories Doll carriage Child-sized stove or sink More dress-up clothes Play food, cardboard cartons Airport, doll house, or other settings with accessories Finger or stick puppets	Simple science books More detailed picture and story books Sturdy record or tape player Recordings of wider variety of music Book and recording sets	Easel, narrower brushes Thick crayons, chalk Paste, tape with dispenser Collage materials

5 and 6 Year Olds

Water toys: food coloring, pumps, funnels
Sand toys: containers, utensils
Harmonica, kazoo, guitar, recorder
Tools for working with clay

Outdoor games: bocce, tetherball, shuffleboard, jump rope, Frisbee, Bicycle

More unit blocks, shapes, and accessories
Props for roads, towns
Hollow blocks
Brace and bits, screwdrivers, screws, metric measure, accessories

More complex puzzles
Dominoes
More difficult board and card games
Yarn, big needles, mesh fabric, weaving materials
Magnets, balances
Attribute blocks

Cash register, play money, accessories, or props for other dramatic play settings: gas station, construction, office
Typewriter

Books on cultures
Stories with chapters
Favorite stories children can read
Children's recipe books

Watercolors, smaller paper, stapler, hole puncher
Chalkboard
Oil crayons, paint crayons, charcoal
Simple camera, film

7 to 10 Year Olds

Modeling materials, papier-mache, wire for sculpture, potter's clay

Jump ropes, roller skates, skate boards, equipment for team sports and ball tossing and catching

Woodworking bench; full range of tools and equipment

Computer games, puzzles, crochet and knitting supplies

Materials for skits and short dramatic activities

CDs, tapes of classical, folk, jazz and popular music
Wide range of fiction and non-fiction books

Full range of materials for easel painting, printing, sculpting, collage, rubbings
Computer programs for graphic design experiences

Appendix G

Puppet Patterns

HAND PUPPET PATTERN

Hand puppets can be an essential part of your curriculum and are fun for children to use. Hand puppets can be made with or without mouths, but puppets with mouths are usually preferable. The following pattern can be adapted to make people- or animal-shaped puppets (see Figure G–1). Encourage the children to use their imaginations to add faces, ears, hair, and clothes. Features can be glued, sewn, or written on the puppet.

MATERIALS:

Felt, upholstery fabric, Velcro fabric
Glue, needle and thread, scissors
Other decorative materials (yarn, feathers, plastic eyes, etc.)

DIRECTIONS:

Cut out two pattern shapes using the type of fabric you choose. Sew or glue them together leaving the bottom open. If you use Velcro fabric, glue or sew the wrong sides together. This fabric will not fray. Velcro hook can be attached to decorative items to change a puppet's personality.

This type of puppet is fun and easy for children to use. Show them how to insert their hand the first time they use one. Keep the puppets in a puppet house in the story corner as well as in the home center for the children to use.

Mittens and Glove Patterns

For each mitten or glove: ½ yard (.5 m) Velcro fabric, fabric glue or thread and sewing machine, scissors.

DIRECTIONS:

Following the patterns (see Figures G–2 and G–3), cut material to the size you need. Place wrong sides together and stitch or glue.

Paste cut-out character's pictures to a sturdy piece of paper (cardboard, poster board). Glue a piece of Velcro hook on the back of each character. Children wear the mitten and attach story characters to them during storytelling.

Child Size

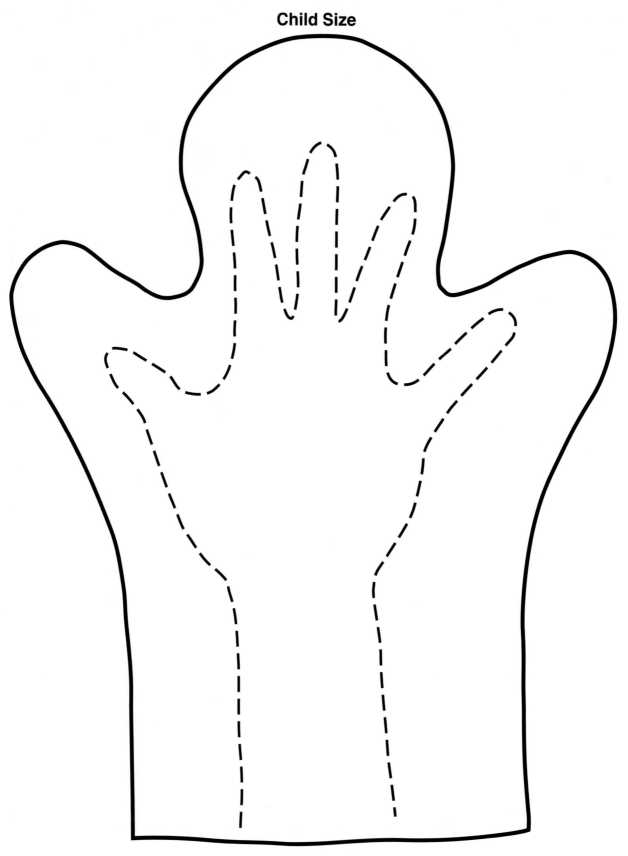

Shorten or lengthen

Figure G-1

Hand puppet pattern.

Figure G-2
Mitten pattern.

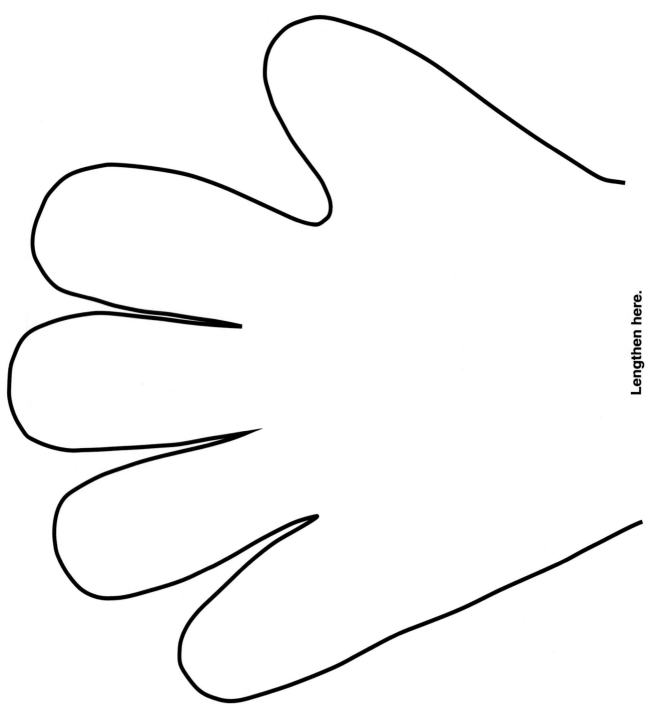

Lengthen here.

Figure G-3
Glove patterns

Appendix H

Software Companies

ActiVision, Santa Monica, CA, 800–477–3650,
http://www.activision.com

Alfred Publishing, Van Nuys, CA, 818–891–5999,
http://www.alfred.com

Alpha Omega Publications, Chandler, AZ, 800–682–7391,
http://www.aop.com

Animusic, Thousand Oaks, CA, 805–402–8219,
http://www.animusic.com

Apptastic Software, Inc., Ontario, Canada, 613–748–7066,
http://www.apptastic.com

Atari, Beverly, MA, 978–921–3700 or 978–921–3372,
http://www.atari.com

Brighter Child Interactive, Columbus, OH, 888–283–2246,
http://www.brighterchild.com

Broderbund, Novato, CA, 800–395–0277,
http://www.broderbund.com

Crick Software, Inc., Bellevue, WA, 866–332–7425,
http://www.cricksoft.com

Davidson, Torrance, CA, 800–747–8697,
http://www.fisher-pricestore.com

Davidson & Associates, Riverdale, MD,
http://www.davd.com

The Discovery Channel School, Silver Spring, MD,
800–678–3343, http://www.discovery.com

Disney Interactive, New York, NY, 800–328–0368 or
800–900–9234, http://www.disneystore.com

DK Family Learning, Collinsville, IL, 877–884–1600,
http://www.dkfbooks.com

Dolphin Don's Music School, Huntsville, AL,
256–881–6565, http://www.dolphindon.com

Dorling Kindersley, Edinburgh, Scotland,
http://stage.dk.com

Edmark, Redmond, WA, 800–426–0856,
http://www.edmark.com

Educational Insights, Rancho Dominguez, CA,
800–858–9914, http://www.edin.com

Electronic Arts, 800–245–4525, http://www.ea.com

Encore Software, Gardena, CA, 800–936–2673,
http://www.encore.com

FanCraftic Press, Santa Rosa, CA, 707–578–3982,
http://www.fancraftic.com

Fisher-Price, East Aurora, NY, 800–747–8697,
http://www.fisher-price.com

Fun for Brains, 954–970–8447, http://www.fun4brains.com

Gallimard Jeunesse, Paris, France, http://www.
gallimard.fr

Global Software Publishing, 646–792–2111, http://www.
learnatglobal.com

GuruForce, Inc., Seattle, WA, 925–283–1146,
http://www.gurusoftware.com

Hasbro Interactive, Beverly, MA, 800–327–8264 or
978–921–3001, http://www.hasbro.com

Hulabee Entertainment, Kirkland, WA, 425–739–2700,
http://www.hulabee.com

Humongous Entertainment, Woodinville, WA,
800–791–7128, http://www.humongous.com

Inspiration Software, Portland, OR, 800–877–4292,
http://www.inspiration.com

Knowledge Adventure, Los Angeles, CA, 800–545–7677,
http://www.vugames.com, http://www.knowledge
adventure.com, or http://www.jumpstart.com

Konami of America, Inc., Redwood City, CA,
650–654–5600, http://www.konami.com

Kutoka Interactive, Montreal, Quebec, 877–858–8652,
http://www.kutoka.com

LeapFrog, Emeryville, CA, 800–701–5327,
http://www.leapfrog.com

The Learning Company/Broderbund, Hiawatha, IA,
800–395–0277, http://www.broderbund.com or
http://www.learningco.com

LEGO Media International, Enfield, CT, 800–835–4386,
http://www.lego.com

Liquid Animation Pty. Ltd., 61 7 3010 7700,
http://www.liquidanimation.com

MagicMouse Productions, 415–669–7010, http://www.magicmouse.com

Make-Believer, Ltd., http://www.make-believer.com

Mekada, Richmond, VA, 804–327–8444, http://www.mekada.com

Microsoft Multimedia, Redmond, WA, 888–218–5617, http://www.microsoft.com/products

National Geographic Interactive, Washington, DC, 800–368–2728, http://www.nationalgeographic.com

Neurosmith, Long Beach, CA, 800–220–3669, http://www.neurosmith.com

PF Magic, Inc., The Learning Company/Broderbund, Cambridge, MA, 800–395–0277, http://www.broderbund.com

Ohio Distinctive Software, Columbus, OH, 614–459–0453, http://www.ohio-distinctive.com

3 Pounds Press, Hayward, CA, 510–733–9877, http://www.3pounds.com

Protozone, Inc., San Francisco, CA, 631–423–1048, http://www.protozone.com

Publix Preschool Pals, Maitland, FL, http://www.publix.com

Quaint Interactive, Cambridge, MA, 617–868–8026, http://www.kidsmusicstage.com

Scholastic, New York, NY, 800–724–6527, http://www.scholastic.com

School Zone Interactive, Grand Haven, MI, 800–253–0564, http://www.schoolzone.com

Sierra, Bellevue, WA, 310–649–8033, http://www.sierra.com

Sierra On-Line, Vivendi Universal, 800–757–7707, http://www.vugames.com

Simon & Schuster Interactive, New York, NY, 888–793–9972, http://www.ssinteractive.com

Sony Computer, Los Angeles, CA, 800–222–7669, http://www.scea.com

Sunburst Technology, Pleasantville, NY, 800–321–7511, http://www.sunburst.com

TDK Mediactive, Calabasas, CA, 800–877–4778, http://www.tdk-mediactive.com

THQ, Calabasas Hills, CA, 818–871–5000, http://www.thq.com

Tiger Electronics (Hasbro), Beverly, MA, 978–921–3001 http://www.hasbro-interactive.com

Tom Snyder Productions, Watertown, MA, 800–342–0236, http://www.tomsnyder.com

Tool Factory, East Dorset, VT, 800–220–8366, http://www.toolfactory.com

Viva Media, New York, NY, 877–848–6520, http://www.viva-media.com

Vivendi Universal, Los Angeles, CA, 310–649–8000 or 800–545–7677, http://www.vugames.com

Wilton Art Programs, 800–458–4274, http://www.wiltonart.com

YES! Software, Las Vegas, NV, 866–312–8049, http://www.yessoftware.com

Glossary

acceptance in teaching music—Teachers should accept more than one kind of response to music activities.

activity centers—A part of the early childhood environment identified by specific activities and materials. In activity centers young children can manipulate objects, engage in conversation and role-playing, and learn at their own levels and at their own pace.

activity pattern—Varying activities so that the new and old are in an interesting as well as developmentally appropriate pattern for young children.

aesthetic movement, the—An artistic movement in the 1880s in the United States. The chief characteristic was its concentration on the "science of the beautiful" or the "philosophy of taste."

aesthetics—An appreciation for beauty and a feeling of wonder. A sensibility that uses the imagination as well as the five senses.

affective readiness (for reading)—A prerequisite to reading involving the child's positive self-concept.

afterimage—After staring at a page of solid color for about 30 seconds, then looking at a dot on a page of white or gray, our eyes will see color on the blank page. The color is usually the complement or near complement of the color first looked upon.

anti-bias curriculum (ABC)—A curriculum developed by the NAEYC to be a starting point for planning an inclusive, anti-bias curriculum.

appropriate music activities—These music activities can only be planned if the teacher understands the developmental levels of the children involved.

art area—An activity center for painting, collage-making, cutting, pasting, etc. It needs to be located near water and light.

arts and crafts—A term that has its origin in folk arts. Examples of arts and crafts are hand-shaped clay pots, original carving, and weaving. A creative activity producing a utilitarian (or craft) item.

assemblage—A three-dimensional art form involving placement of a number of three-dimensional objects, natural or manmade, in juxtaposition to create a unified composition.

associative play—A type of play characterized simply by being present in a group. Example: A child who participates in fingerplays during circle time.

attention span—The length of time a child's interest lasts. Generally, the younger the child, the shorter the attention span.

bag puppet—A common paper bag stuffed with newspapers and fastened shut. A body is made with a second bag attached to the first, leaving room for the child's hand to slip in and work the puppet.

basic forms stage—The stage in the development of art when a child finds, recognizes, and repeats at will basic shapes such as rectangles, squares, and circles.

block-building area—An activity or interest center where young children can create with both large and small blocks, Legos, etc.

bodily/kinesthetic learner—In Gardner's theory, this learner is physically active, prefers hands-on learning, and is talkative. Often called the "mover."

books and quiet area—A place to be alone, quiet in one's thoughts, and to explore the world of books

brayer—An ink roller used with a printing plate. The brayer is rolled in a shallow pan filled with water-soluble ink or tempera paint.

"Capital C" creativity—Creativity that involves bringing into existence something genuinely new that receives social validation enough to be added to the culture. An example of "Capital C" creativity is the invention of the light bulb.

cardboard cylinder puppet—A puppet made by placing a cardboard cylinder, from paper towels or toilet tissue, over the fingers.

cardinal numbers—Number names (examples: one, two, three).

celebration—Used synonymously with the term "holiday" to reflect a broader approach to special days in a child's life.

cephalocaudal development—The pattern of physical development in the human body from head to toe (or top to bottom).

childhood chants—The teasing chants sung by children—and most often heard on the playground—using the words, "You can't catch me!"

classification and sorting—Putting together things that are alike or belong together. One of the processes necessary for developing the concept of numbers.

classroom museum—A collection of items and artifacts on a specific theme. These items and artifacts are brought in by the children for display.

cognitive development theory (of children's art)—Developed by Piaget, this theory holds that children's art is related to their ability to understand the permanent existence of objects.

cognitive readiness (for reading)—The abilities of comprehension, problem solving, and reasoning required in order to learn to read.

collage—A French word meaning "to paste." A two-dimensional art activity involving selection, organization, and arranging materials, and then attaching them to a flat surface.

color—The property of reflecting light of a particular visible light wavelength: the colors of the spectrum are red, orange, yellow, green, blue, indigo, and violet.

color relativity—The color gray appears much lighter when placed on a black background than it does against a white one. This dark/light effect holds true for many other colors as well.

combination of phrase-wise and whole-song method—A method of introducing a song to children where the entire song is presented, but the teacher only asks the children to respond to the easiest parts of it with voices, hands, or an instrument.

communication sites—On the Internet, communication sites allow children to interact with friends, relatives, or classrooms across the street, in another city, or even across the globe.

comparing—A mathematical skill involving the perception of differences in items. (Example: My shoes are bigger than yours.)

contrast—One of the most exciting characteristics (or elements) in all of the arts. Example: The rough bark of a tree in contrast to its smooth leaves.

controlled scribbling—A later point in the scribble stage when the child connects his or her motions with the marks on the page. The child has found it possible to control the marks.

convergent thinking—Encouraging *one* correct answer or *one* way to do things; single-focused.

cooperative play—A type of play marked by mutual involvement in a play activity.

creative dramatics—A form of imaginative play that helps students learn and uses no written dialogue. It is different from performing a play. In creative dramatics, actors create their own words to convey meaning.

creative movement—movement that reflects the mood or inner state of a child.

creative movement activities—Natural activities for children to express their creative selves by physical movement.

creativity—The process of bringing something new into being.

design—The organization of an artwork, including symmetry/asymmetry, repetition, alternation, and variation.

developmental level—Referring to a framework upon which we organize our knowledge and observations of children. Includes four major areas of growth: physical, social, emotional, and intellectual.

developmental levels (of art)—A guide to what a child can do in art at different ages; not a strict guideline.

developmentally appropriate early childhood classrooms—Classrooms that evidence maximum interaction among children; an environment filled with challenging and interesting materials and a variety of independent and small-group tasks.

differentiated instruction—A way of thinking about teaching and learning. Its aim is to maximize each child's growth by meeting each child where he or she is at and helping the child progress from that point.

disordered or random scribbling—An early part of the scribble stage, characterized by the child's lack of control over hand movements or the marks on a page. The marks are random and go in many directions.

divergent thinking—Encouraging many different answers or ways to do things; open-ended.

dramatic play—A free, unstructured form of play in which young children are able to express their inner feelings.

early basic forms stage—The circle and oval are generally the first basic forms. It develops as children recognize the simple circle in their scribbles and are able to repeat it.

early pictorial (first drawings) stage—The stage in art development when a child works on making and perfecting one or many symbols.

ecology—The study of all elements of an environment, both the living and nonliving, and the interrelation of these elements.

emerging literacy—The developmental process involving the time immediately before a child learns to read printed symbols, but also the continuous development of prereading skills that begins at birth. Emergent literacy is preferred over the term "reading readiness," which describes a more narrow range of skills.

emotional brain—The first part of the brain to receive input and the first to react.

enriched—A nutritional term referring to the fact that nutrients lost during processing are replaced.

environment—Refers to two things: manmade and natural things that children meet in their surroundings.

environmental motivation (for picture making)—Children must have the opportunity to reflect on experiences they have in their environment before expressing them visually.

facilitate—To help along, to guide, to provide opportunities, and to be sensitive and caring without interfering.

filmstrips—A series of slides made in a strip of film rather than cut up and placed in slide mountings.

fine motor development—The development of the small (fine) muscles of the body, such as fingers, hands, wrists, and eyes.

finger puppets—Puppets made by using the child's fingers. The include three general types: finger-leg, finger-cap, and finger-face.

flexible thinking—The ability to think of things in many ways; to think of things in the context of change, that not all things are permanent.

flexibility in teaching music—Teachers should adapt music activities based on the various responses received.

folk and traditional songs—Songs that are part of our heritage, sung by children for centuries. Example: "Bingo" and "I'm a Little Teapot."

form or shape—Elements of all artwork. They are combined; made in various sizes; and can be filled, empty, separate, connecting, or overlapping.

formal science—A science experience planned by the teacher to develop particular skills.

fortified—A nutritional term referring to the addition of nutrients to a food after processing.

free play—See "spontaneous play."

functional/physical movement—Movement that serves a practical purpose.

gang stage—Stage of art in Lowenfeld's theory for children ages 9 to 12 when child becomes more aware of how things look in his or her drawings. This awareness is often expressed with more detail in the child's schema. The use of the word *gang* refers to the fact that the peer group assumes more importance to the child at this point.

gross motor development—The development of large (gross) muscles in the body, such as in the neck, trunk, arms, and legs.

hand–eye coordination—The use of hand(s) and eyes at the same time.

holiday—Used synonymously with the term "celebration" to reflect a broader approach to special days in a child's life.

holiday policy—A guide for everyone involved in the program to help them choose, implement, and evaluate celebration activities.

holistically—To look at things in an overall way, as a whole.

housekeeping/dramatic play center—A place for acting out familiar home scenes with various real-life props.

humanettes—See "people puppet."

imaginative play—In Piaget's theory of play, imaginative play is one of the purest forms of symbolic thought available to the young child.

incidental science—The open, unstructured, free exploration of young children of their world.

inclusive environment—An environment that addresses both the daily life realities of cultural diversity as well as the potentially biased attitudes and behaviors that are part of this reality.

individual differences—The unique, different levels of performance present in each child.

informal science—Children explore science on their own with little or no teacher involvement.

information sites—On the Internet, information sites are rich reference resources that teachers and parents can use to model or assist children in answering questions, making new discoveries, and building knowledge.

integrated curriculum—A curriculum in which the artificial divisions among content areas are reduced. Most often an integrated curriculum is designed around a unit of study, centered around a specific theme or project.

interaction sites—On the Internet, interaction sites are similar to software programs, using sound; animation; sound effects; and high-quality, realistic graphics.

interactive (refers to computers)—The computer, when used with young children, provides a vehicle for two types of interaction: child-to-computer and child-to-child.

interest centers—See "activity centers."

interpersonal learner—In Gardner's theory, this learner is group-oriented, extroverted, and communicative, and enjoys interacting with others. Often called the "socializer."

intrapersonal learner—In Gardener's theory, this learner is self-reflective, introverted, and solitary, and prefers learning alone. Often called the "individual."

juxtaposition—Color pigments placed side by side in small repeated strokes are altered by our vision to appear to combine, thus forming a different hue.

later basic forms stage—In the later basic forms stage the rectangle and square forms are made when the child can purposely draw separate lines of any length desired.

later pictorial (first drawings) stage—A later point in the pictorial stage when the child draws symbols more easily and exactly.

left-brained—Using the left hemisphere of the brain as the major learning method.

line—An element of art that is part of every artwork. Every line in a piece of art has length, a beginning, an end, and direction.

linguistic readiness (for reading)—A prerequisite to reading that involves skill at using oral language.

listening—A stage in the development of listening skills when the child reacts through comments or questions.

literacy—A mastery of language—speaking, listening, writing, and reading.

logical/mathematical learner—In Gardener's theory, this learner is inquisitive; experimental; and oriented toward numbers, patterns, and relationships. Often called the "questioner."

mandella—A universal form found most often in the later scribble stage.

manipulative area—A place to enhance motor skills; hand–eye coordination; and mental, language, and social skills through the use of play materials such as pegboards, puzzles, and games.

media—Any material used to create or enhance learning experiences for young children.

modeling—The process of manipulating and shaping flexible material.

modeling behavior—A characteristic of dramatic play in which children imitate what they have observed.

modeling (three-dimensional)—Manipulating and shaping flexible materials.

monoprint—A single-colored print.

motor development—Physical growth; the ability to use one's body.

multicultural activities—Special events in the child's week, separate from the ongoing curriculum.

multimedia artwork—An art form and contemporary art movement that emphasizes the integration of all art forms.

mural—A story-telling picture or panel intended for a large wall space. Another form of picture making.

music center—A place for listening to records, tapes, singing, creating dance, and playing musical instruments.

musical/rhythmic learner—In Gardener's theory, this learner is oriented toward music, rhythmic sounds, and environmental sounds. Often called the "music lover."

National Council for the Social Studies' National Standards—A set of national standards developed for children (K–12) identifying learning experiences that make up a fundamental knowledge of social studies.

National Science Education Standards—A set of national standards on science education, presenting an outline of what students (K–12) need to know, understand, and be able to do to be "scientifically literate" at each grade level.

one-to-one correspondence—A concept basic to rational counting; giving one number per item in a series.

ordering (seriation)—A mathematical skill involving the ability to perceive opposite ends of a series. Example: big to little.

ordinal number—Number that refers to the place of an object in a series of numbers. Example: second book, third window.

organized play—An open, flexible type of play, with some structure provided in terms of materials.

overhead projector—Lightweight machine (hardware) that projects pictures and words on a screen.

paper pulp (papier-mâché)—A clay substitute, easy to work with, made from newspaper and powder paste.

parallel play—A form of play when a child plays side by side with other children with some interaction but without direct involvement.

passive listening—A stage in the development of listening skills when the child just sits, with little or no reaction.

people puppet—Also called humanettes; puppets that are half-person, half-puppet, made by placing a large paper grocery bag over the head. Holes are cut for eyes and other facial features.

perceptual readiness (for reading)—The prerequisite skill to reading involving the ability to associate printed language with spoken language. It also requires the child to discriminate among letters and sounds.

personal celebration—A celebration emphasizing an experience of individual, special significance to a child. (Example: losing the first tooth).

personal creative movement—Movement that reflects the mood or inner state of an individual.

phrase-wise method—A method of introducing a song to children through the use of a brief story, discussion, or question.

pictorial stage—The stage in art development when children have the ability to draw the variety of marks that make up their first representational pictures.

picture making—Any and all forms of *purposeful* expressions, beginning with controlled scribbling.

portfolio—A representative collection of an artist's work including samples from various periods, showing how the artist's talent has developed over time.

prehension—The development of a preferred hand grasp. This means a definite preference for right- or left-handedness.

preschematic stage—A term from Lowenfeld's theory that refers to the basic forms stage. Generally refers to the fact that basic forms are drawn in and of themselves and not to represent a particular object.

pretend reading—Also called "reenactment" or "emergent reading." Children practice reading-like behaviors that build confidence in themselves as readers.

Principles and Standards for Mathematics Children Pre-K–12—A set of standards developed by the National Council of Teachers of Mathematics proposing mathematical content and processes students should know and be able to use as they progress through school.

process over product—The process that leads to originality (exploration and experimentation with materials) is more important than the end product.

proximodental development—The pattern of human growth from inside to outside (or from center to outside).

publication sites—On the Internet the sites can be used as a resource for actually publishing children's work.

quality (in music experiences) vs. quantity—Children develop musical preferences at an early age so listening experiences should include a variety of styles and cultures, not just children's music.

random manipulation—Squeezing clay in an uncontrolled way, comparable to the early scribble stage in drawing.

random scribbling—See "disordered scribbling."

rapport—A warm and friendly feeling and relationship between people.

rational counting—Comprehension of the idea that the last number counted in a sequence of objects represents all the objects in the sequence, the total number of objects counted.

reading readiness—See "emerging literacy." Often used to describe the skills involved in getting ready to read.

representational art—Art in which symbols are used to make a visual representation of something important to the child.

rhythm—The element of art found in repeated shapes, colors, textures, and other patterns.

rhythm instruments—Children learn about rhythm by first listening to the rhythmic pattern of a song, then trying to copy it using rhythm instruments.

right-brained—Using the right hemisphere of the brain as the major learning method.

rote counting—Memorization of a number sequence with no comprehension of what the numbers mean.

schema—An individual way or pattern of drawing. It develops from much practice with drawing symbols.

schematic stage—Another term for the pictorial stage (Lowenfeld's theory) referring to the child's ability to use his or her own special variety of marks or *schema*.

science—A study consisting of two phases that cannot be separated: investigation and knowledge.

science/discovery center—A place to learn about nature and science; to explore the natural world.

scissoring skills—A developmental skill, made up of a sequence of skills, beginning as early as age two, in a child's first attempt at tearing.

scribble stage—The first stage in the development of art beginning with a child's first scribbles, usually at about one and one-half to two years of age.

sensorimotor—Derived from the two words, "sensory" and "motor." Sensory refers to using the five body senses and motor refers to the physical act of doing. Sensorimotor learning involves the body and its senses as they are used in doing.

seriation—See "ordering."

"Small C" creativity—Creativity that involves ideas or products that are new to the person, but only to the person. An example of "small c" creativity is a child's new use of blending finger paint colors.

social–emotional growth—Refers to two kinds of growth. Emotional growth is the growth of a child's feelings and social growth is the child's growth as a member of a group.

software—Collective term for films, tapes, computer disks, and all other materials used on hardware (or machines) as media. Example: The computer disk is software.

solitary play—The form of play in early toddlerhood when the child plays primarily alone.

space—An art element referring to the distance within or between aspects in an artwork.

spontaneous play (free play)—One of the two basic types of play, the other being organized play. A free, unplanned, flexible type of play.

sugar—A nutritional term, generally used to refer to "sucrose," which is refined sugar from sugar cane or beets. Other sources of sugar are fructose, dextrose, lactose, and maltose.

symbol (in children's art)—A visual representation of something of importance to the child.

tableaus—"Frozen pictures" in which groups of students "freeze" or pose to act out a scene, a saying, a book title, etc.

teaching peace—Teaching children a basic attitude made up of trust and consideration toward everyone.

teaching songs from recordings—A method of introducing a song where children respond to the whole song rhythmically, dramatically, and with instruments.

tempera—Powder paint that is mixed with water for use in painting activities.

ten thematic strands of social studies—Developed by the National Council for the Social Studies, these ten themes were developed to point to a fundamental knowledge of social studies for children (K–12).

thinking brain—The part of the brain that thinks logically. It reacts after the emotional brain.

three-dimensional art—Refers to any art form that has at least three sides. Art that is "in the round," which means that one can look at it from many sides.

tourist curriculum—Teaching about cultures only through artifacts such as food, traditional clothing, and household implements.

two-dimensional media—A term used to refer to any art form that is flat, having only two sides—front and back.

varying the rhythm of the music program—A process of adding variety to the music program through choice of music, method of presentation, and lesson planning that helps hold children's interests and makes the experience enjoyable.

verbal/linguistic learner—In Gardener's theory, this learner is oriented toward language, words, reading, and writing. Often called the "word player."

visual acuity—The ability to see and recognize shape and form.

visual spatial learner—In Gardener's theory, this learner is imaginative, creative, and oriented toward colors and pictures. Often called the "visualizer."

whole-song method—A method of introducing a song to children by presenting the whole song in a variety of ways.

INDEX